SOCIOLOGY

A WINDOW ON THE WORLD

SECOND EDITION

SOCIOLOGY

A WINDOW ON THE WORLD

SECOND EDITION

KATHERINA L.P. LUNDY
Late of York University
and
BARBARA D. WARME
York University

Nelson Canada

to Tony and Brett,
and to Paul, Diana, and Karl

Published in 1990 by
Nelson Canada,
A Division of Thomson Canada Limited
1120 Birchmount Road
Scarborough, Ontario M1K 5G4

Canadian Cataloguing in Publication Data
Lundy, Katherina L.P.
Sociology: a window on the world

2nd ed.
ISBN 0-17-603487-0

1. Sociology. I. Warme, Barbara. II. Deutschmann, Linda Bell, 1943- . III. Title.

HM66.L85 1990 301 C89-095117-9

PUBLISHER: Ric Kitowski
ACQUISITIONS EDITOR: David Ward
SUPERVISING EDITOR: Mary Lynn Mulroney
DEVELOPMENTAL EDITOR: Irene Cox
DESIGN: Gail McGowan
COVER DESIGN: Gail McGowan, Lorraine Tuson
COVER PHOTOGRAPHY: Ellen Shuster/The Image Bank
TYPESETTING: Compeer Typographic Services Limited

Printed and bound in Canada

3 4 5 ALG 95 94 93 92

to the memory of Kitty Lundy,
beloved friend and colleague

Barbara Warme

In the classroom with Kitty, students became engaged in sociology and experienced a new view of the world. This direct engagement with students carried over into this book, and her hope was that it would succeed in seizing the imagination and energy of the student in that first encounter with a new field of study.

Larry Lundy

PREFACE

In preparing a second edition, we have had the benefit of criticisms and suggestions from many colleagues and students who were good enough to tell us what they thought worked, and what did not, in the first edition. Besides undertaking the obvious task of updating tables, references, inserts, and suggested readings, we have expanded the discussion to include issues that have more recently begun to engage sociologists. Also, we have added a chapter on organizations, a section on health care in the social institutions chapter, and a section on social control to accompany the chapter on deviance. Throughout the text, we have provided many more references to assist students who wish to explore theoretical and empirical studies in greater depth. As well, we have renewed our efforts to integrate the text with cross-references. We have adhered to our initial decision not to confine the subject of gender, and of "women's issues," to a single chapter of the book but, rather, to demonstrate that the feminist perspective is germane to all areas of sociology. While the basic format of each chapter remains the same, we have enlarged the glossary, included film recommendations, and added to the suggested readings and assignments. Some of the assignments are designed to encourage students to get their feet wet with empirical enquiry of their own, however modest in scope. Many of the suggested readings are literary works, selected not because of a reductionist assumption that literature simply "mirrors" life, but because creative writers explore the rich complexities of the human condition and of human arrangements in ways that force the imagination along unexpected paths. The inserts, drawn largely from newspapers and popular magazines, are intended to invite critical discussion. At no time, perhaps, will students need a healthy scepticism more than in facing the social punditry that will inevitably flourish during the final decade of the second millennium!

In revising and expanding the book, we have continued to be governed by the conviction that an introduction to sociology should not aim for encyclopaedic coverage of the discipline, nor be a compendium of sociological findings. Students should not expect to enter a closed world of established knowledge but, rather, an arena of intellectual play, an arena with traditions, rules, procedures and, yes, "major players," but one in which there are always more questions than answers. The "last word" is an elusive goal being pursued in new books, new articles which are coming off the presses even as I write this preface.

B.W.
February 1990

ACKNOWLEDGEMENTS

Setting out to acknowledge one's indebtedness to others is surely the easiest and most pleasant phase in the writing of a book.

We would like to thank the following people for their generous assistance: Carl Baar, Ellen Baar, Iris Bent, Lenore d'Anjou, Leo Davids, Jack Fine, Jay Goldstein, Linda Grayson, Robert Hetherington, Suzanne Hidi, Elizabeth Julian, Warren Kalbach, Sandra Kirby, Brett Lundy, Vivienne Monty, Dorathy Moore, Graham Morgan, Brendan Murray, Leslie Sanders, June Seel, Earl Stuart, Martin Suitman, Gill Teiman, Hazel Thomas, and Burton Thomas. Bas van Gent eased our work in a variety of ways, lending a practised hand whenever asked. We are also indebted to Kathryn Elder, film and video librarian, York University Library, for her film recommendations.

The editorial staff of Nelson Canada braved the marathon with stamina and spirit. We are particularly grateful for the efforts of Ric Kitowski, Gail McGowan, Mary Lynn Mulroney, Sarah Robertson, Wendy Sedgeman, Dave Ward, and Ben Wentzell. Our editor, Irene Cox, managed to combine firmness with diplomacy, a formula that smoothed the way for all of us.

Linda Bell Deutschmann's contribution in writing the chapter on deviance and social control is self-evident. Our reliance on her expertise was not, however, confined to that one chapter.

Larry Lundy's enthusiasm for the project did not flag throughout the preparation of two editions. We thank him very much for his collaboration.

CONTENTS

CHAPTER 3
SOCIALIZATION 79

CHAPTER 4
STRATIFICATION 113

CHAPTER 5
WORK AND THE DIVISION OF LABOUR 155

CHAPTER 6
ORGANIZATIONS 205

CHAPTER 7
MINORITIES 253

CHAPTER 8
DEVIANCE AND SOCIAL CONTROL 309
by Linda B. Deutschmann

CHAPTER 9
SOCIAL INSTITUTIONS 369

CHAPTER 9A
THE FAMILY 371

THE NATURE OF SOCIOLOGICAL ENQUIRY

It was time for a commercial, and Mary Hunt slipped into the kitchen to fetch the tray of appetizers she had prepared earlier. The Hunts and the Fennels had been getting together to watch Saturday-night hockey games for 20 years, almost as long as either couple had been married. It was usually a simple, relaxed occasion, with easy conversation, much teasing, and mock rivalry. Although not quite in the Gucci and Pucci set, both men had reached financially rewarding stages in their careers, took pride in having attractive wives, and attributed their own trim shapes to racquet sports and summer softball. The two families sported year-round tans as a result of semiannual vacations in the sun and bore many other signs of the good life. Tonight, Bob Hunt had reminded Richard that it would soon be time for their stag weekend at the cottage, and the comment had prompted customary hilarity. When Mary returned to the room with the tray, a commercial was showing a college-age group bicycling in the mountains. She grimaced at the TV set and observed ruefully, ''Why is it that the Beautiful People always seem to be 22 years old?''

QUESTION: What role does advertising play in reflecting and reinforcing dominant cultural values?

That is a sociological question.

It is Saturday morning, and Mrs. Foster makes her way toward the blue-and-white dining room overlooking the wide lawn of Suncrest Residence for the Aged. She has been a resident only since Tuesday but has already decided that the meals are very good and she does not want to be late for breakfast. In the hall, she encounters Jane Kennedy, a member of the staff, and is surprised when the usually affable Miss Kennedy greets her with dismay. "But Mrs. Foster," the employee exclaims, "you are still in your dressing gown! You can't go about like *that*. At Suncrest, everyone gets dressed first thing in the morning. Now be a dear, and go and pretty yourself up."

QUESTION: Whose interests are paramount in the formulation of the rules and regulations of places such as retirement homes?

That is a sociological question.

Raymond always felt a sense of well-being on those days when he found himself alone with his grandfather, sitting out of doors on the back porch and waiting for Gran to call them to lunch. Their chats were about small things and big things, and the old man's calm, so unlike the impatience and urgency of Raymond's father, invited confidences. Today, Raymond was eager to tell him about a decision he had not yet mentioned to anyone, even his best friend. "Gramps," he ventured, "I've decided that Dad has the best job in the whole world. That's what I'm going to be when I grow up." Raymond's father was the chief executive of a large firm. The night before, some other members of the firm had come to Raymond's house for a cocktail party. His grandfather was curious about what had happened at the party to make the job seem so desirable to Raymond. "Don't you see, Gramps, everyone always agrees with him, and everyone laughs at his jokes."

QUESTION: When decisions at the top are never challenged, what are the consequences for the flow of information in an organization and for the efficacy of its decision-making process?

That is a sociological question.

When the small plane landed on the water, almost the entire community was there to greet it and to scrutinize the boxes that would shortly be unloaded on the dock.

Although all comings and goings were of great interest, this was a special occasion, for the priest was returning from a stay in hospital and Harry Mosquito was arriving for a visit on behalf of the National Indian Brotherhood. Several women hurried down to the dock with their groceries from the co-op, and murmured to a group of men who were gathered near the shoreline, playing a stone-tossing game. Some of the younger men were chatting and whittling pieces of wood, seemingly oblivious to the young women standing near the picket fence of the nursing station, clutching the hands of small children.

QUESTION: What social forces have operated in the contact between an indigenous culture and a foreign culture to deprive adult males of their traditional roles without providing adequate new ones?

That is a sociological question.

These vignettes describe only tiny pieces of the endless flow of actual events in the everyday world. One could ask any number of questions about the incidents described. Furthermore, one could ask many sociological questions other than the ones we have chosen. Two characteristics of the nature of the sociological questions posed should be noted.

First, they raise the level of enquiry from particular events to a more general, abstract level. Each asks what the incident observed suggests about the possibility of recurring or similar patterns of behaviour.

Second, each focuses on an issue that involves the individual person in group life in some way. Other social and behavioural scientists, such as historians, political scientists, economists, psychologists, and anthropologists, are also interested in pushing their enquiries up the ladder of abstraction, seeking out the general patterns suggested by individual incidents. However, each type of social scientist would have a different focus, posing different types of questions in an attempt to make sense of what has been observed.

The different points of view of the various social scientists are like the windows of a room. Through each, one can watch the same scene, but from a different perspective. We approached a sample of social scientists from various fields and asked them what questions they might raise concerning today's high unemployment rate among young adults; their responses appear in Exhibit 1.1. You will note that the approaches are not as sharply differentiated as one might expect, reflecting the overlap of interests among the disciplines.

EXHIBIT 1.1

DIFFERENT WINDOWS FOR INVESTIGATING THE SAME PHENOMENON

Phenomenon

Statistics Canada reports that the unemployment rate is higher for 15- to 24-year-olds than for workers 25 years of age and older.[1]

Psychologist

Are there any personality characteristics more prevalent among those young people who respond to unemployment as a challenge to be confronted and overcome than among those who respond with despair? Among young adults, is one's employment status a significant factor in determining one's self-concept and/or self-esteem?

Political Scientist

What is the role of government in relation to the problem? Do certain government policies affect youth employment? Has the government tried to alleviate this problem through specific programs?

If there is government policy addressing this problem, what range of influences internal to the political system led to the relevant government decisions? (For example, what was the role of bureaucracy? federalism? political parties? the cabinet?) And what external forces influenced the policy?

Economist

Is the relatively high unemployment rate among 15- to 24-year-olds a normal characteristic of the current business cycle? Or does it represent a structural change in the Canadian economy?

What will be the effects on the economy 20 years hence of the present high unemployment among young adults?

Anthropologist

What are the sociocultural factors that produce inequalities in the work situation so that some people have jobs and others do not? Is unemployment distributed evenly among ethnic, sex, and other sociocultural categories in the 15-to-24-year-old age bracket?

If we assume that work is as much about social interaction as it is about material production, "unemployment" means not just a lack of income but the loss of a meaningful interactive social group. What are the implications of such an insight?

Historian

What roles did the federal government, the business community, and private philanthropy play in responding to the problem of high unemployment among youth in the 1930s? Compare their responses in the 1980s.

What economic changes since the First World War help to explain the 1986 unemployment rate for young adults?

Sociologist

Why do young people drop out of educational institutions, given the high unemployment rate among the minimally educated young?

What will be the impact of current high unemployment among 15- to 24-year-olds on their future work careers?

The inserts in the book are taken, for the most part, from newspapers and magazines. Many contain opinions and interpretations that we do not endorse. We have selected these inserts to provoke discussion. They are not sociological analyses; rather, they are journalistic descriptions of actual events. We invite students to read these inserts critically, using newly acquired sociological insights.

JOBLESS TEENAGERS ARE PUT TO WORK

By David Crane

Joakim Ostling, an unemployed 18-year-old Swede, heads off each morning to a municipal carpentry shop where he helps build park benches, playground equipment and toys for day-care centres.

He's a member of Sweden's youth teams, a program introduced last year by the government to guarantee work for the country's unemployed 18- and 19-year-olds. It is one of the most innovative work-creation measures introduced by the government and has virtually wiped out unemployment in that age group.

There are roughly 44,000 teenagers in the youth team program at present. They get paid welfare-level wages but, as Ostling says, "It's better than staying at home all day."

Just One Part

The youth teams are just one part of Sweden's highly developed labor market program which also includes intensive job retraining, government make-work jobs and sheltered workshops for the handicapped and hard-core unemployed who cannot get work elsewhere.

While Sweden has a 3 per cent unemployment rate, compared to Canada's 11 per cent, close to another 4 per cent of the labor force is in these various labor market programs, reflecting the importance Swedes attach to giving unemployed people work or training instead of simply welfare.

Maie Kark, a 33-year-old Estonian immigrant, is taking a four-week word-processing course at the Labor Marketing Training Centre in Liljeholmen, a Stockholm suburb, in the hope this will get her a full-time job.

Eighteen months ago she took a 10-month basic office course at the centre. "The problem was that I could only get temporary jobs," she says. "Word-processing machines are so important now. I should be able to get something better because there are lots of word-processing jobs advertised."

And to help students at the training centre seek jobs as they approach the end of their courses, the Swedish employment centre has an office right in the training centre.

At any time, about 38,000 Swedes are enrolled in training centre courses which run from just a few weeks to more than a year. They are paid between $20 and $45 a day in training allowances, depending on past work experience and pay. This amounts to $100 to $225 a week and compares with pay of $245 to $280 a week that a typical Swedish industrial worker earns.

Anna-Greta Leijon, minister of labor and a leading member of the Social Democratic Party, is responsible for the far-reaching labor market programs.

She has a budget of $2.7 billion. Of this, $406 million goes to measures for creating employment, such as relief work and recruitment subsidies, $405 million for special measures for job adjustment and employment, $275 million for labor market training and $178 million for youth teams.

Probably her most innovative measure has been the youth teams, which have virtually eliminated youth unemployment.

"Like many other countries, we have had a problem in Sweden with youth unemployment. And until we introduced the youth teams we had the highest unemployment among 18- and 19-year-olds."

Establishment of the youth teams followed intensive discussions with parents and young people. "We felt something must be wrong when society gives youngsters welfare money but doesn't give them something to do for the money. Everyone thought it was a very poor way to start life."

So the youth teams were set up. "We took the money society was going to have to provide them anyway and used it to provide short-term work, creating a system where we could guarantee work. And society benefits from the work the youth teams do."

SETTING THE AGENDA

To look at the world from a sociological perspective is to discover the fascinating and sometimes surprising patterns of human behaviour. Before going any further, we need a working definition of what we mean by sociology — a definition that will take on fuller meaning as you work your way through the book: sociology is the study of relationships among and within groups. Over time, patterns of relationships crystallize into social structures. These structures constrain group and individual action, and are in turn shaped and reshaped by the push and pull of such action.

As a formal discipline, sociology is of relatively recent origin, having emerged only at the beginning of the 19th century. However, questions about the nature of society and what makes it tick have prompted enquiry since antiquity. For example, in the fifth century BC, Plato was concerned with how social order could be maintained in the light of individual differences. Clearly, there was a need for guardians, but who would guard the guardians? The 14th century Arab historian Ibn Khaldoun wrote about the tension between co-operation and conflict. He recognized that human beings are forced into co-operation in order to survive, but that collective arrangements themselves engender conflict. Theologians attempt to explain the state of the world in terms of particular religious concepts, such as the original sin of Christianity or the birth sin of Buddhism.

As noted in our working definition, sociologists are concerned with the study of groups in society—for example, industrial workers, community college students, or women in the work force—and with the processes of interaction that take place among groups and among individuals. Under what circumstances does dissension arise among groups, and how is it resolved? A labour strike reflects an instance of such dissension between employer and workers. Each group seeks to maximize its share of the benefits; the workers want higher pay and shorter working hours, while the employer wants, say, guarantees that overtime will be worked as required. Religious conflict, such as that now occurring in Iran, and political conflict, such as the dispute over the Meech Lake Accord, become more or less acute at various periods. When the lines of group conflict harden, individuals are significantly affected. A Protestant father may assert that his daughter will marry a Catholic "over my dead body;" white parents in the United States may fight unrelentingly against having their children bussed to racially integrated schools.

Examining the relationships among large groups is called studying society at the macro level. Society can also be studied at the micro level: the relationships within and between small groups, such as particular families or schools. For example, how are relations in the family affected when the wife starts (or stops) working outside the home? What happens when a new element is brought into a formerly homogeneous group—say, a male secretary or a female senior executive? **Macro-sociology** and **micro-sociology** are not different disciplines; rather, they use different lenses to examine what is happening in society. To look at interaction within the family or the peer group, one uses a telephoto lens. On the other hand, a wide-angle lens is a more suitable instrument for recording how labour-contract negotiations are affected by such major forces as changes in technology and economic recession. Different perspectives call for different research approaches, some of which will be briefly discussed later on in this chapter.

CONCERNS OF THE EARLY SOCIOLOGISTS

The sociologists who shaped the discipline in the 19th and early 20th centuries lived at a time of social upheaval, when one change came tumbling after another. Ways of explaining the world that had long been taken for granted were being challenged or appeared to have no further relevance. No longer was it automatic that a son would follow in his father's occupational footsteps. That occupation might be vanishing, as occurred with bellringing, town crying, and blacksmithing. At the same time, new occupations were emerging, creating opportunities but also curtailing the autonomy of workers such as craftsmen. The Industrial Revolution was underway, and this brought in its wake the transformation of society from a rural to an urban one. With the movement of population, people could no longer assume that their lives would be played out on the same little stage. The resultant uncertainty and dislocation engendered anxiety. Many people felt they had lost their sense of direction, though others welcomed the new horizons.

In the past, nature itself had been deemed uncontrollable and unpredictable, as likely to send ideal weather for a bountiful harvest as to deliver an outbreak of plague, destroying whole communities. With the acceleration of scientific breakthroughs, there seemed to be hope that natural forces could be understood and harnessed. The founders of sociology sought, each in a different way, to apply to the study of society the modern spirit epitomized by science. If the mysteries of nature could be deciphered, it was not unreasonable to expect that patterns and regularities could be discovered in society. Once these had been identified, social phenomena would become more predictable and subject to control.

Our purpose in introducing the contributions of some of the early sociologists is not to provide more facts to be memorized. Rather, we want to identify the various streams that have fed into the sociological perspective. Such a perspective is developed by individuals; in turn, each one's perception of the world is influenced by the social context in which he or she lives. At the time of Comte, Marx, Durkheim, and Weber, the explosion of scientific knowledge and attendant technological development were transforming the world and ways of thinking about it.

Two discussions of the development of sociological theory which you might consult are Collins and Makowsky's *The Discovery of Society* (1984) and Swingewood's *A Short History of Sociological Thought* (1984).

A ''BASTARD'' SCIENCE

The term ''sociology'' (made up of the Latin ''socio'' meaning ''groups;'' and the Greek ''logy'' meaning ''study of;'' note that ''logy'' is derived from ''logos,'' the Greek word for reason, implying that study will be conducted along rational lines) was coined by Auguste Comte (1798–1857) who sought to make the study of society scientific by removing it from the realms of philosophy and theology. He divided his study into what he called ''social statics'' and ''social dynamics.'' In the former, he examined the nature and interplay of mechanisms that contribute to stability. He isolated three factors as vital to the maintenance of social order:

- Language, which provides a medium for behaviour.
- Religion, which cements society by providing shared rituals and beliefs.

• The division of labour, which brings about mutual interdependence.

For Comte, the major importance of a particular institution, such as the family or religion, was in the contribution it makes to maintaining society as a harmonious whole.[2] Stability and order were high on Comte's list of priorities, in part, perhaps, because they were conspicuously absent in the society in which he lived. (Just before his birth, the French Revolution had occurred. In its aftermath, France was rocked by a series of further revolutions that wrought extensive social changes in the 19th century.)

Under the heading of "social dynamics," Comte addressed questions of social progress and human evolution. In his Law of Three Stages, Comte argued that every society must pass through the theological and the metaphysical stage to arrive at the positive stage. The dominant mode of explanation in the first stage is religious dogma and, in the second, abstract speculation. The positive stage is marked by the scientific approach, which combines empirical observations and analysis.

Comte believed that, through scientific study, the laws that govern society could be discovered and, from this knowledge, society could be shaped and thus bettered. However, since he did not attempt to test whether the Law of Three Stages applies in the "real" world, he did not put to work the scientific method he advocated.

For Comte, the major significance of any institution was its contribution to the maintenance of society as a harmonious whole.

Comte was, however, the first analyst to lay out a program for investigating society scientifically and to specify the types of enquiry to be used for this enterprise:

- *Observation* within the limits set by his theoretical framework of social statics and social dynamics. Without such a framework, observations are merely a jumble, an aggregation of unrelated items.
- *Comparison* between animal and human societies and among different types of human societies. In this way, the workings of evolution are made apparent.
- *Historical analysis*, since to understand what exists now (for example, a particular family form, such as the nuclear family), one must look back to how it developed.

These three prerequisites may seem obvious today. In Comte's day, however, this was a novel way to approach the study of society. His method has endured and is now taken for granted in the investigation of social issues.

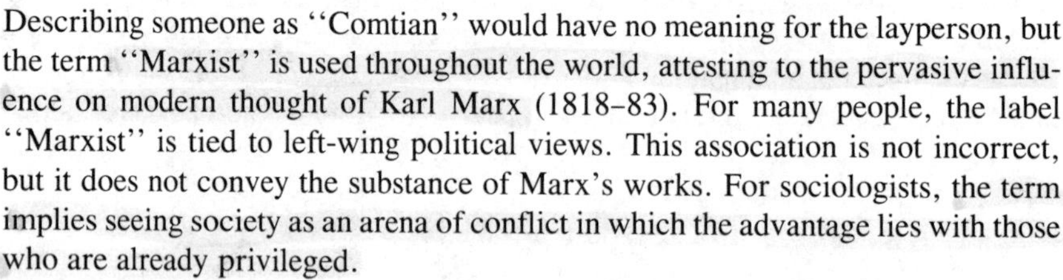

THE STRUGGLE FOR POWER AS HISTORICAL REALITY

Describing someone as "Comtian" would have no meaning for the layperson, but the term "Marxist" is used throughout the world, attesting to the pervasive influence on modern thought of Karl Marx (1818–83). For many people, the label "Marxist" is tied to left-wing political views. This association is not incorrect, but it does not convey the substance of Marx's works. For sociologists, the term implies seeing society as an arena of conflict in which the advantage lies with those who are already privileged.

Marx viewed the history of societies as the struggle for societal rewards (power and possessions) between a dominant group and exploited groups. Exploiter and exploited assume different guises at different points in history, but disparities in power are a persistent characteristic of human societies. In ancient Greece and Rome, the basic struggle was between free men and slaves. Free Romans were themselves divided into the upper-crust patricians and the mass of plebeians, terms that still colloquially connote class differences. However, slaves were the most exploited group; as individuals, they were without power and had minimal civil rights. In mediaeval Europe, the dominant groups were the nobility, the upper clergy, and the landowners (the groups sometimes overlapped). Peasants and serfs were the subordinated groups. Serfs were tied to the land; they could not move about, get married, or make any significant decisions about their lives without the consent of the landowner. Even the nominally free peasants had little latitude in what they could or could not do. In Marx's own time, the unequal contest was between the bourgeoisie and the proletariat. Marx noted that the bourgeoisie owned two of the three **means of production** — land (by which he meant all natural resources) and capital (factories, workshops, machinery, and the money to buy more) — while the proletariat was made up of landless workers who had nothing to sell but their labour.[3] The workers are "exploited" because capitalists pay them less in wages than the value their labour produces. The **surplus value** is appropriated by the capitalists, thus giving them economic power that increases on a cumulative basis.

In each historical case, the power of the dominant group was rooted in its control of the means of producing the goods and services required by society. Marx did not claim that the position of a slave in Roman times was equivalent to that of a 19th-century factory worker. Their similarity is that both were on the lowest rung of the social ladder. Indeed, one of Marx's most important contributions to the social sciences was his insistence that individuals, groups, and institutions must be studied in their social contexts. In other words, to understand the position of a teacher, one must look at the value his or her society places on education, at the way the educational system is organized, at the training required to become a teacher, and at the kinds of individuals likely to have access to this occupation.

Marx viewed the history of societies as the struggle for societal rewards between a dominant group and exploited groups.

The nature of the various contesting groups changes over time; the essential struggle, instead of being between free men and slaves, becomes one between owners and workers, in Marx's view. Changes in these groups attest to changes in society. How does change come about? Marx argued that every social order, every economic system, develops within itself internal contradictions — square pegs in round holes. Over time, these contradictions become so strong that they can no longer be handled within the confines of the existing order; when this occurs, the existing order is overthrown, and a new order comes into being. This new order encompasses new features as well as the remnants of the previous system. However, Marx did not believe that transformations could be predicted on the basis of general laws. Rather, he stipulated that each situation must be analysed empirically, that is, in its specific historical context.

For example, with the accelerating development of technology and other changes in the mode of production, workers had to be able to move to the location of jobs. Thus, it became impractical to have a labour force that was partially tied to the land, so the feudal system became obsolete. However, the capitalist system that emerged was, in turn, to be fractured by internal contradictions that, Marx predicted, would cause the demise of the system. From its ruins would arise communism, in which inequality would be abolished and no internal contradictions would arise. Therefore, the alternation of social systems — the **dialectic** as Marx called it — would end.[4]

Marx was a German by birth, but his revolutionary journalism and other activities led to his living in exile for much of his life. Most of his best-known work was done in England, which, in midcentury, was experiencing the most blatant excesses of the Industrial Revolution. Understanding the political and social chaos he lived in is a requisite to understanding his work.

Marx will be encountered again when we examine the bases on which societal rewards are allocated.

SOCIAL REGULATION AND SOCIAL COHESION

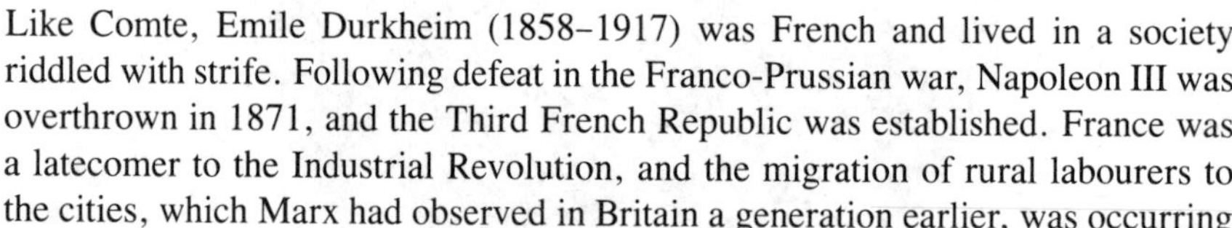

Like Comte, Emile Durkheim (1858–1917) was French and lived in a society riddled with strife. Following defeat in the Franco-Prussian war, Napoleon III was overthrown in 1871, and the Third French Republic was established. France was a latecomer to the Industrial Revolution, and the migration of rural labourers to the cities, which Marx had observed in Britain a generation earlier, was occurring as Durkheim wrote.

When most people had lived in small, homogeneous communities, individuals had performed similar work, engaged in similar lifestyles, and, because of these similar circumstances, held common values and beliefs. This **mechanical solidarity**, as Durkheim labelled it, cemented the social order. In the agricultural society of pre-industrial Europe, each family unit was relatively self-sufficient. However, as the division of labour became more complex and groups of individuals performed specialized tasks, self-sufficiency was replaced by mutual interdependence. Durkheim believed that the mechanical solidarity rooted in similarity would eventually be replaced by **organic solidarity**, an interdependence created by a highly specialized division of labour. Just as the liver, the heart, the brain, and other organs must perform particular work for the body as a whole to function, so must each group carry out its tasks in order for society to operate. In today's world, mutual interdependence is brought home dramatically when an occupational group, such as transit workers or nurses, goes on strike, seriously disrupting everyday life.

In Durkheim's time, the social order was changing so swiftly that the old communal values were eroding before appropriate new values had emerged sufficiently to be held in common. Durkheim described this situation as **anomie**—normlessness, a lack of values and established rules for conduct. As we will discuss in Chapter 3 on socialization, one of Durkheim's important contributions was to elaborate how societal values are internalized (made part of the individual). Social control thus also works in "invisible" ways, and is not solely imposed by external agents. People who have been socialized to one set of values become disoriented if they find themselves in a world in which these values no longer appear applicable. This happened to many new urbanites in the late 19th century; their familiar guideposts had disappeared, and no reliable new ones were available.

Durkheim reasoned that one manifestation of such upheavals would be an increase in the rate of suicide. For him, the group, not the individuals who comprised it, was the appropriate unit of sociological analysis. He contended that one can analyse group phenomena without focusing on the motivations and characteristics of individuals. Consonant with this emphasis, Durkheim studied how suicide rates varied with the state of society and with the extent to which individuals were integrated into a particular group (*Suicide* 1897). It was a brilliant choice of study, for until then suicide had been treated as a phenomenon that could be explained only by the state of mind of the individual who engaged in this behaviour. Durkheim was concerned with suicide as a social fact.

He posited that suicide rates would be higher at times of rapid change, when anomie was likely to prevail, and that they would be higher for people who lacked family ties — those who were single or were married but had no children. The content of religious beliefs, Durkheim believed, would be another important factor. Thus, he predicted that Protestants, whose religion always emphasized individual responsibility for ethical decisions, would be more prone to commit suicide than Roman Catholics, who had available the psychic relief of confession and, moreover, could look to their church as an authoritative guide to conduct. Statistical analysis of suicide rates supported Durkheim's assumptions.[5]

The data, and the statistical tools for analysing them, that Durkheim had available for his study on suicide would be considered unacceptably crude by present-day standards. His vital contribution was a method for analysing social problems, such as suicide, drug addiction, and violence, in the light of the social organization or disorganization of a particular society or group.

Most modern social scientists agree that, ultimately, the person who commits suicide cannot be left out of the equation. Durkheim has, therefore, been criticized for neglecting the individuals who make up social groups in his eagerness to establish the primacy of social facts. Though we believe that there is some justification for this criticism, Durkheim's preoccupation with wholes must be seen as a reaction against the mode of explanation used in his time, which, for the most part, sought reasons for behaviour in the motives and actions of individuals.

SUICIDE RATES IN CANADA VARY FROM PROVINCE TO PROVINCE. WHAT MAKES THE DIFFERENCE?

By Sean Fine

There is something about Newfoundland that makes its residents less likely than other Canadians to take their own lives.

Whatever it is, Quebec and Alberta do not have it, or at least not as much of it.

In 1986, a total of 3,670 Canadians took their own lives (by comparison, 288 died of acquired immune deficiency syndrome).

Despite its high unemployment rate, Newfoundland had an average annual suicide rate between 1981 and 1986 of 5.2 per 100,000 population, only about one-third the national average of 14.1. Quebec, at 17, and Alberta, at 15.9, exceeded the average.

Researchers have ruled out unequal reporting of suicides as a cause of provincial differences. Even when accidental poisonings and "injury undetermined" were added, the picture remained unchanged. The two northern territories generally have the highest suicide rates, but researchers say the figures could be distorted because of the small population.

Why such variation? Is life in one part of Canada so different from life in another? And how does a province's economy affect its suicide rate?

The answers from social scientists, though hesitant, provide a glimpse of regional cultures and their differing social strains, values and strengths.

By some measures, Newfoundland has managed to avoid the malaise — sociologists call it anomie — that has infected much of Europe and North America.

"The people out there don't travel, they don't have big bank accounts, they don't have a lot of cars in their garages. But they're not killing themselves," said Dr. Ronald Dyck, the provincial suicidologist for Alberta—the only one in Canada.

Alberta, on the other hand, has

exceeded each year's national suicide rate for two decades. And Quebec, which in the early seventies rated among the lowest, had the highest levels from 1981 to 1986.

Overall, Canada is in the top half of industrialized countries for suicide, and since the late sixties it has consistently been higher than the United States.

Clearly, some places are more subject to the problem than others. "We should be thinking of some underlying malaise, because provinces high in suicide are high in other problems," said Gus Thompson, an Alberta psychologist and researcher.

He ranks Newfoundland with Prince Edward Island as the least susceptible, in sum, to eight social evils — rape, murder, attempted murder, assault, robbery, divorce, alcoholism and suicide.

These social evils, which some consider signposts of "the decline of Western civilization," are more often encountered as one moves west in Canada.

This was true in both 1981 and 1971, according to a study by Mr. Thompson — British Columbia and Alberta were highest on the index of social evils. Rates in Manitoba exceeded Saskatchewan's in both years, however, and Quebec surpassed Ontario in 1981.

But mere "westerliness" is probably not an important factor, Mr. Thompson said. Social breakdown occurs more often in provinces that are more affluent and more urbanized, have more university-educated people, smaller households, fewer religious people, a greater proportion of immigrants and greater ethnic diversity.

"I don't mean to belittle the effects of poverty," he said, "but poverty is not necessarily the prime cause (of social breakdown), as many of us thought."

In Quebec, rapid social changes since the Quiet Revolution of the sixties has been linked to the increase in suicides. A key is the declining state of the Roman Catholic Church, which views suicide as a sin.

"When they run into trouble, when they are in a position where they don't know where else to turn, they no longer have the threat of eternal damnation," Dr. Dyck said of potentially suicidal people.

As well, political involvement has dropped. "Before, with the strong nationalism in Quebec, people were quite involved . . . not as individualistic as they are today," said Richard Boyer of the psychiatric research unit at Montreal's Lafontaine Hospital.

Quebec, like Newfoundland today, once stood out from the rest of the country with its large families; now it has the lowest birth rate and one of the fastest-growing divorce rates.

For the young, the decline of family, church and political life has been confusing. "There is no very clear goal. They don't see where they're going," Mr. Boyer said. Adults feel "demobilized" and discouraged.

High unemployment and a shortage of jobs for women entering the work force are also cited as factors; Quebec is the only province where the female suicide rate continued to rise after the mid-seventies.

Newfoundland, largely an island province and the last to join Confederation, has not been touched as harshly by change as the rest of Canada. It is more religious, more rural and has larger families.

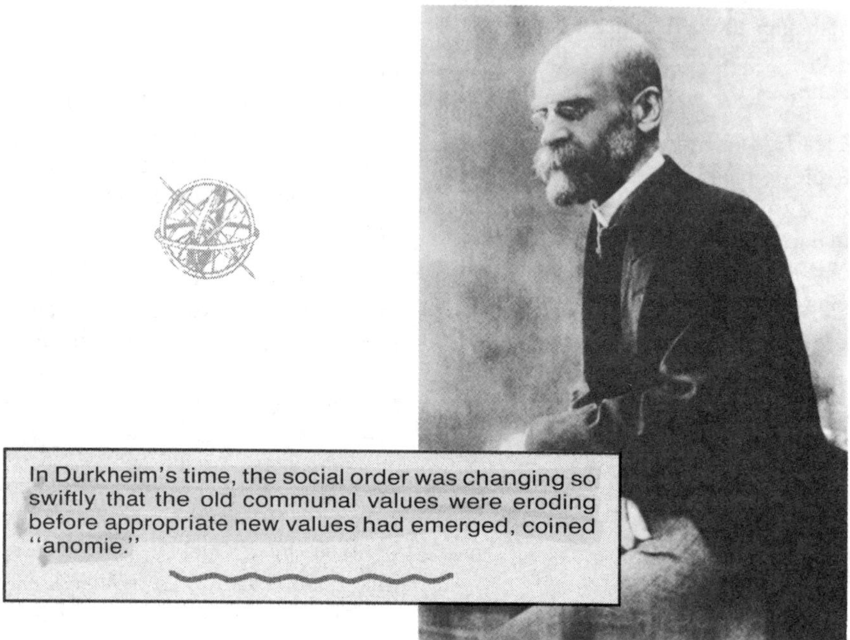

In Durkheim's time, the social order was changing so swiftly that the old communal values were eroding before appropriate new values had emerged, coined "anomie."

THE ESTABLISHMENT OF SOCIOLOGY AS AN ACADEMIC DISCIPLINE

Comte had coined the term "sociology" and attempted to provide the infant discipline with a scientific basis. Marx's controversial theories of how a social order persists and changes had thrust the study of society into the forefront of intellectual and popular debate. It was left to Durkheim to establish sociology as a recognized area of study in university.

In 1913, Durkheim was appointed professor of the newly created chair of the Science of Education and Sociology at the prestigious Sorbonne in Paris. In this capacity, and through his previous long and fruitful association with the faculty of education at the Sorbonne, Durkheim was able to influence the training of teachers and hence the way new generations of students would be socialized. With a group of brilliant young scholars, Durkheim founded *L'Année Sociologique* in 1898. The journal was an instant success in the academic community, allowing Durkheim to communicate his approach to sociology to other social scientists throughout the world.

We will recall Durkheim's formulations again and again in this book: for example, when we look at socialization, at education, and at religion. His impact on so many areas of sociology truly makes him one of its founders.

THE SUBJECTIVE DIMENSION OF HUMAN ACTION 

Like France, Germany was a relative latecomer to the Industrial Revolution. Max Weber (1864–1920) observed the struggle between the landed aristocracy, which still wielded disproportionate political power, and the new urban middle class, which was anxious to obtain some of this power. The tension between tradition and innovation informed much of Weber's research, notably his interpretation of the emergence of capitalism.

What we have noted about Durkheim's influence upon many areas of sociology is equally true of Weber's. Some of his best-known works deal with the characteristics of bureaucracy, an organizational form with which all North Americans are familiar in hospitals, schools, private corporations, and so on. Long before bureaucracies actually became the dominant mode of organization, Weber anticipated this development. Although he believed this form was technically the most efficient one, he was concerned with its potential for depersonalizing and dehumanizing people.

In another important area studied by Weber and summarized in *The Protestant Ethic and the Spirit of Capitalism* (1904–5), he attempted to demonstrate that the collective values and beliefs of individuals were crucial to the emergence of capitalism.

Both these contributions will be examined in some detail in subsequent chapters. Here we will focus on some of the dimensions Weber added to the study of society. He believed that to understand a culture, one has to immerse oneself in it. Knowing the language is invaluable in allowing the researcher to become sensitive to what is going on and to hear not only words but the meaning behind them. (Weber practised what he preached; he had a command of several languages, among them English, Latin, Greek, and Hebrew.) His concept of **Verstehen**, the German word meaning "understanding," is now a basis for all qualitative sociological research methods, such as in-depth interviews and community studies, in which researchers try to think themselves as much as possible into the frame of mind of those they are studying.[6] This kind of stance has pragmatic advantages: consider how much of the goodwill generated by aid projects to third-world countries is dissipated when project personnel are not attuned to the ways in which the native population lives and thinks.[7]

Weber, like Marx, was an historical sociologist. He believed that to understand the characteristics of a society or of an organizational form, such as a bureaucracy, one needs to trace its evolution. Weber was particularly concerned with understanding the meaning that individuals attach to their actions in a particular socio-historic context. An example was his study of the migration patterns of East Prussian tenant farmers. Their large-scale movement away from the estates (where many had worked for generations) into the rapidly growing cities was causing problems for contemporary landowners, who were left without experienced workers. Since most of the migrants did not have skills that were easily marketable in an urban setting, they lived there in abject poverty. In the short run, therefore, they were worse off than they had been. Weber reasoned that their actions had to be viewed in the light of their belief that they were providing their children with the chance of a better life in the long run. In other words, one could not understand the actions or motives of these labourers without knowing the positive value they placed on giving their children opportunities to improve themselves and the belief that this could be accomplished in the cities. (Similar arguments can be put forward to explain the severe hardships many immigrants to North America have been willing to endure.)

Durkheim firmly believed that social scientists have a duty to help strengthen the moral basis of society. In contrast, Weber argued that the task of the scientist was to unravel the interplay of factors that gives rise to a chain of events—for instance, the Industrial Revolution—and to delineate further possible consequences of such occurrences. For Weber, however, prescription (a recommendation of what ought to be done) was inappropriate for someone engaged in a scientific enterprise.

Weber was aware, however, that values enter into the social scientist's choice of what to investigate. Selecting an area for study designates it as important, at least to some segment of society. In North America, for example, the high value placed on the preservation of human life is reflected in the huge resources devoted to medical research and health care. It is in the conduct of the actual research that the scientist must leave personal values aside. To use a hypothetical example: a researcher dedicated to full sexual equality could not simply abandon a study that showed girls to have consistently higher IQs than boys. Similarly, you may be assigned an essay on a topic—say, the abortion issue—on which you have adamant feelings. Nonetheless, since you have been asked to write an essay and not an editorial, you have a responsibility to investigate and present the issue objectively and to avoid value-laden language.

Comte, Marx, Durkheim, and Weber were concerned with the links between the individual and society, and with the tension between the autonomy of the individual and the coercive power of social structures. Marx focused on the role force and "fraud" (the concealment or distortion of various factors) play in keeping society intact, while Comte and Durkheim emphasized the binding function of shared values and beliefs. Weber, too, recognized the importance of shared values, as well as the administrative mechanisms, such as government bureaus and business firms, that establish connections between individuals and the larger society.

Although Weber believed bureaucracy was the most efficient mode of organization, he was concerned with its potential for dehumanization.

PRESENT-DAY APPROACHES TO SOCIOLOGICAL QUESTIONS

The questions addressed by these men and by their contemporaries have continued to exercise the minds of sociologists. Although the range of social phenomena is vast, one can discern patterns in the ways sociologists choose to define and investigate questions.

We will now briefly examine some major modern perspectives, or schools of thought.

FUNCTIONALISM

Functionalism is rooted in the tradition of Durkheim and more remotely in that of Comte. It treats society as a system, which is itself made up of smaller systems, such as armies or families. A **system** can be defined as an arrangement of interrelated and interdependent parts. Each performs functions that contribute to the well-being of the entire system. For a system to operate effectively, each of the component parts must perform its task. Although most functionalists do not take the organic analogy literally, they often cite the human body to illustrate the notion of a system. Clearly, a person cannot survive if a vital organ is out of kilter; heart failure will produce a lethal crisis even if all other vital organs are sound.

Systems, such as an army, possess certain characteristics:

- *Boundaries.* One is either a member of the army or not.
- *Interdependence of parts.* Communication of commands and information, deployment of troops, and distribution of material are interdependent activities.
- *Needs.* An army needs recruits, weaponry, and food supplies.
- *Equilibrium state.* If an army increases in number, as in wartime, supply depots must be enlarged accordingly. For a system to persist, changes in one part must be compensated for by changes in its other parts. The result is a shifting balance called a dynamic equilibrium.

Functionalism has been a prominent orientation among North American sociologists, especially in the 1950s and 1960s, with two of its leading exponents being Talcott Parsons (1902–79) and Robert Merton (1910–). Parsons' writing is not easy to understand, but his work has been highly influential. For a good discussion of what functionalism is (and is not), see Merton's *Social Theory and Social Structure* (1968). Scholars who held this perspective believed that correct identification of the functions assigned to various parts of the social system would facilitate performance of these functions. During the years after the Second World War, there were high hopes that poverty, racial discrimination, and other social problems could and would be eliminated. A society in which all could share in the good life was believed to be just around the corner.

In practice, however, social systems are never in a perfect state of equilibrium. Functionalists tend to view a society as a relatively homogeneous whole, characterized by shared values and beliefs. It is obvious, however, that a large, complex society, such as Canada, contains groups whose interests and values are opposed. Thus, equal-opportunity legislation is functional for such groups as women or native peoples, who have hitherto been denied access to certain prestigious positions. On the other hand, such legislation can be seen as dysfunctional for those (in this case, white males) who must now compete with more contestants for desirable jobs.

Many other criticisms have been levied against functionalism, among them that the kind of harmonious society it posits simply does not exist any longer, if it ever did. A related charge is that functionalism places insufficient emphasis on the importance of power differentials and on their consequences for society, for groups and for individuals. The functionalist perspective has, nevertheless, made important contributions to sociological analysis. First, it has sensitized investigators to those shared values and assumptions often taken so much for granted that they remain implicit rather than explicit in the culture. This "hidden consensus" can be recognized most readily through contact with members of another culture who do not share one's values and assumptions. Thus, the discovery that some societies prize plump women reveals that the ideal of *Vogue* slimness is not a universal one. Second, researchers with a functionalist perspective have undertaken a great deal of research into many areas of social life. William Goode, for instance, did cross-cultural studies of the relationships between industrialization and the ways in which families are structured and operate. (See Goode's *World Revolution and Family Patterns*, 1970).

Although functionalism is no longer the overriding perspective on North American sociology, it continues to exert a strong influence on the work of many present-day sociologists.

THE CONFLICT PERSPECTIVE

Functionalists concentrate on the mechanisms by which society coheres. The **conflict perspective** is rooted in the writings of Marx, though not all conflict theorists accept all of Marx's arguments. Conflict theorists focus on areas of dissent and strife. They look at opposed interest groups and at their attempts to gain (or maintain) power in order to further their own advantage at the expense of other groups. Take, for example, the debate over the elimination of grade 13 in Ontario. Proponents of both positions couched their arguments in terms of what would be most beneficial to the education of students. Conflict theorists point out, however, that beneath this debate smouldered a conflict between secondary-school teachers, eager to keep students in their schools as long as possible to safeguard existing teaching jobs, and community colleges and universities, intent on maximizing their share of the educational tax dollar.

For a society or a group to persist, it clearly needs some consensus, but social scientists disagree as to how this consensus is attained and maintained. Where a functionalist points to shared values, the conflict theorist focuses on the ability of dominant groups to enforce their viewpoint by dint of force and "fraud." Immigrant workers unfamiliar with Canadian laws may, for example, be told by anti-union employers that union membership is illegal or that union dues would take a large bite from the workers' earnings; they may also be threatened, subtly or blatantly, with the spectre of plant closure or with dismissal.

The Hutterites provide a good example of social phenomena that are perceived quite differently when studied by researchers with either a functionalist or a conflict perspective.[8] The functionalists see a group united by shared values and sentiments, with each practice of the group making a contribution to that harmony. On the other hand, conflict theorists note that the group's stability is achieved in large part by its custom of restricting access to power to a minority — mature men. Hence, those who might want to institute changes are deprived of the means of doing so. Thus, some Hutterite women have expressed to researchers the desire to bear fewer children, but lacking money to obtain birth-control devices, they have been powerless to do so.

Among the prominent modern conflict theorists are Ralf Dahrendorf (1929–), C. Wright Mills (1916–62), and John Porter (1921–79), Canada's best-known sociologist. In his *Class and Class Conflict in Industrial Society* (1959), Dahrendorf posits that change, conflict, and coercion are persistent features of every society. In *The Power Elite* (1956), Mills argued that, in the United States, power is wielded by a relatively small group that controls the industrial, military, and government apparatus, and that this group uses power to further its own ends rather than seeking to benefit society at large. Looking at Canada in *The Vertical Mosaic* (1965), Porter traced the many links that interconnect the country's various elites, such as those that exert major influence in large industrial corporations, universities, and the civil service.[9]

It is Porter's claim that an effect of government policies that promote multiculturalism has been to keep the various immigrant groups busy in their own small ponds, while allowing the core Anglo-Saxon group to remain dominant in the central institutions of Canadian society. According to this argument, if one's energy and interests are concentrated on one's own ethnic community, there is little likelihood of gaining access to decision-making positions in the larger society. (We will examine this argument more closely in Chapter 7 on minority groups.)

By definition, conflict theorists are interested in areas of conflict and in the ways in which groups jostle for power so as to maintain or gain an advantage. In some circumstances, such as under slavery or in concentration camps, the power of the dominant group is virtually absolute. In North American society, groups and individuals can enter the push and shove of the political arena more freely, though not always effectively. Human-rights legislation, which includes fair-employment laws, and the establishment of an ombudsman's office in many Canadian jurisdictions, are examples of attempts to equalize power between large collectivities and individuals or subordinated groups.

Power and its deployment are central to a conflict view, just as emphasis on common values informs the functionalist perspective. Theoretical orientation affects whether a bottle is seen as half full or half empty. We have noted in connection with the Hutterites that functionalists may point to an observed consensus, while the researcher attuned to conflict asks at what cost the consensus is brought about. As tools for making sense of social life, both approaches have obvious utility.

ANTI-POVERTY GROUP OPPOSES GAMES

By Sean Fine

The backers of Toronto's effort to play host to the 1996 Summer Olympic Games are upset about plans by a coalition of anti-poverty groups to mount an international protest over the city's bid.

The Bread Not Circuses Coalition announced yesterday it will contact the International Olympic Committee in Lausanne, Switzerland, to express concerns about Toronto's bid to get the 1996 Summer Olympic Games.

"We think quite frankly this will give us a lever to have public acknowledgement of our concerns," Michael Shapcott, a spokesman for the coalition, which includes groups representing women, tenants and anti-poverty workers, told a news conference yesterday.

The group said it is concerned about who will share in the public benefits of the Games, and about the openness of the planning process. It is seeking public funds "in the tens of thousands of dollars" to study the social impact of holding the Olympics.

"We're not trying to blackmail anybody," Shapcott said. "The first priority should be the real needs of Toronto. We shouldn't be building any more palaces until citizens are well-fed and well-housed."

His group's announcement sparked an immediate response from Paul Henderson, chief organizer of Toronto's Olympic bid, who telephoned Shapcott to ask that the group not contact the IOC.

He also pledged to meet coalition members to discuss their concerns.

The coalition, which is endorsed by Metro Toronto councillors Jack Layton and Roger Hollander, also plans to contact the International Bureau of Expositions in Paris to express concerns about Toronto's bid to hold the World's Fair in 2000.

The group was formed three months ago to oppose what it called a Toronto trend to "high-priced extravaganzas," financed at least in part out of the public purse. The big projects include the city's new $400-million-plus domed stadium, which received $60-million from the Metro and Ontario governments, and a proposed opera-ballet house, which is seeking $20-million from Metro Council, and several times that amount from senior governments.

The City of Toronto has placed great importance on unanimous support for its Olympic bid, with one councillor decrying an atmosphere of intimidation to gain unanimity.

Shapcott said singleness of purpose is a key to winning over the international groups that choose the host cities. "We know what they look for: some sort of cohesive community spirit. If they hear that there are groups that have major concerns, we think it will have an impact on the whole process."

Mayor Art Eggleton called the coalition wrongheaded, but said he does not think the protest will affect the IOC's decision.

"I don't think they expect everybody's going to be supportive," he said in an interview.

He said the Olympics will generate spinoff benfits in housing, in transit facilities and in a cleanup of beaches, among other things.

Henderson, head of the Toronto

Ontario Olympic Council, which is spearheading the city's effort to play host to the games, said of the group's protest: "Does it hurt? I would put it the other way. It helps if you've got citizen support."

SYMBOLIC INTERACTIONISM

While functionalists and conflict theorists address themselves to large-scale relationships—for example, those between the values of a society and institutions such as the family or education—symbolic interactionists focus on how individual actors interpret given situations. This is a micro-sociological approach. The assumption is that these interpretations are the basis for subsequent action. In other words, **symbolic interactionism** is concerned with how individuals subjectively react to objective situations. (Note symbolic interactionism's intellectual debt to Max Weber, who also concerned himself with the meanings people attach to events in social life.) The same situation need not evoke the same response in two people or in the same person in different circumstances. For example, a girl may react with pleasure, amusement, fear, or anger to a remark about her appearance, depending on her interpretation of the words.

Symbolic interactionists attribute major importance to **symbols**, which can be defined as signs that have shared meaning to members of a group. Behaviour is then structured in terms of what a particular symbol means. The police officer's uniform acts as a symbol, and people react to the uniform rather than to the person wearing it. For some, the symbol may signify danger, for others safety. Words are symbols that collectively form the most important human symbolic code, language.

In focusing on how people behave in social units, such as families or offices, and in how a unit is shaped by the actions and interactions of its members, symbolic interactionists use the perspectives of both sociology and psychology. They are, therefore, often described as adopting a social-psychological viewpoint.

The theory of symbolic interactionism was first developed by Americans George Herbert Mead (1863–1931) and Charles Horton Cooley (1864–1933). They were intent on showing that human beings differ in kind from other animals because they are able to objectify themselves—that is, each can imagine the effect of his or her behaviour on others and the possible reactions of those others. We will encounter the ideas of these scholars in Chapters 2 and 3 on culture and socialization.

Many present-day sociologists adhere to this perspective, and a large body of research is informed by it. Howard Becker and Erving Goffman, among others, are prominent followers; like many of their colleagues, they study familiar situations and discover they are more complex than they appear. For example, Becker and Geer looked at the processes by which medical students are transformed into full-fledged physicians. Their study *Boys in White* (1961) provides fascinating illustrations of the changes that occur in the ways these students perceive themselves and the ways they are perceived by others, such as instructors and patients. Goffman joined the staff of a state mental hospital while doing his research for *Asylums* (1962), in which he focused primarily on the situation of the inmate who must adapt himself to a role dramatically different from those he played on the outside. Goffman observed the ways in which staff and patients interacted among themselves and with each other. A patient who engaged in behaviour which might have been defined outside the institution as showing initiative or being innovative was likely to be labelled as difficult to manage.

The functionalist and conflict perspectives outline the basic contours of social life; the symbolic interactionist approach shades in the details. Indeed, a criticism of symbolic interactionism is that it is so preoccupied with the trees that it loses sight of the forest. For example, Zeitlin (1975) argued that Goffman focuses on the minutiae of daily life without taking sufficient account of the larger context in which they occur. In other words, to really understand why state mental hospitals operate as they do, observers must look at the society of which these hospitals are a part, and at how that society defines mental illness. For an informative volume on symbolic interactionism, including a chapter on its methodology, see Blumer (1987).

THE ADVANTAGE OF MULTIPLE PERSPECTIVES

By adopting one perspective rather than another, a sociologist illuminates particular aspects of social existence, leaving other aspects in darkness. Therefore, it is useful to take advantage of different viewpoints in order to make sense of the world. People need to know how institutions and the relationships among them are moulded by processes of co-operation and conflict, but it is also important to discover the interpretations individuals attach to situations and the ways in which such interpretations influence behaviour.

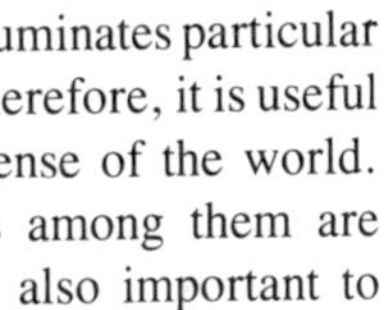

A SCIENTIFIC APPROACH: THE CONDUCT OF SOCIOLOGICAL RESEARCH

The issues that occupy sociologists are in essence similar to those that have puzzled students of society since antiquity. What sociology has sought to add to the study of society is a scientific approach. The root of the word science is *scio*, "I know." Science is a general agreement on one way of looking at the world. It offers a systematic description and explanation of natural phenomena, seeking to map out what the world is like.

Observation and conceptualization (mental pictures) are indispensable to science, and there should be constant traffic between the two. Unless ideas are rooted in factual observations, the thinker is working in the realm of speculation. However, observations must be ordered and interpreted with the use of reason. Without it, they become a meaningless tangle.

Science is a co-operative enterprise in three senses:

- It builds on work already done. Sociologists take into account previous formulations, whether they wish to support, modify, or refute them. In physics, Newton disclaimed total credit for his breakthrough in formulating the law of gravity, pointing to the foundations laid by Copernicus, Keppler, Galileo, and others.
- Much of scientific research is done most effectively by teamwork in which the interplay of minds and perspectives can be brought to bear on a problem. The Manhattan project, which led to the development of the atomic bomb, is a good example from the physical sciences. The extensive research carried out on armed forces personnel during the Second World War exemplifies a collaborative effort in the social sciences (Stouffer *et al.*, 1950).
- Once research is published, it becomes public property and invites challenge or confirmation.

The two main tools that scientists use are: (1) observation of what is occurring in the world, and (2) analysis, which makes it possible to discern patterns in observations. Doing research involves using structured, systematic observation. For example, a study of primary education might include analysing what is taught (which may not be what the curriculum list claims) and the methods by which the subject matter is communicated to students.

Sometimes sociologists take to the streets. Here, Stewart Crysdale is at work in east side Toronto.

In the course of analysis, researchers seek to weld observable data into a meaningful pattern. In fact, analysis precedes as well as follows observation. When a scientist embarks on a research project, he or she has a conceptual framework, an idea of what is sought. It has been observed, for instance, that until junior high school, girls, on the average, do better academically than boys. After puberty, the pattern is reversed. This phenomenon has generally been explained in terms of girls becoming more interested in social graces and appearance than in academic effort. Today a team of sociologists might speculate that the raising of women's consciousness has changed the pattern. In science, such a speculation is referred to as an **hypothesis**, "a tentative statement asserting a relationship between certain facts" (Theodorson and Theodorson 1969, 161). The statement is intended to be tested empirically and either verified or rejected.

In our example, the hypothesis could be tested by selecting a number of high schools across Canada, examining the grades of boys and girls over the last ten years and noting variations in the pattern. The researchers would have to be very careful about reaching conclusions because, after all, they are not looking at the same individuals. If they consistently found changed patterns, they could be somewhat confident that a change had occurred, though they would have to examine possible explanations other than girls' raised consciousness. On the other hand, they might find changes in the west but not in Ontario and Quebec. They would then need to search for reasons for these regional differences and test their explanations systematically.

Disconfirmation of a hypothesis—that is, the finding that a hypothesized relationship does *not* exist—adds to knowledge just as support would. Disconfirmation is not "failure" in the conventional sense of the word; indeed, it provides impetus to rethink the problem, and thus can be extremely productive. Goldenberg's *Thinking Sociologically* (1987) is a useful and clear introduction to pursuing sociology.

THE COMPLEXITY OF SOCIOLOGY AS SCIENCE

Science aims at precision and therefore tends to become increasingly exact and quantitative. Because terms must be used carefully and consistently, each scientific discipline develops a specialized vocabulary, a jargon, to ensure that terms mean the same thing to everyone working in the field. In the emergency room of a hospital, an ambulance attendant might report, "Upon arrival, patient was semi-comatose. BP 60 over 100. Pulse weak and thready. Complaining of pain in chest and right arm. En route, he arrested, and CPR was initiated." All the medical personnel present know exactly what conditions and procedures, in what order, are subsumed in this shorthand report.

Sociology, like all disciplines that are concerned with human behaviour, encounters inherent obstacles to becoming scientific, in the sense of reaching the degree of quantification and precision that physics or mathematics can achieve; this occurs because people are complex and never wholly predictable. You have probably experienced instances in which people you thought you knew extremely well acted "out of character," in a manner quite different from their usual behaviour. In fact, you yourself may respond to an emergency situation in ways you would not have anticipated. In Chapters 2 and 3 on culture and socialization, we will discuss some of the processes that make individuals similar and predictable.

Sociologists can certainly be scientific in the sense of carefully testing observations and seeking to derive general patterns from these data, but the physiological, psychological, and social factors that impinge on human action are so numerous and so complex that there are always exceptions to such patterns.

THE QUESTION OF VALUES

A claim that is frequently made for science is that it is "value-free." Scientists are assumed to be objective, to tell it as it is, without allowing personal values and biases to enter their research. As we noted in our discussion of Max Weber's work, this is both true and not true. Values enter into the selection of what is studied and into the construction of the conceptual framework used to decide what aspects of a problem are relevant. Once the information has been gathered, the scientist must present it impartially, even if it contradicts his or her original assumptions. For example, Lundy (1977) embarked on a study of executive secretaries assuming that a majority of these women yearned for the pay, prestige, and power enjoyed by their bosses. In fact, she found that only a small minority aspired to executive positions.

THE FEMINIST CHALLENGE

Selecting a problem for study means that it is deemed *worthy of study*. Until the recent emergence of feminist scholarship, women's issues were at worst ignored, and at best treated as peripheral. See, for example, Cohen's challenge (1988) to the traditional views of Canadian economic development in the 19th century. However, feminist scholars are not only concerned with selection, but also with method. They argue that the individuals being studied must be brought into the research process, indeed that their experiences should provide the starting point of enquiry. Connell *et al.* write:

> *[A different model of research] should empower the people who are normally just the objects of research, to develop their capacity to research their own situations and evolve their own solutions. It should embody a relationship where expertise is a resource available to all rather than a form of power for a few (1982, 216).*

For a further discussion of what feminist scholarship is attempting to do, see Kirby and McKenna (1989) and Smith (1987).

FORMULATING A RESEARCH PROBLEM

The goal of sociological research is to discover how a group, such as a society, a corporation, or a family, is structured and operates. To put this more formally, research is aimed at increasing knowledge about the structure and functioning of social groups and about relationships among and within groups. Fundamental to investigation is the perception of a problem, of a state of affairs that appears anomalous, "out of sync." In other words, the starting point in a search for answers may be a sense of dissonance.

For example, it has been found that in Toronto, children from lower-class homes are streamed into vocational classes or special-education classes for slow learners far more frequently than those from affluent homes (Wright 1970). In the same vein, Porter (1965; 1973) and others (Harp 1980) have noted that a disproportionate percentage of students in law, medical, and other professional schools come from families in high-income groups. As sociologists, we might want to know reasons for this state of affairs, which runs counter to Canadian society's professed commitment to equality of opportunity.

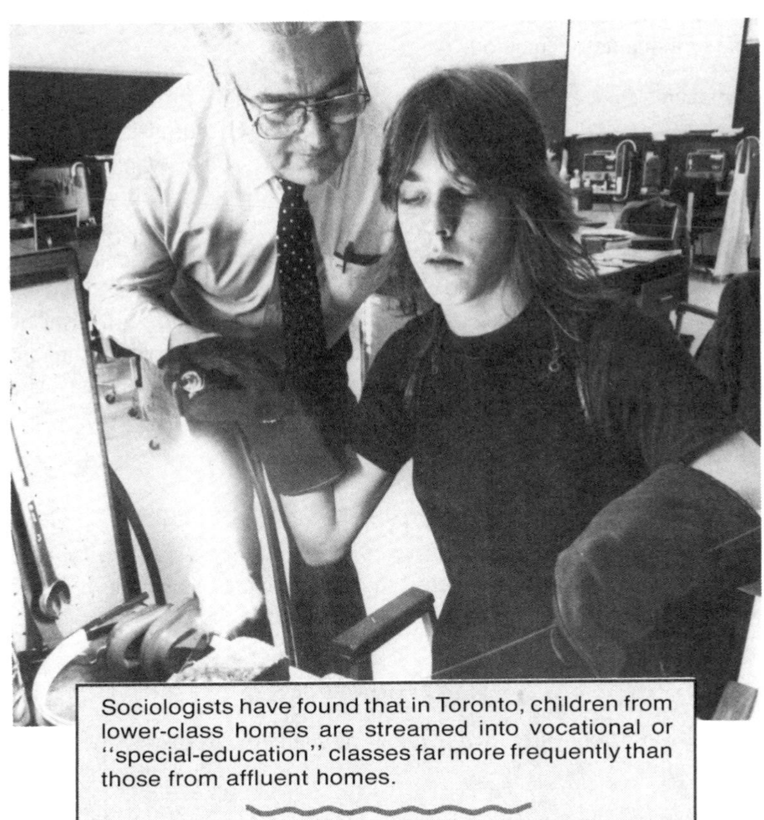

Sociologists have found that in Toronto, children from lower-class homes are streamed into vocational or "special-education" classes far more frequently than those from affluent homes.

To start with, we would look at research that has been done on the relationship between socioeconomic class and formal education. (Remember, science is cumulative.) Among other things, we would want to know what facets of this relationship have been explored by previous researchers and whether the Canadian cases are isolated instances or fall into a more general pattern. What we would find is that it is indeed a frequently occurring pattern that poor children predominate in vocational classes and that affluent students are overrepresented in professional schools.[10]

Various aspects of the relationship between socioeconomic class and educational attainment could now be explored. Depending on the direction we decided to take, we could use **qualitative methods** or **quantitative methods** or a combination. Qualitative methods involve the collection of data through interviews, observation, or analysis of written material. We might speculate that most teachers are middle class and hence find it difficult to relate to lower-class children; they may thus be inclined to view such children as slow learners.[11] To test this assumption, we might conduct in-depth interviews with the teachers and principals of public schools in Toronto that have special-education and vocational classes, in an attempt to find out what criteria are used to assign children to them. In-depth interviews are an example of a qualitative method.

In using quantitative methods, data are obtained in numerical form through enumeration or measurement (as in surveys, for example). If, for instance, we decided to see if the percentage of affluent students in professional schools has changed over time, we would look for the requisite information—say, for 1980 and 1990—in university and other statistical records. Using computers, we could manipulate the data to make several internal comparisons, as between law and medical students, males and females in both schools, and males and females in law schools and in medical schools. We would then try to explain our findings in terms of what we know about inequality in Canada generally and about the relationship between socioeconomic class and formal education specifically. Computer analysis of statistical information is an example of a quantitative method.

RESEARCH METHODS

Qualitative and quantitative methods are the basic tools of sociological research. Here is a brief overview. (For an easily understandable discussion of research in the social sciences see Agnew and Pyke, 1987).

QUALITATIVE METHODS

Some of the most frequently used methods of qualitative research in sociology are described here.

- *Case study* involves an intensive and comprehensive investigation of a single unit, such as a community, a business firm, a prison, or a hospital.[12] Rosabeth Moss Kanter's study of INDSCO, a large, multinational company, focused on the relative positions of men and women, and on the effects of power and powerlessness on managerial behaviour (1977). While chaplain at the Guelph Reformatory, W.E. Mann (1967) examined in rich detail the inmate culture, which stood in stark opposition to the official prison culture. He found that for the prisoners, most of them young and many of them first offenders, the reformatory in fact functioned as a school for crime.

Case studies provide detailed descriptive information and generate questions that cannot be answered by the study itself. They invite study of other cases that are seemingly similar to or clearly different from one another in order to help identify, for example, what characteristics are likely to be present in all institutions in which people are housed involuntarily and those characteristics that are idiosyncratic to reformatories.

- *In-depth interviews* give a researcher the opportunity to talk at length with people whose behaviour they wish to study. This approach can be both intensive and extensive (that is, respondents may be interviewed more than once as well as in more than one setting, such as at home and at the office). In-depth interviews can illuminate areas about which little is known and those areas that cannot be effectively explored through standardized questionnaires. To this end, Lillian Rubin talked at length to working-class women, mostly in their own homes. In her book *Worlds of Pain* (1976), she conveyed how these women live, how they do or do not cope with the frequent crises in their lives, and how they themselves feel about their existence. Peter C. Newman has expanded our knowledge about the other end of the socioeconomic spectrum, those who are part of *The Canadian Establishment* (1975). Newman is an investigative journalist/social historian who learned much about his subjects through in-depth interviewing.

- *Participant observation* permits the researcher to become a part of the group being explored; he or she literally participates in its activities while doing the observing. Prolonged interaction with a group can provide a rounded picture of what it is "really" like. Total immersion allows the researcher to share as closely as possible what the subjects are experiencing. There is the danger, however, that the researcher will become so involved with the group members that objectivity will be impaired.

  William Foote Whyte's study of *Street Corner Society* (1943) bears testimony that it is possible for the researcher to be an acute observer without sacrificing objectivity. While a graduate student at Harvard in the late 1930s, Whyte joined in the activities of a group of young men in an Italian slum in the north end of Boston. He built a rich kaleidoscope of the ambitions, preoccupations, and daily lives of the "corner boys" and the ways in which they differed from those of the "college boys," the inhabitants of the slum who aspired to higher education as a way out.

- *Content analysis* involves the systematic examination of a chosen medium (frequently written materials) to discern perceptions of and attitudes toward certain groups or policies. Such analysis can be used for historical materials, making it possible to draw comparisons between different periods. Thus, in *The Feminine Mystique* (1963), Betty Freidan documented images of women in magazine stories and articles over two decades. She found that during the Second World War, when women were needed in the labour force, they were depicted as competent, able to cope with pressure and with a variety of demands. After the war, when the drive was to get women back into the home to free jobs for returning veterans, stories showed women as dependent, unsure of themselves, and confused, except when they discovered their true roles as wives and mothers. Content analysis can also be used quantitatively. For instance, in analyses of primary school readers, researchers recorded the number of references to male and to female characters. (One can guess which group was mentioned more often.)

Important facets of qualitative research are: (1) description: for example, in what ways do "corner boys" and "college boys" differ from each other? (2) formulation of hypotheses that posit possible relationships between observed facts, relationships that may subsequently be explored by quantitative methods; and (3) making inferences about causal processes: for example, why the image of women in popular magazines reverted to that of homemaker after the Second World War.

Like any other approach, qualitative research has advantages and drawbacks. An important advantage is its fleshing out of data, giving an idea of what life is like for the people being studied. Researchers are able to probe and establish whether the questions being asked address the problems under investigation. In charting out relatively unexplored areas, qualitative research can also provide a basis for larger-scale quantitative studies.

On the negative side, qualitative research runs the danger of interviewer bias; what is observed and recorded represents the researcher's interpretation, both of what is worth recording, and of what it means. Moreover, because the numbers that can be studied by qualitative methods are necessarily small and the cases to be studied must be selected with care, researchers must be cautious in generalizing the findings to ostensibly similar cases.[13]

QUANTITATIVE METHODS

Quantitative research in sociology can vary widely in detail. Two general types are:

- *Experimental design*, which generally entails a systematic comparison of two groups before and after a stimulus has been applied. The immediate goal is to assess the effect of such a stimulus. Suppose we want to test the influence of media propaganda on attitudes toward the "boat people," recent Vietnamese immigrants. We could compose a questionnaire on relevant attitudes and ask a class of students to complete it. Then we would divide the class into two parts, taking care to match the halves as closely as possible for such characteristics as gender, age, and ethnicity. We would apply no further treatment to one half, the control group. The other half, the experimental group, would be shown a movie portraying boat people in a favourable light, describing their plight in Vietnam and showing the ingeniousness and courage that had been necessary for them to get to Canada. We would then ask both groups to complete the same questionnaire they had previously filled out. Our results might be something like those shown in Exhibit 1.2. The control group, as we expected, shows no change. But in the experimental group, we find that 20 students — 10 percent of the population tested — had changed their views.[14] Experiments are generally conducted under artificial (laboratory) conditions; the number of subjects is relatively small, and not representative of the population. Therefore, one must be very careful about making generalizations.

EXHIBIT 1.2

ATTITUDES TOWARD BOAT PEOPLE: AN EXAMPLE OF FINDINGS FROM AN EXPERIMENT

	Favourable	Unfavourable
Control group		
Before	40% (80)	60% (120)
After	40% (80)	60% (120)
Experimental group		
Before	40% (80)	60% (120)
After	50% (100)	50% (100)

NOTE: The figures in parentheses refer to the number of respondents. When percentages are shown in a well-designed table, the number in each category is also shown. An alternative method, often used when the number of cases is the same for an entire column or the whole table, is to write $N = 200$ (the number on which the percentages are based).

- *Survey analysis*, which involves the collection of responses from large numbers of subjects and the statistical manipulation of the information obtained. The Canadian census is an example of survey analysis that provides a large data bank on which sociologists draw for further research. Richmond and Kalbach (1980) used data from the decennial (ten-year) censuses from 1921 to 1971 to show how various ethnic groups and their decendants have fared in Canada. For instance, they were able to compare the educational attainments of members of the same ethnic group at different points in time, of several ethnic groups at the same points in time, and of several ethnic groups at different periods and thus to show how specific ethnic groups fared relative to each other.

The recent, dramatic advances in computer technology have made it possible to handle vast amounts of quantitative data and to extract from them complex information that would have previously been inaccessible. It is, therefore, hardly surprising that sociologists are increasingly using quantitative methods in an attempt to become more scientific and more precise (Cole 1980). Even so, it is rare that the information collected in addressing a particular question is complete; statistics make it possible to carry out research despite this incompleteness.

> *In most problems concerning the administration of business, governmental, or personal affairs, or in the search for scientific generalizations, complete information cannot be obtained; hence incomplete information must be used. Statistics provide rational principles and techniques that tell when and how judgments can be made on the basis of this partial information, and what partial information is most worth seeking. In short, statistics has come to be regarded . . . as a method of making wise decisions in the face of uncertainty (Wallis and Roberts 1962, 13).*

Often, questions that are easily answerable — that is, amenable to quantitative analysis — are trivial in their import. The onus to ask significant questions rests with the researcher.

Ultimately, the kind of method sociologists choose depends on the topic of enquiry and on the resources of labour, money, and time available. The ideal is to have the breadth provided by quantitative analysis *and* the insights qualitative investigation affords.

SCIENTIFIC SIDE OF OPINION POLLS DOESN'T STAND UP

By Conrad Winn

Some years ago, a young man uncertain about his future consulted a scientist he admired greatly. "Become a public-opinion pollster," advised Albert Einstein. "Then you will never be unemployed. We know, after all, that people are ruled by being told tall stories — so the rulers must constantly test and see what they can get away with."

Polling is a growth industry today as Einstein foresaw. Part of its strength is its scientific aspect. People are impressed that polling organizations interview hundreds of people and analyze the results quantitatively and scientifically.

The truth is that polling falls short of an "exact science." Just about every facet of polling has a subjective aspect, even its main feature—sampling.

The scientific basis of polling is that a randomly selected sample of several hundred respondents can mirror the country as a whole. The larger the sample, the better the mirror. Using laws from statistics, a pollster may assert that his poll is "accurate 19 times in 20 within a margin of error of four percentage points." With a statement of this kind, the pollster does not actually claim that his particular poll is valid. He can never know for sure. He is only saying that, if repeated polls such as his own were conducted, only one in 20 would produce results that are wrong by more than four percentage points.

Not random samples

The kind of scientific reasoning used by pollsters might make sense if their polling samples were truly random, but they are not. Many potential interviewees are rarely home and cannot be reached. Others do not speak the language or are too busy, tired, suspicious, ill or inebriated to co-operate.

Another potential source of bias is the format of the interview. Some experimental evidence shows that face-to-face interviews elicit less hostile and less racist feeling than more anonymous formats.

The order of questions in a questionnaire may affect results. Let's imagine for a moment two polls on free trade with the United States. Both polls conclude by asking respondents whether they favor the free trade pact, but each begins with a completely different set of questions.

Poll A starts by asking respondents if they believe Canadians have been sufficiently consulted on the issue, if Americans can be trusted, if Prime Minister Brian Mulroney is sincere and if the respondent has ever had personal economic concerns.

Poll B begins on a more positive note, asking respondents whether international trade can contribute to international understanding, whether the United States is Canada's most important friend, whether the respondent is pleased with Canada's high rate of economic growth and pleased with the success of major Canadian companies in the U.S. economy.

Poll B would probably elicit more favorable attitudes toward free trade because it arouses confident and optimistic feelings while Poll A provokes anxiety and mistrust.

When respondents do not possess strong convictions, they are susceptible to cues in the wording of the question. Imagine three polls on the issue of Sunday closing.

Pollster X says, "There has been a lot of concern lately about whether it is fair that all stores are treated alike, that some stores are allowed to be open on Sunday while others are not. Do you think this situation is completely fair, somewhat fair, somewhat unfair or completely unfair?"

Pollster Y says, "Some corporations want the law changed to let them operate their large stores on Sundays. However, some people, including many employees, say that they really need one regular day to be with their family or friends or just relax after a week at work. In your opinion, should the government (a) change the law right away, as some corporations want, (b) consider changing the law at a later date, (c) consult people more before taking any action, or (d) leave the current law as it is?''

Pollster Z says, ''Some people want the government to allow all stores to be open on Sunday because this would be good for the economy. Other people say that our present law has been good for society, letting people have time away from work to spend with friends and family or time to relax. Still other people say that the government needs to find a compromise acceptable to reasonable people on both sides of the issue. In your opinion, should the government (a) change the law today, (b) leave the present law completely alone, or (c) try to find a compromise that would be acceptable to both sides?''

Pollster X would probably find that a majority does not believe the current law is completely fair. Pollster Y would probably find that a majority does not want an immediate change. Pollster Z would probably find a majority supporting an attempt to find a compromise.

Pollsters can affect history by the way they word questions. During the Watergate period, the big U.S. pollsters repeatedly asked respondents if they wanted Richard Nixon ''impeached and removed from office.'' This was akin to asking people if they wanted an accused to be tried as well as hanged. For almost two years, pollsters reported that most Americans opposed Mr. Nixon's being ''impeached and removed from office,'' and so Congress took little action. In fact, most Americans had wanted the President impeached or tried all along, but they wanted him forced from the presidency only if he were actually found guilty.

Surveys brought action

Congressmen started to take action once better surveys conducted by less well-known pollsters came to their attention. Only 30 per cent wanted Mr. Nixon impeached and removed from office. Relatively unknown Democratic pollster Pat Caddell showed that this figure doubled when respondents were asked if the President should be tried and, if found guilty, removed from office. Then major pollster Louis Harris was found to have clandestine links with the Nixon White House, and he was accused of having rigged his impeachment question.

THE USES OF SOCIOLOGY

Having had some glimpses of the issues that engage the attention of sociologists and of the tools that enable them to pursue their investigations, you may well pose a number of questions. Of what use is the sociological enterprise to society?

Go back to the vignettes at the beginning of this chapter. Can you think of practical applications that might result from answering the sociological questions we have posed? In the case of the nursing home, for example, the question might lead to greater awareness that clients' needs are not accorded priority.

As social scientists, sociologists contribute to knowledge about the myriad variations of human interaction. They do not merely record observations of interactions but seek to order their findings into more general patterns, which can be very useful. For example, when they recognize and call attention to the similarities of apparently disparate cases of minority-group members who find obstacles to career advancement, action to combat the discrimination becomes practicable. Legislation, such as that setting out fair employment standards, may be the result.

Why should students who do not plan to become sociologists bother to study sociology? Even at this stage, your vocational future may be uppermost in your mind. A background in sociology is useful for many types of occupations, such as nursing, teaching, law, social work, architecture and urban planning, business administration, and careers in government service.

The diversity and calibre of jobs of recent sociology graduates is illustrated in Exhibit 1.3.

Most people spend most of their time interacting in groups — in the family, in school, in the workplace, in leisure activities. Studying sociology can sensitize you to dimensions of interaction of which you have been unaware and to others that you could not explain. Perhaps you have watched a male student enter a hitherto all-female group of nursing students and have noticed that the group seemed to become formal and constrained. Before knowing something about sociology, you might have simply regretted the change in atmosphere or attributed it to the personality of the male student, who tended to be somewhat loud and opinionated. In the light of your new knowledge, however, you might consider a number of possible explanations and attempt to test them informally. One speculation is that your new colleague felt insecure as the only male and was trying to compensate by overassertiveness. If you learned that his high school classmates had always found him quiet and unassuming, this explanation, focusing on his group position rather than on his personal characteristics, would gain support. Alternatively, you might speculate that the female nursing students no longer felt free to "let their hair down" now that a new and different element had entered the group.

EXHIBIT 1.3

TABLE 2: OCCUPATIONS OF 1982 SOCIOLOGY GRADUATES IN 1984
(IN PERCENT)

Occupation	Men	Women	Total
Managerial & Administrative	37	18	23
Teaching	18	23	22
Social Science	27	12	16
Health	0	6	4
Other Highly Qualified Jobs	0	4	3
Total Highly Qualified Jobs	82	63	68
Clerical	6	23	18
Sales	8	4	5
Service	3	6	6
Other non-Highly Qualified Jobs	1	4	3
Total non-Highly Qualified Jobs	18	37	32
Column Totals	100%	100%	100%
Number of People	568	1,552	2,120

Source: Canadian Sociology and Anthropology Association, University of Victoria, Department of Victoria, 1988. Opportunities in Sociology.

Another reason for studying sociology is that it sharpens your analytic skills in recognizing ways in which rules, regulations, and legislation impinge differently on groups and individuals in different economic positions. Consider, for instance, a provincial sales tax. The additional eight percent, say, on the purchase of a refrigerator would take a much larger bite out of an income of $15,000 than out of an income of $80,000. In other words, the costs of a flat rate tax are not equally distributed.

Marx aptly noted that human beings make their own history, but not under conditions of their own choosing. The sociological window directs attention to the concrete situations within which individuals and groups must act. The discharged prisoner may be full of good intentions to reform, but if he has few marketable skills and returns to an environment in which criminal activity is customary, the intentions may be thwarted. On the other hand, examples of individuals who have stuck to their resolutions in the light of formidable obstacles show that ultimately each person is responsible for his or her own actions. Groups, too, are constrained by their environment. Think of blacks in the American South. Before the Civil Rights legislation of the 1960s, assertiveness was dangerous; it might result in beatings, or worse. Yet, some braved the risks and strove for change.

To the extent that sociology sharpens people's awareness of the complex processes involved in social intercourse, it allows them to deal with situations more effectively. Inasmuch as it provides insight into why people act as they do, sociology may even help human beings to become more tolerant and compassionate.

SUMMARY

In this chapter, we have mapped some of the ways in which sociology sheds new light on old territory. The territory is large and variegated. It includes society as an entity and the many groups that make up this entity. Sociology calls attention to the continuous interplay between individuals and the social context in which they live out their lives.

The roots of modern sociology lie in the Europe that was shattered by a series of political revolutions and profoundly altered by industrialization and massive migration in the late 18th and 19th centuries. Comte, Marx, Durkheim, and Weber, each in his own way, sought to explain the bases of social stability and the dynamics of change. The insights they brought to the analysis of society have provided an underpinning for subsequent sociological study. In some cases, modern enquiry has followed the paths laid out by the early sociologists. In other instances, sociologists have taken new approaches. In recent years, feminist scholars have challenged both the assumptions and the methodologies of "mainstream" sociological research.

Remember that Comte's goal was to apply to the study of society the tools science was developing in other areas. Central to a scientific way of doing things is a systematic alternation between observation and analysis. Although scientists cannot escape from their own skin—that is, they cannot ignore the values and beliefs that prevail in their own environment—they must strive to honour the canons of scientific investigation.

Sociology uses qualitative and quantitative methods of investigation. Each has advantages as well as drawbacks, with the choice of method depending on the subject matter being investigated. In turn, this enquiry is influenced by the interests and theoretical orientation of the researcher.

One of the most important uses of sociology is to lay bare the connection between the general and the particular. You can recognize, for example, the disadvantaged position of a minority group as one manifestation of inequality in society. If you are aware of the general phenomenon of status passage in a society,[15] you can recognize such occasions as a high school commencement and a black-band dance for graduating nurses as examples of such passages. A sociological perspective enables you to move back and forth between the general and the particular. Since, to a large extent, the everyday and the commonplace provide the grist for the sociological mill, this agility is especially useful for understanding social life.

ASSIGNMENTS

Do one or more of the following assignments, as instructed by your professor.

1 How does a sociological curiosity affect your reading of a literary work? Answer this question in terms of either *A Judgement in Stone* or *The Life of Galileo* (see the Suggested Readings).

2 Using information from the article on polls, discuss the weaknesses of polls, and the political effects they may have.

3 We began this chapter by posing sociological questions about a number of concrete, rather ordinary events. Raise a sociological question about a situation you have encountered in your everyday life. How is the question sociological, and which of the perspectives we have discussed might be useful in exploring it?

4 To get the flavour of doing research, administer the following brief questionnaire probing attitudes toward abortion. Choose six Catholics and six non-Catholics as your respondents; each group should be equally divided between men and women.

What are the differences in responses between the two groups? How do responses differ within each group — for example, between the males and the females? Discuss with your instructor what these responses show about the influence of religion and gender on attitudes.

QUESTIONNAIRE

1 Under what circumstances do you consider abortion permissible? (You can choose more than one alternative.)

a ______ Never
b ______ In cases of dire danger to the mother's life
c ______ When there is a likelihood of the baby being defective
d ______ When there is danger to the mother's mental health
e ______ In cases of economic necessity
f ______ Upon demand

2 Who do you think should make the decision regarding an abortion?

a ______ Hospital abortion committee
b ______ Physician
c ______ Physician and mother
d ______ Both parents
e ______ Mother alone

3 Where should abortions be performed?

a ______ Hospital
b ______ Aborton clinic (such as Dr. Henry Morgentaler's)

4 Should the current legislation (or proposed legislation) on abortion:

a ______ Remain unchanged?
b ______ Become more stringent?
c ______ Become more lenient?

5 Gender:

______ Male
______ Female

Religion:

______ Catholic
______ Non-Catholic

SUGGESTED READINGS

Peter Berger, *Invitation to Sociology* (New York: Doubleday, 1963). Berger outlines the way in which a sociological perspective can provide a clearer understanding of human interaction. One can readily relate to the examples he uses to illustrate his more general arguments. Particularly commendable are his lively style of writing and the absence of sociological jargon.

Bertolt Brecht, *The Life of Galileo* (London: Eyre Methuen, 1981; first published 1939. Can also be found in various collections of plays). Brecht's play illustrates the suppression of scientific truths to support existing belief systems. In the early 1600s, Galileo's observations that the earth revolved around the sun contradicted the Church's teaching that God had created the earth as the centre of the universe. Thus, these observations had to be declared to be in error; Galileo was forced to recant. Brecht, a German with passionate anti-Nazi convictions, wrote his play in the late 1930s, a time when truth was being twisted in the service of political ideology.

Phillip E. Hammond (ed.), *Sociologists at Work* (New York: Basic Books, 1964). Doing sociological research can be a rather untidy process. In these essays, sociologists give a lively account of their research projects and of the snags they encountered. The essays provide a reminder that sociology is both an art and a science, and that imagination, flexibility, persistence, and tolerance for frustration are part of the necessary equipment.

C.W. Mills, *The Sociological Imagination* (New York: Oxford University Press, 1959). In this pungent critique of the sociological enterprise, Mills argues that the sociological imagination should properly be exercised in that territory where "private troubles" and "public issues" meet. That is to say, the social scientist has a responsibility to explore the connections between the experience of individuals and the structural and historical conditions that underlie important social problems.

R. Rendell, *A Judgement in Stone* (London: Avon Books, 1978). The nightmare that an illiterate, stolid housekeeper experiences in the sunny, civilized world of the Coverdale family and the nightmare that she brings into their unruffled lives provide an intriguing example of the chasm that can separate social classes. In this crime novel, illiteracy is shown as a type of social nonconformity that isolates an individual in a way that leprosy might have done in an earlier time.

Anthony H. Richmond and **Warren E. Kalbach**, *Factors in the Adjustment of Immigrants and Their Descendants* (Ottawa: Statistics Canada, 1980). Richmond and Kalbach use census data to give detailed information on the adjustment of immigrants in Canada. The monograph provides comparisons among various immigrant groups on such factors as occupation, income, and percentage of offspring attending postsecondary educational institutions. As well, it traces the progress of several generations within each ethnic group. For example, readers can compare the average educational attainment of German immigrants with that of second- and third-generation individuals of German origin. The book shows what kinds of data can be gathered through survey analysis.

Matilda White Riley (ed.), *Sociological Lives* (Newbury Park: Sage Publications, 1988). Sociology can be useful both for looking outward and for looking inward. This is a small volume of autobiographical essays by several prominent American sociologists, including Hubert Blalock, Jr., Lewis Coser, Rosabeth Moss Kanter, and Alice Rossi. They tease out the interplay between the social contexts in which they have grown up, trained and worked, and their own personal and intellectual lives. You will find interesting illustrations of the ways in which, to use Mills' term, history and biography intersect.

NOTES

1 In 1986, the rate was 15.2 percent for those aged 15-24 and 8.0 percent for those 25 years of age and older (Statistics Canada 1988).

2 A social institution is a patterned way of accomplishing an important social goal or solving an important social problem; it emerges from the interaction of a particular group's beliefs, value system, and coping strategies. Institutions and some common examples thereof — the family, education, religion, law, and health care — are examined in Chapter 9.

3 This process of exploitation does not occur in industrial settings. See, for example, a discussion of Hagan's research in Chapter 9D on law.

4 It should be noted that this very brief overview of Marx's theory of social change does not do justice to the sophistication of the theory. We encourage interested students to refer to some of the Suggested Readings (at the end of the chapter).

5 As an aside, it is amusing to note that Durkheim's powerful intellect did not prevent him from sharing the belief that marriage was more beneficial for women than for men. On finding that recently widowed men were far more likely to kill themselves than recently widowed women, he reluctantly concluded that men might derive greater benefits and stability from marriage than was commonly believed.

6 For good examples of such studies, students can refer to *Street Corner Society: The Social Structure of an Italian Slum* (Whyte 1943) and *Tally's Corner: A Study of Negro Streetcorner Men* (Liebow 1967).

7 The phenomenon has been described over and over again by journalists, economists, and others in recent years. One of the earliest popular dramatizations (which presaged the American disaster in Vietnam) is *The Ugly American* (Lederer and Burdick 1958).

8 The Hutterites are a fundamentalist Protestant sect with a number of rural colonies in western Canada and some adjacent American states. Their traditional, communal lifestyle is deeply rooted in their religious belief, and many aspects of it have changed little in 450 years. The group is further described in Chapter 3.

9 It should be noted that when we identify sociologists as working from a similar perspective, this does not mean that there are no differences in their views.

10 If families with incomes of more than $30,000 form, say, 15 percent of the Canadian population but 30 percent of medical and law students come from such families, we say that such students are "overrepresented" in medical and law schools.

11 In Chapter 9B on education, we examine

this hypothesis and its implications for the assumption of equal opportunity that is common in modern North America.

12 In the course of doing a case study, a researcher may employ in-depth interviews and participant observation (described in this subsection), as well as quantitative data collection.

13 In addition, conducting qualitative research can present the researcher with serious ethical questions. *Tea Room Trade*, by Laud Humphries (1979), is a work that exemplifies some of the problems involved. This study is one of the few accounts to deal with "closet homosexuals," men who have not publicly claimed a homosexual identity. Humphries acted as a look-out to protect men who were furtively using public washrooms for quick, impersonal sex. He surreptitiously observed and recorded their behaviour and also noted the licence numbers of their cars, which allowed him to find out who they were. With this knowledge, he was able to set up interviews with them and thus to collect a great deal of background information about their religion, their families, their relations with their wives, and so on. The second edition of his book contains a very interesting discussion on the morality of doing this research.

14 There is evidence that favourable or unfavourable propaganda material affects attitudes. For example, in a social-psychological experiment testing the effects of violent TV programs on interpersonal aggression among preschool children, Steur, Applefield, and Smith (1971) found evidence of a relationship between the two variables. One group of children was exposed to cartoons of the Saturday-morning type that included violence; another group was shown the same cartoon with the violence removed. Later, children in the first group kicked, choked, and pushed their playmates more than the children in the second group did.

15 Moving from one life phase to another.

2

CULTURE

The girl has never seen her fiancé. She waits in the living room, picks at the spangles on her sweater, sends off her little brother (the karate champion) to investigate. She has bought a dozen roses for the visitor. It is Valentine's Day, 1987.

In the car, steering toward the rendezvous, the boy had been nervous. He is a serious young man, studious, intent. He is tense about meeting his future bride, but not frightened. He talks things over with his parents in the front seat: ''What will she look like? How do I act?'' He tells himself: ''Don't do anything stupid.''

The girl is with a couple of her friends. Again she dispatches her brother with specific instructions: ''Does he have a mustache?'' She has long held visions of her ideal mate: lush, feathery hair, musky cologne, a tuxedo, a diamond earring, a vision from a Stitches store. Or, alternatively, a spiky, sexy Corey Hart of Punjabi extraction, come to fetch her to a life of prosperity and affection, on Valentine's Day in Burlington, Canada. But she has made one law: no mustaches.

The boy is in a grey jacket, a burgundy sweater, slim, his mustache neatly trimmed. He is 23, sells life insurance, plays a little squash, holds his degree in economics. He has made a couple of false starts—correspondence from the parents of an eligible daughter, photographs of three or four candidates—but never has he come this far, to the house of a fiancée he has never seen.

The two families, who know each other because the boy's father was a classmate of the girl's maternal uncle, sit with each other and make small talk. The boy is impressed; the girl's little brother holds more than 100 trophies for his prowess in the martial arts. The boy senses discipline, good upbringing.

The girl, in the living room, gasps: "Oh, God. The time has come." Now they send off the suitor to meet Sunita Sharma, who has known since childhood that this moment would arrive.

Nilesh Shreedhar, who is known as Neil, tells her about his work, his education, his hobbies. He has his own dreams of a woman full of caring—"a total person," a good wife in the Indian sense of the English word "homely"—and he has waited for her to be chosen for him. Sunita, 20, holding the roses, manages four words exactly:
"Sheridan College. Retail management." In her heart, she thinks, "Yes" ("Scenes From an Arranged Marriage," *Toronto* Magazine, June 1989).

The second day a *xwe'xwe* dance with shells was given to me by the chief of Cape Mudge. I gave him a gas boat and $50 cash. Altogether that was worth $500. I paid him back double. He also gave some names. The same day I gave Hudson's Bay blankets. I started giving out the property. First the canoes. Two pool tables were given to two chiefs. It hurt them. They said it was the same as breaking a copper. The pool tables were worth $350 apiece. Then bracelets, gas lights, violins, guitars were given to the more important people. Then 24 canoes, some of them big ones, and four gas boats.

I gave a whole pile to my own people. Return for favours. Dresses to the women, bracelets and shawls. Sweaters and shirts to the young people. To all those who had helped. Boats brought the stuff over from Alert Bay to Village Island by night. (This was to evade the Agent [because potlatching was illegal at the time].) This included 300 oak trunks, the pool tables and the sewing machines.

Then I gave button blankets, shawls and common blankets. There were 400 of the real old Hudson's Bay blankets. I gave these away with the *xwe'xwe* dances. I also gave lots of small change with the Hudson's Bay blankets. I threw it away for the kids to get. There were also basins, maybe a thousand of them, glasses, washtubs, teapots and cups given to the women in the order of their positions.

The third day I don't remember what happened.

The fourth day I gave furniture: boxes, trunks, sewing machines, gramophones, bedsteads and bureaus.

The fifth day I gave away cash.

The sixth day I gave away about 1000 sacks of flour worth $3 a sack. I also gave sugar.

Everyone admits that was the biggest yet. I am proud to say our people (Nimpkish) are ahead, although we are the third [in the Kwakiutl rank structure], *Kwag•uł*, *Mamalelqala*, *Nəmgəs* [Nimkish]. So I am a big man in those days. Nothing now. In the old days this was my weapon and I could call down anyone. All the chiefs say now in a gathering, ''You cannot expect that we can ever get up to you. You are a great mountain'' (Codere 1961, 470–1).

The game had seemed out of reach in the top of the ninth. Tony Fernandez opened it with an infield single against reliever Rob Murphy and the Red Sox summoned stopper Lee Smith from the bullpen to protect the four-run lead.

But a walk and George Bell's double cut the margin to three: A one-out walk loaded the bases for Whitt who hit Smith's 2-1 pitch into the right-field seats to put the Jays ahead.

''I wasn't thinking home run in that situation,'' Whitt said. ''Everyone likes to hit with the bases loaded, but I was just trying to keep the momentum going, trying to get a base hit, just to keep the base runners going.''

Rookie starter Alex Sanchez put the Jays in a hole by allowing four hits, three walks and five runs in one-third of an inning. Three of the runs came on Ellis Burks' seventh homer on an 0-2 pitch. Burks had five runs batted in for the game.

Xavier Hernandez, called up from Syracuse on Friday, did the bullpen a favor by going 6⅔ innings, allowing eight hits and five runs (two earned).

The Jays made four errors, three by first basemen Fred McGriff, playing as if distracted. He committed two errors on the same play in the sixth to allow a run to score and made another that resulted in a run in the third (*Sports* Section, *The Globe and Mail*, June 5, 1989).

''You live all *alone*! Without a friend?'' is what a female foreigner living in a flat hears again and again.

All sorts of helpful suggestions are made, spare nieces and cousins are offered as companion-chaperones. The lady's protests that she *likes* to live alone are either disregarded or taken as a sinister indication that all is not as it should be.

Depending on how one takes it, this can be amusing or infuriating. A woman living on her own, unless she is over 50 and more than commonly plain, is considered to be looking for adventures of the amorous kind. She will not just be gossiped about, she will be actively propositioned! She may get phone calls, self-invitations from male colleagues or acquaintances who think they are on to something easy (Munan 1988, 113).

What do these excerpts from various articles and books have in common? How is the potlatch of the Pacific coast described in the second excerpt similar to the activities in a baseball stadium?

Each of the excerpts refers to an event within a particular cultural setting. You will probably have no difficulty following the baseball account, but may find that the practices of cultures which are foreign to you are ''odd,'' bewildering, or even incomprehensible.

DEFINING ''CULTURE''

Scholars have defined ''**culture**'' in different ways. One of the most widely cited definitions is that of E.B. Tylor (1832–1917):

> *That complex whole which includes knowledge, beliefs, arts, morals, law, customs, and any other capabilities and habits acquired by man as a member of society (1958, 10).*

Members of a particular group or society share a certain way of life and of doing things. Indeed, this sharing of a culture constitutes an important element of group membership.

Each member of Canadian society participates in some ways in a common culture. For example, all Canadians are subject to the same laws and are equal before these laws. All have access to free elementary and secondary education. All feel compelled to wear clothes, even when it is hot. However, since Canada is a complex, geographically dispersed society, there are also many cultural differences based on such factors as geographic location, age, social class, and ethnic group membership.

People often associate the word ''culture'' with highbrow activities, such as attending opera and ballet performances, visiting art exhibitions, and talking knowledgeably about philosophy. However, young people who attend rock concerts, listen to the latest hit recordings, or become ardent fans of Rambo movies also partake of culture, in this case popular culture.

"Culture" is not confined to highbrow activities such as ballet.

MAPPING OUT CULTURES

Group membership involves shared experiences. One of the important factors which provide commonality to a group is language. Language is a symbolic code, in that words make sense only if one knows what they symbolize. Studying such a code is one way of learning what is important to a group. For example, the Inuit have a variety of terms for different kinds of snow, just as Bedouin tribes have many words to describe various types of sand. However, having a command of a language sufficient to translate what is said does not ensure that one will understand, in the deeper sense, what is said. A native English speaker is likely to receive different images if you describe a woman as "aggressive" or if you say she is "forceful," whereas someone whose native tongue is not English may not be sensitive to the distinction.

People who do not speak the same tongue may share some other symbolic code. Mathematicians are one example; chess players are another, as illustrated in the following article.

SYMBOLS MEAN ALL HAVE SAME "LANGUAGE"

By Jonathan Berry

Most forms of cultural expression, such as dancing, singing or writing, manifest themselves with a strong ethnic flavor.

While the forms of expression are universal, a ballet dancer would look out of place at the Highland Games, a western opera singer could hardly undertake a part in a Japanese opera and the world's best novel could remain virtually unknown if not translated from Lithuanian.

However, chess is different. The simple and discrete movements of the pieces form a "language" of their own. A good move in Romania is a good move in Burma is a good move in Peru.

Many players learn Russian or German in order to broaden their chess horizons. Twenty years ago that was vital for the ambitious student because of the lack of serious chess literature in English.

A second or third language is less of a necessity today, not just because of the vast number of serious books available in English, but because of publications that use a sort of language of chess symbols.

The most famous of such publications is Chess Informant, from Yugoslavia. A recent volume, Informant 35, covers the first six months of 1983. Of its 392 pages, 288 are devoted to the best selected games, with moves and commentary in special symbols. The meanings of the symbols are explained in eight European languages and Japanese

(Arabic is to be added soon).

The 'symbolic language' is not complete. For example, there is no expression for "when my opponent saw the move I had made, he fell off his chair." However, "White's counterattack on the king side combined with pressure against the weak square f6 gave him a winning game" could be expressed in seven symbols.

Such books allow chess ideas to spread across the globe without the delay and expense of translation. Each book has the widest possible market, which is a boon for publishers in such countries as Yugoslavia, which are hungry for western currencies. But even such a well-known publisher as Oxford University Press has come out with a series of such chess books.

It is perhaps fitting that the motto of the World Chess Federation, founded in 1924, is 'Gens una Sumus'—we are one family.

Our diagram is taken from the combination section of Informant 35, the game Bagirov-Imanaliev, USSR. The magazine used the following internationally accepted chess symbols: K for King, Q for Queen, R for Rook, B for Bishop and N for Knight. Pawns are noted by the absence of a symbol.

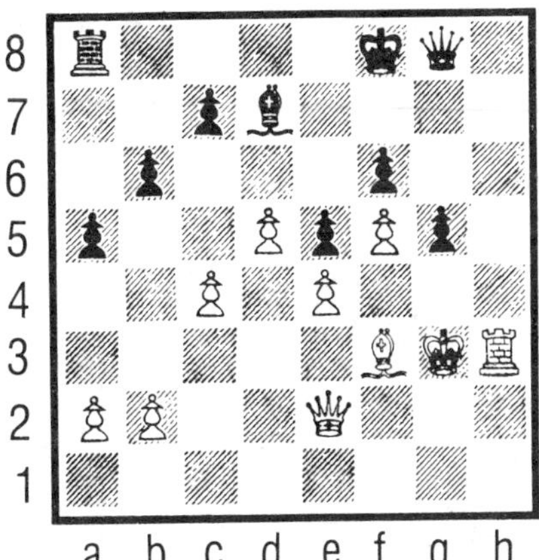

White to move.

The game following the stage depicted in the diagram went 1. d5-d6! (If 1. Qe2-h2 Kf8-e7, with d6 as an escape square) 1 ...c7xd6 2. Qe2-h2 Kf8-g7 3. Rh3-h6 Bd7-e8 (protecting g6) 4. Bf3-h5! Qg8xc4 (if 4....Kg7xh6 5. Bh5-f7 + Kh6-g7 6. Bf7xg8 Kg7xg8 7. Qh2-h6 and wins) 5. Rh6-h7 + ! Kg7-f8 (if 5....Kg7-g8 6. Bh5-f7 + Be8xf7 7. Rh7-h8 + mates) 8. Bh5-e2! and Black resigned.

EXAMINING RADICALLY DIFFERENT SOCIETIES

Much of the seminal research on culture was done by anthropologists, some of whom applied the functionalist perspective of Durkheim that we discussed in Chapter 1. Literally, "anthropology" means the study of human beings, and early anthropologists concentrated their research on societies that were different from western ones in size, traditions, and ways of seeing the world. Ruth Benedict explained some of the reasons why anthropologists chose simple societies for study:

> *Therefore the most illuminating material for a discussion of cultural forms and processes is that of societies historically as little related as possible to our own and to one another. With the vast network of historical contact which has spread the great civilizations over tremendous areas, primitive cultures are now the one source to which we can turn. They are a laboratory in which we may study the diversity of human institutions. With their comparative isolation, many primitive regions have had centuries in which to elaborate the cultural themes they have made their own. They provide ready to our hand the necessary information concerning the possible great variations in human adjustments, and a critical examination of them is essential for any understanding of cultural processes (Benedict 1934, 15–6).*

Another reason for the choice was that the relative simplicity of these societies made it likely that members shared such important aspects of their lives as the kind of work they did, lifestyle, and belief systems. Hence, although there were differences in the way social life was experienced by men and women, the young and the aged, and so on, it was possible to make statements about *the* culture of the Trobriand Islanders or the Kwakiutls with a reasonable amount of certainty. Clearly, it would be inappropriate to make sweeping statements about *the* Canadian or American culture (although politicians, media personalities, and laypeople are not always deterred from uttering such statements).

Bronislaw Malinowski (1884–1942) was an anthropologist who brought a functionalist approach to the study of culture. Malinowski rejected the notion that culture was simply a collection of disconnected traits brought together from disparate sources by historical accident. Rather, he hypothesized that separate aspects of culture interact, contributing to the functioning of society as an integrated whole.

Malinowski was no armchair theoretician; his work was rooted in intensive empirical research that required meticulous observation and systematic analysis of everyday behaviour in the ongoing life of actual human communities. In studying the life of the Trobriand Islanders off the coast of New Guinea, he made detailed observations of their culture and kept pursuing *why* a custom existed by considering what purpose it served in the community. For example, the Islanders seemed to base much of the way they lived on magic. His explorations led him to establish, however, that although a great deal of magic surrounded the hazardous, anxiety-provoking activity of ocean fishing — upon which much of their subsistence depended—there was no such reliance on magic associated with the relatively safe activity of fishing in the sheltered lagoon. Malinowski concluded that magic was an organized response to the sense of impotence and lack of control that these people experienced in the face of an unpredictable, dangerous environment; when uncertainty and danger were absent, this type of response was unnecessary. The Islanders' thinking was not, then, inherently magical.

A.R. Radcliffe-Brown (1881–1955) was also interested in primitive societies and carried out extensive fieldwork in the Andaman Islands. Insisting on the application of scientific procedures similar to those used in the natural sciences, he sought to discover the necessary conditions and laws that govern the functioning of primitive societies as social systems. Drawing upon the intellectual legacy of Comte and Durkheim, he attempted to classify types of societies and to compare their ways of functioning and changing. He examined values, customs, and institutions in terms of the contribution they made to the persistence of the society as a whole.

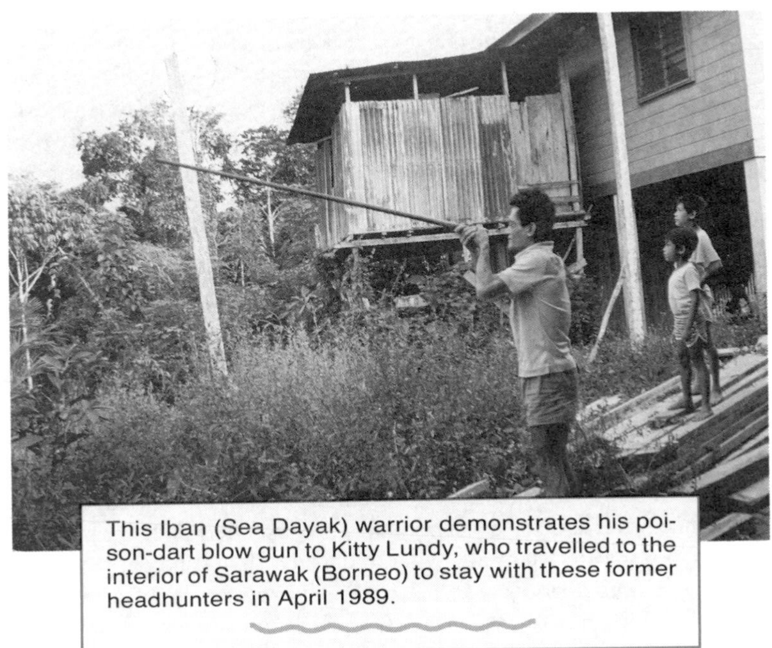

This Iban (Sea Dayak) warrior demonstrates his poison-dart blow gun to Kitty Lundy, who travelled to the interior of Sarawak (Borneo) to stay with these former headhunters in April 1989.

SOCIAL ORGANIZATION

Tylor talks of culture as being a "complex whole." In what way are discrete elements welded into this whole? This welding comes into effect by **social organization**, which Theodorson and Theodorson define as

> *a relatively stable pattern of social relationships of individuals and subgroups within a society or group, based upon social roles, norms and shared meanings that provide regularity and predictability within social interaction (1969, 287).*

The specific meanings that are attached to different behaviours vary from culture to culture. A burp following a satisfying meal is a compliment to the culinary skill of the hostess in some Middle Eastern cultures, whereas in Canadian society, burping is seen as a manifestation of bad manners. This does not mean that Canadians value politeness more highly than do Middle Easterners. It merely demonstrates different conceptions of what constitutes politeness.

For the most part, these conceptions are *shared* by members of a group. Cumulatively, shared conceptions and beliefs are tools a group uses to make sense of the world. One's beliefs have consequences for one's own actions. Believing that traffic will stop at a red light, you walk across the street. You offer a $20 bill for an 82-cent purchase, confident that the store clerk will give you change. The myriad everyday interactions in which people engage, fairly certain about what to expect, lend regularity and predictability to their lives. No such reliable expectations are there to guide a person in a strange culture, a situation vividly depicted in the recent spate of films and television programs on extraterrestrial visitors who constantly misconstrue cultural cues and thus misinterpret their new environment.

ROLE AND STATUS

Individuals play particular **roles** within a social organization. Here, as often happens in the field of sociology, we need to be precise about the meanings of terms that are also used in everyday speech but with quite different connotations. Take the term ''role,'' for example. In everyday language, ''playing a role'' means enacting a public part. You might say of a newly appointed manager, ''She seems a little unsure how to play the role.'' To understand how role is used in sociology, you must understand another concept, that of **status**. Merton delineates status as a ''position in a social system involving designated rights and obligations,'' and role as ''the behaviour oriented to the patterned expectations of others'' (1959, 110).

Status and role are closely linked. Status refers to position in the social structure, while role is the active dimension, the behaviour stemming from occupancy of a certain position. Thus, to be a father is a type of social status. Associated with it are prescriptions for the behaviour expected of a father in a given group. In western society, for example, there is an expectation that a father will give his children economic and moral support; many people would now say that emotional support belongs on this list, although a few decades ago this obligation was often viewed as falling mainly within the mother's purview.

In other societies, many of the obligations of the father's role are met by the mother's brother. Thus, Lowrie notes:

> *Among the Hopi the mother's brother is vested with disciplinary functions, which parents rarely exercise, and in general he takes care of his sister's children. His advice is essential as regards the choice of a girl's future husband, and he helps prepare the wedding garments. From among his nephews he chooses one as his successor in ceremonial*

office and teaches him the requisite sacred knowledge (1948, 73).

Each individual in a society has many statuses—for example, wife, mother, lawyer, volunteer for the Cancer Society, daughter, tennis player—and each status has role relationships attached to it. The role of the mother involves a woman with her children, their friends, perhaps their friends' parents, teachers, sport coaches, and others. This web of relationships makes up social organization at the micro level. (Later in the chapter, we will discuss social organization at the macro level.)

A person who successfully executes the roles associated with many statuses is described as versatile: "I don't know how he finds time to hold down a responsible job, coach the pee-wee hockey team, build an addition to his house, and be knowledgeable enough to beat us at Trivial Pursuit!" Conversely, when an individual engaged in a variety of activities performs some of his obligations less than adequately, you may remark, "He is spreading himself too thin." Often high school students, eager for independence and spending money, devote more and more time to paid work. Their lower marks then reflect the reduced time they invest in the obligations associated with the role of student.

This situation can also be seen as an example of **role conflict**, a clash between the obligations accruing from two or more roles. The case of the working mother, frequently cited as the classic example, is just one of the many individuals who experience role conflict. For example, should Mario Minelli stay at the office to finish his departmental report or go home to make himself available to his teenage son, Tony, who after two years of being uncommunicative is showing signs of wanting to talk to his father? And when will Mario find time to lend support to his wife, who is being driven to distraction by her mother?

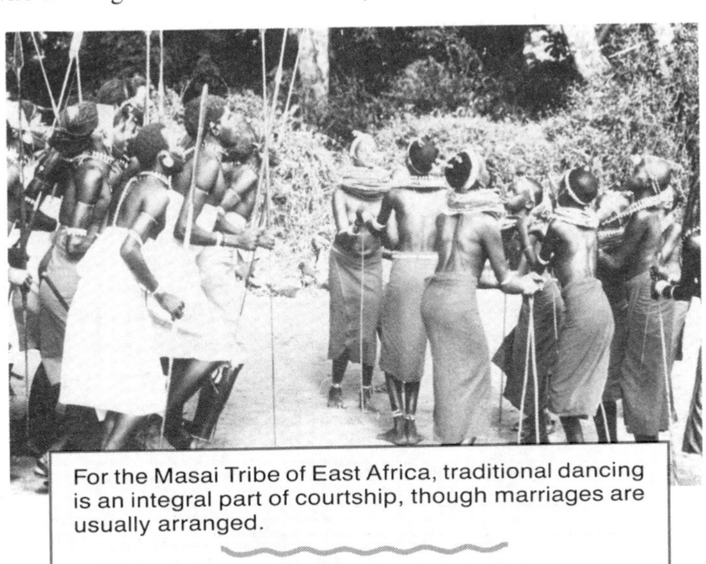

For the Masai Tribe of East Africa, traditional dancing is an integral part of courtship, though marriages are usually arranged.

ASCRIBED AND ACHIEVED STATUS

Since status refers to position in the social organization, it can be something that the individual simply has or else it can be "earned" in some way. In all societies, certain statuses are ascribed. An **ascribed status** is a characteristic such as gender, race, or religion, that is bestowed at birth. One is born male or female into a particular family that lives in a particular place. Some ascribed statuses, such as one's religious status, can be changed, but most remain with the individual for life. However, social expectations of the role behaviour associated with a status may change. For example, 50 years ago, the status of Japanese Canadians in British Columbia was quite different from what it is today.

Achieved status depends more on individual action. Education, occupation, and club membership are a few of the many possible examples.

SALIENT STATUS AND RANKING

Every individual holds many statuses. One is a **salient status**, also called a **master status**, which becomes the source of his or her identity. In earlier times, people derived their identities from kinship and regional affiliations. One identified oneself first as a member of a family or clan and second as living in a particular village or region. In industrialized societies, a man's salient status has generally been his occupational one. When meeting someone new, people tend to ask not "Who are you?" but rather "What do you do?" Being a wife and mother were until recently (and are even still in some cases) the salient statuses for most women. Hence, unmarried women have been pitied for lacking these identity-bestowing positions.

Each culture invariably ranks statuses. But the criteria for high and low status vary over time and space. For example, Clarke found that in Canada there has been a considerable decline in the status of the clergy during the last century. (Evidence of the decline can be found in such indices as the percentage representation of clergy relative to other professionals.) Clarke argued that this reflects the changing orientation of Canadian society from a predominantly religious to a mainly secular one (1981, 215–22). (Recall, from Chapter 1, Comte's attempt to systematize such changes into the Law of Three Stages.)

The criteria for evaluating statuses change, and so do the patterned expectations of appropriate role behaviour for the "incumbent" of a particular status. Exhibit 2.1 contrasts guidelines for the role of a public teacher as set by the Ontario school board in 1898 with guidelines from the Ontario Education Act of 1983. Note that the 1898 list mainly addresses the teacher's behaviour as a person, whereas the modern one emphasizes the teaching function, and how it is to be carried out. It is also interesting, however, that some things have changed very little. Moral overtones can be detected in both lists, and, in both, the weight of the organizational control to which teachers are subject is readily apparent.

VALUES, NORMS, FOLKWAYS, AND MORES

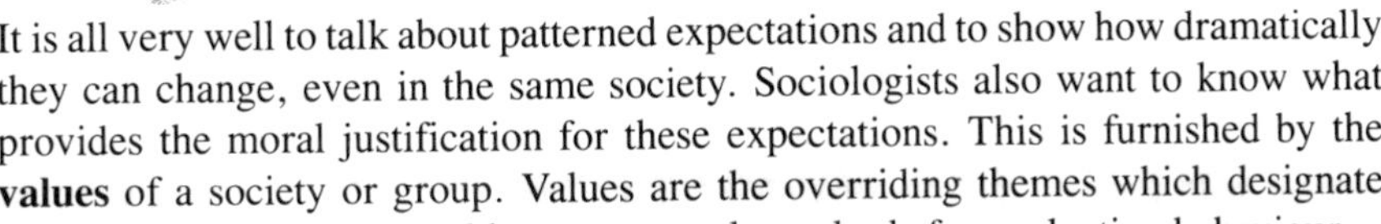

It is all very well to talk about patterned expectations and to show how dramatically they can change, even in the same society. Sociologists also want to know what provides the moral justification for these expectations. This is furnished by the **values** of a society or group. Values are the overriding themes which designate goals worth striving for and lay out general standards for evaluating behaviour.

EXHIBIT 2.1

CHANGES IN ROLE BEHAVIOUR FOR TEACHERS

OBLIGATIONS OF A TEACHER AS DETAILED BY AN ONTARIO SCHOOL BOARD, 1898

MALE

1. The teacher shall light the fire in the schoolhouse no later than 7:30 a.m. (firewood supplied by the Board), and fill the water pails.
2. The teacher shall dress conservatively, preferably in black, and conscientiously avoid any distracting colours.
3. The teacher shall instruct the young in religion and morals not only through daily readings of the Good Book, but by example.
4. The teacher shall not associate with members of the female persuasion except on Sunday, when the Board graciously extends courting privileges.
5. The teacher shall not smoke or drink on pain of instant dismissal.
6. The teacher shall be firm with the children but not brutal. Strapping is permitted, but caning and beating with oaken switches are forbidden.
7. The teacher shall not appear on the streets after dark, but spend his time preparing lessons to the profit of the children.
8. The teacher shall not engage in rancorous quarrels with the citizens.

Should the teacher be **FEMALE** she is exhorted to obey the following instructions:

1. She will not wear fewer than 3 petticoats nor shall her dress from the floor be removed in excess of 3″.
2. She will wash the schoolhouse floor each morning before the arrival of her charges.
3. She shall not be seen abroad with a male other than her father or brother except on Sunday afternoons between the hours of 2 and 5 p.m.
4. Privies should be inspected daily during times when they are unoccupied. Materials for purifying will be supplied by the Board.

Be it so ordered by all these present in the year of our Lord, 1898.

GOD SAVE THE QUEEN!

EXHIBIT 2.1

DUTIES OF A TEACHER AS SPECIFIED BY THE ONTARIO EDUCATION ACT OF 1983

It is the duty of a teacher and temporary teacher,

To teach diligently and faithfully the classes or subjects assigned to him by the principal;

To encourage the pupils in the pursuit of learning;

To inculcate by precept and example respect for religion and the principles of Judaeo-Christian morality and the highest regard for truth, justice, loyalty, love of country, humanity, benevolence, sobriety, industry, frugality, purity, temperance and all other virtues;

To assist in developing co-operation and co-ordination of effort among the members of the staff of the school;

To maintain, under direction of the principal, proper order and discipline in his classroom and while on duty in the school and on the school ground;

To conduct his class in accordance with a timetable which shall be accessible to pupils and to the principal and supervisory officers; to participate in professional activity days as designated by the board under the regulations;

To notify such person as is designated by the board if he is to be absent from school and the reason therefore;

To deliver the register, the school key and other school property in his possession to the board on demand, or when his agreement with the board has expired, or when for any reason his employment has ceased; and to use and permit to be used as a textbook in a class that he teaches in an elementary or a secondary school,

(i) in a subject area for which textbooks are approved by the Minister, only textbooks that are approved by the Minister, and

(ii) in all subject areas, only textbooks that are approved by the board. R.S.O. 1980, c. 129, s. 235 (1); 1982, c. 32, s. 58.

(*Ontario Education Act*, 1983 Printing)

Social relationships are cemented by shared values and beliefs. They are also regulated by the exercise of power. Weber has defined **power** as the ability to impose one's will on others, to force groups or individuals to act in certain ways, even against their will. Power may be wielded subtly, crudely, or in a manner falling between these extremes. For example, employers cannot wield power as crudely as they did in Marx's day; nevertheless, power relationships remain a pervasive facet of work life (also see the discussion in Chapter 1 on the conflict perspective).

Authority is power that has become legitimated and institutionalized in a society or other social group. Because, from infancy on, individuals are conditioned to comply with authority, they may be unaware of the extent to which everyday life is fueled by external authority, most prominently by the authority of the state. This authority is expressed in laws, regulations, and ordinances — to pay taxes, to declare goods purchased abroad, to obey traffic signals, to keep dogs leashed.

In small groups, such as the family, most children accept parents' authority most of the time. The team coach directs the activities of players; not every player may agree with the directions, but they usually comply with them because the coach's authority is seen as legitimate (see chapter 6 on organizations for a discussion of the bases on which authority may be legitimated).

IDEOLOGY

The values of a group or society are clustered into ideologies. Theodorson and Theodorson define **ideology** as:

> *a system of interdependent ideas (beliefs, traditions, principles, and myths) held by a social group or society, which reflects, rationalizes, and defends its particular social, moral, religious, political and economic institutional interests and commitments. Ideologies serve as logical and philosophical justifications for a group's patterns of behavior, as well as its attitudes, goals and general life situation (1969, 195).*

An important component of our societal ideology is individualism. Thus, for instance, success is seen not only as attainable, but also as being primarily dependent on individual *efforts*. This ideology pays scant attention to the impact of the environment; one must compensate for an unfavourable environment by trying harder—just look at those who made it against tremendous odds. The dominant values in Canadian society involve individual freedoms—freedom of speech, freedom of choice with respect to religion, occupation, area of residence, and marriage partner. Success, as the result of individual effort, moving onward and upward in a particular field—whether this be occupation, athletics, or artistic endeavour—is one of the most pervasive values.

What is deemed a fundamental goal varies from society to society. Values are very basic, and conflicts over the priorities assigned to them arouse strong feelings. For example, the controversy surrounding the National Security Bill (C-157) represented tension between individuals' right to privacy and the need to safeguard the nation from internal and external subversion. Indeed, the issue of civil liberties versus perceived threats to national security is a longstanding one in western society. The McCarthy era of the 1950s was one in which civil liberties were firmly subordinated in order to "keep America safe from Communism."

Values, then, are general ideas of what is good or bad, desirable or undesirable. **Norms** are the signposts that regulate everyday behaviour, the concrete ways in which the abstract conceptions of values are put into practice; the set of rules guiding the behaviour expected of teachers is one example.

What would these two 1912 bathers think of the modern beach scene below?

In turn, norms can be divided into folkways and mores. **Folkways** are informal norms, usually not encoded in law, that change quite frequently. Folkways include etiquette, fashions, minimum standards of politeness, and other everyday practices. One is not supposed to push ahead of others in a line-up or cut into a conversation. Sanctions for violations may include teasing or a verbal reprimand: "Well, you certainly are in a hurry" or "Some people just have no manners." Victorians referred to trousers as "unmentionables." To present-day North Americans, this is an example of quaint prudery. For women, smoking in public used to be quite unacceptable, and then it became commonplace. Today, smoking is becoming increasingly unacceptable for both men and women. In fact, in some places smoking is prohibited by law.

Mores are the norms that are salient in a particular culture. In an industrialized society like Canada, mores form the basis of most laws, such as those that safeguard people against such violations as murder, rape, or physical assault and those that protect property against robbery, theft, and embezzlement. However, mores are not always a matter of law. For example, adultery was never illegal in Canada, even when it was regarded as an unspeakable act (for a woman, at least) that provided grounds for divorce.

Transgressions against mores meet with far harsher sanctions than do the breaking of folkways. Penalties include ostracism, fines, imprisonment, or death. Sanctions may go well beyond those imposed by law. In jails, people who have been convicted of crimes deemed especially repugnant—child molesters, for example—often have to be isolated from other prisoners for their own safety. The other inmates may demonstrate their sense of outrage against violation of such a sacred norm by attacking or even murdering the offenders.

TYPES OF CULTURES

Culture provides the overarching term to describe the particular way in which the elements of social organization cohere. If sociologists compare several cultures, they are likely to find that the elements of social organization in each one form a particular configuration that permits identification of the *type* of society. For example, an Israeli kibbutz, in which property is held collectively, presents quite a different configuration of characteristics than that of a North American community, with its emphasis on private property and individualism.

It is useful to distinguish among types of societies by contrasting their complexity and the ways in which members typically relate to one another. Given the vast array of ways in which the discrete cultural elements can be combined to form different societies, a variety of classification systems is possible. One that we will examine in this chapter is the Gemeinschaft and the Gesellschaft. These terms, which were coined by the German sociologist Ferdinand Tönnies (1855–1936), can be translated respectively as "community" and "society." However, the original German terms are frequently used by sociologists.

Tönnies depicted a **Gemeinschaft** as a small, homogeneous, mainly rural society. The group has a high degree of self-sufficiency, and the division of labour is simple. The members share values; in Durkheim's terms (see Chapter 1), they are tied by mechanical solidarity. The belief system holds that it is a duty to conform to god's will (however god is conceptualized), and that certain aspects of existence are beyond human understanding and must simply be accepted.

Relationships in this type of small community are close and overlapping. Individuals interact within their economic activities, working co-operatively or exchanging skills and resources; they also pray and play together. Relationships are permeated by both positive and negative emotions; friendships that provide warmth and security may co-exist with intense feuds, such as the famous one between the Montagues and the Capulets, dramatized in *Romeo and Juliet*. Ascribed statuses weigh heavily in determining the functions each member performs. People are expected to behave in accordance with the norms prescribed for their positions. Since expectations are known and clearly understood, individuals can feel sure of doing the right thing and can predict how others will act. However, there is little tolerance for deviation, and those who do not fit smoothly into their assigned places must face community sanctions. For example, among the Amish, complete ostracism, which they refer to as "shunning," is meted out to those who have severely offended communal standards. The Hutterites are an example of a present-day group that approximates a Gemeinschaft (see the Suggested Readings at the end of this chapter).

Mennonite communities provide an example of Gemeinschaft in today's Canada.

The polar opposite of the Gemeinschaft in Tönnies' schema is the **Gesellschaft**. It is a large, heterogeneous society that has been urbanized (where the bulk of the population has shifted from the countryside to the city). The division of labour is highly specialized, creating interdependence among members; this is organic solidarity in Durkheim's terms. Although the Gesellschaft, like any society, has certain overriding values, there is room for a diversity of worldviews. In modern Canadian society, individuals can live together peaceably most of the time even though they hold opposed values on such important issues as capital punishment or the deployment of nuclear warheads.

In the Gesellschaft, achieved status is normatively the salient one. Ideally, it matters more what one has achieved by way of education and occupation than whether one was born male or female, Indian or white. The vital question is what one has done. (In practice, of course, one's ascribed characteristics bear on what one is able to do and on the obstacles one must overcome.)

In this kind of society, relationships are typically segmented, which means that one's co-workers or fellow parishioners are not necessarily one's personal friends. The 200 tenants of a high-rise building live in close proximity, but their contact with each other may be minimal or nonexistent. Emotional involvement is reserved for personal relationships. Minding one's own business, not getting entangled in the affairs of outsiders, is positively valued. Sometimes this attitude can reach horrifying extremes, as in the case of Kitty Genovese, who was murdered in New York while close to 50 people heard her scream.

In contrast to the high degree of consensus that regulates behaviour in the Gemeinschaft, the Gesellschaft has no unequivocal prescriptions of what constitutes appropriate behaviour. This uncertainty engenders a high degree of anxiety. A father may agonize over choosing among the roles of being a disciplinarian, an advisor, or a buddy to his children. However, members of such a society have some leeway in what they do and how they do it. They can choose to attend religious services or not, consume alcoholic beverages or abstain, become politically active or remain indifferent to political life.

It is worth noting that the Gesellschaft and Gemeinschaft types, like many of the constructs of sociological theory, are abstract concepts. In Weber's term, they are **ideal types**, ideas rather than real things. They can be used as measuring devices so that one can examine how actual communities, past and present, conform to or deviate from the model.

SEVEN BRIDES FOR SEVEN BERBERS

By Peter Bax

Every year in a remote valley deep in the Moroccan Atlas mountains, Berbers of the Ait Hadiddou tribe gather at a Moussem, the equivalent in

Morocco of a country fair. There, they sell their sheep, goats, mules or camels, and buy shovels, plastic buckets, tea, sugar and other supplies to support their lonely existence in the mountains for another year.

Many tribesmen also take this opportunity to look for a new mate — either a first or a replacement. This is carried out on a big scale: divorce is common and the average person may have eight spouses. The gathering is known as the Moussem des Fiancailles or, loosely translated, the Brides' Fair.

The Moussem lasts only three days, in which one must make and seal a match. Men and women, who appear to enjoy equal status among the Berbers, roam the vast fairground in small groups of twos or threes, meet, chat, hold hands, look into each other's eyes and maybe decide that this is it. In which case, the couple will spend the remaining time wandering round hand in hand and usually looking very pleased with themselves. Alternatively, one side or another will snatch a hand away and walk off to search further.

To help in the process, for there is a huge crowd of people intent on other business, tribesmen seeking a bride wear a white turban. Prospective brides wear all their jewelry of silver and amber. Some are veiled, but most dispense with this and show off their beauty, enhanced with rouge for their cheeks and kohl for their eyes. They wear a rounded spangled headdress if they have never been married before, or a pointed one if they are divorced or widowed.

Searching for a new mate is only one feature of the fair. The main purpose of such a large gathering of the normally widely dispersed tribesmen is, of course, trade. Merchants come to buy the sheep, goats and such and in turn sell the supplies that the Berbers need. The huge encampment of tents is organized into separate small souks: there is an area for the sellers of carpets, another one for such hardware as pots and pans. Animals are bought and sold in satellite souks around the main encampment, each species having its own area. There is even a gambling section where all the universally known games, such as the shell game, serve to part the Berber from his hard-earned cash, dirham by dirham.

On the last day of the Moussem, the newly joined couples celebrate with traditional songs and dances, swaying and chanting to the beat of hand drums and the shrill sound of pipes. An official drives in from outside to register the new arrangements and to try to weed out the 12-year-old girls pretending to be 18. Then the new husbands and wives depart on their donkeys for their remote villages — perhaps to return and try again next year.

SUBCULTURES

By definition, a heterogeneous society contains groups and individuals who engage in a variety of lifestyles and have different sets of goals and priorities. When a group exists within mainstream society but differs from it in patterned ways — for instance, in language, norms, or customs — we describe it as a **subculture**. Sociologists do not clearly agree on the criteria for designating a group as a subculture. However, most would categorize an ethnolinguistic group as a subculture. Torontonians refer to certain districts as "little Italy" or "little Portugal." The implication is that for the immigrants who inhabit these areas, life runs as closely as possible along the lines of the old country.

To the extent that an occupation provides an all-encompassing context for everyday life, it, too, can be described as a subculture. Examples are the world of the military or that of circus artistes. In both cases, members and their families have limited opportunities to interact with outsiders on a continuing basis. Therefore, the development of distinctive ways of living and of looking at the world can proceed relatively unchecked.

The very rich and the very poor have also been described as constituting subcultures. The very rich are not easily accessible for investigation by social scientists, though some studies have been done. Lundberg, for example, wrote about *The Rich and the Super Rich* (1969), and Peter C. Newman did research on the Canadian establishment (1975) in general and on some of its members in particular (1981). The poor have been studied in greater detail. Oscar Lewis developed the concept of the culture of poverty, based on his research in North-American and Latin-American slums. He argued that in severely deprived environments, people develop orientations of passivity, fatalism, and a short-term rather than a long-term perspective.[1] Ironically, these very orientations hinder escape from poverty.

> *Poverty becomes a dynamic factor which affects participation in the larger national culture and creates a sub-culture of its own. One can speak of the culture of the poor, for it has its own modalities and distinctive social and psychological consequences for its members (Lewis 1959,2).*

Subcultures can be summed up as the collective responses of individuals who share certain traits that set them apart from their society at large. A **counterculture** also meets this specification, but its members have joined the group as a form of protest against prevailing societal values and norms. Thus, the flower children of the 1960s manifested their dissatisfaction with the existing state of affairs by emphasizing community and rejecting material possessions. Punkers, whose dress and behaviour contravene accepted standards, can also be viewed as forming a counterculture.[2]

Members of a counterculture share certain traits that set them apart from their society at large. Joining the group is, in itself, a form of protest against societal values.

BRAZIL SEEKS TO BURY MILLENNIA-OLD CULTURE

By David Suzuki

If you read newspapers very carefully, you noted recently that South American Indians were blocked from entering a Brazilian court because they were improperly dressed. It is worth looking into the story that is hinted at by those brief news reports to understand the current plight of Brazil's indigenous people.

The Kaiapo Indians live in the Amazon rainforest much as they have for thousands of years. The Kaiapo are warriors who wear fearsome war paint and whose primary weapons are bows and arrows and a deadly club. But the same as aboriginal peoples around the world, they are under increasing pressure from people they refer to as the "civilized" ones.

Brazilian Indians are wards of the state and officially treated as "minors" by FUNAI, the government's Indian agency. Native culture is not valued in Brazil, so FUNAI's goal is to assimilate the Indians into the general population as quickly as possible. Of course, assimilation also frees Indian land for other uses. Mining, farming, logging and hydroelectric dams have polluted the rivers, cleared the forest and squeezed the Kaiapo into an ever shrinking area. Brazilian Indians are threatened with extinction as much as the Amazonian flora and fauna.

The Brazilian constitution guarantees protection of Indian land, yet logging, farming, mining and flooding have steadily cut into Kaiapo territory that had not yet been demarcated. In 1985, angered by the mining going on in their land, a young chief named Paiakon led a force of 125 warriors on an 8-hour hike to the mine site. There they discovered a massive operation, with 5,000 miners protected by armed guards.

Under cover of night, Paiakon and his tiny group seized the airstrip and seven planes, overwhelmed the sentries and their weapons and then captured the entire mining force! The Indians expelled the miners, occupied the camp and held officials captive until, three months later, the government recognized the reserve boundaries, put the Indians in charge of the mine site and gave them a 5 percent royalty on all gold taken from their land. It was an incredible victory achieved without the loss of a single life.

This January, Darrel Posey, an ethnobiologist who has worked with the Kaiapo for more than 11 years, accompanied Paiakon and chief Kube-i, to a conference in Miami on tropical rainforests. Through Dr. Posey, the two Indians spoke about the forest and rivers, what they mean to their way of life and the terrible effects of massive development projects.

The chiefs were especially concerned about the effects of a series of dams being built on the Xingu River. Costing $10.6-billion (U.S.), the dams will flood 7.6 million hectares, 85 percent of it Indian land. The World Bank was preparing to give a $500-million loan to Electrobras, Brazil's power company, to finance the dams. In Miami, the Indians were urged to go to Washington to talk to politicians and representatives of the World Bank. The chiefs did, and had a widely publicized meeting with politicians and bank officials.

Upon returning to Brazil, Dr. Posey and the Indians were arrested for "criticizing Brazilian Indian policy" and "denigrating the country's image abroad." All three were charged under a law that forbids foreigners from getting involved in issues of Brazilian national interest. Thus, indigenous people of the Amazon were legally classified as foreigners! Their first court appearance was scheduled in the town of Belem on Oct. 14.

That morning, soldiers arrived in front of the courthouse armed with shields, guns, rifles, clubs and bulletproof vests. Dr. Posey came early with his lawyer and they went into the courthouse. Around 8:30, buses pulled up and disgorged about 250 Indian warriors fully dressed in war paint and spectacular feather headdresses and armed with clubs and bows and arrows. Paiakon and Kube-i came in a car as the warriors filled the street.

The Indians began to sing and dance in front of the phalanx of soldiers in a powerful demonstration that evoked the emotional impact of drumming and chanting by Canadian Indians. One of the "civilized" spectators in the court muttered contemptuously, "How quaint." When Paiakon and Kube-i attempted to enter the court, they were stopped because, the judge said, they were "semi-nude." He ruled that they must dress to show respect for Brazilian law. When the Indians replied that they were wearing their traditional attire, the judge replied that they must follow Brazilian formalities and should strive to become Brazilians.

Dr. Posey commented to me later that the judge's policy was tantamount to genocide. The Indians waited 10 minutes for the judge to change his ruling. When he did not, they departed peacefully, leaving word that the court could contact them in their forest homes. Suddenly and quietly, they were gone.

Brazilian Indians are a repository of thousands of years of accumulated folk knowledge about the forest, which can never be replaced. They are now fighting a desperate battle to save the remaining bits of their home, which happens to be the richest ecosystem on the planet. Their fight is ours, because that great biological jewel is a part of the world's vanishing natural treasures.

CULTURAL RELATIVISM AND ETHNOCENTRISM

In our discussion of various cultures and subcultures, we have sought to demonstrate that individuals may behave in ways that other people deem morally wrong or nonsensical but that make perfect sense in the context of their own cultural values. Being married to more than one person at the same time is a legal offence in Canada whereas, in many Middle Eastern countries, having many wives is a symbol of high status. The regular consumption of meat denotes affluence in western societies, while eating meat is a violation of a sacred dietary taboo for orthodox Hindus. To acknowledge and respect such diversity is to accept the principle of **cultural relativism**.

The logical opposite to cultural relativism is **ethnocentrism**. Literally translated, it means placing one's own culture at the centre. It is the view that one's own culture is inherently superior and other cultures are, by definition, inferior. Different food habits, modes of dress, and family structures are evaluated in relation to one's own ways, and found wanting. Carried to an extreme, ethnocentrism incites hatred of everything that is foreign and therefore different. Some of the worst examples of inhumanity have been rationalized on the basis of ethnocentrism.

When a group is under threat from outside, as in time of war, leaders deliberately invoke ethnocentric sentiments to ensure that members will be willing to defend "our way of life." Analogously, Québécois leaders, ranging from the men who refused to join the American colonists in revolution in 1776 up to the politicians who drafted its language legislation, have partially justified their actions in terms of saving French culture from extinction.

CULTURAL CHANGE

In our discussion so far, we have focused primarily on some of the building blocks of culture and on ways in which they are combined into different cultural forms. However, cultures are dynamic systems involved in a continuous process of change. How does change occur?

When the world's means of transportation were rudimentary and travel both cumbersome and hazardous, groups that were off the beaten track lived in relative isolation from each other. Their cultures were slow to change. Other peoples, especially those living near waterways, have had extensive contact with outsiders since antiquity and their cultures are relatively fluid.

Sometimes groups become closed in on themselves because of circumstances. The collapse of the Roman empire, for example, isolated Europe during the so-called dark ages, from about the 5th to the 12th centuries. Then the crusaders, who set out from Europe to enlighten the "infidels" in the Middle East, were dazzled by the thriving society they found there. They brought back with them a host of innovations, such as new techniques in weaving, dyeing, and metal-working, which then became integrated into the existing European cultures. Slowly, communication and travel both within Europe and with the outside world improved. With the Renaissance and the voyages of discovery, such as those of Christopher Columbus and John Cabot, contact between cultures greatly increased. Voyages to the Americas introduced Europeans to potatoes, tobacco, and corn. Quite rapidly, these items became staples of everyday life. This process is called **cultural diffusion**.

Generally, material items that pass the test of usefulness are accepted more readily than cultural symbols and rituals. Many of North America's native peoples, for example, were using horses, iron tools (including guns), and woven cloth soon after their first contact with Europeans. This century's immigrants to Canada have been quick to adopt cars and labour-saving devices but have clung to certain old-country practices, such as those relating to courtship behaviour. In traditional Macedonian families, for instance, a young man brings his girlfriend home to meet his family only after the couple has decided to get married.

With the advent and growth of the mass media, there has been a dramatic speed-up in the rate and the extent of cultural diffusion. Coca-Cola and jeans have become part of the youth culture of societies as geographically and ideologically removed from each other as the Soviet Union and Sri Lanka.

Cultural diffusion facilitates **acculturation**, the process by which groups or individuals who are in contact exchange cultural traits and acquire new ones. Since Canada is a nation of immigrants, it provides a ready laboratory for observing acculturation. Raymond Breton (1964) has noted that not all immigrant groups become acculturated at the same rate. If they live in ethnic enclaves within which they can worship, shop, and eat, and if they have access to newspapers and other mass media in their native tongue, acculturation is likely to be slow. An example of slow acculturation was relayed to one of the authors by an elderly German professor, when he reminisced about his childhood in Milwaukee in the early 1900s. When he started school, he and his friends knew no English. They picked that up quickly enough, but within earshot of their elders, the children were forbidden, under threat of physical punishment, to speak anything but German. Apparently, the elder generation was anxious to retard acculturation.

Acculturation cannot be staved off permanently or completely, however, unless the group opts for isolation, as do the Hutterites, some Mennonite sects, and ultraorthodox Hasidic Jews. Most children of immigrants go to Canadian schools, learn a new language, and meet youngsters from other groups. Language plays an important part in acculturation because it helps to shape ideas as well as to express them. The more completely the children come to function in the new language, the more removed they become from the culture of their parents. Male immigrants also tend to have at least some contact with the new society at large, even if they work mainly with compatriots. It is the stay-at-home wives who are least likely to be acculturated. (See for example "Maria in Markham Street," Rayfield 1970).

In an encounter between two cultures, which one is more likely to adapt to the other? As we will examine in Chapters 4 and 7 on stratification and minority groups, the direction of acculturation is strongly influenced by differences in power. The dominant group has the capacity both to resist change and to impose the group's ways of living and thinking on others. Porter (1965) and others have observed that, in Canada, this has translated into the dominance of Anglo-Saxon ways of seeing and doing things (see Chapter 4).

Even so, acculturation is by no means a one-way street. In our society, the popularity of ethnic restaurants, or the burgeoning interest in soccer, show that the host society also adopts culture traits from incoming groups.

"FOR EVERY NORTH AMERICAN INDIAN WHO BEGINS TO DISAPPEAR, I ALSO BEGIN TO DISAPPEAR"

By Wilfred Pelletier[3]

Being educated in white schools was a painful experience for me as for most Indian kids. I have therefore given a lot of thought to the Indian way of learning. I believe that it has a lot to do with our difficulties in your schools.

I grew up in a community where kids were allowed to discover everything for themselves, by personal observation rather than formal instruction. Nobody said to us "this is a desk," we learned that that was a desk by other people using the word, calling it "a desk." We began to use that word, too, but we related to that desk in our own way, not because somebody told us that was a desk and that's what you do with it, you write at it, or that is a table and you eat off a table, and this is a chair and you sit on a chair. We probably used chairs in many different ways, like most kids, but we also knew that you could sit on that chair. We made the discoveries that other people had made centuries before us, but they belonged to us, they didn't belong to some despot or expert, someone who tells you, I've got the answers, so you quit being curious, quit exploring. That didn't happen to me until I went to school, from then on it was a matter of suppression.

I don't much like looking back at what happened to me at school. It seems to me that the only thing I enjoyed was playing hooky and running away. One of the difficult things I had to cope with was something called "time." The teacher would talk about wasting "time." I didn't know what that meant, I didn't know how you could waste "time." And then she would say you could make it up, you could make up "time." She'd read us a story in school and then she'd say we've lost all that "time," so now we have to hurry and make it up. I couldn't figure out what that meant, either. There were all kinds of things about time that really bewildered me. I did not understand what all this clock watching was about, because in our community we ate when we were hungry and slept when we felt tired. We did not do things on any kind of schedule, yet that never presented a problem. The things that were necessary always got done.

I discovered gradually that white people lived in two kinds of time, the past and the future. Indians, on the other hand, live in an eternal present. Our history only ran back to the oldest member of the community, so there was no way we could live in the past or in the future, we could only live in the here and now. When we become like you people, dealing with the past, trying to live some kind of a future that doesn't exist, then we'll have taken ourselves completely out of the present. That's what happens to me when I switch from our language to English. After I have been out in white society for a while, speaking English, I find myself having a really difficult time when I go back to an Indian community. I don't know how long it takes me to readjust, and I don't realize when it happens, I just find myself flowing in that community again, forgetting about that abstract time outside.

White educators always complain that Indian kids have difficulties with abstractions. I, too, had that problem. It is hard for us Indians to make sense of the segmented approach to learning taught in the schools, to study "Chemistry" or "Math" or "French" without relating them to each other and to some larger whole. We Indians approach things the opposite way. We start with the whole and examine every part in relationship to that whole. This is because our way of life was total, nothing was outside it, everything was within. So we didn't begin to explore in the same way you people began to explore; we look for answers within ourselves, but always related it to the natural order that we saw ourselves part of.

This affected our politics as well as our education. I can remember as a boy, when we sat in council, we came to unanimous decisions. Everyone agreed, and if one person objected, we didn't suppress that person. What we did was ask ourselves a question: "Is it possible that we don't see this thing the same way as the other person? Let's explore ourselves." I see white people attempting to use the same method, but they cannot make it work. For what they do, if one person disagrees, they begin jumping on that person trying to change that person's mind and to suppress him. They say, you're holding up the works, there is only one person who disagrees, so you must be wrong, because the majority cannot be wrong. I don't think that it works out that way, because it is quite possible for the majority to be wrong. I look around at the majority culture around me, and at all the suffering it has caused both in this country and abroad, and I am very sure that something is wrong.

CULTURE LAG

When Comte evolved his Law of Three Stages, he envisioned all sectors of society changing simultaneously, making for a smooth transition. In real life, however, cultural change happens in a piecemeal way at different times and at different rates. More than 60 years ago, Ogburn (1922) noted that material culture — the technological realm — changes more quickly than other elements of social life. It takes time before adjustments are made in these other areas. Ogburn referred to this delay as **culture lag**. This phenomenon is even more common today, given the great explosion of technological advances. Look, for example, at the vast nuclear build-up. The lag in developing commensurate control mechanisms may well prove fatal for humanity. Look, too, at automation, which has the potential for increasing productivity and hence overall well-being. But no effective policies have as yet been developed for the redeployment of displaced workers.

Technology is not the spearhead for change in every instance. Sometimes behaviour changes before institutional support mechanisms have been put in place[4]. For instance, increasing numbers of married women, many of them mothers of young children, have entered the labour force, but the availability of good, affordable day care has lagged far behind (Cooke 1986). In part, this lag can be attributed to the entrenched value that a mother's rightful place is at home with her children. In turn, the notion of a mother's "proper" place allows various levels of government to downplay the urgency for action on day care. This ideological stance flies in the face of the fact that many women are obliged to work for economic reasons, and that others choose to work.

SUMMARY

In this chapter, we have used Tylor's definition of culture as the sum total of a group's way of life, including knowledge, beliefs, morals, customs, and law. To acquaint oneself with a particular culture, one must become familiar with its language and other symbolic codes.

The common aspects of a culture are most often apparent in the small homogeneous societies studied by early anthropologists. As outsiders, these investigators could take nothing for granted, as people tend to do in familiar surroundings. Precisely because they could take nothing for granted, anthropologists, such as Malinowski and Benedict, painstakingly examined discrete elements and their place in the total culture.

Social organization is the process by which cultural elements are integrated into a relatively stable and predictable social system. Key to this organization are the twin concepts of status and role. Status is the stationary aspect of role, and role is the behavioural dimension associated with a particular status, which may be ascribed (an accident of birth) or achieved. In all groups, each individual occupies one status that is considered his or her salient — most important — one. Thus, in South Africa, racial status, whether black, colored, or white, supersedes all other statuses. The rights and obligations associated with a certain status, and expectations regarding appropriate role behaviour, change over time and space.

The "oughts" and "ought nots" of conduct form a hierarchy which includes societal values and norms, with norms subdivided into mores and folkways. Mores are cultural imperatives, whereas folkways constitute a code of etiquette. The relative importance of mores and folkways is reflected in the sanctions applied when they are violated, sanctions that may range from death to a raised eyebrow.

The elements of social organization are combined into different configurations, permitting us to refer to types of societies. Two such modes are Gemeinschaft and Gesellschaft. These societal types differ in size, in complexity, in their bases of solidarity, and in the ways individuals relate to each other. Another notable difference is that one can describe a Gemeinschaft — a small, homogeneous community — as having *a* culture, whereas no such claim can be made for a large, heterogeneous society such as Canada.

The latter embraces a variety of subcultures, each of which represents a distinctive way of life. Subcultures form along lines such as age, ethnicity, occupation, and socioeconomic status. A subculture that constitutes a rebellion against values and norms is called a counterculture. The lines that distinguish a subculture or a counterculture may be blurred.

For a culture to survive, its members must deem it worthy of preservation and transmission. In this sense, then, ethnocentrism — literally, the assignment of a central place to one's own culture—is a positive force. It becomes negative when people regard their culture as inherently superior, and diminish other cultures. To avoid this judgmental stance, one must interpret particular cultural elements in their overall context.

Custom, habit, ethnocentrism, and the myriad unarticulated ways in which people live out their culture every day are powerful forces for its preservation. However, there are always counteracting forces pressing for change. Prominent among these forces is the process of cultural diffusion, by which artifacts and ways of thinking penetrate an existing culture and become part of it. As this occurs, both old and new cultures undergo modification. When groups are continually exposed to one another, cultural traits are exchanged, resulting in acculturation. Generally, this exchange favours the adoption of the dominant group's ways. Cultural change tends to proceed at different rates in various sectors of a society. Culture lag occurs when one sector, often the technological one, moves ahead before the changes can be effectively integrated with other aspects of social organization.

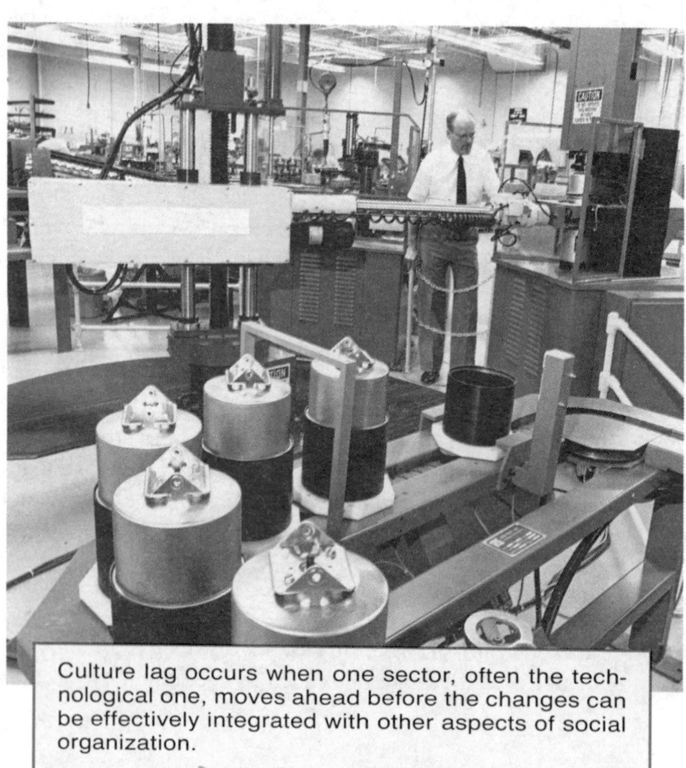

Culture lag occurs when one sector, often the technological one, moves ahead before the changes can be effectively integrated with other aspects of social organization.

ASSIGNMENTS

Do one or more of the following assignments, as instructed by your professor.

1 Select a religious group that is unfamiliar to you (for example, Jehovah's Witnesses or Hare Krishna). Do some library research to learn about the group, and then attend one of its services. Be alert to the rituals, and listen carefully to the points stressed in any sermon or impromptu speech. How do your observations fit with what you read?

2 Television is central in propagating values that serve the interests of powerful groups in society. Watch two programs and identify the cultural values reflected in each. Pay careful attention to the commercials. What kinds of behaviour do they encourage, and whose interests are best served by this behaviour?

3 Seek out an elderly person and invite him or her to reminisce about growing up in an era different from this one. What are the main differences this respondent perceives? How does he or she feel about them?

4 Interview five members of a subculture that is accessible to you. Find out how belonging to that subculture affects their work and leisure activities activities. If you live in a large city, you might be able to talk to gay activists. If there is a military base near you, you could conduct interviews with those stationed there and with members of their families.

5 Opponents of Canada's free trade agreement with the United States have argued, among other things, that the pact poses a major threat to Canadian culture and to the nation's cultural industries. What do you think is distinctive about Canadian culture? As well, are there distinctive ways Canadians promote and attempt to preserve this culture?

SUGGESTED READINGS

Bruce Chatwin, *The Songlines* (Markham, Ont.: Penguin, 1987). "He went on to explain how each totemic ancestor, while travelling across the country, was thought to have scattered a trail of words and musical notes along the line of his footprints, and how these Dreaming tracks lay over the land as 'ways' of communication between the most far-flung tribes." The book is an enthralling record of Chatwin's search for the pathways, or "songlines," of the hunter-gatherers of precolonial Australia, as they lived out their lives in perpetual travel across a vast continent. Along the way, Chatwin ponders the question: why have we come to assume that living a sedentary life, in a house, is "normal," and that a wandering existence is aberrant?

E.L. Doctorow, *Billy Bathgate* (New York: Random House, 1989). *Billy Bathgate* is a fictionalized account of the reign of underworld kingpin "Dutch" Schultz. To Billy, who had grown up in an East Bronx tenement, gaining an entrée to the glitz and glamour of Schultz's gang was like a dream come true. Poverty and the Depression seemed a long way off.

As Billy is more deeply drawn into the tightly insulated subculture, he learns that the values and norms of the world outside are simply not relevant.

Alan Fry, *How a People Die* (Toronto: Doubleday, 1970). In this graphic novel documenting the west coast Indians' grim task of accommodating to life in the white world, Fry raises numerous sociological and ethical questions without attempting to provide pat answers or to assign blame. Staged in a small British Columbia community, the encounter between two "worlds" is uncompromising, violent, and inevitably painful for both sets of participants.

Pauline Gedge, *Child of the Morning* (Agincourt, Ont.: Gage, 1977). Well-written historical novels provide you with an opportunity to immerse yourself in the ambience of other cultures, in other eras. Here, Gedge weaves a rich tapestry depicting ancient Egyptian civilization during the reign of Egypt's only woman Pharaoh, Hatshesput, whose temple in Deir-el-Bahari can still be visited.

T. Kroeber, *Ishi in Two Worlds* (Berkeley and Los Angeles: University of California Press, 1962). In August 1911, the last known survivor of the Yahi tribe, emaciated and close to exhaustion, walked into a small California town. He was named Ishi, meaning "man" in Yana, by the two anthropologists who befriended him. Ishi spent his remaining few years in San Francisco, living and working at the museum attached to the University of California. The book is a fascinating account of a now extinct culture and of how its last member experienced modern life.

H. MacLennan, *Two Solitudes* (Toronto: Macmillan of Canada, 1945). MacLennan dramatizes classic clashes of worldviews in Quebec. First, there is the conflict between the village priest, committed to the traditional way of life, and Athanase Tallard, who wants to bring to his community the advantages of technological progress. But Tallard, in turn, is not culturally equipped to function in the cold, impersonal business world of Montreal, where profit is the overriding consideration. (We alert students to MacLennan's references to the French and English as different "races." As sociologists, we would describe them as different "ethnic groups," both of which are of the caucasoid race.)

Peter C. Newman, *Bronfman Dynasty* (Toronto: McClelland and Stewart, 1978). From a bootlegging operation in the Depression, the Bronfmans built

Seagrams into the world's largest distillery company. *Bronfman Dynasty* lets the reader look in on life at the top. Like the very poor, the super rich live in their own subculture. Residences in many parts of the globe, travel by private jet, and a large personal staff are taken for granted.

NOTES

1 Critics of this formulation (for example, Becker 1967) counter that, when circumstances change, the attitudes and behaviour of the poor change more readily than the notion of a culture of poverty would suggest.

2 Ironically, countercultures, conceived in rebellion against community standards, often demand strict conformity to their own standards.

3 It is interesting to realize that the meaning of a concept as seemingly straightforward as that of "time" varies across cultures and subgroups. See Forman's *Taking Our Time: Feminist Perspectives on Temporality* (1989) for a discussion of the ways in which females experience time differently from males. See also Burman's fine chapter on the experience of time among the unemployed in *Killing Time, Losing Ground: Experience of Unemployment* (1988).

4 For a definition of institutions, see Chapter 1, Note 2, and the opening of Chapter 9.

3

THE LITTLE ENGINE THAT COULD

There was a little town in the big hills. It was a pretty town, but it was sad. It was sad because the children who lived in it were sad, and when children are sad, no town can be happy.

Now all of the children were sad because for a long time no toys had come to the town. You see, to get to the town, trains had to come over the hill, and it took a big engine to pull a train over the hill. But big engines had no time for toys.

The mothers and fathers didn't like to see the children look so sad. One day the mothers and fathers called a man who made toys.

"Our children want toys," they said. "Please put some on a train and get them to us as fast as you can." The toy man thought of all the toys that he could get for the children. There were tops, balloons, jets and rockets, toy animals, and clowns. He had every toy you can think of.

The toy man put all his toys on a train with an old, old engine, and it headed for the town. The toys were happy. At last they were on the way to the children who wanted them! The cars and the old engine were happy too.

Suddenly—
Crash! CRASH!!

The wheels fell off the old engine.

Oh, how sad the old, old engine was.

"Oh, my!" he said, "I did want to take the toys to the children. But I have no wheels."

The cars looked at the old, old engine.

"Oh, no!" they cried. "Now we can't take the toys."

The toys were sad and some of them were crying.

Just then the toy clown jumped out of one of the cars.

"Come, come," he said. "Don't give up. Many engines whiz by here. Maybe one of them would help us."

• • • • •

Then came a little engine. The clown called to it.

"Yes," it said. "What can I do for you?"

"Please, little engine, would you help us?" he asked. "We want to get to the town on the other side of the hill. The toy man wants to give toys to the children there. Please help us get to the town."

"I'm very little," said the engine, "but I think I can do it. I can try."

The little engine looked at the hill. My, how big it was! Could he make it? He took the old cars and pulled.

He pulled and pulled and pulled.

As he climbed, he said over and over,

"I think I can. I think I can. I think I can. I think — I—can. I think—I can. I——think——I——can."

Then, with one last pull he was at the top of the hill. The toys all laughed and shouted. The toy clown cried, "I thought you could do it."

Then the little engine rushed down the other side of the hill to the waiting children. And as he rushed down, he said,

"I thought I could. I thought I could. And I DID!"

In the previous chapter, we established that there are striking differences in the ways groups of people order their lives. These differences are partially rooted in imperatives of the environment: for example, what does the group do with the old and infirm when it must migrate annually under harsh conditions? Differences are also rooted in the values assigned to forms of behaviour, determining what is seen as good, polite, pleasurable, or disgusting.

Anthropologist Clyde Kluckhohn said that in some ways all people are alike and in some ways no two people are alike. To be more specific, all human beings share a basic biological make-up, as well as certain needs, for survival; groups of people share understandings and customs. At the same time, each human being has a particular combination of physical, psychological, and cultural characteristics that makes him or her unique. In this chapter, our focus is on how people come to be alike in certain ways, and on the processes by which common understandings and practices evolve. Consider *The Little Engine That Could*. Even popular children's stories are repositories of societal values and common understandings. Note, for example, that the little engine triumphs by his very own efforts. In what ways could this storyline be seen to relate to political and economic ideologies?

BASIC SOCIALIZATION AND ITS AGENTS

For a culture to survive, its patterns of thinking and acting must be passed from one generation to the next. This process of transmission is known as **socialization**.

Basic socialization is the process by which the baby is shaped into a member of its group and inducted into the ways and "secrets" of its society.[1] The young child is attuned only to its own needs; gradually and painfully, it is trained by example and by reward and punishment to conform to the expectations of others. Socialization goes on throughout the life cycle. Every time you enter a new group or assume a new role—for instance, when you become a college student, start a new job, or get married—you undergo a period of preparation for this new role. Basic socialization has particularly far-reaching effects because it is carried out on very young children, who by nature are physically and mentally helpless.

THE FAMILY

Who does the socializing or, to put the question more formally, who are the **agents of socialization**? In our society it is somewhat taken for granted that early socialization takes place within the **nuclear family**—that is, the father, the mother, and their children, who share the same dwelling. Increasing numbers of children in Canadian society, however, are growing up in families in which there is only one parent, or at least only one biological parent (see Chapter 9A). In other societies (and in North American society in previous generations), children are brought up in large households that include grandparents, parents, and children, not to mention uncles, aunts, and their children. Such a household is referred to as an **extended family**.

All known societies train their young in the ways of the group, although there are wide variations in what these ways are (cultural content) and in the training methods used (form of socialization). In every society, there is a wide range of methods for moulding a child's behaviour. Children learn by example, imitation, and direct teaching. They learn by being praised when they follow group norms and by being shamed, perhaps by exposure to ridicule, when they deviate from prescribed standards. They also learn from the withdrawal of love and from corporal punishment. Many societies, including our own, use a combination of these methods.

Unlike simple societies in which all members substantially share the same values, beliefs, and way of life, complex industrialized societies are made up of a variety of subcultures, divided along economic, ethnic, and religious lines. Particular subcultures often favour some methods of child-rearing over others. For example, several studies (Bronfenbrenner 1959; Kohn 1963) have shown that North American middle-class families state that they disapprove of corporal punishment (even though they may resort to it in practice). On the other hand, working-class families are more likely to affirm that they physically chastise their children, and groups such as the Hutterites see physical punishment as a positive value.

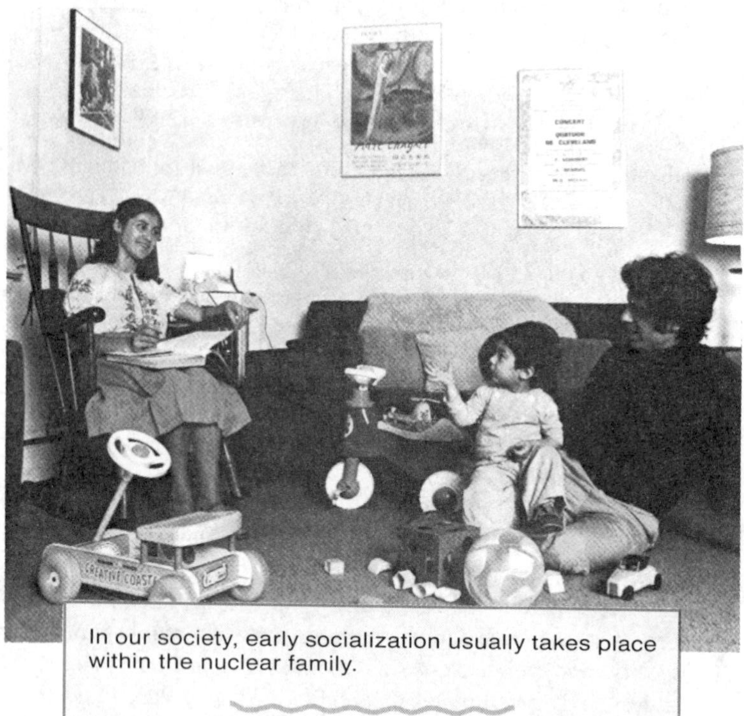

In our society, early socialization usually takes place within the nuclear family.

THE NEW EXECUTIVE FATHER

By Rona Maynard

The guilt was getting to Peter McCrodan, a stockbroker with Nesbitt Thomson Deacon Inc. in Toronto. His sons, Andrew, 3, and Graeme, 18 months, had no use for their new day-care centre — and they made it all too clear when McCrodan dropped them off each morning. "Graeme would get a death grip on my suit jacket and I'd have to peel him off me," he says, recalling in painful detail the standoffs last August. "He'd bawl his head off as if to say, 'Why are you leaving me, Daddy?' Meanwhile, I'd have Andrew clutching my pants until the teacher managed to get him interested in a car. Then he'd ignore me while I dealt with Graeme. The message was, 'If you're going to do this to me, Daddy, I'd rather you didn't exist.' "

After two heart-wrenching weeks, McCrodan, 34, started wondering whether hustling stocks justified his children's distress. His business, which had earned him $167,000 in his headiest year, had been hit so hard by the previous October's stock market crash that he estimated his 1988 income at $26,000 — much less than his wife, Shirley, made analyzing computer hardware for the Royal Bank of Canada. With his career at a turning point and the family home paid for, he figured the time was right for a stint as a full-time father. Now on an open-ended leave of absence, McCrodan likes his new life just fine. Even when he returns to work, there will be limits on his zest for making deals. "Enamored as I am of high finance," he says, "I have a family and I want to see them."

Meet the new professional father, whose commitment to his kids is breaking all the rules that have long determined corporate success. He ducks out of meetings to watch school track meets, turns down promotions to protect family time or reduces working hours to help nurture his baby. He won't dodge weekend work when a crisis demands it, but refuses to let 60-hour weeks become routine. And like McCrodan, he may even risk his hard-won career if it threatens his family's well-being. Although few men yet take fatherhood quite *that* seriously, all signs point to a changing work ethic — one that prizes family harmony over perks and power.

Women have been juggling kids' dental appointments with rush assignments ever since they entered the workforce. But for men, this kind of thinking is nothing short of revolutionary. And in offices across the country, it's causing an unprecedented conflict between family needs and business priorities. For managers, it means major headaches because, while fathers' hearts may have softened, the bottom-line realities facing companies are tougher than ever, thanks to intensified competition at home and abroad. Even the most enlightened bosses are bound to have mixed emotions about their staff putting families first. Absenteeism can result in postponed meetings, frustrated clients and extra work for resentful colleagues. "The business day is still intuitively defined by business people as something before 9ish to something after 6ish," comments

Dave Sanderson, marketing vice-president of The Sports Network in Toronto and a father of two. "So a 6 o'clock departure for a school play or a recital is not OK. It's just that there are more people like me who say we are going anyway."

With his navy-blue suit and jammed leather briefcase, today's corporate father may look the part of the traditional go-getter careerist. In fact, he and his boss come from different worlds. When the men who run Canada were launching their careers 30 years ago, 70% of families looked like Beaver Cleaver's, with mom in her apron and dad in his workday tie. Men could retreat into their easy chairs after a tough day at work, confident that scrubbed and smiling kids would soon be summoned to a home-cooked dinner. Now that more than half of women with children at home hold jobs, just 7% of families fit this picture, and men face as much pressure in their own living rooms as they do at the office. And many of their older bosses are unaware of the trend. At a 1986 Harvard University seminar, senior business executives vastly overestimated how many of their employees had traditional homes where only dad worked. Their guesses ranged from 40% to 70% of employees. The actual figure was 10%.

Although survey after survey has found men shouldering far less than half of the household load, their overburdened wives are out to change that. Kitchen-table conferences to split up parental and household duties between spouses have become commonplace. And the pressure takes its toll. One recent U.S. study showed 36% of the fathers at a large public utility reported "a lot of stress" keeping their public and private lives in sync—compared with 37% of the mothers. Another study showed that men forced to miss work by a child's illness experience more stress-related symptoms than do women in the same bind.

Men are aware that while employers grudgingly tolerate the tug of parental obligation in women, they see it as the mark of a wimp in men. "Employers are getting more accepting when women ask for flexibility," says Bruce O'Hara, director of Work Well, a Victoria information centre that helps employees sell their bosses on flexible schedules. "But they're only beginning to look at giving men the same privileges."

Yet companies can't simply ignore the problem. Painfully aware that do-or-die slogging no longer guarantees a job, much less a six-figure salary or a shot at the top, employees are not as willing to sacrifice personal time. The reward they prize most is job flexibility—and employers who can't deliver risk losing some of their best people.

SCHOOLS AND EARLY CHILDHOOD INSTITUTIONS

Parents and parent surrogates, such as babysitters and day-care personnel, are paramount among agents of socialization. In complex societies, institutions have come to play a major role in preparing children to become full-fledged members of society. Day-care centres are becoming more prevalent because of the increase in single-parent families and the growing participation of women in the labour force. In the day-care centre, looking after the child is a paid job, carried out with greater detachment than is usual in a mother-child relationship. Instead of being the main focus, the child is one member of the group. Of course, in a family with many children, the child is also accustomed to being a member of a group.

In Canada, the moralistic conviction that young children should be taken care of by their mothers serves as a barrier to the development of adequate day-care facilities. This is an example of a situation in which the prevailing ideology, that mothers with small children ought to stay at home, is at odds with the practical reality that many must work and that others prefer to do so. Mackay and Clifford have reflected on this dilemma:

Day-care centres are becoming more prevalent because of the increase in single-parent families and the growing participation of women in the labour force.

> *Economic necessity and the demand for equal rights for women have propelled women into the paid work force. Now that it is more common for mothers to work than stay at home with children, who will look after the children? In contrast with other western industrialized nations, Canada, Britain and the United States have yet to demonstrate that they really care about childcare; these three countries do not have "family policies". . . .*
>
> *Attitudes toward quality of daycare must also change. But first, we will have to change our values. Do we really care more about cleanliness than child development? Have we our priorities in the right order when we pay four times as much for housecleaning as for childcare? In the most formative and impressionable pre-school years, do we really want to pay daycare workers one-third the salary received by primary school workers? (1982, 44).*

Women's groups have long lobbied for more day-care facilities; government task forces have acknowledged the need for expanded services, and these were promised by the federal government prior to the 1988 election. Yet, the gap persists between the demand for day care and the facilities available. Initiatives by a few private-sector employers have narrowed this gap only marginally, and good private day care is a luxury few can afford.

Even for children whose mothers are not in the work force, the time of leaving the home may come long before the age at which they must start school. Parents may organize play groups or simply trade off on the care of small children to give each other a break. Three- to five-year-olds may attend a nursery school or kindergarten for periods ranging from two hours to all day. In these situations, children are encouraged to share and to become oriented to what other children do. It is often their first experience of being exposed, on a continuing basis, to people outside the immediate family. Thus, teachers and other children become a significant part of the child's environment.

A present, only a minority of Canadian children experience day care and/or nursery schools. By contrast, it is obligatory for all children to attend educational institutions from the age of 5 or 6 to 15 or 16—a period of at least ten years, and for many it is longer. Historically, as we will discuss in more detail in Chapter 9B, free public education was introduced in the wake of industrialization. It was intended not only to impart basic literary, mathematical, and social skills but also to pass on characteristics suitable for an industrial work force, such as obedience, time-consciousness, neatness, personal hygiene, and tolerance for performing repetitive, routine tasks. Since then, formal education has been greatly expanded, both in duration and in the scope of the curriculum.

When a child goes out from the home—to school or simply to the homes of friends—it finds that things are not always done or thought of in exactly the same way as they are at home. In other words, the child's universe expands—a necessary kind of growth. However, socialization is likely to proceed most smoothly when there is no marked disparity between the values and customs espoused at home and those taught at school. In that fortunate event, conflict is minimized, since it becomes quite clear to the child what is considered right and what is considered wrong. In a nation of immigrants such as Canada, however, few children make the transition from home to school and home again with ease, at least not until they learn to tailor their behaviour to the specific context. For example, the child reared in a highly disciplined immigrant home may experience confusion and feelings of ineptitude in a classroom situation that rewards initiative, innovation, and independent thought. The opposite situation is also often true.

Ethnic origin is not the only factor that both differentiates children at school and influences many children's school experience. Social-class background (see Chapter 4 on stratification) can also be a bridge or a barrier between home and school. Many analysts (Martell 1974; Bowles and Gintis 1976) view schools as middle-class institutions. If indeed they are, it follows that they attempt to impose middle-class values and patterns of behaviour, which may be quite foreign to students from other social classes. Those from the upper class are for the most part shielded from such discrepancies by attending elite private schools, but lower-class children must each day confront an alien world (Sennett and Cobb 1972). What does one offer during show-and-tell on Mondays when one's weekend was spent playing around the lane or the apartment building, rather than visiting grandma and grandpa in the country or going to a puppet show at the local library? By the same token, homework may have to take second place to looking after younger brothers and sisters.

VISION OF QUALITY DAY CARE IN ONTARIO CLOUDED BY RACE FOR SPACE

By Andrew McIntosh
and Ann Rauhala

It is not an analogy that inspires much confidence:

"We're working at three or four cliff edges all at the same time," said John Sweeney, Ontario's Minister of Community and Social Services, describing in an interview his ministry's efforts to meet simultaneously a frantic demand for child care and an urgent need to maintain quality.

In Canada in 1987, according to the National Council of Welfare, there were 1,937,163 children under the age of 13 whose parents worked or studied outside the home. There were 243,545 licenced child-care spaces.

Ottawa has promised to spend $6.4-billion to create 200,000 spaces over seven years, with about $4-billion of that sum destined for sharing costs that the provinces incur to build or renovate centres or to run them.

In Ontario in 1987, there were 766,751 children under 13 who needed care while their parents worked outside the home or attended school. There were 94,000 licenced spaces. (This number reportedly has increased to about 100,000.)

Mr. Sweeney, whose ministry will spend more than $300-million on day care from 1988 to 1990, described the increase in the number of spaces in Ontario as "the kind of growth that has never happened before."

Yet demand for child care continues to far exceed supply throughout Canada, posing a logistical puzzle both for families trying to obtain care and for governments — federal, provincial, regional and municipal — trying to create a coherent social service out of a mishmash of babysitters, parents' co-ops and small businesses.

A Gallup poll conducted last month found that 54 percent of Canadians surveyed believe that governments should share responsibility for providing child-care facilities; 48 percent said they favored increased government spending to provide subsidized spaces for preschoolers.

The question about day care is no longer whether it is necessary but how it can best be provided and by whom. But every twist of the puzzle raises another debate, whether it is ideological, constitutional or financial.

Should child care be a non-profit social service, a commercial industry or a mixture of both? With the regulation of child care primarily a provincial responsibility, to what degree can Ottawa use cost-sharing dollars to build a genuine province-wide institution.

Who will guarantee safety and quality? And who will pay?

An examination by *The Globe and Mail* of more than 1,600 government day-care inspection reports from across Ontario in 1987 and 1988 revealed that the province's race to provide more spaces may be sacrificing quality.

About 38 percent of the centres for which inspection documents were available had some problem — poor record-keeping, dirty carpets and bedding, worn-out toys and playground equipment, failure to observe fire safety regulations or inadequate food.

More than 22 percent of the centres failed to keep basic records of attendance and information about children. About 14 percent were in environments that were unclean or potentially unsafe.

About 11 percent lacked toys and equipment, and about 10 percent did not check fire extinguishers or conduct regular fire drills.

A smaller number of the 1,643 centres examined had other difficulties, including poor food, unlocked drugs, inadequate liability insurance, insufficient or unqualified staff or irregular sanitary inspections.

Not surprisingly, a Decima Research Ltd. poll conducted for Health and Welfare Canada in June, 1987, found that 59 percent of those surveyed rated the quality of day care in Canada as fair or poor. Metro Toronto residents gave their city's day care the worst marks in the country—67 percent rated the quality as fair or poor.

Laurel Rothman of the Ontario Coalition for Better Day Care, which supports non-profit child care, said *The Globe*'s findings showed a fragile, vulnerable network of services. "I thought to myself: We wouldn't allow anybody to run schools that way. We wouldn't allow anybody to run hospitals that way."

PEER GROUPS

A **peer group** consists of individuals who occupy a roughly similar status and who tend to identify with each other. A German proverb states, "Willst Du wissen wer Du bist, frag' wer Deine Gesellschaft ist" ("If you want to know who you are, ask who your companions are.") As the child spends more time away from home, children of its own age group, as well as older ones, become important **role models**. Theodorson and Theodorson (1969, 335) define a role model as "a standard used by the other person in determining the appropriate attitudes and actions of an occupant of the role." In other words, if Johnny's fourth-grade friends are interested in little but hockey, Johnny may quickly abandon his previous interest in gymnastics, which they call sissy, and take up the game even if he doesn't like it much.

As the child spends more time away from home, the peer group and older youngsters become important role models.

As the child reaches adolescence, the peer group becomes markedly more important, touching all areas of life. In a major study of American high schools (1963), James Coleman found that peer attitudes toward academic achievement profoundly affected whether students put forth their best efforts in academic work or withheld them for fear of being labelled teacher's pets or even more derogatory terms. The effects of such peer pressure can be lasting indeed because, as we will demonstrate later, educational attainment is crucially linked to occupational and social status and to many other aspects of existence.

Influences which are less permanent, but very strong at the time, are apparent in the tyranny of teenage dress codes, music idols, the use of slang, and the countless fads to which teenagers are prey. Advertisers take advantage of teenagers' susceptibility to peer-group pressure, through the use of mass-advertising campaigns. The major objective of such a technique is to establish one brand of sports shoe or soft drink as *the* brand, the use of which will demonstrate conformity and hence not jeopardize acceptance by the group.

Sociologists have commented that a striking facet of modern North American society is the extent to which age groups are segregated. In part, this is because of the attrition of the extended family. This segregation is most pronounced throughout the age-graded school system. In human groups generally, homogeneity (sameness) *within* groups enhances the potential for conflict *between* groups. In the case of age groups, the conflict is most evident between teenagers and their elders. For example, parents may strongly disapprove of their teenagers' choice of clothing, hairstyle, and music, such as heavy-metal rock. School administrators and students come into conflict over such issues as punctuality and restricted smoking areas.

As more and more high school students go on to attend postsecondary educational institutions, such as community colleges and universities, the adolescent subculture is perpetuated. At those universities where fraternities and sororities are a highly visible and vocal minority, peer-group pressure is intensified. Since each fraternity and sorority seeks to recruit students who are similar to one another in many respects, conformity with group norms is easier to enforce. The same is true of teenage gangs, even though the group norms enforced within gangs may be very different from fraternity norms.

It is apparent that the content of the norms, and the means by which they are enforced, may vary in youth subcultures as in other human groups. But the phenomenon of seeking conformity remains constant. Approaching this phenomenon theoretically, Cohen has commented:

> *Every one of us wants to be a member in good standing of some groups and roles. We all want to be recognized and respected as a full-fledged member of some age and sex category. . . . For every . . . role there are certain kinds of action and belief which function, as truly and*

> *effectively as do uniforms, insignia and membership cards, as signs of membership. To the degree that we covet such membership, we are motivated to assume those signs, to incorporate them into our behaviour and frame of reference. Many of our religious beliefs, esthetic standards, norms of speech, political doctrines, and canons of taste and etiquette are so motivated (1963, 56–7).*

Here is a demonstration of the particular window sociology opens on the world: it directs our attention to similarities in situations that are ostensibly quite different. At first glance, would the similarities between fraternities and street gangs seem obvious?

THE MASS MEDIA

In discussing peer groups, we focused on factors which internally link members of a group, at the same time bringing about differentiation among groups. The mass media provide a powerful countervailing influence to the forces of differentiation. For one thing, they permit mass advertising to millions of people, which tends to bring about a levelling of taste and prefabricated standards of what is desirable. Homemakers in Vancouver and Charlottetown, in mansions in Westmount and in public housing in Riverdale, tend to agree that "ring around the collar" and "greasy french fries" reflect adversely on their competence.

Modern media permit mass advertising to millions of people, tending to bring about a levelling of taste and prefabricated standards of what is desirable.

Mass-media advertising facilitates mass consumption, which creates a superficial sameness. For example, based on the clues afforded by appearance, it would be difficult to make accurate judgements about the income levels of spectators at a movie theatre or a football game.

Mass-media advertisers don't simply sell products; they also promote lifestyles which lead to the consumption of their products. This creates a paradox. On the one hand, the existence of social classes (see Chapter 4 on stratification) is obscured because most Canadians are portrayed as leading quite similar lives. The image is that of the "average" Canadian family, the "average" North American teenager or child. On the other hand, the lifestyles depicted as average are really affordable by only a small portion of the population. Ironically, then, the majority of people, those who cannot engage in the "average" Canadian lifestyle, are conditioned to think of themselves as a deprived minority.

From "cathy" by Cathy Guisewite.

Thus far we have looked at agents of socialization. Not unexpectedly, their relative importance has varied, both within particular cultures and among different cultures, at various points in history. We have noted that in Canadian society, the extended family is not as significant among agents of socialization as it was a century ago, or as it may be in less industrialized societies today. Conversely, the media have become increasingly important as socializing agents in our society.

THEORIES OF SOCIALIZATION

In this part of the chapter, we will examine various explanations of how social influences transform the biological organism into a functioning human being. This question has long engaged the attention of those who study social life, and a variety of theories has resulted. All such theories must address a basic problem for social scientists: the relative impact of nature (the endowment with which one begins life) and nurture (what one experiences in living). Thus, they all contain implicit or explicit assumptions about the nature of the biological organism, which is the newborn baby, as well as about the ways in which it becomes socialized and develops a personality. We will briefly examine some of these theories and their implications.

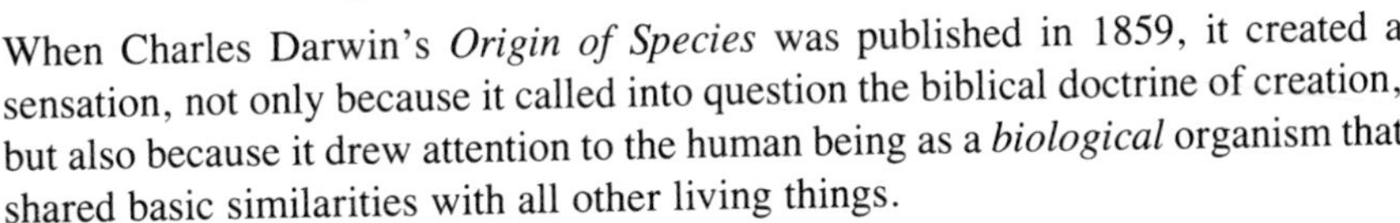

BIOLOGICAL DETERMINISM

When Charles Darwin's *Origin of Species* was published in 1859, it created a sensation, not only because it called into question the biblical doctrine of creation, but also because it drew attention to the human being as a *biological* organism that shared basic similarities with all other living things.

At that time, there was an enormous gap between the rich and poor, and many of the poor lived under abysmal conditions. Darwin had talked about the "survival of the fittest," that is, the survival of those organisms able to adapt to changing conditions. Such a concept seemed a tidy explanation of differences between rich and poor, since the poor were obviously less fit. The idea that organisms were given divergent endowments by nature also made it perfectly reasonable that Europeans should conquer and dominate so-called inferior races. Having a seemingly scientific rationalization available was patently useful for justifying the upsurge of colonialism that took place in the late 1800s.

At the level of the individual, **biological determinism** (also called **social Darwinism**) held that each person was born with a certain temperament and with certain abilities and that these could be changed only within a narrow range. That is to say, one cannot make a silk purse out of a sow's ear. Logically, this argument assigns socialization a limited role in the development of a human being.

William McDougall (1871–1938) elaborated a theory of biological determinism that attributed behaviour to instincts, each of which was paired with an emotion. People behave differently, he said, because their instincts vary in intensity. However, since followers of this school could not agree on what characteristics were instinctual, let alone how these could be studied in a scientific manner, the theory fell into disrepute in the mid-1920s. It is mentioned here merely for historical interest.

More generally, biological determinism demonstrates that the assumptions of a theory are often consonant with the beliefs of the particular society. In this case, the belief was that genetic endowment of individuals and of groups of people is the major determinant of how they will fare. As the political climate has shifted to the right during the 1980s, arguments containing some of the pernicious assumptions of biological determinism have again surfaced.

BEHAVIOURISM

Biological determinism holds that little can be done to change and upgrade individuals. By contrast, **behaviourism** regards the infant as infinitely plastic; apart from basic biological needs, individuals can be moulded to fit desired patterns.

Faith in the power of conditioning was given a boost by the experiments of the Russian physiologist Ivan Pavlov (1849–1936). He showed that when a stimulus, such as food, was consistently paired with another stimulus, such as the ringing of a bell, a dog would eventually salivate at the sound of a bell even if the ringing was not accompanied by food. This phenomenon is known as classical conditioning.

Pavlov's work attracted great attention, and physiologists and psychologists have since experimented with variations in conditioning processes — notably, operant conditioning, in which the desired behaviour is reinforced by rewards, and attempts are made to extinguish undesired behaviour by punishment. The work of B.F. Skinner (1904–) in teaching rats to run mazes is a famous example. A rat was rewarded by a food pellet for choosing the correct turn and punished by an electric shock for going astray.

Clearly, similar ideas are implicit in many current child-rearing methods, both at home and at school. The good student is rewarded with a star or a prize, while the disobedient one is subjected to various forms of punishment. According to behaviourist theory, learning takes place through a continuing process of operant conditioning.

The main tenets of behaviourism are:

- Psychology is basically a study of animal behaviour. Observations made on animals can be applied to human beings. If certain methods are effective in teaching rats to run mazes, they should be effective in teaching children how to read.
- Only overt behaviour can be studied. The behaviourist is not concerned with why Maggie smashes windows, but merely with her actions.
- Apart from basic biological needs, the infant is adaptable—a clean slate.
- Behaviour can be understood as stimulus and response. Desirable and undesirable behaviour can be respectively reinforced and extinguished. (Note the lack of explanation of how certain behaviours arise in the first place.)

Behaviourism has many current adherents and many practical applications. For example, it is used in treating alcoholics. In such programs, alcohol is paired with a substance that induces violent vomiting; the hope is that, in time, the very idea of drinking alcohol will cause revulsion.

Behaviourism de-emphasizes the significance of heredity and hence dismisses such concepts as the natural inferiority of certain individuals and groups of people. However, it replaces biological determinism with environmental determinism, a view that claims individuals are essentially at the mercy of their environment. The assumption underlying environmental determinism, that individuals can be shaped and reshaped by their environment, has been put to sinister use. For example, trainee guards for Nazi concentration camps were often given a pup. The individual would care for the dog and spend a great deal of time with it. After six months or so, he would be ordered to kill the animal. Immersion in this brutal training environment was intended to inure recruits against the horrors they would be expected to perpetrate in their work setting.

Neither biological nor environmental determinism, then, makes allowance for the active, creative dimension of individuals, a product of the dynamic interplay between innate characteristics and social experiences that makes each person unique.

THE FREUDIAN VIEW

A psychodynamic perspective of socialization, based largely on clinical observation and focused on the development of various internal characteristics and processes, was provided by Sigmund Freud (1856–1939). Freud's major contribution to thinking about personality and its development was the notion that human behaviour has unconscious (hidden) meanings. He claimed that the mind is like an iceberg; the tip showing above the water represents the region of consciousness, and the much larger mass below the water level represents the region of unconsciousness. For example, a person who had hypercritical parents might experience lifelong difficulty accepting *any* criticism, however justified. The idea of a hidden dimension to behaviour was revolutionary in Freud's time, though it is taken for granted in today's thinking.

Freud hypothesized that the personality is made up of three major systems—the id, the ego, and the superego—and that behaviour is almost always the product of an interaction among the three. The id consists of those forces and instincts that are inherited (and therefore present from birth). They provide a reservoir of psychic energy that is sexual and aggressive, causing the infant to be impulsive, selfish, and pleasure-seeking. Gradually, the acquisition of culture represses some aspects of the id so that the individual can deal more appropriately with the objective world of reality. What emerges is the ego—the "executive of the personality"—whose job it is to mediate, through intellectual and cognitive processes, between the individual's instinctual requirements and the conditions of the social and physical environment. The superego, often referred to as the conscience, is the third system of the personality and the last to develop. What the superego involves is the internalization of society's values (morality), which first occurs through the rewards and punishments imposed by the child's family. The superego is oriented to the ideal world, rather than to the actual environment, and pushes the individual to strive for perfection rather than for pleasure.

> *Under ordinary circumstances, [the id, the ego and the superego] do not collide with one another nor do they work at cross purposes. On the contrary, they work together as a team under the administrative leadership of the ego. The personality normally functions as a whole*

rather than as three separate segments. In a very general way, the id may be thought of as the biological component of personality, the ego as the psychological component, and the superego as the social component (Hall and Lindzey 1963, 35).

Freud attributed great importance to the early years of infancy and childhood, believing that the child passes through a series of stages. He defined each stage in terms of its emphasis on a particular zone of the body. In the oral stage, the mouth is the principal locus of attention, affording great pleasure through sucking and biting. The anal stage is centred upon the bowels, and the toilet training that is initiated at this time gives the child its first major experience with the external regulation of an instinct. The consequences of this training can thus have far-reaching effects on personality formation. In the phallic or Oedipal stage, the focus changes to the sexual and aggressive feelings associated with the genital region, leading to the development of gender identity and the appearance of the Oedipus complex, whereby the child wishes to possess the parent of the opposite sex and to remove the parent of the same sex. The hostility felt toward the parent of the same sex is gradually resolved through a process of identification with that parent. Thus, the mother becomes a role model for girls and the father for boys. If the resolution of this conflict does not ensue, the child may continue to experience difficulties in dealing with relationships in later life. Between the ages of five and twelve, the latency period, children's sexual interests as well as their aggression are assumed to be relatively muted.

The genital stage begins at puberty, when the individual's narcissism (self-love) expands to include those interests and activities that are characteristic of a mature, reality-oriented, socialized human being. The emergence of the adult self is not, however, a simple process, for it may be impeded by difficulties experienced in the earlier phases of development. Thus, all five stages contribute to the organization of the personality.

Many criticisms have been made of Freud's theories, even by those who have been greatly influenced by his thinking. It is alleged, for example, that his ideas were culture-bound, based on data obtained from his upper-middle class, adult patients in the Vienna of the 1890s and early 1900s. There is no question, however, that his emphasis on the unconscious dimension of human behaviour has had an enormous impact on modern thought.

THE SYMBOLIC INTERACTIONIST APPROACH

As noted in Chapter 1, symbolic interactionism is a general perspective on how society functions. Here, we are mainly concerned with the explanations this school of thought offers concerning the steps by which the individual becomes a functioning member of society.[2]

GEORGE HERBERT MEAD

Freud saw the personality as being divided into three parts, which generally operate in concert. At times, however, the id and the superego engage in a power struggle in which the ego — more or less successfully — acts as arbitrator. George Herbert Mead (1863–1931) also viewed the self as made up of separate parts:

- The *I* (somewhat akin to Freud's id) is unreasoning, impulsive, and pressing for immediate gratification of its wishes. It constitutes the innovative, creative dimension of the organism.
- The *me* represents the aspects of culture absorbed in the course of socialization.

The agents of socialization in this theory are the **significant others**, those who are important to the individual at various life stages — parents, teachers, peers, colleagues. These people transmit the parts of the culture they deem important and relevant to successful functioning in society. The content of what the child absorbs, then, depends on the values of the society as a whole, particularly on those which are dominant in the specific group or subculture—ethnic, religious, socioeconomic — of which the significant others are members. Thus, the child of an orthodox Jewish or Muslim family learns in whose house it may or may not accept food.

Mead's theory, unlike Freud's, gives considerable weight to the importance of culture in socialization. It does not depict the individual as totally constrained by genetic endowment or by social environment; neither does it represent the individual as entirely a creature at the mercy of impulse. The socially created "me" makes possible action which is independent of one's impulses, while the "I" ensures individuality. (After all, even children socialized in the same family do not become identical.) Instead of thinking, "I must not lie because Dad says it's wrong," the child comes to see lying as wrong. That is, the child internalizes the group's norms as its own.

Where Freud emphasized the fundamental conflict between the individual and society, with the energy for social activity obtained at the cost of repressing the urge for constant pleasure, Mead saw the individual and society as two sides of the same coin. They are inseparable. The very notion of what it means to be human presupposes the existence of a social group. Children raised in isolation lack the attributes associated with humanness.

Mead saw people as different in kind from other species. For him, two factors were crucial in accounting for this difference: language and self-awareness.

Language is an elaborate symbolic code that allows response to symbols rather than to actual stimuli.[3] The words "I am angry" convey a clear message that need not be supplemented by jumping up and down and waving one's fist (though sometimes such behaviour accompanies the words). Self-awareness yields the ability to empathize with others, to put oneself in someone else's shoes. To phrase the matter differently, individuals can become objects to themselves, imagining how another views their behaviour. They can mentally relive situations, savouring a successful performance in a job interview or chastising themselves for having said the wrong thing at the wrong time. They can also fantasize how they would react in some totally different situation. For example, you can imagine having a date with a famous film star. The Danny Kaye movie *The Secret Life of Walter Mitty* provides an example of a man enjoying fantasy existences that bear little resemblance to the drabness of his real life.

According to Freud, emotional development proceeds in a number of stages, which follow each other in a set order. Mead, too, delineated stages of development, but he was mainly concerned with cognitive development — that is, the process by which the child learns to place itself in a social environment and to interpret this environment. Mead posited the following process:

- *Imitation stage.* The infant has no conception of itself as a separate being. It simply apes the gestures, words, and facial expressions it observes in its environment.
- *Play stage.* Some time between the ages of two and three, the child begins to conceive of itself as a separate being, an object, and to experiment with assuming various roles. "Lucy is a good girl," says the child, displaying her ability to conceive of herself as an entity separate from her environment. Children together may play house, successively pretending to be themselves, their parents, and their siblings.
- *Game stage.* The child learns to respond to several others at the same time. For example, a hockey player must adjust his actions to those of all the other players; he cannot simply concentrate on what the goaltender is doing. During this stage, the child begins to categorize people and situations, which makes it possible to develop guidelines for behaviour based on situations that have been experienced previously and that are defined as similar. For instance, teacher, police officer, and rabbi may be grouped as "authority figures."
- *Generalized other.* The values and norms of the group have been internalized, and behaviour is guided by an internal monitor, the conscience (similar in some ways to Freud's superego), as much as by external control.

CHARLES HORTON COOLEY

Charles Horton Cooley (1864–1929) was a contemporary of Mead. Indeed, Mead, in developing his ideas about the emergence of the self, made use of many insights Cooley had gleaned from systematic observation of his own children. Cooley, too, saw the self as a social product that is formed in the process of interaction within primary groups. Cooley's **primary group** is small; its members are in frequent face-to-face contact and bound by common values and beliefs. The group is suffused with emotion, which tends to be strong and can run the gamut from love to hate. These groups are also primary in time. Most children's earliest experiences take place in primary family groups, subsequently supplemented by peer groups. Moreover, such groups are primary in importance, because the child forms its basic conceptions of self within them.[4]

Cooley pointed to the emergence of self-perception by referring to the **looking-glass self**, which can be defined as "a person's perception of himself as determined by the way he imagines he appears to others" (Theodorson and Theodorson 1969, 236). The individual eventually sees himself or herself, overall, as a competent person or a ne'er do well, as a worthwhile person or a failure, according to the responses given by significant others. The girl who is frequently told she is clumsy, sloppy, and plain will come to think of herself in those terms. Conversely, good feelings about oneself result from approval and admiration. Since one can only surmise what the other person really feels, misinterpretation is possible and often occurs. For example, parents may withhold praise for fear of making the child conceited, thus conveying a distorted impression of their views. Or they may mention only things that displease them, being too busy to vocalize pleased reactions. Sadly, many people who developed negative self-images in childhood never entirely shed them, even in the face of strong contrary evidence.

Once again, we note the lasting importance of early experience. It is, indeed, primary in its impact.

The Victorians beat their children as a matter of course.

DOES PUNISHING CHILDREN CAUSE A VIOLENT SOCIETY?

By Janet Watts

"I am afraid," says professor Michael Freeman of University College, London, "the British are rather keen on beatings." He is the mildly-spoken expert in family law who was surprised last week to find himself at the centre of public debate for saying something he has been saying for years (and has just said again): there should be a law to forbid any adult from striking any child. Even their own.

"As someone who has spent much of the last 15 years thinking, writing and lecturing on child abuse, and much of the last 10 years thinking and writing about children's rights—both as a lawyer and a moral philosopher—the link between corporal punishment and child abuse just seems to me blindingly obvious," he says. In an article in *Childright*, the magazine of the Children's Legal Centre, he writes: "Children are persons, not property. If it is wrong to hit persons, then it must also be wrong to hit children. If we are concerned to eliminate the evil of child abuse, we must ultimately accept that corporal punishment of children is child abuse."

The British have in this decade been obliged to admit themselves to be a nation whose adults on occasion ignore, neglect, beat, batter, burn, starve, bite, bugger, rape and murder their children. But when such behaviour reaches the newspapers and the criminal courts, we can wrap it in the familiar label of child abuse and comfort ourselves that it belongs only to monsters and psychopaths. We pay less attention to that level of acceptable behaviour that never makes headlines or case histories for the NSPCC, but which gives certain observers grave concern.

Valerie Yule of Aberdeen University made a simple and striking study of the way British adults treat their children in the streets, shops and buses in 1985. She just watched them. She watched 85 adult-child pairs in these settings for three minutes each, and compared what happened with the behaviour of 85 adult pairs. She found that in the time allowed, four-fifths of the adult pairs conversed, looked or smiled at each other.

Things went rather differently with the adults accompanying children. In the same time, less than half of them had any communication at all with their children; and in two-fifths of the cases, what took place was negative. Children were told off, told to shut up, and to stop what they were doing. Other children were smacked. Five children were yanked by arm or hand across a road. One child was cuffed for misbehaving at a bus stop. More than half of the children were ignored whatever they did: whether they cried, played, or tried to talk to the adult.

The father of a six-week-old baby told Valerie Yule proudly: "We know other parents who smack their babies to keep them quiet. We think that is terrible. All you need to do is shake them."

Dr. Alice Miller, a psychoanalyst and

writer now living in Switzerland, has for decades worked to change the way people view and treat children. She believes that the violence and cruelty in our society have their roots in the way a traditional upbringing teaches a child "not to feel;" and demonstrates how a cycle of punishment and violence is continued by adults who were hurt and humiliated by their own (often well-intentioned) parents.

The pain, anger and sadness of the hurt child are unbearable, and hurt children (as Alice Miller believes most adults are) do not continue to bear these feelings. They obliterate and forget them. And when hurt children become parents themselves, they in turn hurt and humiliate their own children. They can't remember their own pain, and they genuinely believe that such parental behaviour "never did them any harm."

"The English person," says Alice Miller (who was born in Poland), "has to take everything with humour, and not complain. But so many of them were beaten as children in English schools. When you say that caning is dangerous, they say: Oh, no, it was good for me—I became a professor or lawyer! They don't want to see how damaging it can be."

"I see it as my task," she says, "to *repeat* that each kind of beating, caning and spanking of a child is a humiliation and is a serious damage for his whole life. The tragedy is that people treated this way pretend this treatment was necessary. They reserve the right to do the same to their children and are reluctant to pass laws forbidding spanking."

In Britain's prolonged refusal to legislate against corporal punishment in schools (at a time when no one listened to Professor Freeman's proposal to forbid all corporal punishment), she perceives the effect of a tradition of child abuse so ingrained that we have ceased to notice it. Even humane and intelligent people can fail for a long time to see something which is wrong. Dr. Miller hopes to open the eyes of people who are blind to the damage they do to their children, as they have blinded themselves to the damage that was done to themselves as children. It is not unlike another revelation of children's suffering made to adults who for decades unquestioningly condoned it. Frederic Leboyer, like Alice Miller, was at first ridiculed for pointing out that a newborn baby may suffer great pain if its first experience after birth is to be upended and slapped.

GENDER SOCIALIZATION

Since earliest recorded times, gender has been one of the main bases for the division of human labour—that is, for the ways in which tasks are allocated among members of a group. Even in hunting and gathering societies, which had little specialization, it was clear what work was appropriate for women. The activities considered suitable for males and females vary from society to society, but everywhere, culture takes account of the unalterable fact: only women can become pregnant, give birth to babies, and nurse them.

Given a gender base for the division of labour, sociologists would expect to find differences in the ways in which males and females are raised. Further, these differences are likely to be most pronounced when boys and girls are being prepared for sharply differentiated roles. As roles become more interchangeable, upbringing for the two sexes becomes more alike. For example, in most Canadian jurisdictions today, boys may take courses in home economics while girls enrol in shop classes, something unheard of 15 years ago.

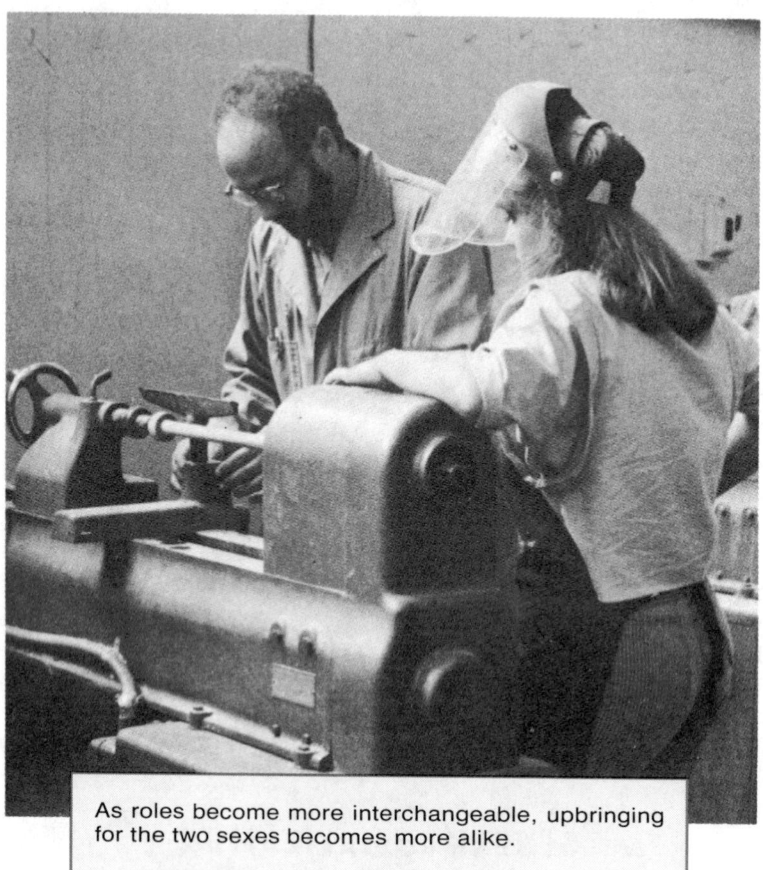

As roles become more interchangeable, upbringing for the two sexes becomes more alike.

Gender socialization does more than prepare youngsters for the kinds of tasks they will perform. Additionally, it seeks to inculcate the values, attitudes, and patterns of behaviour that are deemed desirable for men and women in society. From babyhood on, boys and girls are distinguished from each other, often by the colours worn, by the kinds of toys they are given, and by the kinds of people they are encouraged to emulate. As the child grows older, gender socialization is continued by parents, teachers, peers, and the media. Many adult Canadians (themselves socialized along sex-specific lines) think that it is fine for boys to get dirty and sweaty playing soccer, but that girls should be "sugar and spice and everything nice." "Don't be forward, dear," mother may admonish Kirsten, who wants to solicit babysitting jobs, but Nils receives praise for his initiative in asking the new neighbours if they need help cutting their lawn.

During adolescence, sex-specific patterns of thinking and acting become firmly ingrained. Walshok noted:

> *Not only the activities that boys engage in, but also what adolescents value in people and situations, is differentiated along gender lines: girls value physical attractiveness, co-operation, kindness, ability to get along with people, neatness and passivity; boys value strength, competitiveness, toughness, power and drive or aggressiveness. In adolescence, boys and girls begin committing themselves in earnest to activities and roles that express these socially prescribed and valued characteristics (1981, 88).*

Although the distinctions between men and women have always been less rigid in North America than in many societies, such as India or Saudi Arabia, where women have been expected to not leave their homes unaccompanied, the roles are clearly demarcated nevertheless. Today relationships between the sexes and sex-stereotyped roles are undergoing some change.[5] Messages transmitted in the home are echoed by the school. However, what is said may carry less weight than the reality children see around them. Despite much current talk of equal opportunity and the assurance that girls can become anything they want to be, children cannot help but observe that, even in the school environment, most people in authority, such as vice-principals, principals, and school superintendents, are male.[6] Moreover, although efforts have been made to eliminate sex stereotypes from school reading material, this does not magically change the attitudes of teachers, who may have been brought up themselves with more traditional attitudes and expectations. Furthermore, when agents of socialization act consciously, they generally seek to prepare the young for the world that exists now, rather than for one that may emerge. It is understandable, therefore, that school guidance counsellors may attempt to steer male and female students into occupations that have traditionally been socially appropriate for them.

Clearly, bringing about social change is often a slow and obstacle-ridden process because one is moving against the weight of tradition. Such tradition is especially hard to break in areas which carry a heavy emotional weight, such as attitudes and expectations pertaining to the relative position of men and women in society. As a number of recent studies have demonstrated, gender socialization is marked by both continuity and change (Baker 1985; Kostash 1987; Luxton and Rosenberg 1986; Martin 1986). In a national study of high school students, Baker found that, while girls may have high career aspirations, they rarely develop strategies for pursuing them. At the same time, they envision playing traditional familial roles, and show little awareness of potential conflicts between family and career.

Martin's participant observation study of female mine workers in the Yukon demonstrated both women's ability to carry out non-traditional work, and the resistance they encountered.

NO BOYS IN MATH CLASSES SO GIRLS CAN MAKE PASSES

By Regina Hickl-Szabo

When it is time for mathematics class at A.Y. Jackson Secondary School in North York, the boys go one way and the girls go the other. They take the same course, but they are taught in separate classes.

The pilot project started in fall 1984 for 300 grade 10 students and it is designed to help girls overcome what educators call their fear and dislike of mathematics.

The school is combatting what high schools across Canada and the United States have been witnessing for decades with increasing alarm—the dropping of mathematics by most girls by the time they get to Grade 13.

Educators and researchers generally agree that boys are taught to believe they will do well in mathematics and girls are brought up to think the world of theories and numbers is a male domain.

''What we should be aiming for is to make math seem more relevant for more women,'' says Mary Alice Guttman, a psychologist at the Ontario Institute for Studies in Education.

''Most girls would probably welcome a (teaching) situation that is particular to them with the proviso, of course, that the course content is not watered down.''

The danger inherent in the girls' high drop-out rate is that girls are effectively cutting themselves off from many careers ranging from accounting and merchandising to medicine and engineering, says Warren Hyland, principal at A.Y. Jackson.

He acknowledges that administrators are running the risk with this project of making girls feel singled out and less able than the boys.

However, none of five female students interviewed said they thought the project had anything to do with their ability to understand mathematics and none felt they were being isolated because they are not as capable as their male counterparts.

"It feels more relaxed," says Heather Taylor, a 15-year-old student taking part in the program. "I can get into math more."

Five boys interviewed about the project said they felt more comfortable studying mathematics without girls around. "This way the girls aren't there to distract us," one youth said. "Maybe (the school) should do the same thing with English class."

Splitting up the girls and the boys removes at least one obstacle that may be impeding girls from enjoying mathematics, researchers say.

"The speculation is that there's an intimidation factor having boys in the class," says Karl Kinzinger, director of education at the North York Board of Education.

"What we're trying to do is reduce the sexual competition in the class and try and get girls to realize they can do as well as boys in math."

Mary Lynn Jefferies, head of A.Y. Jackson's mathematics department, say studies show women do better in mathematics when boys aren't around.

Girls often feel they have to "put on a show" when they are with boys, she said. "It's sex rearing its ugly head. It's a time when women are just finding out about their sexuality."

She's reluctant to say they are intimidated by boys, "but the fact is they often don't want to speak out and appear stupid."

Dr. Guttman, who has focused her studies at OISE on young women's career aspirations, says she sees the school's project as a step in the right direction.

At the same time, however, school boards should be looking for more women mathematics teachers or male teachers who have a better understanding of women, she said. "Many male teachers just don't know how to reach female students."

Similarly, mathematics text books should not be as obviously geared to boys as they are, she said.

The girls' mathematics course at A.Y. Jackson will be identical to that of the boys except that they will be shown films the boys won't see about women in careers that need a background in mathematics, Mrs. Jefferies said.

"There are still a lot of girls around who think they don't really have to have a career. I show the film in Grade 10 but I'd like to show it in Grade 6."

Mr. Hyland said if the project gets good results at the end of the year, it will be carried on in Grades 11 and 12 and might be extended to the sciences as well.

After their first major mathematics test, the girls did better than the boys, Mrs. Jefferies said. "It's a good sign, but it's too early to say anything yet."

ANTICIPATORY SOCIALIZATION

As the previous section suggests, the socialization process is intended both to enable the individual to function in a socially acceptable way in the present and to prepare for future roles. Elena scolding her doll for spilling the orange juice is anticipating the maternal role.

Anticipatory socialization can be defined as the process by which individuals prepare themselves for roles to which they aspire but which they do not yet occupy. It differs from basic socialization in that there is some conscious motivation on the part of the learner or apprentice to acquire the trappings of a given role. In the work world, for example, learning the ropes includes far more than mastering technical skills. Think of the fate of imposters (such as "physicians" without actual credentials). Even though they might be able to carry out most technical aspects of the role, they might eventually be unmasked by their unfamiliarity with a certain bit of lore. Greenwood has described what is entailed in becoming a professional:

> *Mastery of the underlying body of theory and acquisition of technical skills are in themselves insufficient guarantees of professional success. The recruit must also become familiar with and learn to weave his way through the labyrinth of the professional culture. Therefore,the transformation of a neophyte into a professional is essentially an acculturation process wherein he internalizes the social values, the behavior norms, and the symbols of the occupational group (1965, 520).*

Secretarial colleges not only teach shorthand, word processing, and bookkeeping, but also alert students to what constitutes suitable modes of dress. Garish clothing and jewellery are definitely out for the aspiring executive secretary. On the factory floor, apprentices learn not only the basics of their trade but also the norms of the group: how much respect to give the shop steward and the boss, how fast to work so as not to incur the wrath of either the group or the manager.

Anticipatory socialization is not confined to the occupational world. A small-town adolescent intent on joining an urban clique prepares himself by adopting the mannerisms, habits, and attitudes of the clique, hoping to become acceptable to its members in the process.

One of the greatest difficulties in being a pioneer stems from an absence of signposts which would familiarize that person with the rights, obligations, expectations, and viewpoints of its social role. A male kindergarten teacher or a female welder will likely experience some uncertainty concerning just what to anticipate.

Related to the concept of anticipatory socialization is that of the **reference group**. A reference group provides a model of values, attitudes, and behaviour that one seeks to emulate. In traditional societies, membership groups, both familial and occupational, also serve as reference groups. In our society, which is more fluid, moving to a new neighbourhood or receiving a substantial promotion may mean that a person has selected new Joneses to keep up with. In other words, he or she chooses a new reference group.

RESOCIALIZATION

Incorporated into every socialization process are forces of coercion. These influences can be seen in their most extreme form in the case of **resocialization**, which is aimed at stripping the individual of his or her identity and replacing it with a new one. The armed services provide a good example. The stripping process that takes place on entry assumes both physical and psychological dimensions. The recruits are issued new clothing, and men must have a regulation haircut. They must learn to adapt their thinking, behaviour, and priorities to conform to army expectations. In his book *Asylums* (1962), Goffman analysed the ways in which a **total institution**, such as a mental hospital, concentration camp, prison, or boarding school, seeks to ensure conformity. Goffman categorized as total institutions those that control every aspect of an individual's existence. Here is another example of the way in which the sociological perspective enables one to pinpoint similarities among institutions which at the same time are strikingly different.

Resocialization is not confined to such dramatic experiences as entering a total institution; it entails experiences that teach a person a different way of looking at the world. Resocialization becomes necessary, for example, each time one starts a new job (see Chapter 5 on work), joins a club, changes marital status, or emigrates to another country. In *Men and Women of the Corporation* (1977), Kanter noted that secretaries who were promoted into the executive stream not only had to learn ways of relating as peers to individuals who were formerly their superiors but were also expected to dress differently. These expectations were rarely set out in formal rules; they were, nevertheless, widely understood. Becoming familiar with these understandings constitutes the essence of successful resocialization.

SUMMARY

In this chapter, we have noted that socialization is a universal process, even though its form and content differ from culture to culture. Socialization begins with the first years of life and continues throughout the life cycle. Acceptable behaviour is learned by example as well as through deliberate indoctrination. Learning, then, proceeds by what is caught as well as by what is taught.

In Canadian society, the main agents of socialization are parents, parent surrogates, peers, teachers, and a variety of mentors or authority figures, such as hockey coaches and camp counsellors. To the extent that the values transmitted by these various agents are not consonant, the individual being socialized may experience uncertainty and discomfort. On the other hand, such mixed messages may provide an advantage in that no one particular lifestyle comes to be seen as the only possible one.

As the child gets older, peer groups become increasingly influential. In the school setting, membership in a particular group may affect whether a student chooses to direct his or her main efforts to academics, athletics, or social activities. In part, the strength of the peer group's influence stems from the fact that children spend an extended period of time in an age-graded school system. The media have emerged as powerful socializing agents, with the growth in literacy and the increasing availability of printed material and television sets.

We examined a number of theories about the process by which the human organism is transformed into a social being. Underlying these explanations are different views of homo sapiens. For example, biological determinism treats the individual's development as tightly constrained by genetic endowment. According to behaviourism, on the other hand, the infant is a clean slate to be written on by environmental influences. Freud was a pioneer in drawing attention to the unconscious motivations that affect behaviour and to the lasting effects of early-childhood experience. These effects were also of central concern to Mead and Cooley, who have come to be identified with the symbolic interactionist perspective. For them, society and individual are inseparable. They noted that the very notion of humanity presupposes interaction with others. Where Freud focused on stages of emotional development, Mead traced cognitive development, marking the child's growing ability to order situations into categories. For example, it learns to group school and church as places in which one is expected to sit still and be attentive.

Gender socialization is the process by which individuals are prepared to function as men and women in society. If the group expects men and women to assume widely different statuses, this difference will be reflected in the attitudes and behaviour they are expected to acquire. As North American society moves toward greater equality between the sexes, students are less likely to be steered into sex-stereotyped careers. Growing participation by women in the work force and in more demanding jobs may entail the need to restructure the division of labour in the home. In turn, changes in work life and domestic life are liable to affect socialization practices.

Anticipatory socialization is the process by which individuals prepare themselves for new roles. Clues about what constitutes acceptable behaviour are gleaned from those who are already members of a group one aspires to join. Perhaps the most difficult aspect of preparing for a new role is to become familiar with the subtleties that give it texture. For example, a good police officer must master far more than the technical skills outlined in the official job description.

Resocialization involves being divested of an existing identity and acquiring a new one. The clearest examples occur in extreme circumstances, such as prisons or mental hospitals, where all aspects of the individual's existence are subject to control. However, resocialization is not confined to total institutions. In *Pygmalion*, Eliza Doolittle was carefully transformed from a Covent Garden flower seller to a society lady.

ASSIGNMENTS

Do one or more of the following assignments, as instructed by your professor.

1 Discuss the following situation. During a lunch-hour conversation at KTT Appliances, a group of shipping clerks were discussing their children. One of them said that what he wants to teach his children in the first instance is obedience. In a similar discussion among executives at Brascan, one insisted that self-discipline is the quality he most wants his children to have. How would a sociologist attempt to explain the differences in the two men's perspectives? If you have taken psychology courses, consider how a psychologist would attempt to explain the differences.

2 Discuss the following situation. Mr. and Mrs. Mendez came from Portugal eight years ago, and both hold full-time jobs. The two older children are at school, and Juan, age 3, goes to a babysitter during the day. When Juan had measles, Mrs. Mendez had Maria stay home from school to look after him. Mrs. Robinson, the school attendance officer, came to the house after Maria had missed three days' school. She suggested Mrs. Mendez did not care about her daughter's education as she was causing her to miss classes. Using the sociological concepts presented in this chapter, examine the values and priorities that underlie the different perspectives of the Mendez family and the school authorities.

3 If a 14-year-old girl who wanted to become a surgeon asked for your advice, what would you tell her? Frame your response in sociological terms.

4 Examine the costs and rewards for an individual who becomes a pioneer. For example: a male nurse; a female heavy-equipment operator; Jackie Robinson, the first black to play in major-league baseball (who got his start on a Montreal farm team).

SUGGESTED READINGS

Maya Angelou, *I Know Why the Caged Bird Sings* (New York: Bantam Books, 1971).

Annie Dillard, *An American Childhood* (New York: Harper and Row, 1987).

These two autobiographies present a fascinating contrast. Angelou and Dillard spent their childhood and adolescence under drastically different circumstances of class and race. Yet, both went on to win international recognition as creative writers — a reminder that an "oversocialized" view of human beings must be regarded with a measure of scepticism, since it does not leave room for sheer gutsiness and the individual capacity to "sing."

Ruth Benedict, *Patterns of Culture* (New York: Mentor, 1934). Aided by anthropological field work in different parts of the globe, Benedict illustrates the great diversity of cultures. The culture in which one is socialized plays an important part in moulding personality. Cultures should not be ranked in value terms. Rather, each one has great significance for its members, just as yours has for you.

Erik Erikson, "The Eight Stages of Man," a chapter in *Childhood and Society*, 2nd ed. (New York: Norton, 1963). Erikson provides an elaboration of Freud's theory of emotional development. It places in the foreground human beings' adaptive behaviour, taking into account both innate and environmental factors, in contrast with Freud's original emphasis on the innate. Erikson shows how a particular culture directs psychological predispositions into particular channels.

Erving Goffman, *Asylums* (Chicago: Aldine Publishing, 1962). Goffman's sociological analysis is mainly based on participant observation in a state mental hospital. The book describes what life is like for patients in a total institution, a setting in which every aspect of existence is controlled. Attempts by a patient to resist resocialization, to adhere to behaviour that is appropriate in the outside world, are interpreted as signs of recalcitrance or as symptoms confirming the diagnosis of mental illness. The author notes that the absolute conformity that is expected is likely to make readjustment more difficult when the patient is discharged.

Aldous Huxley, *Brave New World* (London: Penguin; first published 1932). *Brave New World* is Huxley's nightmare of a fully regulated and totally closed society. By means of genetic engineering, individuals are prepared, even before birth, for their assigned stations in life. The family has been abolished, and cohorts of equals, such as Alphas or Betas, undergo a continuous and intensive process of socialization. They are taught to think of their society as the best possible one and of their particular place in that society as yielding the optimum degree of happiness.

Myrna Kostash, *No Kidding: Inside the World of Teenage Girls* (Toronto: McClelland and Stewart, 1987). Kostash documents the 1980s' dreams (economic self-sufficiency, a career, romantic marriage and children) of teenage girls, yet makes it clear that these dreams are unrealizable for most in the absence of a fundamental restructuring of economic, social, and political relationships. There are many teenage worlds in Canada, not just one, and they mirror the underlying class, ethnic, and racial divisions of the wider society. This book's strength lies in the riveting words of the girls whom Kostash interviewed, as they tell their own stories about coming of age in Canada.

George Bernard Shaw, *Pygmalion: A Romance in Five Acts* (Harmondsworth: Penguin, 1965; first published 1913 and available in many editions). This play, which was the source of the musical *My Fair Lady*, portrays a dramatic instance of resocialization. With the help of relentless drilling by Professor Higgins, Eliza Doolittle is transformed from a Covent Garden flower girl into a society lady. The process involves much anguish on her part and the realization that acquisition of a new identity makes it impossible to resume one's former life.

NOTES

1 The reference to a child as "it" may sound awkward to you. The usage is common in the social sciences, partly to avoid the clumsiness of "he or she" when the gender of the child is beside the point.

2 The main emphasis of the symbolic interactionist perspective is on the interaction between individual and environment and the symbolic interpretation attached to behaviour at any stage of development. For example, in *The Silent Language* (1959), Edward Hall vividly portrays the differences in meaning attached to time and to punctuality in Middle Eastern and western society. The symbolic significance of these concepts varies crossculturally. (See the Pelletier insert in Chapter 2 on culture.)

3 Human beings may not be unique in this respect. Recent research on whales and dolphins indicates that these species may use sophisticated symbolic codes. As yet, scientists have not fully broken these codes; some scholars do not accept their existence.

4 Today, many social scientists find the concepts of primary and secondary groups useful. The primary group is usually defined as involving face-to-face contact, knowledge of who the other group members are, several kinds of joint activities, and inter-relationships involving some emotion or personal feeling. For example, people who work together may form a primary group (and some personnel managers hope they do). A secondary group is much less personal and focuses on some common object; its members may not meet or know each other. A large corporation and a mammoth introductory sociology class are examples of secondary groups.

5 The changes are more evident in some groups of society than in others; thus, generalizations must be treated with extra caution.

6 It is the well-known strength of gender socialization that gives pathos to the following passage from the autobiography of J. Morris, who eventually underwent one of the first sex-change operations:

> *A moment of silence followed each day the words of the Grace—"the grace of Our Lord Jesus Christ, and the love of God, and the fellowship of the Holy Ghost be with us all evermore." Into that hiatus, while my betters I suppose were asking for forgiveness or enlightenment, I inserted silently every night, year after year throughout my boyhood, an appeal less graceful but no less heartfelt:* "And please, God, let me be a girl. Amen" (*1974, 20*).

STRATIFICATION

Stratification is the division of a group—a society, a business firm, a clan, a school—into strata (horizontal layers). Groups and individuals who occupy different strata in the same system receive rewards to varying degrees. The benefits may be **material rewards**, such as money, or **symbolic rewards**, such as power and prestige. It is important to recognize the circularity of the relationships among these rewards. Power itself is a scarce and valued commodity. Powerful groups are able to obtain access to money and prestige, and to ensure the continuity of such access. Thus, physicians receive higher incomes than ward orderlies, are accorded greater prestige, and wield more power. One's position in the social hierarchy affects virtually all aspects of an individual's life: how much education one is likely to receive and, therefore, what work one will be qualified to perform, one's life expectancy, and one's participation in political and voluntary associations, to note just a few.

To the extent that the difference in rewards is a shared and accepted expectation among a significant proportion of the group's members, one can describe the stratification system as institutionalized. Most Canadians expect the physician to earn more than the orderly and agree that she *should* earn more because of her higher expertise and the greater responsibility she carries. (This does not mean, of course, that there is consensus on how much more the physician should earn. In other words, even though you may deem some inequality acceptable, you may be dismayed at the degree of inequality.)

Tumin has listed some important dimensions of stratification:

- It is a social phenomenon; that is to say, it exists within a group.
- The criteria according to which a group is stratified, and according to which rewards are distributed, follow a pattern that is known to the members of the group.
- Stratification, in varying degrees of rigidity, has existed in all societies past and present.
- Stratification can assume diverse forms.
- *Where* individuals are placed in the hierarchy of stratification has fateful consequences for them (1953, 65).

As we noted, one can examine the stratification of groups ranging from a club to a whole society. Our discussion in this chapter will focus primarily on the level of *society*.

RICH CITY

By Peter Cheney

If the city of the rich has a heart, it's Rosedale, the old Toronto neighbourhood whose name has become a synonym for Canadian wealth and privilege.

There are neighbourhoods like The Bridle Path, whose denizens may actually have more money, but in the Canadian consciousness Rosedale is still The Blue Chip Neighbourhood, a central column in the Canadian Establishment.

Not for decades has Rosedale had the patina it currently enjoys — the counterculture '60s are long gone. Wealth is back in style with a vengeance and the neighbourhood runs with the quiet

POOR CITY

By Kim Zarzour

Forget the moneyed side of Toronto. There's an underground tour that offers a very different view of the city.

It's called A Guide To The Real Toronto, and it's put together by the BASIC Poverty Action Group. It's not pretty. It's the city's underbelly: the world of the penniless and working poor, the losers in a city infatuated with success.

This tour group skips the regular sightseeing fare of the CN Tower and upscale shops, and heads right to places such as Regent Park. It's only a few blocks from the yuppified Cabbagetown, but the people here even *walk* elegance of a Rolls Royce, driven by the sheer financial horsepower of its residents.

Rosedale is the kind of place people picture when they dream about what would happen if they were suddenly made richer, more powerful . . . more *elegant*.

Devoid of life

Sometimes, it seems so quiet as to be devoid of life. On a midweek afternoon, the streets are still. For minutes at a time, there is no movement at all . . . then a uniformed maid emerges from a home the size of an embassy carrying a bag of garbage.

Though there are no doubt struggling *arrivistes* who have stretched themselves to their financial limits to be here in Rosedale, this is by and large a neighbourhood for people who have risen above — or were never part of — the general financial fray.

Through the houses' window frames, an observer can partially glimpse the splendors of the interiors — fabulous, decorated kingdoms primped and arranged with the care of Fabergé eggs.

Great curving sofas and grand pianos are set off with vases of fresh flowers and accessories that have the look of art treasures, illuminated by carefully arrranged lighting. The rooms stretch away into the hidden interiors.

Even the world of the vast middle class seems far away. News about people who can't afford to live in the city has the distant ring of reports about Third World hunger.

differently: slower, with gloveless hands crammed in pockets, staring at the sidewalk.

It's not a private place to live: a kaleidoscope of windows — half covered in tinfoil and sagging curtains knotted in the middle — stare into each other and down on to the busy streets.

Litter bag

Nor is it very quiet: a garbage truck heaves in the parking lot. A litter bag snagged to a tree branch snaps in the wind like a flag. Ambulance and fire trucks idle noisily and flash their lights at one entrance as police run in to the latest emergency call.

Inside the echoing yellow corridors, a lone black woman in housecoat and slippers drags two garbage bags to the bin. The stairwells and elevators here reek with fear — of crack deals, violence and abandoned needles. Residents say.

If you live here, you probably lie on your job applications, says David Kidd, today's tour guide.

Kidd, a community worker with Central Neighbourhood House, points out the grates and parks where the homeless huddle, the government buildings that take care of welfare and family benefits, shops tailored to the neighbourhood like Mary's Coin Laundry, and greasy spoons with names such as Tom's Lunch and Alfie's Burgers.

Within walking distance, there are five cheque-cashing offices — "vultures," Kidd says, who hover over poverty and feed on those who are end-of-month

There is no hunger here, no struggle to provide the basics of life. Instead, there is a struggle for Quality — there is the quest for the correct cornice moulding, the perfect end table, the tasteful accent for the drawing room. Life is comfortable, tasteful, organized. People can afford the finest things and the services to maintain them.

Over on Bloor West, the rich shop at Holt Renfrew, Creeds, and a few other perfumed refuges that are to the wealthy what K-Mart is to the masses. But here there are no masses. In a Darwinian selection of the financially fittest, the clientele is pared down to those with the wherewithal to buy such items as a $3,000 skirt or a silver dog bowl.

There are more than a few people who can afford such things, and who are willing to pay the lofty premium for buying The Best.

Creeds' owner Jack Creed explains it simply: "When a customer buys here, it's a pleasure," he says. ". . . the staff aren't trying to ram something down your throat . . . for some customers, price just doesn't matter."

Over on Avenue Rd., Downtown Fine Cars sales manager Gerry Peterson is selling Porsches at such a rate that most models are now back-ordered until 1990. Peterson's clientele, he says, is "like a who's-who." But he doesn't name names. If there's anything the rich hate, it's indiscretion.

For that reason, no one really knows just how much money there really is in Toronto — except that there is a great deal more concentrated here than anywhere else in the country.

short-of-cash because they're stuck with post-dated government cheques. The cheque-cashers take off 6 per cent from each cheque; it amounts to one week's food for many of their clients.

Regular snowsuits

Just north of here, in another public housing area, lives "Jane Black." She's just a few blocks from Rosedale. "I bet half the stuff they put in their garbage would furnish all of St. Jamestown," says the single mother of four.

This harsh city tour also includes a drive past the temporary employment agencies that offer short-term, often low-paying jobs. And the men's hostels — intimidating-looking brick buttresses that provide a roof, but little safety and no privacy for the homeless. You learn to tie your boots to your bed or keep them under your pillow if you don't want them stolen, Kidd says.

Just one poor neighbourhood? Cross Yonge St. and head west to the poorer part of Parkdale for another view of the *other* Toronto.

Demanded fence

It's a mixed area, not far from High Park. At one point the upscalers demanded an eight-foot concrete fence around the public housing, Hartling says.

In the heart of Parkdale is Stop 103, one of 140 food banks in Metro.

The hungry sit around a table, waiting for their name to be called.

At the opposite end of Metro, not part of the tour and not part of the glossy

Demographers say that the gap between the rich and the poor has widened sharply in recent years, and nowhere is the difference more stark than in major cities such as Toronto.

''These are people who can spend a lot of money,'' says Alann Cohen, a Toronto retail analyst. ''But you have to know how to deal with them—they have very specific tastes, and they're picky. They expect the best.''

tourist brochures either, is the Jane-Finch neighbourhood. Here ''Sandi Norton'' begins another frazzled weekday morning rush in public housing.

A separated mother of two who has bounced back and forth between government support and minimum-paying jobs for seven years, she just landed a two-year contract co-ordinating a housing program, making $24,901 a year. But money is still tight.

From ''Doonesbury'' by G.B. Trudeau.

VARIATIONS IN SOCIAL STRATIFICATION SYSTEMS

A variety of criteria are used to place individuals in the hierarchy of their society. Skin colour, gender, number of children (or spouses), occupation, and wealth are only a few of the possibilities. Recall, however, the requirement that the criteria for placement follow a known pattern. Implicit in this statement is the group's acceptance of the criteria, an acceptance that may be reinforced by the authority of tradition, religion, or some other form of moral sanction. Caste societies, estate societies, and class societies are examples of different stratification patterns.

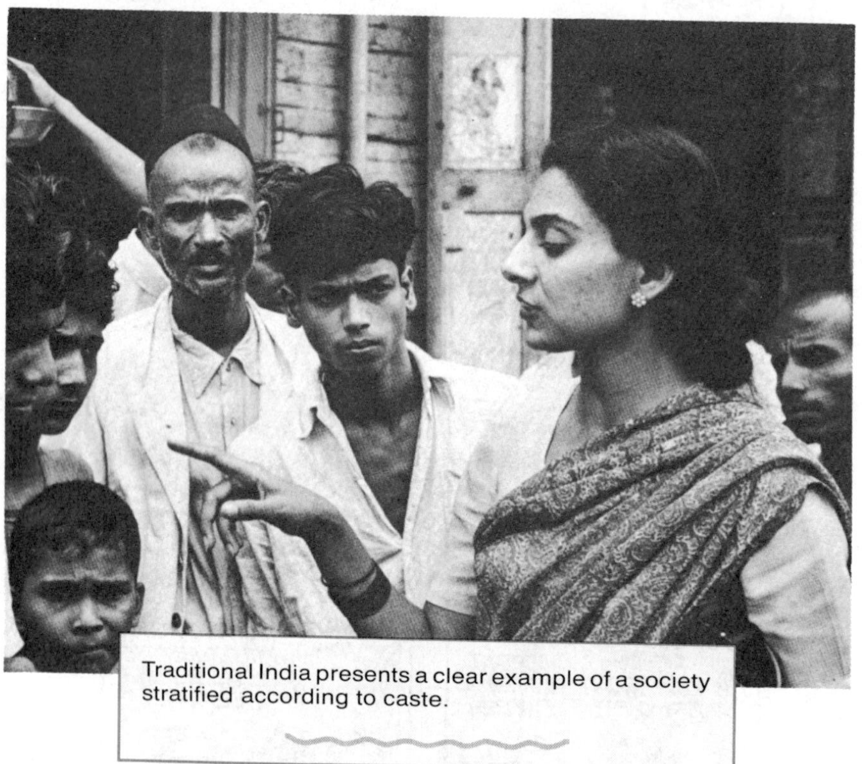

Traditional India presents a clear example of a society stratified according to caste.

CASTE SOCIETIES

Traditional India presents a clear example of a society stratified according to caste,[1] which Theodorson and Theodorson define as "a closed social stratum based on heredity that determines its members' prestige, occupation, place of residence, and social relationships" (1969, 38). One is born into a caste, which is further divided into subcastes, and one lives and dies within the confines of this subcaste.

In other words, status is ascribed. Each subcaste has a monopoly over certain occupations and engages in a lifestyle, every detail of which is minutely prescribed. Rigid taboos forbid social interaction between members of different castes; intermarriage with a member of a lower caste results in both partners becoming "outcastes" in the literal sense of the word.

Anthropologist Oscar Lewis described the operation of the caste system in Rani Khera, a village near Delhi, where he did field work in 1953:

> *The caste system divides the village and weakens the sense of village solidarity. The caste generally represents a distinct ethnic group with its own history, traditions and identifications, and each caste lives in more or less separate quarters in the village. There are separate wells for the Harijans, or Untouchables; dining and smoking between members of higher and lower castes are still taboo; low-caste persons . . . will not sit together on the same . . . cot with a Jat or Brahman, and when government officials come to the village to explain the new community development projects, the Harijans may attend, but they stay off to one place in the audience and "know their place" (1955, 156).*

The tenets of Hinduism furnish the moral sanction for the caste system. The doctrine of continuous reincarnation holds that, provided one conscientiously carries out the duties of one's caste position, one may hope for elevation to a higher caste in a future life. Conversely, failure in one's obligations may result in being reborn in a lower caste or even as an animal. The belief system makes no provision for movement between castes during one's lifetime, even though exceptional individuals may, in fact, move.

As long as such a system is widely accepted as morally right, it provides stability for the society as a whole. On the other hand, since positions are allocated by ascription, the talents of individuals may not fit the tasks they are called upon to perform. Socialization from birth is an important mechanism in directly preparing people for their future roles. Individuals know what is expected of them; they are not under constant pressure to better themselves, as are members of a society such as Canada's, in which upward mobility is possible and seen as desirable. But people born into occupations for which they have neither interest nor aptitude are likely to become bitter and frustrated.

A caste system suggests a commitment to tradition that makes it difficult to bring about change. An example is the Indian government's continuing battle to curb population growth, a problem shared with many third-world countries. Use of birth control is resisted because it runs counter to the prestige and security in old age associated with having many children, especially sons.

If one places societies on a continuum from "open" to "closed" in terms of the individual's ability to move up and down the stratification ladder, a **caste society** is nearest to the closed pole. But society is not completely static because castes and subcastes are differentiated internally. Some members of the same subcaste may be much better off than others, so that there is some room, at least, in which to improve one's condition.

ESTATE SOCIETIES

Estate societies were the prevalent form of social organization in Europe through the Middle Ages until the beginning of the modern era. Membership in an estate was hereditary (and therefore ascribed).[2] The main divisions were the nobility, the clergy, and the peasantry; the peasantry included both free peasants and serfs. The latter were tied to the land and in many respects "belonged" to the landowner, who himself might hold his land through several levels of fealty in the complex web of rights and obligations that constituted the feudal system. Since each estate comprised a variety of occupations and socioeconomic levels (Theodorson and Theodorson 1969), mobility within an estate was easier than mobility between estates. Some premium was placed on individual ingenuity and achievement, however, as demonstrated by the law that a runaway serf who remained undetected for a year and a day was to be set free.

The priest, the soldier, the peasant, and the magistrate were the key elements in the estate societies that dominated social organization in Europe throughout the Middle Ages.

In the later mediaeval period, more people were attracted to the burghs (towns) that sprang up around castles. Within these burghs arose clusters of artisans, merchants, and professionals. Some of these individuals became wealthy and aspired to partake in the privileges reserved for the nobility.

Members of each estate were governed by different laws, which set out their rights and obligations. These laws, which varied considerably from place to place, impinged on every aspect of daily living. In her work on the 14th century, Barbara Tuchman recounts a few of them:

> *Proclaimed by criers in the county courts and public assemblies, exact gradations of fabric, color, fur trimming, ornaments, and jewels were laid down for every rank and income level. Bourgeois might be forbidden to own a carriage or wear ermine, and peasants to wear any color but black or brown. Florence allowed doctors and magistrates to share the nobles' privilege of ermine, but ruled out for merchants' wives multicolored, striped, and checked gowns, brocades, figured velvets, and fabrics embroidered in silver and gold (1978, 19).*

In estate societies as in caste societies, formal and informal rules regulate the interaction of individuals located in different strata. Caste societies, for example, have precise prescriptions about who can prepare food for whom and who can eat with whom.

Moral justification for the estate system in mediaeval Europe was provided by the Roman Catholic Church, to which virtually everyone belonged. It taught that god had assigned each person's station on earth, and each had a duty to live within the rights and obligations attached to this station. To the extent that the populace accepted these teachings, the motivation for individuals to seek change in their own condition was minimized.

Moreover, those in power used every means at their disposal to resist changes in a system that granted them such a disproportionate share of societal rewards. Dominant groups generally have the power to block legislative and economic changes that they define as disadvantageous to themselves. They are also able to shape ideologies, a term we defined in Chapter 2 on culture. In the estate societies of Europe, the belief system stressed the importance both of tradition and of life in the hereafter. Between these poles, the way people existed in the here-and-now was de-emphasized, and change was made difficult.

Although the balance of rights and prerogatives clearly favoured the superior group, its members had certain obligations toward inferior groups, as reflected by the term *noblesse oblige* ("privilege entails responsibility"). The nobles had some responsibility for those who lived on their land: to succour orphans, the sick, and the aged; to provide protection from marauders and unfriendly armies; to hold local courts; and to sponsor various publicly used lands and buildings.

CLASS SOCIETIES

The feudal estate system gradually disintegrated because it could not meet the needs of the burgeoning, industrializing society. Two important needs were a labour force that was geographically mobile (able and willing to move where work opportunities were available) and strictly economic employer-employee relationships, untinged by tradition or sentiment.

By the late 18th and early 19th centuries—the era when sociology was founded—western society was stratified, as it is today, by classes, which are categories made up of individuals and families who have similar socioeconomic status. In the classic Marxian definition, class membership is based on strictly economic criteria. What class one belongs to is defined by one's relationship to the means of production—in other words, by whether one is an owner or a wage-earner. In analysing class membership, other sociologists also consider factors such as prestige and lifestyle, as well as being interested in how variables like education and attitudes interact with social class.

In class societies, what class one belongs to is defined by one's relationship to the means of production—in other words, by whether one is an owner or a wage-earner.

Membership in a class is not hereditary, though the position held by the family into which one is born significantly affects one's life chances. Insofar as status is predominantly achieved, mobility is possible.[3] Individuals who are exceptionally gifted (and lucky) can indeed go from rags to riches. Professional athletes and movie stars provide outstanding examples. Many well-known political figures—for example, John Diefenbaker, Harry Truman, Brian Mulroney, and Jean Chrétien—had humble beginnings. But numerous studies (Rogoff 1953; Teppermann 1975; Warner *et al.* 1963) have shown that a much more common pattern is one of gradual movement: the able and determined children of working-class parents receive a higher education and become nurses, teachers, or administrators, and sometimes lawyers, architects, or physicians. The movement from manual worker to full professional frequently spans two or more generations.

Not everyone in a **class society** experiences mobility, however, even in North America, where the ideology assumes a completely open society. According to the tenets of this belief system, there is equality of opportunity; whether individuals improve their positions and how far and how fast they move is a function of ability and motivation. This ideology ignores structural barriers, such as regional variations in educational and economic opportunities, as well as the effects of the social characteristics of race, ethnicity, religion, and gender.

Because the ideology is validated by the success of the few, the many who are unable to surmount the obstacles facing them tend to attribute their failure to personal shortcomings. Hence, they are less likely to challenge the prevailing system. Think of a race in which the contestants have different starting points. Theoretically, everyone can reach the finish line, but what entails merely routine effort from the front runners demands extraordinary qualities from those at the back. Thus, the architect's son does not have to sprint as far to the finish line of a law degree as does the labourer's son. Yet if the latter does not reach his goal, he may blame himself rather than the conditions of the race. Sennett and Cobb commented on this tendency:

> *The possibility of failure is the most uncomfortable phenomenon in American life. There is no room for failure in our schemes of respect, unless the failure is found to result from some cataclysmic event like the Great Depression. There is, as well, indifference to those who do not move ahead. Failures and static people—the nobodies Sammy Glick so feared—are seen as having undeveloped personalities; the uncomfortable feelings about those who do not "make something of themselves" when they have a chance come out of an assumption that men can be respected only as they become in some way distinctive, as they stand out from the mass (1972, 183).*

In industrialized societies, it is assumed that optimum utilization of human resources is a prerequisite for general well-being and progress. Hence, it is seen as crucial that key societal positions be filled by the most able individuals, regardless of their ascribed status. To the extent that this ideal is achieved in practice, our ''open'' class society offers its members an opportunity to fulfil their potential, thus benefiting themselves and the group as a whole. However, there is a wide gap between what ought to be and what is. An example is provided by a respondent in a study of postwar German immigrants who reported that her father was returning to Germany because ''he could not attain the goal he had set himself here. It was just too large'' (Lundy 1972). Recall the discussion, in Chapter 3, on the role of the media in fuelling such frustration by bombarding the public with success images.

In class societies, such as Canada and the United States, people are differentiated mainly according to economic criteria. However, there also exist categoric divisions usually associated with caste societies, which cannot be breached by the abilities and efforts of individuals. Historically, and to some extent still, some of the most important of these divisions have been based chiefly on race. Being nonwhite has meant fewer opportunities on all fronts, a fact of life of which blacks in the American south have been only too aware: ''It takes a lot of preparing before you can let a child loose in the white world. If you're black in Louisiana it's like cloudy weather; you just don't see the sun much,'' a respondent told Robert Coles, a psychiatrist who was doing research on the first black children to attend racially integrated schools (1964, 337).

In Canada, too, nonwhites generally and native peoples in particular have been consistently disadvantaged. Because the majority of Native Indians and Inuit live on reserves or in remote communities, many Canadians have been unaware of just how severe these disadvantages are. Doing participant observation research in a northwestern Ontario railway town, Stymeist found:

> *The economic and social position of Native people in Crow Lake has not changed significantly over the years. Although greater numbers have settled in town, secured jobs there and intermarried, for most Indians Crow Lake is still just a place to trade, to buy automobiles, outboard motors, guns, axes, boats or clothing. . . . In Crow Lake Indians are still regarded as outsiders, as people who have no real place in the community (1975, 64).*

8,500 POOR HUDDLE TOGETHER IN CITY-WITHIN-A-CITY

By June Callwood

Vancouver has done something unusual with its homeless people—they live in a city of their own called Downtown Eastside, population 10,000, formerly known as Skid Row, on a choice neck of land three blocks wide between Burrard Inlet and False Creek.

The community is a sociological curiosity. Though 8,500 of the residents live in desperate poverty, the Downtown Eastside is the second most stable community in Vancouver. The poor have gathered there and most will remain until they die because the area contains more than 50 rundown hotels where they can rent cheap shelter.

Few of Vancouver's destitute live in the open, as do millions of impoverished people in the world's major cities. Only a handful choose to take up permanent residence in home-made shacks near the railway tracks; most of Vancouver's homeless have shelter. However, they fit within the United Nation's definition of homelessness because they have no security of place. British Columbia offers the hotel-dwellers of the Downtown Eastside none of the protections other tenants receive. They are vulnerable to being evicted without cause or notice, their property can be seized for invented reasons, and they are subjected to such petty tyrannies as being charged a fee for having a guest in their room.

Vulnerable as they are, Downtown Eastsiders are attached to their community. During Expo 86, when 500 people, most of them elderly, were evicted from repairable hotels to make room for tourists, one old man stopped eating and died six weeks later, one man jumped to his death from his hotel window, and another threw himself under the wheels of a truck.

"These are fragile people," says Jim Green, 44, a burly former longshoreman who heads the Downtown Eastside Residents Association, known as DERA.

Last Tuesday was a cold, rainy morning on Main Street in the heart of the ghetto. Two doors from a strip joint rated high by international sailors is the Downtown Eastside Women's Centre. A big woman, shapeless in a windbreaker and sweater, jeans and construction boots, is stepping quickly from one foot to another, staring blankly at the rain, waiting for the staff to arrive and unlock the door.

She wears a blue cotton Greek fisherman's hat, which she thinks helps disguise her sex. She is concerned, as are all the women of the Downtown Eastside, about rapists. She will spend most of the day in the narrow, shabby, cluttered and friendly drop-in centre, keeping to herself and rarely speaking to anyone.

Later, a coffee mug in her hand, she felt like talking about survival. Her monthly welfare allowance is $429, out of which she pays $210 for a cockroach-infested hotel room that contains a small sink. Down the hall is a room with four toilets, another with a bathtub and another with a shower. Her room contains a bed, bedside tables, a small refrigerator, an electric frying pan, an electric coffee pot, a record player she bought for $25 at a pawn shop, and two chairs.

FOUR SISTERS PROJECT A HAVEN OF SANITY AND REPOSE

By June Callwood

The residents of the Four Sisters in the part of Vancouver that used to be called Skid Row have just finished harvesting their rooftop garden.

The garden, which grows flowers, corn and tomatoes, is off the solarium where house plants owned by the residents are awaiting a visit from a volunteer plant doctor. Down the hall, past an area where people can sit by a huge window and admire Vancouver's spectacular scenery, is an outdoor park.

Below is a superbly landscaped courtyard, fully enclosed and secure, where a woman is sitting with her baby. And over there are the townhouses with their private backyards, and a laneway, fenced in for children to play safely.

Welcome to the future for public housing for vulnerable people. In a country that offers the whole range of possibilities — from sleeping under bridges to seedy rooming houses to quarrelsome house-sharing to high-rises whose addresses shame the occupants — Vancouver's Four Sisters, which opened this year, is the model of the future.

First, and most important, it is run by the residents. Jim Green, head of the Downtown Eastside Residents' Association, which had a lot to do with the concept and the political struggles that ensued, heard on every side that winos and welfare bums did not know how to live in a decent place and would trash it in a week.

What has happened in Four Sisters, as he predicted, is that it is spotless. To save money, there is no maintenance or cleaning staff, so the carpeted halls are vacuumed by the people who live there, fingerprints left by children are washed by residents, and littering is unthinkable.

The building, an architectural pleasure, conveys a sense of sanity and repose. It took its tone from the 90-year-old, five-story Fleck warehouse, a dirty eyesore, which was converted to form the main building, with additions that spread over a half-block and seem, by matching the soft, rosy old brick and simple lines of high-tech windows, to be of the same vintage.

Four Sisters — named for Vancouver's four sister cities, Odessa, Edinburgh, Yokohama and Guangzhou — contains 153 units; 105 of them with rent subsidies are occupied by people on some form of social assistance.

Those residents are the most vulnerable in society: elderly men without families from the infamous hotels of the neighbourhood, now known as the Downtown Eastside of Vancouver; women depleted and frail from a lifetime of violence; single-parent families led by women; disabled singles; and — 40 per cent of them — elderly Chinese, some of whom are not comfortable in English. All notices at Four Sisters are bilingual: Chinese and English.

Four Sisters was built at a cost of about $18-million with the help of Canada Mortgage and Housing Corp., on land leased by the City of Vancouver in a tidy deal that will see the city own the entire project in 60 years. The apartments, under the administration of DERA and another non-profit group, Building Independent Living with the Disabled, abound in ingenuity and charm. Almost all have spacious balconies and handsome kitchenettes.

The hard part was finding people paying market rents of up to $600 a month who would want to move into the building with the much-scorned Downtown Eastsiders as neighbours. Mr. Green, a former union man himself, appealed to trade unionists, a group he thought would be sympathetic and supportive. Hundreds applied and were carefully screened for their attitudes.

"We made a mistake or two," he admits, "but mostly it has been a roaring success."

The country has had 40 years since the Second World War to try every way it can imagine to provide shelter for what are known in the trade as hard-to-house people. Across the country, everyone who works on the front lines with fragile homeless people is talking about the latest concept: independent living so that people have a chance, in a stable environment that respects their dignity and the need for privacy, to put their lives together. No project anywhere looks as good, or works as well, as Four Sisters.

GENDER INEQUALITY

In each of the stratification patterns we have discussed, and in numerous others, gender has played a significant role in the placements of individuals. Commenting on studies of Indian (caste) society, Caplan notes:

> *Although the dominant ideological norms of both Hinduism and Islam can only be followed by the upper castes and classes, women are relegated, ideologically at least, to the domestic sphere—the private rather than the public; the reproductive rather than the productive. Women's work in this sphere, as has been frequently and forcibly pointed out, is not only unpaid, but is usually devalued too (1985, 11).*

In estate societies, also, **patriarchy** (literally rule by the father, or male head of the household) was upheld by law, ideology, and institutions such as religion and the family. A substantial, and growing, body of literature documents gender stratification in modern class societies (Acker 1980). Sociologists are examining the ways in which the intersection of patriarchy and capitalism has perpetuated the disadvantages imposed on women as a social category (see the 25th anniversary issue of the *Canadian Review of Anthropology and Sociology*, May 1988).

Note that patriarchy is a remnant of earlier social orders, most recently feudalism. That it persists is consistent with Marx's observation that, at any given time, the current social order incorporates aspects of previous systems (see Chapter 1).

THEORIES OF STRATIFICATION

So far, we have looked at three bases according to which societies are stratified and have pointed to disjunctions between ideals and actual practice in "open" class societies. Now we will briefly examine some theoretical approaches to the study of stratification.

CLASS: THE ECONOMY AS SUBSTRUCTURE

In the first chapter, we described Marx's view of how social change occurs and, specifically, of how societal forms succeed each other. A central theme of Marx's writings was inequality, which he viewed as inevitable under capitalism. It is helpful at this point to note some important features of capitalism:

- The means of production are owned by a relatively small group of entrepreneurs.
- Workers are free to sell their labour to the highest bidder and must be able and willing to move to where work is available. Hence, it is impractical to have slaves, or serfs, or people unwilling to leave the ancestral burial grounds. Wages fluctuate with supply and demand, but are always lower than the value of what the workers produce. This surplus value accrues to the capitalists, and continues to augment their economic power.
- The maximization of efficiency and the ever-increasing accumulation of money are important social values. The mediaeval church preached that it was easier for a camel to pass through the eye of a needle than for a rich man to get into heaven.[4] Capitalist ideology, by contrast, equates wealth with virtue.

Marx saw society as divided into two main classes. The **bourgeoisie** own and control the means of production. The **proletariat** is made up of landless labourers, who have nothing to sell but their labour. Marx and his friend and collaborator, Frederick Engels (1820–95), were aware of internal differentiation within these classes, and of the existence of groups that did not fit into either class. However, their main focus was on the relations *between* the two main classes.

For Marx and Engels, the typical mode of production of an era—whether peasant agriculture under feudalism or factory wage-labour under capitalism — and the relations of production associated with this mode underlie all other societal institutions. Thus, education, religion, culture, and law are strongly influenced by the nature of the prevailing economic system. Those who control the means of production also control the definition of what is acceptable and unacceptable, moral and immoral, desirable and undesirable (see Chapter 8 on social control).

At the level of the individual, this schema means that economic position is the most fateful factor of one's existence. It influences income and, therefore, where and how one can live—indeed, how long one is likely to live and in what state of health. The head of the household's place in relation to production (that is, whether he is an owner, a labourer, or a free professional) affects how much and what kind of education his children receive and hence the kind of work that will be open to them.

Belonging to a class does not automatically bestow on its members awareness of their common fate and interests. Marx believed that this awareness was present among the bourgeoisie, who were a relatively small group. Despite internal differences, they were able to present a united front to outsiders and to act in support of their class interests. At first, the workers were not aware of their commonality. However, as they spent long hours herded together in factories and shared the experience of exploitation and similar deprivations, Marx predicted that they, too, would develop consciousness of kind and become a class *for itself*. Over time, members of the proletariat would come to realize that their common interests demanded the overthrow of capitalism, and they would unite to accomplish this.

Thus, in the Marxian schema, class membership has an objective dimension in that it is determined by one's relationship to the means of production. But it also has a subjective dimension: recognition of shared objectives with one's fellow class members, which evolves through similarity of life experience. This recognition spurs action that supports mutual interests.

''CONSORTIUM OF INDIFFERENCE'' FRUSTRATES LEWIS

By Jim Cody

Western governments are arrogantly sitting back and allowing developing African nations to be crushed under the weight of immense foreign debt, creating incredible social hardship and spiralling infant mortality rates, says Stephen Lewis.

Mr. Lewis, a former Ontario NDP leader and Canadian ambassador to the United Nations, said Wednesday night in Charlottetown it drives him crazy to see Canada not standing up to rectify this situation and have the debt forgiven. Instead it has joined the ''consortium of indifference'' along with the other richest Western nations.

''How can Canada engage in the laceration of its (foreign) aid budget?'' he also questioned, pondering the humanitarian principles it must compromise to do so.

PACKED HOUSE

Mr. Lewis, who serves as special advisor on Africa to the UN, was speaking to a packed house at the Prince Edward Convention Centre. His visit was organized by the fledgling P.E.I. branch of the United Nations Association of Canada.

He credited the United Nations International Children's Emergency Fund

(UNICEF) with being the ones to chronicle the human tragedy which western-imposed development policies were having on sub-Saharan countries in Africa.

Of the 45 countries, he said some 34 doggedly pursued an African economic reform policy dictated by the west through the World Bank and International Monetary Fund in an effort to save themselves. The U.S. insisted on free enterprise principles being terms of the agreement.

"What essentially happened is African countries moved heaven and earth to fulfil their share of the bargain," he said, implementing the "Reaganite" programs agreed to, which resulted in devaluated currency, public sector lay-offs and removal of consumer subsidies which led to rioting in the streets.

Children are the world's most vulnerable citizens, notes a 1989 UNICEF report which endeavours to provide the African children with a voice because hundreds of thousands of children are paying for the African debt crisis with their lives, and more are malnourished with bodies and minds unable to grow properly.

EVERY CENT

These African nations are having to spend every cent of their export earnings to service the debt to the detriment of their people, especially children, women and the unemployed, Mr. Lewis indicated. UNICEF says the rich got the loans and the poor got the debts.

Because people are paying with their lives, UNICEF says the debt crisis "should not be discussed politely." It is an "outrage" against a section of humanity and allowing the world economy to function against children is "the antithesis of all civilized behaviour."

Mr. Lewis said the UNICEF report is courageous and speaks the truth with passion and clarity which risks offending its major donor countries which are represented on the UNICEF board.

Its report tells the World Bank to alter its African policy in favour of "structural adjustment with a human face," and he said he was surprised the organization responded with compassion, though the IMF did not. In the past two years there has been a change, but it doesn't begin to approximate the need.

"We're not getting anywhere," he said, and among the economically-preoccupied western countries there is "no concern it has to be changed."

The African countries are attempting to move from the "swamp of famine," he said, to long-term durable economic recovery. And how has the west responded? Investment has become negligible, its share of trade is down from 7 per cent to 3.9 per cent and debt-service obligations are strangling these countries, he said. It is the "betrayal of an agreement reached honorably" following the famine crisis of 1984.

U.S. aid to the sub-Saharan countries has been cut to $1.3 billion, down $700 million in 1988, and Canada is cutting its foreign aid $1.8 billion over five years. Only a handful of Nordic countries are fulfilling a .7 per cent of gross national product foreign aid commitment, while Canada's has gone from .49 per cent to .43 per cent.

The African nations debt is owed to western governments. The whole thing could be written off, he said, much easier than the Latin American debt because that is owed primarily to private lending institutions.

In one day, the stock exchange lost four times the African debt and yet "capitalism is still limping along," he noted wryly.

With so many good things happening in areas of disarmament talks and the struggle for rights and freedoms of the world's people, he said there is "a sense of hope and movement in the world."

However, in terms of "north and south" the dialogue has stopped and the north is allowing the gulf between developed and developing nations to become the widest ever, banishing them to poverty with an arrogance "which takes the breath away."

"In my lifetime, I have never seen worse."

CLASS, STATUS, AND POWER

It is often said that the writings of Max Weber constitute a dialogue with the ghost of Karl Marx. Since the work of Marx dominated so much of later 19th-century thought, it was not surprising that Weber, who was age 19 when Marx died, felt that the latter's views were something with which he had to contend. His work came to provide a significant critique of Marxian formulations, most notably of Marx's heavy emphasis on economic determinants.

Though Weber conceded that one's role in the market place had a fundamental effect on the degree of power one wielded in society, he maintained that Marx was simplistic in believing this factor was the sole basis for differentiating people. He viewed social power as a multifaceted phenomenon; people are sorted in a hierarchical way, on more criteria than just property, ownership, and wealth. Weber said that social inequality flowed from three interacting factors: class, status, and party.

By "**class**," Weber meant essentially what Marx meant by the term: the conditions of life and the social position derived from one's relation to the processes of production in society. Weber did not underrate the significance of wealth in determining what he called the life chances of an individual. In an analysis compatible with Marx's, Weber saw economic position as influencing access to such fateful and socially valued goods as material possessions, education, health, and the opportunity of living a long life in the mainstream of society.

Weber discounted the likelihood of class consciousness, however, claiming that the existence of other sources of social power tended to obscure people's awareness of belonging to an economic interest group. Unless individuals of equal ranking, according to wealth and property ownership, *recognized* their commonality and experienced it as the central feature of their life, he said, they would not tend to pursue class interests per se. Thus, he did not agree with Marx that society would become polarized into the bourgeoisie and the proletariat.

Weber also drew attention to the emergence of a range of middle classes, consisting of people who do not own extensive property but who, unlike the lower classes, have more than mere labour power to sell in the market place. These middle-class people may own modest businesses or small farms, or they may have valued skills gained through education and specialized training. (In this latter category fall, for example, lawyers, physicians, musicians, and craftspeople.) Weber argued that Marx's analysis of the class structure failed to place sufficient emphasis on this middle range. Weber's keen interest in bureaucracy as a key feature of modern society led him to recognize that the distribution of people throughout hierarchically ordered administrative systems provides a strong check on the simple dichotomization of classes described by Marx.[5] (It must be remembered that during the half-century separating Marx from Weber, both the number and the size of bureaucracies had grown, creating a large group of people who comprised an intermediate class between the bourgeoisie and the proletariat.)

Weber's most important contribution to the analysis of social stratification, however, lay in his recognition that prestige or social honour—in other words, **status**—is a major source of power and influence. In turn, this power and influence can be used to attain a favourable economic or class position, thus enhancing the life chances of one's descendants. This hereditary transmission of privilege is a powerful factor in channelling social relations and in rigidifying the social hierarchy. Weber recognized that class position is a factor in determining the social deference or degradation one receives, but he did not see it as the only determinant. An artist, a university president, a scientist, or a senior government official might not possess much property but could enjoy the same amount of prestige and manifest the same social comportment as the owner of a large firm. By the same token, a group of people from formerly wealthy families might continue to feel superior to a wealthier group whose riches were newly earned.

The third facet of association and social differentiation Weber identified was participation in the political sphere in groupings he referred to as "**parties**." Political power constitutes an important basis of command over the resources society values. A political party may represent the interests of a particular class or status group, but this is not inevitably so. One party may draw members from several classes or status groupings.

In brief, Weber's approach to the issue of power was pluralistic in that he saw power deriving from three spheres of social life—class, status, and party. His analyses of social life and of conflict in society, more than that of Marx, took into account the complex matrix in which human interaction unfolds. Although it allowed for a certain predictability within human events, Weber's work did not allow a simplistic scenario of social change. See Gerth and Mills' discussion of Weber's approach in their *From Max Weber: Essays in Sociology* (1946).

INVESTIGATING SOCIAL CLASS EMPIRICALLY 

Weber broadened Marx's economic analysis of stratification by adding social and political dimensions to the placement of both groups and individuals. Marx and Weber were theorists; it was left to future sociologists to flesh out the theoretical frameworks with empirical data. W. Lloyd Warner (1898–1970) and his associates set themselves the task of investigating how class membership manifested itself in a contemporary American community. The famous Yankee City studies (See Warner *et al.* 1963) were carried out during the 1930s in Newburyport, Massachusetts, a small industrial town north of Boston.

Warner and his associates conducted a series of in-depth interviews with informants who occupied a variety of positions in the Yankee City social hierarchy. Respondents were asked to identify what they perceived as the town's strata, to place each of various individuals in one of these strata, and to describe the salient characteristics of these individuals. When the ratings of the various informants were compared, a high degree of consistency emerged as to who was classified as "one of the people who look down at everyone else," "hard-working common people," and those who lived on the wrong side of the tracks and behaved in ways that put them outside the pale of respectability. These subjective evaluations were supplemented by an "Index of Status Characteristics." Each member of the sample group was allocated an ISC score calculated according to a formula that took into account occupation, source of income, and type and area of residence.

On the basis of these findings, the sociologists proposed a six-level classification scheme: the upper, middle, and lower classes, with each subdivided into an upper and lower segment. Thus, for example, they spoke of the upper-upper class, the lower-middle class, and the lower-lower class. Warner found that membership in the upper-upper class could not be obtained just by being rich; the wealth had to be inherited over generations. In fact, the members of the lower-upper class often had more money, but it was "new" money, and, like whisky, good money apparently needed aging. "Nouveau riche" is a derogatory term still used to describe those who are perceived to engage in conspicuous consumption by virtue of newly-gained wealth. On the lowest rung of the hierarchy were the unskilled labourers, employed in marginal jobs only sporadically and dependent on public welfare when they were not working.

Warner's approach has been criticized on the grounds that it defines class not according to strictly objective criteria but merely by what people say it is. Warner's classes, then, do not correspond to the Marxian concept of class, since members of any one class do not necessarily share the same relationship to the means of production. Another criticism of the work is that the method cannot be universally applied; the method of ranking families and individuals is clearly impracticable in large cities, where people may hardly know their neighbours, let alone be able to decide in what social category residents of a specific area should be placed.

Nonetheless, Warner's findings drew attention to the fact that members of a community were aware of social differences among themselves, and that they substantially agreed on the hierarchy. At the time Warner worked, the belief in a classless America stood unchallenged by empirical research. He showed that people believed classes existed and that, contrary to the rags-to-riches myth, upward mobility between classes typically proceeded in small increments, if at all. For example, although the descendants of Irish immigrants had lived in Yankee City for several generations, none had penetrated into the upper-upper class and very few into the lower-upper. Despite criticisms and problems with Warner's classification, it has stood the test of time and continues to be meaningful to sociologists and laypeople alike.

THE FUNCTIONALIST PERSPECTIVE – AND ITS CRITICS

In our discussion of various perspectives within sociology, we noted that functionalists view society as an integrated system of interdependent parts which all make some contribution to the total system. The central question posed by functionalists is how societies remain stable and persist over time. Thus, what captures their interest is continuity rather than change. This focus leads to concentration on those mechanisms that achieve consensus, rather than on what provokes conflict.

The functionalist approach to stratification, then, centres on what contribution the universally-apparent phenomenon of inequality makes to the maintenance of social order and survival. The essence of their answer is that unequal distribution of income, prestige, and power provides incentives to ensure that people are available to assume society's most vital tasks. Rewards, they argue, are necessary as motivating factors to bring forth the abilities and the hard work that are required to carry out these tasks. It is assumed that, if such rewards were not forthcoming, a pool of talent would not be available, and the appropriate distribution of people in whatever division of labour the social system calls for would not occur. According to this view, an individual would hardly be willing to undertake a long and arduous program of medical education unless he or she could be assured of ultimately receiving a higher income and higher prestige than, say, a postal clerk.

This view, of which Kingsley Davis (1908–) and Wilbert Moore (1914–) are well-known exponents, has been challenged by those, such as Melvin Tumin (1919–), who argue that many variables are involved in the rankings assigned to individuals in the stratification system, and that there is no empirical one-to-one relationship between the rewards of a job and its societal importance (Davis and Moore 1945; Tumin 1970). Does society need rock musicians, who receive fame and wealth for the entertainment they provide? Are professional baseball players more valuable than farmers? Furthermore, how does one determine the appropriate differential in rewards? To put the question differently, just how much inequality is necessary?

It is important to note that the functionalist perspective on social stratification emerged in a specific context — the United States, where the ideology of individualism and equality of opportunity stresses the value of ambition and hard work. Further, such an ideology assumes the absence of a rigid social system in which people are sorted mainly according to ascriptive characteristics, such as race and kinship. The social system is seen, rather, as fluid or open, allowing motivated individuals to acquire those attributes, such as education, that they need to achieve the best-rewarded positions.[6]

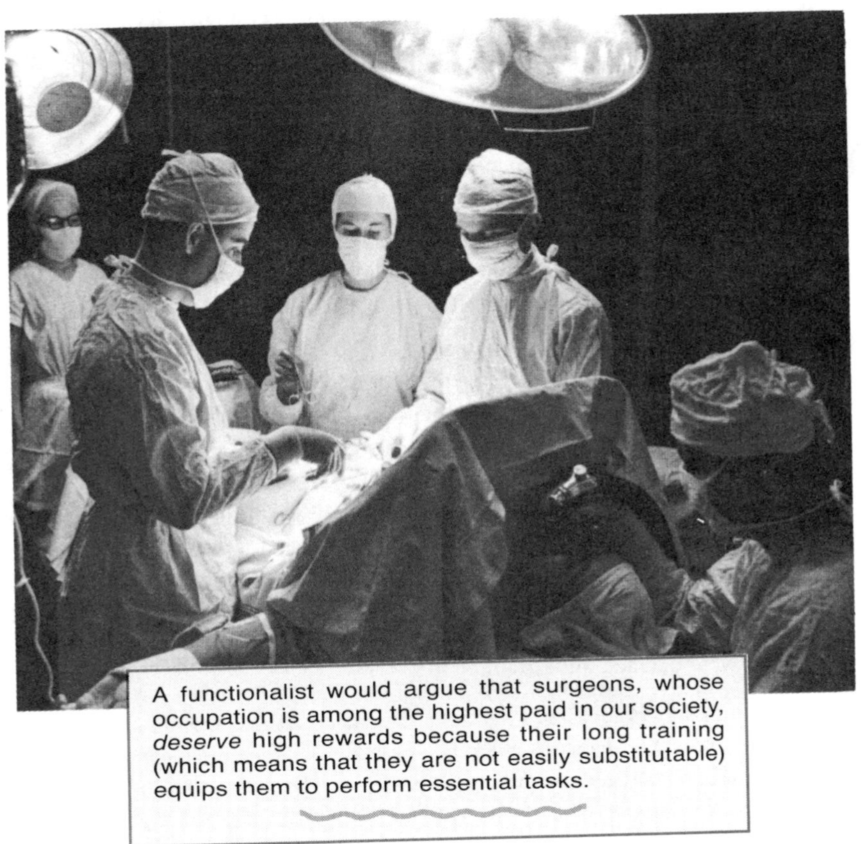

A functionalist would argue that surgeons, whose occupation is among the highest paid in our society, *deserve* high rewards because their long training (which means that they are not easily substitutable) equips them to perform essential tasks.

Conflict theorists argue that the functionalist view serves to legitimize social inequality by providing a rationale for serving and perpetuating the interests of the privileged (Dahrendorf 1959; Poulantzas 1978). They point out that inequality persists because powerful groups are able to claim the lion's share of rewards, while thwarting any changes to the system. The difference between the two schools is clearly a matter of emphasis; neither would argue that there is a perfect fit between talent, effort, and reward. Many theorists, including Lenski (1966), have sought to reconcile the conflict and the functionalist perspectives in order to provide a more comprehensive explanation of the way stratification systems work.

STRATIFICATION IN CANADA

Lloyd Warner was in the vanguard of those demonstrating that class divisions were alive and well in the "classless" United States. Assumptions of classlessness have been made about Canada, too. However, here again sociologists have found that the assumptions do not fit the reality of social stratification.

A VERTICAL MOSAIC

John Porter (1921–79), in a major work making extensive use of statistical data on such factors as education, occupation, and income (1965), showed how stratification was manifested in Canadian society. He found a great deal of evidence that contradicted the image of Canada as a classless society or as a middle-class society without extremes of poverty or wealth.

Canada is a nation of immigrants. At several times in our history, the authorities have deliberately attracted immigrants for economic reasons. Even at other times, there has been little shortage of people who, fleeing political strife, persecution, or economic hardship, sought entrance to this country with its vast natural resources. But immigration to Canada has never been for everyone. Using various criteria, the authorities have selected candidates based on their presumed ability to meld into the mainstream of Canadian society. In the days of Nouvelle France, colonists had to be Roman Catholics (a requirement that prevented the entrance of the Huguenots, even during the times when these French Protestants were tolerated in France itself). For many years, orientals, East Indians, and blacks, and sometimes Jews were deemed undesirable.[7]

Immigration in the United States has been similar in outline, though not in detail. That country, however, has long championed the ideal of the **melting pot** in which acculturation is to proceed as quickly as possible. The very motto of the United States—*e pluribus unum* ("one from many")—suggests that goal. Canada, on the other hand, has espoused a philosophy of pluralism in order to legitimize the creation of a **cultural mosaic**. Theoretically, groups are able to maintain their heritage and traditions; immigrants become "hyphenated Canadians." (The concepts of the melting pot and the cultural mosaic are further discussed in Chapter 7 on minority groups.)

Porter titled his book *The Vertical Mosaic* because he argued that while Canada may be a mosaic, the parts that constitute it do not enjoy equality. Economic position (class) and ethnicity have a significant relationship.[8] The decennial censuses from 1931 to 1961 consistently revealed those of British origin to be overrepresented at the top of the occupational and income hierarchies, whereas native peoples were grossly overrepresented at the bottom. The other groups of the ethnic mosaic ranged between these poles. Drawing on Blishen's analysis of the 1951 census data, Porter commented:

> *Within the total occupational system the vertical mosaic can be summed up as follows: ". . . the proportion of British in each class generally increases from the lowest to the highest class whereas the reverse is true for the French. The Jewish group follows a pattern similar to that of the British whereas all other origins follow the French pattern" (1965, 90).*

This inequality in class position both reflected differential educational attainment by the head of the household and influenced the educational opportunities of his children. Thus, class differences and inequality are perpetuated, even though the educational system makes mobility possible. In 1961, as shown in Exhibit 4.1, only 14 percent of all family heads age 35 to 65 were in professional occupations, but significantly higher percentages of students in arts and science, law, and medicine had fathers in such occupations. By contrast, only a small percentage of law and medical students were the children of labourers, who constituted 5 percent of all family heads.

EXHIBIT 4.1

DISTRIBUTION OF UNIVERSITY STUDENTS BY FATHER'S OCCUPATION

Father's occupation	Arts and science	Law	Medicine	All family heads age 35-65 years
Professional	19.8%	26.4%	29.5%	14.2%
Managerial and proprietary	27.0	26.3	22.2	8.0
Clerical	4.2	5.4	5.7	7.1
Commercial	8.0	7.3	7.5	5.1
Service	6.2	5.4	2.3	8.6
Transport	5.7	3.2	4.5	6.6
Craftsmen	14.3	12.7	13.2	29.1
Labourers	1.6	1.1	2.9	4.5
Others	13.2	12.2	12.2	16.8
Total	100.0	100.0	100.0	100.0

SOURCES: Dominion Bureau of Statistics, *University Student Expenditure and Income in Canada, 1961–2* (Ottawa, 1963), table 16; and *Census Canada 1961*, vol 2: 1–3, as reported in Porter (1965).

Of course, various conclusions can be drawn from such figures. On the one hand, they show that the children of professionals, managers, and proprietors were overrepresented among university students. This would support the argument that class differences, though not hereditary, are transmitted between generations. On the other hand, it should be noted that more than half of all university students and close to half of the law and medical students had fathers who did not fall into the professional or managerial category. Are these students moving up the social ladder?

Uncovering the extent and the form of inequality in Canada was one major thrust of Porter's enquiry. A second, related objective was to examine the structure of power. Porter defined power as "the recognized right to make effective decisions on behalf of a group of people" (1965, 201). Who exercised power, what was the composition of the elite (power-holding) groups, and how did they interact with one another?

The economic elite, which Porter defined as individuals who held directorships in one or more corporations employing at least 500 people, was dominated by those of British origin. Francophones constituted a mere 6.7 percent, and "ethnic groups of neither British nor French origin, which made up about one-fifth of the general population, were hardly represented at all" (1965, 286).

Members of the economic elite shared more than ethnic origins, Porter found. They were from similar class backgrounds, overwhelmingly the upper or middle class. Many had attended the same private schools and summer camps, and nearly all had been to university. Similar background was reinforced by a similar lifestyle: membership in private clubs and geographic proximity of both city and vacation homes, respectively. Jointly, these characteristics helped to create a socially homogeneous group, aware of its shared origins and goals.

Economic elites hold no monopoly on power—it is also wielded by those at the apex of other societal sectors, such as the federal bureaucracy, the universities, the judiciary, organized labour, and the mass media. Porter did not argue that these elites are identical, though he did point out that Canadians of British ethnic origin and high social-class background were overrepresented in all of them. What is important, he said, is that members of these elites have access to each other. Their relations are intermittently marked by conflict, but there is also much co-operation.

> *Whom else would political leaders consult but business leaders, labour leaders, higher bureaucrats, and newspaper proprietors? Sociology often has to deal with obvious facts, and the task here has been to show that within the overall structure of power in society elite groups co-ordinate their own activities, and the complex social activities of the institutions they command. A confraternity of power develops among them, and this in turn is reinforced by the establishments of kinship and class (1965, 540–1).*

Overall, Porter found strong relationships linking ethnicity, class, and power in Canadian society. He predicted that they would persist and that the "historical pattern of class and ethnicity will be perpetuated as long as ethnic differentiation is so highly valued" (1965, 558).

Porter provided a fresh way of looking at stratification in Canada. In the 1950s and 1960s, the functionalist perspective, in which society was seen as a smoothly operating system of interlocking parts, was especially prominent. Social scientists focused on the bright side of opportunity and mobility. Porter shifted attention to the roadblocks that stood in the way of mobility. He pointed to the wasted potential of those who did not manage to get ahead because they were born in the wrong province or had the wrong class or ethnic background. Porter's work has spurred continuing research into the issues of power and inequality in Canadian society. See, for example, The John Porter Memorial Lectures 1984–87.

ELITES: GETTING THERE AND STAYING THERE 

Wallace Clement (1949–) had been one of Porter's students, and both were interested in the study of **elites**. An elite can be defined as a set of persons who hold the top positions in any institutional hierarchy. In his study *The Canadian Corporate Elite*, published in 1975, Clement frequently used Porter's findings as bases of comparison, contributing important dimensions to the older man's work.

To analyse how much equality of opportunity exists in a society, Clement noted, one must first establish the extent to which there is equality or inequality of "condition." According to capitalist ideology, one's condition (that is, position attained and possessions accumulated) is the result of individual ability and effort. Hence, inequality of condition does not run counter to the societal credo. However, Clement and many other analysts hold that inequality of condition necessarily results in unequal opportunities:

> *The accumulation of privilege associated with dominant positions affords their incumbents advantages which are transmitted to their kin but not available to other members of society. This is transmitted by differential access to the means of mobility such as private and post-secondary education, inherited wealth, career openings, social contacts and a series of advantages perpetuated through class institutions such as private schools and private clubs. This leads to differential class opportunities in favour of the privileged (1975, 6–7).*

Porter's data on the social composition of elite groups supported the existence of such "differential class opportunities." However, major changes had occurred in the interim between the time Porter's and Clement's research was done. The number of firms had been reduced through mergers and acquisitions, concentrating ownership. Foreign, particularly American, ownership of Canadian firms had become more extensive and more recognizable. The much-publicized "war on poverty'' had been launched, and there had been explosive growth in Canadian postsecondary education. How, if at all, did these developments affect recruitment into the elite stratum, and the ways in which elites exercised power?

Canada has often been described as a ''branch-plant economy,'' which makes Clement's analytic distinction of three types of elites useful:

- *Indigenous elites.* Canadian directors and executives of predominantly Canadian-owned corporations (for example, the chartered banks).
- *Comprador elites.* the upper managers of largely foreign-owned companies in Canada (for example, the top executives of GM Canada).
- *Parasite elites.* those who govern the foreign-owned multinational corporations from their head offices (for example, the Dutch-based management group of Shell Oil).

Since policy is handed down from head offices, comprador elites have administrative rather than policy-making power. This means that outsiders make decisions which vitally affect the Canadian economy and the fate of Canadian workers; this does not necessarily have an adverse effect on the indigenous elite, though, most of whom are concentrated in the commercial sectors of finance, trade, and transportation. Indeed, Clement noted:

> *The position of the traditional indigenous elite is reinforced by the industrial development occurring with U.S. direct investment. It is the smaller Canadian entrepreneurs based in industries which have not established themselves as dominant who feel the squeeze of U.S. penetration (1975, 121).*

Although conflicts undoubtedly arise, Clement viewed the interests of the indigenous-commercial elite and the parasite-industrial elite groups as inherently compatible and largely harmonious. This view was confirmed by the massive support the business community gave to the 1988 Free Trade Agreement between Canada and the United States (Campbell and Powell 1989).

As indicated by the title of his book, Clement's analysis was confined to the corporate elite: those who held directorships or senior executive posts in one or more of the 113 corporations he categorized as ''dominant'' (based on capital assets and sales). He also restricted his analysis to individuals domiciled in Canada.[9]

Porter had used a number of criteria for his definition of class background, including family connections to the elite, private schooling, university education, and father's occupation. On the basis of these indicators, he deemed 82 percent of the corporate elite to have upper-class origins in 1951. By 1972, when Clement did his research, the figure had risen to 94.2 percent.[10] Clement concluded that the elite had become less accessible to those people from the working class.

Like Warner and Porter, Clement stressed the multiple ties that link those at the top. Shared origins and shared life experiences reinforce the consciousness of commonality. Close-knit groups become resistant to penetration because they fear that outsiders will spoil the cozy, familial atmosphere. As we discussed in connection with primary groups, the more homogeneous a group, the easier it is for members to predict each other's reactions and the more likely they are to resist change.

We have already quoted Marx's statement that human beings make their own history, though not under conditions of their own choosing. Clement examined the conditions in Canadian society that constrain the history individuals can make for themselves. Powerful vested interest groups defend structured inequality, and only a few exceptional people are able to breach these defences. With little likelihood that inequality would decrease in Canada, Clement could hold out little hope that the ideal of equal opportunity would ever be widely realized.

In his 1977 study, Clement went on to examine the connections between corporate elites in Canada and those in the United States. He argues that although these elites are part of a continental economy, the balance of power resides with American industry.

LEVELLING INFLUENCES IN MODERN CLASS SOCIETY

Over the last two centuries, industrialization and urbanization have consolidated the hold that economic class maintains as the pre-eminent cause of stratification in North American society. Canadian policies to redistribute income through the taxation and social welfare systems are attempts to reduce inequality and thus to reshape societal stratification. They have been only marginally successful.

In the preceding parts of this chapter, we have shown that classes are more than artifacts of definition, since differences in lifestyle, in behaviour, and in attitude are associated with membership in a class. However, we must not let these differences blind us to the factors that cut across class lines and serve to homogenize, at least superficially, the bulk of Canadian society. Consider sports, television serials, or the youth culture with its rock idols.

One important levelling influence is mass education. Except for the small proportion who attend private schools, Canadian children experience prolonged exposure to essentially similar schools. Variations in curricula and in the availability of such facilities as science laboratories and audiovisual equipment are connected with differences in school systems and regions, rather than with class differences. Within schools, students meet youngsters and teachers with social backgrounds different from their own. This homogenization has been weakened by the exodus to the suburbs of the middle class, which has increased residential segregation and reduced opportunities for the mixing of social classes within schools. The controversial bussing program in the United States was designed to counteract the effects of such residential segregation along racial lines. Recently, however, there has been a return of middle-class families to inner city neighbourhoods, such as Toronto's Cabbagetown and Vancouver's Kitsilano, increasing the chances of "mixed" classrooms.

As we will discuss in Chapter 9B on education, students from different class origins do not fare equally in the schools. But for the moment, we are emphasizing the commonality provided by going to school for many years, by being expected to complete specified tasks on time, and by attending assemblies, sports days, and school dances.

Modern technology has made possible mass production. In turn, mass production has resulted in real income gains for a majority of workers.[11] The combination of these two factors has brought about mass consumption. Ownership of such goods as cars, radios, television sets, and electric refrigerators is broadly diffused throughout Canadian society. Mass consumption is spurred by the ongoing barrage of media advertising and by the ready availability of financing.

The consumption of many goods that are fundamentally alike, if varying in quality, veils class differences. In all strata, jeans and running shoes are the uniform of the young. Cheaper versions of high fashion filter down quickly. Within hours of Princess Diana's wedding, Londoners were able to buy facsimiles of her dress. Most of the time, you probably do not encounter people who look vastly different from yourself. The juxtaposition of obvious, abject poverty and ostentatious wealth is more muted in Canada than, say, in Rio de Janeiro, where shanty towns overlook the luxurious Copacabana Beach. Much of the severe poverty in Canada is hidden in rural areas and remote native reserves. Recently, however, increasing numbers of homeless persons in our cities demonstrate that poverty is a serious problem in Canada (Ontario Government Report on Homelessness, *More Than Just a Roof* 1987).

The well-known sociologist W.I. Thomas (1863–1947) noted long ago, "If men define situations as real, they are real in their consequences" (quoted in Merton 1968, 475). One important consequence of Canada being defined as essentially a middle-class society is the belief by much of the populace that this is in fact the case. The discovery by social scientists of widespread inequality of condition, bringing in its wake inequality of opportunity, makes few dents in this belief.

ENDLESS POVERTY LIKELY FUTURE OF POOR CHILDREN, STUDY SHOWS

By Graham Fraser

Poor children are caught in a vicious cycle that makes poverty even more likely to continue when they grow up, according to researchers who have studied poverty in Canada.

"The drop-out rate for young people is twice as high in poor families as in non-poor families," David Ross told a news conference yesterday. He is co-author of The Canadian Fact Book on Poverty published by the Canadian Council on Social Development.

"We consider this to be a self-perpetuating situation," he said. "Poor education leads to poor incomes, and poor income leads to dropping out (of school) by children in these families."

The study found education to be the most significant common factor in poverty levels. Non-poor households have more education than working-poor households, who have more education than poor households without employment.

The study concluded that poverty in Canada strikes hardest at children, the most vulnerable people in society. The children of single mothers — who fare much worse in Canada than in many other industrialized countries — are hurt the most.

This was one of a number of conclusions which Mr. Ross and his co-author, Richard Shillington, drew from a study of the statistics on poverty.

"Relative to the poverty rates among children in other industrial countries, the rates in Canada and the United States are dismal, especially with respect to children in lone-parent families," the study said. "In Sweden, for example, the rate of child poverty among all lone-parent families in 1981, the most recent year for which a figure was available, was 9.8 percent; the Canadian rate was 51.2 percent, and the U.S. rate (in 1979) was 60 percent."

The study found that over the past 15 years, poverty has proportionally shifted from the elderly toward children and young families.

"In 1972, a young family faced a 16 percent chance of being poor. By 1986, however, and in spite of a fall in the over-all rate of poverty, the rate among young families had almost doubled."

Mr. Ross and Mr. Shillington found that the proportion of poor families (20 percent) had remained unchanged from 1973 to 1986, but that the number had increased by 366,000. But of those living in poverty, the proportion who are employed has increased.

Mr. Ross and Mr. Shillington pointed to the emergence of two-income families as a factor that distinguishes poor families from non-poor families. "In 1986, 72 percent of married women in non-poor families had some employment, compared with only 39 percent in poor families," they wrote.

However, they pointed out, this has had

serious implications for those who cannot rely on more than one wage-earner: single individuals and single parents.

The minimum wage should be increased immediately in order to deal with the growing problem of child poverty, said Terrance Hunsley, executive director of the council.

He also called for an increase in the income support level for children by tripling the child tax credit.

In the House of Commons, New Democratic Party Leader Edward Broadbent called on the government to respond to the problem of poverty as outlined in the report by increasing the minimum wage.

Prime Minister Brian Mulroney responded by saying that the number of Canadian living in poverty had fallen by 549,000 since 1984, and that 1.4 million jobs had been created in the same period.

Finance Minister Michael Wilson said that during the same period, the child tax credit had increased from $367 to $559.

''It's sad complacency that the reality of four million Canadians living in poverty—amongst them a virtual doubling of young families living below the poverty level — should be dismissed as it was by the Prime Minister,'' Mr. Broadbent told reporters outside the House. ''The government was just acting as if we were talking about a cloud in the sky.''

SOCIAL MOBILITY: CHANGING PLACES

As we have noted, one of the characteristics that distinguish types of societies is their degree of openness — that is, the extent to which there is mobility up and down the hierarchy. Here, we will examine the concept of mobility more closely, first defining the relevant terms.

Vertical mobility refers to movement up and down a hierarchy. Since occupational and social position are closely linked within Canadian society, mobility generally means occupational mobility. Traditionally, this has not been the case for women, for whom mobility has typically come through marriage. The secretary who marries her boss is considered upwardly mobile.

Vertical mobility can be divided into **intergenerational mobility** and **intragenerational** (career) **mobility**. A lawyer whose father was a plumber has experienced intergenerational mobility—mobility between one generation and the next. If he starts as an associate in a large law firm and becomes a partner, he is also upwardly mobile intragenerationally—within his own work life. Intragenerational mobility need not take place within the same occupation. For instance, a nurse may retrain as a physician. Intergenerational downward mobility is exhibited by the executive's daughter who becomes an unskilled cleaner. The teacher who has an alcohol problem, is dismissed, and drifts into casual work is downwardly mobile within his career.

Intergenerational mobility is difficult to measure accurately because the occupational structure itself changes and because the parents and also the child may experience career mobility. Sociologists have traditionally treated movement from blue-collar or farm occupation to white-collar occupation as upward mobility (Rogoff 1953). This assumption may have to be re-examined in light of the significant income gains made by unionized blue-collar workers and the narrowed scope of the lower-echelon white-collar labour force, which, significantly, is made up mainly of women (Lowe 1981).

Horizontal mobility is exhibited when a person moves among jobs which are at roughly the same level. For example, someone in car sales may switch to selling real estate, a bank teller may become a clerk typist, or a nurse may retrain and practise physiotherapy.

As we have already noted, **geographic mobility** is frequently a necessary condition for moving up. To get a better job — or even any job — people come to North America from Europe and Asia; others move from rural areas to the city, or from one region of the country to another. In Canada since Confederation, this movement has been predominantly westward, from the Atlantic provinces to central Canada. During the heady years of the oil boom in the 1970s, Alberta was seen as the promised land.

Structural mobility is brought about by changes in the economy that either facilitate or constrict opportunities for occupational advancement. In industrialized societies, technology helps to eliminate many menial and routine jobs — for example, loading and unloading heavy cargo — and creates a host of new, higher-level ones.

The most dramatic recent technological developments have been computer-related. Programmers and analysts are needed, as well as technicians to service sophisticated hardware and software, and all these tasks must be co-ordinated by skilled personnel. When economic activity expands more quickly than the population, structural mobility occurs.

Demographic trends are important here. Historically, industrialization has been accompanied by lowered fertility rates, a decrease which has become much sharper with the availability of reliable birth control. Smaller family size has been positively correlated with socioeconomic status. Put simply, those on the top tend to have fewer children than those at the bottom, as noted in the adage "the rich get richer and the poor get children." This has the effect of increasing structural mobility. Tepperman has commented:

> *Thus as industrialization adds new occupational positions at the middle and top of the job hierarchy, low fertility at the top diminishes the likelihood that sufficient candidates for such positions will be found in families in the top social classes. Stated otherwise, the ratio of higher born children to higher status jobs declines with industrialization; this means that the likelihood that higher status jobs will be filled by children from lower classes will increase. This phenomenon illustrates the working of a combination of resource mobility—an upgrading of the occupational structure—and demographic mobility—a change from too few higher class children (1975, 38–9).*

The effect of industrialization on mobility can be seen as two-pronged. The shift in available positions pushes the occupational structure upward. At the same time, the insufficient number of offspring produced in the higher classes creates a force that pulls up some well-qualified children from the lower classes.

Mobility rates are based on statistical calculations; they say nothing about the individuals who actually move up and down, those who get better jobs, and those who must make do with worse jobs (or perhaps with none at all). It cannot be assumed that workers displaced from routine jobs will be capable of obtaining the new jobs. In fact, they may be relegated to the ranks of the marginally employed, or unemployed. In a study of the effect of plant closures on the careers of displaced workers, Grayson (1986) found that a majority of those who did find new jobs experienced de-skilling, lower earnings, and greater job insecurity. The next question to be addressed is, who moves up? In other words, we are changing the emphasis from developments that affect a society as a whole to the fate of individuals.

In their book *Who Gets Ahead?*, Christopher Jencks and his colleagues recounted their investigation of the "relationship between personal characteristics and economic success among American males age 25 to 64," for which they used several large-scale surveys, focusing on "family background, cognitive skills, personality traits, and years of schooling" (1979, 3).

In practice, of course, some of these characteristics are related; those from a favoured family background are more likely to develop and enhance their cognitive skills (as measured by IQ tests, for example), and both of these factors positively influence the numbers of years of schooling an individual completes. However, by sophisticated statistical analysis, it is possible to weigh separately the effect of each of these factors on earnings and occupational status.

Jencks' findings showed that family background had a significant impact on advancement (as measured by earnings and occupational status):

> *If we define "equal opportunity" as a situation in which sons born into different families have the same chances of success, our data show that America comes nowhere near achieving it (1979, 82).*

Cognitive skills (that is, academic ability), as well as such noncognitive personality traits as motivation and leadership potential, were found to influence occupational success, even when family background and education were constant. In other words, the researchers found differences in earnings and occupational status in comparing respondents who had the same number of years of schooling and similar family backgrounds but differed in academic ability or personality traits. In connection with the latter, Jencks and his colleagues concluded, "Non-cognitive traits contribute more to individual achievement that previous research indicated" (1979, 158).

Conventional wisdom has long held that getting an education is the most reliable means for getting ahead. Jencks' findings do not contradict this, but they show that it is postsecondary schooling, rather than just high school completion, that provides the real upward push. (See Exhibit 4.2 for Canadian data on earnings and level of education.) As an increasing percentage of the population has completed high school, the relative advantage has diminished.

> *Our findings place a number of widespread presumptions in doubt. The most significant of these is that high school dropouts are economically disadvantaged largely because they fail to finish school. Our results suggest that the apparent advantages enjoyed by high school graduates derive to a significant extent from their prior characteristics, not from their schooling. Unless high school attendance is followed by a college education, its economic value appears quite modest (1979, 189).*

Earlier in this chapter, we noted that family position plays an important part in the likelihood of a person's attending college or university. If the advantages accruing from education are largely reserved for such persons, the possibility of upward mobility for lower-class individuals may actually diminish, except for those who manage to obtain a higher education.

In answer to the question of who moves up, we tentatively conclude that a combination of favourable characteristics accounts for success. Thus, Exhibit 4.2 demonstrates the favourable effect on earnings of being a male university graduate. However, two cautionary notes are indicated. First, individual success is strongly influenced by structural conditions. It is a lot easier to get ahead in a period of economic expansion than in a recessionary climate. For example, Harvey and Kalwa (1983) examined the effects of socioeconomic background, educational achievement, and labour-market conditions (as indicated by the unemployment rate) on the occupational status attainment of five "cohorts" of men and women who gradúted from selected Canadian universities between 1960 and 1976.[12] The findings showed that "changing labour market conditions appear to be much more important than the standard socioeconomic and educational attributes" (1983, 446).

The second cautionary note is that the same personal attributes may not produce the same results for blacks and whites or for men and women, again as Exhibit 4.2 demonstrates. We will discuss the effects of ascribed characteristics on life chances in the chapters dealing with work, with minority groups, with organizations, and with social change.

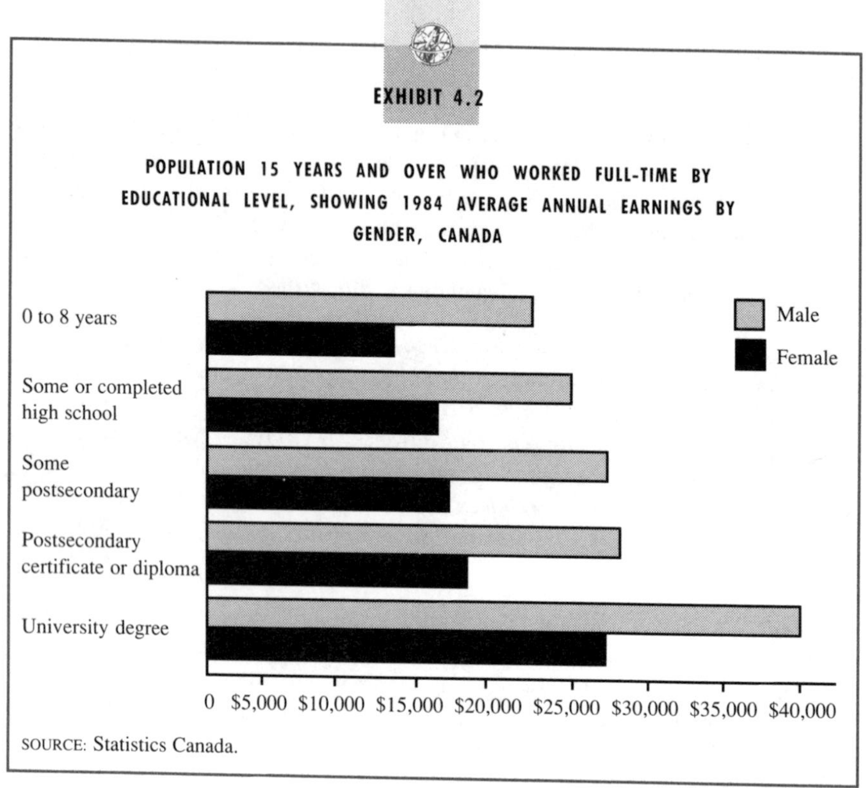

EXHIBIT 4.2

POPULATION 15 YEARS AND OVER WHO WORKED FULL-TIME BY EDUCATIONAL LEVEL, SHOWING 1984 AVERAGE ANNUAL EARNINGS BY GENDER, CANADA

SOURCE: Statistics Canada.

SUMMARY

In this chapter we have examined society's sorting of people into levels or strata that carry with them unequal rewards. Those in the higher strata obtain both higher material and symbolic rewards. Some societies are more open than others. Caste and estate societies are more or less closed; status is ascribed, movement between levels is difficult, and interaction among individuals situated at different levels is regulated by formal and informal rules.

A class society is more open. An individual's class position is held to be determined by achievement. However, in class societies, particular regions and racial or ethnic groups are consistently overrepresented in such indices of disadvantage as minimal education, poor health, and marginal employment. Such overrepresentation demonstrates that inequality cannot be satisfactorily explained in terms of individual attributes. Even in open class societies, there is substantial gender inequality. Despite an ideology that proclaims equal opportunity for those of equal ability and rejects the notion of a frozen hierarchy, considerable structural inequality exists in Canada.

Social thinkers substantially agree that inequality exists in virtually every society. Disagreement centres on the causes and consequences of this inequality. Marx's analysis centred on economic inequality: how it is created and preserved, and how it affects the lives of individuals. Weber acknowledged the importance of economic factors but expanded his focus to the social and political dimensions of inequality. In this sense, Weber's is a pluralistic approach to the study of stratification.

Is inequality necessary? To Marx, the function of inequality was clear: it serves the interests of the dominant group. To structural functionalists such as Davis and Moore, unequal rewards benefit the society as a whole by providing able individuals with incentives to make the efforts required for performing society's vital tasks.

Until empirical research was conducted, the notion prevailed that class differences did not exist in the new world. Studies, such as those by Warner in the United States and by Porter and Clement in Canada, have challenged the myths that class is not a significant variable in these societies, and that rapid upward mobility can be easily achieved.

Class differences are obscured by levelling influences that make for superficial similarity among people and create the impression of a common lifestyle. The widespread acceptance of this view discourages the emergence of class consciousness and makes conflict less apparent.

Even though mobility is hampered in modern class societies, it does occur. The mobility of the few keeps alive faith in mobility for all. How much mobility takes place is influenced by such macro factors as the expansion or contraction of the economy, and technological advances which reorder the occupational structure. Personal attributes do play a part in determining who will move up or down and who will remain stationary. In all instances, however, mobility is constrained or facilitated by conditions beyond individual control.

ASSIGNMENTS

Do one or more of the following assignments, as instructed by your professor.

1 Read *The Tin Flute* and *The Women of Brewster Place* (see the Suggested Readings), both of which describe poor families. Compare and contrast

the ways in which people cope, or fail to cope, with being poor. You may wish to choose two other novels as the basis for the assignment.

2 Chart your family tree as far back as you can go. See what, if any, patterns of mobility you can identify between and within generations. Explain your findings in sociological terms. For example, a skilled tradesman coming from Europe may have to start work as a labourer in Canada because his formal qualifications are not recognized here (downward mobility).

3 What would a day spent in upper-class activities be like? List these activities and try to determine the origin of your notion that such things are upper class. You may have actually engaged in such activities, or you may have derived your notion that such activities are upper class from television programs, such as *Dynasty*, or from magazines and books.

4 Re-read the article "Rich City: Poor City." Write an account, after careful observation, of the two extremes of the social hierarchy in your home community or in the community in which you are studying.

SUGGESTED READINGS

Charles Dickens, *Oliver Twist* (Oxford: Oxford University Press, 1978; first published 1837 and available in many editions). Marx insisted that analysis be specific to the economic and social situations of the times. Similarly, Marx himself should be read with some knowledge of the times in which he wrote. Some of the best pictures of the social evils which followed from the Industrial Revolution in England come from the contemporary novels of Charles Dickens, who wrote in part to encourage reform.

In this novel, Oliver, born in a workhouse (the mid-19th-century equivalent of social assistance), flees from its cruelty; almost the first kindness shown him is by a gang of pickpockets. Throughout the book, the focus is on the upper classes' degrading treatment of the poor and on the way such treatment breeds crime.

E.G. Grabb, *Social Inequality: Classical and Contemporary Theorists* (Toronto: Holt, Rinehart and Winston, 1984). Grabb offers an overview of writings by several theorists on the subject of social inequality. Although the material he covers is complex and not always easy to grasp at first reading, his simple, clear writing style lightens the task. This book is especially recommended to students who intend to pursue studies in sociology.

J. Hawkesworth, *Upstairs, Downstairs* (New York: Dell, 1973). This is one of several books based on the highly successful British television series of the same name. In the early part of this century, the rich and the poor occupied radically different worlds in Britain, even though they often lived in the same house. This practice conformed to the ideology that one's station in life had been allotted by the Lord himself, and one had better make the best of it. Students will note that this ideology differs from the one prevailing in our society.

A.A. Hunter, *Class Tells* (Toronto: Butterworth, 1981). Hunter provides an informative discussion of causes and manifestations of social inequality in Canada. He traces the historical development of classes here and examines the relationship between class membership and power as well as the extent to which Canadians are aware of the existence and the consequences of the class structure.

Karl Marx, *The Communist Manifesto* (New York: Modern Library, 1932; first published 1848). *The Communist Manifesto* was written on the eve of the 1848 revolutions against the oppressive regimes that held most of Europe in thrall. The revolutions failed, but *The Manifesto* survived, a superb example of polemical writing. The ideas expressed in it have given impetus to revolutions in the present century.

In *The Manifesto*, Marx briefly traces the evolution of the bourgeoisie into the dominant class and spells out, with remarkable accuracy, the trend toward large, multinational enterprises. Not all Marx's predictions with respect to the condition of the working class have come true. In industrialized countries at least, workers today enjoy a standard of living greatly improved from that of the mid-19th century.

G. Naylor, *The Women of Brewster Place* (London: Penguin, 1983). What is it like to be poor, black, and female in contemporary America? The consequences are overwhelmingly negative — one's life chances and those of one's children are limited. One is likely to live in a run-down neighbourhood; the traditional nuclear family with a working father and a stay-at-home mother is something one sees in television programs rather than in one's own life. Yet, people keep going and keep trying to make things a little better. Without downplaying frustration and failure, Naylor's book testifies to the resilience of the human spirit.

B.D. Palmer, *The Character of Class Struggle: Essays in Canadian Working Class History, 1850–1985* (Toronto: McClelland and Stewart, 1986). This is a collection of essays examining changes in the organization of work, and in the relations between workers and employers. The contributors look at the struggle for power from the workers' perspective and address issues such as regional differences, gender, and trade union leadership.

Gabrielle Roy, *The Tin Flute* (Toronto: McClelland and Stewart, 1947). It is the Depression, and the Lacasse family, with its many children, barely manages to survive in the slums of Montreal. Being poor and trying to cope with it is a grim reality for all members of the Lacasse clan, and for the community of St. Henri generally. Volunteering for military service in the Second World War is the first opportunity for many St. Henri men to make a living. Ironically, it is a living that exposes them every day to the possibility of dying.

R. Sennett and **J. Cobb**, *The Hidden Injuries of Class* (New York: Random House, 1972). This book is based on in-depth interviews with blue-collar workers during the early 1970s. Sennett and Cobb's respondents offer poignant testimony to the way the disjunction between the ideology of equal opportunity and the reality of structured inequality is experienced by those who perceive themselves as not having "made it."

NOTES

[1] The Indian government has now outlawed many aspects of the caste system. However, much of it persists in some rural areas — a good example of society's simply ignoring laws it does not agree with, as well as of the fact that it is the group, not some outside authority, that sets the criteria for stratification.

[2] "Estate" comes from the Old French *estat*, derived from the Latin *status*. The word is still current in the phrase "the fourth estate" as a name for the press.

[3] One of the chief developments of the modern class system has been its increased emphasis on achieved status. In the 19th century, as we see in novels such as those of Jane Austen, the newly rich, especially those who made money in less acceptable occupations such as "trade" (merchandising), were of lower status than those whose wealth came from inherited land or even the professions (see the Suggested Readings for Chapter 10). This point is further discussed in the sections on Weber and Warner later in that chapter.

[4] Most biblical scholars now say that this reference is not to a literal needle but to a very low gate to the city of Jerusalem. A camel could go through it, but only with great difficulty.

[5] A bureaucracy is a rationally patterned organization, hierarchical in structure and run on predictable principles. The theory and application are further discussed in Chapter 6.

[6] Many people, including blacks, hispanics, and native peoples, would challenge the actuality of this ideal. But few would deny that this is the ideal and that many Americans believe it to be at least partially true.

[7] Today, the basic criterion for immigration is employability — in other words, education and work skills.

[8] Notwithstanding the melting pot ideology, such a relationship has also existed in the United States. See for example Christopher's *Crashing the Gates: The De-Wasping of America's Power Elite*, 1980.

[9] Membership in Clement's corporate elite cuts across his indigenous, comprador, and parasite elites. In other words, the president of the Royal Bank (indigenous) would be a member of the corporate elite, as would the president of GM Canada (comprador) and a director of Exxon Corporation (parasite) who lives in Connecticut.

[10] It should be noted that this comparison did not take into account the fact that university attendance was becoming more widespread. It may have been a less reliable class indicator in 1972 than it was in 1951.

[11] Real income gains refer to increased purchasing power, rather than to enlargement of incomes to match inflation.

[12] A cohort is a group of people who share some statistical characteristic or set of characteristics (age and/or sex, for example) in a demographic study. One speaks, for example, of the cohort of Canadians born in 1967 or the cohort of North American women born between 1935 and 1939.

5

WORK AND THE

DIVISION OF LABOUR

The variety of work covered in the selection of advertised employment opportunities at the beginning of this chapter reflects the highly specialized **division of labour** in Canadian society. The division of labour refers to the bases on which tasks are allocated to individuals in a group. These bases vary among societies; some societies use caste, for example, some use race or gender, and in some the main criteria are training and expertise.

How work is divided in a society is an important indicator of its state of development. An advanced society is one that has access to sophisticated technology, whose division of labour is complex, and whose work force is relatively well educated. Experts — individuals who have knowledge that is typically acquired during long years of formal training — are deemed vital to the continuing well-being and development of society. Experts are generally highly rewarded, both in terms of material rewards — in our society, pay and perquisites (perks) that have a monetary value — and in terms of symbolic rewards, such as power and prestige. Workers who possess few or only simple skills are the most easily replaceable and usually receive the least rewards.

Sociologists often refer to the cluster of pay, power, and prestige as the three Ps.

The same work is not equally valued in all societies or within the same society at different points in time. For example, in the 18th and early 19th centuries, hospital nursing was a lowly occupation, performed for a pittance by the lowest-class women, who were often untrained and regarded as little better than prostitutes. Today nursing is a profession whose practice requires considerable postsecondary education, often at the college or university level. The work is integral to the operation of modern hospitals, and the occupation is a respectable, even "traditional" one for women of all classes who meet the educational requirements.

The central place that work holds in our lives today makes it difficult to realize that the view of work itself has varied over time and space. For example, many societies, including those of the western world, have for much of their history regarded work, especially manual labour, as a punishment for some sin committed by the individual or by humanity in general (think of the story of Adam and Eve). Therefore, not having to work, especially not having to perform manual labour, became a sign of high status. To take the matter a step further, outdoor work results in tanned skin for most caucasians; therefore, fair skin has been a symbol of high status in many societies.[1]

HISTORICAL CHANGES IN THE DIVISION OF LABOUR

In considering culture in Chapter 2, we discussed simple and complex societies, the Gemeinschaft and the Gesellschaft, and commented on some basic differences between them. Here, it is useful to examine very briefly the transformation from simple to complex society and the corresponding changes that occurred in the division of labour.

PRIMITIVE SOCIETIES

Since the earliest societies left no written records, there is little evidence of the ways in which they functioned. So, anthropologists speculate backward from the primitive societies studied in the 19th and early 20th centuries, as well as from the few that exist today (for example, the tribe discovered in a Philippine jungle during the late 1970s).

Primitive societies are assumed to have been hunting and gathering societies in which:

- The division of labour was minimal, except for the gender division necessitated by the demands of pregnancy, lactation, and care of young children. Women tended to be confined to working near their home. Everyone was more or less equal and did similar work, limited only by the biological factors of extreme youth or age, and illness.

- Nobody was totally free from physical labour. Those who had special talents, perhaps as healers or magicians, practised them in addition to their daily tasks; hence, these "specialists" were not radically different from everyone else. Using modern terminology, we would say that they were merely "moonlighting."
- The minimal technology available did not allow the production of a surplus; therefore, the group was always on the edge of survival. A sudden change in the climatic pattern, leading to extreme drought or flooding, might bring widespread disaster and even destruction of the group.

ANTIQUITY

Eventually, the domestication of animals and the development of rudimentary technology increased food production. When it was more or less possible to predict a surplus, some people could be excused from food procurement for more specialized tasks. The earliest indications of a priesthood come from naturally fertile areas, such as Egypt, Mesopotamia, and parts of Central America.

The Old Testament chronicles the shift from a transient to a sedentary, agricultural society in which land and property (primarily livestock) were valuable assets. These assets had to be defended, so warriors became important—and another stage in task specialization was accomplished.

Many of the material and intellectual achievements of the ancient world were made possible by the enslavement and forced labour of conquered peoples.

Many of the material and intellectual breakthroughs of the ancient world were made possible by the enslavement and forced labour of conquered peoples. Achievements during the "golden age" of Greece were facilitated by the presence of a large helot (slave) population, which freed the citizen class from physical labour. The higher prestige accorded to mental work is a carry-over from that time. In Greece, mental effort was not regarded as work at all, but rather as intellectual exercise. As Krause noted, increasing division of labour was accompanied by increasing social differentiation.

> *The primary mark of the citizen was his leisure. Choice of vocation—the division of labor in the citizen elite—was by talent and by intrinsic interest of the citizen. One did what could gain the most honor in the contest system of social competition for prestige. Another main function of the citizens was to fight in the army. Slaves were prohibited from fighting because of the risk of desertion and because of the honor-bestowing functions of battle, an opportunity that could not be offered to slaves (1971, 14–5).*

At the bottom were the slaves, forced to perform the hardest and most dangerous tasks—for example, rowing galleys and digging in the salt mines. The group of free citizens consisted of patricians and plebeians. The latter, artisans and tradespeople, performed relatively mundane jobs. In contrast, the patricians possessed specialized knowledge; they were the warriors, the statesmen, and the philosophers. For an insightful and readable account, see Bowra's *The Greek Experience*.

In the Roman empire, disparities between patricians and plebeians were maintained and even widened. However, in that large, far-flung empire, there was a continuous need for able soldiers and administrators. Although the constraints on mobility were greater than those of today, those plebeians, or even slaves, who were competent and lucky could move up by capitalizing on their special skills. Exceptional individuals, such as Julius Caesar, could rise from obscurity and go very far, very fast. Carcopino (1962) provides a vivid description of life in Rome when that city was the centre of the ancient world.

THE MEDIAEVAL WORLD, THE RENAISSANCE, AND THE REFORMATION

As the Roman empire disintegrated, a process which culminated in about 400 AD, the dark ages descended on Europe. The loss of much effective government and trade meant that a great deal of effort again had to be devoted to just staying alive—producing food, clothing, and shelter and then staving off people who threatened to take these necessities away. The division of labour did not vanish, but it became broader, and other skills became important. Literacy all but disappeared, even among the aristocracy, except in the church, whose monasteries became the protectors and producers of intellectual work for most of the next thousand years.

In the face of continuing warfare and raiding, successful warriors became highly valued. They were rewarded by grants of land from kings and overlords, who were themselves unable to provide much protection for the people on their land. Note that the people who lived on the land "came with it," as it were. They became serfs, obligated to render services to the landholder in return for his protection. Soon, the lord not only became entitled to most of the products of the serfs' labour but also acquired rights over their persons. Serfs were forced to accompany their lord on campaigns, could not leave the land on their own volition, and could be beaten. Serfdom persisted for a long time, especially in eastern Europe and Russia.

Society was overwhelmingly rural, with just incidental towns. Slowly, this state of affairs changed as burghs sprang up outside the manors or castles, although the burghs remained close to them for protection. At first these setttlements grew slowly, but a number of developments helped to accelerate their growth. In these rudimentary cities, groups of artisans, merchants, and professionals began to aggregate in order to pool their knowledge and to exchange skills. Once more, the division of labour became more complex.

These developments received an unanticipated boost from the crusades, a series of expeditions organized between 1096 and 1291 to conquer the holy places of Christianity and, at least theoretically, to free them from "infidel" rule. The societies of the Middle East were thriving at the time, and the crusaders marvelled at the techniques for weaving, dyeing, and painting, and at the vigour of the cultural and intellectual life they encountered. They brought back much new knowledge, including a rediscovery of Greek learning which had been lost in the west.

Meanwhile, the gradual growth of towns plus the increase in trade were disrupting feudal society. Warfare was still common (inspiring technological innovation), but raiding was better controlled and systems of government more extensive. Travel was safer and thus more frequent. Universities had been created. Members of the aristocracy and even some merchants had amassed vast fortunes, and a few were willing to sponsor artists and scholars. As the "new" learning spread through the upper and artisan classes, the interplay of these significant changes gave rise ultimately to the Renaissance era, literally a "rebirth" of enquiry, of learning, and of experimenting with new ideas and techniques. A spirit of discovery was kindled, which led some individuals to search for new continents and others to re-examine physical phenomena, questioning traditional explanations.

The supremacy of the Catholic Church was undermined by the Protestant Reformation, which began in the early 15th century. As discussed further in Chapter 9C, on religion, the Reformation had important consequences in terms of ushering in another new era.

What happens when old and new social orders collide? The play (and film) *A Man For All Seasons* dramatizes the confrontation between Henry VIII and Thomas

More over Henry's desire to divorce Catherine of Aragon and marry Anne Boleyn. Thomas More insisted on the Catholic position which stated that divorce was unacceptable.

Mediaeval Catholicism had generally viewed the world as a vale of tears that one had to traverse en route to everlasting salvation in the hereafter. Much of Protestantism considered the world to be the lord's vineyard, where one must work as hard as possible for his greater glory. Work, then, became a "positive good" rather than a necessity for survival.

THE INDUSTRIAL REVOLUTION

Over the next 300 to 400 years, the feudal order was shattered; by the beginning of the 1700s, the Industrial Revolution had begun, gathering momentum during the 1800s. In its wake came rapid urbanization, the shift of the population from the countryside to the cities.[2]

The revolution was really an evolution in that the progression was gradual. At first, artisans working in their own homes or shops were responsible for the entire manufacturing process, whether their products were cloth, furniture, or wagon wheels. The artisans bought the necessary materials, made the articles, and sold them to purchasers. Gradually, intermediaries entered this sequence: they supplied the raw materials, provided exact specifications for the articles to be produced, and handled the sale of them. They became the entrepreneurs — the owners and controllers of the means of production.

With the growth of population and the improvement of facilities for exporting goods, the volume of business increased, and it became more economical to move production into centralized premises owned by the entrepreneurs. Workers were provided with tools and paid a wage based on the number of articles produced or on the number of hours worked. Gathering workers into the same premises facilitated control over them and made it possible to fragment tasks. No longer did a worker produce a finished article. Each performed one operation and passed the article to the next person, who took the product one stage further toward completion. By the mid-1800s, the transformation of independent artisans into factory labourers was in full swing. Anthony has noted that in the *Inquiry into the Nature and Causes of the Wealth of Nations*, which was written in 1776 but is still regarded as seminal in economic thought, Adam Smith dwelt on the increased productivity attainable by task specialization:

> *The detailed division of labour is carried to its highest point in industrial production, says Smith. It is a most important principle because it explains and is required by increases in productive capacity. . . . It combines three advantages. It leads to an increase in the dexterity of workmen, it leads to the saving of time by avoiding the workers having*

> *to move from one place to another, and it leads to the development of machines "which facilitate and abridge labour"* (1977, 54).

A less rosy picture emerges when factory work is examined from the viewpoint of those recruited into it:

> *Hard and fast rules replaced the freedom of the small workshops. Work started, meals were eaten and work stopped at fixed hours, notified by the ringing of a bell. Within the factory each had his allotted place and his strictly defined and invariable duty. Everyone had to work steadily and without stopping, under the vigilant eye of a foreman who secured obedience by means of fines or dismissals, and sometimes by more brutal forms of coercion* (Mantoux 1961, 375).

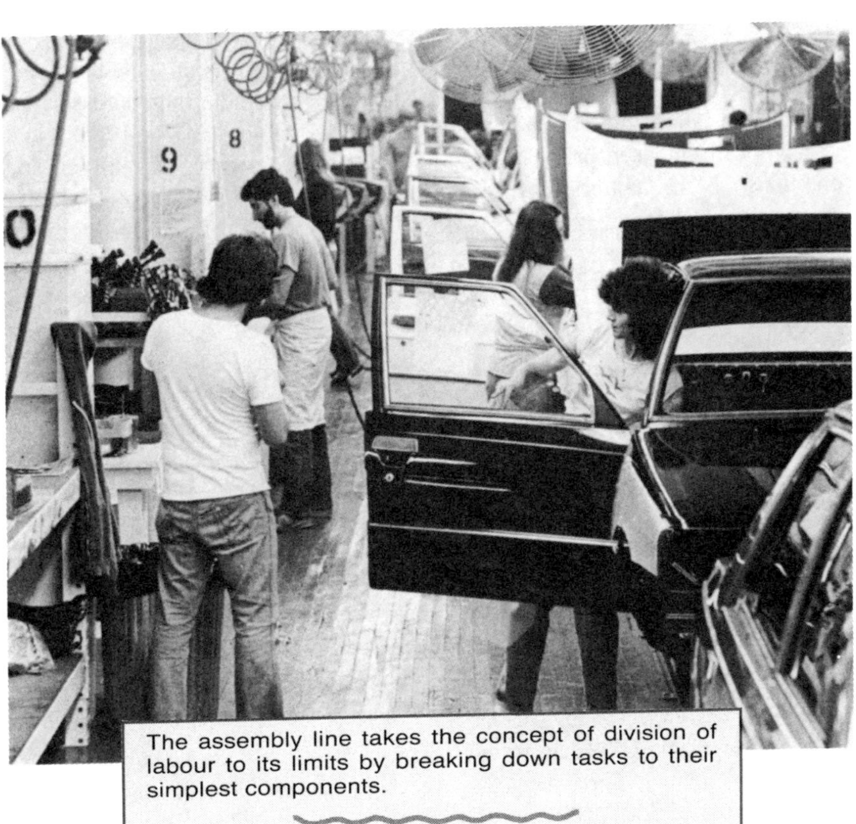

The assembly line takes the concept of division of labour to its limits by breaking down tasks to their simplest components.

Once production had been broken into simple, repetitive components, it did not take employers long to establish that many tasks could be performed by women and children.[3] They could be paid much less—after all, they were supplementary wage earners—and they also tended to be more docile than men. Moreover, before public schools were established, employers could rationalize that they were keeping children off the streets by putting them to work.

At first no legislation regulated wages, hours of work, or working conditions. In Britain, there was bitter opposition to the 1833 Factories Regulation Act prohibiting the employment of children under age 9 in textile mills and limiting those under age 11 to nine hours of work per day (Anthony 1977, 58). Disabling accidents were common, but no compensation was available, except from unusually charitable employers.

The appalling condition of the working class spurred self-help in the form of attempts at unionization; it also aroused the concern of reformers, including some members of the clergy. By a slow and piecemeal process, developments such as universal education, full enfranchisement, the right to collective bargaining, and technologically-induced increases in productivity led to better pay and working conditions.

The shift from pre-industrial to capitalist modes of production, and its far-reaching impact on how people work and live, is a fascinating story. There is a voluminous literature on the subject; we recommend Beaud (1983), and Miller and Form (1980).

SHIFTS IN LABOUR-FORCE DISTRIBUTION

An important change in countries undergoing industrialization has been a continuous shift in labour-force distribution (the proportion of people engaged in various kinds of work).[4] As evident from the Canadian data tabulated in Exhibits 5.1 and 5.2, this shift in distribution has occurred from the **primary sector** (agriculture, fishing, mining) to the **secondary sector** (manufacturing) and most recently to the **tertiary sector** (services). The decline in the number of farm workers is especially striking. In 1911, this group constituted 34.1 percent of the labour force; by 1987, it had shrunk to 3.1 percent. In contrast, the percentage of professionals has grown steadily since 1911. Overall, the proportion of blue-collar or manual workers has dwindled, while that of white-collar workers has grown.

A further far-reaching change in this century has been in the labour-force participation of women. This change has occurred because of economic need, the availability of reliable birth control methods and domestic appliances, and the encouragement provided by the women's movement.

The labour-force participation rates for all women increased each year between 1966 and 1980, but the major shift involved married women. By 1980, the gap between the participation rates of all women and those of married women had narrowed to 1.4 percent.

EXHIBIT 5.1

WORK FORCE BY OCCUPATION, 1911–61

	1911	1921	1931	1941	1951	1961
Total	2 725 148	3 173 169	3 927 230	4 195 951	5 218 596	6 305 630
Owners and managers	8.0%	8.3%	5.6%	5.4%	8.1%	8.6%
Professionals	3.1	5.5	6.0	6.7	7.3	10.0
Clerical and sales	8.3	12.3	11.9	12.4	16.3	19.7
Operatives	34.3	31.4	36.2	43.5	45.7	46.5
Farmers and farm workers	34.1	32.8	28.7	25.8	15.9	10.3
Labourers	11.2	9.7	11.3	6.1	6.3	4.7

SOURCE: Adapted from Statistics Canada (1978).

EXHIBIT 5.2

WORK FORCE BY OCCUPATION, 1971–89

	1971	1981	1989
Total	8 626 925	12 005 320	13 159 000
Managerial, administrative, and related occupations	4.3%	6.8%	12.5%
Professional	11.7	13.6	14.6
Artistic, literary, recreational, and related occupations	0.9	1.4	1.9
Clerical and sales	25.4	27.8	25.6
Service occupations	11.2	11.9	13.6
Manufacturing	14.0	14.2	13.4
Contruction and transport	10.5	10.2	9.8
Materials handling	2.4	2.0	2.5
Other crafts and equipment operating	1.3	1.2	1.2
Fishing, hunting, trapping, forestry, logging, and mining	1.8	1.6	1.3
Farming, horticultural, and animal husbandry	5.9	4.2	3.1
Occupation not stated	8.5	3.5	0.5
Others, not listed elsewhere	1.9	1.5	0.5

NOTE: The categories are not strictly comparable with those in Exhibit 5.1. This is due to changes made by Statistics Canada in recording information on occupational categories.
SOURCE: Adapted from Statistics Canada (1989).

Despite the dramatic increase in women's participation rates which had reached 54.3 percent by 1985 (Statistics Canada 1987), little change has occurred in the ghettoization of women. Their occupational status and earnings continue to lag behind those of men. Clerical work has become the leading female job ghetto. See Armstrong and Armstrong (1984), Fox and Fox (1987), Krahn and Lowe (1988), Walby (1988), as well as our discussion in Chapter 10 on social change.

THE LANGUAGE OF WORK: AN ISSUE IN CANADA

The language in which work is conducted is a feature of the work setting that is often taken for granted. Yet is has consequences for those who must learn to function in a language other than their own. For the majority of the Quebec labour force, French has been the native tongue, but for over a century, those who sought advancement found it necessary to learn English in an economy dominated provincially, nationally, and internationally by anglophones.

In the course of the Quiet Revolution, the Quebec educational system, especially the postsecondary sector, underwent substantial expansion. The new cadres of educated francophones were increasingly vocal about their dissatisfaction with the pre-eminence of English. The language of the work milieu became a significant aspect of the more general language issue.

The francophones were not only asking to be addressed in their own language — they were asking for recognition of their culture. As the Royal Commission on Bilingualism and Biculturalism stressed in speaking about the importance of bilingualism in institutions:

> *It is important to understand the difference between individual and institutional bilingualism. A bilingual institution is not necessarily an institution made up of bilingual individuals; it may also be one that contains groups of unilingual persons working in their own language, as well as a number of bilingual individuals. An institution is bilingual not solely because individuals speaking two languages are involved in it, but also because members of both language groups and cultures are able to work and participate in their own language at all levels of the institution (1969, 113–4).*

As we will discuss further in Chapter 7 on minorities, language has continued to be a bone of contention in Canada.

GARMENT INDUSTRY NEEDS TO MEND ITS WAYS

By June Callwood

On Sept. 28 last year, the 149 employees of a Toronto east-end garment factory, Lark Manufacturing Inc., went to work in an uneasy mood. The signs of plant closure had been plain for several weeks, as company trucks hauled away equipment and supplies. When the axe fell, as it did that day, they angrily demanded that the company president, Raymond Lan, pay their wages. Some stalling and evasions followed, after which it became clear that he would not.

Almost nowhere in Canada can a work force be found that is easier to cheat than the people who worked at Lark. Most of them are poor immigrant women, earning close to the minimum wage, who speak no language but Chinese.

An appalling element in the Canadian garment industry, by long tradition the employer of destitute newcomers to Canada, is meeting its current economic crisis by being brutal to helpless people. Owners close the plants suddenly, and wages, benefits, severance pay and holiday pay remain unpaid. If there are assets, the banks, as the secured creditors, will seize them and like the villains in a 1890 melodrama leave the workers without a penny.

The workers, if they are not in a union, and most garment workers are not, don't know what to do about it. Usually their documents are so botched that they have difficulty getting unemployment insurance. If they are able to find another job in the garment industry, sometimes with the same employer who oddly enough seems to be continuing in another location, their seniority will have vanished and they will start with bottom-line wages.

Something different happened when Lark closed. The plant happens to be near what used to be Woodgreen United Church, which, like many urban downtown churches, has now grown to be a community centre. Moreover, because it is in an area where Chinese-speaking newcomers have concentrated, Woodgreen had the good sense to become a Chinese-Canadian resource, complete with a Chinese-speaking staff. That September day last year more than 100 Lark workers walked to Woodgreen and told their stories to John Lau, a counsellor. John Lau, a lean, respectful young man, patiently listened and sifted through the tangle of separation slips, pay stubs, and T-4 slips.

With this documentation, he went to the Metro Toronto Chinese and Southeast Asian Legal Clinic, situated in the heart of one of Toronto's largest Chinese-speaking business districts. Ontario's legal-aid plan was skeptical in the beginning that such a clinic was needed, but no one questions its usefulness any more. At the clinic, Gary Yee, a brilliant, up-and-coming lawyer who also is president of the Chinese Canadian National Council, took on the case. On behalf of 119 Lark workers, he is suing the owners in the District Court of Ontario for unpaid wages and vacation pay.

Unhappily, termination pay and severance pay cannot be pursued by this route. Also regrettably, because a class-action suit isn't possible, only those workers who indignantly made the trek to Woodgreen and told their stories stand a chance of benefiting, an injustice to the 29 workers who humbly accepted their fate.

A court action would seem an odd way to proceed in a province with relatively enlightened labour laws, but the fact is that the Employment Standards Branch of the Ministry of Labour is widely viewed by workers as a hopeless instrument for redress of wrongs. The ESB proceeds in a contemplative manner, giving long and deep thought to complaints before making a languid move, and it almost never prosecutes. Its staff has been reported by Mark Holmes, a lawyer who studied the branch's disconcerting lethargy, to make such comments as, "No one ever died from wages not being paid."

The unpaid money owed to the workers at Lark exceeds $300,000. The case has generated a tumult of activity. David Reville, NDP member of the Ontario Legislature, raised the matter at Queen's Park and wrung from Labour Minister Gregory Sorbara admission that the money is owing. Lark workers demonstrated at Queen's Park and Parliament Hill, in front of banks and factories, and kept pressure on the ESB.

Last week, they played another card. The Basic Poverty Action Group under David Kidd organized an all-day inquiry, featuring David Reville and Toronto Councillor Jack Layton on a panel that listened to reports of the garment industry's resolute march back to sweatshops.

By a remarkable coincidence, only the day before the panel met, David Reville was advised that the ESB, which eight months ago issued an order that Lark ignored, has decided at last to prosecute. When the news was translated for their benefit, Lark workers in Woodgreen's auditorium cheered.

THE STUDY OF WORK AND WORK RELATIONSHIPS

So far, we have provided a cursory historical overview of the division of labour in the western world, and have drawn the rough contours of the present-day situation. We now proceed with a brief examination of contributions made by analysts of society to the study of work and work relationships.

As we have noted in previous chapters, Marx, Weber, and Durkheim all concerned themselves with the interaction between the division of labour and other societal spheres. Marx was a **materialist** in the sense of regarding the economy as the substructure for all other societal spheres, such as law, education, and religion.[5]

For Durkheim, task specialization provided the cement of mutual interdependence that caused society to cohere. However, in the France of his day, that cement was clearly inadequate to effect coherence. As a substitute, he proposed occupational associations that would bring together people with common work, common life-styles and presumably, therefore, common values.

Weber elaborated theoretically the kinds of formal organizations best suited for the administration and co-ordination of an increasingly complex division of labour. We will look at some of Weber's formulations later in this chapter.

Each of these theorists adopted a broad perspective that encompassed the way the division of labour influences and is influenced by the overall structure of society. However, none lost sight of how individuals' lives are affected by their economic placement.

Marx's discussion of alienation is relevant here (See Boltomore 1956). **Alienation** means literally ''estrangement.'' Marx argued that in performing repetitive, meaningless tasks to earn a survival wage, workers become estranged on several levels:

- Working on the employer's property, using the employer's raw materials and tools, and performing partial operations rather than turning out a completed article result in the *product* of the worker's labour being alienated from him or her.
- The wages the employer pays represent only a fraction of the value the worker produces. The difference, which is called surplus value, is converted to money by the employer. The more money employers make, the more their power increases. Since Marx saw capitalists and workers as irreconcilable enemies, he assumed the employers would use this increased power to oppress the workers yet further. Thus, the very products of the workers' labours are turned against them as an alien force of oppression.
- By using their hands to perform tasks that do not engage their hearts or brains, workers become alienated from themselves.
- Each person is a ''species-being,'' a member of the human species. Hence, anyone alienated from himself or herself becomes, by extension, alienated from humanity as a whole.

Marx first wrote about alienation in the 1840s, a time when the excesses of the Industrial Revolution weighed heavily on British workers. Oppression of workers continued for an extended period. The New England textile industry in the early 1900s provides an apt example:

> *Everywhere, men, women and children were fixed to the fast pace of the machines, until they too seemed just pieces of machinery, anonymous, uniform, and interchangeable in the tiring din (Gambino 1981, 199).*

Though wages and working conditions have improved since, there has been little abatement in alienation for those doing routine, monotonous jobs, as is the lot of textile-mill operators, workers on assembly lines or video-display terminals (VDTs), as well as many others.

The pivotal role of work in society and in the lives of individuals is reflected in social scientists' interest in the alienation engendered by work (Blauner 1964, Rinehart 1987), and in the impact of this alienation on other areas of life.

The three perspectives to which we now turn have been important in shaping enquiry into work and relationships within the work setting.

SCIENTIFIC MANAGEMENT

Devising effective means for improving labour productivity became a major concern for entrepreneurs, as the coercion of workers had to be tempered in the face of union pressure, increasing public awareness of working conditions, and government legislation. Also, employers had made large capital investments in machinery and wanted to maximize returns on these investments. The **Scientific Management** approach, spearheaded by F.W. Taylor (1856–1915), was based on the premise that the interests of workers and employers can be reconciled if pay

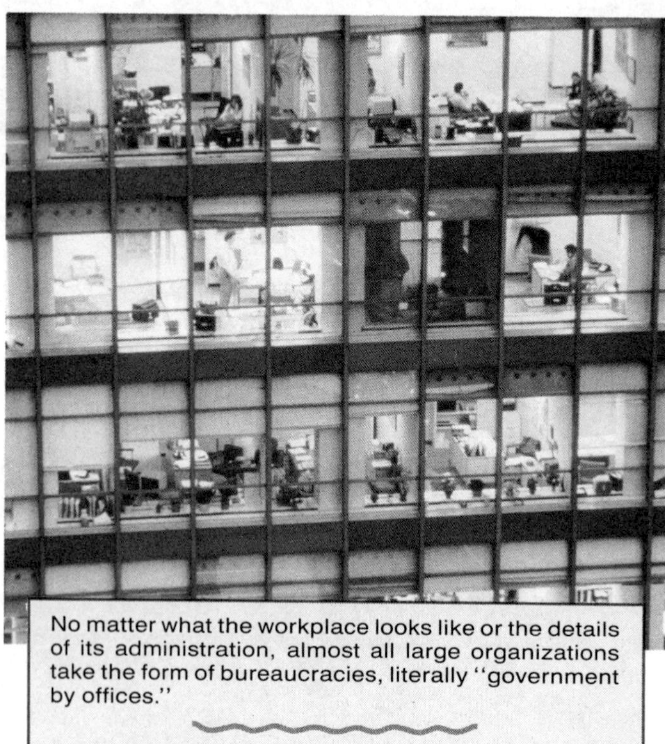

No matter what the workplace looks like or the details of its administration, almost all large organizations take the form of bureaucracies, literally "government by offices."

is tied to productivity. Taylor has been called the father of the assembly line because his time-and-motion engineers observed factory tasks with a view to breaking them down to their simplest components. Taylor recommended that each individual execute only one or two subtasks, become highly proficient at them, and be rewarded on a piece-work basis. Thus, he said, workers would be able to increase their earnings and the organization would enjoy greater productivity and higher profits (Taylor 1919).

Taylor and his colleagues considered workers to be motivated solely by economic rewards. They ignored the facts that work also meets social needs and that people do not want to spend their days pitted in relentless competition against their co-workers. Scientific Management methods did enhance productivity but not to the extent that had been anticipated.

THE HUMAN RELATIONS SCHOOL

During the First World War, as is generally the case in times of labour shortage, employers had to make concessions to workers. Unions were able to entrench their position. With the return of the veterans after the end of the war, the balance of power shifted as, once again, there were more workers than available jobs. Even so, employers were anxious not to provoke overt industrial conflict.[6] In part as a response to the limited success of the Scientific Management approach, Elton Mayo (1880–1949) and his colleagues at Harvard University developed the **Human Relations School**, which focused on developing better human relations within industry. The hope was that providing more pleasant surroundings and getting workers involved in decisions about their hours of work and fringe benefits would counteract the alienation engendered by doing intrinsically meaningless work in large, impersonal organizations. Lower turnover rates, less absenteeism, and less industrial sabotage—and, therefore, higher productivity—would be the concrete manifestation of happier workers (Mayo 1945).

At the Hawthorne plant of Western Electric, a study based on the assumptions of the Human Relations perspective was to become a classic. The initial study, during the 1920s, considered the impact changes in lighting had on the productivity of a group of female mica splitters. To their surprise, the researchers found that, regardless of whether they increased or decreased the lighting, output rose. The same pattern was observed when they tried other variations, such as introducing coffee breaks, lengthening or shortening them, or removing them altogether. The conclusion was that the workers were reacting positively to having attention centred on them.

Another team of investigators engaged in long-term observation of a small group of workers who assembled telephone sets. The researchers found that the workers evolved their own norms, which frequently ran counter to the official ones, and enforced them with positive and negative sanctions. For instance, the group set its own output quotas. Workers who continually exceeded the quotas, thus showing up everyone else, were labelled "rate busters;" consistent underproducers were known as "chisellers." If individuals persisted in violating group norms, they were ostracized by fellow workers. The findings furnished empirical support for Durkheim's argument that working together gives rise to shared values or, using his term, to mechanical solidarity (Roethlisberger and Dixon 1939).

The primary goal of both the Scientific Management and Human Relations approaches was increased productivity. This does not mean that no importance was attached to the benefits workers would receive. Indeed, both approaches sought to demonstrate that management and labour were partners rather than adversaries. Also, both focused on organizational analysis, examining how various characteristics of the work setting affected worker output and morale.

The premises of both approaches are evident in today's work settings. Braverman (1974) has argued that Taylor's principles of subdividing and deskilling work have moved from the factory to many other workplaces, notably the office. The decline in status and the increasing regimentation of white-collar workers were addressed by C.W. Mills in his major work, *White Collar* (1956). Suggestion boxes, workers' membership on some corporate committees, flexible hours, company picnics, and other amenities represent today's human-relations emphasis. Another strategy has been to institute stock purchasing plans that allow workers to buy the company's shares through payroll deductions. It is hoped that ownership will give workers a direct stake in higher productivity and higher profits.

THEY OWN THE PLACE

By Frederick Ungeheuer

In thousands of U.S. companies large and small, the employees are starting to act as if they own the place. Well, they're entitled, because they do. Meet the new breed of hard-driving capitalist: the employee stockholder. At Oregon Steel Mills in Portland, the chairman's secretary has earned $500,000 in company stock, and a few of her colleagues have become paper millionaires. At Quad/Graphics, a Wisconsin printing company, the average five-year employee owns shares worth $250,000. In Avis car-rental offices across the U.S., employees are touting their stake in the company with lapel buttons that put a new twist on their old "We Try Harder" slogan: OWNERS TRY HARDER.

Employee stock-ownership plans, or ESOPS, are rapidly gaining adherents among corporate managements in the U.S. and are beginning to catch on in Western Europe and Asia. Ten million U.S. workers, about one-fourth of all corporate employees, are enrolled in an ESOP, up from 3 million only a decade ago. More than 9,800 American companies offer such programs, including 1,500 in which employees own the majority of the stock. By giving workers a stake in the company's success, enthusiasts say, the programs boost morale and productivity. But the popularity of ESOPs, which date back to the 1950s, has been fueled in the 1980s by an unintended and somewhat controversial application: as a double-edged tool useful for both financing corporate takeovers and staving them off.

Thanks to hefty tax breaks that Washington allows for ESOPs, investors who launch a takeover can reduce their borrowing costs if they set aside part of their stock for employees. At the same time, U.S. corporations seeking to repel raiders can use an ESOP as a way to put a chunk of the company into relatively friendly hands. "Every corporate treasurer is looking at it," says Paul Mazzilli, a principal at the Morgan Stanley investment firm. In recent months, three major corporations — J.C. Penney, Ralston Purina and Texaco — spent a total of $1.75 billion on ESOPs to shore up their takeover defenses. Procter & Gamble announced plans in January to spend $1 billion to boost its ESOP from 14% of outstanding shares to 20%, partly to ward off raiders.

The most hotly contested use of an ESOP is at Polaroid, which has put 14% of the company's stock into employee hands as a defensive ploy in its bitter six-month battle against a takeover bid by Shamrock Holdings. Because Massachusetts-based Polaroid is incorporated in Delaware, where an anti-takeover law requires that bidders must get 85% ownership of a target company to gain control, the ESOP is leaving Shamrock with almost no room to manoeuver. When a Delaware court rejected Shamrock's challenge to the ESOP, Polaroid's workers "jumped up and down with joy," said Nicholas Pasquarosa, chairman of the employee committee. Shamrock is appealing the decision.

Pioneered by Louis Kelso, a San Francisco lawyer and economist, ESOPS were slow to catch on. But Kelso began to create a fertile financial climate for them by enlisting the support of Russell Long, the populist U.S. Congressman from Louisiana. Before retiring from the Senate Finance Committee in 1986, Long initiated more than 20 bills to encourage creation of ESOPS.

One tax incentive allows a company sponsoring an ESOP to deduct not only the interest on the loan to buy stock for the plan but also the principal. Another tax break gives banks and other lenders a 50% deduction on income from ESOP loans, enabling them to charge lower interest rates to companies that borrow for such programs. Because Kelso's method of paying for the stock-purchase plans was to borrow against corporate assets, ESOPS gave rise in the U.S. to the leveraged buyout. But Kelso never intended his technique to be used for buyouts that would put all a company's stock in the hands of a few investors and top managers. "That is a perversion of my idea," says Kelso, 74. "Instead of making economic power more democratic, they make it more plutocratic."

The idea of mixing ESOPs and leveraging, thereby giving ordinary employees the same access to capital and credit enjoyed by people who control companies, has been exported only to Britain. Roadchef, a caterer to highway restaurants, borrowed $2.3 million two years ago to buy 12% of the stock for its employees. It has since added a further 15%. Just as in the U.S., the shares are held in a trust and distributed to employees as the loan is paid off. But there are only 14 companies, involving about 20,000 workers, that have experimented with ESOPs in Britain. All of them were privately owned previously, and British tax law does not yet recognize the concept.

In Japan employee stock-ownership plans began to take off in 1968 as a means of fending off foreign buyers. Today 1,738 companies, more than 90% of all firms listed on Japan's eight stock exchanges, have some kind of ESOP. But these have rarely granted more than 1% of their shares to employees and have never borrowed money to buy the stock for them. In Japan, says Koji Danno, chief of the employee-savings service at Nomura Securities, "the company becomes a father giving part of his savings to his children." For the 2.2 million Japanese employees with shares in their companies, the average holding amounts to $12,200.

In West Germany, where employee stock ownership is subsidized by the government, the average holding is nonetheless lower than in Japan, because annual allotments are limited to $500 per employee. But even those small stakes have lifted employee morale. The plan is aimed at strengthening the equity base of West German firms and making worker participation in management more meaningful.

If a company thrives, ESOP participants can accumulate a nest egg far beyond the means of most wage earners. At Wisconsin's Quad/Graphics, which prints hundreds of catalogs and magazines, including a regional edition of *TIME*, the value of ESOP shares has risen from 6¢ each in 1975 to $5 currently. In the case of Stone Construction Equipment, a small firm in Honeoye, N.Y., annual revenues have jumped from $12 million to $30 million in two years, and the loan to buy the company's $4.5 million worth of shares will be paid off out of profits in ten years. But for all their promise, ESOPs can mean sacrifices for workers. In many instances, U.S. employees have accepted wage concessions in return for their stock. The United Steelworkers of America has saved dozens of failing mills in such wage-for-stock tradeoffs. In distressed industries faced with low-wage foreign competition, says James Smith, a U.S.W. staffer in Pittsburgh, "one of the ways American workers can compete is by having some investment income along with a lower labor income."

The ESOP surge has raised some eyebrows in the U.S. Congress. For one thing, ESOPs were never intended as a way for corporate managers to entrench themselves against takeover bids or for corporate raiders to enrich themselves. For another, the cost of providing the tax breaks is running as high as $3 billion a year, when deficit cutting is urgently needed.

But in Washington the ESOP seems politically secure for now, while in Britain a growing number of politicians on both sides of the House of Commons support the concept and would like employees to be cut in on Margaret Thatcher's program for selling off publicly owned enterprises. Even China's Communist reformers are studying the ESOP as a possible way to boost workers' competitive spirit.

E.C. HUGHES AND THE CHICAGO SCHOOL

E.C. Hughes (1887–1981) and his colleagues and students at the University of Chicago focused on occupational task complexes — what people actually do in carrying out their work roles. Hughes contended that the limits of an occupation can never be assumed but, rather, must be discovered.

Hughes saw occupations as containing prestigious as well as demeaning elements, and he observed that members dwell on the prestigious ones. For example, in interviewing apartment janitors, Gold (1964) was able to elicit only with difficulty that they had to sort and separate tenants' garbage for appropriate disposal. Analogously, Lundy (1977) found in her study of executive secretaries that they emphasized activities such as scheduling meetings and preparing background material, rather than tasks such as taking dictation and typing, which were categorized as mundane.

Members of the **Chicago School** also did a great deal of research on adult socialization — that is, on the ways in which individuals are prepared to assume occupational, especially professional, roles. A well-known study of this type is *Boys in White* (Becker *et al.* 1961), which traces the transformation of medical students into full-fledged physicians. Through professional socialization, the aspiring practitioner gains confidence in his own competence and conveys this to "legitimating audiences" — namely, his superiors, colleagues, and patients.

Thanks to Hughes and his students, we have learned a great deal about what work people actually do as members of certain occupations, and how they regard their membership and their specific duties.

THE SORTING PROCESS: WHO DOES WHAT?

What are the formal and informal criteria that determine who gets to do what? Before the Industrial Revolution, occupational inheritance was the norm. The sons of farmers farmed, those of blacksmiths ended up in the smithy. A daughter who was not entirely occupied with household tasks and child care helped in her father's, then in her husband's, business. Changes in the occupational structure and the broader availability of education have been important factors in changing this pattern; there are very few blacksmiths today.

Modern North American ideology proclaims that work is allocated to individuals on the basis of their competence and achievements. However, as we saw in Chapter 4 on stratification, changes in the level of work performed by different generations of the same family have been less dramatic than the myth of continuous upward mobility would lead us to expect.

To some extent, occupational mobility is inhibited because the sorting-out process begins long before the allocation of work begins. Recruits are selected, and select themselves, for the preparation necessary to assume certain occupational roles.

> *Ascription continues to play an important role in the allocation of tasks, and in the definition of what kinds of persons are suitable for performing certain work. . . . Categorization has far-reaching consequences for steering individuals into certain types of work, while excluding them from others. Once in existence, this sorting process operates at many levels. It is perpetuated through socialization which transmits a certain level of expectations, and by vocational training which prepares people for positions consistent with their anticipated status. Individuals thus raised are unlikely to challenge the legitimacy of the sorting process, and to test the strength of barriers (Lundy and Warme 1981, 60).*

A combination of socialization, socioeconomic class, education, gender, membership in an ethnic or racial group, and, of course, personal characteristics influences what kind of work a person will do. (Of course, chance also plays a part.) A girl from a poor Greek immigrant family may excel at science, but even if financial assistance for university is available to her, it is unlikely that she will pursue the advanced studies that would lead to a high-level scientific career.[7] If Melina attains postsecondary education at all, she is apt to choose the shorter training to become a laboratory technician or perhaps a science teacher. The likelihood of becoming a scientist is much greater for Andrew, who has equal intellectual endowment and whose father is an executive in a large corporation.

From a logical perspective, membership in a racial group would not be relevant to one's placement in the division of labour. In fact, however, race does exert an influence. Henry and Ginzberg (1985) provided empirical evidence that non-whites had disproportionate difficulty in finding work in Toronto.

NOT WORKING AT ALL: UNEMPLOYMENT

Marx argued that capitalism would be plagued by recurring boom and bust cycles, and that the latter would produce massive unemployment. The Depression of the

1930s demonstrated the accuracy of these predictions when millions of unemployed roamed the continent in search of work, any work. One consequence was that governments felt compelled to create minimal safety nets for these contingencies, such as unemployment insurance. These measures acknowledged that unemployment was a public issue, not merely the result of personal fecklessness—but their design was also based on the assumption that unemployment was a temporary condition (Drummond 1986; Struthers 1983).

However, it has become clear that some unemployment is a permanent feature of industrial society because of such structural factors as technological displacement (for example, by robotics), corporate consolidation (the recent merger between Canadian Pacific Airlines and Wardair is an example), and, in the era of a global economy, exportation of jobs to countries where wages are lower (think of how many clothing items are manufactured in South East Asia).[8]

Even in boom times, workers who are minimally educated, old, or living in depressed regions (for instance Atlantic Canada) can be found in the ranks of the chronic (hard-core) unemployed. They are then subjected to the deprivations that accompany this status—poverty, loss of self-esteem, and estrangement. Burman explores the perspectives and problems of the unemployed in his study *Killing Time: Losing Ground* (1988).

MOST DERELICTS WANT JOBS, MONTREAL STUDY SHOWS

By Andre Picard

The 15,000 homeless men living on the streets of Montreal have, on average, 15 years work experience, according to a new study.

Only 15 per cent of the men interviewed by sociologist Pierre Simard had left their jobs voluntarily. Most had been laid off or fired because of illness or addiction to drugs or alcohol.

While 81 per cent of the derelicts depend on welfare as their primary source of income, 65 per cent are willing and able to work.

"Derelicts aren't lazy. They want to work," Mr. Simard said. He said his study contradicts the commonly held belief that people live on the streets by choice.

In fact, Mr. Simard's study showed that only 4 per cent of homeless men had chosen their way of life voluntarily, and 63 per cent did not enjoy being street people.

He said the men remain on the streets because no treatment is available to control their addictions, and no job training to get them back to work.

More than half the men interviewed became street people in the past three years, and Mr. Simard said the homeless population is growing at a rate of 2,000 annually.

''It's an explosive situation,'' he said.

The average age of derelict men in the city is 35. More than half have served time in prisons, while nearly as many had come from broken homes.

On the other hand, homeless women, who make up about 40 per cent of street people, are younger, with an average age under 30, according to a study by the Quebec Status of Women Council.

That study, released last week, reported that derelict women do not fit the stereotype of the elderly bag lady, and are far less visible than their male counterparts.

Françoise-Romaine Ouellette, the study's author, said women are driven to the streets by sexual violence, poverty, and alcohol and drug dependency. Many depend on prostitution to survive.

''With the homeless men, it was usually their careers that was their downfall,'' she said. ''But with women it is usually family violence, incest and poverty that drives them away.''

Ms Ouellette's research was not as in-depth as Mr. Simard's, who conducted lengthy interviews with 101 men in downtown Montreal shelters.

Mr. Simard said poverty hits the francophone population particularly hard: 75 per cent of street people are French-speaking, compared to 60 per cent of the general population in Montreal.

WORK CONTEXTS

In the western world before the Industrial Revolution, ''going to work'' was a rare practice. The majority of people lived and worked on the land. For many tradespeople, the workplace and living quarters were the same location, and apprentices frequently boarded with the artisan's family. Industrialization changed all that, though in the beginning workshops and factories tended to be small. Both Marx and Weber accurately foresaw that the multitude of small enterprises would be diminished through bankruptcies, mergers, and takeovers and that the search for greater efficiency would lead to the corporate giants that dominate the business world today. Growth in the private sector has been accompanied by rapid expansion of the public sector, namely government and related agencies.

BUREAUCRACY

Whether public or private, large organizations take the form of **bureaucracies**, literally ''government by offices.'' From his research on earlier societies, Max Weber observed that their organizations shared certain characteristics and themes. From these common features, Weber drew up a model of an ideal bureaucracy—

one that would be free from the distortions that occur in the actual functioning of real-world bureaucracies.[9] It has several key characteristics:

- Members are recruited on the basis of competence, usually attested to by formal qualifications. Thus, a hospital cannot hire a nurse who does not have the requisite credentials (B.SC.N., R.N., R.N.A.). Promotion is based on merit. Frequently, further training and examinations are required, as for teachers aspiring to become vice-principals or principals. In other words, achievement, rather than ascription, is the determinant for recruitment and promotion.
- The organization is arranged according to hierarchical principles. The incumbent of each office knows where he or she fits in the chain of command. Positions and their relationships to each other are set out in the organization chart.
- Each office carries with it rights and obligations. In theory, it is immaterial what individual occupies it. Rules set out the mandate for the office of police inspector or vice-president of marketing, not for Marion Carter or Sushi Huy.
- Authority, too, inheres in the office, not in the incumbent.
- The official carries out duties without "anger or passion." Faced with an abusive motorist, the police officer does not counter with verbal or physical abuse.
- Rules and administrative decisions are recorded in writing. Files are an integral part of bureaucratic organization because they can be consulted for guidance on precedents.

Weber believed that bureaucracy was the optimal form of organization because it provided:

- *Specialization.* Individuals are slotted into a division of labour in accordance with their skills and expertise.
- *Predictability.* Each individual is constrained by the mandate of the office and bound by precedent.
- *Impersonality.* Decisions are made on the basis of objective criteria, rather than personal whim.

In practice, of course, bureaucracies deviate from the ideal. Who one knows may be more important in getting a job than what one knows; evaluating merit is a subjective exercise, and the predilections of a particular official may have an impact on decisions. Separation of jurisdictions leads to buck passing, the claim that "this is not my department." Emphasis on predictability tends to stifle experimentation, and impersonality engenders depersonalization, thereby reducing people to ciphers.

Though Weber was well aware of these serious drawbacks, he was unable to conceive of an alternative form of organization that could effectively cope with large-scale administration and co-ordination. The quest continues but has been largely unsuccessful. Moreover, although the frustrations of trying to cope with red tape are only too familiar, it must be conceded that most bureaucracies function reasonably effectively most of the time. Student grades are processed and transmitted, income tax refunds are received, and VISA payments are credited to the correct accounts. Only when something goes awry do individuals tend to become lost in the bureaucratic maze. Indeed, it is a sobering exercise to contemplate how a complex society such as ours would function without bureaucracies.

However, in an age when quick adjustments are necessary to remain competitive in a rapidly changing economy, some large corporations, hampered by bureaucratic rigidities, are becoming dinosaurs. This state of affairs has prompted a body of research devoted to rethinking the optimal structure of organizations and of work processes (see Chapter 6 on organizations).

EXHIBIT 5.3

THE PATTERN VARIABLES OF RELATIONSHIPS

In primary groups	*In secondary groups*
ascription	achievement
affectivity	affective neutrality
diffuseness	specificity
particularism	universalism
collectivity orientation	self-orientation

RELATIONSHIPS IN THE WORK WORLD: ON WHAT BASIS DO PEOPLE INTERACT?

Weber's work was translated into English by several North American scholars, among them Talcott Parsons, whose work we mentioned in the discussion of functionalism in Chapter 1. Parsons reasoned that in Weber's ideal type of bureaucracy, individuals would develop particular ways of interacting with one another. Accordingly, he constructed the **pattern variables**, opposites that represent different patterns in which people typically relate to one another in specific situations (see Exhibit 5.3). Parsons argued that different behaviour is expected and accepted in primary- and **secondary-group** settings.[10] Within modern society generally and in the work context in particular, impersonal relationships prevail.

- *Ascription—achievement*. Achievement is the normative determinant for hiring and promotion in a bureaucracy. It is also the underlying premise of human-rights legislation and fair employment standards. To the extent that ascription (*who* you are) supersedes achievement (*what* you are) in deciding the individual's fate at work, the situation deviates from bureaucratic norms. Today it also often deviates from societal norms as expressed in law. Canadians who believe they have been discriminated against on the basis of ascriptive factors such as race or gender can seek redress from the human-rights commission or labour-relations board in their jurisdiction.

- *Affectivity—affective neutrality*. ''Affective'' means that which pertains to the emotions. Superiors and subordinates, officials and clients, physicians and patients relate to one another in an affectively neutral manner. Emotion is not supposed to enter these relationships.
- *Diffuseness—specificity*. Work relationships are circumscribed in the bureaucracy; they do not spill over into one's total existence. A subordinate's private life is of no concern to his or her superior, unless it impinges on job performance. Teacher/student interaction is centred on academic issues. To some extent, the concept of specificity is captured by the aphorism ''business and pleasure don't mix.''
- *Particularism—universalism*. Individuals are treated in accordance with general, universal criteria. All students follow the same procedure in registration. You do not pluck your niece from the line-up and allow her to proceed ahead of everyone else. Likewise, the rest of the staff are likely to resent a secretary's enjoyment of special privileges because of a particularistic relationship with the boss. The concept of equality before the law embodies universalism.[11]
- *Collectivity orientation—self-orientation*. In Parsons' scheme, self-orientation is normative in the Gesellschaft.[12] In other words, it is accepted that individuals consider their own interests ahead of the group's just as a business puts profit-making ahead of community concerns. However, the self-orientation that is expected both in society generally and in business does not apply in the ideal public bureaucracy, or in the interaction between professionals and their clients. The interests of the clients, the ''collectivity,'' are expected to take precedence. Revenue Canada personnel are supposed to search for tax overpayments with the same zeal that they devote to finding shortfalls, even though the latter may be of greater help in career advancement. Dentists are not supposed to recommend root canal treatment because they are in need of cash.

Parsons formulated each pair of variables as dichotomous and mutually exclusive. In practice, it is useful to think of each set as a continuum, with interaction tending to fall toward one or the other pole. Typically, the relationship between customer and salesperson is specific, oriented to concluding a commercial transaction. However, if the same customer has repeated contact with the same salesperson, elements of diffuseness are likely to arise. Thus, the two may exchange information about their work, families, and hobbies. Can you think of examples from your own experience? The Hawthorne and other studies demonstrated that primary groups develop in the midst of vast, bureaucratic organizations. Within these groups, relationships are personal or, in Parsonian terms, diffuse, affective, and particularistic.

Like Weber's bureaucracy, the pattern variables represent an ideal type that never exists in its pure form in the real world. Again, however, they can be used as standards for measuring bureaucratic action. A theoretical measuring stick alerts us to the disparities between the conceptual and the real. A major goal of professional socialization is to replace affective involvement with detached concern, a form of affective neutrality. Studies have focused on ways of effecting this transformation among such practitioners as nurses, social workers, and physicians (Becker *et al.* 1961; Lundy 1969; Merton *et al.* 1957).

In what ways might the pattern variables help you to study occupations? Think about kindergarten teachers, for example, and how difficult it might be for them to not betray their likes and dislikes in the classroom. Can you examine this situation in terms of particularism and universalism?

OUTSIDE BUREAUCRACY

Although modern North American society has been aptly described as an organizational society, not everyone works in a bureaucratic setting. Relatively small businesses continue to exist, despite the predominance of large corporations. Small firms are likely to provide a more personal work atmosphere. On the negative side, however, such firms are highly vulnerable to economic fluctuations and have high mortality rates. They tend to exist in what is often called the ''peripheral economy'' (Krahn and Lowe 1988). Thus, their workers have less job security, lower earnings, and fewer fringe benefits than employees of large firms.[13]

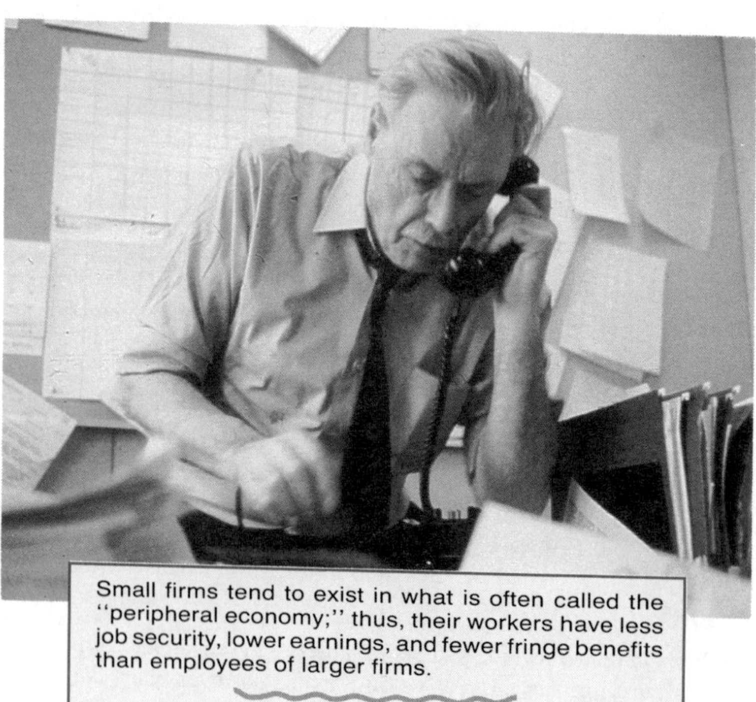

Small firms tend to exist in what is often called the ''peripheral economy;'' thus, their workers have less job security, lower earnings, and fewer fringe benefits than employees of larger firms.

Another way to avoid working in a bureaucracy is to run one's own business. The dream of being independent persists among many people. The few small entrepreneurs who attain success help to sustain the belief that it can be realized with perseverance, hard work, and a little bit of luck.

Ironically, the dream is particularly strong among those who are least well equipped for success. Using findings from a study of Ontario industrial workers, Knight noted:

> *We find that expectations for self-employment are greatest among the older workers, among those with the least education, and among those with the least resources and opportunities to become successfully mobile by commencing and pursuing a bureaucratic or professional career (1981, 287).*

A further irony is that many small businesses, such as convenience stores and gas stations, are now franchise operations. Although they ostensibly provide opportunity for independent entrepreneurship, in actuality what can be sold, at what price, during what periods, and often in what manner is stipulated by the franchiser, who typically operates in a highly bureaucratic manner.

Often a small business, whether franchised or independent, is run by the whole family, who must work long hours for relatively low returns. Nevertheless, there is less regimentation and more autonomy than is afforded to those who work in the lower echelons of large corporations, and this may be most important to someone aspiring to be his or her own boss.

SOLO PRACTICE

Professionals are another occupational group often thought of as working in solo work settings, free of bureaucratic constraints. In fact, many professionals (especially dentists) do continue to be in practice by themselves or to work in small partnerships, but as Hall has noted:

> *The country doctor heeding the call of the sick or working in his laboratory, the individual lawyer searching for support for his client's position, or the architect developing original and controversial designs have been discussed and celebrated in fact and fiction. Although central to many conceptualizations of professional work, this type of setting is in actuality a disappearing phenomenon (1975, 82).*

Solo practice affords autonomy, but in the case of lawyers, engineers, or architects, it generally entails exclusion from large projects. Clearly, an undertaking like the West Edmonton Mall requires the resources of large engineering and architectural firms. Major corporations use large law firms that have access to an array of legal specialists. In studying solo lawyers, Carlin (1962) found that their work is for the most part routine and professionally unchallenging, though it may be lucrative financially. Hall commented:

> *These lawyers tend to deny their low status by stressing their independence and the fact that they are in the general practice of all facets of the law. The feeling of autonomy, however, does not overcome the fact that these lawyers also feel insignificant in the overall structure and are frustrated because their high ambitions have not been realized, even though they are professionals (1975, 87).*

Our overview of work settings indicates that the majority of workers are employed by organizations in the private or the public sector. Even those not directly employed there tend to depend on organizations. For example, small merchants depend on their suppliers. Similarly, a solo medical practitioner would be severely handicapped without hospital privileges.

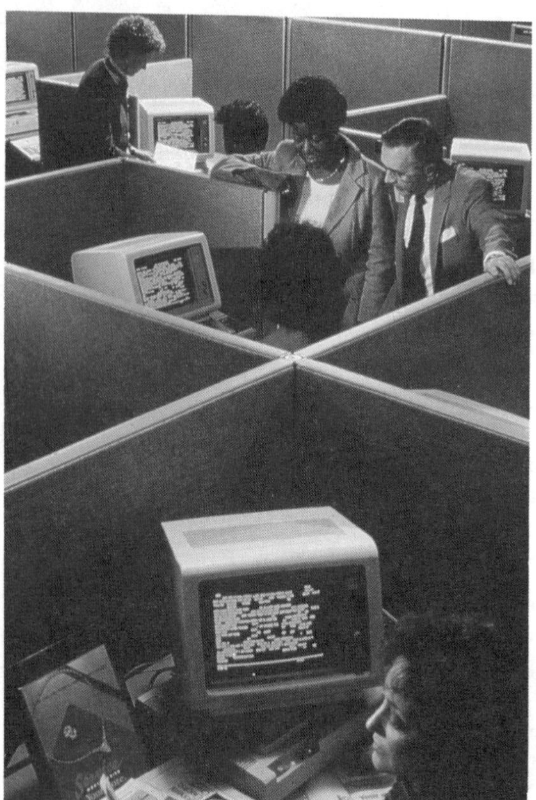

A crucial variable affecting social participation is the work people do and the context in which that work occurs.

OCCUPATIONAL TYPES

In the developed world, work has become perhaps the most vital link between the individual and society. A crucial variable affecting social participation is the work people do and the context in which that work occurs.

For this reason, sociologists and other social scientists have continued to be intrigued by the study of occupations. To obtain a profile of a single occupation requires the exploration of numerous dimensions, as suggested by Exhibit 5.4.

EXHIBIT 5.4

CHECK LIST FOR THE ANALYSIS OF AN OCCUPATION

- What type of occupation is it? What is the broader category (or categories) to which it belongs (profession; service occupation)?
- How does the occupation rank in terms of prestige? What kinds of social rewards does it receive? What kind of lifestyle does it tend to be associated with?
- What kinds of skills are required? How are the skills—and the "appropriate" occupational attitudes — acquired (on-the-job training; trade schools; university education)? Does that socialization process tend to be short or long?
- What are the components of the self-image that emerges during the socialization process?
- How are people recruited to this occupation; in other words, who, theoretically and in fact, has access to the occupation?
- What kinds of groups protect and advance the interests of the occupation? Is there a well-developed sense of occupational community?
- How is the occupation structured? On what basis is prestige allocated within it? What is the division of labour (specialization) within the occupation?
- Is there a typical career line associated with the occupation? What kind of mobility is possible, and what is typical?
- What is the nature of the work setting (large-scale organization, clinic, small firm, solo practice, freelancing)? Is more than one setting common (say, private practice and the hospital)? In what ways does the setting influence the occupation?
- What is the nature of the occupation's relationship to other groups in society (related occupations, government, pressure groups)?
- How have the nature of the occupation and the functions it performs for society changed over time?

Clearly, such analysis encounters many problems. As researchers from F.W. Taylor to E.C. Hughes to present-day scholars have discovered, it is often difficult to even say exactly what a worker does. The problem is not helped by variations in job titles. A ''registered nursing assistant'' in some jurisdictions is a ''licensed practical nurse'' in others; a ''superintendent'' in some parts of North America is a ''janitor'' in others. Conversely, the duties of a ''secretary'' may vary widely from firm to firm and even from department to department in the same firm.

It is a continuing challenge for researchers to categorize occupations in ways that maximize similarities within a category and differences between categories. No generally accepted typology has been developed.[14] Here we will use a modified version of the Canadian census classification system:

- Professionals.
- Executives, proprietors, and officials.
- White-collar workers.
- Skilled blue-collar workers.
- Semiskilled workers.
- Unskilled workers, including farm labourers.

It is easy to point to differences between, say, university professors and assembly-line workers. There are clear contrasts in the qualifications required, in power, and in prestige.[15] However, classification schemes tend to obscure internal variations within each category. The category ''executives, proprietors, and officials'' encompasses not only executives of major corporations and senior civil servants who exercise considerable influence over the implementation of policy decisions, but also the owners of family stores who have little power or prestige and may end up with much smaller net incomes than plumbers or electricians.

The difficulty here provides one example of a general problem for all sociologists —indeed, for all human beings. It arises from the phenomenon of **labelling**, which can be defined as the practice of defining groups, individuals, or activities on the basis of one overriding characteristic, thus obscuring internal differences. Labelling is undoubtedly necessary for analysis, perhaps even for thought, but it obscures internal differences. For example, the term ''white-collar work'' says nothing about the diversity of tasks included in the category.

With this caveat in mind, we will briefly examine each of the major groupings.

PROFESSIONALS

Law, medicine, social work, teaching, and nursing are some of the occupations included among the **professions**. Practitioners have specialized expertise, based on extensive formal training, which gives them power to make decisions affecting their clients. Many modern analysts, such as Freidson, have argued that professionals are vital to the knowledge industry, which forms a linchpin of modern societies. Hence, professionals have power within society generally.

Autonomy (literally ''self-regulation'') is a jealously guarded privilege of professional groups, though it is realized in varying degrees. The elementary-school teacher has less autonomy than the university professor regarding course content and teaching methods. The physician is more autonomous than the social worker in developing a plan of action for a client.

Professional autonomy is crucially affected by the work setting. The majority of teachers, librarians, and nurses as well as increasing numbers of engineers, pharmacists, and architects work in organizations in which they are subject to the bureaucratic authority of superiors who may not be professionals or of the same profession. Although, as we noted earlier, the professional in solo practice is becoming rarer, physicians and lawyers tend to work in relatively small partnerships in which hierarchical distinctions are downplayed. Alternatively, they may work in ''professional'' organizations, such as hospitals or large law firms, in which the practitioner is subject to administrative authority in such matters as scheduling operating time, but is autonomous in making professional decisions regarding the handling of a case.

Members of professions are generously rewarded in terms of the three Ps—pay, power, and prestige. However, the rewards received by members of different professions vary considerably, and variations also exist within each professional group. Certainly, the Wall Street lawyers studied by Smigel (1964) had far more power and prestige than Carlin's solo practitioners (1962). More recently, a study of the legal profession in Toronto found that the profession is ''stratified by classes that are defined in terms of power relations'' (Hagan, Huxter, and Parker 1988, 50).

The professional community seeks to ensure that its members adhere to normative ethical and performance standards. As we mentioned in our discussion of the pattern variables, professionals are expected to put client (collectivity) interest ahead of self-interest. This apparent self-denial, coupled with specialized expertise, legitimates the high rewards most professionals enjoy.

> *The advantages enjoyed by professionals thus rest on evaluations made by the larger society, for the professional community could not grant these advantages to itself. That is, they represent structured relations between the larger society and the professional community (Goode 1957, 196).*

EXECUTIVES, PROPRIETORS, AND OFFICIALS

The chief characteristics of executives, proprietors, and officials are their ''middle to high positions in organizations of all types'' (Hall 1975, 137) and their relatively high socioeconomic placement. Executives and officials are employed by organizations, whereas, by definition, proprietors own enterprises, which range from the vast holdings of the Eaton or Reichmann family to the small dress or hardware store. Since we have already referred to small-business owners, we will concentrate here on the people who run organizations in the private and public sectors.

The vast majority of executives and officials are university-educated. The crawl from stockroom to boardroom celebrated in Horatio Alger stories (see the Suggested Readings) has all but disappeared today. Aspiring managers are generally recruited from university campuses. Whereas some of the professions, such as nursing and teaching, are numerically dominated by women, the ranks of executives and officials are overwhelmingly filled by white males.

Whereas some of the professions, such as nursing and teaching, are numerically dominated by women, the ranks of executives and officials are overwhelmingly filled by white males.

In her study of Indsco, Kanter found:

> *Managers at Indsco had to look the part. They were not exactly cut out of the same mold like paper dolls, but the similarities in appearance were striking. Even this relatively trivial matter revealed the extent of conformity pressures on managers. Not that there were formal dress rules in this enlightened company, like the legendary IBM uniforms, but there was an informal understanding all the same. The norms were unmistakable, after a visitor saw enough managers, invariably white and male, with a certain shiny, clean-cut look (1977, 47).*

Similarly, Porter commented on the homogeneity of senior bureaucrats in Canada's federal civil service:

> *It is similarity of social type which makes an elite a cohesive group distinct from those at the top of other institutional hierarchies. Homogeneity results from common socialization processes and from common interaction. These senior civil servants have, by and large, a common background in the social class and educational systems of Canada. Their high level of education and their link with the universities would suggest commonly held intellectual values. It is likely also that the recruitment of outsiders tends to select those who have similar views about the role of government in national development (1965, 447).*

Since those who manage organizations must be able to agree on decisions, corporations have traditionally placed a high value on homogeneity. However, such sameness also has drawbacks, in that innovativeness and new departures are stymied, sometimes with disastrous effects. In an account of his experiences as a top executive at General Motors, John DeLorean (Wright 1979) noted that during the 1970s GM executives simply ignored the trend toward more fuel-efficient, compact cars, dismissing the rising number of imports as catering to "the teacher trade." It was, of course, this trend, combined with the overall economic slowdown, that plunged the North American car industry into a massive crisis in 1981.

In the next chapter, we look at the ways in which members of an organization are socialized to its culture, to "how things are done around here." Socialization is facilitated because recruitment is selective (see also Chapter 3 on socialization).

Managerial careers offer the possibility of significant upward mobility, accompanied by increasing rewards in terms of pay, power, and prestige. But given the pyramidal shape of bureaucratic organizations, only a few individuals can go all the way to the top.

WHITE-COLLAR WORKERS

The category of white-collar workers is a highly diverse one, encompassing groups such as secretaries, bookkeepers, clerks, salespersons, data processors, and programmers. Preparation for white-collar jobs is generally short and may be augmented by on-the-job training. Autonomy is limited in that the nature of the tasks and the manner in which they are performed are defined for workers.

The relative rewards of white-collar workers have declined since 1900 for a number of reasons:

- At the turn of the century, this group formed a small proportion of all workers, so its members were special. As the white-collar category has grown to the single largest occupational group, this exclusivity has been lost.

- Some high school education was a requirement when only a fraction of the population had such education. Now that almost everyone attends high school, white-collar workers no longer enjoy the advantage of being better educated than the rest of the population.
- The introduction of office machinery, specifically of the computer, has made it possible to break down tasks into simple, repetitive components, thus making office workers more easily substitutable and their output subject to precise measurement. If workers can be exchanged for one another easily, there is no reason to offer special incentives to retain them.
- White-collar work has become heavily feminized. By January 1989, women constituted 80.4 percent of clerical workers and 48.6 percent of sales workers (Statistics Canada 1989). Since the overall status of women in society is low, their large representation among white-collar workers has depressed the status of the group.
- Unionization has been retarded because white-collar workers have traditionally identified with management.[16] Even though few actually moved up significantly, this identification has been deliberately reinforced by corporations. Krause has suggested:

> *The typical relationship between high-level management, lower-level office management, and the white collar work force is dramatized by a careful gradation of responsibility and an ideology of the potential for upward mobility with every secretary identified by management as part of itself. This deliberate management policy aims at the satisfaction of status and dependency needs by lower-level clerical personnel and the avoidance of a militant class consciousness by the white collar work force. Relations between management and white collar groups are probably, in most settings, characterized by more care and politeness than in any other intra-management relationship pattern. Given the size of the white collar work force in modern corporations, the political motivation behind this politeness and care should be obvious (1971, 245).*

The numerical predominance of women with their more tenuous attachment to the labour force (although this is changing) has further retarded unionization. Hence, white-collar workers' relative earnings have declined vis-à-vis those of the more extensively unionized blue-collar labour force. In 1901, clerical workers earned $116 for every $100 of average earnings in the total labour force. In 1987, male clerical workers earned $96 for every $100 of average earnings in the total labour force; female clerical workers earned $102 (Statistics Canada 1988). Overall, however, the average earnings of women lag far behind those of men. In 1967, the average of women's earnings was 58 percent of every dollar males earned, by 1977 this had increased to 62 percent, and by 1987 to 68 percent (Statistics Canada 1988). The gap is narrowing, albeit slowly.

As formal degrees or diplomas are becoming required entrance tickets to managerial careers, the barriers to moving from clerk to executive, from salesperson to buyer, are becoming less penetrable. Clerical and sales workers can and do move into management, but their numbers are few.

SKILLED BLUE-COLLAR WORKERS

Skilled workers, such as tool and die makers, electricians, plumbers, and millwrights, are the elite of the blue-collar world. Their training is accomplished through lengthy, formal apprenticeships. Therefore, they are not easily substitutable and command expert power. (Anyone who has had a drain back up on a weekend can attest to ''plumber power!'')

Skilled workers enjoy the highest prestige of all blue-collar workers. Indeed, they are often labelled the ''professionals'' of the blue-collar world. They are also generally well paid. Although the work is defined for the individual, the manner of execution is left to the worker on the assumption that he (or she) will internalize adequate performance standards during apprenticeship.

Craft workers have always jealously guarded access to apprenticeships in these occupations. Therefore, members of certain groups, such as blacks, orientals, and women, have been substantially excluded. With today's legislation on fair employment practices and with raised consciousness among minorities, this situation is slowly changing.

In *Blue-Collar Women*, Mary Walshok has documented women's experiences in entering blue-collar jobs, many of them skilled. Those who succeeded were exhilarated by the feeling of mastery obtained from performing skilled work; they were also happy with earnings far higher than those obtainable in most traditional female jobs. One of Walshok's respondents explained:

> *I'm doing it for the money and I'm doing it because I need a skill that I'm going to be able to get jobs at wherever else I decide to travel to. I'm saving a lot of money on my job. It's about the most secure job I could have gotten. It's not the job I thought I wanted but it's turned out to be the right one. I've had to fight for my training and I mean fight for it, but I really think they now want to keep me because I'm willing to do anything they give me and I've learned the job, I mean I love to weld, I really do (1981, 196).*

Also changing is the availability of these jobs. Because skilled workers are expensive and not easily substitutable, industries have striven to de-skill the jobs, breaking down one complex task that requires a skilled worker into several simpler ones to be carried out by semiskilled or unskilled labour. Clement commented on these developments at the International Nickel Company (INCO):

> *Tradesmen become more expendable as companies develop means to teach limited aspects of their trades rapidly to unskilled workers (1980, 294).*

Skilled craft workers were the first workers to form successful unions in Britain and North America, despite vigorous opposition from employers. As the union movement as a whole has consolidated its power, craft unions have maintained an important position, even though the proportion of skilled workers in the labour force has been shrinking.[17]

SEMISKILLED WORKERS

The large majority of factory workers, and service workers such as cabdrivers, bartenders, and waiters and waitresses, are categorized as semiskilled. It is assumed that the skills needed for a specific job can be learned easily and quickly, usually on the job. Hence, selection procedures are not rigorous, and candidates need not have prior formal training. (This does not mean, of course, that individuals do not differ in how quickly or how well they learn their tasks or that experience does not enhance proficiency.) Prestige within the larger society is not great.

For these workers, not only the job is defined but also, in most cases, the manner in which it must be carried out. Assembly-line workers are the most regimented in this respect, since even their work pace is governed by the speed of the line. Because they cannot move from their stations, the opportunity for social interaction is drastically curtailed.

Semiskilled workers employed in large unionized industries, such as the steel and automotive ones, enjoy high earnings and benefits. Technology has benefited these workers by eliminating some of the hardest and most hazardous tasks. On the other hand, automation and robotics threaten to eliminate vast numbers of semiskilled jobs. (We will discuss the role of technology in greater detail in Chapter 10 on social change.)

Whereas the power of craft unions is based on their members' skills, that of industrial unions, such as the Canadian Auto Workers (CAW) or United Steelworkers (USW) is based on numbers. Even though the individual worker can be easily replaced, large numbers cannot.

Semiskilled workers employed in the service sector generally lack the protection and benefits of unions. Wages are low, often supplemented by tips, and job security is minimal. On the other hand, these jobs offer opportunities for social intercourse, and the work is not as regimented as that of factory operatives.

UNSKILLED WORKERS

Unskilled workers are at the bottom of the occupational hierarchy in terms of pay, power, and prestige. Technology has reduced the number of jobs available, so many such workers are employed only sporadically, hired on a day-to-day basis for clean-up jobs or for moving equipment, materials, or furniture. Rarely is there an expectation of permanence or a mutual commitment between employer and worker.

Hughes has emphasized the "moral" aspect of the division of labour. (For example, see *Men and Their Work*, 1958.) How work is regarded and rewarded depends not only on how much skill is required but also on the value a society gives to that work at a given time. For instance, domestic servants and migrant farm labourers are categorized today as unskilled and relegated to the lowest rung of the occupational hierarchy, although it takes a lot of time to acquire the skills for efficient performance. This low evaluation of domestic and migrant farm work has made it difficult to recruit other than individuals from disadvantaged groups. Thus, devalued work and low status of workers have interacted to keep these occupations in the lowest category. Turrittin's study of West Indian domestics in Canada (1981) provides an apt illustration.

We note once more that fitting the vast array of occupations into a handful of categories conceals significant variations within each category. Small-town teachers, partners in large engineering firms, and physiotherapists are all categorized as professionals but share few work experiences. Being the only bookkeeper in a small office is different from monitoring computerized accounts receivable at Sun Life. The bookkeeper for the small business performs a greater variety of tasks and probably enjoys greater autonomy but may be isolated and probably receives a lower salary and fewer fringe benefits than the employee of the large corporation.

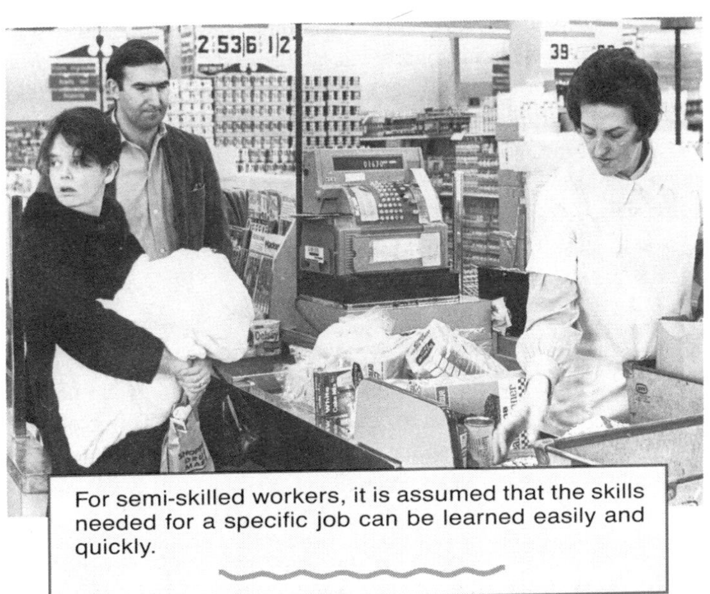

For semi-skilled workers, it is assumed that the skills needed for a specific job can be learned easily and quickly.

ALTERNATIVE WORK PATTERNS

Not all employed persons work according to a five-day week, nine-to-five pattern. We review here a few of the alternative patterns of labour-force participation.

PART-TIME WORK

The part-time labour force has grown at a dramatic pace in the past 20 years, finally outstripping the growth in full-time workers. The number of part-time workers in Canada has increased at an average annual rate of seven percent since 1953. This figure is more than three times the growth rate of the full-time labour force (Coates 1986, 6).

Part-time work has a number of advantages for persons at certain stages of the life cycle. It permits individuals to earn money while at the same time having the freedom to study or retrain, to meet domestic commitments, to phase into retirement, or to supplement income in old age. In other words, it is a form of employment that offers flexibility to the worker. More than seven of ten part-time workers are female, reflecting women's need to juggle paid work with family responsibilities.

But what are the costs of this flexibility? Part-time jobs are concentrated in service industries. These jobs are traditionally characterized by low pay, few or no fringe benefits, little job security and few opportunities for advancement. Unions have resisted the creation of part-time jobs because they have been seen as a threat to the supply of full-time work, and there is a low rate of unionization among part-time workers themselves. The advantages for employers are clear. Parcelling out work in this way permits firms like banks or departments stores to extend hours of business at less cost. Universities and colleges, too, use part-time instructors as a cost-saving strategy (Warme and Lundy 1988).

Do individuals choose part-time work to suit their own needs? That is to say, are they voluntary part-time workers? Statistics indicate that many are not, but accept these jobs because they are unable to obtain full-time work. This group is referred to as the involuntary part-time labour force, and it is growing at a more rapid rate than the voluntary group (Akyeampong 1987).

For full discussions of the advantages and disadvantages of part-time work, see Coates 1988; Duffy, Mandell and Pupo 1989; Kahne 1985; Wallace 1983.

IRVING INC. SAYS PEOPLE WORKING PART TIME SHOULDN'T BENEFIT

By Canadian Press

Part-time workers should not be entitled to the fringe benefits full-timers receive, a spokesman for the Irving industrial empire has told the New Brunswick Legislature's public accounts committee.

The committee is studying planned changes to the Employment Standards Act that would extend some new rights to part-time workers and provide all employees with new benefits, such as leaves of absence for new parents.

"By removing qualifying periods for vacation pay, vacations and statutory holiday pay, the legislation is ignoring the realities and necessities found in business enterprises," said Gary Sudul, director of corporate human resources for J. D. Irving Ltd.

Industries require part-time workers and should not have to pay extra benefits to have them on their payrolls, he said.

Mr. Sudul said the new law would allow an employee who works only one day a week to qualify for vacation pay and paid time off during statutory holidays.

"Surely this is not the intent of the legislation," he said.

Mr. Sudul also disapproved of the plan to force companies to grant leaves of absence for childbirth and adoption.

"Even if the leave is characterized as unpaid, that does not mean there is no cost attached to the leave itself," he said. "Replacement costs such as training, lower productivity and benefits are all to be experienced when filling a temporary vacancy."

JOB SHARING

Job sharing is a work arrangement engaged in voluntarily by employees who seek the flexibility that working less than full-time gives them. Under such an arrangement, two persons fill an equivalent full-time position and receive partial pay and benefits (for instance, pensions). Job sharers may divide the working hours in a number of ways; for example, they may each work two-and-a-half days per week, or they may each work a full week in alternate weeks. Such scheduling provides them with more leisure time, more time for domestic commitments, or time to upgrade their education.

It is an opportunity for women to maintain their skills, contacts, and career prospects during the period in their lives when child caring responsibilities are heaviest. Although there are no statistics on the extent of job sharing in Canada, Wallace found that job-sharers tend to be women with post-secondary education and young children at home (Wallace 1983). For employers, the main advantage is that they obtain the skills and commitment of two employees for the price of one. However, it is more expensive to fill a position with job-sharers than with part-time workers, because of the costs of benefits and higher pay.

It is interesting to note that job sharing first emerged for professional and managerial women. What obstacles can you think of regarding its implementation for workers lower down on the occupational hierarchy? What are the advantages to employers of merely packaging positions into part-time jobs instead of allowing them to be job-shared?

NOW JOB-SHARING IS CATCHING ON . . .

By Violet Johnstone

Job-sharing is a little like marriage, according to Dr. Jane Maxim, of the National Hospitals College of Speech Sciences. You have to like each other and trust each other, and it's probably better if the two of you have different temperaments. Her job-sharer, Dr. Sheila Wirz, agrees: "Like marriage, once you get it right, you stick with it."

Sheila and Jane have a lesson for those who long to job-share: ask and you may get. They put up the idea to their superiors and, what is more, used it to gain promotion.

The secret is to do one's homework. Jane and Sheila obtained an information pack from *New Ways to Work*, a small charity in England that promotes job-sharing. This enabled them to present a convincing case, setting out costs and considerations to their employers.

Jane, short, fair and introvert, and Sheila, tall, dark and extrovert, are an unusual example of this growing trend towards working in partnership. First, they are both well-qualified, with PhDs in clinical linguistics, and they share a high-level job: co-ordinator of the BSc degree at the College of Speech Sciences, one grade down from Principal. They are in charge of 200 undergraduates, teaching, taking part in clinical work and doing research. They have been awarded a grant to research motor-neuron disease, and communication needs.

Second, their reason for sharing is not, like most women, to have more time to spend with their children — Jane has none and Sheila's are grown-up. Both simply want more time to pursue their outside interests. For Sheila this means, for example, being a Parliamentary wife — her husband, Andrew Rowe, is Conservative MP for mid-Kent and one of the leading opponents of the Channel Tunnel rail link. She is also involved in a publishing venture. "I like the business buzz as well as the academic life," she confesses.

Jane is writing a book on language and the elderly. She adds: "My husband is a solicitor and specialises in company law. Now instead of both of us returning home exhausted, only he does, and it makes for a better home life."

She would love him to job-share too, but it's a concept that hasn't yet taken off with men. Is this because men's self-image is more tied up with their work-image? "Well, that's what feminists would argue, but I'm not sure that I totally agree," says Sheila. "It would be difficult for many families to survive if the breadwinner was on only half a salary."

Each has a particular interest in the clinical field. For Jane, it is how language changes with age, and whether research in this could help to diagnose various types of dementia. For Sheila, it is dysphasia (the after-effects of strokes). So double the expertise is being channelled into the one job.

"I think initially the college didn't like the idea because they felt we were not putting our careers first," recalls Sheila. In reality, they are very much "full-time types." In their first year they found each was doing the same number of lecturing hours as her full-time colleagues. "You have to be very careful not to take on more than your half."

Their contract has been carefully worked out: for example, should one of them wish to leave, the other will first be offered the job full-time, then either accept another sharer or resign.

Gradually, after two years, more and more correspondence is addressed "Dear Sheila/Jane," but colleagues still feel the need to repeat to one what they have already told the other. "They don't trust our communication system," says Sheila. And it is communication that is the crux of successful job-sharing.

How long will it be before more employers take this view? A dwindling workforce may compel them to do so. Employees, for their part, can take heart that such schemes are no bar to promotion. It's possible to job-share at the top.

HOMEWORK

Working in one's own home has been treated as a way for women with young children, or disabled persons, or older workers, to have paid employment without the requirement of "going to work." Homework can provide an opportunity for increased control over one's life, and the flexibility to integrate work with other activities. Sewing on a piecework basis is one example. Traditionally, homeworkers have been almost exclusively women (Huws 1984) about whom it can scarcely be said that they have gained "increased control." The price for working at home has generally been lower pay than office or factory-based counterparts, no benefits, no assurance of a steady flow of work, lack of union protection, and extreme isolation. For a discussion of the difficulties involved in traditional homeworking, see Johnson and Johnson's *The Seam Allowance: Industrial Home Sewing in Canada* and Brown's *Sweated Labour: A Study of Homework.*

Huws' study of the "the new homeworkers" in Britain (1984), chiefly engaged in word processing, found that there are advantages and disadvantages both for employers and employees. On the positive side, employers cited increased productivity, lower overheads, and flexibility. Furthermore, the new technologies themselves allowed management to monitor a remote workforce. On the other hand, employers complained of higher administrative costs and the problem of a less committed workforce. As do traditional homeworkers, the new homeworkers saw flexibility to juggle work and family responsibilities as a major advantage. On the negative side, homeworkers found pay rates lower than for similar work on-site, felt they had no promotion prospects, and complained of isolation as the chief drawback.

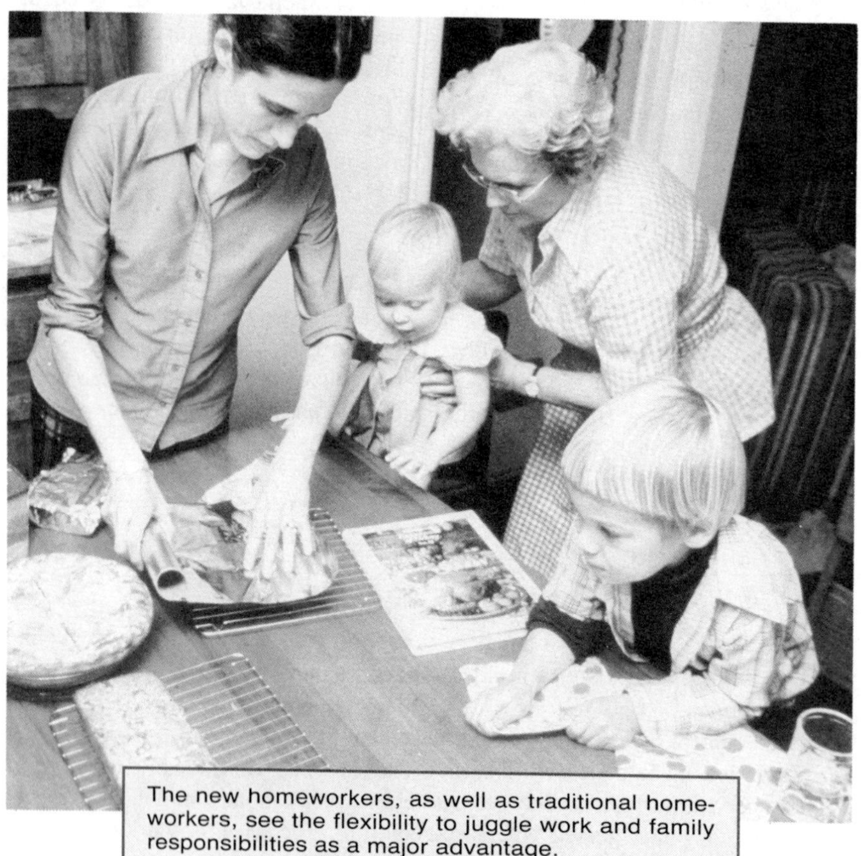

The new homeworkers, as well as traditional homeworkers, see the flexibility to juggle work and family responsibilities as a major advantage.

In the future, it is likely that the demand for alternative work patterns will increase. Technological advances and the push for economy are likely to ensure that the availability of such work is also likely to increase. However, the search for a ''fit'' between the needs of workers and those of employers is a process that will no doubt entail heightened conflict over the ways that the costs and benefits of these work options are to be distributed.

THE OCCUPATIONAL HIERARCHY

An occupation's place on the occupational hierarchy is affected by many variables. Generally, lengthy education and training yield high rewards. Sociologists want to know how high, and here they encounter a problem. Material rewards — pay and fringe benefits — are quantified and thus easy to measure. But how does one compare such symbolic rewards as power and prestige?

One way is to determine the relative standing of a number of occupations. One of the earliest and best-known studies was that conducted by the National Opinion Research Centre (NORC) in 1947. A sample of almost 3000 people across the United States was asked to rank 90 occupations on a five-point scale, ranging from ''excellent'' to ''poor.''[18] The respondents ranked justices of the U.S. Supreme Court first. Professionals such as physicians, architects, and ministers were all placed in the top quartile, while taxi drivers, waiters, and street sweepers were in the lowest. (No predominantly female occupation, such as nursing or secretarial work, had been included on the list.)

When the study was replicated in 1972, the rank order of occupations remained substantially unchanged. Interestingly, studies in other countries, including third-world countries, produced similar rankings, especially with regard to professional and white-collar occupations. A notable exception is the relatively low rank accorded to physicians in the Soviet Union. Once can speculate that the numerical dominance of women among Russian physicians has lowered the group's prestige.

In 1967, Pineo and Porter published the results of their study on occupational prestige in Canada, the first such national study undertaken in this country. It was also designed to make rigorous U.S./Canadian comparisons. Canadian and American prestige rankings showed no major differences. Professional and executive occupations received the highest scores, and unskilled work was at the bottom.[19]

In 1976, Blishen and McRoberts published a socioeconomic index for occupations in Canada, in which occupations of the male labour force were rated on a combination of three variables: education, income, and prestige ranking. Among 500 occupational titles, ''administrators, medicine, and health'' was first, followed by ''nuclear engineers'' and ''dentists.'' ''Newsboys'' ranked 497th, while ''locomotive engineers and firemen'' and ''photographers and cameramen'' were in the upper half at 209th and 175th respectively.

Blishen, in collaboration with Carroll and Moore, revised the index using 1981 data. The revised index takes into account socio-economic stores, education (job preparation), income levels, and gender composition for census occupations. However, the authors caution that:

> *. . . the present index is most applicable in situations where access to data is limited to occupational titles and where one desires a unidimensional, contextual indicator which locates individuals in the Canadian occupational hierarchy at a given point in time. Sociological analysis of structured inequality, however, may be advanced most effectively if, where feasible, the full range of methodological options is considered. In addition to the use of a socio-economic index, these options include the disaggregation of occupational income and education, the assessment of conditions on the level of the individual, the use of other contextual levels such as the workplace, the examination of class relations, and the investigation of occupation, gender, and class as interdependent historical products (1987, 473).*

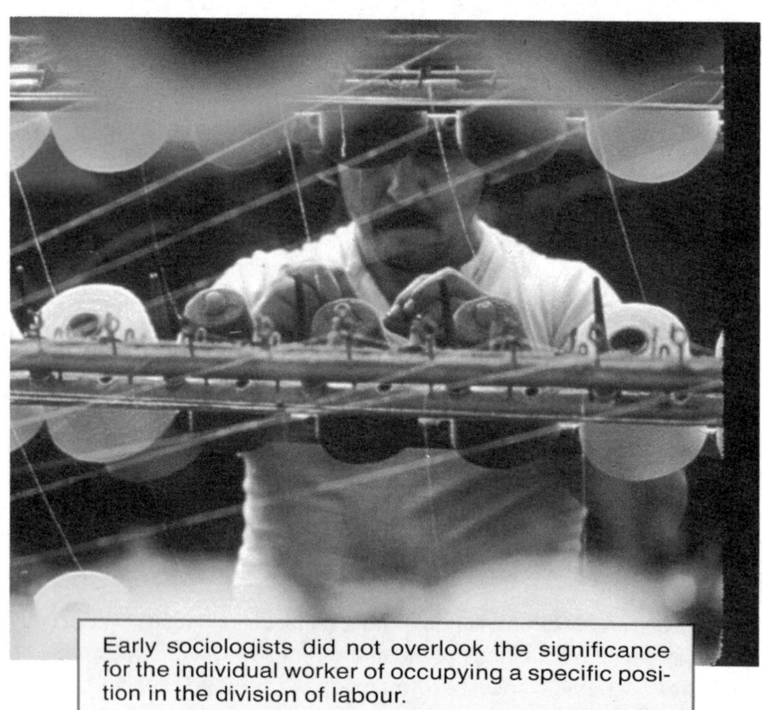

Early sociologists did not overlook the significance for the individual worker of occupying a specific position in the division of labour.

EXHIBIT 5.5

HE WORKS, SHE WORKS

BUT WHAT DIFFERENT IMPRESSIONS THEY MAKE!

The family picture is on HIS desk:
Ah, a solid, responsible family man.

The family picture is on HER desk:
Hmmm, her family will come before her career.

HIS desk is cluttered:
He's obviously a hard worker and a busy man.

HER desk is cluttered:
She's obviously a disorganized scatterbrain.

HE'S talking with co-workers
He must be discussing the latest deal.

SHE'S talking with co-workers:
She must be gossiping.

HE'S not at his desk:
He must be at a meeting.

SHE'S not at her desk:
She must be in the ladies' room.

HE'S not in the office:
He's meeting customers.

SHE'S not in the office:
She must be out shopping.

HE'S having lunch with the boss:
He's on his way up.

SHE'S having lunch with the boss:
They must be having an affair.

The Boss criticized HIM:
He'll improve his performance.

The boss criticized HER:
She'll be very upset.

HE got an unfair deal:
Did he get angry?

SHE got an unfair deal:
Did she cry?

HE'S getting married:
He'll get more settled.

SHE'S getting married:
She'll get pregnant and leave.

HE'S having a baby:
He'll need a raise.

SHE'S having a baby:
She'll cost the company money in maternity benefits.

HE'S going on a business trip:
It's good for his career.

SHE'S going on a business trip:
What does her husband say?

HE'S leaving for a better job:
He recognizes a good opportunity.

SHE'S leaving for a better job:
Women are undependable.

By Natasha Josefowitz

SUMMARY

We have briefly traced the route by which the division of labour in our society has reached its present complexity. The centrality of work to societal functioning, and its impact on the individual, were recognized by early sociologists. Marx, Weber, and Durkheim focused primarily on the macro level but did not overlook the significance for the individual worker of occupying a specific position in the division of labour.

When unionization and government regulation of employment made workers somewhat less exploitable, employers attempted to find incentives for enhancing productivity and worker morale. The Scientific Management and the Human Relations schools provided different approaches to this quest. Both schools remain influential today. Under Hughes, the Chicago School pioneered in-depth exploration of individual occupations, a focus that continues to inform research.

Who gets to do what is affected by a combination of many factors. The societal ideology of equal opportunity for those of equal ability is confounded by the ongoing significance of ascriptive characteristics, such as sex, race, and ethnicity.

Changes in the nature of work have been accompanied by changes in the contexts in which work is performed. The number of small enterprises and solo practices has declined. Although the ideal bureaucracy conceptualized by Weber does not exist in practice, more and more work is carried out in bureaucratic settings. Such organizations seek to make task performance rational, predictable, efficient, and impersonal. These features have come to be seen as characterizing interaction in modern society generally and in the workplace specifically. However, more traditionally patterned relationships continue to prevail in the world of small business.

Given the high degree of specialization in the labour force and the rapid emergence and disappearance of occupations, their grouping poses an ongoing academic and practical challenge. In our discussion, we roughly followed the categorization of occupational groups adopted by the Canadian census. The occupational structure forms a hierarchy in terms of education required and rewards allocated. Pay, power, and prestige are not necessarily commensurate. For example, a plumber working in construction may earn more than most members of the clergy but have less prestige and less individual power.

The prestige rankings of occupations have remained remarkably stable since social scientists started to measure them more than 50 years ago. Furthermore, rankings are similar across industrialized countries generally. These patterns of stability and similarity reflect the extent to which advanced societies depend on expertise.

White-collar occupations continue to enjoy greater prestige than blue-collar ones, even in the face of the former's declining relative earnings. In part, this may be a continuation of traditional values according to which manual work is devalued and assigned to low-status groups.

ASSIGNMENTS

Do one or more of the following assignments, as instructed by your professor.

1. Select an occupation and analyse it in terms of at least five of the questions included in Exhibit 5.4.
2. From the viewpoint of white-collar workers, discuss some of the advantages and drawbacks of being employed in a large bureaucracy.

3 Read *Few Choices: Women, Work and Family* and *Pink Collar Workers* (see Suggested Readings). What light do these books shed on the ways in which women combine work and family obligations? What conflicts do the women experience? What strategies do women use for resolving them? How do these conflicts differ at different stages of the female life cycle?

4 Using concepts presented here, analyse the advertisements at the beginning of the chapter in terms of work, its content and context. What inferences can you draw about these positions on the basis of information provided or not provided?

SUGGESTED READINGS

Horatio Alger, Jr, *Silas Snobden's Office Boy* (New York: Doubleday, 1973; first published in *Argosy*, 1889–90). In the late 1800s, Horatio Alger was a prolific writer whose books were eagerly awaited. Their plots ran along similar lines: after a series of adventures, the poor, honest, hard-working hero emerged triumphant on the road to riches. Frank Manton, Silas Snobden's office boy, is no exception. Alger's message, which has been incorporated into modern ideology, is clear: virtue and personal effort lead to occupational success. (See also *Iacocca* in Suggested Readings for Chapter 6 on organizations.)

A. Duffy, N. Mandell and N. Pupo, *Few Choices: Women, Work and Family* (Toronto: Garamond Press, 1989). To stay at home full-time, to work for pay full-time, or to work part-time? These are the the options that women with domestic obligations confront. Their choices are constrained by social, economic, and political forces, yet the solutions they find, and attempt to make sense of, are personal. The authors draw on interviews with Canadian women to explore the costs and benefits of each option, and argue that the structure of the family, and the nature of paid employment, should be re-conceptualized to provide greater flexibility for both women and men.

L.K. Howe, *Pink Collar Workers* (New York: Avon, 1978). Even though an increasing number of women are making breakthoughs into traditionally male jobs, the majority are trapped in low-paid service and clerical work. Through her report based on participant observation and in-depth interviews, Howe affords us a look at the lives of a few such women. Most of them must fit in home responsibilities as best they can while keeping up to scratch at work, where they know they are easily replaceable. Yet, interaction with co-workers and a feeling of accomplishment in a job well done bring some satisfaction to their work.

R.M. Kanter, *Men and Women of the Corporation* (New York: Basic Books, 1977). *Men and Women of the Corporation* is a case study of a large multinational corporation. Kanter focuses on three variables that impinge on corporate careers: opportunity, power (defined as the ability to mobilize resources), and numerical representation of particular social types (for example, are women 1, 15, or 50 percent of the managerial group?). Her discussion of the "token" experience is germane to all those who form a small minority in their work group. Examples are female managers who must function in a predominantly male environment, male nurses, and native peoples in senior government positions.

Studs Terkel, *Working* (New York: Avon Books, 1972). Terkel, who speaks almost entirely in the voices of the people he interviews, sought out workers in a vast range of jobs across America. He invited them to describe the way they experience their work, their frustrations, disappointments, and satisfactions, and how the daily job affects the meaning of their lives. Although we hear pride, contentment, and hope in some of the voices, the overwhelming impression is one of emptiness, boredom, unfulfilled dreams, and a sense of waste. As one respondent stated, "I think most of us are looking for a calling, not a job. Most of us, like the assembly line worker, have jobs that are too small for our spirit. Jobs are not big enough for people." The book is worth skimming as a richly detailed chronicle of the way in which a variety of people spend the major portion of daily life.

C.L. Vincent, *Policeman* (Toronto: Gage, 1979). This study of the Windsor police force is based on participant observation. Vincent's theoretical perspective is a symbolic interactionist one, and his main focus is on the socialization process that converts the rookie into a full-fledged police officer who thinks and acts in accordance with the norms of his peer group. Because the police officer is isolated by unusual work hours, by the uniform, and by public perceptions, peer-group support and approval are especially important.

NOTES

1 Compare North American society's admiration of sun tans. One can speculate that because so much work in North America is performed indoors, a tan symbolizes the availability of leisure time or, in the winter, the luxury of travel to southern climes.

2 It should be noted that the dates cited refer to developments in Britain, where the Industrial Revolution had its start. Some parts of Europe, as well as the United States and Canada, reached similar stages of industrialization somewhat later.

3 The concept did not lack legitimacy; women and children had previously worked in cottage industries.

4 As defined by Statistics Canada, the labour force includes the residents of all Canadian provinces (but not the territories) who are age 15 or older; are not members of the armed forces, inmates of an institution, or residents of an Indian reserve; and are either employed or unemployed. An unemployed person is one who is without work but available for it and who has actively looked for work in the past four weeks, has been on layoff for less than 26 weeks, or has a job due to start within four weeks.

5 In contrast, an idealist regards a society's values, beliefs, and attitudes — its ideas — as the substructure.

6 In fact, the period immediately after the

war was one of bloody confrontation, of which the 1919 Winnipeg General Strike is an example.

7 Individuals have done just that, so "unlikely" does not mean "impossible." However, we are discussing statistical probabilities rather than individual biographies.

8 National unemployment rates are calculated by dividing the number of persons out of work and seeking work by the total number of labour-force participants (including the unemployed). These rates conceal variations among regions of the country, among occupational groups and industrial sectors, among age groups, and between gender groups (for a fuller discussion, see Gonick 1978; Krahn and Lowe 1988).

9 Clearly, such an organization can be found in pure form in real life. It is "ideal" in the sense, described in Chapter 2, of representing ideas rather than reality.

10 For an explanation of primary and secondary groups, see Chapter 3, footnote 6.

11 Equality under law is by no means universal. Membership in a racial group determines legal status in countries such as South Africa and Malaysia. The Canadian criminal courts distinguish among adults, youthful offenders, and children. But within each such group, individuals are supposed to be treated equally.

12 We described the distinction between a Gesellschaft and a Gemeinschaft in Chapter 2. Primary-group settings are typical of the Gemeinschaft, while secondary-group settings are a distinctive feature of the Gesellschaft.

13 The mortality rate for new businesses, most of which are small, is extremely high. Ten years after inception, only one business in five survives, a figure that shrinks to one in ten after 20 years. On the other hand, during the last few years *job creation* has taken place entirely within small firms. From 1978–84, 781,147 jobs were created in firms with 100 employees or less. During the same period, the number of jobs in companies with 500 or more employees declined by 8,495 (Statistics Canada 1988).

14 A comparison of Exhibits 5.1 and 5.2 suggests some of the ways an organization, such as Statistics Canada, adjusts its classification system over time. Changes in subgroups are even more frequent.

15 The gap in pay may be less pronounced, especially if the assembly-line workers are employed in the automotive or steel industries.

16 In Canada, white-collar workers are extensively unionized in the public (government) sector. Attempts to unionize white-collar workers in the private sector have not met with much success to date.

17 See, for example, *The Rise and Fall of the Toronto Typographical Union, 1832–1932: A Case Study of Foreign Domination* (Zerker 1982). Also note Heron's short history of The Canadian Labour Movement (1989), in which he chronicles the ups and downs of unions and the bureaucratization of the labour movement.

18 "The final rankings were obtained by a scoring system that gave an occupation that received 100 percent excellent a score of 100, and those that were unanimously rated as poor a score of 20. None achieved unanimity, of course" (Hall 1975, 246).

19 For example, the mean score for 21 professional titles was 72.04; 15 titles for proprietors, managers, and officials in large organizations showed a mean score of 70.42; 18 titles of unskilled work produced a mean score of 23.46 (Pineo and Porter 1967, 35). The scoring was much like that of the 1962 NORC study, whose design Pineo and Porter adapted. (The mean score is simply the arithmetic average of a group of scores.)

6

ORGANIZATIONS

Since learning is a messy business, let's start this chapter with a rather messy exercise. Think about your activities of the past week. How many involved organizations, directly or indirectly? Make a list of these organizations. (Remember that even solitary pursuits such as reading a book or watching television depend on organizations that publish books and beam television programs into your home.)

Before reading about organizations, the concept may not be entirely clear to you and you may feel uncertain about what to include in the list. Hence, you will likely make changes to the list as you read the chapter.

As Canadians, all of us live in an organizational society. Most Canadians are born in an organization, they are educated in organizations, are likely to work in an organization, and die in an organization. Even religious, political, and leisure activities are carried out in organizations (stepdance groups, bowling centres, duplicate bridge clubs, environmental lobby groups). From cradle to grave, organizations are prominently featured in our existence, shaping more of our attitudes and behaviour than we may realize.

The pervasiveness of organizations in contemporary society has spawned a vast literature by sociologists and other organizational analysts. Most of it has been concerned with large complex organizations, and our discussion focuses mainly on dimensions of structure and process that are relevant to these types.

We want to caution students, however, that leadership and decision-making, for example, may take different forms in less hierarchical organizations, such as a small athletic club, a gourmet cooking school, or a community food bank. Furthermore, the appropriateness of the ways in which bureaucratic organizations operate is being challenged. It is possible that we are moving toward greater openness, more flexibility, more consensual decision-making, fewer hierarchical barriers, and less impersonality in organizational life.

In this chapter, we deal with the following topics: the problem of definition; structure; organizational culture; communication; power and conflict; organizations and the individual; and the reciprocal relationships between organizations and the environment.

DEFINING ''ORGANIZATION''

Any cluster of relatively continuous, goal-directed activities, from a ''Mom and Pop'' variety store to General Electric, from a local credit union to the Prudential Insurance Company, would be classified as an organization. Hence, it is difficult to construct a definition that encompasses this wide range—we are unaware of a perfect definition. Hall's version, though cumbersome, has the merit of being general enough to subsume different types and sizes of organizations, while specifying characteristics that distinguish organizations from other collectivities, such as a rock concert audience or guests at a wedding.

> *An organization is a collectivity with a relatively identifiable boundary, a normative order, ranks of authority, communications systems, and membership co-ordinating systems; this collectivity exists on a relatively continuous basis in an environment and engages in activities that are usually related to a set of goals; the activities have outcomes for organizational members, for the organization itself, and for society (1987, 40).*

Since the definition is complex, we will elaborate some of the components—an exercise that will at the same time demonstrate problems associated with defining terms, since it is difficult to define the components themselves in a way that encompasses wide variations.

- *Identifiable boundary.* Just where this boundary is drawn is often difficult to establish. For example, do we include or exclude the *students* when defining the university as an organization? What input should students have in the formulation of university policy (for example, to sell off a parcel of land in order to cope with higher costs and tighter budgets)? Likewise, do we include or exclude patients—the clients—in a definition of the hospital?

- *Normative order.* In Chapter 2 on culture, we discussed values and norms. In an organization, written and unwritten rules specify acceptable types of behaviour for individuals both inside and outside the organization. For example, in Canada, physical sanctions or racial or sexual slurs are not "normatively" acceptable—though the latter two occur with distressing frequency.

- *Ranks of authority.* Generally, those at higher levels define what those at lower levels must do, and how it is to be done. Even though you may dislike your immediate supervisor, you accept instructions from her because she is in a *position of authority*. The team coach can discipline a player who misses practices. When one joins an organization, whether it be a bank or a musicians' union, one implicitly *accepts* the ranks of authority and *expects* that this authority will be exercised in accordance with the normative order. Hierarchy, and hence authority, are likely to be de-emphasized in collegial and co-operative organizations.

- *Communications systems.* An organization has both official communications systems (memoranda, newsletters, proclamations) and informal ones — "the grapevine." An informal warning may circulate in the plant that the president is coming to inspect it and that "he is on the warpath about litter." One may be excluded from the informal communications because one is unpopular (a reason based on individual characteristics) or because of group membership (for example, gender or race). Exclusion can be very damaging. For instance, one may be denied all the informally transmitted information so crucial to both "learning the ropes" in a job, as well as to becoming a likely candidate for promotion. Can you think of useful tips you have acquired from fellow workers that you would never have gleaned from official communications?

- *Membership co-ordinating systems.* Those in authority use communication as one way of co-ordinating the efforts of an organization's members. For example, when the United Way embarks on its fund-raising campaign, canvassers must be allocated territories, and know both when, and to whom, to hand in their pledges for the organization. No large fund-raising campaign could proceed in the absence of such co-ordination. When foul-ups occur, we say that the effort was "poorly co-ordinated."

- *Continuity over time.* The Moscow Circus still exists between performances. Members of the Yellowknife Choral Society may not rehearse during the summer, but the society continues as an organization, as does the Montreal Expos baseball club in the winter season.

- *Environment.* Each of the characteristics we have looked at is influenced by the environment. For instance, extreme physical sanctions were accepted in Nazi Germany's concentration camps. In another example, unequal pay for women doing jobs comparable to those held by men has been a practice not challenged until recently.

- *Set of goals.* Organizations are established for specific purposes (usually set out in the charter), and activities are geared toward achieving these purposes. *Catalyst* is an organization founded in New York in the 1970s to promote job sharing arrangements for managerial and professional women, so that they will not have to abandon careers while raising children. The ultimate goal of a business is to show a profit (even though this goal may be de-emphasized in communications with the public—for example, in advertisements by loan institutions and insurance companies).

  Organizational goals may be incompatible with one another. Prisons are a case in point. Their goals include the protection of society (hence tight security is desirable) and punishment, but also rehabilitation of wrongdoers, so that, on release, prisoners will become law-abiding citizens. However, many of the features of a prison which are oriented toward security and punishment (restriction of visiting hours, absence of conjugal privileges, isolation) further remove prisoners from normal society, and erode their ability to function in it. As organizations become "settled," the dominant goals tend to become institutionalized, and organizational participants develop the additional goal of perpetuating the status quo. Thus, a new warden with a more therapeutic and rehabilitative orientation (as opposed to a custodial or punitive one) may encounter considerable resistance from the staff.

  In some cases, there may be agreement about the goals themselves but disagreement about the means of achieving these goals. School administrators, for example, share the goal of wanting to graduate individuals who are well-adjusted, literate, and motivated. However, there may be a great deal of disagreement over how this is to be accomplished.

- *Outcomes—for organizational members, for the organization itself, and for society.* In a work organization, members first of all earn a living. This living may be deemed adequate or inadequate by the employee. As well, the work and the work environment may engender challenge and commitment for some, apathy and frustration for others. In an organization dedicated to formal learning, different individuals experience various outcomes in relation to their personal objectives. Thus, you may be pleased with the intellectual stimulation provided by academic work, but apprehensive about whether it is directly preparing you for a job.

There is a reciprocal relationship between the outcomes for individuals and for the organization. An apathetic or alienated work force is likely to depress the productivity (and ultimately threaten the viability) of a business; a failing business will not provide a happy work environment. A community college in which academic standards are high, and in which relations among students, faculty, and administration are harmonious, will provide largely positive outcomes for the organization and for its members.

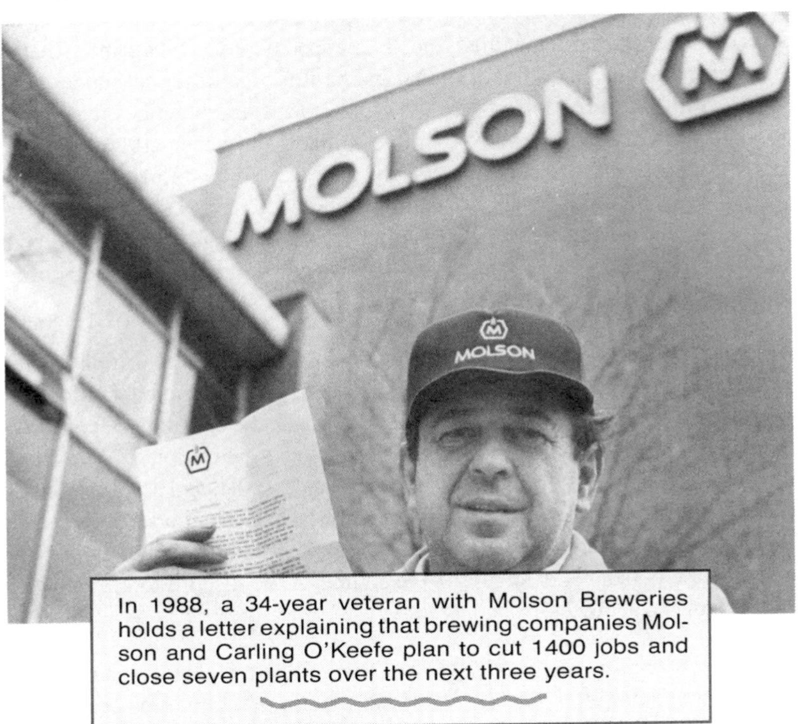

In 1988, a 34-year veteran with Molson Breweries holds a letter explaining that brewing companies Molson and Carling O'Keefe plan to cut 1400 jobs and close seven plants over the next three years.

What happens to organizations and to their members affects society. Consider the impact of a plant closing, especially in a one-industry town. Elliot Lake, Ontario, became a virtual ghost town when the uranium industry slumped in the 1970s. The large-scale expansion of a college may change the demographic profile of the town in which it is located, due to an influx of young people.

In summary, elaborating the components of Hall's definition of an organization has alerted us to such problems as where boundaries should be drawn, and incompatibility among organizational goals. We have also found that what happens inside an organization is influenced by the environment in which it is located. In turn, the environment is affected by the outcomes for the organizations themselves, and for their members.

Research has increasingly shown that there is no one best way to design an organization. What works best is contingent on a number of factors—technology, the degree of uncertainty within the environment (for instance a fluctuating inflation rate), and the degree of competitiveness over the market, or "target group," for a particular product or service. Competition is much stiffer in the garment industry than in the oil industry, which is dominated by a few giants (see Lawrence and Lorsch 1967; Woodward 1965).

Hall's definition emphasizes the "**formal organization**." This term refers to those aspects of an organization that are typically mapped out in its blueprint. What does not appear in the blueprint, but is an integral part of organizational functioning, is the "**informal organization**"—the everyday norms and practices that flesh out the organization in action (see, for example, Clinard and Yeager 1986—*Corporate Crime*). For instance, the chief millwright may ask the parts manager for some bearings "right now" to repair a machine, adding, "I'll send over the requisition later." Thus, informal practices can facilitate getting things done. They can also subvert organizational goals—think of the output restrictions researchers observed at the Hawthorne plant (see Chapter 5 on work).

As we noted in the first chapter, social phenomena can be viewed through different "windows." When sociologists study organizations, they look at interaction among organizations (such as the Provincial government and the Manitoba Medical Association), between the environment and a particular organization or organizations (for example, the impact on society of the Alaska oil spill), and among individuals and groups of individuals within an organization. They might pose such questions as: why is it that the conflict between the production and the sales units persists even when the personnel changes? Is the source of the discord to be found in the organizational structure?

Likewise, new employees generally learn from fellow workers which rules can be safely ignored most of the time, but someone deemed untrustworthy or undesirable (for example, a male nurse in an all-female nursing unit) may not be privy to this information.

It is important to note that the bulk of organizational research has focused on large enterprises, such as corporations, government departments, and hospitals. Small organizations, such as self-help groups or co-operatives, have not attracted the same attention. Somewhat analogously, women's economic, social, and cultural contributions have been given short shrift in historical records. Both instances demonstrate how a society's dominant values affect research.

Delegates to the Council of Yukon Indians annual assembly met in 1987 to put together their negotiating position for resumption of the 15-year talks on native land claims.

ORGANIZATIONAL STRUCTURE

By ''organizational structure,'' we mean the framework or anatomy of an organization (for example, the number of ''units,'' meaning groups of people whose work is organized around distinctly different tasks). These images are somewhat misleading, however, because, as Hall notes, ''organizational structures are constantly evolving as a consequence of the activities that take place within them'' (1987, 56).

The structure of an organization is closely related to how that organization functions. Task allocation, communication, and decision-making are handled differently in a family-owned scrap metal business than in a ''tall'' hierarchy such as the Ministry of Health. Here, we will examine three structural features: complexity, formalization, and centralization. We have chosen to concentrate on these features because, analytically (though not in practice), they can be separated from organizational processes.

Complexity refers to both the extent to which the organization is divided into subunits so as to carry out the work, and to the ways in which these parts are distributed across horizontal and vertical dimensions. Just as living creatures differ in complexity (compare the simply structured starfish with the highly structured chimpanzee) so, too, do organizations. Furthermore, an organization that on first glance appears to have a simple structure may in fact be highly complex.

For example, you may discover that your community synagogue has a more complicated structure than the small manufacturing plant located near it. In other words, one cannot make inferences about how simple or complex an organization is merely by knowing its main function. One must examine its anatomy, and map out what work gets done, and by whom; as well, one must know the kinds of relationships the organization has with other collectivities. (The synagogue may interact with other religious institutions in the area, and with the local hospital, police, youth groups, seniors' groups, and anti-poverty coalitions, to name a few possibilities.)

As we noted earlier, the concept of complexity has several components. If one looks at an organizational blueprint, one can often observe that the work is divided along a *horizontal* axis. (At General Motors, for example, each division has its own research, manufacturing, marketing, and accounting department—and these departments are at the *same structural level* as those in other divisions.) Additionally, tasks are divided *vertically* in terms of ranks of authority. Spatial dispersion refers to the different geographic locations at which work may be carried out—think of the wide dispersion of such organizations as the National Action Committee on the Status of Women or the Canadian Society of Muslims.

These factors influence both the ways in which work must be co-ordinated and how information and instructions are communicated. They also affect the extent to which different employees can identify with the "larger picture" of what gets done.

People who work at the lowest echelon of a **complex organization**, those at the "bottom," are likely to have little or no contact with those who function at the upper levels. The degree of complexity influences whether "the boss" is someone familiar, readily accessible, and on a first-name basis, or a distant figure who pays a ceremonial visit to the annual staff party.

Weber argued that bureaucratic rationality is best achieved through: specialization; rules which provide predictability; and impersonal procedures. In his ideal type, rules and procedures are written down in minute detail and carried out to the letter. (Review the discussion of bureaucracy in Chapter 5 on work.) This is what we mean by a high degree of **formalization**. In practice, however, the extent to which rules and procedures are articulated and carried out in actual organizations varies both among organizations, and within any single one.

For individuals, formalization is perhaps the most significant structural variable, because it strongly influences the extent to which their daily behaviour is controlled by the organization. Discipline imposed by the clock is an obvious example. Does one have to punch in on arriving at work at 8 a.m. and punch out on leaving at 4 p.m.? Or is one free to come and go at one's own discretion, provided that the work gets done?

The first situation is likely to pertain to jobs that are highly routine and require a low level of skill (salespersons in a department store, for example). The second is more characteristic of professional and managerial positions. In those instances, it is assumed that discipline has been *internalized* in the course of adult socialization. However, the distinction by level of skill is not invariant. The neurosurgeon is as constrained by the operating room schedule as the cleaning staff; the same is true of airline pilots.

Formalization has both a positive and a negative side; rules and procedures both constrain and protect. In defining what the employee must do, rules also circumscribe what the organization can demand of the employee, thus regulating the behaviour of both parties. However, channelling behaviour too narrowly can dampen the creativity which leads to innovation, and can inhibit necessary change. Mechanisms for altering rules and procedures are necessary, because they enable organizations to adapt to changes in society. The Ford Motor Company came close to bankruptcy following World War II, because Henry Ford was unwilling to implement the changes necessary to function in a highly competitive environment for selling cars. To some extent, this is true of the North American car industry generally; firms like General Motors were too set in their ways, too convinced of their ability to manipulate consumer demand, and chose to ignore evidence during the 1970s that gas guzzlers were "out" and that imports were making increasing inroads in the market. Organizations may also play a *proactive* role in society. For example, they may take the initiative in choosing to package their products in ways that pose fewer hazards to the environment. Some hospitals have instituted counselling services for those infected with AIDS, thus changing the environment by heightening public awareness of the difficulties people with AIDS confront.

Centralization refers to the ways in which decisions are made, and to how power is distributed among an organization's members. We say that an organization is centralized when all major decisions are made by those at the top of the hierarchy. If authority to make decisions is delegated to positions at lower echelons, the organization is said to be de-centralized. However, if lower-echelon "decisions" are largely dictated by organizational policies that are already in place, then these are not decisions in the true sense, and a high degree of centralization remains. For example, the police officer on patrol has considerable latitude whether to *charge* an individual with a particular offence; by contrast, the welfare worker cannot "decide" that a person is eligible to receive Family Benefits if she clearly does not meet the official criteria.

Participation in the decision-making process does not automatically imply delegation of power. People at lower levels of a hierarchical organization may be widely consulted, but their input is merely advisory (for example, contributions to a Suggestion Box)—that is to say, final decisions are still made at the top. Each organization, therefore, must be carefully examined to determine whether participation in decision-making is real or illusory.

The issue of centralization is a sensitive one, because it concerns points of view on the capacity of individuals to make proper decisions, and on their right to do so. How organizations are run in a particular country may be closely tied to its political system. In a centralized country like the U.S.S.R., organizations are likely to reflect this centralization. On the other hand, such countries as Yugoslavia and Israel have sought to introduce democratic forms of organization (worker-run factories or kibbutzim) in order to broaden the traditional political structure (Weingarten 1959). Some organizations are structured from the beginning on a horizontal rather than a vertical basis, to promote mutual goals (for example, the P.E.I. Farmers' Co-operative). Nevertheless, in order for such organizations to survive, they must face many of the same imperatives as hierarchical organizations, imperatives such as effective communication.

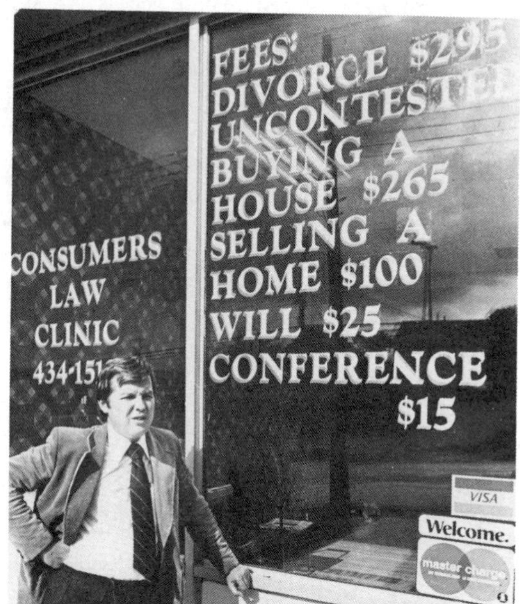

Dartmouth, Nova Scotia lawyer Ted McFetridge advertises his legal fees in the window of his law office, to the dismay of the provincial barristers society which is seeking to suspend him for this practice.

THE GUNS OF AUGUST

By Barbara Tuchman

"Now, on the climactic night of August 1, Moltke was in no mood for any more of the Kaiser's meddling with serious military matters, or with meddling of any kind with the fixed arrangements. To turn around the deployment of a million men from west to east at the very moment of departure would have taken a more iron nerve than Moltke was disposed of. He saw a vision of the deployment crumbling apart in confusion, supplies here, soldiers there, ammunition lost in the middle, companies without officers, divisions without staffs, and those 11,000 trains, each exquisitely scheduled to click over specified tracks at specified intervals of ten minutes, tangled in a grotesque ruin of the most perfectly planned military movement in history.

'Your Majesty,' Moltke said to him now, 'it cannot be done. The deployment of millions cannot be improvised. If Your Majesty insists on leading the whole army to the East it will not be an army ready for battle but a disorganized mob of armed men with no arrangements for supply. Those arrangements took a whole year of intricate labor to complete' — and Moltke closed upon that rigid phrase, the basis for every major German mistake, the phrase that launched the invasion of Belgium and the submarine war against the United States, the inevitable phrase when military plans dictate policy — 'and once settled, it cannot be altered.' "

ORGANIZATIONAL CULTURE

In our discussion of culture (Chapter 2), we noted that culture is an important element of group membership, part of the cement that bonds individuals into a coherent and cohesive whole. Organizations, too, are held together not only by their structure, but also by their culture. We will examine the relationships between organizations and culture from two perspectives:

- The impact on the organization of societal culture.
- Culture within organizations.

Organizations do not function in a vacuum; they are constrained by the larger society in which they are situated. For example, in Third-World societies, delegation of authority may be discouraged because the status systems often do not define subordinates as people capable of making appropriate decisions. The subordinates have been socialized to this view of themselves, and are therefore reluctant to accept responsibility for decisions. In this instance, we could say that both sets of participants share a view of the way things *ought to be*.

What constitutes acceptable behaviour by organizations varies among societies; it also changes within the same society over time. Conservation of the environment is an example. Until a few years ago, this was seen as an issue that should not be allowed to interfere with the central task of maximizing corporate profits. Now, organizational policymakers are under increasing pressure from government bodies, from environmental groups, and from consumers to manage environmental resources more carefully. (In western Europe, political parties for whom environmental concerns were central obtained seats in parliaments.)

The 14th-annual Economic Summit, held in Toronto in 1988, was attended by leaders of the world's seven major industrialized nations and the commissioner for the European Economic Community.

When corporations in a particular society are especially successful, those in other countries want to emulate the characteristics they believe to be responsible for this success. Currently, some Canadian and American industries are attempting to adopt "the Japanese way" of operating. This is not always easy because the practices of Japanese industry are rooted in a culture which is quite different from that dominant in North America. (Given regional cultural disparities in Canada and the United States, it is an oversimplification of talk about "a" dominant culture.) Morgan describes the Japanese concept of work and relations between workers and their organizations:

> *The organization is viewed as a collectivity to which employees belong, rather than just a workplace comprising separate individuals. The*

> *collaborative spirit of a village or commune pervades work experience and there is a considerable emphasis on interdependence, shared concerns and mutual help. Employees frequently make lifelong commitments to their organization, which they see as an extension of their family (1986, 58).*

On the other hand, the North American way is characterized by an ideology of competitive individualism. Economic life is seen as a game which has winners and losers: ''he just didn't have the necessary drive;'' ''she would not give up.'' The emphasis on individualism and competition also permeates relationships *within* organizations. Consider, for example, ''employee-of-the-week'' contests. Thus, Japanese methods conflict not only with the traditions within organizations, but also with expectations, in the larger society, of what are appropriate modes of interaction. (The film *Gung Ho* depicts what happens when a defunct American car plant is taken over by a Japanese firm.) Cultures can and do change—we are merely pointing out that time and effort are needed.

Organizations are affected by the culture of the society; in turn, the culture of organizations makes itself felt within society at large. We will expand on this point further on in this chapter when we discuss the reciprocal relationships between organizations and the environment.

''The way things are done around here'' is a shorthand definition of **organizational culture** (Ford *et al.* 1988, 455). This culture subsumes the values, norms, folkways (see Chapter 2), symbols, rituals, and traditions that permeate the organization. As we discussed earlier, values designate the goals that are worth striving for. Within organizations:

> *For those who hold them, shared values define the fundamental character of their organization, the attitude that distinguishes it from all others. In this way, values create a sense of identity for those in the organization, making employees feel special. Moreover, values are a reality in the minds of most people throughout the company, not just the senior executives. It is this sense of pulling together that makes shared values so effective (Deal and Kennedy 1982, 23).*

The dominant values of a company are likely to be reflected in the organizational structure. If cost control is a central value, then the financial vice-president and the comptroller will be major players in top management. If the company's values are geared primarily to the marketplace, the marketing vice-presidents are likely to play key roles. Slogans tell us a lot about a company's central values; for example:

- Sears Roebuck: ''Quality at a good price''—mass merchandising.
- Du Pont: ''Better things for better living through chemistry''—stressing that Du Pont's strength lies in innovation.

- McDonald's: "QSCV," i.e., Quality, Service, Convenience, and Value—emphasizing that providing a fast food service does not mean sacrificing standards.

Organizational norms include both *mores*, which cannot be violated with impunity (for example, releasing confidential information concerning people's earnings), and *folkways*. The latter include such practices as shaking hands or not shaking hands, modes of addressing others, and dress codes. Folkways are rarely set out in writing, but members of organizations generally conform to them nonetheless. Dress codes are an example: management trainees soon learn that jeans and sweaters, the standard college uniform, are not acceptable in the bank or in the downtown law firm.

Organizations that prize a strong internal culture emphasize rituals. For example, all across Japan, Matsushita workers recite the company song every morning. At IBM's annual meeting of sales people, participants reaffirm their allegiance by singing the IBM song:

That's the spirit that brought us fame!
We're big, but bigger we will be
We can't fail for all can see
That to serve humanity has been our aim
Our products are now known in every zone
Our reputation sparkles like a gem
We've fought our way through and new
Fields we're sure to conquer too
Forever onward IBM

To outsiders, the words may seem naive and corny; for insiders, singing them in unison reinforces their commonality (in Durkheim's terms, their "mechanical solidarity").

Like complex societies, complex organizations usually have subcultures that manifest the value systems at different organizational levels, and perhaps in different locations. Things are not done the same way in the Geneva headquarters of the International Red Cross as in Red Cross outposts in the Sudan or Borneo. In his study of the restaurant industry, William Foot Whyte (1948) found marked status differences between the kitchen staff and those waiting on tables. He described the relations between the two groups as "cultural warfare."

If subcultures become too numerous, and if their goals differ too sharply from those of the organization as a whole, the survival of the organization is threatened. It must develop strategies for dealing with internal conflict, since consensus is unlikely to be achieved under such conditions and there are limits to the effectiveness of coercion. The same is true of societies—recall Lincoln's argument prior to the American Civil War that a "house divided" cannot stand. (Lincoln was referring to the fact that in the North the economy was based on wage labour, while slavery prevailed in the South.)

''Organizational culture'' has become a catchphrase in the present era. However, cultures are slow to change, and new ones cannot be created overnight. Change is the hallmark of the environment in which contemporary organizations operate. The culture of an organization, then, can have characteristics that promote speedy adaptation, or it can stand squarely in the way of change.

During labour-management negotiations in 1987, Canadian Auto Workers leader Bob White, lower left, helped forge the first made-in-Canada contract for workers at General Motors, Ford, and Chrysler.

HANDS ACROSS THE WORKPLACE

By Marguerite Michaels

''What we're looking for is good kaizens.''
''Watch that muda.''
''We have to nemawashi *this.''*

Those are U.S. autoworkers talking about building a car. They talk like that, in a mixture of Japanese and English, because they work for the Japanese, who now have more companies in the U.S. that manufacture cars than America does. What they are saying is: let's discuss (*nemawashi*) how to keep making improvements (*kaizens*) and avoid waste (*muda*).

This is not how they talked — or worked — when General Motors ran this factory six years ago. At the time GM closed its Fremont, Calif., plant in 1982, it had one of the worst labor-relations records in the country. ''We were fighting with GM all the time,'' says United Auto Workers committeeman Ed Valdez. ''The product was going down the line with no one paying any attention to it. 'Ship it! Ship it!' they said.'' Today, working for New United Motor Manufacturing, Inc., a joint venture formed by GM and Toyota in 1983, the same workers are producing almost defect-free Chevrolets and Toyotas with a higher efficiency rating than any GM plant in the U.S.

GM is represented by 17 management-level employees at NUMMI, while Toyota has 36, including the president and executive vice president. One of the first things the Japanese did was eliminate executive perks such as reserved parking places and a separate cafeteria. Then they turned the top-down style of American management — the tradition of the industrial engineer having the first and last word on how a car is made — on its head. As NUMMI president Kan Higashi says, ''The person who does the job knows it best.''

The Japanese production system is based not just on high-tech robotics. An employee is a ''team member.'' A foreman is a ''group leader.'' Teams in the plant consist of six to eight members who rotate jobs, with each unit headed by an hourly team leader. Three to five teams are led by a salaried group leader. Their task: to work together in an atmosphere of ''mutual trust.'' ''The main reason American industry has lost competitiveness,'' Higashi observes, ''is distrust. I said to American management, 'On this we must go down the stairs to the people. They won't come up to us.' ''

Since NUMMI's creation, every one of its 2,500 employees has had hundreds of hours of training, and nearly 500 have been sent to Toyota City in Japan. ''U.A.W. workers are thirsty to be treated as intelligent,'' says former personnel coordinator ''Nate'' Furuta. But Furuta was discouraged at first — and American executives are still embarrassed—by the lack of basic educational skills among U.A.W. workers, especially in the area of simple math.

While the NUMMI plant is considered better than some factories in Japan, it is still less efficient than the operation in Toyota City. American team leaders who were sent to Japan took one look at the ''young wiry kids'' working at great speed on the assembly line and said, ''No way.'' ''Japan was scary,'' says Ed Valdez. ''We work to live,'' says assembly-line worker Jackie Romero. ''They live to work.''

At NUMMI, by contrast, the Japanese have ''loosened up,'' says assistant plant manager Jesse Wingard. ''You can get them to break for a cup of coffee, and there's a lot of joking on the line.'' Furuta's successor, ''T.J.'' Obara, thinks his compatriots have learned something from the Americans. ''It is more cheerful here than in Japan,'' he says. ''It's phenomenal.'' Executive vice president Osamu Kimura feels this is a valuable lesson. ''The current way is not a good way. We need a more dynamic, creative society. So we tell our colleagues here from Toyota City to work hard *and* enjoy California.''

Whenever he has the chance, Kimura spends time with his family on what he describes as ''going around landscape.'' Popular spots are California's Napa Valley, Monterey and Carmel, Arizona's Grand Canyon and Nevada's Reno. Ultimately, however, nothing beats golf. In California, greens fees for 18 holes are less than half what they are in Japan, and good golf equipment sells at a fraction of the Japanese price. There is a lesson in NUMMI: not one American involved has failed to learn the new ways. ''We have to regroup,'' says Wingard, ''and come out fighting to regain our share of the market.'' Such a transformation, all agree, will take years to accomplish. In the meantime, says Bill Childs, a NUMMI vice president, there is an ironic parallel trend. ''Look to the younger Japanese. They don't accept authority automatically any longer. They are more like us. They are our only hope.''

COMMUNICATION

The Oxford Dictionary defines **communication** as ''the act of imparting news; the science and practice of transmitting information.'' At the very least, such an act involves two actors, the communicator and the intended recipient. The ability to communicate is predicated on organizational literacy—that is to say, on basic assumptions that are shared. A red traffic light means ''stop;'' in the hospital setting, the call ''Code 99'' means that a patient has suffered cardiac arrest. A ''CVA'' is the shorthand term for a cardiovascular accident (a heart attack, in lay language).

Organizational structure delineates the path that *formal* communication follows. **Formal communication** can be divided into *vertical* and *horizontal* communication. **Vertical communication** occurs *between* levels of the hierarchy. A communique from the plant manager announcing an immediate change from a two-shift to a three-shift schedule is an example of vertical communication (recall that in Weber's ideal-type bureaucracy, commands are passed down the hierarchy). On the other hand, **horizontal communication** takes place *within* levels of the organization. In our example, the plant manager's memorandum will activate horizontal communication—for instance, among the shift supervisors as to how workers are to be rotated.

Formal communication is supplemented by **informal communication**, especially if the recipients believe they have not been given sufficient information — for example, about the reasons for the change in shift schedules. Generally, the ''grapevine'' flourishes in proportion to the degree of uncertainty that exists in a given situation. The process of socialization conditions us to seek predictability. When this is hard to come by via official sources, rumours and speculations fill the gap. Although these often contain much of the truth, they foster embroidery and inaccuracy because it is difficult to ascertain "who said or did what" when nothing is committed to writing. Hence, bureaucracies place importance on "having it in writing."

Organizational leaders must walk a tightrope between swamping members with communication—"Oh no, not another memo!"—and withholding too much information. Either extreme may detract from the organization's ability to realize its goals. In the first situation, members may be overwhelmed by the mass of communication and have insufficient time to carry out their functions effectively. (One need only listen to the complaints of those working in public sector bureaucracies!) In the second case, effective functioning may also be impeded, but this time inaction, or improper action, may result from a lack of understanding of what is required. Imagine merely being instructed to "write an essay for next Wednesday."

When we think of a foul-up, in organizational functioning as well as in personal interaction, we usually find that, somehow, somewhere, there has been a brakedown in communication. Let's say a business associate calls you in great annoyance: "We waited for you for more than an hour, but you did not show." You check your diary and find you have marked the lunch date for *next* Wednesday. This is a simple misunderstanding (though it may leave your associate with a feeling that you are "disorganized"). Both dates had been mentioned, but different conclusions had been reached regarding what date was agreed upon. In this case a confirmatory note, so beloved by bureaucracy, would have averted the mix-up.

Other barriers to communication are not as simple, because individuals become attuned to a specific organizational language. Thus, in the armed services, commands are unequivocal: "Report at 20:00 hours." The individual who moves from the Air Force to the more relaxed atmosphere of a management consulting firm may therefore not understand that the request "to prepare a report within the next few days" nevertheless requires prompt action.

STATUS BARRIERS TO EFFECTIVE COMMUNICATION

For a number of reasons, status differences make communication problematic:

- A lower-echelon employee receiving instructions may be unclear about something but be afraid to seek clarification (especially in a group situation), lest he appear "slow" or "thick." He may subsequently ask his peers, who may or may not have understood the instructions themselves. (Sadly, this is also true of learning environments. Too often, students are reluctant to seek further explanations because they do not want to risk seeming ridiculous.)

- Someone in a position of authority may phrase questions in a way that makes it clear what answer is expected. In a real-life situation, the owner of a chain of recreational centres (during visits to individual locations) often asks/tells the manager: "Everything is alright with your centre? No problems?" Most managers respond in the manner they sense is expected. As a result, problems are often swept under the rug, where they fester rather than disappear.
- The error-correcting function of communication is impaired when subordinates do not challenge and correct their superiors' errors or inaccuracies. In a study of private secretaries, Lundy (1972) found that more than half the respondents would simply "type as dictated" a report they *knew* to contain factual errors.
- There is a "hierarchy of credibility" in the sense that statements from individuals low on the totem pole tend to be discounted. Awareness of this fact may prevent these workers from making suggestions — "They would never listen to me anyway." Likewise, despite greater societal awareness of child abuse, children may not be believed when they report sexual advances by family members or friends.

Organizations generally have a "hierarchy of credibility," meaning that statements from individuals low on the totem pole tend to be discounted.

At the top, too, there are barriers to communication, in that leaders are furthest removed from the sources of much of the information on which they must base their decisions. One way to combat remoteness is to manage "by walking around," as Peters and Waterman advocate in their book *In Search of Excellence.* As communication travels, it becomes distorted both accidentally and deliberately, as individuals at key junctures seek to slant it in a way most favourable to themselves. For example, an executive comes up with an idea to reduce parts inventories by means of just-in-time delivery as a cost-saving measure. Yet, he may not include in a report expenses such as the increase in air freight charges for parts that are not in stock but are needed in current production.

Workers at the bottom of an organization are frequently included in official communication networks only on a need-to-know basis. On the other hand, massive "information overload" prevails at the top. Hence, communication must be stripped to essentials in the form of digests or synopses. The preparation of these reports involves having the subordinates who write them make judgments about what is important to include.

As already noted, what is included — or omitted — may be motivated by self-interest. However, another factor needs to be considered. We tend to be most comfortable with those who most resemble us; again, it is the effect of socialization — remember Professor Higgins' plaintive question in *My Fair Lady*, "Why can't women be more like us?" Hence, there is a tendency to hire as assistants those whom Bennis (1979) calls "Doppelgänger" (literally, one's doubles), or clones. Homogeneity, however, can have serious drawbacks. If only one type is dominant in management (hitherto, generally Anglo-Saxon males), vital information may go unnoticed because nobody is sensitized to it; shared ways of seeing mean that there are also shared ways of not seeing. Recall the film *Tootsie*, in which it took a man's being disguised as a woman for him to become aware of the myriad little indignities to which women are routinely subjected.

Individuals, organizations, and nation-states function most effectively in a stable environment, one that allows some planning. Since environments contain varying degrees of uncertainty, organizations seek to reduce the level of uncertainty by obtaining "reliable" information. Industry organizations (such as the Canadian Manufacturers' Association), lobbyists, and formal and informal contacts all have, as one of their tasks, the obtaining of information that will facilitate the organization's ability to plan. For instance, organizations like the Salvation Army or the Canadian Opera Company will find out the dates of the United Way campaign before making their own fund-raising plans. If there were a clash in dates, potential donors might balk at repeated requests for funds in such short order.

In large organizations, whole departments are devoted to disseminating appropriate information about the enterprise. The Public Relations department is charged with releasing communications about the organization that will put it in the best possible light. It is important that such official communication not be contradicted by the ways in which the organizational personnel actually interact with the public. A university's publicity efforts to recruit "non-traditional" students (those without the academic prerequisites) may be undermined if applicants are made to feel inferior by the Admissions Office staff.

Organizations may resort to covert measures to detect, and eliminate, such discrepancies. For instance, Townsend advises executives to telephone their firm incognito to find out what kind of reaction a caller might get:

> *When you're off on a business trip or a vacation, pretend you're a customer. Telephone some part of your organization and ask for help. You'll run into some real horror shows. Don't blow up and ask for name, rank and serial number—you're trying to correct, not punish. If it happens on a call to the Dubuque office, just suggest to the manager (through channels, dummy) that he make a few calls himself (1984, 25).*

One important function of the Employee Relations department is to maintain a dialogue between the organization and its employees. This has both formal (such as communiques, newsletters) and informal dimensions. In theory, any employee can discuss any work-related problem with the personnel staff (for example, an unsatisfactory relationship with the supervisor). In practice, one or more of the obstacles we discussed earlier may impede real communication.

The other side of the communications coin is secrecy, noncommunication. In modern societies, whole organizational complexes are devoted to preventing certain information from being communicated (CIA, RCMP). Espionage and counter-espionage basically revolve around one country's quest to obtain the secrets of other countries. Most espionage activity takes place on a national level, but industrial espionage—getting a jump on a competitor—is not uncommon. Corporations are conscious of this and make every effort to safeguard their own "secrets."

Less dramatically, organizations, political parties, corporate departments, interest groups, and individuals seek to minimize communication about their activities that could be used either against them or in favour of a rival.

It is ironic that in their anxiety to cover themselves by having everything in writing, bureaucracies become vulnerable to the leaking of secrets. Once something is in writing, or in the computer memory, it is potentially retrievable by unauthorized persons (computer crime is the growth industry of white collar crime). Interestingly, secretaries (Latin—*secreti*), despite their lowly status in the organizational hierarchy, have a vital role in the preservation or leaking of secrets.

For the individual, the degree of access to information within the organization is a key indicator of status. Being dropped from a circulation list may presage a demotion or sidelining. Conversely, appointment to the executive committee means, among other things, that one is now privy to communication available only to the chosen few. In highly sensitive areas, as for example in the defence industry or in the Department of External Affairs, access to communication is formalized, with only a few persons being given unlimited clearance.

ENVIRONMENT GROUPS FACE A CRISIS OF IDENTITY

By Craig McInnes

After decades of guerrilla action from the fringes of society, Canada's environment groups are facing an identity crisis precipitated by the success of their struggle to enlist the public in their crusade to save the planet.

Their success is redrawing the lines in what began as a straightforward battle between a few thousand lonely environmentalists on one side, business and government on the other.

''Looking back 20 or 30 years . . . there were no departments of the environment, there were no environmental vice-presidents in big corporations, there were no environmental studies in any institutions, there wasn't anything at all,'' said Donald Chant, chairman of the Ontario Waste Management Corp. and one of those who founded Pollution Probe, Ontario's largest environmental group, almost 21 years ago.

''Essentially, the job of the environmental groups was stirring things up, dramatizing, bringing to the public's attention, to politicians and the media, that things were in a very bad way,'' he said. ''Clearly that's been very, very successful. What we are seeing now . . . is very much the product of the work those groups did.''

Public opinion surveys show Canadians are concerned about their world and are ready to join the fight for its preservation. Politicians and business leaders, too, have been persuaded to cross the line and pick up the green banner.

It is those new recruits who are obliging environmental groups to rethink their role in the battle to save the planet. They represent both a tremendous opportunity and a threat to traditional environmental groups.

For a movement that cut its teeth on confrontation, the prospect of riding side by side with traditional foes has proved deeply troubling. Many longtime warriors mistrust the motives of the late converts and doubt the value of the new alliance.

Others say they must recognize the new political climate and abandon the ''us'' versus ''them'' mentality if groups are to make progress on the real problem —cleaning up the environment.

''An anti-authority mentality really doesn't have any place any more. Sometimes you have to go up against authority, but that must be a deliberately chosen tactic, not just acting out hostility,'' said Michael Perley of the Canadian Coalition on Acid Rain.

''Now, instead of having to throw

rocks, environmentalists can throw new ideas across the boardroom table,'' said Gary Gallon, senior policy adviser to Ontario Environmental Minister James Bradley and formerly the head of SPEC, a Vancouver-based environment group. ''That approach is very effective today.''

Within some groups, the new political environment is causing divisions. The main fear is that developing ties with polluting industries and government agencies will limit their ability to act and undermine their credibility.

''Your objectivity and your credibility are one of the main things that you possess if you are an environmentalist,'' Mr. Perley said. ''To give any appearance of being in some ongoing commercial relationship with a company of any kind whose activities have any impact on the environment is just very risky.''

The debate erupted publicly in Ontario during the past few weeks as Pollution Probe was hit by a staff revolt over a decision to endorse the Loblaw supermarket chain's ''Green'' brand of disposable diapers.

Pollution Probe's executive director, Colin Isaacs, had long sought to enlist the power of business in the fight for the environment, but many in the organization felt he had gone too far, too fast. He has since resigned, and Probe's endorsement of the diapers, for which it received a 1 per cent commission on sales, will be allowed to lapse.

Just as there are more people calling themselves environmentalists now, there are more environmental groups, further complicating the issue. The Canadian Environmental Network lists 1,800 groups, and national co-ordinator Martin Theriault estimates there are another 1,000 that are not associated with the network.

Although there are no firm estimates of how many people belong to the groups, it seems likely that they attract money from more Canadians than the traditional political parties do.

Greenpeace alone has received contributions from 100,000 Canadians during the past 18 months, according to Michael Manolson, executive director of the Canadian section of the international organization. In comparison, the ruling Progressive Conservative Party of Canada counted fewer than 70,000 donors in 1988.

Support for the environmental groups has been mushrooming. Donations doubled last year, Mr. Manolson said, and they are expected to double again this year. Other organizations are experiencing similar increases. But as their support increases they are having to consider how they can increase their influence and avoid irrelevancy as the ranks of the self-professed environmentalists grow.

''I think life now becomes much more complex for environmental groups,'' Mr. Chant said. He believes they will have to specialize.

''Some should keep up the stirring up . . . other groups will have to monitor the system,'' he said. ''Here we have all these politicians and developers saying 'Me too, me too, we're all in favor of sustainable development, environment is the number one issue.'

"OK, over the next five years these people are going to have to . . . deliver on that commitment. We haven't seen very much of that yet."

Even with government environment departments coming into being in the past decade, non-governmental groups will still be needed to urge them on, said Julia Langer of Friends of the Earth in Ottawa. "The pace of government action on the environment has been so slow that if we were to wait for government on its own to solve the problem, we would be mired in pollution and overwhelmed by natural resource exploitation. They have to be kept on their toes."

Environmentalists who work for the government agree that they cannot supplant the groups that got the movement started.

"You still need the rock-throwers" such as Greenpeace and Earth First (a radical U.S. environment group), Mr. Gallon said. "As well, you need the activist organizations like Friends of the Earth and Energy Probe, to continue to strongly criticize the institutions — government and industry — who have not moved on issues.

"And then you need environment groups such as Pollution Probe and the Institute for Research and Public Policy . . . to go into the boardrooms to fight it out with the CEO and the ministers."

Most groups have not determined where they fit into the changing political environment, Mr. Chant said, but it is a decision they will have to make soon.

THE INTRINSIC AND EXTRINSIC POWER OF ORGANIZATIONS

Power, or more precisely, the exercise of power, keeps organizations functioning. The ways in which power is exercised depend on the culture of both the society and the organization, as well as on the structure of the latter. Power cannot be exercised in the absence of communication. Imagine an army field commander, cut off from the rest of his unit, having to rely on sending scouts who may never make it back! Power and access to communication are closely linked; access to information is a reflection of power (being privy to confidential knowledge), and endows individuals, as well as organizations, with power.

Power can be defined as the ability to get a person to do something, even against that person's will. This definition emphasizes the coercive aspects of power. An adult has *power* over a child in part because of superior physical strength. However, power is by no means based only on physical strength. Think of economic power — "the power of the purse."

Whereas power implies coercion, **influence** is based on persuasion. An advisor to a political candidate may persuade her to curb the stridency of a campaign speech. The advisor has no power to do so but, rather, has influence.

Authority is legitimated power. Weber constructed a typology of the bases on which authority is legitimated.

Charismatic authority (the word "charismatic" is derived from the Greek term meaning "grace") inheres in the personal characteristics of a leader—for example, Mother Theresa or Martin Luther King. Religious and secular social movements are often founded by charismatic individuals. Hitler is an example. If the movement becomes established, authority becomes vested in an official position. From 1933 on, Hitler's authority was based on his being Germany's chancellor.

Traditional authority is legitimated by an ascribed position. Monarchies are the clearest example.

Rational-legal authority is authority that is vested in the office; it is typical of bureaucracies. Even though you may have a low opinion of your supervisor, he has the authority, by dint of his position, to give you instructions.

These three types are analytically distinct; in practice, they overlap. Personal charisma makes it easier to obtain rational legal office (authority). Think of people like Pierre Trudeau, John Kennedy, or Jean Drapeau.

Personal charisma, such as that of former Montreal Mayor Jean Drapeau, makes it easier for a leader to obtain rational-legal authority.

Although overt and covert coercion is prevalent in organizations, and in society generally, so, too, is co-operation. This dimenson is highlighted in Kanter's definition of power as: "the ability to get things done, to mobilize resources, to get and use whatever a person needs for the goal he or she is attempting to meet" (1977, 166). Given the specialization that prevails in modern society generally, and in bureaucracies in particular, this definition alerts us to the fact that the exercise of power is usually contingent on enlisting co-operation. The most brilliant surgeon cannot perform an operation without access to support staff and facilities (hence physicians' preoccupation with obtaining "hospital privileges"). A surgeon who is arrogant may find that access to resources becomes mired in petty obstacles and rigid adherence to rules.

In any organization, the manager or leader who can rely on her team to come through will gain a reputation for getting things done, broaden her access to resources, and increase her power. In turn, this allows her to mobilize resources on behalf of employees and help them to achieve their personal objectives—a pay increase, educational leave, attendance at an international conference. Thus, a "benign circle" is set up, in which the actions of persons at all levels reinforce each other to give an individual greater *de facto* (and eventually greater positional) power. The obverse also applies. Individuals who cannot elicit the co-operation, rather than the mere passive compliance, of those who work for them, and who unjustly blame others for missed deadlines or botched presentations, will lose credibility—and power—in relationships with those in the organization to whom they themselves are accountable.

The very concept of power implies that it is exercised over an individual, a group, an organization, or a nation. Most of the time, the response to the exercise of power is compliance. Why?

In the course of socialization, we learn that in general conformity brings rewards, such as approval from others which serves to affirm our feelings of self-worth. As noted earlier, each time we enter a new group, the "right" way of doing things must be learned. The same applies within organizations, not only in terms of formal rules, but also in terms of general demeanor, the "presentation of self." Thus, the super salesman who is promoted to management may find that he must realign his ideas about the clothes he should wear and the jokes he may tell.

Conformity to an organization's formal rules is rewarded most fundamentally by having a job, and also by promotion, pay increases, and symbols of approval such as awards or mention in the newsletter. Sanctions for violations of rules run the gamut from being warned to being sidelined or fired. Transgression of informal rules, too, exacts a price. In the novel *Doctors*, Erich Segal dramatizes what happens when a young physician complains to the director of a major teaching hospital that a baby died because no oxygen was on hand when the child went into respiratory failure:

> *Dr. Caldwell leaned across the desk and said: ''But it is a cardinal rule that one doctor never impugns another'' . . . ''And what if you see a mistake that's so egregious that you can't accept this 'article of faith?' I mean, if someone, say, saw a drunken surgeon kill a healthy patient?'' ''Don't be absurd, Laura. Then of course you would report that to his superior . . . but never in writing'' (1988, 513).*

In many instances, organizations attempt to ensure conformity by recruiting the ''right'' people. For example, life in the armed forces is unlikely to attract people who look for flexibility, tolerance for individuality, and opportunities for exercising initiative. If such persons were to apply, it is unlikely that they would be selected. Recruiters who visit university and college campuses look not only for high performers, but also for men and women who will ''fit'' into the organization.

The adjustment process between the individual and an organization continues after recruitment and, indeed, may persist throughout a lifelong career (Schein 1978, 4). In many instances, attempts to ensure a proper fit between the needs of the organization and the individual are the objectives of in-house training efforts. What occurs via this process may be supplemented by informal pressure from peers as well as from more obvious directives from management.

Quite frequently, those who are blatant misfits are cast out in one way or another. Either the person realizes that he or she is in the wrong spot and leaves or requests a transfer, or the organization initiates a change or termination— ''we made the wrong choice.''

Over time, then, homogeneity and the thrust toward conformity within an organization tend to increase, and with these rise the risks of rigidity and incapacity for innovation. At the same time, conformity is never total because it is impossible to eliminate unpredictability from human behaviour.

Even though many factors both separately and together contribute to conformity, some degree of **conflict** is a fact of life—in the family, in the work group, within and among organizations and countries. Inherently, conflict is neither good nor bad; whether it is beneficial or harmful depends on the situation. Conflicts revolve around issues that directly and indirectly relate to power.

Organizations are repositories of vast power, and hence are frequently the arenas where conflicts are played out. Perrow notes:

> *Organizations are tools for shaping the world as one wishes it to be shaped. They provide the means for imposing one's own definition of the proper affairs of humankind and others. The person who controls an organization has power that goes far beyond that of those lacking such control . . . Such power is naturally contested. People attempt to achieve control of organizations or even of part of an organization in order to gain that power (1986, 11-2).*

A classic example of institutionalized or structured conflict is found in management/labour relations. Conflict centres around the allocation of resources, money, and benefits, as well as around the amount of control various people hold over the work process. Conflicts may result in strikes — withdrawal of labour (by, for example, steelworkers, nurses, or professors), and the employer's response of locking workers out. Conflict may centre on whether certain practices should be instituted (AIDS testing of immigrants and of military or government personnel) and, if they are, how they should be carried out. Conflict may also arise over whether the relationship between certain groups is to remain intact or change (for example, should landlords have the power to evict a tenant and, if so, on what grounds?).

Major conflicts are generally associated with change. Conformity means adherence to a set of rules. If the rules change, new patterns are called for—and often resisted. For instance, the 1965 Hall-Dennis Report advocated fundamental changes in the Ontario educational system. It called for flexibility rather than rigid structure in the classroom, and for freedom of expression rather than for regurgitation of the material taught. Many of the teachers who had been socialized to the old norms resisted the changes, and the Ontario education system went through a period of turmoil.

Conflict among and within organizations often involves jurisdictional disputes. Thus, in universities, there is an ongoing tug-of-war over whether departmental faculties should unilaterally be able to fill new appointments (since they are qualified to judge expertise), or whether the administration (who control funds) should have the final say.

Some conflicts are not resolved. They become routinized and are taken into account during interaction. A good test of whether conflict is structural or interpersonal is to see whether it persists when new actors take over.

AN UPHILL BATTLE: VOLUNTARY AFFIRMATIVE ACTION PLANS DON'T SEEM TO BE WORKING

By Ann Rauhala

This summer, a team of federal employees has the unenviable task of rooting through pages of documents filed by banks, transportation companies and crown corporations. The Department of Employment and Immigration will be checking to see how well the makeup of the 1988 workforce is reflected in about 400 federally regulated enterprises.

Social critics and human rights advocates expect the Government will discover what they have been saying all along: voluntary affirmative action does not work.

"Theoretically, there's nothing wrong with voluntary affirmative action," said Constance Backhouse, a law professor whose report on female faculty set off fireworks at the University of Western Ontario this spring. "The problem I see with it is that most institutions develop programs that just aren't successful. They don't set their goals high enough, or there's not much pressure to reach the goals they do set."

In her study of the Western faculty, Ms Backhouse found that the university's voluntary affirmative action plan—one that had won a prize—had made only a negligible difference in the number of women on the teaching staff.

Two other reports on women at universities demonstrated that Western's small ratio of female faculty members—14 per cent of the total—was by no means unusual.

The Council of Ontario Universities noted that 5.7 per cent of full-time professors and 14.4 per cent of associate professors are women, while a Statistics Canada report found that women professors made up only 17 per cent of full-time faculty across the country and were concentrated in lower-ranking, lower-paying jobs. The Ontario Council noted, too, that since 1982 more women than men have been graduating from Canadian universities.

Although the universities have attracted the most attention recently, the situation in many other workplaces is not much brighter. Even in fields where women are in the majority, or that are supposed to be under federal regulation, most of the best positions are still held by men.

- Of 120 diplomatic missions abroad, 10 are headed by women.
- Of 4,538 managers in the public service, 481 are women.
- Of 22,702 scientific and professional personnel in the public service, 5,563 are women.
- Of 4,378 public and separate school principals in Ontario, 692 are women.
- Of 86,364 members of the armed forces, 8,222 are women.
- Of 1,101 lieutenant-colonels, seven are women.
- Of 366 colonels, five are women. Of 87 brigadier-generals, one is a woman.
- Of 112 newspaper publishers, three are women.
- Of 728 federally appointed judges, 58 are women.
- Of 211 directors on the boards of Canada's major banks, 12 are women.
- Of 698 chief executive officers of health-care operations, 189 are women.
- Of 57 directors of the major department stores, five are women.

Despite evidence that affirmative action may be desirable, Canadians have been ambivalent about it—if for no other reason than that many are confused about what it means.

"Among employers you don't even hear the term affirmative action any more," said Ray Brillinger, a spokesman for the Canadian Manufacturers' Association. "Affirmative action itself is loaded with all kinds of connotations. One of the reasons for shedding the term was that it had come to connote the setting of quotas.''

Affirmative action has changed since the sixties and seventies, when the first efforts to assist women and visible minorities began. It quickly became apparent that to be effective it had to do more than push pre-ordained quantities of women, visible minorities and the disabled into places where they were not welcome.

In her influential 1984 federal commission report on Equality in Employment, Rosalie Abella called for a broader understanding of the factors that keep some groups at a disadvantage in the workplace, and articulated what changes could be made.

For women, she wrote, equality in employment had to include equal pay for work of equal value, accessible day care and increased training opportunities. For natives, equality meant policies shaped to geographic and cultural differences. For visible minorities, it meant attacks on racism and a method for assessing foreign qualifications.

Interestingly, Judge Abella, now head of the Ontario Labor Relations Board, rejected hiring quotas. But she wrote that voluntary measures were ''an unsatisfactory response to the pervasiveness of systemic discrimination in Canadian workplaces.''

Nevertheless, Ottawa has adopted two measures recommended in the Abella report that critics say are a far cry from mandatory affirmative action.

Under the Employment Equity scheme, federally regulated firms with 100 or more employees—a fraction of the labor force—had to report by June 1, 1988 on the number of women, visible minorities, natives and the disabled they hire, fire and promote. The data will be made public and will be turned over to the Canadian Human Rights Commission, which can initiate a complaint against firms that will not make an effort to change their ways.

Another initiative, the Federal Contractors Program, applies to any company with 100 or more employees bidding on federal Government contracts worth $200,000 or more. The firms are supposed to give a signed promise to demonstrate a commitment to employment equity.

But Marnie Clarke, director-general of the employment equity branch of the Department of Employment and Immigration, sounds proud of the work she and a staff of about 30 are doing collecting data on federally regulated firms. Of 380 companies that should have reported, she said, 96 per cent have done so.

Ms Clarke knows that some human rights activists think the two federal initiatives are too little and too slow, but she sees a need to balance a desire for change on one side against strong opposition on another. ''There are people who think affirmative action is a gross interference in the labour markets.''

Behind the ambivalence about mandatory affirmative action lies much anxiety and confusion. Employers may believe it is too expensive and time-consuming to develop a program. They may worry about being open to charges of reverse discrimination. Or they may simply be reluctant to give up the privileges that have gone with being a white, able-bodied male.

"It's a legitimate concern," said Raj Anand, chief commissioner of the Ontario Human Rights Commission. "There's little co-ordination, and there should be more."

But Mr. Anand believes employers still are not aware of the advantages of workplace measures, including quotas in some cases.

"They think that devoting resources to advancing women or visible minorities will put them at a disadvantage. The experience in the United States has been that the long-term gains outweigh the short-term costs."

Those gains include the obvious, such as the availability of a wider pool of talent and creativity and an enhanced public image, and the not so obvious, such as improved morale and an inroad into untapped markets.

"The guys who saved affirmative action in the United States (when it was under attack from the Reagan Administration) were AT&T, IBM, GE and GM," said Rhys Phillips, chief of the employment equity division of the Canadian Human Rights Commission.

"They found it gave them a real edge in business, that productivity increased. But they also noticed that if you were an employer that treated blacks right, you were an employer that blacks took their business to."

Interestingly, that message does not appear to have been relayed to the Canadian operations of some of these firms. IBM Canada Ltd., though it uses management techniques similar to those of its U.S. counterpart, does not have hiring targets. The firm told the Abella commission it favoured voluntary affirmative action only, an IBM spokesman said.

Voluntary affirmative action is a relative term, Mr. Phillips said. "Voluntary affirmative action in which all you get for failing to comply is a nasty letter may not do much. But voluntary affirmative action in which failure results in a serious sanction — then you'll get action."

"IBM might *volunteer* to make a change if AT&T has just paid a $50-million fine for not making one."

LEADERSHIP

Like power, **leadership** is a relational concept—without followers, the concept of a leader is meaningless. Within this broad framework, Hall notes that "it is the persuasion of individuals and innovativeness in ideas that differentiates leadership from the sheer possession of power" (1987, 152).

Etzioni, too, focuses on the influence dimension, on the ability to elicit voluntary compliance based on the personal qualities of the leader. To him, leadership is "the ability, based on the personal qualities of the leader, to elicit the followers' voluntary compliance in a broad range of matters. Leadership is distinguished from the concept of power in that it entails influence, i.e., change of preferences, while power implies only that subjects' preferences are held in abeyance" (1965, 690-1).

Leaders who possess *charisma* or have a skill in consensus building are likely to find it easier to exercise leadership, to persuade subordinates or followers to "change their preferences." However, the leeway given to leaders of large organizations is circumscribed by bureaucratic rules and regulations. In the case of democratic governments, there are also built-in checks and balances. In part because of factors such as these, researchers have been unable to produce clear-cut evidence of exactly how leaders affect an organization, because so many situational variables comes into play, such as changes in the economic or political climate. Even so, there is currently an interest among social scientists in how charismatic leaders operate, and in making an assessment of the impact of leaders on organizations. Perhaps some of this interest was spurred by Chrysler's dramatic turnabout after Lee Iacocca assumed the presidency.

FUNCTIONS OF A LEADER

Drawing on Selznick's conceptualization, Hall (1987, 151-2) places critical leadership tasks into four categories:

- Defining the organizational role. In a dynamic environment, the organization that does not adapt will be left behind. When the Salk vaccine drastically reduced the incidence of polio, the March of Dimes organization had to redefine its objectives in order to remain visible (see Sills' *The Volunteers*).
- Deciding on the means, on the policies that will achieve the desired ends. Just as the scientist must "operationalize" a research project (decide on the research instrument, questions to be asked, subjects to be sampled, and methods of data analysis), corporate executives must make it possible for a new policy to be put into effect—for instance, Volvo's changeover from the assembly line to "quality work teams."
- Defending the organization's integrity, both by motivating organizational members to work toward the attainment of goals, and by creating an accepting climate within the larger environment for the organization. Thus, child welfare agencies may have to convince the public that families with a history of child abuse must be closely monitored when a new baby is born, even though this may be construed as an infringement of the parents' civil liberties.
- Dealing with internal conflict that is a threat to the organization as a whole. Jurisdictional disputes abound in public as well as in private organizations.

Woodward (1987) describes how branches of the vast American intelligence network refused to share knowledge or sources of knowledge. This resulted in duplication of cost and effort, and in certain information being passed to the Administration either too late or not at all.

Each of the categories of tasks we just discussed entails decision making. In *The Functions of the Executive*, a book still regarded as a classic, Chester Barnard (1938) pinpointed decision making as the essence of the executive role. Barnard was concerned with *critical* decisions, those that cannot be made at lower levels. For example, while it would be an executive decision whether General Electric should move some of its operations offshore to take advantage of lower labour costs, decisions such as switching ads between trade magazines or changing the wording of an advertisement are to be made at lower levels.

However, top leaders may not find it easy to concentrate on critical decisions. Warren Bennis (1979) argues that leaders, whether in charge of a nation or of a university, have difficulty in "leading," in concentrating on far-reaching decisions, because they are overwhelmed by routine "management" matters.

Being a leader entails the need to make unpopular, and often painful, decisions: to send soldiers into battle where, in all likelihood, a significant percentage will be killed or maimed; to bring in new technology that will enhance the company's competitive position but will put people out of work.

On the other hand, a leader cannot allow herself to become paralysed and make no decisions because she is aware of adverse consequences. It is impossible to please everybody all the time, and those who attempt this find that they end up pleasing nobody in the long run. Politicians are notorious for avoiding unpopular decisions, because these are likely to jeopardize their chances of re-election.

Organizational analysts have not been able to identify one style of leadership that is successful in all situations. Rather, they have found that a number of variables affect whether authoritarian, democratic, or an intermediary form of leadership is likely to succeed. These variables include: the position of the organization in the social and economic environment (a day-care centre or a small high-tech firm just starting up will require a different type of leadership than IBM), the nature of the work, the organizational culture, and the education and expectations of the organization's members.

In practice, leadership styles tend to lie along a continuum, with leaders veering toward either the democratic or the authoritarian pole. A leader is unlikely to be successful if he implements a style that is alien to a particular setting—for instance, trying to impose the rigid routine of a prison on a liberal arts college.

Non-authoritarian leadership styles are more likely to occur in organizations consisting of members who define themselves as "a community of equals" — for example, a university department, a collective, or women's political groups such as the Icelandic Women's Party. In such settings, the practice of rotating the leadership may be adopted to downplay hierarchical distinctions.

One component of rational-legal authority is that, to some extent, leaders and followers share goals. Nonetheless, the leader must tread a fine line by pursuing organizational or personal goals without exceeding the willingness of subordinates to follow along.

Kanter and Stein cite the story of *The Little Prince* who asked the ''King of the Universe'' how the king was able to perform his miracles. He replied that ''it was all a matter of what to ask for and when to ask for it'' (1979, 7). Especially in an environment where a modicum of democracy is expected, leadership without consent of the led is not feasible in the long run.

In the hands of hostile workers, the rules and regulations that are intended to ensure organizational effectiveness and efficiency can in fact become powerful tools for creating chaos. Work-to-rule campaigns are intended to be disruptive. Even workers at the bottom of organizations exercise discretion in interpreting rules, often without thinking about it. Postal workers usually forward mail addressed to ''Toronto, Manitoba'' rather than returning it marked, ''Can't be delivered — no such address.'' In the extreme case, leaders who consistently violate people's need to act as sentient beings rather than as robots will be unable to lead or govern.

THE INDIVIDUAL AS ORGANIZATIONAL EMPLOYEE

It was one of Durkheim's axioms that the group is different from, and greater than, the sum of its parts. In terms of organizational study, this means that we cannot understand how organizations function by merely examining the characteristics of their members. However, organizations are comprised of individuals who subjectively experience their environment, in the process helping to shape this environment.

People's experiences are affected by their position in the organizational hierarchy — an airline pilot's reality differs from that of the crew who cleans planes. Conversely, one's organizational placement crucially affects one's life chances (see discussion in Chapter 4 on stratification).

LIFE AT THE BOTTOM

For most people, being at the bottom means that their work is tightly controlled — by machines, by close supervision, or by both. Assembly-line work, which we briefly discussed in Chapter 5, is a case in point. The private in the army is another example: the smallest details of everyday life are regulated — how one ties one's shoes, makes one's bed, or cuts one's hair. A computerized cash register tallies the number of items supermarket check-out clerks punch in over a given timespan. The productivity of a telephone operator can be closely measured (see Braverman 1974).

Marx noted that the bargaining power of Britain's proletariat was undermined by the "reserve army of the unemployed." In the 19th century, people were forced to either take work at any wage or to endure the horrors of the poorhouse. Nowadays, this need is moderated by programs such as unemployment insurance and welfare. However, the assumption persists that workers at the bottom are easily substitutable, and that it is therefore unnecessary to create conditions that will induce them to stay. Short or nonexistent training programs for many jobs reaffirm the notion that "anybody can do it."

Bottom level jobs also offer few opportunities for upward mobility. Whether we look at factories, at offices, or at service organizations such as the police, we find that there are few first-level supervisory jobs. Furthermore, mobility increasingly requires advanced education. For example, a 27-year-old secretary who had been working for nine years told Lundy: "I am at the top of the secretarial ladder now; there is nowhere else to go unless I take a degree in Business Administration" (1977, 142).

 BEING IN THE MIDDLE 

The middle of an organization usually contains the largest number of people, and the greatest diversity in terms of education, areas of expertise, and hierarchical position. First-level supervisors, assistant vice-presidents, and members of the health department would all fit somewhere in the middle.

One can arrive in the middle by dint of promotion from the bottom. More commonly, one is recruited, perhaps as a management trainee, or to fill a staff slot, for instance as a psychologist in the Human Resources department. *Entry* positions, by definition, offer opportunities for promotion. Hence, organizations expend more resources (tests, reference checking, personal interviews) on recruitment and selection of middle-level employees than they do in their hiring procedures for low-level jobs.

Being hired is the first step on an escalator that may move individuals a long way up or, for a number of reasons, strand them at quite low levels. For example: the economy may turn sour, as in the 1981–2 recession; government departments may cut programs and staff; or reorganization may make a position less central or even redundant. Company politics and social-psychological characteristics (combined with various other factors) all influence how far and how fast someone advances.

Being in the middle means being dependent on those above, who control access to rewards and advancement, as well as on those below, who can subvert effectiveness by stonewalling or actively undermining a boss. Policies set at the top of an organization are translated into administrative procedures in the middle, and carried out by workers at the bottom. The latter are likely to direct their resentment about unwelcome changes toward the middle-level personnel charged with enforcing the changes—for instance, docking the pay of anyone who clocks in more than five minutes late.

Large organizations used to take for granted full commitment from middle-level employees; an employee's automatic acceptance of a transfer without regard to the upheaval in family life was one way to show loyalty and commitment. The organization manifested its loyalty by virtually guaranteeing lifelong employment (except for those who were clearly incompetent or dishonest). Things have changed.

If the employee to be transferred has a working spouse (in the majority of cases, this means wife) who is unwilling just to drop her career, this makes geographic mobility more problematic. Lifelong job security has been eroded by organizations' discovery of the virtues of "downsizing" and becoming "lean and mean"—strategies that have been spurred by the large number of mergers and takeovers. (For example, Canadian Airlines' buyout of Wardair entailed the loss of more than a thousand jobs.)

MANAGERIAL CLASS GETS ROUGHED UP

By Steven Prokesch

Anna H. Jones lost her job as vice president for information systems when the Gilman Paper Company consolidated its staff and moved its headquarters from Manhattan to St. Mary's, Ga., to cut costs.

A decision that the operating divisions could handle their own personnel matters cost Stephen C. Rexford his job as corporate vice president for human resources at Continental Can.

The cutbacks that followed Coleco Industries Inc.'s severe problems in computers and electronic toys landed Harold Cohen, a retail sales manager, on the street.

And the acquisition of the Pacific Lumber Company rendered Robert E. Giusti, a Pacific executive, redundant: the acquirer, Maxxam, already had its own vice president for employee relations and had no need for another.

As thousands of managers and professionals have learned the hard way, the days when white-collar workers could assume that their jobs were for life is no more true nowadays than it always has been for blue-collar workers. After more than three decades of adding to corporate headquarters staffs and creating one new layer of management after another, major corporations are now doing an abrupt about-face. In the last six years Xerox, Exxon, General

Electric, Kodak, Ford and scores of other major companies have done all they can to shrink the size of their white-collar work forces.

A handful of companies — such as the International Business Machines Corporation, which, according to one IBM personnel executive, decided it had 20,000 workers too many — have been paring their staffs by offering attractive severance or early-retirement packages to entice people to quit.

But most other businesses are not so kind. Such companies as Unisys and Exxon have told employees that if a sufficient number of them do not jump through the "golden window" while it is open, the choice of leaving will no longer be theirs to make — and the severance might not be as generous.

At least three major factors have caused the change:

- The rise of formidable foreign competition beginning in the 1970s, coupled with recession and deregulation, leached business from the American market and made it clear that the management costs at American companies were too high.
- Improvements in computer technology decreased the number of workers needed to carry on many business operations.
- The wave of mergers, acquisitions and corporate restructurings in recent years has resulted in wholesale eliminations of middle- and top-management layers.

 WHAT IF THE DREAM COMES TRUE?

Realistically, very few people can reach the top because the number of positions is small. But what is it like for those who do? We have already mentioned some of the dilemmas leaders must confront. Those at the top must not only function in a climate of uncertainty, but they are also under constant scrutiny. Kanter aptly notes that "the room at the top is all windows" (1979, 35). One's family-life, friendships, and social activities must all be subordinated to organizational priorities. To a considerable extent, the boundaries between business and private life disappear. Golf games form the venue for a business chat; a dinner party becomes a forum for informally sounding out one's bankers as to how they might react to a new share offering that would raise capital for expansion.

Individual aspirations and expectations are formed in a concrete social matrix. In our society, success is perhaps the most pervasive value, and for most people (especially for men) this means success in one's work. It was one of Marx's crucial insights that one's position in the division of labour influences all other aspects of life. Those at the top are not only liberally endowed with material goods, but they also enjoy symbolic rewards — power, prestige, respect, deference.

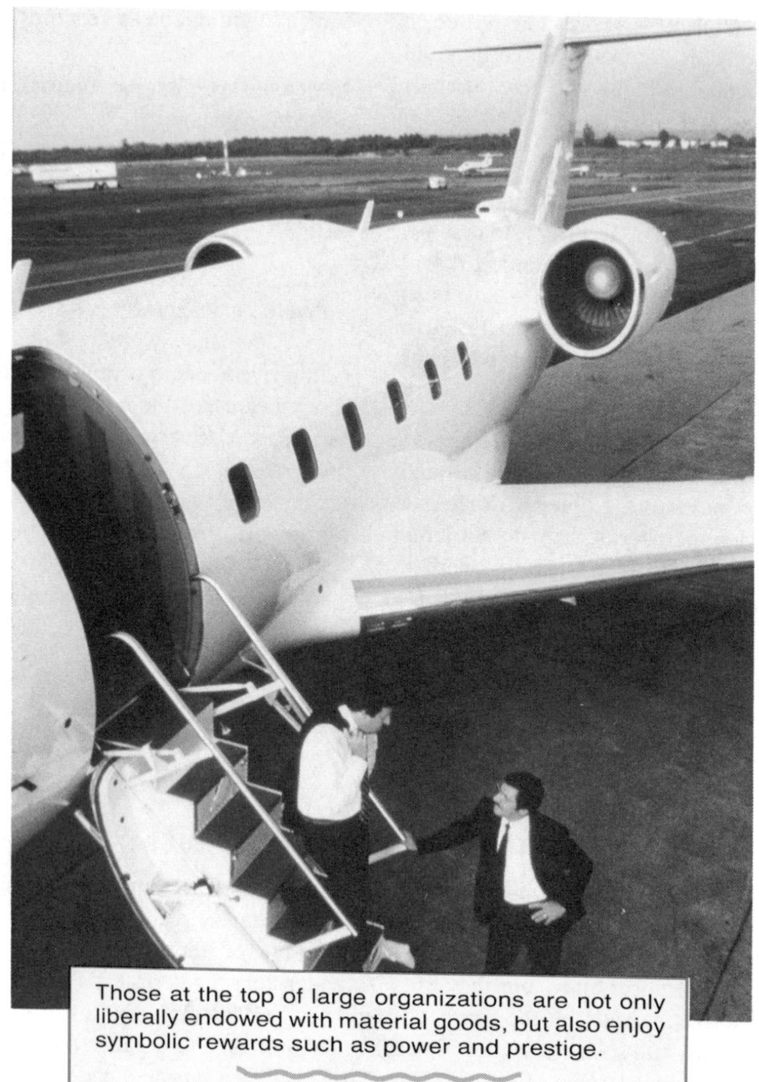

Those at the top of large organizations are not only liberally endowed with material goods, but also enjoy symbolic rewards such as power and prestige.

At every turn, top executives are reassured of their own importance—in the first class section of planes, in expensive hotels and restaurants, in the office, in social interaction. By way of contrast, Coleman (a college president who spent his sabbatical year doing a number of blue-collar jobs) notes that hardly anyone paid attention when he walked through the restaurant in his white chef's uniform. This was very different from his experience as president of Haverford College:

> *At the college I have become accustomed to being noticed when I walk in a room. I sense a slight stir, a turn of the head here and there, even*

> *a calm sometimes that I never noticed before I took the presidency. I don't think I just imagine this awareness, happy or not, that "Jack Coleman is here." I know that part of my pride stems from having a job for which there is wide respect and which attracts attention to itself. So esteem feeds on esteem, and I become in part what people think I am (1974, 157).*

Being in a position of power makes it possible to try out one's ideas and to experience a sense of accomplishment when an idea proves fruitful. One *initiates* action rather than carrying out policies or tasks that have been designed by others. Though subject to the environmental and organizational constraints we have discussed, one has significant influence over the direction an organization takes.

Whether one sees the top as a desirable goal, given the improbability of attaining it and the heavy costs entailed in the attempt, is an individual predilection. If one values privacy, wants to devote time to family and friends, and puts a premium on popularity, then a "good job" may be more rewarding than the pressure cooker atmosphere of the boardroom. On the other hand, if "winning isn't everything, it's the only thing" is one's value scheme, the drive for the top may be worthwhile.

We will discuss some general issues relating to women in Chapter 10 on social change. Here, we merely include a brief explanation for why the proportion of women in the upper ranks of organizations is so small.

Because the time and energy demands on top executives are so heavy, a sound infrastructure is crucial. Executive assistants and secretaries fill support roles at work; wives have traditionally done so at home. It is hard to concentrate on a merger when one has to worry about picking up the laundry.

Other factors may be even more crucial to the paths of women's careers. Kanter (1977) argues that individuals' aspirations and expectations are influenced by the "opportunity structure" they encounter in the work environment. In the past, and to a lesser degree now, discriminatory practices have impeded women's chances of climbing to the top. There is evidence that awareness of this, coupled with the absence of the home front back-up that men have enjoyed, has depressed women's expectations of success in their careers. For instance, in her study (conducted from 1981–3) of the 82 female graduates of the 1975 Harvard MBA class, Gallese found that only one was aiming for the top, and very few were aspiring to what a professor at the Harvard Business School described as "simply a good job." To him, this meant something like "vice-president in charge of a division—running something big." Gallese "did a double take . . . Of the eighty-two women I had interviewed, only a handful were striving for such a goal" (1985, 79).

Of course, our discussion of barriers to success is based on traditional definitions of what constitutes success in our culture. For example, in the university, standards for tenure and promotion are based on a male career model that is not appropriate for women—thus creating a "glass ceiling" that is not obvious but nevertheless exists. The question must be raised: is it possible that prevailing notions of success will come to be redefined in a more humanistic way, so that the all-consuming demands of ''greedy institutions'' will be restrained?

Job satisfaction is of concern both to individuals and to the organizations in which they are employed. Most people in the paid labour force — and often those who are not, such as full-time homemakers—spend most of their waking hours at work, or commuting to and from work. How they feel about their jobs spills over into home and social life. For example, Luxton's study of housewives in Flin Flon, Manitoba, demonstrated that a man's work experience had consequences for his wife and children. One woman who was regularly abused by her husband explained to Luxton that: ''He hates his job. He's got all this mad locked up inside with nowhere for it to go. So sometimes he takes it out on me and the kids. Well, I sort of don't blame him I guess'' (1980, 70).

Ever since the Human Relations approach became popular in the late 1920s, organizations have assumed that *satisfied* workers are more productive workers. In fact, no conclusive evidence has been adduced that job satisfaction gives rise to higher productivity. Perrow notes that ''one reason it was not possible to clearly establish that high morale led to high productivity is that the relationship often goes in the opposite direction: high morale may be due to high productivity, rather than the reverse (1986, 97).

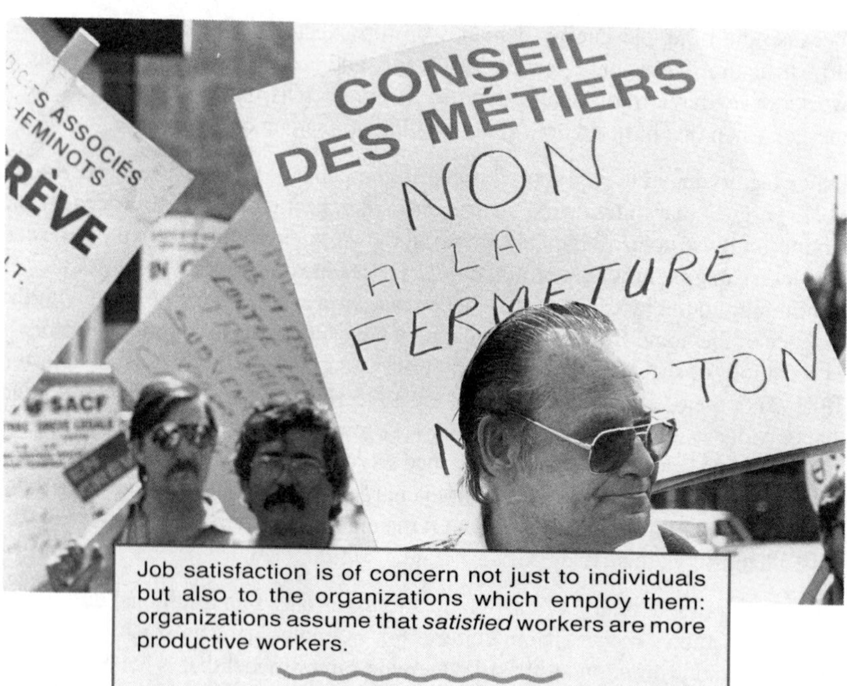

Job satisfaction is of concern not just to individuals but also to the organizations which employ them: organizations assume that *satisfied* workers are more productive workers.

What influences job satisfaction? Structural factors affect how people feel about their work. Routinized, monotonous jobs that workers perceive as meaningless foster alienation and squelch job satisfaction (Blauner 1964, MacKinnon 1981). Other influences are the physical ambience and atmosphere of the work setting, as well as relationships with superiors and peers. A pettifogging supervisor can make the job miserable for the most dedicated nurse or social worker, even though the work may be intrinsically rewarding; a mundane clerical job can be transformed by a group that is congenial and shares leisure activities, such as going to lunch or curling on the same team.

The degree of job satisfaction is further affected by the fit between what one wants and what one gets, and by psychological disposition—the same bottle can be seen as half full or half empty.

THE INDIVIDUAL AS ORGANIZATIONAL CLIENT

On the one hand, specialization and compartmentalization are vital; without job boundaries there would be chaos. On the other hand, some matters fall between the cracks and, as a result, clients may be shunted from department to department. Jurisdictions may be clear to those who work in the organization, but not to outsiders. Imagine a rural migrant who is stranded in Montreal without money or shelter. To him, the procedures to get emergency funds—procedures that would entail filling out forms he may have difficulty understanding—may seem quite overwhelming.

Goal displacement may also come into play. Meeting the needs of their clients is supposed to be the primary goal of service organizations (colleges, libraries, hospitals). Often these needs become subordinated to the personnel's desire to have the organization run smoothly. For instance, hospital patients may be awakened at the crack of dawn to be washed and have their beds made, so as to facilitate the switch-over from night staff to day staff.

Everyone can think of horror stories that demonstrate how organizations ride roughshod over their clients, especially if the latter belong to a powerless group, such as welfare recipients. Fundamental to the interaction between organization and client is the power differential, which essentially puts the client at the mercy of the organization and its representatives. In private-sector profit-making enterprises, the client has the option of taking her business elsewhere, but this is not necessarily helpful in the short run. If the staff at a bank refuses to cash your cheque and you need money now, it is scant consolation that you can "punish" the bank by withdrawing your account.

It is also the case that most client contact occurs between the clients and the workers in the lower echelons of organizations. Such employees may themselves be aliented, less concerned with providing service than with following rules to the letter so that they cannot be blamed if anything goes wrong — the ''cover your ass'' strategy.

Of course, not everyone has negative experiences all the time, nor are all organizational employees disinterested in helping clients. There is most likely to be good service if there is a strong commitment to service from the top. Peters and Waterman (1982) are convinced that the drive for excellence, in service as in other organizational functions, must begin at the top and percolate through the ranks.

It should also be stressed, however, that consumers are not entirely powerless. Businesses have been known to yield under pressure from consumer associations or determined individuals.

ORGANIZATIONS AND THE ENVIRONMENT

It is somewhat confusing to speak of ''organizations and the environment,'' since the environment itself is largely a web of other organizations (such as government regulatory agencies, unions, and occupational associations). Organizations attempt to negotiate the complexity of this environment both by planning and by maintaining the flexibility to make quick decisions.

Some feminist organizations have the controversial mandate that the entire organization be run by females, considered affirmative action by some people and reverse discrimination by others.

However the environment may be conceptualized, organizations influence the environment both directly and indirectly. As we noted earlier, the organizational experiences of individuals influence their self-perceptions as well as their expectations. Members of marginalized groups, on the basis of gender, race, or disability, who have had a taste of power by dint of their organizational position, are likely to resist discrimination in their lives outside the organization. If such people are numerous, more liberal practices may filter into the society generally.

Indirectly, then, there is a continuing interchange of influence between organizations and the environment, because changes in the environment in turn feed back, affecting organizations. Educational institutions provide an example. On the one hand, their environment influences what is taught and how it is taught. On the other hand, educated people are more prone to both question societal practices and have the skills to try to change those they deem unacceptable.

It was Marx's hope that shared experiences and deprivations would forge workers into "a class for itself," conscious of its common interests. Labour unions are such "class" associations, but in North America only a minority of workers are unionized. Even in Marx's day, private sector organizations were conscious of their own interests, and this consciousness has remained strong. Corporations engage in "purposive" action to mold the environment, and their vast collective power has ensured considerable success for their endeavours.

Sampson describes the ways in which the world's largest oil companies influenced the affairs of entire nation states. More important than competition was collaboration to safeguard their collective interests:

> *The band of sisters had been led by two giants, Exxon and Shell, who for the past sixty years had been the prototypes of the sophisticated international company. Their rivalry across the continents had been a long subplot to modern history, financing whole nations, fueling wars, developing deserts. Their commercial ambitions were fraught with diplomatic consequences: the revolutions in Iraq, the separatist movement in Scotland or the civil war in Nigeria (1984, 9).*

On the domestic front, the lack of progress in developing a commercially viable electric car is in large part attributable to the oil lobby's success in stifling funding for research and development. While oil was plentiful and could be obtained for a fraction of its selling price, the oil industry was determined to quash potential competition.

The oil industry is not an isolated case. Richardson (1988) argues that the recent takeovers of several trust companies by conglomerates (Canada Trust by Imasco, Royal Trust by Brascan) have increased the power wielded by large corporations, as well as their ability to shape the environment in ways that favour their interests —often to the detriment of other groups in society.

A frightening aspect of the power of organizations to shape the environment is the limitation of real choices. Perrow reports that, in 1983, six firms accounted for 85 percent of all sales of recorded music. This concentration makes it possible to control tastes: "In keeping with increasing concentration in the industry, the format is the rise of stations broadcasting only the Top 40 hits—if this is all you hear, it is all you can purchase" (1986, 188).

Such examples raise the question: "Why is this allowed to go on; why doesn't government stop it?" Anti-monopoly legislation is on the statute books in Canada as well as in the United States but, first, such legislation does not have real "teeth," and, second, organizations have contrived to prevent rigorous enforcement.

One reason for this ineffectual legislation is the flow of personnel between large corporations and government. For instance, a former federal deputy minister of finance is now chief executive officer of Molson Breweries; Prime Minister Mulroney was formerly president of the Iron Ore Company of Canada; ex-U.S. Secretary of State Alexander Haig became president of United Technologies. In other words, elites in the private and public sectors tend to be staffed by individuals of similar background and experience, who "see things the same way" (see John Porter's argument in Chapter 4 on stratification). Hence, there is no tight curb on the power and influence of corporations. One need not subscribe to the Marxist argument that the capitalist state is a "tool" of major corporations to recognize that they play a significant part in shaping the environment.

SUMMARY

Living in an organizational society such as Canada makes it important to have some understanding of organizations—their structure, how they function, and how they are influenced by the larger environment and in turn help to mould this environment.

Organizations are established to attain a set of objectives. These objectives are often incompatible, as in the case of prisons. Rehabilitation and punishment are not easily accomplished within the same institution at the same time.

The organizational culture, a term that subsumes values, norms, folkways, and "language," affects what strategies are selected to achieve organizational goals. In turn, the culture is built on the strategies selected. Communication within the organization, as well as with societal agencies and with individuals, is also coloured by this culture. An organization may prize openness, information on a need-to-know basis, or else secrecy wherever feasible.

In democratic societies which emphasize the rights of individuals, power in organizations cannot be exercised effectively without enlisting the co-operation of subordinates. Even low-level workers can paralyse a system by refusing to exercise discretion.

For a number of reasons, the exercise of power is met by conformity most of the time. From infancy on, we learn that conformity is rewarded (and deviance punished); organizations expend a lot of resources to recruit the "right" people, who will "fit in." The fit between organization and individual is fine-tuned by formal and informal socialization within the organization.

Despite these efforts, conflict can never be eliminated. Since organizations are the major repositories of power within society, conflict revolves around the distribution of this power. In some settings, the inevitability of conflict is recognized and mechanisms are instituted to deal with it.

How to exercise power in ways that fulfil the organization's goals, as well as those of its members, is a major component of leadership. Leaders must deal with constant dilemmas because, as mentioned earlier, these goals frequently do not coincide. It is therefore hardly surprising that "good" leaders are a rare breed. Numerous studies have failed to identify the exact combination of personal characteristics and leadership style that will be successful in all situations.

While organizations cannot be analysed merely by studying their members, they are comprised of individuals whose experiences and motivations help to redefine the organization itself. People in different hierarchical positions perceive and experience organizations differently. Working at Loblaws is a different experience for the president, for the manager of a store, and for a cashier.

Individuals interact with organizations not only as workers, but also as clients. At some time, all of us deal with hospitals, government agencies, and private sector corporations such as stores, banks, or insurance companies. Most of these interactions are asymmetrical, because the organizations command greater power and more resources.

Concentration of power means that organizations have a major impact on society as a whole. Tastes in food, in music, or in clothes are shaped by what is available, and by the ways in which these goods are portrayed in the media. Choice is constrained because of limited variety in product or service.

The flow of high-level personnel between public and private sector organizations militates against stringent enforcement of legislation that controls how corporations act and interact with one another. Homogeneity of these elites facilitates giving corporate interests favourable consideration in public policies.

Most research has been carried out on large-scale hierarchical organizations, so that knowledge of smaller and less stratified organizations is only beginning to accumulate.

ASSIGNMENTS

Do one or more of the following assignments, as instructed by your professor.

1 Visit two fast food restaurants in the same neighbourhood. List any differences you notice that might reflect different organizational cultures — for example, the treatment of clients, cleanliness of the premises, visual attractiveness of the food. Why is it important for you as a researcher that both restaurants be in the same neighbourhood?

2 Examine each of the barriers to effective communication described in this chapter. Can you think of (a) situations in which you have been involved where one or more of these barriers impeded communication? (b) situations that would contradict what has been said about these barriers?

3 At the beginning of this chapter, you made a list of the organizations with which you were involved over the period of a week. Review the chapter. Wherever we have given examples of organizations to illustrate a point, substitute an organization from your own list. Explain why each substitution is appropriate.

4 Authors of textbooks are not infallible, nor can they be all-inclusive. Our discussion of organizations has largely focused on corporations and large-scale public bureaucracies. Consider a small organization (for example, a club) with which you are familiar. In what ways would our discussion regarding power, leadership, decision-making, and communications have to be modified to explain how your organization works?

5 Imagine that you have worked as a clerk in a large corporation for a number of years. You are being offered a first-level supervisory position, with opportunities for further promotions if you perform well and are willing to upgrade your education or training. Explain why you would or would not accept the position.

SUGGESTED READINGS

J. Callwood, *Twelve Weeks In Spring* (Toronto: Lester and Orpen Dennys, 1986). Not all organizations exist on a "relatively continuing basis," nor are they all large and hierarchical. Callwood describes how sixty individuals organized themselves to provide home care for an elderly woman with terminal cancer. In fact, this *ad hoc* organization was created precisely because Margaret Frazer dreaded the idea of dying in the impersonal environment of a large hospital.

L.R. Gallese, *Women Like Us* (New York: Morrow, 1985). 1975 was the first year in which women constituted 10 percent of the students in the Harvard MBA program. Gallese interviewed the 82 female graduates from 1981–3 to find out what had attracted them to the program, how they felt about their experiences in it, and to what degree their aspirations and expectations had been realized.

Overall, Gallese found that even these "elite" women were neither as ambitious nor as successful as men with the same backgrounds. Nevertheless, as a group they appeared satisfied that they had gone to the Harvard Business School and "that they had taken the risk to reach for their dreams" (p. 252).

L. Iacocca, *Iacocca* (Toronto: Bantam, 1984). Iacocca is a stunning example of the American Dream come true. The son of Italian immigrants, he became an engineer, won a scholarship for advanced study at Princeton, and began working for Ford in 1946. He rose to the presidency, but was fired by Henry Ford in 1978. Iacocca was not unemployed for long; he became chairman of Chrysler and played a major role in restoring the moribund company to robust health.

The book is interesting and entertaining but, remember, it is written from Iacocca's perspective. Others might interpret his actions and the events surrounding them quite differently.

M. O'Malley, *Hospital* (Toronto: Macmillan of Canada, 1986). O'Malley is an investigative journalist who has turned to freelance writing. His study of Toronto General Hospital is not a sociological one. Rather, it offers a bird's-eye view of how the many parts of the hospital function — from the emergency department to the operating theatre, from plant maintenance to the administrator's office.

By personalizing each vignette, O'Malley raises our awareness of the *people* who make up the vast organizational complex known as Toronto General Hospital.

T.J. Peters and **R.H. Waterman, Jr.,** *In Search of Excellence* (New York: Harper and Row, 1984). At a time when the lustre seems to have worn off North American companies, and when they are under siege from foreign competition, Peters and Waterman set out to find excellent companies, and to isolate the characteristics that make them excellent. The authors discovered that such firms believe in and encourage willingness to experiment, employee commitment to the organization and to its clients, and open communication between both management and staff and between the company and its clients.

Furthermore, "the excellent companies seem to abound in distinctly individual techniques that counter the normal tendency toward conformity and inertia" (p. 121).

R. Townsend, *Further Up The Organization: How To Stop Management From Stifling People And Strangling Productivity* (New York: Knopf, 1984). The title conveys the flavour of Townsend's book. He advocates the elimination of such corporate "sacred cows" as "assistants to," central purchasing departments, and reports couched in esoteric language that displays the sophistication of the authors, but often makes the documents incomprehensible to those who are supposed to be guided by them.

7

In the heyday of colonialism, a popular British poet wrote for his compatriots:

Take up the White Man's burden—
Send forth the best ye breed—
Go bind your sons to exile
To serve your captives' need;
To wait in heavy harness,
On fluttered folk and wild—
Your new-caught, sullen peoples,
Half-devil and half-child. . . .

Take up the White Man's burden—
The savage wars of peace—
Fill full the mouth of Famine
And bid the sickness cease,
And when your goal is nearest
The end for others sought
Watch sloth and heathen Folly
Bring all your hopes to nought. . . .

From "The White Man's Burden"
by Rudyard Kipling

Considering the problem of filling the vast prairies of the new nation of Canada with economically productive immigrants who would work the land, Minister Clifford Sifton considered eastern Europeans ideal:

''I think,'' he [Sifton] said ''a stalwart peasant in a sheepskin coat, born on the soil, whose forefathers have been farmers for ten generations, with a stout wife and a half dozen children is good quality'' (Lower 1977, 427).

In the 1930s, Director of Immigration Frederick Charles Blair explained his vehement opposition to Jewish immigration:

''I suggested recently to three Jewish gentlemen with whom I am well acquainted, that it might be a very good thing if they would call a conference and have a day of humiliation and prayer, which might profitably be extended for a week or more, where they would honestly try to answer the question of why they are so unpopular almost everywhere. . . . I often think that instead of persecution it would be far better if we more often told them frankly why many of them are unpopular. If they would divest themselves of certain of their habits I am sure they could be just as popular in Canada as our Scandinavians. . . . Just because Jewish people would not understand the frank kind of statements I have made in this letter to you, I have marked it confidential'' (Abella and Troper 1982, 9).

A character in the novel *A Gathering of Old Men* reflects on the experience of returning to Louisiana after serving overseas in World War I:

''I was the only man from this parish ever fit with the 369th,'' Coot said. He didn't even look at Mapes. He was over by the garden fence, looking down the quarters toward the fields. ''The 369th was a all-colored outfit. You couldn't fight side by side with these here white folks then. You had to get your training in France, take orders from French officers. They trained us good, and we helt our ground. Boy Houser, Minnycourt, Champagne — we helt our ground. We got decorated, kissed on the jaw — all that. And I was proud as I could be, till I got back home. The first white man I met, the very first one, one of them no-English-speaking things off that river, told me I better not ever wear that uniform or that medal again no matter how long I lived. He told me I was back home now, and they didn't cotton to no nigger wearing medals for killing white folks. That was back in World War One. And they ain't change yet—not a bit. Look what happened to Curt's boy when he come home from World War Two. Because they seen him with that German girl's picture, they caught him — and all y'all remember what they did to him with that knife. Korea — the same thing (Gaines 1983, 103-4).

We begin this chapter with passages expressing attitudes toward members of minority groups. Such generalizations ignore individual differences, but provide the basis for the ways in which individual members of the group are perceived and treated.

Each of the groups referred to above has one or more characteristics perceived as negative. These negative views may, in varying degrees, continue to be held. Yet today, at least in North America, it is no longer socially acceptable to declare such sentiments publicly, much less officially, nor to act openly on them.[1] It is precisely because biased attitudes and behaviour have tended to go underground that it is important to recognize the ways in which they persist and continue to shape the experiences of groups and their individual members.

Biased attitudes can be defined as **prejudice** (literally "pre-judgement") based on **stereotypes**, which are generalizations about categories of people based on beliefs that are validated by emotion rather than by reason. Stereotypes are often shared with members of one's particular reference group and are resistant to modification: conflicting evidence is explained away as the "exception proving the rule." Attitudes that involve stereotypes often lead to behaviour that involves **discrimination**, "the unequal treatment of individuals or groups on the basis of some, usually categorical, attribute, such as racial, ethnic, religious, or social-class membership" (Theodorson and Theodorson 1969, 115).

It should be noted that prejudice and stereotypes can be positive or negative. An example of a positive stereotype is the perception of the Dutch as being extremely clean (hence the brand of scouring powder called Dutch Cleanser). However, in this chapter we focus on groups that have been negatively stereotyped, namely minorities.

DEFINING "MINORITIES"

In defining a **minority**, we have made use of Kallen's concept (1982, 109–10). A minority is a social category, within a society:

- that is defined by the majority as incompetent, inferior, abnormal, or dangerous;
- whose members experience "categorical" (as a group) and "systemic" (rooted in the way institutions and organizations are structured) discrimination by the majority, thus being restricted in or denied fundamental human rights;
- whose members are to some degree denied political, economic, and/or social power and human dignity;
- and that comes to occupy a disadvantaged and stigmatized position in society.[2]

Notice the differences between this sociological definition and conventional usage. In the latter, "minority group" describes a group that is numerically smaller than another group or less than half of the whole. For instance, a political party that is a minority in Parliament is one that has fewer seats than some other party. The sociological definition we are using does not refer to numbers; rather, it draws attention to the relative standing of different groups and the ways in which they interact. The very concept of a minority group that is discriminated against implies the existence of another group or groups that enjoy disproportionate power and access to desired goods and services. Such a **majority** or dominant group may be a small numerical minority. Whites in South Africa are a dramatic example.

Power is pivotal to understanding majority/minority relationships. According to Kallen, the majority exercises "the greatest degree of political, economic, and social power in the society and [is] able to control the life destinies of minorities" (1982, 110). This ability of the majority to define laws, values, and informal norms leads the minority to experience some degree of "oppression (denial of political power), neglect (denial of economic power), and/or discrimination (denial of social power and human dignity)" (1982, 1).

Once the minority status of a group becomes entrenched in the social structure, the ability of the group's members to manipulate their own fate is constrained. If the group's access to educational and occupational opportunities is restricted, individuals find it very difficult to get ahead. Moreover, minority status may set in motion a **self-fulfilling prophecy**, which is:

> *a belief regarding a social situation, which, because one believes it and one acts upon it, actually manifests itself as truth, further strengthening the belief. If, for example, an outgroup is believed to be hostile, and if people act as though it were hostile, the outgroup will most likely show hostility in response (Theodorson and Theodorson 1969, 375).*

The group's members internalize negative stereotypes of themselves, thereby adding internal barriers to external ones.

In the past, sociologists have usually focused on minorities in terms of racial and ethnic groups, subjects that are still of particular interest in pluralistic societies, such as Canada and the United States. A considerable literature has accumulated, for example, on the experience of the black racial minority in the United States. Also of much interest, with respect to treatment of ethnic minorities, have been differences, both in policy and ideology, between the United States and Canada. The Americans have pushed for quick assimilation—a melting pot—while Canadians have promoted slower assimilation and a multicultural society—a cultural mosaic. (These contrasting concepts and the reality of their application are considered later in this chapter; also refer back to Chapter 4 on stratification.)

Although in Canada, relationships among ethnic groups—specifically between the French and the English—have been pivotal, we examine racial groups first because their minority status is visible and permanent (at least in the short run and in the absence of continuing intermarriage) and because they have suffered the most severe discrimination.

In addition, we look at some groups you may not have thought of as minority groups. During the last 20 years or so, sociologists have become increasingly aware of minorities other than those based on race and ethnicity. Women, children, the aged, the disabled, and homosexuals are social categories that have been subjected to varying degrees of discrimination. Human-rights legislation, and events such as the Year of the Child and the Year of the Disabled, have been designed to improve the lot of people in the particular categories. Accordingly, in this chapter we will widen our scope beyond race and ethnic groups to include a brief examination of the poor and the aged.[3] For a discussion of three other groups that fit the definition of minority (alcoholics, disabled, gays/lesbians), see Kallen (1989).

HOMOSEXUAL RIGHTS: A MODERATE MAJORITY ACCEPTS GAYS

By Nora Underwood

On election night in the Vancouver-area riding of Burnaby-Kingsway, the newly re-elected MP, New Democrat Svend Robinson, acknowledged a thunderous ovation from 400 supporters and declared, "I share this victory with my brothers and sisters, with lesbians and gay men across this land." Robinson's election in the ethnically diverse working-class party stronghold marked the first time that a publicly declared homosexual had been elected to Parliament. The development came at a time when Canada's estimated 2.5 million homosexuals have become increasingly vocal and, according to the annual *Maclean's*/Decima poll, when Canadians are in a mood to accept homosexuals in politics or at work. But there were reservations among the 1,500 respondents about homosexuals in three professions: teaching, medicine and dentistry.

On the political front, respondents were asked what they would do if they found out that a senior politician in their party was a homosexual. Fully 76 per cent said that they would "leave things as they are," 12 per cent said that they would work to remove the politician, and 10 per cent said that they would join another party. As for discovering that an employee was a homosexual, 82 per cent said that they would leave things as they were. Typical of such respondents was Carol Ferguson, 44, who owns a catering business in Parry Sound, Ont., and has two adopted children, aged 14 and 18. She told *Maclean's* in a follow-up interview that she considers herself to be tolerant of homosexuals. "I feel that it is their life," declared Ferguson. "They don't tell me how to live my life, and I don't tell them how to live theirs. Who am I to judge?"

A significant minority of poll respondents, however, did express concern about homosexuals who teach their children or serve as their doctors or dentists. Thirty-five per cent of those polled said that if they discovered their child's teacher was a homosexual, they would either try to remove the teacher or move their child to another class. An even larger number — 44 per cent —

claimed that they would take similar action if their doctor or dentist were a homosexual. But in all three instances, more of those respondents said that they would opt for a more moderate course rather than seeking removal of the professional: 19 per cent would move their child to another class, and 39 per cent would change their doctor or dentist.

Experts said that they were not surprised by the results of the poll. Richard Burzynski, executive director of the Ottawa-based Canadian AIDS Society, said that because AIDS has become closely linked with the homosexual community — despite its increasing spread to intravenous drug users — there is a tangible rise in discrimination against homosexuals. For his part, Toronto lawyer Peter Maloney, who has a very large homosexual clientele, believes that many people use AIDS to justify their irrational prejudices. Said Maloney: "More people rationalize their feelings by talking about AIDS, because it's no longer acceptable to talk in negative stereotypical images."

Still, in the follow-up interviews, many poll respondents cited AIDS — especially in the area of health care—as the reason for their fears. Respondent Katherine Reed, a 25-year-old retail manager in Halifax, told *Maclean's* that she would be concerned about having a homosexual doctor or dentist. Said Reed: "I wouldn't want a homosexual doctor or dentist for the obvious reason that they have closer contact with your body and bodily fluids during an examination." But in all other respects, she added, she is open-minded about different lifestyles. Declared Reed: "Who you prefer to have as your lover is your choice."

Karl Hartig agreed with many poll respondents. Hartig teaches technical and vocational subjects to students in grades 11 and 12 in the Edmonton suburb of Sherwood Park and says that he sees no harm in having a homosexual teacher in the classroom. "As long as he sticks to his teaching, there's no problem," said the father of six. But Hartig voiced concerns about homosexual health care workers. Added Hartig: "I would change my doctor or dentist because I am in intimate physical contact with him."

In general, answers to the questions on homosexuality differed notably according to age of the respondents. Older respondents — especially those 65 and over—voiced a greater measure of concern about homosexuality. Only 41 per cent of those over 65 said that they would not take any action against a homosexual teacher, compared wth 72 per cent between the ages of 40 and 44, and 71 per cent of the 30- to 34-year-olds. Similar findings emerged on the question of a homosexual employee: 32 per cent of those 65 and older said that they would replace the person, compared with only 10 per cent of respondents between the ages of 30 and 34.

Concern also appeared to be directly linked with the respondents' education. Of those with university education, 71 per cent said that they had no significant concerns about a homosexual teacher, compared with 54 per cent with some high-school education and only 43 per cent of respondents with elementary school. Similarly, 87 per cent of the postsecondary group said that they would do nothing if they discovered that an employee was homosexual, compared with 65 per cent of respondents with an elementary-school education.

Attitudes about homosexuality also varied according to the gender and political affiliation of the repondents. Sixty-four per cent of female respondents said that they would continue to go to a homosexual doctor or dentist, compared with only 48 per cent of men polled. Similarly, 82 per cent of women said that they would continue to support a party in which a senior politician was homosexual, compared with 71 per cent of men. Of those who said that they identified with the NDP, 83 per cent said that a homosexual politician would not change their support for their party, compared with 72 percent of Conservatives and 78 per cent of Liberals.

New Democrat Robinson received the backing of leader Edward Broadbent after Feb. 29, when he publicly declared that he is a homosexual. As a result, Robinson — who was a grand marshal on Lesbian and Gay Pride Day in Toronto in June — has given homosexual-rights activists their first high-profile political representation. And Robinson, 36, does not appear to have suffered for his admission. Indeed, in the Nov. 21 election, he beat Conservative John Bitonti by a comfortable margin of more than 7,000 votes.

RACIAL MINORITIES

A racial group comprises people who share physical characteristics, such as skin- and eye-pigmentation (see Exhibit 7.1). Many physical scientists voice serious doubts as to whether the concept of **race** is a useful device for sorting human beings, since there are no pure races and since so much overlap in characteristics exists. Social scientists point out, however, that scientific validity aside, people do use race as a major criterion for sorting other people, and thus sociologists must deal with the concept.

By definition, racial groups constitute *visible* minorities. Therefore, differences from the majority group cannot disappear, even if the minority-group member is prepared to assimilate into the dominant culture. Talking about this dilemma, David Suzuki likened his own Japanese-Canadian group to bananas, "yellow on the outside, but white on the inside." In other words, members of a racial minority may act and think like the dominant group, but they remain physically different.

All skin colours are represented in Canadian society today: native peoples, orientals, and blacks. Each is sharply subdivided along tribal or national (ethnic) lines, but other people often see only the physical characteristics of race and do not realize the difference between, say, Chinese and Koreans or Haitians and Jamaicans. During the 1970s and 1980s, aided by changes in immigration laws, the percentage of non-white immigration increased markedly. Exhibit 7.1 documents this increase:

EXHIBIT 7.1

PERCENT DISTRIBUTION OF IMMIGRANTS TO CANADA, BY ETHNO-RACIAL-RELIGIOUS GROUP AND DECADE, BEFORE 1901 TO 1971–1980

Ethno-Racial-Religious Group

	Before 1901 #	1901–10	1911–20	1921–30	1931–40	1941–50	1951–60	1961–70	1971–80
Asian	5.6	1.8	2.1	.7	.8	.6	1.7	9.1	29.2
Chinese	4.2	.6	1.7	.4	0*	.5	1.4	3.2	7.6
East Indian	.3	.3	0*	0*	.2	.1	.2	2.4	7.4
Japanese	1.2	.8	.4	.3	.6	0*	.1	.3	.5
Vietnamese	*	*	*	*	*	*	*	*	3.6
Black	.2	0*	.1	.1	.1	.1	.3	4.2	11.5
British	53.5	40.9	39.1	40.9	40.6	41.2	25.8	22.9	12.8
Central & So. Am.	*	*	*	*	*	*	*	*	6.7
Czechoslovak	*	0*	.1	2.3	3.7	1.1	.4	.3	.3
Dutch	.3	.3	.4	.9	.6	6.3	7.1	1.5	1.0
Filipino	*	*	*	*	*	*	*	*	1.4
Finnish	*	.7	.6	1.4	.3	.2	1.0	.4	.2
French	2.0	1.0	.7	.4	.7	1.3	2.1	3.0	1.4
German	6.7	1.2	1.1	5.9	3.0	3.2	14.3	4.4	1.5

SOURCE: Statistics Canada.

Herberg comments further on changes in these immigration patterns:

> *The 1970s brought other major alterations in the immigration flow. Asians came to comprise almost one-third of all immigrants—including a new group, the Vietnamese. There were also some new groups: Central and South Americans, Lebanese and Filipinos. From widely separated parts of the globe, these three new categories together represented almost one-eighth of the immigrants to arrive here between 1971 and 1980. Another group, not new by any means, but much greater in their relative share in the process were blacks (mostly West Indians), who made up almost as great a proportion of immigrants as the British.*

If one uses a rather restrictive definition of "visible minorities" as including only Asians and Blacks (the number and proportion of immigrant Indians and Inuit to Canada have been infinitesimal), then visible minorities represented less than 1% of immigrants before 1960 and only about 13% in the 1960s. In the decade 1971–1980, however, they made up about 41% of all immigrants here. If, moreover, the definition of visible minority is expanded to include Filipinos, Lebanese, and Central and South Americans — as many of these peoples perceive themselves to be in Canada and as many "white" Canadians declare them to be — then the visible minorities made up 54% of immigrants to Canada in the period 1971–1980. Immigration to Canada, then, has become increasingly variegated in the post-war era (Herberg 1989, 72).

THE SOCIAL SIGNIFICANCE OF RACE

Although race is based on physical differences, its significance has been social. Membership in a particular racial group can affect every aspect of an individual's life. Being a Native Indian in Ontario meant, until the 1950s, that one could not buy liquor in a liquor store. Native peoples who wanted to drink had to do so in hotels during licensed hours. Hence, any who became intoxicated did so in public view and were likely to come to the attention of the police, thus inflating statistics on Indian drunkenness. Before civil rights legislation took effect in the 1960s, blacks in the American south had to learn the locations of "colored" washrooms on venturing into a strange city. As recently as 1980, football star Hershel Walker could not attend a banquet celebrating his Georgia high school's football championship because the local country club did not admit blacks.

KINDS OF RACE RELATIONS

Pierre Van den Berghe (1967) has posited two models of race relations: paternalism, typical of the Gemeinschaft, and competition, typical of the Gesellschaft.

PATERNALISM

Paternalistic race relations are typical of pre-industrial societies. Dominant and inferior groups live in close proximity, but interaction between them is ritualized. Rules spelling out appropriate behaviour for each group are generally understood. Only menial tasks are allocated to the inferior group. The colour line is impenetrable, except to those whose physical characteristics allow them to "pass." (Since women from the minority race are deemed sexually available to dominant men, the number of individuals who can "pass" increases over time.)

Members of the dominant group view minority individuals as immature, irresponsible, and impetuous, as children who need the guidance of a father. Like well-behaved children, docile minority-group members are rewarded with kindness and little treats. *Gone with the Wind* depicts an idealized picture of a society based on paternalistic race relations. The minority's acquiescence to their depressed status reduces overt conflict.[4]

Paternalism is not a thing of the past; it continues to play an important part in majority/minority relations today. Consider the way the elderly are treated. Similarly, a paternalistic view of native peoples is embedded in Canadian public policy.

COMPETITION

Competitive race relations are characteristic of modern industrialized societies. Because such systems of **competition** depend on utilizing talent within the society, race can no longer be the exclusive determinant of the individual's place in the division of labour (although it continues to affect one's position). The rules for intergroup relations become fuzzy. Informal mixing is minimized by spatial segregation — for example, black ghettos, whites-only neighbourhoods, and Chinatowns. Dominant-group members view minority individuals with hostility rather than with condescending tolerance, because they are now seen as competitors for such valued goods as education and jobs.

Thus, a continuing struggle is waged between the dominant group, which seeks to defend its privileges, and the minority, which wants its piece of the pie. "Our time has come" was the banner cry of Jesse Jackson, a black candidate for the 1984 Democratic nomination for president of the United States, but in 1988, when Jackson again ran for the nomination, that time had still not come.

NATIVE PEOPLES

Canada's native peoples are the Inuit, the Indians, and the Métis.[5] Because these racial minorities differ so much, umbrella terms such as "native peoples" impose an artificial similarity on quite diverse cultural and linguistic entities. Almost the only thing that Baffin Island Inuit share with members of the Six Nations Reserve near Brantford, Ontario, is that their ancestors inhabited this country long before those of white Canadians. We use the term "native peoples" merely for simplicity, without implying any uniformity among them.

Relations between Europeans and Native Indians were largely peaceful in the beginning, despite the occurrence of conflict when Europeans took sides in Indian tribal hostilities. Peace was advantageous to the Europeans, since the Indians had valuable expertise in trapping and hunting animals whose furs were in great demand in Europe. Systematic oppression of natives became widespread, however, as European settlement expanded. The Indians inhabited vast lands that the whites coveted. Because Native Indians had no conception of private ownership of land, they often did not understand that in signing treaties they were giving up their land forever. Land that Indians did not give up peaceably was taken from them by force. Frequently, it was deemed most efficient simply to kill the Native Indians whose territory was desired.

> *By 1800 the Beothuk population of Newfoundland had reached a critical point. Increased settlement had upset the delicate balance of their nomadic way of life and they were being indiscriminately slaughtered by the whites and their Micmac fur-trade allies, who were encroaching on Beothuk territory. Evidence suggests that about this time three or four hundred Beothuk were herded onto a point of land near their favourite sealing-site and shot down like deer (Such 1973, vii).*

Gradually, but inexorably, the Indians were pushed onto reserves, most of which did not permit self-sufficiency but at least provided escape from imminent starvation. The natural resources of the land had been depleted, often by needless waste as in the case of the Plains buffalo herds. Other employment opportunities were minimal, because many of the reserves were in remote areas far from industrial activity and also because most Indians lacked the education, training, and skills needed in the society Canada was becoming.

In brief, Canada has no reason to feel proud of its record in dealing with the Indians or other native peoples. They fared poorly in the past; their present situation is scarcely better. As Canadians have plunged into native peoples' wilderness, regarding its riches as a prime opportunity for economic growth (in fact, as the "last frontier"), the foundations of native cultures have been undermined by the increased contact with whites, the depletion of their resources, and the disruption of traditional pursuits. Grescoe describes the appalling health conditions among Native Canadians:

> *The wretched physical and mental health of Native Canadians is a national disgrace. Native deaths come quicker. The infant-mortality rate among Canadian Indians and Inuit is four times the national average, and the average age of death for Indians, 42.4 years, is nearly 24 years younger than that of the general population. Among native people between the ages of 20 and 39, death by violence (homicide, suicide, and accidents) is almost four times more common than among whites. And the brief lives they lead are far less healthy. Tuberculosis, supposedly under control, has had a slight resurgence in the North and is still seen in the South: ten new cases of TB appeared last year among the four hundred residents of the house-poor, pollution-rich Stoney Creek reserve near Vanderhoof, British Columbia (Grescoe 1987, 127-8).*

Cultures can be regarded as patterns of living designed to allow group survival in a particular environment. When the environment changes as drastically as it did for Native Canadians, many of these patterns become irrelevant, if not maladaptive. Hunting lore may be painstakingly passed on to one's son, but what use is it when the herds to be hunted have been decimated, and when survival depends on welfare doled out by strangers? The result can only be Durkheim's anomie: internalized values and norms are no longer effective for dealing with the realities of existence. For instance, Chance noted that the Inuit of North Alaska who were engaged in wage labour soon realized that:

> *Their success on the job depends largely on individual rather than co-operative effort and, as such, conflicts with much of their past experience and cultural outlook (1966, 76).*

The manifestations of anomie among native peoples form a litany of woes: a high incidence of drunkenness, fatalism, family violence, and suicide, to name only a few. In urban environments, native peoples are strikingly over-represented among prisoners, welfare recipients, and the homeless.

Along with cultural dislocation, most Native Indians face substandard "shelter" conditions, on and off reserves. Writing in the late 1970s, Krauter and Davis noted:

> *Indian families working for ranchers often live in shacks on the property. Those who are transient labourers in the larger cities usually find housing in slum areas because either landlords will not rent to them elsewhere or they can afford no better. The situation is particularly acute in western urban centres (1978, 20).*

Things are hardly better for the Métis, who continue to exist on the social and economic fringes of western communities. Howard Adams has described what it was like growing up as a Métis in Saskatchewan during the Second World War:

> *Although the majority of the population were Métis—French and Cree—not a single business was owned or operated by us. We remained the casual and unskilled labourers, the depressed and powerless people. The hotel, garage, store, lumberyard, and cafe were all run by white Frenchmen. A few Anglo-Saxons ran other small businesses and had importance and power in the community quite out of proportion to their small numbers. Dotted along the back roads were more half-breed shacks, log and mud houses used as permanent dwellings throughout the year, built to accomodate large families and withstand the severe sub-zero Saskatchewan winters (1979, 23).*

Canadian government policy with regard to native peoples has never been clear-cut. On the one hand, the reserve system was used to deal with the Indian "problem," presumably in the hope that problems that are made "invisible" would disappear permanently. (The Inuit were already "invisible," since there were relatively few of them and they lived in remote northern areas.) On the other hand, there was the desire to assimilate the native peoples into Canadian society. An important means to this end was residential schools, operated by Christian denominations but supported by government funding. In a case study of one such institution, *The School at Mopass*, King found that the school sought to strip students of their traditional ways but did not provide them with the social and academic attributes to make it in mainstream society.

> *The fact that children always wait for directives, even in the most routine situations, is somehow not connected by Whitemen with the fact that these children are never encouraged to make personal decisions or choices among real alternatives. It is taken as prima facie evidence that directives are needed. "They're only children; even their parents are just like children in so many ways . . . " is a common theme. "You have to tell them what is right." Over a period of many days, such directives constitute the totality of verbal communication from most adults to the children (1967, 75–6).*

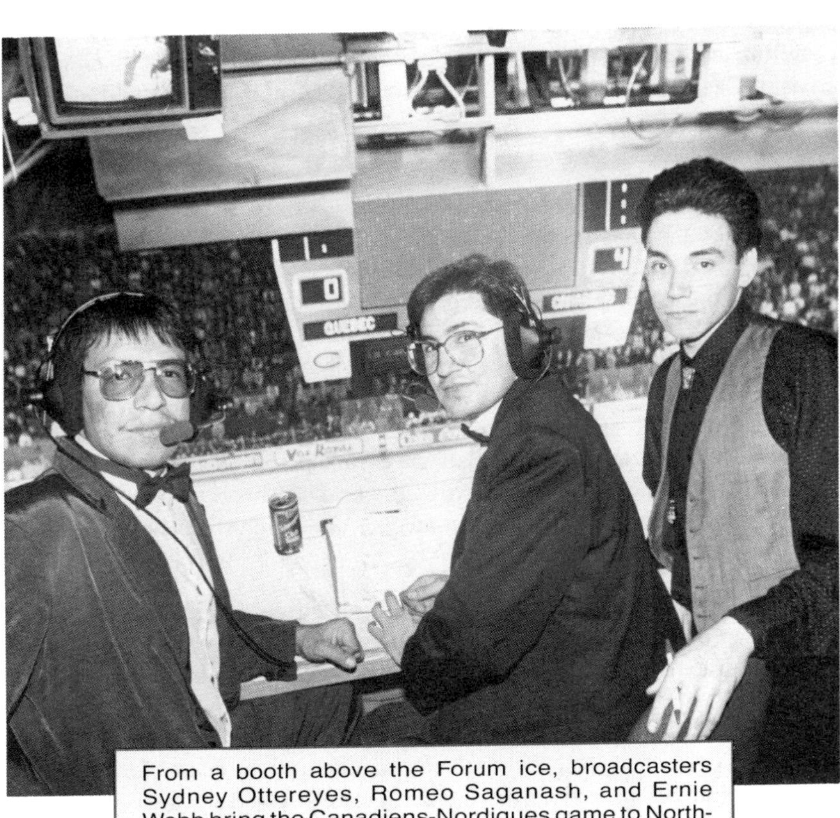

From a booth above the Forum ice, broadcasters Sydney Ottereyes, Romeo Saganash, and Ernie Webb bring the Canadiens-Nordiques game to Northern Quebec radio listeners in the Cree language.

In other words, the view of Indian children (and of Indians generally) as needing constant, detailed directions means they are given little opportunity to use their own initiative. Hence, self-direction remained unpractised. The prophecy that Indians could not act autonomously thus becomes self-fulfilling.

Today such self-fulfilling prophecies are being challenged by the emerging militancy of native peoples. The example of the civil rights movement and of the new phase of the women's liberation movement during the 1960s sparked the mobilization of other minority groups that were no longer willing to accept inferior status. One important consequence is that Native Canadians no longer necessarily accept the dominant group's definition of various situations. Native-rights movements are seeking a rebirth of aboriginal cultures. They are facilitating this change by taking control of their schools, by insisting on self-administration of government funds allocated to them, and by pressing for cash settlements which they claim to be due under various treaties. Furthermore, native peoples are questioning whether industrial and technological development of the north would really be to their benefit in the long run. They are also asserting the right to reclaim land in some areas of Canada — for example, the Haida in British Columbia and the Inuit in Labrador.

In the 1970s, the quest for new sources of energy fostered pressure for the construction of a pipeline to transport arctic gas southward. For the first time since colonization, native peoples, in collaboration with environmental conservationists, were able to exert effective counterpressure. The result was the appointment of the Berger Commission, whose report was titled *Northern Frontier: Northern Homeland* (Berger 1977). Although its chief recommendation — that no construction should be started for ten years — was ignored, the hearings themselves achieved a breakthrough in race relations in Canada. Indians and Inuit were able to voice their concerns in their own languages, in their own communities, to whites in positions of authority who were willing to listen. (This is the kind of approach we described in Chapter 1, in the section on "The Feminist Challenge.")

As is often the case with groups categorized under a broad label, native peoples are divided by the conflicting goals of subgroups. Yet, they have a strong and growing awareness of their shared identity and common interests as a minority group. Self-assertion has reversed their former invisibility. Native peoples remain a discriminated-against minority, but they are no longer a passive one. However, as Ponting points out, their ability to command resources and to force change is extremely limited. In view of the Canadian state's reluctance to accede to rapid change, Ponting predicts that native peoples will resort increasingly to such tactics as civil disobedience, international embarrassment, and a selective use of the courts (1988, 640).

NATIVE BANDS SIGN MUTUAL DEFENCE TREATY

By Canadian Press

Some of Canada's most militant Indian bands have signed a mutual defence pact after a year of confrontations with authorities which—as one native chief put it yesterday — are "tearing us to pieces."

The treaty, signed Thursday by nine bands from across the country, calls on signatories to send reinforcements when requested and to support each other in endeavors such as making complaints about the Canadian government to the United Nations.

The signing was announced here at the annual meeting of the Assembly of First Nations, the umbrella group for Canadian aboriginal people.

"We can't always sit back and watch the other side tear us to pieces," said Alberta Lubicon Cree Chief Bernard Ominayak, who pushed for the treaty.

Land claim

The Lubicon, who have been trying to settle a land claim in northern Alberta for 50 years, watched helplessly as the RCMP dismantled a barricade they erected last fall on the land they claim.

Asked if the defence treaty marks a step on the road to armed confrontation with authorities, Ominayak said: "I wouldn't recommend to anybody we go in that direction, but it's hard to say where it could go."

Quebec Indian Affairs Minister Raymond Savoie was less than keen about the treaty.

"These things have to be hammered out at the negotiating table, not hammered out with kids and gun-toting individuals on a line somewhere," he said.

Savoie had to negotiate personally with rifle-carrying Mohawk Indians last year after they blockaded a bridge leading from Montreal to their reserve to protest an RCMP raid over the alleged illegal sale on the reserve of duty-free cigarettes.

Grand Chief Matthew Coon-Come, representing Quebec's 10,000 Cree, said he signed the treaty because "all avenues have been exhausted" with the government.

"The federal and provincial governments continue to renege on their obligations, continue to authorize forestry and mining operations on our land," he said.

Mass arrests

"We tried the courts, to no avail. The government is not sincere. They just want to give the impression of negotiating."

The treaty was also signed by Chief Daniel Ashini of the Labrador Innu, whose band members were arrested en masse in September for blocking a runway used for low-level military flights the Indians say disrupt their lifestyle.

However, Denis Ross, a Montagnais band chief, said the defence treaty concept of sending reinforcements to the scene of a confrontation would not have helped a 10-hour standoff with police on his reserve last month.

At Les Escoumins, a village 250 kilometres northeast of Quebec City, provincial police used tear gas on 30 Indian demonstrators blocking the exit of RCMP officers who had seized band documents as part of a fraud investigation.

Ross said the band knew it was more a symbolic blockade, set up in an effort to assert sovereignty over the reserve, and that reinforcements from other tribes would not have changed the outcome.

ORIENTALS

Historically, relations between whites and orientals in Canada have clearly fallen into the competitive model of race relations outlined by Van den Berghe. The dominant group used its political and economic power to maintain lucrative and prestigious activities for itself. Opposition to such monopoly was minimized because of widespread prejudice based on negative stereotypes. Hence, for many whites, attitudes of prejudice against orientals were consonant with discriminatory behaviour.[6] Illustration can be provided with a brief history of the experience of Canada's two main oriental immigrant groups, the Chinese and the Japanese.[7]

THE CHINESE

The first Chinese are believed to have come to Canada during the Fraser River gold rush of the 1850s. Once any given mine was exhausted, some returned home, but most remained in British Columbia and found work as domestics, gardeners, and laundrymen. When the Canadian Pacific started construction of the trans-Canada railway, it petitioned the federal government to import the labour needed to work in the unpopulated west; about 17,000 Chinese were brought here. Since only males were permitted to come and relationships with white women were sanctioned severely, the government constantly reiterated that their stay was meant to be temporary. However, because they had received only meagre wages, most of which had to be used to pay for food and board, many of these workers had insufficient savings to pay the return fare to China when the railroad had been completed; nor could they afford to bring over wives and children from China. The Canadian Pacific and the federal government were unwilling to pay the return fares, though reduced rates were available and men over age 60 were transported at government expense.

In the 1870s and 1880s, some 17,000 Chinese labourers were "imported" to help build the Trans-Canada railway in the unpopulated West.

Most of the Chinese stayed around Vancouver, where they formed a pool of cheap labour. In the absence of government programs, such as unemployment insurance or welfare, they had to accept whatever wages employers chose to offer. The Chinese were, therefore, regarded as unfair competition by white workers, who reacted vehemently. In 1878, the whites formed the Workingman's Protective Association, and, in a related move, "respectable" citizens united against the "oriental threat" and succeeded in having a $10 annual cue tax levied on every Chinese male over age 18 who wore long hair. Soon the federal government, too, responded to anti-Chinese feeling by imposing a head tax on every Chinese person who entered Canada.

Although these taxes escalated steadily, they did not manage to halt Chinese immigration. The Chinese Immigration Act in 1923 did halt immigration. Meanwhile, Orientals, both Chinese and Japanese, had been barred from voting in provincial and municipal elections in the western provinces. In 1919, this ban was extended to federal elections on the basis that anyone barred from voting in provincial elections because of race should not vote federally either.

Disenfranchisement affected employment opportunities. In British Columbia, for example, orientals could not obtain a license to sell liquor or practise law or pharmacy, because entrance to these professions was limited to those who would be eligible to vote when they attained the age of majority. The Japanese were excluded from teaching in British Columbia, and orientals could not perform work under public works contracts (Davis and Krauter 1978).

Such blatant discrimination is no longer legal in Canada, and the emphasis in immigration legislation has shifted from racial and national origins to the educational and occupational qualifications of applicants. Many Chinese have taken advantage of the more liberal immigration policies instituted in 1967.[8] Once in this country, they have tended to take advantage of educational opportunities. At the time of the 1971 census, 49 percent of young (19- to 24-year-old) Asian Canadians, of whom the Chinese form a significant proportion, were in full-time school attendance (Richmond and Kalbach 1980, 271). The rising educational standard is reflected in a changing occupational distribution, with more Chinese in administrative and professional positions. This does not mean that prejudice has disappeared, but it does mean that Chinese-Canadians, both immigrant and Canadian-born, are now able to fight discrimination more effectively than they could in the past. For a well-documented study of the effects of institutional racism, see Li's *The Chinese in Canada* (1988).

THE JAPANESE

For much of their history in Canada, which began about 1885, the Japanese were subject to somewhat less discrimination than the Chinese, in part because there were fewer Japanese here and in part because they were represented in this country by articulate organizations, and enjoyed some protection by the Japanese government. This situation changed drastically with the outbreak of the Second World War, particularly following the Japanese attack on the American navy base in Pearl Harbor and the occupation of Hong Kong (in which a large number of Canadians were taken prisoner).

Almost all the Japanese in Canada had settled on the west coast. In 1942, most Canadian residents of Japanese origin, regardless of citizenship or place of birth, were removed to camps in the Canadian interior, some as far east as Ontario. There they spent the rest of the war. In *Obasan*, Joy Kogawa (1981) has hauntingly portrayed the experience of family members torn from their home and separated from each other.

Depriving citizens of all legal rights was officially justified on the basis of national security. However, longstanding prejudice against the Japanese and their "clannish, foreign ways" had prepared the ground for general acceptance of such action. It is also significant that by 1942 many Japanese had established successful market-gardening and fishing enterprises, the forced sales of which, it is said, benefited white business people.

In 1942, most Canadian residents of Japanese origin, regardless of citizenship or place of birth, were removed to camps in the Canadian interior, where they spent the rest of the war. These children are being escorted to the infamous Hastings Park camp.

The experiences of 1942 and 1945 changed the settlement patterns of Japanese Canadians. Many did not return to the west coast, and they have avoided clustering in cities in which they have settled. Those born since the war have rates of out-marriage so high as to threaten the survival of the Japanese as a distinct group in Canadian society; that few Japanese have immigrated to Canada since 1945 increases the likelihood of this occurring.

In many ways, the Japanese have fared well in Canada since the war. The Brazilians have a saying that "money blanches" — dark-skinned individuals become quite acceptable if they are rich enough. A somewhat similar process has been operative in the case of Japanese people in Canada. Their image has been enhanced by Japan's spectacular economic success in recent decades. Japan is now a major player in the world economy and one of Canada's important trading partners; the establishment of subsidiaries of Japanese corporatons in the West is eagerly pursued. On the other hand, the ability of Japanese industry to outperform North

American firms has heightened economic competition and, with it, awareness of the "we/they" dichotomy.

ACKNOWLEDGEMENT

As a people, Canadians commit themselves to the creation of a society that ensures equality and justice for all, regardless of race or ethnic origin.

During and after World War II, Canadians of Japanese ancestry, the majority of whom were citizens, suffered unprecedented actions taken by the Government of Canada against their community.

Despite perceived military necessities at the time, the forced removal and internment of Japanese Canadians during World War II and their deportation and expulsion following the war was unjust. In retrospect, government policies of disenfranchisement, detention, confiscation and sale of private and community property, expulsion, deportation and restriction of movement, which continued after the war, were influenced by discriminatory attitudes. Japanese Canadians who were interned had their property liquidated and the proceeds of sale were used to pay for their own internment.

The acknowledgement of these injustices serves notice to all Canadians that the excesses of the past are condemned and that the principles of justice and equality in Canada are reaffirmed.

Therefore, the Government of Canada, on behalf of all Canadians, does hereby:

1) acknowledge that the treatment of Japanese Canadians during and after World War II was unjust and violated principles of human rights as they are understood today;

2) pledge to ensure, to the full extent that its powers allow, that such events will not happen again; and

3) recognize, with great respect, the fortitude and determination of Japanese Canadians who, despite great stress and hardship, retain their commitment and loyalty to Canada and contribute so richly to the development of the Canadian nation.

Brian Mulroney
Prime Minister of Canada

JAPANESE CANADIANS WIN APOLOGY TO "CLEANSE" PAST

By Canadian Press

Here are the highlights of the $291 million compensation package for Japanese Canadians interned during World War II:

☐ About $252 million for tax-free payments of $21,000 to each of the 12,000 survivors;

☐ $12 million to the Japanese Canadian community for educational, social and cultural activities;

☐ $24 million for a new Canadian Race Relations Foundation to foster racial harmony among all racial groups in Canada;

☐ $3 million to the National Association of Japanese Canadians to implement the package. The group will help Ottawa in tracking down survivors, through newspaper advertisements.

The government will also give Canadian citizenship to eligible people of Japanese ancestry who were expelled from Canada or had their citizenship revoked during the war. They were convicted of violations of the War Measures Act and the National Emergency Transitional Powers Act.

BLACKS

In the United States, relations between blacks and whites have been one of the most explosive issues in its history. From its very inception as a nation, the U.S. has had to try and reconcile, on the one hand, an ideology that proclaimed everyone to be entitled to life, liberty, and the pursuit of happiness with the reality of slavery followed by gross, often legally entrenched discrimination against blacks. In a monumental study, Gunnar Myrdal labelled this problem *An American Dilemma*.

In Canada, this dilemma was mitigated by the small number of blacks. Slavery existed here but it never became widespread, in large part because there was no plantation agriculture suited for slave labour. Furthermore, the harsh climate made it expensive to house, feed, and clothe slaves. Canada was still a relatively unpopulated, undeveloped area when the British Parliament passed the Emancipation Act of 1833, abolishing slavery.

During the Revolutionary War of 1775–83 and again in the war of 1812–4, the British promised to free any slaves who escaped from the United States to Canada. These refugees and those who came later by way of the Freedom Railway certainly desired political freedom, but they also needed economic opportunities, which proved sparse. As Krauter and Davis commented, on the pattern of land grants in Nova Scotia,

> *Certainly, in every instance where acreage was granted to both Black and white settlers, Blacks received less. For example, while Blacks were given one-acre lots in Digby, whites were granted from one-hundred to four-hundred acre lots throughout Annapolis County. Moreover, only Blacks who settled in Chedabucto Bay or in Preston township*

> *were not completely segregated. Most of the Black settlements eventually failed; as a result many former slaves, now freed in Canada, continued to work as hired or indentured servants (1978, 42).*

During the 1840s and 1850s, American abolitionists organized the Freedom Railway to help slaves escape, and blacks clustered at its terminal points in Canada. Sizeable settlements were established near Chatham, Ontario and in Nova Scotia. The most famous was Africville, a part of Halifax. This community existed for more than one hundred years, until it was demolished in the 1960s as part of an urban renewal plan. By that time, Africville had become a notorious slum.

The story of Africville is an apt example of a self-fulfilling prophecy. Because blacks were negatively stereotyped, their community was last in line for services from the city. Africville never obtained water or sewage systems, its roads were not paved, and its snow and garbage removal were inadequate. Small wonder, then, that it deteriorated, allowing white Haligonians to cluck their tongues and deplore "the way these people live."

Many American slaves escaped to Canada during the 1840s and 1850s and settled here to live in freedom but in de facto segregation. In 1910, this group of students posed by their school near Chatham, Ontario.

Substandard housing, an inferior and segregated education system, and hence, lack of access to good jobs kept most Africville residents enmeshed in a web of deprivation. In turn, this deprivation made it very difficult to mount an effective campaign for positive change. Clairmont and Magill wrote that:

> *Africville residents were always poor. The historical pattern was that the males worked as labourers on the docks or in small industries and businesses near Africville, and the females worked in low-paid service jobs as domestics in homes or in nearby institutions. Africville residents of Halifax had been petitioning the City for services available to other residents of Halifax since the middle of the nineteenth century, but successes were few (Clairmont and Magill 1974, 62).*

Blacks in Canada remained small in number until well past the Second World War. With liberalization of the Immigration Act in 1967, however, numerous West Indians began to arrive. Since then, factors in the Caribbean such as poverty, unemployment, political unrest, and the lack of opportunities for advancement have remained powerful ''push forces'' for West Indian emigration.

Most West Indian immigrants to Canada have settled in large, urban centres, the majority in Toronto. The 1986 census showed 106,040 individuals living in the area who came from the Caribbean and Bermuda (1986 Census of Canada). Many, possessing limited education and few occupational skills, had been forced to take whatever menial jobs were available. Most also encountered prejudice and discrimination. Many of those who came with expertise, and intellectual and creative skills, have successfully established themselves in Canadian society, even though they too have suffered discrimination.

SOUTH AFRICAN BLACKS TAUGHT FROM CHILDHOOD THAT ''EQUALITY'' IS NOT FOR THEM

By Emil Sher

A black child who reaches adulthood in South Africa can expect a lifespan nine years shorter than a white person's. Hector Petersen never even made it to 15.

He was one of the thousands of students who, 13 years ago today, marched through the dusty streets of Soweto. At stake was the language of instruction in their classrooms: Afrikaans had been imposed in place of English. Fists were raised, stones were thrown. The police opened fire. Hector Petersen was among the first to die.

His death sparked the Soweto uprisings, a popular movement that permanently altered the political landscape of South Africa. The students' anger fuelled countryside protests that continued into the following year. Up to 1,000 people were killed by police, many of them school children.

''Natives will be taught from childhood

that equality with Europeans is not for them,'' Minister of Native Affairs H.F. Verwoerd had declared in 1953, the year that control over black education was transferred from the hands of missionaries to the government. . . .

Last week the South African regime renewed the state of emergency, as it has every year since first declaring it on a regional basis in 1985 and nationally a year later. Police and other authorities will remain immune from prosecution. Government opponents can be detained indefinitely.

Children have cause for fear, considering the legacy of previous states of emergency. According to official figures, 312 youngsters were killed by police from 1984 to 1986. This excludes those run down by police vehicles, those who died in custody and those in the ''independent'' Bantustans, the tribal homelands where many live.

At the same time, 18 000 were arrested on charges arising out of protest activities and a total of 173 000 were in detention pending trial.

Most children arrested are charged with ''public violence.'' This includes everyone from stone-throwers to the nine children between 11 and 16 who were arrested after they chased a soccer ball onto a road.

Police seem to have little patience for conventional approaches to education. When they want to teach a lesson, they prefer a sjambok (leather whip) and a bare back to chalk and a blackboard. A 1987 account in The Johannesburg Star told of police stoning eight naked boys lined against a wall. A hit to the genitals or head was worth 100 points.

Birdshot replaced bullets in the February, 1985, attack on a 7-year-old boy who ventured too closely to a group of youths singing freedom songs and paid dearly for his guilt by association. When the police arrived, he froze while older boys ran off. Doctors later removed 15 pellets from his body.

Some children don't wait for doctors. A 1986 press report told of a doctor who ''knew of children who cut out bullets themselves with penknives, rather than come to the clinic for fear of arrest. Police had raided the clinic and taken the medical records of people treated for gunshot wounds.''

Children detained under the state of emergency face a Pandora's box of tactics. Delegates to the 1987 International Conference on Children, Repression and the Law in South Africa were told of detainees subjected to ''unspeakable conditions and treatment . . . routine but pervasive practices'' that include electric shocks, beatings by fists, sjamboks and rifle butts, severe deprivation of food and sleep, sexual abuse and attempted strangulation and suffocation.

The Detainees Parents' Support Committee (DPSC) — restricted under emergency regulations in February, 1988 — documented the case of a 16-year-old girl, one of seven children accused of burning a policeman's house, who was beaten and blindfolded. ''Then I felt the shocks at the top of my spine. This seemed to go on for about 10 minutes. When this was being done, I was sitting on the floor. While the shock treatment continued, one of the police put his feet on my knees to keep me still.'' She was released after two months.

''Growing pains'' take on a sinister meaning for children who have been detained. The DPSC's list of the psychological consequences of detention include a general loss of interest in life, shattered self-esteem, suicide, psychic numbing, anxiety and fear.

''Some of the children we have seen will never be able to organize their lives adequately,'' the DPSC reports.

Children have phrased it in other ways. ''Life nowadays is like a sick butterfly,'' 12-year-old Bothale writes in Two Dogs And Freedom—Children of the Townships Speak Out. ''To many of us it is not worth living when it is like this. The little kids don't understand why they have been put in jail.''

Perhaps Canada's Prime Minister Brian Mulroney knows something they don't. In 1985 he pledged total sanctions against South Africa if fundamental changes were not made to the apartheid system. There have been no changes. What is he waiting for?

Mr. Mulroney would do well to heed the words of Olof Palme, the late Swedish prime minister: ''A system like apartheid cannot be reformed, it can only be abolished. If the world decides to abolish apartheid, apartheid will disappear.''

It's an idea so pure and simple that it could have come from a child.

RACIAL MINORITIES IN CANADA TODAY

Since 1967, changes in immigration legislation have resulted in a significant increase in visible minorities in Canada generally. In addition to the Chinese and blacks, recent immigrants have included diverse East Indians, such as Pakistanis and Indian nationals, as well as some Koreans and Vietnamese (the ''boat people''). The East Indian group was swelled by an influx of refugees from Uganda following President Amin's expulsion of Asians from that country in 1971. (This event demonstrates that **racism**—discrimination on the basis of race—is not practised only by whites.)

As visible minorities have increased numerically, so have incidents of discrimination, harassment, and outright violence. The Toronto subways, for example, have been the scene of a number of attacks on East Indians. These attacks became sufficiently serious to arouse public concern and spurred the appointment of a task force to study race relations in Metropolitan Toronto. Its findings, reported in 1977, were in line with those of many other studies of racial interaction in North American cities. The initiators of physical attacks against minority-group members tend to be young, male, uneducated, and frequently unemployed. The victims perceive the police as not particularly helpful. The researchers described what happens when the police are called following an incident of vandalism:

> *This particular type of vandalism . . . causes a great deal of ill-will between the minority and the police. When the police arrive at his home, the complainant, because of his fear and anxiety, is often highly excited. The only organization to which he can turn for help is the police. He demands action—the police must do something. At the same time the policeman is exceedingly frustrated. There are no leads to follow and he knows that there is little he can do. He must cope with the very excited civilian who may be extremely critical of him. The consequence is a loss of confidence in the police by the minority on the one hand, and the reinforcement of the police stereotype image of the South Asian as demanding and with high expectations (1977, 133–4).*

Today, more than a decade after this study was conducted, relations between law enforcement agencies and visible minority groups continue to be problematic.

No institution is immune to racism in a racist society. Thus, schools often become vehicles that transmit racism to the next generation. The task force found that many children spoke of nonwhite immigrants as being ''dirty'' and ''smelly'' and as ''taking away our jobs'' (1977, 174). Nonwhite parents perceived the schools as ''de-motivating'' their children by channelling them into vocational rather than academic streams, thus depriving them of opportunities for upward mobility.

By 1986, Canada's nonwhite minorities included approximately 2,219,660 persons and made up 8.8 percent of the population (Statistics Canada 1986). That many Canadians believed race relations to be unsatisfactory was reflected in the establishment, by the Federal Government, in June 1983, of a commitee under the chairmanship of Bob Daudlin. This committee conducted a nationwide investigation into race relations, and provided recommendations for improving relations between nonwhite and white Canadians.

In its 1984 report, *Equality Now*, the committee noted a connection between the depressed economy and curtailed opportunities for visible minorities. This is a particular instance of a general phenomenon. When economic conditions deteriorate, discrimination against out-groups increases as the groups in power make every effort to conserve scarce opportunities for themselves. Since power in Canada is overwhelmingly wielded by whites, visible minorities are given short shrift.

Minorities also furnish ready scapegoats for majority members who suffer economic and social dislocation. This phenomenon is not new. For instance, around the turn of the century, lynchings of blacks in the American south fluctuated with the price of cotton, which was the mainstay of the southern economy. When cotton prices were low, the number of lynchings increased as people vented their frustration and helplessness against the even more helpless blacks.

Across Canada, the Daudlin committee rediscovered discrimination against nonwhites:

> *Visible minorities encounter a variety of systemic discriminatory practices in the workplace. Minority workers are denied access to employment by such recruitment, ''Canadian experience'' criteria and culturally biased testing procedures and interviews. Barriers also exist for advancement and promotion through relegation of the minority persons to low status and low income positions, through seniority policies, and through limited exposure to new job openings (1984, 33).*

On the positive side, the researchers noted several initiatives aimed at remedying this situation. Examples were special programs instituted by Nova, An Alberta Corporation as well as by Hydro Québec, at its James Bay project, to train native peoples for skilled positions.

This overview of the experiences of some visible-minority groups in Canada leads us to conclude that physical attributes, which in themselves have no effect on an individual's character or competence, have resulted in far-reaching negative consequences. Reaction to physical differences is exacerbated by cultural differences, another characteristic of racial minorities.[9] The fact that discriminatory attitudes and practices are defined as a social problem, a state of affairs deemed to be in need of change, inspires some hope that the vicious circle of prejudice will be broken. In the mid-80s, the Commission on Equality made recommendations for modifying institutional practices both to prevent the multiple disadvantages experienced by racial and other minority groups and to compensate for the disadvantages they have faced in the past. This two-pronged strategy of prevention and remedy is referred to as ''**affirmative action**'' (Abella 1984). While the concept is gaining acceptance, its implementation remains highly controversial.

ETHNIC MINORITY GROUPS

Race, as we have noted, refers to a way of classifying human beings according to physical characteristics. In contrast, **ethnicity** distinguishes various cultural categories. Theodorson and Theodorson define an ethnic group as

> *a group with a common cultural tradition and a sense of identity. . . . The members of an ethnic group differ with regard to certain cultural characteristics from the other members of their society. They may have their own language and religion as well as certain distinctive customs. Probably most important is their feeling as a traditionally distinct group (1969, 135).*

In other words, the members of an ethnic group share cultural attributes. These similarities are apparent to others in the society and serve as a basis for categorizing the individuals as belonging to a particular group. For instance, if you see a man in a broad-rimmed, black hat driving a horse and buggy, you likely put him under the rubric of Mennonite (and thereby engage in a form—sometimes a useful one—of stereotyping). Equally important is the subjective dimension of ethnicity. Members of an ethnic group conceive of themselves as being alike and identify with each other: ''We Greeks [or Jews or Québécois] must stick together.'' Indeed, the main function of ethnic associations, such as language schools, social clubs, and publications, is to preserve group traditions while strengthening members' identification with them. For a sociological history of the Mennonite and Amish community in the Waterloo area, see Fretz (1989). See also Baar's study (1983) of Mennonites in the Niagara region.

FRENCH/ENGLISH RELATIONS IN CANADA

When the British North America Act was signed in 1867, the Canadian Constitution remained in Britain. Following several unsuccessful attempts, it was patriated to Canada in 1982, but Quebec refused to become a signatory. The stalemate continued until the 1987 Meech Lake Accord, which restored Quebec to the constitutional fold and recognized it as a distinct society within Canada. The Accord was to be ratified by each province no later than June 1990. If a consensus were not achieved, the agreement would become null and void. (In the United States, the Equal Rights Amendment that guaranteed women and other minority groups certain rights ''died'' when it was not ratified by two-thirds of the 50 states within the stipulated time period.) How did one Canadian province come to see itself as a ''distinct society?''

History books have often referred to the French and the English as Canada's ''founding races.'' This is an erroneous statement, since French and English share membership in the caucasoid race. However, they are (at least technically) distinct ethnic groups, since they differ in language, in traditions, and frequently in religion. The French are overwhelmingly Roman Catholic, whereas most early British settlers belonged to Protestant denominations.[10]

The complexities of French/English relations within Canada are clearly beyond the scope of this book, but some historical background can aid in an understanding of ethnic relations between the two groups in present-day Canadian society.[11] Following the signing of the Treaty of Paris in 1763, most members of the French elite returned to France. The bulk of the population, heavily concentrated in Quebec, carried on their agricultural way of life. Their linguistic and religious rights were guaranteed by the 1774 Quebec Act and eventually entrenched by the British North America Act in 1867.

The clergy were an active force in government. The local parish was, in fact, the basic social-political, as well as religious, unit. The importance of family, land, and church was proclaimed from the pulpit and emphasized by the schools, which were controlled by the Catholic Church (a control that was not completely relinquished until 1964).

As early as the 1830s, high birth rates among the Québécois meant that not everyone could continue working the land. Thus, the children of the habitants had to migrate. During the 19th and early 20th centuries, some were able to duplicate their way of life on Quebec's frontiers—the Gaspé, Lac St-Jean, the Laurentians—and some took up land in the west. Others had to adapt to a more industrialized life in cities and towns dominated by the English: Montreal, Quebec, and other Canadian cities; the burgeoning northern communities of Ontario, such as Sudbury and Timmins; and the factory towns of New England. For most of the migrants to urban areas, the move meant accepting minority status.[12]

John Porter (1965) has argued that Canada's policy of multiculturalism has been a means of maintaining British dominance. This argument is relevant to the French/English question. While the French tilled the land, went to church, and produced children, most of whom received only minimal education, the British group was consolidating its economic power in the industrialized society Canada was becoming. French workers were integrated at the lowest rungs, and a confluence of external and internalized obstacles kept them from going up the ladder. For most, moving up meant having to give up the mother tongue as well as values that placed domestic loyalties ahead of occupational advancement. Discrimination by the British, based on negative stereotypes of French workers and on the wish to monopolize desirable positions, was an important external factor. In a study of "Cantonville," a Quebec textile town, Everett Hughes perceptively analysed this phenomenon:

> *When the subject of French foremen is raised, the answers come in stereotypes, of which these are the common ones: "The French have to be told what to do and therefore cannot be trusted with jobs requiring initiative and the meeting of crises." . . . "They are so jealous of one another that they do not yield to the authority of one of their own number." . . .*
>
> *These clichés become painfully familiar to anyone who talks about this problem in Quebec. . . . It is evident that those who have the power to appoint foremen in Cantonville think that ethnic differences are significant and that the English are superior (1971, 55–6).*

Hughes' observations on language in a predominantly French community are also instructive:

> *The executive and technical language of industry in our community is English. Since, in addition, the persons in authority are English, it is but natural that English should percolate downward among the French workers. The pressure is on the subordinate, whose mother-tongue is French, rather than upon the superior, whose language is English (1971, 82).*

This pattern is typical. Where ethnic groups co-exist in a society, the language of the superior group becomes the dominant one. In the polyglot Austro-Hungarian empire, Poles, Czechs, and Hungarians who wanted to get ahead had to learn German. Knowledge of English was mandatory for ambitious Indians and Africans living under colonial rule; by contrast, many British administrators did not speak a native language.

During the 1950s and 1960s, life changed among the Québécois. They remained attached to their language and to other aspects of their culture, but a world view emerged that focused on individual success rather than on traditional values. This altered orientation in French Canada manifested itself in many ways. Control of education passed from the Catholic Church to the Quebec government. More francophones attended institutions of higher learning. Higher education veered from its classical bent (geared to turning out lawyers, physicians, and theologians) to a more technical one. Members of the emerging stratum were educated, eager for achievement, and aware of the disadvantages francophones suffered in the labour market. They wanted to change this state of affairs, to be "masters in their own house." Their increasing refusal to accept minority status, combined with determination to preserve French culture, created pressure for greater bilingualism both in the federal government and throughout Canada, so that francophones outside Quebec would be able to conduct official business in their own language.[13]

Meanwhile, fears had arisen about the survival of French culture in Quebec itself. Since the British conquest, Canada's francophone population had hovered at about 30 percent of the total, even though the French-speaking group had been confronted with relying on natural increase to maintain its numbers. The percentage remained constant; the strong tendency of immigrants to opt for English was balanced by the high francophone birth rate — and because its birth rate was very high — the well-known "revenge of the cradle." In the 1960s, however, the francophone birth rate dipped sharply as reliable birth-control methods became readily available and Québécois women, less obedient to the dictates of the Catholic Church, became eager to use them.

Moreover, Montreal became home to a flood of immigrants in each postwar decade. A majority chose acculturation into the anglophone group, thus inspiring fear among the francophones that even their own members might receive the message that their children's route to advancement lay in anglicization.

In response to these fears, Quebec passed successively more stringent language laws, aimed at giving primacy to the French language and at forcing immigrants to adopt French rather than English. Ironically, Quebec's insistence on becoming a unilingual francophone province has made anglophones fear becoming a minority that is discriminated against on the basis of language.

When Quebec passed a *Charter of the French Language*, one section of which mandated that "public signs and posters and commercial advertising shall be solely in French,'' Anglophones sought a court declaration that these restrictions violated the *Canadian Charter of Rights and Freedoms* and Quebec's own *Charter of Human Rights and Freedoms*.

The Supreme Court of Canada, in its decision rendered on December 15, 1988, held that Quebec's ''sign-law'' was a breach of its own *Charter of Human Rights and Freedoms*. The Court found that the ''freedom of expression'' guaranteed by Quebec's human rights *Charter* included the right to express oneself in the language of one's choice since language is one of the means by which a group is able to express its cultural identity. The Court further decided that commercial, free speech is to be accorded the same constitutional safeguards as political speech because commercial speech ''serves individual and societal values in a free and democratic society.'' Following this reasoning, the Supreme Court struck down Quebec's ''sign law.'' Within one week, the Quebec government responded by passing new legislation which also placed restrictions on the use of languages other than French on public signs. The government shielded this new law from court scrutiny by stating that the new law would operate notwithstanding the protections of Quebec's *Charter of Human Rights and Freedoms* and the *Canadian Charter*. The *Canadian Charter* allows a government to opt out of the enshrined guarantees merely by expressly stating that it is doing so. The Quebec government chose to exercise this option with respect to the ''sign law'' legislation.

By this Montreal store which displays a bilingual sign, French CEGEP students protest the Supreme Court's 1988 ruling that struck down the sign provision of Quebec's language law.

THE IMPORTANCE OF LANGUAGE

Why all the commotion over language? First, it is one of the principal ingredients in the quality of life: not just a medium of expressing oneself but also, as Bill 101 calls it, a medium for living—at home, on the job, in recreation. The individual's whole identity is wrapped up in it.

Moreover, the vitality of a language is essential for the survival of a culture. Traditions and group history are transmitted from one generation to the next through language. In the case of Quebec, there has been an historic coincidence of Roman Catholic affiliation and the French language. Language affects a group's access to power and its participation in political life. One can't be heard if one does not speak the language. Language also affects participation in economic life (see Chapter 5 on work). To date, francophones continue to be underrepresented in the upper levels of Canadian corporations.

The depth of emotion that surrounds language rights in Canada attests to the widespread awareness of their importance. The struggle is by no means evident only in this country. It is being waged in Belgium between the Flemish and the economically dominant, French-speaking Walloons. There is agitation for broader usage of Welsh in Wales and of Gaelic in Scotland. Minority groups are increasingly aware that protection of language, economic well-being, and cultural survival are interrelated.

EUROPEAN IMMIGRANTS IN CANADA

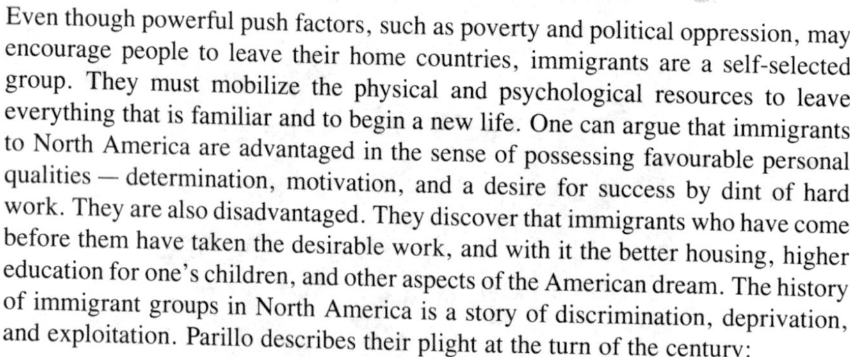

Even though powerful push factors, such as poverty and political oppression, may encourage people to leave their home countries, immigrants are a self-selected group. They must mobilize the physical and psychological resources to leave everything that is familiar and to begin a new life. One can argue that immigrants to North America are advantaged in the sense of possessing favourable personal qualities — determination, motivation, and a desire for success by dint of hard work. They are also disadvantaged. They discover that immigrants who have come before them have taken the desirable work, and with it the better housing, higher education for one's children, and other aspects of the American dream. The history of immigrant groups in North America is a story of discrimination, deprivation, and exploitation. Parillo describes their plight at the turn of the century:

> *As unskilled workers, most found employment in the low-status manual labor jobs in the factories, mines, needle trades, and construction. At that time the worker had no voice in working conditions, for labor unions had not yet become effective. The fourteen-hour day, six-day*

> *week for low wages was common. There were no vacations, sick pay, or pension plans. Child labor was the norm, and entire families often worked to provide family income. Lighting, ventilation and heating were poor; in the factories, moving pieces of machinery were dangerously exposed. There was no workers' compensation if, as was likely, someone was injured on the job. A worker who objected was likely to be fired and blacklisted (1980, 156).*

Yet, for the descendants of many immigrants, the story had a happy ending in that they were able to triumph over obstacles and become full-fledged, even prominent Canadians and Americans. Here we must note a significant difference between visible minorities and others. In the absence of continuing intermarriage, racial characteristics are permanent and trigger prejudice and discrimination. Members of European ethnic groups are gradually absorbed into the mainstream of society and are able to become more or less equal participants. The Irish are an example of a group that experienced severe discrimination when large numbers arrived, virtually destitute, in the wake of the famines of the 1840s. "No Irish need apply" proclaimed notices on job postings in Protestant-dominated Toronto. Although some anti-Irish prejudice was evident in Ontario until the 1950s, being of Irish ancestry today has little direct impact on one's life chances.

In the United States, the thrust has always been toward rapid assimilation, producing the melting pot in which the constituent parts blend into a new amalgam. The immigrants (or at least their children) were to shed their distinguishing characteristics and become "real," not hyphenated, Americans. (One reason for pushing assimilation was the need for patriotic citizens, given the many armed conflicts in which the United States has been involved during its relatively brief history.) In practice, ethnic groups have not disappeared in the United States. Cities such as Chicago, Philadelphia, and Buffalo have large, active ethnic communities. Social scientists—for example, Michael Novak in *The Rise and Fall of the Unmeltable Ethnics: Politics and Culture in the Seventies* (1971)—have argued that the melting is by no means total. Indeed, during the last two decades, there has been a revival of ethnic consciousness.

In Canada, large-scale immigration took place later than in the United States, and immigrants were ranked and granted entrance in accordance with their perceived ability to assimilate. Those from Britain were deemed most desirable, followed by Germans and Scandinavians. Writing in 1909, J.S. Woodsworth categorized Germans as being, on the whole, "among our best immigrants" (1972, 84). Scandinavians were similarly described:

> *Taken all in all there is no class of immigrants that are as certain of making their way in the Canadian West as the people of the peninsula of Scandinavia. Accustomed to the rigors of a northern climate, clean-blooded, thrifty, ambitious and hard-working, they will be certain of success in this pioneer country, where the strong, not the weak, are wanted (1972 [1909], 77).*

Woodsworth was not equally sanguine about all immigrant groups. Some had worrisome tendencies toward "clustering:"

> *Not only are they less open to Canadian ideas, but, closely united, they can control the entire community. The social, the educational, the religious, the political life is dominated by alien ideas. It would seem a wise policy to scatter the foreign communities among the Canadians, in this way facilitating the process of assimilation (1972 [1909], 234).*

It should be remembered that Woodsworth, who was the founder of the Co-operative Commonwealth Federation (CCF), was deemed an enlightened, concerned Canadian, not a racist bigot.

Apart from admitting some immigrants more readily than others, Canada has never pursued assimilation with the amount of zeal exhibited by the United States. As already noted, Porter (1965) argued that the British charter group encouraged the maintenance of ethnic boundaries because they helped the group itself to remain dominant. However, it is really only since the end of the Second World War that Canada has espoused a policy of deliberate multiculturalism, the promotion of a cultural mosaic in which the constituent parts remain visible and distinct. From a practical standpoint, the vast number of immigrants who arrived over a relatively short period of time in the postwar era could not be assimilated. As Reitz explained, other factors also contributed to the new orientation:

> *The ideology of multiculturalism has evolved in Canada at a time of increased tension between the dominant linguistic communities, English and French. Following the post-World War II Quiet Revolution in Quebec, the federal government tried to improve English-French relations by setting up a Commission on Bilingualism and Biculturalism in 1963. At this time, pressure grew to recognize "the cultural contribution of other ethnic groups" (1980, 10).*

Multiculturalism has positive as well as negative consequences for members of ethnic groups. Socialization to the values and norms of the ethnic community allows individuals to feel secure as part of a "we-group." However, the individual continues to be an outsider in the society at large, a situation that can entail heavy social and psychological costs. Rayfield focused on some of these costs in a sensitive work based on participant observation of women in an English-language school:

Being different from the surrounding society can have positive consequences for members of ethnic groups. Here an ethnic business provides work — and meals that recall the old country.

As her children progress in the Canadian school system, they soon speak only English to each other at home. When spoken to in Italian they answer in English. Maria feels this as a rejection of her as a mother, sometimes even as a deliberate rejection. She feels that the children do not want her to know what they are talking about. This is another vicious circle. The more isolated the mother is from the world outside her family, the less the children are able to communicate with her. Even if they speak the same language, they feel they have nothing to talk about. So the children, who might have been a contact between the mother and the outside world, involving her through the school and their friends in a wide network of associations, have just the opposite effect. They increase her diffidence about venturing outside the social world of the family at the same time as they break communication within the family network.

As we noted in Chapter 3 on socialization, the Canadian-born children of immigrants may also face difficulties as they attempt to reconcile the differences between the values and practices of the home and those they encounter at school and in other social institutions.

On the positive side, as Reitz's study of 10 ethnic groups in five large Canadian cities showed, ethnic communities provide economic opportunities that may not be readily available within the larger society. This is especially important for the minimally educated.

> *Having a good education is completely unrelated to income mobility in the minority setting. The irrelevance of education in such settings may be attributed to the job involved; expertise provided by the school system may be unnecessary to effective job performance. To be productive in such jobs, knowledge of the ethnic language and the ability to maintain relationships with other ethnic members as co-workers or as customers, clients and suppliers, may be more important than education (1980, 164).*

Anderson made similar points in her study of Portuguese immigrants, specifically noting the role of ethnic networks in securing employment for compatriots:

> *Networks function to allow the possibility of job mobility for persons in our society who might not otherwise risk career or geographical changes. They enable the persons to ''try out'' for different jobs, in situations where they are assured assistance in learning new skills and role requirements in a congenial and supportive atmosphere. The employer can locate new employees rapidly and with minimal expense and trouble, by merely asking his present employees if they know of suitable workers. He is thus assured of a reasonably congenial work group who will exert peer group pressure for adequate job performance. New immigrants experience a cushioning effect by working among kin and friends, so that the adverse effects of culture shock are minimized (1981, 331).*

Once again, we alert students to the wide variations concealed by umbrella terms such as ''ethnic groups'' and ''immigrants.'' However, a general discussion of race and ethnic relations is essential because it provides insight into the overall struggle for power in society. A large sociological literature addresses the history, problems, and current position of specific ethnic groups. For studies of a wide variety of racial and ethnic groups, see *Generations: A History of Canada's People*, a series under the general editorship of Jean Burnet and Howard Palmer (1988).

THE POOR

The poor in Canada constitute a minority, according to our use of the term in a sociological sense. The poor are a powerless group of people whose participation in the social, economic, and political life of the country is low and whose life chances are severely restricted. They are subject to prejudice because of the societal attitude that failing is a symptom of individual inadequacy (lack of ambition, unwillingness to adapt to market conditions, and weak character), and they experience structural discrimination, even at the level of government policy. Such discrimination makes it difficult, if not impossible, for most people to break out of the cycle of poverty, and it becomes a condition that is then perpetuated from one generation to the next (see Ryan 1972).

The problem of income security has been a persistent one throughout Canadian history, especially since industrialization has increased the concentration of people in urban centres (see Herbert Brown Ames' *The City Below the Hill* [1972; first published in 1897]). Although Canadians have now achieved one of the highest standards of living in the world, many Canadians live at the margins of society. Since the Second World War, a massive and complex structure of social welfare programs has been created, entitling Canada to be referred to as a welfare state.

Despite the responsibility for social security that Canadians have assigned to government at both the federal and provincial levels and despite massive infusions of money into programs designed to bring about income redistribution, income disparities have not, in fact, been substantially reduced. Disparities persist among classes, among regions of the country, among sectors of the economy, and among age, gender, and ethnic groups. Exhibit 7.2 attests to this, indicating relative shares of the national income over a 16-year period. In 1971, the two lowest groups in the income hierarchy received 13.9 percent of total income, while the two highest groups received 69.9 percent. By 1987, there was a slight narrowing of the gap. In his analysis of the redistributive role played by the Canadian state, Banting notes that it has been a modest one, below the norm for industrialized countries and "representing a restrained response to the social insecurities of industrial life" (1987, 311).

WHO ARE THE POOR?

How does one define poverty? It can be defined in absolute terms (**absolute deprivation**): does the individual have enough on which to subsist—to obtain the basic necessities of life, such as food, clothing, and shelter? Poverty can also be defined in relative terms (**relative deprivation**): does the individual's economic well-being fall short of community standards?[14] In this sense of the term, one asks how the person or family fares in relation to others in society. Those who are poor by relative standards tend to be those who, because of low education and lack of job opportunities, cannot participate fully in community life.

Who are the poor? Their characteristics vary widely. Some are rural and some are urban. Contrary to popular belief, most do work. The working poor are concentrated in the most precarious and vulnerable sectors of the economy, where employment is irregular, low paying, and lacking in fringe benefits. Ross noted:

As the National Council on Welfare concluded, ''It is not their ages, education or geographic distribution that distinguish low-income workers. The single common factor which sets the working poor apart as a group within our society is their jobs.'' Not only do the wage-earning poor hold low paying jobs and suffer more and longer spells of unemployment, but they also tend to have hard, dirty, boring and low-prestige jobs with little or no chance for advancement. These jobs in most instances do not represent the career and income opportunities that play such a central economic and social role in the lives of most Canadians. They are simply dead-end jobs that barely permit the holder to scratch out a living (1981, 23).

EXHIBIT 7.2

INCOME OF FAMILIES AND UNATTACHED INDIVIDUALS

	Bottom Quintile	Second Quintile	Middle Quintile	Fourth Quintile	Top Quintile
1971	3.6	10.6	17.6	24.6	43.3
1972	3.8	10.6	17.8	24.9	42.9
1973	3.9	10.7	17.6	25.0	42.7
1974	4.0	10.9	17.7	25.1	42.5
1975	4.0	10.6	17.6	24.9	42.6
1976	4.3	10.7	17.4	25.1	42.9
1977	3.8	10.7	17.9	25.6	42.0
1978	3.9	10.4	17.7	25.5	42.5
1979	4.2	10.6	17.6	25.3	42.3
1980	4.1	10.5	17.7	25.3	42.4
1981	4.6	10.9	17.6	25.2	42.8
1982	4.5	10.7	17.3	25.0	42.5
1983	4.4	10.3	17.1	25.0	42.2
1984	4.5	10.3	17.1	25.0	42.0
1985	4.7	10.4	17.0	25.0	42.0
1986	4.7	10.4	17.0	24.9	43.1
1987	4.7	10.4	16.9	24.8	43.2

NOTE: Quintiles are equal 20-percent slices of the population ranked according to whatever is being measured. (Here the ranking is by percentage of total income.) The definition of income used here includes virtually all sources of cash income — for example, wages, interest payments, transfer payments, pensions — and is calculated on a before-tax basis. Post-tax analysis changes the trend very little.
SOURCE: Statistics Canada. Canada Year Book 1988. 1987, 5-30 and Statistics Canada Income Distributions by Size in Canada 1987. 13-207.

Women are more likely than men to be poor at some time in their lives, particularly in the later years. The increasing risk of poverty borne by women is a trend referred to as the **feminization of poverty**. Women face a much higher risk of poverty than men and constitute a larger percentage of the poor. During the 1960s and 1970s the feminization of poverty escalated. By 1980 it was entrenched and persisted largely unabated through most of the 1980s. In 1980 the rate of poverty was 46.6 percent for families with female heads who were under the age of 65; this was five and three-quarters times the rate for families with male heads. By 1987 the rate for families with female heads was still very high, i.e., 40.3 percent or 4.9 times the rate for families with male heads. For older females who were unattached individuals of 65 years and over, the poverty rate in 1980 was 65.4 percent but by 1987 was reduced somewhat to 43.8. Exhibit 7.3 shows how the burden of poverty falls unevenly, with females bearing the far greater share. More than half (56.1 percent) of all low-income Canadians are female, as are 71.7 percent of the elderly poor. Further, women constitute the great majority (82.3 percent) of the unattached aged who have low incomes (National Council on Welfare 1988).

What about children? One Canadian child in six (17.6 percent) is poor. Of these, 60.1 percent live in two-parent families, 35.5 percent are in single-parent families headed by women, and 4.4 percent are in families headed by men (National Council on Welfare 1988).

Our discussion of native peoples indicated that most of them live in a condition of severe poverty. Here too is an example of mutual reinforcement between the stigma of being poor and the stigma of belonging to some other minority group.

THE STIGMA OF POVERTY

One of the many costs of poverty is that it engenders individuals with a significant stigma—a social mark of unworthiness or discredit—that affects their social identity. As Goffman has observed:

> *Our society appears to have several basic types of stigma. There are "tribal" stigmas, arising from unapproved racial, national, and religious affiliations. There are the stigmas attached to physical handicap, including—to stretch the term—those associated with the undesirable characteristics of female sex and old age. And there are stigmas pertaining to what is somehow seen as a decay of moral responsibility, including those persons who are unemployed or who have a known record of alcoholism, addiction, sexual deviation, penal servitude, or who have been committed to a mental hospital (1962, 196).*

In Chapter 4 on stratification, we noted that people start the social race at different points on the track. Thus, the social system does not merely have winners and losers—it helps to create them. However, the blame-the-victim approach, which has influenced Canadian public policy toward the poor, presumes that individuals are personally responsible for success or failure; the policy thus seeks to change the behaviour of individuals rather than attempting to find long-term solutions in the social structure itself. Assistance to the poor is delivered on a short-term, crisis basis, and programs are designed not only to encourage self-reliance and hard work but also to discourage dependence and lack of effort. Canadian society attaches a heavy stigma to being poor and dependent but, as we have noted, cannot seem to find an effective way to reduce poverty and dependence.

EXHIBIT 7.3

POVERTY TRENDS

	Families		Unattached Individuals			All persons
	All families	Female heads under 65 years	All individuals	All 65 years and over	Females 65 years and over	
1979	13.1	43.9	40.3	66.3	68.8	15.7
1980	12.2	46.6	39.6	61.5	65.4	15.1
1981	12.0	40.5	37.8	58.6	62.2	14.7
1982	13.2	44.7	37.4	56.2	60.1	16.1
1983	14.0	47.1	41.3	57.5	60.6	17.1
1984	14.5	46.1	37.8	49.6	51.7	17.3
1985	13.3	46.7	36.8	46.8	51.0	16.0
1986	11.8	39.4	34.6	43.0	46.8	14.5
1987	11.3	40.3	33.5	39.4	43.8	14.1

Rates of poverty in percents.

NOTE: These estimates are based on low income cut-offs using the 1978 base which is updated each year according to changes in the cost-of-living as measured by the Consumer Price Index.

Excerpted from: Statistics Canada: Income Distribution by Size in Canada, 1987 (13-207). table 72. Incidence of Low Income.

THE AGED

In the normal course of events, most North Americans can anticipate being old before they die. How then is it appropriate to discuss the aged as a sociological minority?

There is little consensus in the sociological literature as to the validity of such a label. On the one hand, the aged are highly visible, are stereotyped by other groups, and experience powerlessness, prejudice, and discrimination. They are excluded from most occupations, and if they work, they tend to receive lower-than-average pay. They are often segregated both socially and physically. They typically respond to their subordinate status with defensiveness and negative self-concepts. On the other hand, the aged are not socially organized as an independently functioning subgroup. Rather, they are engaged, through family ties, with other age groups. They exhibit wide diversity in socioeconomic status, state of health, degree of participation in mainstream life, amount of prestige traditionally bestowed on them in their own ethnic communities, and the degree to which they experience discrimination and loss of dignity.

In our opinion, the arguments that favour viewing the aged group as a minority are more compelling than those against. Diversity need not keep social scientists from exploring what individuals have in common. The minority perspective sensitizes people to many aspects of life for the aged in Canadian society that might otherwise be overlooked.

AN AGING SOCIETY

The study of aging as a field of enquiry is referred to as gerontology; it brings together the perspectives of a wide variety of disciplines, such as economics, demography, political economy, epidemiology, and sociology. It is also receiving growing attention from applied disciplines, such as nursing, medicine, social work, health administration, and health planning. The fact that the first Canadian text (Marshall) devoted to the social aspects of aging was published in 1980 points to the very recent nature of the interest in this field.[15]

The area has considerable importance in Canada today because the country has, in recent years, become an aging society, with a striking increase in the number and proportion of older people. Historically, high birth rates, declining rates of infant and child mortality, and the large influxes of immigrants made the average age of the population relatively low. Exhibit 7.4 documents the direction of the population shift, and Exhibit 7.5 sets forth the projected changes to the year 2031.

This upward shift in the proportion of the population over age 65 raises concerns for policymakers. How does society plan to cope with the financial implications of having a large group of people who can no longer support themselves through working? How will social and economic necessities be made available? Alterations in the age structure of society also raise questions for social scientists about changing patterns of social interaction and shifting balances of power. Some analysts predict that, as the enormous baby-boom cohort ages, Canadian society will experience heightened intergenerational conflict. The capacity to forecast and plan is, at the present time, severely hampered by the dearth of scientific knowledge available on all aspects of aging.

EXHIBIT 7.4

CANADIAN POPULATION AGE 65 AND OVER

	Total population	Males	Females
1851	2.67%	2.80%	2.53%
1871	3.60	3.96	3.35
1891	4.55	4.67	4.42
1911	4.66	3.99	4.87
1931	5.55	5.49	5.62
1941	6.67	6.63	6.72
1951	7.75	7.77	7.73
1956	7.73	7.64	7.84
1961	7.63	7.31	7.95
1966	7.69	7.13	8.26
1971	8.09	7.24	8.93
1976	8.71	7.65	9.76
1981	9.70	8.38	11.00
1986	10.66	9.08	12.20

SOURCE: Jarvis (1972, 605).

EXHIBIT 7.5

POPULATION PROJECTIONS FOR CANADA, PROVINCES AND TERRITORIES 1984–2006

Low growth scenario				
	0–17	18–59	60–64	65+
1991	6.4	17.0	3.2	26.6
2001	5.7	18.2	3.9	27.8
2011	4.9	18.8	4.5	28.2
2021	4.5	17.5	5.9	27.9
2031	4.0	15.7	7.1	26.8
High growth scenario				
	0–17	18–59	60–64	65+
1991	6.8	17.1	3.2	27.1
2001	7.7	18.7	3.9	30.3
2011	8.2	20.3	4.5	33.0
2021	8.6	21.2	5.8	35.6
2031	9.4	21.5	7.2	38.1

derived from table 14 (millions)

SOURCE: Statistics Canada May 1985 Cat 91-520.

NEW PENSION LAW WON'T BRING NEEDED REFORMS

By John Deverell

Robert Dickie, former metalworker and machine parts inspector, is 71. He was making $2,200 a month plus overtime when he retired six years ago.

Now he gets a company pension of $146 a month.

Consumer prices have gone up 36 per cent since Dickie left Hawker Siddely Canada in 1983. The pension, meagre then, hasn't risen a penny.

Like many seniors, Dickie knows why his pension at retirement was small. The pension plan wasn't set up until late in his working career. That he regrets.

But the tiny pension also buys less and less every year. That he resents.

Most of Ontario's 600,000 workplace pensions have shrunk with inflation during the 1980s. At the same time, Ontario's $65-billion workplace pension pot has piled up investment gains far above the long-term average.

One result has been the dramatic reduction in current pension contributions by employers. The contradiction—growing pension funds, shrinking pensions—has bedevilled provincial politicians ever since Conrad Black drew public attention to it with his spectacular raid on Dominion Stores pension fund surpluses in 1986.

Financial Institutions Minister Murray Elston now says he will be ready to bring forward a new pension law later this month.

All signs indicate that when Elston is finished, Dickie and most other current pensioners still won't be able to count on regular pension increases to protect them from rising consumer prices.

The Liberal plan continues to allow employers to use pension fund surpluses to offset their required annual contributions—the so-called employer contributions holiday.

There will be some partial pension indexing in the Peterson government's scheme, but its limited help won't be completely realized by retiring workers until the year 2020.

Meanwhile employers, unions and the courts are still wrestling with the need for some kind of pension reform in the here and now.

The variation in workplace pension practice is enormous.

There are thousands of small, private-sector workplaces with no pension plan. At the other extreme is the Rolls-Royce of retirement programs at Shell Canada. The oil company makes the contributory, indexed pension plans of teachers and civil servants look modest.

Since 1975 Shell has built a huge pension fund financed entirely by the employer. The payout is 2 per cent of average final earnings multiplied by years of service. Thus a 25-year employee's pension is set at half the earning rate at retirement.

These generous pensions are fully guaranteed against consumer price inflation of up to 10 per cent yearly.

"We do it to attract and retain top-notch people," says John Ritchie, Shell's pay and benefits manager. "Our executives felt indexation would come to Canada eventually, and we wanted to be far-sighted."

Shell's guaranteed indexing, combined with an early retirement plan that allows 25-year employees to take unreduced pensions as young as age 50, is expensive. The Shell pension fund already holds a stunning $1 billion in assets to take care of just 6,200 active workers and 2,700 retirees — an average of $111,000 apiece.

By way of comparison, General Motors of Canada allows early retirement at reduced pensions and provides partial inflation protection without guaranteeing it.

GM's $1.1-billion pension fund covers 39,000 active workers and 8,400 retirees, an average holding of $23,000 apiece.

Shiraz Bharmal of the management consulting firm of Towers, Perrin, Forster and Crosby says the Shell plan is unrivalled and the General Motors plan is better than most in the private sector.

The standards aren't overly demanding. To avoid the costly pre-funding rules of pension law, employers who offer defined pension benefits usually wait to see how much damage inflation does to retiree pensions. Then sometimes they provide partial repair — and sometimes they don't.

A Towers Perrin survey of non-union employers with pension plans shows that for employees who retired in 1973, only 4 per cent of employers had granted increases that fully preserved the purchasing power of the pension to Jan. 1, 1987.

A similar number, 4 per cent, made no pension adjustments whatsoever. During the 14-year period consumer prices nearly tripled, slashing the pensions' purchasing power by two thirds.

About three quarters of the employers granted adjustments to pensions that offset half or less than half the increase in consumer prices over the period. In other words, even with adjustments, most private pensions lost one third of their value or more.

General Motors, for example, sent its 1973 retirees out on a company pension of $245 a month. By Jan. 1, 1987, that had been increased to $474 a month. Despite the adjustments negotiated by the Canadian Auto Workers, the pension was buying only half what it did 14 years previously.

THE AGED IN CANADA TODAY

Some statistical data are, however, available on aged Canadians today. Their economic situation, as a group, is not enviable. Relative to that of other Canadians, the income of people aged 65 and over has improved since the early 1970s, a change which can be largely attributed to the growth of the Canada and Quebec Pension Plans. However, as Exhibits 7.6 and 7.7 show, the income of the elderly remains well below that of the rest of the population. The issue of security in old age should be seen in relation to "lifetime earnings." Thus, the problem of income for elderly persons begins long before they reach old age. Since the risk of poverty is strongly linked to labour-force attachment, it is not surprising that elderly women bear the highest risk. The price of never having worked, or of having worked intermittently in low-paying jobs that did not entail pension benefits, is one that becomes particularly heavy for women in their later years. For a detailed analysis of the sources of public and private income for the aged in Canada, see Lindsay and Donald (1988); for the economic situation of elderly women, see Dulude (1978).

EXHIBIT 7.6

AVERAGE REAL INCOME OF HUSBAND-WIFE FAMILIES, BY AGE OF HUSBAND, 1971–1986

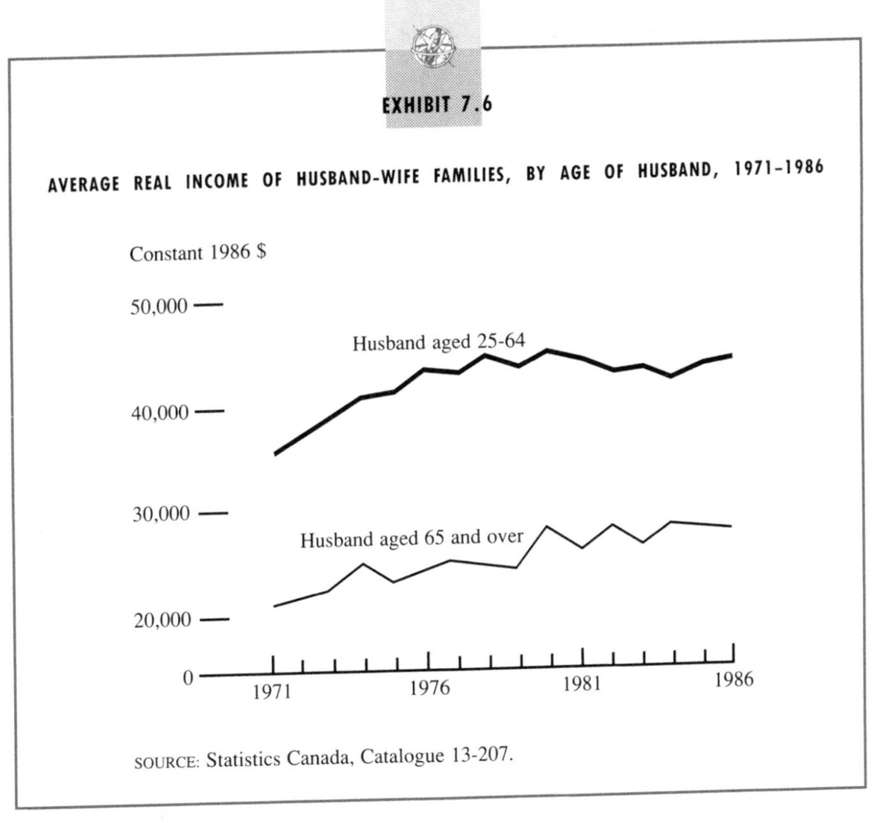

SOURCE: Statistics Canada, Catalogue 13-207.

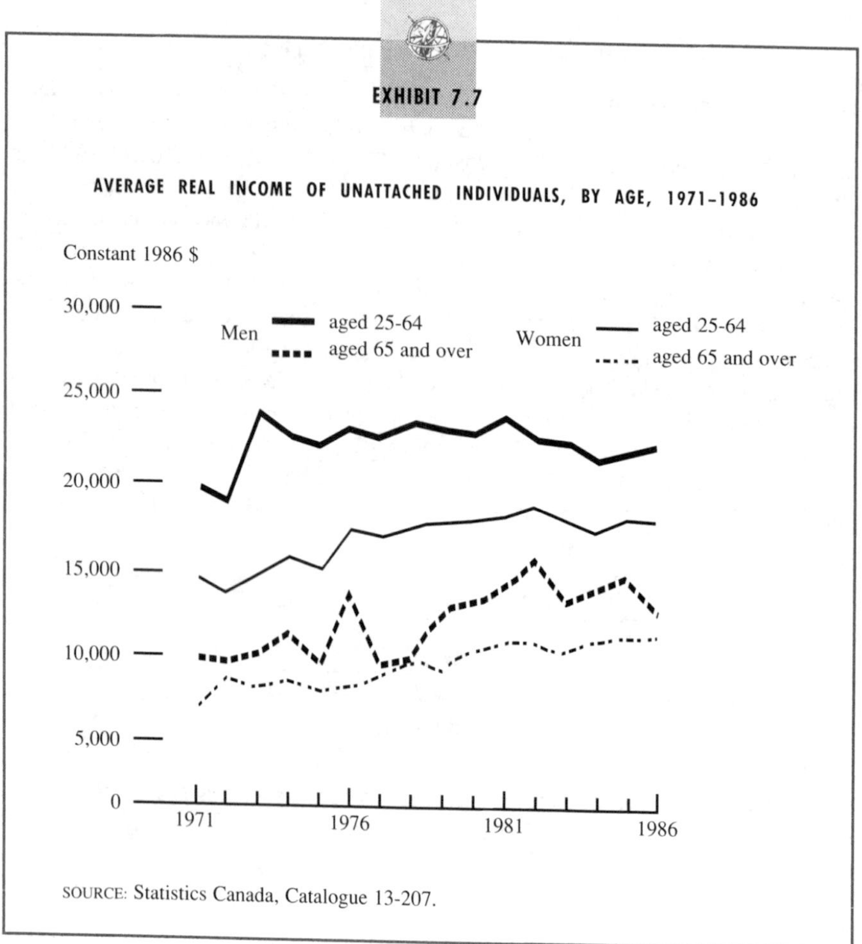

SOURCE: Statistics Canada, Catalogue 13-207.

We have already explored the ways in which poverty itself confers minority status on individuals, one of these ways being a drastic reduction in social participation. For the aged, this reduced participation is further exaggerated by their forced departure from the labour force, by lack of access to transportation, and by physical infirmities that restrict their activities. Jarvis has noted that the quality of housing for the aged is markedly below average even though many own their own homes; with lower incomes, they have difficulty paying property taxes, are unable to provide adequate maintainence and repairs, lack conveniences such as modern appliances, and cannot afford to move if the neighbourhood deteriorates (1972, 65). At the same time, the rate of institutionalization of the elderly in Canada is one of the highest in all industrialized countries. Schwenger (1974) has pointed to a pronounced tendency in Canada to institutionalize people, such as criminals and invalids, who vary from the societal norms.

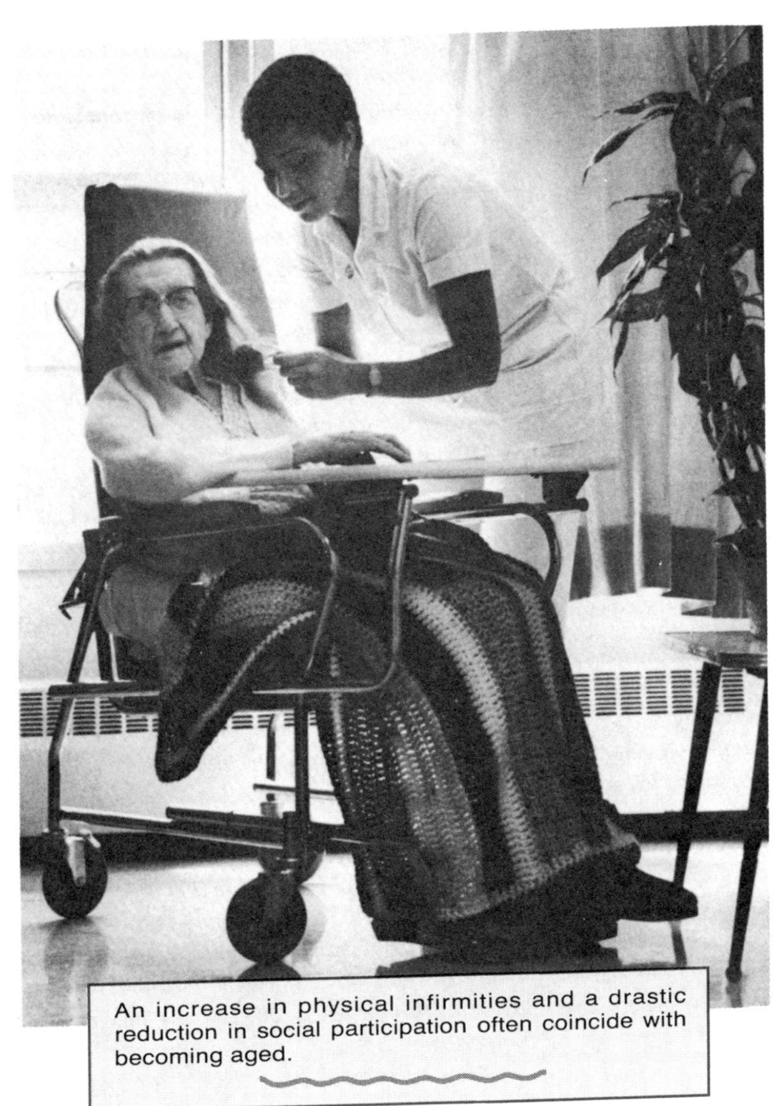

An increase in physical infirmities and a drastic reduction in social participation often coincide with becoming aged.

THE STIGMA OF AGING

It is widely recognized that the aged are subject to considerable stigmatization in a youth-oriented society. Posner has argued that this is especially true for aged women, who experience what she calls the ''double whammy'' of being both old and female, two attributes that are socially depreciated (1980, 80). The negative stereotypes of the elderly increase social isolation, causing individuals to confine their contacts to a shrinking pool of age peers, and to avoid contact with the majority.

Perhaps the most enduring of all stereotypes are those between old and young. Contrary to most stereotypes differentiating social categories, time and interaction do not lead to the decay of youth-age stereotypes and the misunderstandings which result. As most people get older, communication progressively withers. Old people even look repulsive to the young. This revulsion is heightened when intimate physical contact is required. This may affect an old person's chances for something as fundamental as life itself. One intern in the emergency ward of one of the hospitals which Sudnow studied indicated that he could not stand to give mouth-to-mouth resuscitation to an old woman who came in and was later pronounced dead. On a less dramatic basis, consider the difficulty in getting people to care for old people who have lost the ability to control their urination and defecation (Jarvis 1972, 620).

The physical changes that accompany aging are perceived negatively in a society that extols youth, beauty, and physical vigour to such an extent as to devote whole industries to the promotion, display, and perpetuation of these qualities.

Barring premature death, passage through the life cycle seems inevitable. It is not surprising, therefore, that the young find the presence of the aged an unwelcome reminder of a dreaded fate.

As aging occurs, the old person become something more than old and unattractive to the young. He becomes a grim reminder of the young person's own future. He does not let us forget that all life ends in death. In a society which isolates itself from unpleasant events such as death, poverty, and disease, is it not to be expected that the youthful would encourage the natural tendency of the old to isolate themselves from too frequent contact with others? Special homes, special communities, special activities, special housing, special organizations are encouraged by the younger population. Although the manifest motive is to provide better care and social life for the aged, is there not also a latent objective in concealing the aged from view, removing the reproach of the elderly and often poor from sight? (Jarvis 1972, 620–1).

Becker decribed a master status (salient status) as that status of a given person which overrides this person's other statuses in determining how other people treat the person (1963, 33). Typical social interaction with the elderly demonstrates that age itself confers the master status, leading to the attribution of a great many other characteristics that make up the stereotype. Have you ever found yourself raising your voice when talking to an old person, on the assumption that he or she is hard of hearing? Or described your grandmother as "amazing" or "cute" because she is able to make witty observations, contradicting the image of the old as confused or senile? Have you assumed physical frailty in the absence of evidence? Have you ever challenged the assumption that it is delightful for you to have a late Sunday breakfast in your dressing gown but sensible that the elderly in nursing homes should dress before being served an early breakfast? These are not frivolous questions. One of the greatest risks involved in the aging process is that the elderly themselves will consent to the stereotype and, unnecessarily, begin to confirm it with their own behaviour. The self-fulfilling prophecy may thus launch an irreversible downward spiral.

Jennifer Griffiths, shown with seeing-eye dog Sunshine, has worked at the Advocacy Resource Centre for the Handicapped since September 1986.

SEEKING FULL RIGHTS IN THE WORK FORCE

By Susan Reid

A big blonde dog dying for attention is one of the first things people notice at this office's reception desk.

And then the voice. A woman's voice, friendly and welcoming, directing the visitor to a chair. But first, "could you just give Sunshine a pat, then he'll be quiet."

The woman's seeing-eye dog has his harness off while he's off duty — "so he thinks he can act silly." He shakes an old blue bath mat and dares the visitor to pull it from his clenched teeth.

Jennifer Griffiths and Sunshine have been coming to work at the Advocacy Resource Centre for the Handicapped since September, 1986. She's the first person visitors meet when they come to talk to a staff lawyer or counsellor and sometimes she surprises people who don't know how to react to her blindness.

"I usually say, 'Can I help somebody?' I don't know if there is one person there or two . . . most people respond," said Griffiths.

"But one time a group of lawyers came in and I asked if I could help. I asked again and again until I was like a stuck record. Finally, I stomped over, put my hands on my hips and asked: 'In which capacity can this clinic help you?'

"I don't know," she says, "Some people probably think that if you can't see, you can't talk."

Employment of people with disabilities in Canada is dismal, according to the Canadian Human Rights Commission's 1988 annual report. They make up only 1.6 per cent of the work force.

People have become so frustrated about job prospects that many have stopped seeking employment.

In Ontario, over 80 per cent of the 35,200 employable people with disabilities severe enough to restrict daily activity have stopped looking for work, the Canadian Paraplegic Association has found.

Of all the complaints it received last year, the Ontario Human Rights Commission reported 41 per cent were related to disabilities and most were about employment.

Griffiths, 33, who has lived on her own for nine years and takes public transit to work every day, knows what it's like to try to convince employers that a disabled person is capable.

"One place didn't want me because I would have had to take coats and get coffee," she said. "What an awesome responsibility. I get my own coffee every day."

Now, she feels "gainfully employed." But it's hard to persuade other people of her independence.

"People over-help you; they kind of get all over you like wet paint," she said. "Sometimes one woman on my bus shouts: 'Will someone give this blind person a seat?' I don't like that.

"One guy put his hands on my eyes and said he wanted to heal me," she said. "I said, 'Get your hands off my eyes.'

"It's a struggle for me to get self-esteem anyway, I don't need that. I think people think less of you if you have a disability, whether it's subtle or overt."

Groups, such as the Canadian Paraplegic Association, People United for Self-Help in Ontario, and the Advocacy Resource Centre for the Handicapped, are pushing to get people with disabilities into the work force.

The advocacy centre, with four lawyers who work under the Ontario Legal Aid Plan, deals only with disability issues.

There's also an articling law student, Gregory Sones, a specialist on employment who hopes a case now before the Canadian Human Rights Commission will improve the outlook for people with disabilities.

The commission is investigating the complaint launched in December by Sones' client, Disabled People for Employment Equity, he said.

The group charges that nine large companies discriminate against people with disabilities by not hiring them and not making accommodations for their disabilities in job interviews and at the workplace.

It looked at the records of many companies and chose nine of the largest: Bell Canada, Canadian National Railways, Canada Post, Canadian Broadcasting Corp., Bank of Montreal, Scotia Bank, Toronto Dominion Bank, Royal Bank and Canadian Imperial Bank of Commerce.

Sones said that in 1987 only 94 of 14,000 positions in these companies across Canada went to people with disabilities.

"The employers will likely say people aren't applying for the jobs," Sones said. "But that begs the question why. Is it because they know there's no accommodation for them?"

Under the Employment Equity Act employers are directed to remove barriers to employment, he said, but they are only expected to report on their progress, with no mandatory setting of goals.

The act puts the onus on workers to enforce it through the time-consuming process of filing a human rights complaint, he said.

SUMMARY

In looking at stratification in Chapter 4, we noted that inequality cannot be adequately explained in terms of individual differences; rather, one must take into account structural factors that create and perpetuate social inequality. In this chapter, we have investigated the significance of minority status for the individual's life chances and position in society.

Traditionally, the term "minority" has been used to describe racial and ethnic groups. The dimensions of the definition we use permit us to include, under this umbrella term, other groups that experience prejudice and discrimination. The aged, like women and the disabled, are found in all class strata. However, these collectivities are often categorized on the basis of one negative characteristic: being female in a male-dominated society, being old or physically impaired in a culture that extols youth and physical perfection.

These negative categorizations give rise to discriminatory treatment that impedes access to political, economic, and social power. Lack of such power entails a disadvantaged position in society.

In recent history, developments within society have made it easier for certain minority groups to secure more equitable treatment. They have become more aware of their rights and are determined to continue fighting for them. For the struggle to succeed, however, the dominant group must be willing to acknowledge minority rights. Experience has shown that acknowledgment of these rights, and the action to back it up, are more easily obtained in good economic times than in bad.

ASSIGNMENTS

Do one or more of the following assignments, as instructed by your professor.

1 The sociological perspective permits us to discern similarities among groups that are ostensibly not similar at all. Using such a perspective, discuss two of the following in terms of minority status: children, the physically disabled, homosexuals, and former inmates of prisons.

2 It is difficult to think sociologically about one's own ethnic or racial group because one takes its behaviour patterns for granted. Visit a celebration or festival of a group different from your own. Compare and contrast the event with a similar one in your own group. (Chapter 4 on stratification will have alerted you to the fact that ethnic differences may be cross-cut by class.)

3 Over a two-week period, make a file of newspaper clippings on the topic of native peoples. Review Chapters 2, 4, and 7 on culture, stratification, and minorities, and analyse the information you have collected in the light of conceptual material discussed in each of these chapters.

4 Minority groups do not necessarily accept discrimination passively. In recent years a number of grey-power (and other) groups have emerged in Canada to represent the interests of old people. Their efforts have met with some success. For example, the federal government was induced to reinstate full indexation to old-age pensions in the 1985 budget.

Do some research on one or more of these groups. Use the library as a resource. If such a group is active in your community, speak to some of the people associated with it. Find out how they got involved, how the group is organized, what its objectives are, and how members go about achieving those objectives.

SUGGESTED READINGS

David Freeman, *Creeps* (Toronto: University of Toronto Press, 1972). This play centres on a sheltered workshop where disabled people are employed to do repetitious, simple jobs at token wages, ostensibly to be kept occupied and to be able to feel useful. That they feel diminished, exploited, and restless, yet fearful of the outside world which some of them nevertheless dream of entering, becomes evident as the drama unfolds and as the obstacles to their leaving the security of the workshop become clear. The self-fulfilling prophecy so typical of minority-group behaviour takes on flesh with Freeman's trenchant characterizations.

E.J. Gaines, *A Gathering of Old Men* (New York: Knopf, 1983). When a white planter is killed in rural Louisiana, a group of old black men come forward, each claiming to be the killer so as to shield the real culprit. For generations, they bore silently the humiliations and injustices inflicted upon them, but this one time they have found the courage to assert themselves.

Gaines writes with sensitivity and compassion, but his book is a searing indictment of the inhumanity of which some people are capable.

Erving Goffman, *Stigma: Notes on Management of a Spoiled Identity* (Englewood Cliffs, N.J.: Prentice Hall, 1962). In one way or another, each person bears attributes he or she fears will be discrediting in the eyes of others. Goffman looks at individuals who suffer discrimination in society because of a salient, negative characteristic that ''spoils'' their social identities. Members of minority groups, such as Indians, blacks, gays, or the handicapped, are exposed to such stigmatization.

Joy Kogawa, *Obasan* (Toronto: Lester and Orpen Dennys, 1981). Kogawa was a child of six in 1942 when Japanese Canadians were summarily removed from the west coast and located in camps in the interior. Many had been born in Canada; they were punished not for anything they had done, but for their national origin. By telescoping a sad chapter in Canadian history into an account of one family, Kogawa allows us to experience this outrage vicariously.

In September 1988, when Prime Minister Mulroney extended a formal apology to the Japanese-Canadian community and announced a lump sum compensation payment, Kogawa was among those invited to the ceremony.

P. Kreiner, *Contact Prints* (Toronto: Doubleday Canada, 1983). For Joe, going north to teach in Fort Henrietta-Maria meant ''going abroad again,'' albeit in his own country. Economically, socially, and culturally, Fort Henrietta-Maria's small population is divided between native peoples and whites; the whites are split internally along linguistic lines into English and French factions.

The novel vividly conveys the various stages of culture shock, the sense of isolation, and the fear of going ''stir-crazy'' that are common among immigrants from Canada's south.

Margaret Laurence, *The Stone Angel* (Toronto: McClelland and Stewart, 1964). Stubborn, proud Hagar Shipley survives, at 90, with her wry humour, steely-mindedness, and sheer crankiness intact. Laurence's portrait offers an understanding of a long life and of old age in a way that no social-scientific discussion of gerontological issues can match. At the end of her life, Hagar's outspokenness discomfits, outrages, and nurtures those around her. "What do I care now what people say? I cared too long."

V.S. Naipaul, *An Area of Darkness* (Markham: Penguin, 1968). With humour, impatience, and despair, Naipaul describes his attempt to understand the India which his family left for the West Indies two generations ago. Now living in England, he contrasts his experience of growing up Indian in the multi-racial society of Trinidad with his experience of living as an "outsider" during a one-year stay in India. Of his arrival in Bombay, Naipaul writes:

> *And for the first time in my life, I was one of the crowd. In Trinidad to be an Indian was so distinctive. To be anything there was distinctive; difference was each man's attribute. To be an Indian in England was distinctive . . . Now in Bombay I entered a shop or a restaurant and awaited a special quality of response. And there was nothing. It was like being denied part of my reality . . . I might sink without a trace into that Indian crowd . . . I felt the need to impose myself, and didn't know how.*

Gabrielle Roy, *The Fragile Lights of Earth* (Toronto: McClelland and Stewart, 1982). This is a collection of short pieces (newspaper articles and what Roy refers to as "memories") that appeared in various publications between 1942 and 1970. Roy's accounts of visits she made to small ethnic settlements, especially in western Canada, are full of rich details about people and places. Travelling with her, the reader enters the modest homes of Hutterites, Mennonites, Doukhobors, pioneer Jewish farmers, Sudeten Germans, Ukrainians, and French Canadians in communities that seem vastly removed from the urban Canada of today.

NOTES

1 For example, the title of Agatha Christie's mystery *The Little Nigger Boys* was changed to *Ten Little Indians* to eliminate the pejorative reference to black people.

2 Stigmatized means to be given a mark of discredit; its significance for social identity varies both with the severity of the stigma and with the way it is perceived in a particular culture. Stigma is further discussed later in this chapter and in Chapter 8 on deviance.

3 Although, numerically, women constitute half the population, they have had to wage a continuing struggle to escape minority status. We will discuss women as a minority group in Chapter 10 on social change.

4 Note that the term "majority" is used here to designate a *numerical* majority.

5 The little-known history of slave revolts testifies that acquiescence by black slaves was by no means universal.

6 The Métis are descendants of European fur traders and Indian women, who emerged as a distinct and self-conscious group on the Prairies about the beginning of the 19th century. Their culture combines native and Euro-Canadian values and norms; for example, although most are Catholic, they retain many spiritual beliefs and customs of their Plains Indian ancestors. And although most speak English, they also use a distinctive Métis language that combines Cree and English words in a French base (see *The Canadian Encyclopedia* 1985, 1124–5/1127).

7 Sociologists wage an interesting but as yet inconclusive debate about whether people act first and then develop attitudes to fit the action or whether actions follow from attitudes. In this case, the question is whether discrimination follows from prejudice or whether prejudice is developed to justify discriminatory behaviour.

8 Recently, there has also been some immigration from Korea and Vietnam.

9 In part, their immigration can be explained by push factors: for example, the uncertain political situation in Taiwan and Hong Kong and the overcrowding of Hong Kong. The student-led movement in 1989 to bring democracy to China, and the ruthless suppression of these efforts, have swelled the number of would-be immigrants from Hong Kong. These push factors coincide with the Canadian government's current emphasis on encouraging "business immigrants."

10 An overarching term such as "visible minority" tends to divert attention from the cultural differences that exist among various racial minorities. For example, Sikh culture is markedly different from West Indian culture. Indeed, there is no *one* West Indian culture; customs and even language vary from one island to the next just as the colonial experience varied. Furthermore, the customs, habits, and languages of visible minorities differ in varying degrees from mainstream Canadian culture. Adolescents in Hindu families are not allowed the kind of freedom that is taken for granted in some other groups in Canada (see Kostash 1987).

11 In fact, the arrival of large numbers of anglophone, but Catholic, Irish in the mid-19th century changed the face of Canadian society in areas such as southern Ontario, Montreal, the Eastern Townships, and Newfoundland, because it represented the introduction of a third ethnic group.

12 For an analysis of the social, economic, and political transformations that have occurred in Quebec, see McRoberts 1988.

13 "Minority" is used here in the sociological sense previously defined. The French were also a numerical minority in the cities of English Canada and even in Montreal from about 1831 to 1867.

14 The 1985 Supreme Court order that Manitoba render all statutes and government documents in both French and English started with the 1976 complaint of Georges Forest that his $5 parking ticket was printed only in English.

15 See Osberg, *Economic Inequality in Canada* (1981) for a full description of these measures.

8

DEVIANCE

AND SOCIAL CONTROL

By Linda B. Deutschmann

Johnny lives in a disorganized neighbourhood that has few recreational facilities. He drifts into spending his spare time with several other youths who live in the same high-rise. They frequently roll drunks and vandalize their area.

Mary, an unemployed single mother with three preschool children, hears voices that tell her to do dangerous things. Several of her relatives have been diagnosed as schizophrenic.

Mark comes from a culture in which it is normal for males to playfully pinch unescorted females. He is arrested for sexual assault and is unable to speak the language well enough to explain his behaviour. He is sent to a psychiatric hospital.

Alison feels tired most of the time. She cannot live up to the expectations of her school, family, and friends, and she cannot accept their accusations of laziness. Just living is a great effort.

Joe, James, and Jack are suspected of a violent act. Joe looks fat and slow; James is skinny and wears glasses; Jack is wiry and athletic. The judge doesn't find it difficult to decide which of them should be sent to a training school.

Arthur's father is a successful businessman who respects only high achievers. Arthur escapes into drugs and alcohol.

Susan dreads the day her friends find out that her family takes its holidays at a nudist camp.

The meat inspector looks at his book of rules and knows that if he takes the time to follow all of them, he will be fired for being too slow. So he skips some of the required procedures and finds himself facing criminal charges for having bypassed regulations; the prosecutor claims that Christmas gifts and favours were bribes to entice him to do so.

Each of the situations described in the opening of this chapter is an example of deviance, which is a subject many sociologists have studied intensively, seeking to understand how such behaviour is engendered and shaped.

WHAT IS DEVIANCE?

Most people think of **deviance** as something intrinsically bad or evil or at least rude. Sociologists, however, have found that deviance is best described as a special label put on behaviour (or appearance) that violates a society's **salient norms** (mores). By salient norms, we mean the rules actually in effect, as opposed to those "on the books" or regarded as ideals. The **deviant** is a person who is not just different: he or she is different in a norm-violating (moral) way. In an aggressive, warlike society, the young man who prefers to read and think is considered deviant. In another society, he may be highly respected. Thus, his behaviour is not bad in itself. It is deviant in the warlike society because it violates the salient norms.

But surely, you might think, some behaviour—say, murder—is bad in itself, it is not just a label. Murder is, in fact, a deviant act in all societies. Not all killing of human beings is called murder. The label "murder" tells us that a particular taking of life is wrong or wrongly done. Killing may be approved (not called murder) when it is done for humane purposes or justified by some higher view. The taking of life on the battlefield, for example, is usually not considered murder.[1]

BELIEFS AND VALUES

Norms which define deviance are usually related to group values and group beliefs. If the group believes, for example, that touching some object angers the gods and brings disaster, anyone who even comes close to the object evokes a strong negative reaction. When coffee was first introduced into Europe, it was treated as a religious intoxicant in some places and banned as a politically dangerous potion in others. Coffee-drinking was deviant.

The actual harmfulness of deviance is often difficult to assess. Many types of behaviour are outlawed because they would harm the existing social order, not because they would do any physical damage to people or things. This is one reason why the killing of hundreds of people by unsafe products, by pollution, or by exposure to hazards in the workplace often receives much less attention than a single murder in the street. The gunman in the street is more clearly violating common values and so is more readily labelled deviant. This may be changing as environmentalists are becoming more influential and environmental norms are becoming more salient (Ermann and Lundman 1978).

Definitions of deviance are always bipartite. One part is the action or condition that is attributed to the deviant; the other is the negative response of the group. If these two parts do not occur together, there is no deviance. Exhibit 8.1 outlines some common pairs. Since each kind of deviance exists as a violation of some normative standard that is actively supported in the society, rule-violating behaviour is no longer judged deviant when this support declines.

The duality of deviance has led some people to assume it could be abolished just by eliminating rules. True, the result would be no deviance, but there would also be no society.

A deviant is a person whose appearance or behaviour is seen as rule-violating, but normative standards do change.

EXHIBIT 8.1

DEVIANCE AS THE LABELLING OF NORM VIOLATION

Deviant label	Normative standard
Heretic	Religious orthodoxy (beliefs)
Sinner	Religious regulation (acts)
Traitor	Loyalty
Homosexual	Gender roles
Dangerous Driver	Highway Traffic Act
Robber	Criminal Code
Absentee, alcoholic	Reliability, self-control
Slow learner, "egg-head"	Group's desired level of intellectual achievement
Deformed person, freak	Group's definition of desirable physical appearance

CROSS-CULTURAL VARIATION

History and anthropology provide many examples of the variability of human society. No matter how awful an act may be in terms of one culture, another has likely permitted or even demanded it. In North American society, for example, infanticide, suicide, child abuse, and theft are regarded as seriously deviant. Some cultures (particularly those that exist in harsh environments) regard infanticide as a normal form of population control. In highly-regulated societies (such as that of traditional Japan), certain situations call for ritual suicide as a moral duty. At various times in Europe and North America, treatment so severe as to amount to child abuse has been justified as strengthening children, providing survival of the fittest. Plains Indian societies rewarded youths who could demonstrate the ability to sneak into camps and steal horses (Wallace and Hochel 1952).[2]

To see the point differently, ask yourself who is considered different, immoral, or dangerous. According to Jerry Simmons, the range would include

> *the Plains Indian youth who was unable to see visions, the big-breasted Chinese girl, the early Christian skulking in the catacombs, the Arab who liked alcohol instead of hashish, the Polynesian girl who didn't enjoy sex, and the medieval man who indulged himself by bathing too frequently (1969, 4).*

CULTURAL INTEGRATION

Although rules may vary from society to society, they are not arbitrary nor interchangeable. Rules and the deviance they define are integral parts of established systems. In North America, a person who buys goods in one city and sells them at a higher price in another is considered a resourceful entrepreneur. Such acts fulfil the norms of capitalism and help the capitalist economic system to operate. The same behaviour in Albania would disrupt the government-controlled plan for the distribution of goods; it would not help the bureaucratic socialist system to function smoothly. Thus, in one society, seekers of individual profit may win awards, while in the other they may be subject to severe punishment.

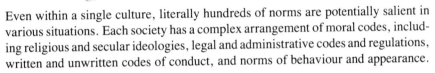

THE UNIVERSALITY OF DEVIANCE

Even within a single culture, literally hundreds of norms are potentially salient in various situations. Each society has a complex arrangement of moral codes, including religious and secular ideologies, legal and administrative codes and regulations, written and unwritten codes of conduct, and norms of behaviour and appearance.

As we noted in Chapter 2, these various moral orders may conflict or cross-cut each other, creating role conflict. You have probably noticed, at school and at work, that the norms of your peer group sometimes conflict with the norms of the institution. Adhere to one too closely, and you are a friendless ''browner.'' Adhere to the other, and you will not be promoted. Compromise too much, and you are a spineless ''nerd.'' It is unlikely that a perfect balance can be maintained in this or any situation.

Similarly, as society adapts to internal development and external change, following yesterday's rules may not work to get you to your goals or even to the goals that you've been told you should achieve. Many young women, for example, feel obligated to find appropriate husbands but find that their parents' rules as to what is appropriate, developed in another culture or another time period, seem to interfere. Similarly, many middle-aged men in North America today complain that they do not know what behaviour is appropriate in marriage and in the workplace because the women's movement has changed the rules.

TOLERANCE

Not all behaviour that strays from the straight-and-narrow path is labelled deviant. Some normative demands are uniformly enforced, but most have a **margin of tolerance**. This margin is usually wider for higher status members of the group. Societies also set aside certain times and places during which all but the most stringent rules are relaxed or even overturned, providing release from the pressure of regular conformity. (Since the relaxation of control becomes a norm on such occasions, management of these events often calls for specific police training beforehand.)

Tolerance varies with the value system. In a society in which the church steeples are the highest buildings, religious deviation is the kind least tolerated. If the banks have the tallest structures, economic deviance calls forth the strongest reproach.

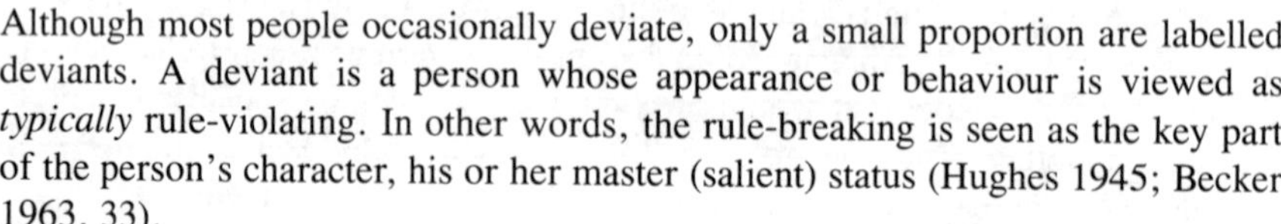

DEVIANCE AS A MASTER STATUS

Although most people occasionally deviate, only a small proportion are labelled deviants. A deviant is a person whose appearance or behaviour is viewed as *typically* rule-violating. In other words, the rule-breaking is seen as the key part of the person's character, his or her master (salient) status (Hughes 1945; Becker 1963, 33).

Consider the following statement: John X is a friendly, hard-working, talented ex-convict.

Would you hire John X? How did "ex-convict" change your impression of John's other qualities? Criminal conviction tends to create a master status. Everything else you know about the person is reinterpreted in the light of that one piece of information.

This reinterpretation has been documented in many types of situations. For example, the employee who is eager to work overtime is seen positively until it is discovered that she is stealing from the company; then her eagerness is reinterpreted. The man who acts "like a gentleman" on dates with women may find his behaviour reinterpreted when someone accuses him of homosexuality.

The fall from respectability is often sudden and dramatic, since people tend to assume that the deviant has been hiding his or her "true" self. The label "murderer" can be earned permanently by a single act, even though most such people kill only once. The same is likely to be true of "child molester" or "welfare cheat." In recent years, increasingly vigilant attention by media and "watchdog" agencies has led to exposés of prominent politicians and business leaders detailing conflict of interest, patronage, and fraud; their fame and fortune were suddenly seen in a new light. Thus, the discovery of a deviant element in a person's behaviour may have overwhelming consequences. One occasion, one brief moment may result in a complete reinterpretation of the person's moral character. Everything about him or her is now reinterpreted in the light of this new evidence about what others think he or she really is (and, by implication, has been all along).

IDENTIFIERS

Deviant identity may be sought out or resisted. Erving Goffman (1963, 44) has delineated the roles of **identifiers** and **disidentifiers**, signals that people use intentionally to negotiate a position in society. They are visible signs that suggest, to those who know them, membership in a social role. A tattoo on the forearm, black leather equipment, metallic jewellery, a style of haircut (or the lack of one) can instantly communicate all you need to know about a person's beliefs, commitments, and behaviour. Underworld slang can also serve in this way. Since much deviant behaviour survives by hiding from official control, deviant identifiers tend to change once they become common knowledge.

Unwilling deviants may use disidentifiers to counter the effects of their handicap or deformity. Just as identifiers proclaim identification with less respectable society, disidentifiers announce that the individual is not really an outsider. The dwarf who wears a beard and carries a cane is using them to identify with the normal adult world (Truzzi 1971). Many people who are visibly different from others go to great lengths to do "normalizing" things. These disidentifying signs may overcome the master-status effect of their deviance.

BIKER FUNERAL: "Colours" (Satan patch and sleeveless leather jacket) identify full-fledged members of a biker club. These identifiers are highly valued within the group.

DEVIANTIZING: A POWER GAME

Deviantizing is the interactive process by which deviant labels are applied. The process is a political one that can occur in the smallest of small groups and the largest of government or corporate organizations. Rules are proposed and debated, accepted or not.

Sometimes the process is democratic; quite often it is not. Even in democratically-led groups, some members have more influence than others. Occasionally, special-interest groups successfully bring pressure on the power-holders to do things their way. Thus the rules of a group or a society rarely, if ever, reflect the interests of all its members equally.

Similarly, when the rules have been made, another continuous political process determines the extent to which they are enforced. It is not surprising that, in most societies, the less politically powerful members, those people who have the least say about the rules, are over-represented among those who are punished and controlled. At school, at work, or in the courtrooms, it is mainly these outsiders who are suspended, fined, or jailed.

MORAL ENTREPRENEURS

Deviantizing may come about in many different ways. One pattern that has attracted a great deal of attention is the pattern of moral entrepreneurship. **Moral entrepreneurs** are people who actively crusade for causes. According to Becker, there are two kinds: the rule-makers, who take seriously the statement "there ought to be a law," and the rule-enforcers, who commit themselves to seeking out and punishing offenders. Both groups try to convince power-holders that society would be improved if new rules were made and enforced. They hope to create a more moral society by removing temptation and raising the costs of immoral behaviour (1963, 147–55).

In North America, moral entrepreneurs have campaigned to stop (among other things) drinking, swearing, bribe-taking, and polluting. Others have tried to make everyone participate in what they consider worthwhile practices, such as religious observance and voting, or to reduce or eliminate what they see as temptations, such as drugs and topless bars. In the Middle East, some have denounced working women and kissing in public. In England not long ago, one group tried to put pants on cows and horses. In North America today, moral entrepreneurs work to gain seat-belt legislation, make available fair housing, clean up the air, and stop (or else protect) the seal hunt.

The term "moral entrepreneur" is used to suggest that these people usually have an economic or social stake in the rules they propose. They are not just interested in saving everyone else. For example, in *Symbolic Crusade*, Joseph Gusfield (1963) interpreted the temperance (anti-alcohol) movement as an effort by native-born, white, rural, Protestant North Americans to preserve their way of life over that of the growing majority of immigrants and urban dwellers. This group's major achievement in the United States was the Volstead Act of 1919, which banned the sale of beverages having more than 0.5 percent alcohol. Prohibition in Canada followed the same pattern.[3]

In both countries, the banning of alcohol was the result of political pressure exerted by an unrepresentative minority. These unpopular laws proved unenforceable. Breaking them became a source of challenge and amusement for ordinary citizens and a source of unparalleled revenue for gangsters. It was in this period of "bathtub gin" that organized crime made its greatest gains. Criminals provided liquor to the rich and powerful, who in turn rewarded and protected their sources.

The failure of Prohibition illustrates the major weakness of moral engineering, as well as the way in which rules are integral to society: effective lawmakers must take care not to go too far beyond what the majority of citizens are willing to support. Legislation to make people behave ''better'' — fair housing laws, gambling restrictions, automobile safety-belt rules — is a gamble. If enough people support it, it becomes legitimate. If it is flouted, it may encourage other kinds of rule-breaking and bring law, and law enforcement, into disrepute.

CANADIAN NARCOTICS LEGISLATION

By E.W. Vaz

Shirley Cook emphasizes three prominent groups in Canada who were involved with drugs earlier in the century: the medical profession, whose members were commonly prescribing medications containing opiates, the Chinese pedlars of opium, and the general public among whom there was widespread use of medicines containing opiates. Admittedly the Patent and Proprietary Medicines Act was introduced to control the indiscriminate use of harmful drugs by physicians and others, but the penalties for violation of this Act were much less drastic than those for violation of the Opium and Narcotic Drug Act. In the end it was the Chinese who were the losers; they, rather than the physicians, were designated deviants. Cook suggests that the decision to consider narcotic users as criminals clearly reflects the stratification order and power differential between groups at the time.

Secondly, the moral reformers ''had the arena of social legislation-making to themselves.'' Because it was largely a ''hidden type conflict,'' there were no opposing views, their moralistic testimonials and writings went unchallenged, and there was no need to arouse public opinion. They encouraged belief in the ''dope fiend'' image of the drug user, they condemned the use of drugs which they said encouraged the ''natural depravity of man,'' and they strongly advocated protection for the moral fiber of the citizenry. It is noteworthy that these views were ''espoused by the superordinate group who made and enforced the rule,'' and that the absence of public debate successfully neutralized any objection.

Another factor was the long-standing hate and hostility directed against Asian immigrants, especially the Chinese and Japanese, in Canada. In the 1922 narcotics debates, the ''moral ruin of innocent young people'' was attributed to the ''foreign inferior race,'' an allegation which heightened the moral indignation of the legislators and led to stiffer penalties. Had this racial hatred been non-existent, Cook suggests that the moral indignation against drug users, and with it stringent law enforcement, would have waned, as it did against the manufacturers of tobacco and alcohol, many of whom were of British ancestry. Their high social standing helped immunize them from the kind of intense vilification that was directed against the Chinese. Until after World War II, the Chinese remained a despised social group because of immigration restrictions, their occupational skills, and their "high social visibility."

The evidence makes quite clear that the Canadian Narcotics Legislation was engineered by groups of resourceful "moral entrepreneurs." Neither rationality nor the opinions or sentiments of the majority were evidently involved. The positions of power held by the crusaders, their freedom from countervailing views, and their intense hatred of Asians greatly influenced the content of the legislation.

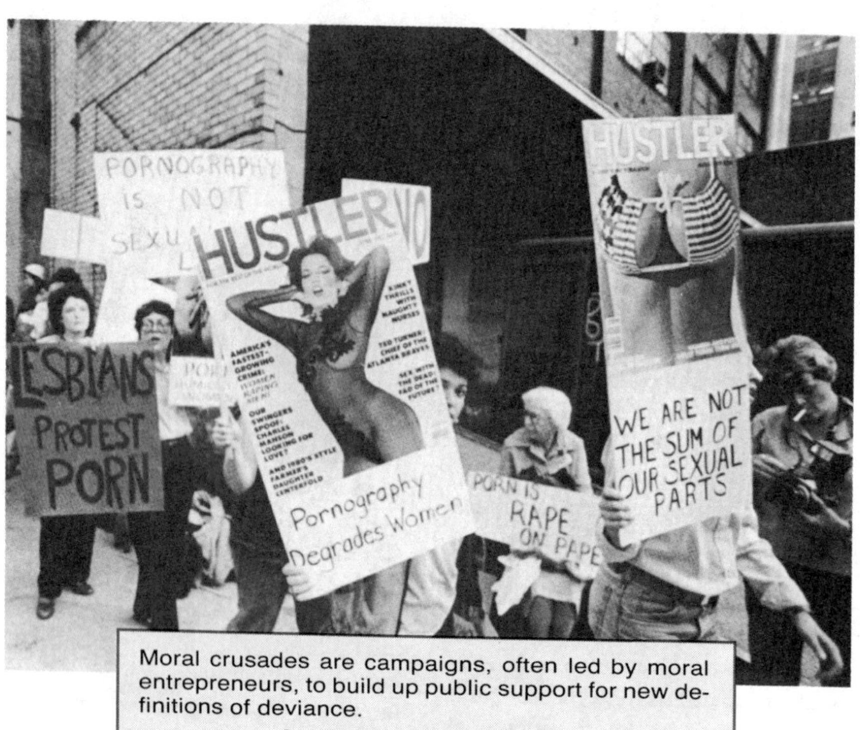

Moral crusades are campaigns, often led by moral entrepreneurs, to build up public support for new definitions of deviance.

MORAL CRUSADES

Moral crusades are campaigns, often led by moral entrepreneurs, to build up public support for new definitions of deviance (Becker 1963, Chaps. 7 and 8). Child abuse, wife beating, and drunk driving, for example, have been redefined in recent years — they have been increasingly deviantized. Both the official penalties and unofficial censure have increased in the light of campaigns by women's groups and victims' families to increase public awareness and change social values. Anti-smoking, anti-polluting, and anti-discrimination movements have all gained considerable influence in North America in the last decade. They have created new categories of deviants.

Moral crusades often employ propaganda to get public attention and sympathy. The 1930s film *Reefer Madness* was made to support the anti-marijuana cause. It shows a young man going totally berserk after a mere whiff of pot. Similarly, a recent film made to support the anti-abortion movement has been criticized as a deliberate distortion of fetal development. Although not all the information put out by moral crusades is incorrect, its onesidedness and its attention-getting features often distort the issues.

POLICE ARREST 6 SANTAS, 2 ELVES DURING PROTEST AGAINST WAR TOYS

By Janis Hass

Six Santas and two elves were arrested during the weekend after trying to declare a Metro Toronto toy store a ''war toys free zone.''

''Santa's here to take war toys away,'' shouted one of those arrested, a woman who asked to be identified only as Santa Claus.

The Santas, saying they had travelled from the North Pole to remove toys of which Santa would not approve, stuffed toy rocket launchers, soldier dolls, plastic grenades and guns into garbage bags, then left the bags in the store's aisles.

The Santas and elves, members of the Alliance for Non-Violent Action, decided to stage the demonstration on Saturday afternoon at the Toy City store at Dufferin Street and Lawrence Avenue West after two sets of protest letters sent to managers at 40 stores across Metro did not elicit any response, another arrested Santa said.

''Everyone has a right to their opinion, but they shouldn't infringe on others,'' said Toy City's acting manager, Mario Addesa.

Mr. Addesa, who said it was his first day back at work after a sick leave, said he received notice of the demonstration 15 minutes before the Santas and their half a dozen helpers descended on the toy store.

He said he put extra clerks in the war toys section, but, after watching a heated discussion between a guitar-carrying elf and one of the clerks, he decided to call the police.

While most shoppers appeared confused over the cause of the commotion, some said they were happy that Santa

Toronto Police arrest Santas at a store on Saturday. Santas were removing violent toys.

was doing something about the sale of war toys.

"What do children need to learn from war toys?" asked Mirella Serpe, a preschool teacher.

Cathy MacDonell, 25, also applauded the protesters' action but thought they had picked the wrong place to do it. "The store manager just sells toys that sell." She said the toy manufacturers would have been a better target.

Some Santas and elves sang protest songs and distributed handbills and candy canes. Others pulled war toys from the shelves and put them into bags as store staff tried vainly to stop them.

Constables from 32 Division escorted the Santas and elves out of the store after they refused to leave when asked.

"You're really putting on a good show for the kids, Santa — being put in a police car," shouted clerk Enzo Addesa, 19, the manager's cousin.

The Santas and their helpers were detained for several minutes inside police cruisers, charged with trespassing and released.

They said they were unsure whether they would pay the $53.75 fine or fight it in court.

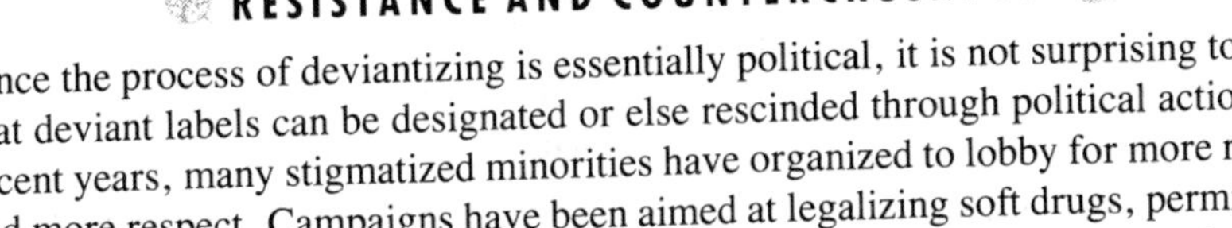

RESISTANCE AND COUNTERCRUSADES

Since the process of deviantizing is essentially political, it is not surprising to find that deviant labels can be designated or else rescinded through political action. In recent years, many stigmatized minorities have organized to lobby for more rights and more respect. Campaigns have been aimed at legalizing soft drugs, permitting Sunday shopping, permitting homosexuals in the armed forces, and enforcing job rights for all kinds of deviant minorities.

These advocates often find, however, that it is more difficult to rescind a rule than it was to make it in the first place. Those who come out to protest a particular rule—for example, the banning of marijuana—may find themselves labelled as people who do not respect the law or even as people who are users.[4] In times of religious revival, whole societies can be caught up in a spiral of increasing moral restriction, while opponents find themselves classed with the devil.[5]

Unofficially and often officially, negotiation and bargaining take place between the deviants and those who would control them. If the labellers take on a group with strong organizational and media access, they may not only fail to reach their goal but may also find themselves on the receiving end of the labelling process. For example, people who attempt to censor sexually explicit material in books and films have often found themselves stereotyped as frustrated, interfering old biddies, "the third sex," who lack the ability to enjoy themselves and want to make sure no one else does either.

INSULTS FLY AS TV HOSTS DEFEND RIGHT TO BE KINKY

By Associated Press

Morton Downey Jr. found the shouting distasteful, Phil Donahue settled upon an epitaph ("occasionally he went too far") and Geraldo Rivera proclaimed that the real Geraldo is three different men. And Larry King defended their right to be kinky. The occasion was a raucous, 90-minute debate Wednesday pitting the four talk-show stars against print media luminaries over what constitutes responsible journalism and good taste. The videotaped show, for airing over public television, opened the annual meeting of the American Society of Newspaper Editors.

King rejected the notion that anyone should be reined in. "It's a big pie," said the USA Today columnist and CNN talk-show host. "Geraldo's producers may decide they want to do a lot of sex on their programs, or they want to do things that may be kinky. So what? I don't have to watch."

The program was produced and moderated by former CBS News chief Fred Friendly, now with Columbia's Graduate School of Journalism. He showed an excerpt from a program Rivera did on sex surrogates, telling his former student: "It seems to me that what you're concentrating on is that 'kinky' business."

Rivera: "I do lots of different programs. You are talking about 10 per cent of what I do."

Friendly: "Mr. Rivera, I looked at a hundred of your programs. I could have run a hundred of them and made the same point . . . Who are your role models?

Rivera: "There's a lot of (Walter) Winchell in what I do. There's also Edward R. Murrow, and Merv Griffin."

Jack Nelson, Washington bureau chief of the Los Angeles Times, snapped that Rivera and the others are "more show biz than you are journalists." Tom Shales, television critic for the Washington Post, said, "We're not talking about what's journalism and what's not journalism. We're talking about what's good taste and what's bad taste, what's good manners and what's bad manners. And I think television now is overrun with bad taste and bad manners."

The audience was shown another excerpt, from Downey's program, in which a young member of the audience challenged the host's views on prison furloughs by noting that "one of the central tenets of Christianity is forgiveness."

Downey was shown retorting, "Let me tell you something. More people have been killed in the name of Jesus . . . by guys like you." Downey and the young man wound up screaming "Murderer!" at one another 10 times over. Downey concluded by raising his arm and inviting the youth to "suck my armpit."

Donahue said, "I do not apologize for wanting to draw a crowd. I'm as interested in ratings as the people in the room are interested in circulation." Besides, he added, "I think it's a pretty good epitaph for somebody: 'Occasionally, he went too far.' " Toward the end, virtually all the panelists were trying to be heard over each other. "I find it extremely distasteful," said Downey, "to listen to shouting."

STIGMA: SOCIAL DISTANCE AND DISHONOUR

North American society punishes people who are "bad," uses therapy to curb the disruption of the mentally or physically sick, and invokes re-education (training) to deal with the inadequately socialized. All of these groups, the bad, the mad, the sick, and the misguided, experience **stigma**—a mark of discredit or unworthiness, the opposite of a status symbol.

The Greek word *stigma* originally referred to a physical sign that marked a ''polluted'' individual, warning good citizens to avoid close contact with the person. Body cuts or brands were used to identify the bearer as a slave, criminal, or traitor—an unworthy person. Later, clothing was used to the same effect. For example, in Nazi-controlled Germany, Jews, labelled by the power-holders as evil deviants, had to wear large yellow stars of David, which warned obedient citizens not to associate with them, buy from them, or give them employment.

In earlier times, stigma was not always artificially created. People who were abnormal mentally or physically were held to be stigmatized by god. Their affliction and suffering were taken as an indicator of sin committed earlier in their lifetime or in a previous generation or a previous life.

The message was often ambivalent, though, since being touched by god, even in the negative sense, was something special. In Christian theology, for example, suffering is associated with purification and redemption (the crucifixion) and god's favour (the story of Job). Thus, stigma has a dual meaning. Those who have been stigmatized have been treated mainly as moral lepers, but occasionally as sacred. Although the religious meanings attached to stigma have not entirely disappeared, they are much less common now.[6]

Today stigma is usually experienced as punishment. It generally has the effect of producing **social distance**, a lack of closeness in social interaction. This distance, in turn, induces discrimination and reduced life chances. Stigmatized people are handicapped in the competition for power, prestige, and wealth. They may have difficulty obtaining and retaining essentials, such as employment and housing, and they may also be excluded from the respect that their achievements would otherwise earn them. The few individuals who are able to overcome the stigma enough to make major contributions (being a crippled master musician or a dwarf college professor, for example) often experience the problems of **status inconsistency**. Some people judge them by their deviance, while others respect them for their achievement; they can never be quite certain which treatment to expect.

DEVIANCE DISAVOWAL AND STIGMA MANAGEMENT: A STUDY OF OBESITY

By John Evans and Alexander Himelfarb

Those who feel that their stigma is invisible to others will generally employ techniques to keep it so; while those who feel that their stigma is visible to others will attempt to reduce its visibility, assert normality in spite of it, or actually discount it.

Since we are concerned with the role of the actor, it is important to point out that visibility is seldom a clear-cut issue. That is, depending on the situation, the actor may be quite uncertain as to how others see him. For example, one obese person commented, "Almost every morning I have to ask my wife whether I look fat today. I can never tell. She usually says no, but I don't always believe her." In addition, many fat people commented, "Some days I wake up and feel fat while other days I feel fine." . . .

Perhaps the most widespread technique for the management of obesity consists of attempts to hide or minimize the appearance of fatness. The most obvious and the most frequently used technique is to cover it. For the obese person his coat is his shield:

> *Being fat is so embarrassing that I wear my coat almost everywhere I go —even in the movies where it's dark.*

Or, as a Weight Watchers' member describes her first appearance at a meeting:

> *I registered with all my fat tucked into a coat and oh! did I feel sloppy when I took that coat off to be weighed.*

For many fat people their entire wardrobe seems to reflect this shielding function. Baggy pants, baggy sweaters, long skirts, and waistless dresses are always "in." More sophisticated camouflage involves making use of patterns and tailoring to "increase" height and "decrease" width; hence the preference for vertical stripes over checks in the selection of clothing. It seems unnecessary to emphasize the role of foundation garments in compacting fat.

However, one of the difficulties with props such as clothing is that there are occasions when one is expected to remove them. What begins as a relatively simple management technique becomes more complex and affects more and more areas of the individual's life:

> *I joined the "Y," but didn't enjoy it because I couldn't undress for the shower.*
>
> *I used to swim, but now I can never go to the beach.*
>
> *What's a bikini!*

It is perhaps ironic that many of the activities we engage in to keep trim are out of bounds for the obese. Thus, joining a gym group, swimming, and exercising in public are avoided by many of the obese.

Regardless of the camouflage, there is a generally held belief that numbers don't lie. For example, many obese people do not like to be measured for clothes. This may mean, as many of our informants report, that the obese person will frequently send someone else to purchase his clothing. For much the same reason, many obese people find mail-order houses useful. The obese are also reluctant to reveal clothing size. One respondent protected herself from inadvertent disclosure by tearing off all her clothing labels. When discussion of clothing size cannot be avoided, many of our informants report that they lie about it. In fact, there seem to be size barriers beyond which many are reluctant to go: "When I got to size 40 I stopped buying pants.'' What seems to be an extreme example of this same concern for numbers occurs when individuals ''fit'' into clothes which they themselves consider too small: ''I was so happy to get into a size 14, I didn't mind not breathing.''

STIGMA AND THE SELF-FULFILLING PROPHECY

A common consequence of stigma is a negative spiral into deviancy. By acting as if someone is deviant (whether true or not), we limit his or her legitimate opportunities. Stigma becomes the basis for the self-fulfilling prophecy (Merton 1949, 179–95). There are many jobs ex-convicts cannot get. Upon getting out of prison, they are stigmatized as dangerous or untrustworthy, and now face even greater difficulty in making it in the straight world. They may choose a deviant path partly *because* of the stigma society has attached to them.

Other examples are common. People with histories of psychiatric illness may have to face the stress of being denied responsible work, stress that may make them behave strangely. People with physical handicaps may be denied entry into training for ''normal'' jobs, either by explicit policy or by lack of appropriate facilities, making it impossible for them to engage in ''normal'' work.

Thus, although the desire to avoid stigma may motivate people to conformity, once stigma is present, it tends to increase the deviance of those stained by it.

Stigmatized people may find acceptance in deviant subcultures. Here their deviant record, appearance, behaviour, or attitude is a kind of membership card. Here they may find an alternative social system, one that rewards them with respect and support. In comparison to the mainstream, however, these alternative systems are usually quite limited in their range of positions and paths to upward mobility. Most career criminals, for example, operate at the semiskilled level at best. Workshops for the handicapped are even more limited.

UNDERWORLD CAREERS

Everyone has a career in the sense of having a life course. While some people devote their main energies to conventional, ''legitimate'' activities, others pursue deviant ones. For the latter, deviance (often criminal deviance or deviance that supports criminal activity of others) is primarily a way of making a living. They become professional thieves, arsonists, terrorists, or paid killers with a place in an underworld occupational hierarchy.

Professional killers, for example, commit murder as a job to be done. Killing may gratify them, but personal gratification does not guide their choice of time, place, or victim. These choices are business strategy, designed to intimidate competition, eliminate informants, or meet the needs of paying clients. The occupation itself is deviant.

Most criminal deviance is not occupational in this sense. Rather, it arises out of psychological or interpersonal conflicts or pressure to cheat at a legitimate job. Occupational criminals often express disdain for such a deviant, who, in their opinion, acts out of weakness. They dislike "amateurs" who make mistakes and "bring down the heat." Professional criminals like to present themselves as exploiters of opportunities that others are too stupid or too afraid to try. They hide their activities not because of shame or guilt, but because other people might inform on them or get in their way. For them, getting caught is just another business risk, not a personal disaster (Nettler 1982; Miller 1978; Dietz 1983).

Criminal occupations, like legitimate ones, evolve as society changes. McIntosh (1971) has outlined changes in the form and structure of the practice of thieving from the early days of piracy and highway robbery through pickpocketing and second-storey work to modern high-stakes projects, planned for months and carried out with military precision and military equipment. Changes in the occupation adapt it to the changing social order.

EXPLAINING DEVIANCE: THEORIES AND PERSPECTIVES

Deviance has preoccupied parents, priests, and politicians since earliest times. Authorities have tried to understand and control it. Deviants themselves have sometimes tried to explain or justify it. As explanations and solutions have been proposed and tested, knowledge of deviance has become more refined.

No one theory of deviance today, however, has a monopoly on truth. Of course, you can find books that claim it is all caused by biological deficiencies or faulty mothering or capitalism. Such simplifications are often popular, but they cannot deliver what they promise. A careful look at the research record shows that deviance, like conformity—indeed, like all behaviour—involves biological, psychological, and sociological elements that combine in different ways. There are many paths to the same destination (Nettler 1982).

Over the years, various theories of deviance have been proposed, tested against reality, and changed. Older theories often persist alongside the newer ones, occasionally in some revised form.

DEMONIC THEORY: "THE DEVIL MADE ME DO IT"

The earliest theories blamed deviance on supernatural forces—trolls, the snake in the Garden of Eden, or, more directly, the devil. The magical beliefs of early religions included the threat of curses, spells, possession, enthrallment, and other ways in which external forces were thought to make ordinary or weak people do evil things. Naughty children were sometimes seen as changelings (evil substitutes for human babies stolen in the night). The mentally ill were viewed as possessed or cursed. Deviance was a state to be detected through magical signs, whether in trial by ordeal, trial by battle, or compurgation.

With evil-doing blamed on supernatural forces, the cure was sought not in reform of the society or the individual but in rituals of conversion, prayer, penance, and sacrifice. Or the evil might be exorcized (driven out by magical forces), which was often a dangerous, painful, or even fatal exercise for the person "possessed."

Demonic theory has only a minor influence in the field today, but continues to imbue popular conceptions of deviant motivation. Unusual or compulsive behaviour is sometimes attributed to possession by evil spirits (see Scott Peck's *The People of the Lie* [1983]).

RATIONAL SELF-INTEREST

By the 1700s, philosophers were developing a new image of humanity that was free of demonic influences (Scheleff 1981; Pfohl 1985). People were now seen as self-interested beings whose deviant behaviour was based on a rational calculation that they would gain more by breaking the rules than they would lose.

Deviance was believed to emerge when the chance to gain an advantage by rule-breaking was greater than the likelihood of being caught, or else when the punishment was light enough to be worth the risk; based on these beliefs, the solution to criminality seemed to lie in improving law enforcement and designing punishments that would fit the crime. Capricious, vindictive punishments were to be avoided, since they interfered with the ability to calculate the cost of actions (Becarria 1819).

Reforms were introduced, but they did not reduce the amount of deviance. No amount of punishment served to deter crime. Some theorists began to question the normality of criminals.

EARLY PHYSIOLOGICAL EXPLANATIONS OF DEVIANCE

Try to imagine a fairy tale in which the villain is handsome and the heroine ugly. It works only as a joke. This reflects the underlying monism of most cultures: good is beautiful, bad is ugly.

Unfortunately, life is not so simple. The sadistic Dr. Mengele, the "angel of death" who ran medical experiments in the Auschwitz concentration camp during the Second World War, was described, even by his victims, as an extremely handsome man. Eichmann, the Nazi official whose efficient arrangement of transportation kept the death camps full, even when German troops desperately needed trains, was a very ordinary-looking bureaucrat (Arendt 1964). Yet there remains a powerful tendency to find connections between physical characteristics and moral quality, and this desire has often entered into the hypotheses of researchers.

BORN TO BE CRIMINAL

One of the best-known early theorists to link criminality with biology was Cesare Lombroso (1835–1909). He studied the cadavers of prisoners who had died in Italian prisons and found they differed from the bodies of noncriminals in many ways. Unusually large jaws and cheekbones, abnormal dentition, and long arms and legs with large fingers and toes were among the ''signs'' of abnormality.

Consequently, Lombroso (1895, 1918 [1899]) posited the existence of a ''born criminal,'' an example of **atavism**. The criminal's body and his or her criminality were signs of a genetic throwback to traits characteristic of a more primitive stage of human evolution. The criminal man was ''an atavistic being who reproduces in his person the ferocious instincts of primitive humanity and inferior animals'' (Lombroso 1895).

Lombroso's theory was a popular one and attracted a great deal of attention, although his critics were quick to point out that the variations he found might result from the physical effects of prison life, the high proportion of disadvantaged minorities (such as Sicilian migrants) in the prison population, and the tendency of judges to lock up people who did not seem as civilized as others.[7]

Today Lombroso is chiefly important for his role in having inspired research. In considering deviance, he and his followers (and their critics) began to use empirical rather than philosophical enquiry. Thousands of ''caught'' criminals were studied and compared with noncriminals. Although modern researchers criticize the way in which this was done, it helped to give empirical substance to the study of deviance and criminality.

Ernest Hooton, an American follower of Lombroso, extended the theory that criminals were inherently inferior men and women who were unable to resist the natural temptations of the normal social environment:

> *Crime is not rampant in savage and retarded human societies. Crime flourishes rather in rich cultures where production is varied and abundant, so that constitutional inferiors are coddled and fostered, inevitably to bite the hands which have fed them (1939, 388–9).*

The environment, he said, could not be improved to a point at which these ''flawed and degenerate human beings'' would be able to succeed in honest social competition.

Although Hooton did not blame criminals for their inadequacy, he challenged society to rid itself of them. Thus, he argued for the elimination or at least complete separation of the physically, mentally, and morally unfit. While some of his followers recommended only physical training to strengthen these inferiors, others called for sterilization and euthanasia. The basis of a gas-chamber approach to deviants had been laid.

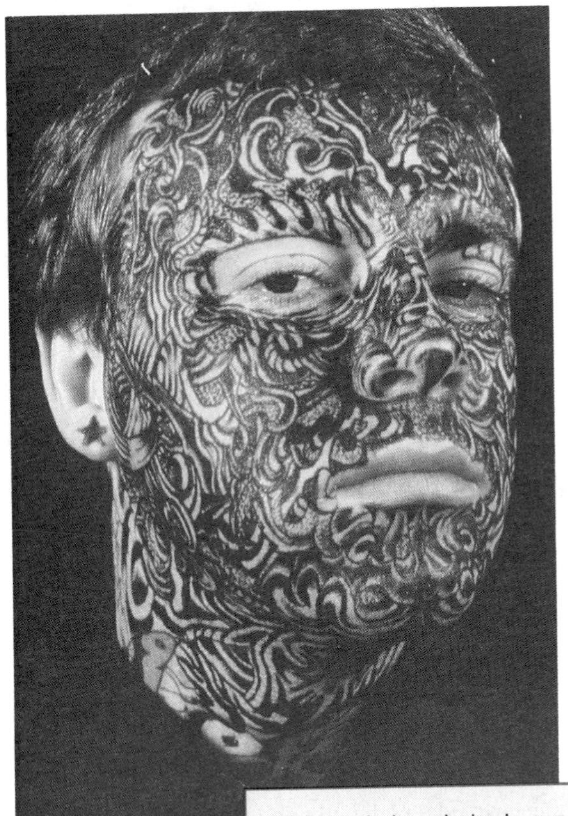

Are atavistic criminals more likely to adorn themselves with tattoos? Lombroso thought so.

BODY SHAPES AND DELINQUENCY

The belief that form makes function was the basis of early body-type research. Between the wars, social scientists worked out a tripartite system of body types (see Exhibit 8.2), saying the shape of the body indicates how it will be used. It was found that mesomorphs (individuals with an athletic build) were over-represented among juvenile delinquents. Researchers such as Sheldon (1948) argued that people with such bodies were more likely to have an imbalance of impulses and impulse controls that would lead to acts of delinquency.

EXHIBIT 8.2

BODY TYPES AND CHARACTER

	Physical traits	Character traits
Endomorphic	round soft	easy-gong sociable indulgent
Mesomorphic	rectangular hard	restless energetic
Ectomorphic	lean fragile	introspective sensitive nervous

The mesomorph is thought to be better adapted to delinquent activities than the soft endomorph or the fragile ectomorph.

SOURCE: Adapted from Sheldon (1948).

Later writers, such as Glueck and Glueck (1956), argued that mesomorphic youths are more likely to be treated as delinquents by authorities and by other young people. In this view, the body is not the source of deviance but a cause of labelling and also a factor in opportunity. Mesomorphs, said these anlaysts, are the people most likely to be pushed into or attracted to delinquent roles. Thin, short-sighted ectomorphs may be motivated to deviance, but they are much less likely to be recruited by others or convicted if they are caught.

MODERN PHYSIOLOGICAL THEORIES 

A century of research has not uncovered any directly observable biological characteristic that distinguishes deviants from the rule-abiding. No modern theorist argues that criminals are atavistic, constitutionally inferior, or of a particular body type. But the search for physiological factors in antisocial and violent behaviour continues. It has simply shifted to less visible phenomena, such as chromosomes, body chemistry, and brain waves.

XYY: THE JOLLY GREEN GIANT OR BIG BAD JOHN?

In 1969, John Farley, a 203 cm, 109 kg giant of a man, confessed to having beaten, strangled, raped, and mutilated a New York city woman. Usually a good-natured fellow, he was subject to sudden fits of violent temper. He was defended as insane; the basis of the plea was that he had a chromosomal deviation called the XYY genotype (Jarvik, Klodin, and Matsuyama 1973).

The XYY man has two male (Y) chromosomes, rather than one. Although the condition was recognized by the 1920s, it was not linked with deviance until the 1960s, when it was correlated with "supermaleness" — tallness, acne, aggressiveness, skeletal deformities, and mental deficiencies. By the 1970s, however, when genetic testing had become easier and more widely used, it was found that few convicted criminals had the extra male chromosome and that many men who did have it remained out of trouble (National Institute of Mental Health 1970).

BODY CHEMISTRY

In the 1950s, pharmacologists brought out many new drugs to help control moods and behaviour. Mental patients who had lived under restraint in the back wards of asylums could now be kept well enough (or peaceful enough) to live in the community. At about the same time, it was discovered that certain drugs, such as the stimulant Ritalin, increased conformity and achievement scores in children who were overactive and disruptive in the standard classroom. The hyperkinetic syndrome became recognized as a "distinct medical entity" (Pfohl 1985, 114–23).

Many observers now feel that since chemicals seem to relieve deviant symptoms, chemical imbalances may cause them. For example, violent or disruptive behaviour has been blamed on sensitivities to sugar or food dyes. In an American court case, a man blamed his violence on the junk food he had been eating. The jury acquitted him. Lawyers quickly labelled this the "twinkie-bar defence."

AROUSAL LEVELS

Researchers have recently reported that deviants are less sensitive to stimuli, such as pain, and have lower arousal rates (as revealed by brain-wave patterns, galvanic skin response, and other physical measures). Analysts theorize that this insensitivity may impede socialization in two ways. First, such children would be less responsive to threats or promises. Second, the lower arousal might be experienced as boredom, as a craving for danger and excitement. According to this theory, deviants do not learn good behaviour because "normal" socialization does not get through to them, and they seek out stimulation because time goes much more slowly for them than for other people (Lykken 1982).

But which comes first? Researchers have also shown that people can change their body chemistry by changing their behaviour. Do deviants somehow *become* less sensitive and less easily aroused? Or are these traits inborn? Can a normal pattern of arousal be developed through therapy?

It seems unlikely that any purely biological theory will be sufficient to explain much of human deviance. It is clear, however, that any explanation of deviance must take into account the ways in which energy levels, strength, and mental balance may enter into behaviour, either by directly motivating and providing opportunity or by eliciting controlling responses from others.

PSYCHIATRY AND DEVIANCE

The psychoanalytic theories of Sigmund Freud and his followers have had a substantial impact on explanations of deviance. As we discussed in Chapter 3 on socialization, psychiatrists see each individual as having strong, biologically rooted drives—the id part of the personality. Society, represented in the personality by the superego developed through socialization, demands that the primitive urges of the id be curbed and channelled. The ego balances these demands and keeps the individual in contact with both inner reality and the reality of the environment. Thus, deviance can be blamed on a particularly strong id (violent behaviour), an overly repressive superego (neurotic behaviour), a weak ego, or a combination of the three. Specifically, it may be a symptom of conflicts unresolved during one of the stages of human development: the oral, anal, genital, and phallic.[8]

The interpretation of deviance as the externalization of inner conflicts was recently exemplified in the case of a provincial cabinet member who explained to the news media that he deliberately set himself up to be caught shoplifting because he was unable to resolve the discrepancy between his deviance (disavowed homosexuality) and his high position (Mackenzie 1983).

Psychoanalytic explanations may be insightful. When deviants understand the way in which their behaviour relates to unmet needs, they can often be helped to find more acceptable ways of meeting these needs. When they realize they are fighting out conflicts dating from many years ago, they may be freed to face the present. On the other hand, some observers feel psychoanalytic explanations are merely "inciteful" (Samenow 1984). That is, they give the deviants further excuses for their behaviour, removing the penalty of guilt. It is the fault of society if the culture is too repressive, and the fault of parents if they have not loved well and sensitively. When criminals "use" psychiatry this way, they perceive punishment as further persecution and become bitter instead of reformed.

PSYCHOLOGY AND DEVIANCE

Psychologists have also focused on the mind/body connection, but compared with psychiatrists, they have been much more concerned with the development of theories that can be empirically tested. The modern social psychology of deviance tends to focus on cognitive styles (ways of thinking) and on individual temperament (personal style). Psychological theories of learning have become well integrated with sociological theories.

FRUSTRATION/AGGRESSION

The frustration/aggression theory is rooted in the Freudian view that social living is inherently frustrating and that such frustration may be met by defence mechanisms, such as displacement (attack on a safe and available target, instead of the real source of anger) or reaction-formation (an attack on people who represent disowned parts of the personality). Thus, a person who is unsure of his own manhood may react violently to young men who seem homosexual or effeminate (Dollard *et al.* 1939).

Frustration/aggression theorists have documented an increase in aggression against out-groups when the political or economic system fails to meet expectations. One of the strengths of this approach is that it helps to explain aggression against innocent targets. When minorities are attacked or buildings vandalized, the "real" cause may be frustrating social conditions.

THE CRIMINAL MIND

Another theory, that of the criminal mind, argues that the thought processes of criminals are fundamentally different from those of other people (Yochelson and Samenow 1976). When ordinary people enter a drug store, they assess how easy it will be to find what they want and pay for it. When criminals enter, they assess how the cash register is protected and where the exits are. They do this automatically, even if they are not currently planning to rob the store.

According to Stanton Samenow (1984), this type of thinking can be traced to the criminal's earliest childhood. He has argued that people with criminal minds can be trained to behave normally but will always differ from normal, moral people.

This theory, which resembles the disease theory of alcoholism (the alcoholic is always an alcoholic, even if he or she stops drinking), has been popular among people who would like to believe that criminals are born, not made. There is no reason to improve society or waste time understanding deviants, they think.

TEMPERAMENT AND LEARNING

Social-psychological theories of temperament and learning have also played an important part in explanations of deviance. There is mounting evidence that temperament does not change a great deal during an individual's life unless changes in the environment are drastic and longlasting (Nettler 1982). People may reform themselves, but revolution—complete transformation—occurs only when they are cut off from their roots and brainwashed. This does not mean that people are born criminal. The temperament that makes for a successful astronaut may also make for a successful leader of an urban gang.

Theories of learning have also been integrated with some of the sociological perspectives discussed in the next subsection.

SOCIOLOGICAL THEORIES OF DEVIANCE 

FUNCTIONALISM

Can deviance be a good thing? It is not difficult to see how it can be harmful. The alcoholic pilot endangers passengers, the mentally ill social worker cannot help clients, the terrorist undermines citizens' trust in the existing social order, and the drug-using musician makes conformity to standard values look foolish, unnecessary, or even hypocritical. These consequences, which are counter to the survival of individuals or the society, are negative manifest (intended, recognized) functions.[9]

Functionalists, such as Talcott Parsons and Robert Merton, have shown that not all functions are manifest. The persistence of deviance, they say, shows that it serves some positive function in the society. Research has involved looking for the actual consequences of deviance, including its latent (unintended, unrecognized) functions.

Consider, for example, the effects of prostitution. Kingsley Davis (1961) has argued that prostitution helps to maintain the family. How? It provides men with a way to express their gender role (the search for variety) but to do so with women ineligible for marriage, so the family is not threatened.[10]

FUNCTIONALIST BEGINNINGS: DURKHEIM

One of the earliest functionalist theories of deviance was sketched out by Emile Durkheim (1947; first published 1893). He argued that when society was simple and everyone in it had very similar life experiences, rules were few and well supported. Violators were expelled or severely punished. As society became more complex and was held together by interdependence, instead of by common beliefs and lifestyles, rules became more pragmatic. No one person could ever know all the rules, much less know the experiences that gave rise to them. Very few rules could be supported with the moral fervour of the simpler society.

As we noted in Chapter 1, society in Durkheim's time was rapidly changing. Deviance might occur because the rules were unknown or unclear and people lacked a sense of the right path. Durkheim argued that given this state of anomie—unclear guidelines in a fluid society—much rule-breaking had a positive function in that it made people decide which rules ought to be supported and which needed to be changed. Deviant behaviour would reveal some rules to be weak, harmful, or inadequate, often anticipating social change. Today's deviance became tomorrow's conformity.

How can responding to deviance increase social solidarity? Consider what happens when people gather together to express their anger and indignation, to take action against an offender, or to force the authorities to do so — social interaction increases. Shared sentiments are confirmed, and common concerns are identified. People increase their sense of belonging, solidarity, and commitment. They draw clear lines between themselves and outsiders. They are more willing to work for the group and make sacrifices for it. All this usually makes the group stronger. If, in addition, the deviant suffers an unpleasant penalty, the value of conformity is further enhanced.

How would Durkheim analyse the behaviour of Henry Morgentaler, who for years has operated abortion clinics in clear defiance of Canada's Criminal Code? Can anything be socially beneficial about such rule-violating behaviour? Morgentaler challenged the morality and practicality of a set of rules that were frequently violated in secret, though officially upheld. Because of his challenge, citizens learned about the actual effects of the rules and began to weigh them against more recently salient values of respect for individual choice and equal rights (including equal access to medical services). The battle led to new rules to clarify the meaning of the law and to establish proper procedures for enforcing all laws.[11] It also led to increased religious solidarity and attention to theology. Ordinary citizens learned a great deal about politics, the law, law enforcement, and citizenship, as well as about abortion. Many people who normally avoided controversy and politics were drawn into active participation.

Thus, functionalism reveals that a certain level of deviance, like conflict, is a necessary part of social life and that its positive consequences for the social system co-exist with the negative ones (Coser 1962).

Henry Morgentaler successfully challenged the morality and practicality of a set of rules that were frequently violated in secret.

EXHIBIT 8.3

FUNCTIONS OF DEVIANCE

1. May cause an unknown or unclear rule to be specifically and clearly stated (aids predictability, planning)
2. May cause a group to unite in support of the value violated (ritual affirmation of values, commitment of members)
3. May cause a group to realize rule is a "bad" one (e.g., "test cases")
4. When deviant punished, the value of conformity is enhanced
5. Scapegoating/vote getting (e.g., politicians who attack juvenile delinquency instead of white-collar crime)
7. May serve as an alternate means of obtaining goals such as wealth, power, recognition (organized crime/antibureaucracy)
8. May act as tension release at group or personal level

DYSFUNCTIONS OF DEVIANCE

1. Can cause breakdown due to interdependency of parts (e.g., alcoholic who cannot perform work, family roles)
2. Can affect other peoples' motivation to conform (e.g., effect of "punk" lifestyles)
3. Can destroy trust in the system (e.g., terrorism)
4. Can cause personal suffering
5. May lead to loss of socially useful talent

ANOMIE THEORY AND ITS EXPANSIONS

In the anomie theory of Robert Merton (1957), the society provides culturally accepted goals, such as a college degree, a car in the driveway, and 2.2 children. It also provides culturally institutionalized means for achieving these goals: study well, work hard, or marry the boss's daughter. **Anomia** (Merton's term for anomie) occurs when the accepted goals are not matched by available means.

The middle-class child with normal intelligence and a few strings to pull usually has no difficulty accomplishing these goals. The disadvantaged child absorbs the same TV version of the good life but may not find an open path to it. The school is a middle-class institution, and so are most successful businesses. Managerial jobs, for example, tend to be open to those who can look and act like members of the middle class.

Merton set out a paradigm of deviance-producing situations to show that deviance is a product of the social structure, not of individual biology or psychology (see Exhibit 8.4).

- *Innovation*. When an individual accepts the culture's goals but chooses a different means of reaching them, the result is innovation. For example, the embezzler may fully accept the suburban ideal but chooses an illegal way to obtain it.

- *Ritualism.* When the individual loses sight of the goals but systematically goes through the approved means, the result is ritualism. The bureaucrat who makes you fill in 20 forms and then tells you the service you want is unavailable is providing an example of ritualism.

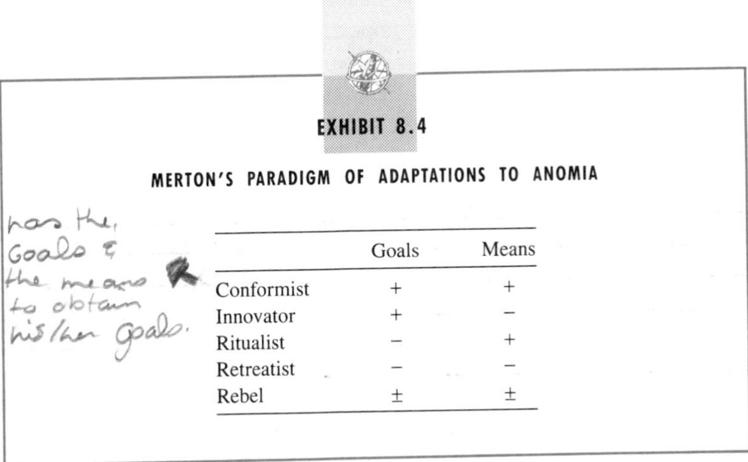

EXHIBIT 8.4

MERTON'S PARADIGM OF ADAPTATIONS TO ANOMIA

	Goals	Means
Conformist	+	+
Innovator	+	−
Ritualist	−	+
Retreatist	−	−
Rebel	±	±

- *Retreatism.* When the individual has neither the cultural goals nor the desire to pursue them, the response is called retreatism. The heroin addict, who seeks the pleasant relief from reality that the drug temporarily provides, may fit this category (although the desperate search for supplies may undo the effect).
- *Rebellion.* When the individual rejects the approved goals and means and seeks a new system, the response is called rebellion. It can range from adolescent rebellion against parental dictates to mature political rebellion against the current economic or political order.

Other theorists have expanded this framework. Albert Cohen, for example, also began with the problem of goals and means but interpreted them differently. Where Merton had spoken of individual deviance, Cohen (1966) described social-class responses to unequal opportunity. Lower-class boys want recognition just as much as do middle-class boys, but find themselves effectively excluded from the middle-class institutions, mainly the school; their drive for identity and autonomy leads them to develop an alternate status system in which they can succeed. This alternate system is a **counterculture**, a reversal of the middle-class one they were rejecting. Its central values are disrespect for property and for property rights.

Another development from Merton's anomie theory was the work of Richard Cloward and Lloyd Ohlin (1960). They developed their own set of categories, similar to Merton's but including the possibility of illegitimate opportunities. In their paradigm, the social order offers illegitimate goals that, like legitimate ones, can be open or closed, accepted or rejected. It is possible to succeed in either world —to become prime minister or the "boss of all bosses"—or be a loser in both, a double loser. A great deal depends on the degree to which the illegitimate opportunities are available and organized into a system that allows upward mobility. In neighbourhoods characterized by organized illegal enterprises, such as loan-sharking, racketeering, and gambling, researchers have found that young people were provided with more illegal than legal opportunities; many of the illegal ones could lead to large incomes and considerable social power. In other areas, there were few avenues of any kind to success. Here, deviance often took the form of bands of fighting gangs in which status was based on toughness and violence (Spergel 1964).

Other theorists have focused on subcultures as the source of values that conflict with the dominant, middle-class ones. Miller (1958) argued that the lower class generates the values of trouble, toughness, smartness, excitement, fate, autonomy, and hedonism, which lead young people into law-breaking activities. The middle-class values—ambition, discipline, deferral of gratification, control of aggression, respect for property—encourage conformity. Each set of values works in its own milieu and is therefore not countercultural. Thus, in Miller's view, many delinquents are not reacting to rejection by the middle class (in the school, for example). Rather, they are acting out lower-class cultural norms.

Notice that all these theories presume that there is more deviance in the lower classes than in the classes above them. Not all modern theorists agree that this assumption is legitimate. More "caught" and "labelled" deviants come from the lower classes, but this prevalence may reflect the nature of the rules and the way in which they are enforced.

DIFFERENTIAL ASSOCIATION: "IT'S NORMAL PRACTICE AROUND HERE!"

Edwin Sutherland (1961) argued that people are not born deviant and they do not commit deviant acts merely because they are stressed or have easy opportunity. They act as they do because they have learned, from their environment, that this is the normal way of doing things. Such values, said Sutherland, are found in all strata of society, not strictly, nor even predominantly, in the lower classes. (His research focused on deviance in white-collar occupations.)

Sutherland maintained that most deviance is learned in small intimate groups that communicate not only attitudes favourable to crime, but also techniques and rationalizations for it. The heart of the theory is the idea of **differential association**. A person becomes deviant when the environment to which he or she is exposed provides more definitions favourable to rule-violation than definitions favouring conformity.[12]

The greatest impact of Sutherland's work was on the study of white-collar crime, the kind of violation of criminal and administrative laws that occurs as an everyday matter in some organizations, including large, reputable corporations. When caught, such offenders claim that the deviant practices were already in place when they began to work, that these practices were simply normal business practices that happened to be against the rules (Ermann and Lundman 1978).

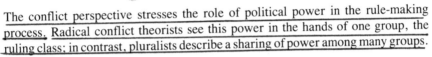

CONFLICT THEORIES 

The conflict perspective stresses the role of political power in the rule-making process. Radical conflict theorists see this power in the hands of one group, the ruling class; in contrast, pluralists describe a sharing of power among many groups.

In radical Marxist and neo-Marxist theories, the ruling class comprises the owners of the means of production, who control the political, social, and physical environment for everyone else. According to the radical theory of history, more and more people fall into the disempowered groups, leaving fewer and fewer people in control. To put off the inevitable overthrow of the social order, the powerful minority at the top must find ever-increasing means for controlling those below them. These controls, which include the rules of welfare agencies as well as overt policing, mean that more and more people are deviantized, receive punishment or therapy, or are controlled by regulatory agencies. In such theories, therefore, deviance is the result of exploitative regulation.

Pluralistic forms of conflict theory see the competition for social power as occurring among a variety of groups, which may be divided in many cross-cutting or reinforcing ways: religion, region, age, income, ethnicity, or any other parameter of life. Each group fights for political power in order to protect its particular interests. As the groups compete, the rules for the society are worked out. If only one group had all the power, it would be able to impose its rules as the societal rules, without compromise. In all modern societies, though, groups are forced both to compete and to compromise with each other.

Pluralistic conflict theories do not contain an over-riding theory of history, except, perhaps, the conviction that conflict is endemic to every social order; all that changes is the form these conflicts take.

Thus, all conflict theories see social rules, including laws, as tools used to further the collective interests of the politically powerful. Rules reflect these interests *except*:

- when laws are passed to reduce the manifestation of conflict among social classes;
- or when there is internal conflict among members of the dominant class.

Conflict theorists point out that this reality is often obscured by the claims of the lawmakers. For example, in *The Child Savers*, Anthony Platt (1969) argued that juvenile courts were not established to benefit youngsters, even though the separation of young offenders from hardened criminals seems benevolent. In his view, the juvenile court is, like the schools, simply another mechanism whereby urban youths can be coerced into working-class conformity.

NIGERIA'S GRUESOME WAR ON CRIME

By Angela Cobbina

Nigerian authorities are turning to draconian measures in the face of an escalating crime wave.

The most gruesome of these is in Niger state where the governor, Col. David Mark, has ordered that armed robbers be executed from the feet upwards. Firing squads start with the condemned person's ankles and work their way up to the heart with five-minute intervals between shots.

''By intermittent shooting the armed robber will not only pay dearly for his crime but suffer to the death,'' a Niger state spokesman said.

But few believe the punishment will reduce the crime—and the evidence so far seems to bear them out.

Public executions have been held in several Nigerian states and reporters invited to take photographs of the condemned and to record their final utterances — all to serve as a deterrent to others.

The other side of the equation is Nigeria's tattered economy: It has created many hardships and the perfect climate for crime to flourish. The result is that city dwellers live in constant fear of gunmen.

Many homes have at least four lines of defence: the padlocked iron gates around the compound; the guard armed with a cutlass; steel-girded doors and windows; and finally, if the robbers gain entry, a stash of money to be handed over in the hope that lives will be spared.

Broad daylight

Here in the sprawling, densely populated capital of Lagos, where robbery is most widespread, almost everyone has a mugging story—either involving themselves or someone they know.

Few venture out in the dark, though even that is no guarantee since gunmen frequently strike in broad daylight.

An 18-year-old armed robbery suspect, who was killed while trying to escape prison, once boasted to police that he ran his ''business'' from a flat in London. His gang of four specialized in embassies.

One of the most spectacular raids was on the Egyptian embassy two years ago in mid-morning in Lagos' heavily-guarded diplomatic sector. Two women were raped and more than $8,000 stolen.

At first, the armed robbers confined their activities to Lagos, which is often compared with New York in terms of violence. But now the crime wave has spread to other cities, including the less developed north, hitherto regarded as a safe haven.

Violent crime first made regular headlines during the civilian government of Shehu Shagari, when the oil boom began to fizzle.

While the "haves" continued to enjoy and flaunt the fruits of their wealth the "have nots" — including thousands of rural people who had flocked to Lagos in hope of sharing the bonanza — suddenly found themselves destitute.

The profligacy of the Shagari government eventually led to its overthrow. The ensuing military government tried to cut the waste of previous years with mass cuts in the ranks of factory workers and civil servants. The result was a rapid rise in unemployment.

Death Penalty

Other well-meaning policies created additional hardships. Thousands of people were made homeless by an environmental clean-up campaign when bulldozers demolished "illegal structures," the official euphemism for the ever-expanding shanty towns of Lagos.

The number of recorded armed robberies jumped from 271,240 in 1982 to 311,961 in 1984, while killings increased from 93 to 159 in the same period.

Under his much-publicized "war against indiscipline," former president Muhammadu Buhari introduced the death penalty for armed robbers. The 19 Nigerian states averaged five executions each in 1984.

Thieves were joined on death row by a number of cocaine and heroin smugglers, mostly caught at airports in possession of relatively small amounts of drugs.

But the harsh penalties and widespread publicity appear only to have made gunmen even more desperate and daring. Since armed robbery carried the death penalty, there seemed to be nothing to lose by also murdering the victims.

Many believe that executing hardened criminals at least represents some action. That explains why, despite head of state Ibrahim Babangida's much-heralded human rights policy, there was little outcry over Governor Mark's slow execution announcement. Criticism was confined mostly to left-wing university intellectuals; the press declined to comment.

LABELLING THEORY

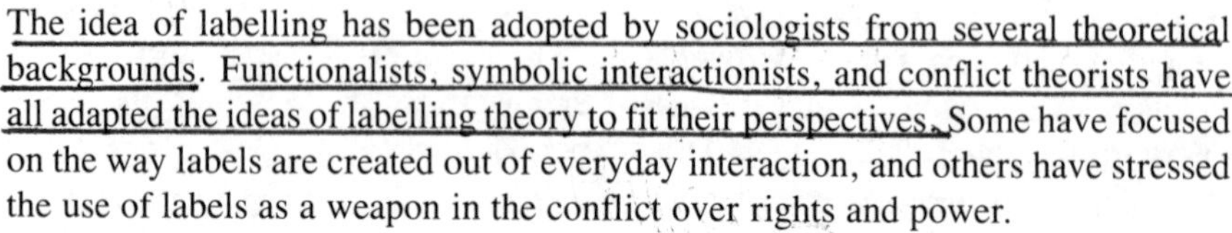

The idea of labelling has been adopted by sociologists from several theoretical backgrounds. Functionalists, symbolic interactionists, and conflict theorists have all adapted the ideas of labelling theory to fit their perspectives. Some have focused on the way labels are created out of everyday interaction, and others have stressed the use of labels as a weapon in the conflict over rights and power.

Edwin Lemert (1951, 1967) introduced two of the best-known concepts of labelling theory: primary and secondary deviation. **Primary deviation** comes from many sources. It is seen as temporary and nonrecurrent and can even be accidental. Most people do, at one time or another, deviate: they hit a child or write a cheque for a sum greater than is, at that moment, in their bank account. Such lapses, even if they evoke a societal response, do not usually produce a deviant identity. Most people commit any number of small offences in the course of a day and do not attract any sustained attention.

Secondary deviation, on the other hand, is caused by societal reaction to deviance (or the belief that it has occurred). Secondary deviation is prolonged. It results from a change in status (produced by stigma) and becomes a role that is knowingly (and sometimes willingly) played by the deviant. This role becomes a part of his or her self-concept. Frank Tannenbaum observed, in 1938, that part of the solution to juvenile delinquency ''is through a refusal to dramatize evil. The less said about it, the better'' (1938, 20).

CONTROL THEORIES

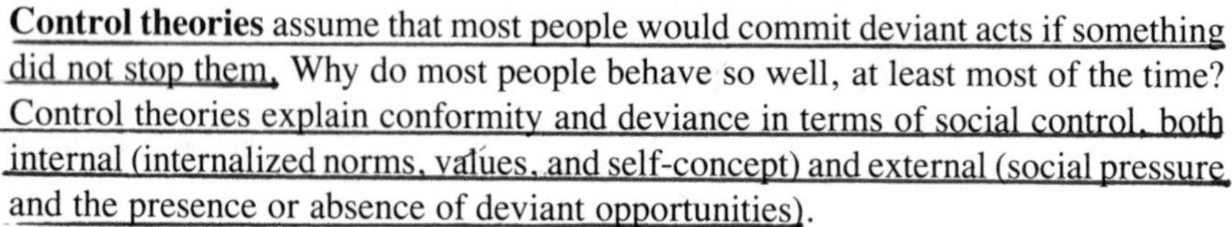

Control theories assume that most people would commit deviant acts if something did not stop them. Why do most people behave so well, at least most of the time? Control theories explain conformity and deviance in terms of social control, both internal (internalized norms, values, and self-concept) and external (social pressure and the presence or absence of deviant opportunities).

The forerunners of control theories were members of the Chicago School, which developed in the 1920s. These writers argued that deviance emerged amid the disorganization of rapidly changing urban society. In a well-organized society, they said, each person's socialization has provided internalized norms that serve him or her well. When society becomes disorganized, by rapid technological change, immigration, war, or other factors, the normative system is disrupted. Socialization is less effective, and individuals grow up with weakened internal and external restraint (Pfohl 1985, Chapter 5).

These works convinced public authorities to invest in ambitious projects, such as the Chicago Area Project, that were intended to revitalize inner-city communities. Unfortunately, these projects were not set up as scientific experiments, and experts are still arguing about whether they reduced delinquency or, by helping to organize gangs, actually increased it.

Modern control theorists have moved away from the grand-scale projects of the Chicago School and now build their work on that of social psychologists, such as Travis Hirshi. Hirshi (1969) identified four "controls" that create a bond between an individual and the rules of his or her society:

- *Attachment.* Feelings of empathy, sympathy, and sensitivity to the opinion of others. People who are not capable of this are sometimes labelled psychopaths.
- *Commitment.* Investment in the group norms, so that doing things differently would mean sacrificing something of value, such as one's status, job, or reputation.
- *Involvement.* Participation in conventional activities, which leaves little opportunity for deviant ideas or behaviour to flourish.
- *Belief.* Allegiance to the values of the group.

When these bonds are strong, they contain and prevent deviance. Society may, however, not provide the environment that supports such bonds.

TECHNIQUES OF NEUTRALIZATION

It is also possible that deviants reinterpret social reality to exempt themselves from the rules. Gresham Sykes and David Matza (1957) proposed five techniques of neutralization that deviants use to release themselves from compliance with norms. They may sound familiar to the reader.

- *Denial of responsibility.* "I was drunk and upset, and I come from a broken family."
- *Denial of injury.* "I was just borrowing it. This was just a private quarrel. No harm was done."
- *Denial of victim.* "He was just a bum. He deserved it."
- *Condemning the condemners.* "Who are you to call me bad? At least I'm not a hypocrite about it."
- *Appeal to higher loyalties.* "A guy has to stand up for his friends. I stole only for the family."

These techniques permit the deviant to engage in rule-breaking behaviour without defining him- or herself as a bad person. They permit the delinquent to commit robbery in the street, and the manager to commit fraud in the executive suite, all in more or less good conscience (Matza 1964, 1969).

PHENOMENOLOGICAL THEORIES

Phenomenological theories of deviance are grounded in philosophy. They focus on the way in which people construct notions of deviance and how they decide *who* (or *what behaviour*) fits these categories. Official records do not accurately describe actual events; these records have to be partial and selective. Cicourel, for example, described the routine conviction process in juvenile court as one in which the judge and other court personnel share a concept of "normal" crime. Their goal in the courtroom is to find details that make the reported event make sense in terms of the way the court understands crime. Events that cannot be reconstructed in this way are pushed out of the system, and the juveniles involved are not officially labelled delinquent (Cicourel 1969; Sudnow 1965).

Another example of this approach is Arlene K. Daniels' research (1970) into the philosophy of combat psychiatry, which, she showed, sharply restricts the definition of mental illness compared with the definition used in civilian psychiatry. Very few symptoms are taken to indicate a need for relief from duty, and even these few are ignored if malingering has ever appeared in the soldier's record. Thus, "mental illness" is revealed as a social construct that varies acccording to the situation in which the judgement is made.

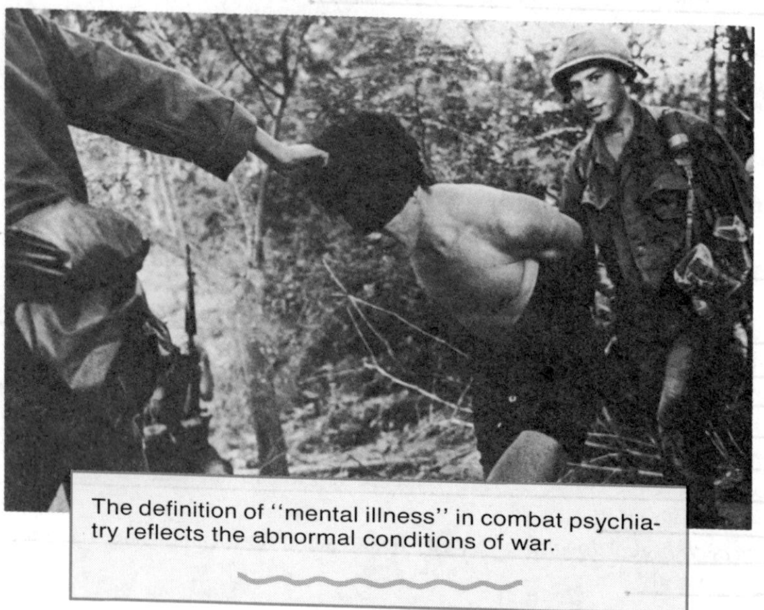

The definition of "mental illness" in combat psychiatry reflects the abnormal conditions of war.

These analysts have exposed some previously unexamined assumptions of the processing of deviants. They do not attempt to tell us anything about the causes of deviance or the causes of labelling, but they have shown that current "understanding" of deviance is a product of social process, one that is not infallible.

EXPLANATIONS OF DEVIANCE: CONFUSION OR CONSOLIDATION?

At this point, you may well feel that we have offered too many explanations for deviance. Whatever type of deviance one looks at, some people assert that its primary cause is biological or psychological or sociological. Even within each of these disciplines, there is debate over which variables are most important and how they are related to each other. The only way that these issues can be resolved is through research.

STUDIES OF DEVIANCE

Scientific study of society is always difficult, and the study of deviance has special difficulties. How is the social scientist able to study deviant action when, as a scholar, he or she represents authority? How can one understand the behaviour of people whose values and experiences are radically different from one's own? How can the researcher get past the defensive barriers of the deviant subculture?

Deviants, particularly those who live within the closed circle of underworld societies, usually have more to lose than to gain by being studied. There is always the danger that the research data will wind up being used as evidence in a court case or fall into the hands of enemies. No one who works hard to maintain a false front wants to have it exposed. Deviants are unlikely to think that furthering scientific knowledge is a particularly important goal.

If you want to find out when a man last beat his wife, how much a person drank before an accident, or what kind of regular customers a prostitute has, you need innovative research methods—or flexible ethics.

Because of these difficulties, early sociological studies on deviance relied heavily on official sources of information. Lombroso, as we have noted, studied the cadavers of convicted criminals who had died in prison. Until the late 1960s, most researchers used statistical information collected by authorities, such as school principals, police, and other public agents. Some relied on questionnaires or interviews with people who were already caught up in the official net.

In 1967, a book by Ned Polsky, *Hustlers, Beats and Others*, helped to initiate a new trend in research. Polsky argued that official statistics are biased and that data obtained from ''caught'' criminals are not accurate.

> *These are data that are much too heavily retrospective; data from people who aren't really free to put you down; data involving the kind of cooperativeness in which you get told what the criminal thinks you want to hear so that you will get off his back or maybe do him good with the judge or parole board (Polsky 1969, 115–6).*

Deviants who come to the attention of authorities may not only be uncooperative or dishonest—they are also atypical. They are disproportionately the losers, the inept, and those who do not care enough to avoid detection. Deviants who seek out the help of social workers or psychiatrists are even less typical of the underworld in general.

Yet for each type of deviance, the most readily-available informants are the failures and drop-outs. Most studies of homosexuals, for example, have used men who have come to psychiatrists or been arrested. These tend to be promiscuous men rather than those who have formed long-term stable relationships. Psychiatrists' studies of disturbed homosexuals can shed little light on those who are comfortable with their lifestyle or who hide their identities successfully.

Thus, Polsky's challenge was to go into the field, despite its dangers and discomforts. Many sociologists have now done so. They have entered into, recorded, and analysed the underworld life of organized crime, of the drug world, prostitution, and con games and have thus contributed to the understanding of the deviant and of deviant cultures. In many cases, these studies have been done by insiders who became sociologists (rather than the reverse). Howard Becker (1964), who studied the marijuana use of jazz musicians, had himself been a jazz musician for several years. Ned Polsky had spent years playing pool with pool-hall hustlers before he began to study their behaviour.

Participant observation (or covert observation) is, however, an option open only to sociologists with special contacts and lots of time. Several alternative approaches exist:

- *Insider reports* are books and articles written by deviants and people who hang out with them.[13] The quality of these reports varies. Some are detailed and insightful descriptions of "the path less travelled." However, the main motivation for many of these writings is access to the mass market. They romanticize, sensationalize, or even advertise. Some are elaborate efforts at self-justification; Mafia bosses come out looking like responsible, even philanthropic, businessmen, and prostitutes are treated as warm, compassionate social workers.
- *Victimization reports* are data gathered from the potential victims of deviants. They can provide much information about certain kinds of deviance, since most people are willing to answer questions about whether they have been mugged, burglarized, or annoyed by others. They may not be quite so willing to admit that they have been fooled by a con man, cheated by a prostitute, or have received bad drugs from a supplier.
- *Self-reports* are anonymous questionnaires used to find out about the kind and amount of deviance within particular groups. A researcher might ask subjects who are drug users, for example, to indicate whether they use particular drugs, how often, and whether they have ever been caught. These questionnaires are usually administered in group contexts (a school, for example) with elaborate precautions to ensure anonymity. Even so, the questions never ask for details such as, "Who is your supplier?"

Self-reports and victim studies have shown that deviance is more common than the records indicate and that those apprehended are not a representative sample of those who offend. They have been particularly useful in correcting the impression that lower-class youths commit more crimes than do those from the middle or upper class.

SOCIAL CONTROL

Social control includes all those aspects of social life by which we are enticed, cajoled, or coerced into particular patterns of behaviour.

INTERNAL AND EXTERNAL CONTROLS

Edward Ross (1896) described social control as "the moulding of the individual's feelings and desires to suit the needs of the group." This definition stresses the role of socialization, and the importance of **internal social controls**. In the process of socialization, we learn the rules of our culture and the degree to which various types of rules need to be respected. We learn to be guided mainly by our inner convictions, or we develop a strategy for responding to the demands of others. These internalized controls act as a kind of gyroscope which guides our personal action across a wide variety of specific contexts.

Many of the rules that we are expected to follow are not fully internalized. Every society supplements socialization with **external social controls**. External controls include open and obvious measures, such as the making and enforcing of official rules. They also include the blatant arsenal of peer group pressure.

Generally, external social control is based on the principles of reward and punishment. Although we tend to focus almost exclusively on threat and punishment, rewards are a more important part of conformity than punishments. Rewards such as belonging, respect, attention, and admiration combine with practical incentives such as income and privileges to make most citizens feel that conformity is worthwhile most of the time. The social control literature, however, documents our preoccupation with forms of punishment.

- *Revenge.* Although revenge is generally no longer accepted as a legal principle (except possibly in the notion of "punitive damages" awarded in civil courts), it still exists in our relations with one another. Revenge occurs when the injured person causes the guilty person to receive a punishment greater than the original offence.

- *Retribution.* Unlike revenge, retribution sets punishment at a level equivalent to the offence. The "eye for an eye" regulations outlined in the Book of Exodus, for example, reflect the historical transition from revenge to retribution. The idea of retribution is gradually giving way to the idea of compensation, whereby the offender is required to "make good" the offence, usually through a fine or community service work.

- *Rejection.* There are many forms of rejecting the deviant, including avoidance, shunning, or expulsion. Sending hard-to-manage children to boarding school, or violent adults to jail, is physical expulsion, but sometimes the rejection is symbolic instead. The ''silent treatment'' can be very effective. Some tight-knit communities will treat an offender as if she did not exist. There may even be a funeral for the person, who is now ''dead'' in the eyes of the community.

- *Ridicule.* A form of control practised in relatively homogeneous communities is public humiliation. In early Europe, an offender may have been mounted backward on a donkey and driven through the town while fellow villagers pounded on pie pans to make a loud noise. In colonial times, many towns made use of stocks, in which offenders would be displayed in humiliating positions and forced to endure the comments (and rotten fruit) thrown at them. In countries such as China and Japan, where the family is a strong force and maintaining ''face'' is very important, humiliation is still used as an official control tactic.

- *Repression.* Ideas or actions can be repressed in a variety of ways. Censorship, denial of licenses, and intimidation of leaders have been used to force deviance underground.

- *Restraint.* Restraint and incapacitation are often used to curb deviance. The defiant teenager may be ''grounded'' until he shows signs of being able to resist deviant peer-pressure. Bad drivers may lose their cars or their licence to drive. In Paris, some taxis have been equipped with 52,000 volt Israeli-made ''hot seats'' which are intended to stun an aggressive passenger, and allow the driver to disarm or remove the passenger from the car (Ganley 1987). Under the Sharia (Islamic Law), a thief might have his right hand cut off—a rather effective way of preventing similar offences, even if it fails to deal with the causes of theft.

- *Resistance.* Crime and deviance can be reduced by making them more difficult. When the wearing of motorcycle helmets was made mandatory, the number of thefts declined. The new regulation ''hardened the target,'' making it more difficult to steal. Similarly, steering wheels that lock when the key is removed help to prevent car theft, and passwords and codes help to protect computers from hackers and spies.

Resistance sometimes takes the form of fortification. When a small community near Miami, Florida experienced three burglaries, one rape, and an aggravated assault one Sunday afternoon, it responded by closing off six of the seven roads into the town. Exits from the State highway were blocked with steel pilings, and mounds of earth and sections of pavement were ripped up. An armed guard was hired to control the town's one remaining entrance (Conniff 1982).

- *Restriction.* Often the response to deviance has involved restricting it to particular places, rather than attempting to eliminate it. Zoning regulations may be used for restriction, or informal arrangements with police may have the same effect. The police will leave you alone as long as you are in the appropriate area, but will act quickly if you misbehave outside it. For example, police have often tolerated soft drug use at rock concerts, but would arrest the same people for the same act if it were done elsewhere.
- *Surveillance.* Sneaks and cheats are often controlled by the threat of exposure. Protest groups have used this tactic to reduce industrial pollution and the sale of unsafe products. Recently, the U.S. Securities and Exchange Commission added a new twist to this by ordering two Canadian-owned companies (which had violated regulations in the United States) to hire an independent regulator. This "consultant" would have to be acceptable to the SEC, and would closely monitor the company's activities for the next three years and prepare regular reports to the Commission (Fisher 1989). Perhaps some day, criminals may be forced to pay the salaries of correctional officers.

THE CHANGING SHAPE OF SOCIAL CONTROL

Types of social control favoured by a society are related to its explanations of deviance. As we have seen, when the devil causes evil, exorcism is practised; when deviance is caused by self-serving calculation, then carefully graduated deprivations and punishments will be practised. Similarly, pathological explanations have drawn forth medicalized and treatment-oriented programs.

THE U.S. DEBATE ON "CRACKDOWN" IS A CONTEST TO SEE WHO CAN PROPOSE MORE SPENDING

By Associated Press

Crack, which is smokable cocaine, is highly addictive and is widely used because it is so cheap, about $10 for a "rock" good for one high. It is generally sold in ghetto neighborhoods, in crack houses or open-air drug "marts." The violence associated with the turf wars and debt collections usually occurs in and around these areas, and a primary goal of the drug strategy is to retake the streets from such operations.

But the policy does not address the chronic despair and poverty in many of those neighborhoods. The immediate environment of the addict is the critical factor in weaning a person from crack.

"We're not talking about rehabilitation with most of these people, it's a question of habilitation," said Herbert Kleber, a professor of psychiatry who is on leave to serve as drug policy adviser William Bennett's deputy.

Addicts need the support of social structures such as family and other groups to succeed, he says, and for many crack users such support has never been part of life.

With crack, as with heroin in the past, the best predicator of a person's ability to shake addiction is whether he or she has a job.

What distresses some critics of the drug war proposals is that there is no sign the Bush administration has any intention of dealing with these factors.

"Drug profits are the major economic mobility program for ghetto youth in this country," said Ira Glasser, director of the American Civil Liberties Union. "And as long as that is the case, this silly strategy is not going to work.

"People are not shooting each other over drugs in our inner cities, they are shooting each other over the $300 a day they can earn. We do not have a drug problem, we have a money problem."

Indeed, conspicuous consumption among black youth in some areas of Washington and other cities is astonishing. Range Rovers and Jeep Cherokees are the vehicles of choice, because their four-wheel drive capabilities are admirably suited to fleeing over the lawns and parking barriers of public-housing areas. Heavy gold jewelry and European sportswear proliferate, and thousand-dollar leather jackets are de rigueur.

"It's a pretty powerful inducement when the alternative is $3.50 an hour at McDonald's," observed Eric Sterling, head of the Criminal Justice Policy Foundation.

He, like a number of other U.S. experts in the field, suggests that decriminalization would take the fantastic profits out of the drug business, and that the methods employed to reduce tobacco use could be adopted in the war against drugs. As even the most ardent legalization proponents acknowledge, however, it is not an option that has any hope of adoption in the near future.

Nor should it, argues Mr. Shain of the Addiction Research Foundation, who says that in the long run, neither those who argue for legalization nor those who delight in applying military metaphors are helpful.

"Drug use is a response to anxiety and depression; they provide control and confidence in a society where those are in short supply."

This applies equally to the ghetto user and the Manhattan stockbroker, whose insecurities can seem as real as the genuine lack of security experienced by a welfare mother.

Cocaine, with its stimulant effect, is ideally suited to addressing those feelings, but the patterns of use have long been part of human culture. The gin-soaked denizens of East London taverns in the nineteenth century have their present counterparts in the crack houses of southwest Los Angeles.

Such outbreaks tend to be cyclical, Mr. Shain said. Indeed, recent research at Yale University seems to show that the U.S. cocaine epidemic at the turn of the century was even more widespread than the current one.

What Mr. Shain finds more troubling is the trend towards a chemical society, in which every ache and pain, physical or psychic, can be treated away.

On the one hand, stress creates drug use as North Americans try to escape the increasing pressures of life in a modern industrial society. On the other hand, there is the rootlessness of North American life, where the traditional social structures — families and organized religion most notably — have eroded.

Mr. Shain suggests that determined "national introspection" would be far healthier than a drug war.

"I don't know that we want to go back to the old days," he said of the theory that a restoration of old-fashioned values is needed, "but there is no question we have lost our way spiritually as a culture."

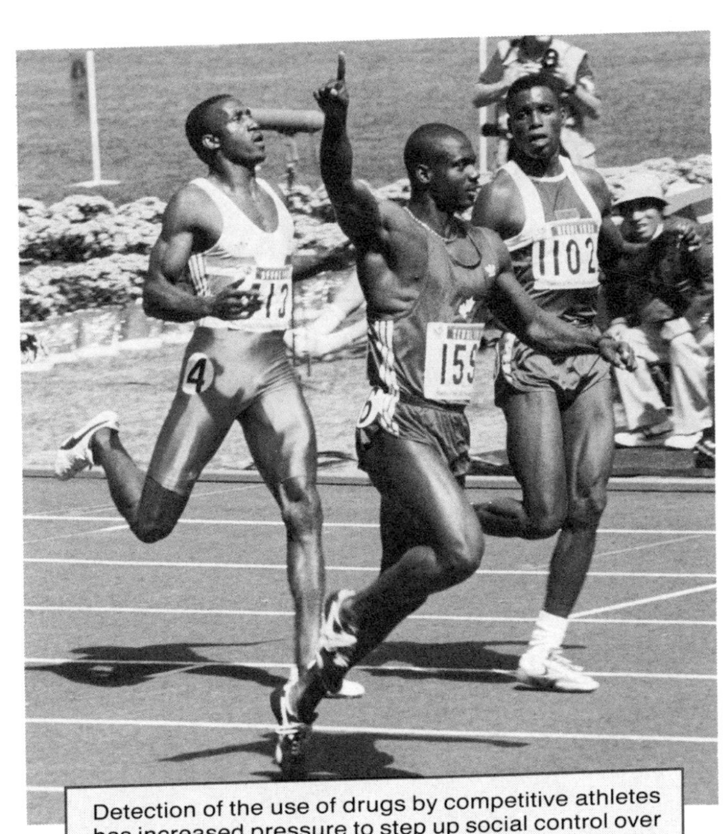

Detection of the use of drugs by competitive athletes has increased pressure to step up social control over this practice; the high cost of laboratory tests is one factor restricting an effective campaign.

EVOLUTION OF PUNISHMENT

In 1757 a man named Damiens attempted to assassinate the King of France. The court ordered a punishment that was intended to be horrifying. It ordered that he be taken to his place of execution in a cart, wearing nothing but a shirt and holding a torch of burning wax. There,

> *"the flesh will be torn from his breasts, arms, thighs and calves with red-hot pincers, his right hand, holding the knife with which he had committed the said parricide, burnt with sulphur, and, on those places where the flesh will be torn away, poured molton lead, boiling oil, burning resin, wax and sulphur melted together and then his body be drawn and quartered by four horses and his limbs and body consumed by fire, reduced to ashes and his ashes thrown to the winds." (Foucault 1976, 3–6)*

The actual execution proved to be even more terrible than that envisioned by the court.

Horrific punishments were common during this period, and often meted out for crimes which were minor, or even in cases in which the only evidence against the "criminal" had been obtained by anonymous denunciation and judicial torture (Weisser 1979).

Such punishment was not meant to reform the person who was punished. It was meant to terrify and horrify those who saw it. It made men "see" the seriousness of the offence, and it demonstrated the absolute power of the authorities over the lives and bodies of the people. Executions, whippings, and mutilations were public. Heads of executed criminals were displayed on city walls, bodies of highwaymen were hung in gibbets along the roadway.

The displacement of this form of "correction" was hastened by the rise of the urban mob. The crowd occasionally rescued prisoners and attacked officials; they often indulged in unrestrained revelry and riot. The crowd also saw to the efficiency of the execution—a bungled one at times meant death to the executioner. In 1783 executions were moved behind prison gates, and in 1868 [in England] they ceased to be public (Ignatieff 1978, 21–2). The presence of pickpockets in the crowds who gathered to see other pickpockets hanged demonstrated the futility of this way of dealing with crime.

The use of horrifying public spectacles was gradually replaced by what Foucault has graphically described as "The Great Confinement" (1965). The poor, the unemployed, the criminal, and the insane were gathered together in "hospitals" or asylums. At first, little distinction was made between various categories of "deviants." Anyone who begged or seemed to be without support or legitimate occupation could be committed to an institution, and subjected to whatever control (including stakes and chains) was deemed necessary. This general incarceration gradually evolved into the differentiated institutions of the asylum (for the mentally ill), the work house (for the indigent), and the prison (for the criminal).[14]

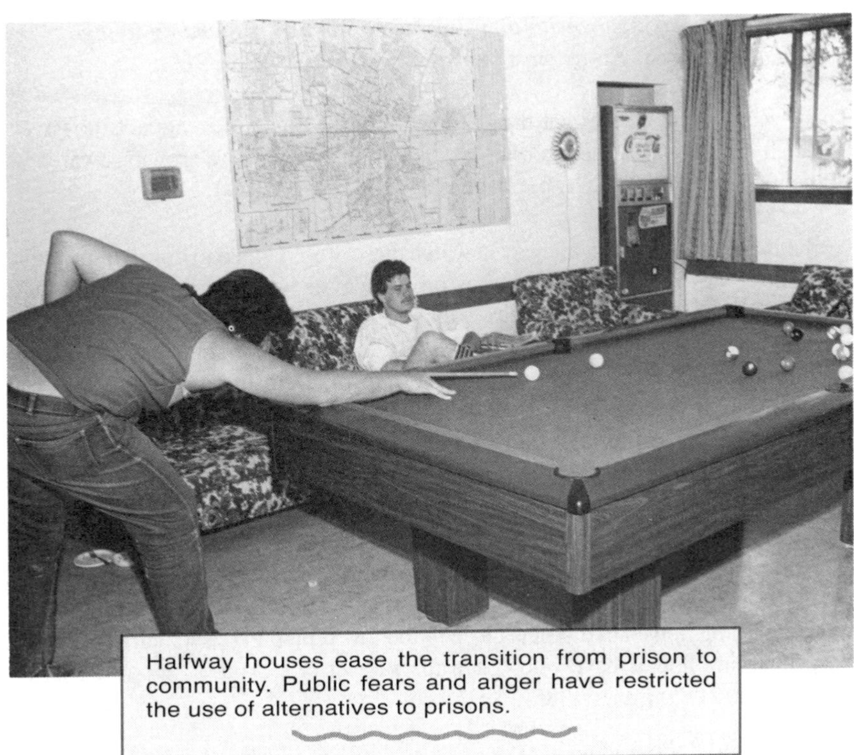

Halfway houses ease the transition from prison to community. Public fears and anger have restricted the use of alternatives to prisons.

DEINSTITUTIONALIZATION

In modern times, the catchword has been ''decarceration'' or ''**deinstitutionalization**.'' Both of these terms refer to reversing the ''great confinement,'' through ''mainstreaming'' people who used to be segregated because of their behaviour or appearance.

PSYCHOPHARMACEUTICALS

A major factor in deinstitutionalization has been the introduction of psychotropic drugs in the mid-1950s. The initial effect of psychotropic drugs was to change the quality of life within psychiatric institutions by reducing the need for restraints and permitting patients enough control over themselves for other therapies to work. An early experiment in a Canadian hospital produced the following report:

> *Within two weeks of commencing treatment, a striking change had taken place. The patients on Frenqual had become more sociable, they*

> *were neater, cleaner, and tidier. . . . For the first time, the patients would read books and magazines instead of tearing them apart. . . . Some who had previously banged their heads against the walls and covered their heads with their overcoats stopped responding to their hallucinations. It was most impressive (Bowes 1956, 532).*

There was some concern that drugs might take the place of treatment, however, especially in nursing homes and similar institutions, as well as a growing awareness of their side-effects (such as permanent tics and mannerisms).

By the 1960s, emphasis on the way in which these drugs helped to improve custodial institutions was replaced by emphasis on the way in which their calming effects allowed former inmates to be released into the community. Most of our psychiatric facilities were antiquated and overcrowded, costs were rising, and the use of institutions was meeting with increasing criticism. Deinstitutionalization seemed the best solution. From 1955 to 1975, there was a dramatic reduction in the size of mental health institutions, not just in Canada, but also in the United States, Britain, and Europe.

Inmates of psychiatric institutions were transferred to nursing homes and chronic care hospitals, a change which did not necessarily mean an improvement in the quality of their lives. Many others gravitated to privately operated, quasi-institutional boarding homes in districts close to the few remaining psychiatric facilities. Such boarding homes have often been the subject of ''exposé'' reporting in the press (Flynn 1985; Silzer 1985).

At least a few students reading this text will have come through the educational system while taking Ritalin, a drug which helps to control ''hyperactivity'' in children so that they can sit down, concentrate, and learn. Ritalin has been helpful, but many people believe school programs should be adjusting to meet the needs of children, rather than adjusting the children to fit the programs.

DEINSTITUTIONALIZATION AND COMMUNITY CORRECTIONS

The same drive to reduce the institutionalized population has affected the practice of imprisonment, but to a somewhat lesser degree. The demand from the public to be protected from criminals and to see justice done (i.e., punishment meted out) has slowed the process of deinstitutionalization. In fact, most of the efforts to find a substitute for prisons (through probation, parole, and community service orders) have only expanded the number of people who come under the supervision of the correctional system. The prisons continue to function as our main means of controlling criminal deviance, even though they are demonstrably expensive, inefficient, and often counterproductive.

AGENCIES OF CONTROL

Nearly everyone participates in social control, simply by responding to the behaviour of others. Some members of the society are more consciously and continuously involved in social control than others. Who are they? They include the police, private security guards, and probation and parole officers. They also include teachers, priests, doctors, psychiatrists, therapists, social workers, and even apartment superintendents.

New **agencies of control** emerge to meet new needs. Insurance companies have become increasingly involved in the area of social control. Their need to establish the legitimacy of claims has made them specialists in the investigation of arson, car theft, and other forms of deviance. Their regulations for certain kinds of coverage may encourage the use of seat belts and curtail "bad habits" such as smoking and drinking.

The provision of social welfare has also added a whole layer of social control which affects mainly the poor, the disabled, and the dependent population. The poor and needy are policed by agencies that are set up for their welfare. These agencies must establish exactly which people are entitled to their help, and must account for the way in which the support is given and used. This involves a degree of regulation and supervision. Public housing, for example, may be denied to people who have used their apartments for drug dealing. Patients in homes for the elderly or handicapped may be denied the right to smoke, have alcohol, or entertain persons of the opposite sex.

FEAR OF CONTROL

Although most people want to live in a reasonably orderly society, they don't want to be watched all the time, or subjected to more control than is necessary for the maintenance of public order. People fear the type of society in which some "Big Brother" can observe the everyday thoughts and actions of each and every citizen.

In early England, the government refused to establish a police force until the 1830s, despite a high and rising level of criminal activity. An ordinary citizen had to sleep with a weapon by his bed, and those who were wealthy went through the streets with armed escort. Englishmen seemed to feel that disorder was the price of freedom (Fowler 1979). Only when the London mob threatened the safety of Parliament itself was an official police force, with very restricted powers, created. Even then, the new police force was only slowly accepted.[15]

Many modern controls are frightening because they are hidden, making resistance to or modification of them quite difficult. Propaganda and censorship, for example, control us by controlling our understanding of the world. Social control is often concealed in architectural designs, street layouts, and product displays, most of which affect people without their conscious awareness. Many stores, for example, provide counter layouts that encourage impulse buying; planners of urban residential areas lay out winding streets that discourage speeding. The wide avenues of central Paris were created as a means of preventing the building of barricades by street mobs. Churches and courtrooms tend, by architecture and interior design, to induce solemnity and respect for authority.

Less common, but potentially controversial, are the more subtle tactics of control, such as subliminal messages hidden beneath soothing music or within the frames of popular movies.

On the whole, people seek a *level* of control at which dangers as well as serious nuisances are avoided, but at which freedom and social change are possible. Unfortunately, they do not agree about what that level is. There is always pressure to increase the control on undesirable behaviour, and there is always pressure to eliminate unnecessary rules and excessive monitoring of the actions of ordinary citizens. The public media play a powerful role in shaping these debates. Should there be more control on hockey violence? Should police be allowed to install cameras in men's washrooms? How much information about the private citizen—credit ratings, social insurance data, census and taxation data, social security police checks—should be kept in centralized computer banks? Every day the newspapers carry items about disputes over control: how much control should we have over the mess on the neighbours' front lawn? Where should cigarette smoking be allowed, tolerated, and prohibited? How much information should the government be allowed to collect about us, and how can this information be used?

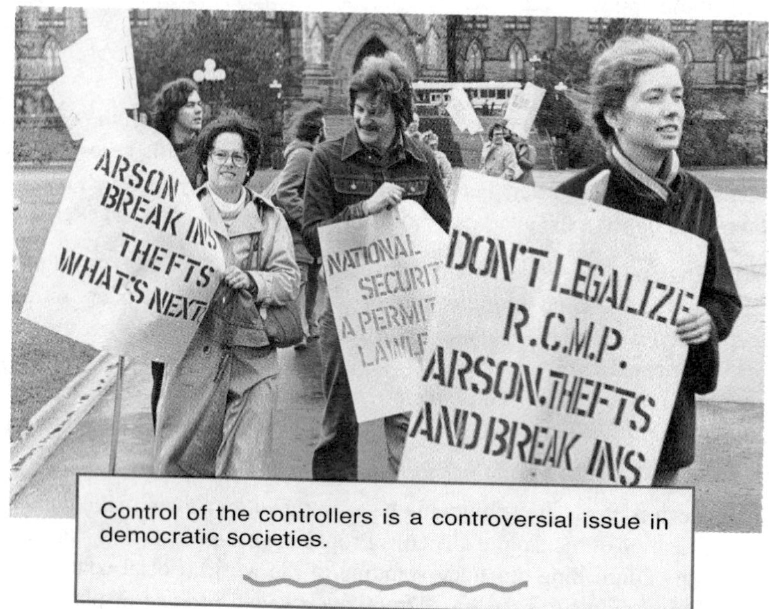

Control of the controllers is a controversial issue in democratic societies.

Most people accept a high level of intrusive surveillance at airports due to fear of terrorist acts. Armed guards and body-searches are neither welcome as a long-term solution to the problem nor expanded beyond the airport.

CONTROL THAT CAUSES DEVIANCE

Controls can be excessive, they can threaten freedoms, and they can actually create more deviance (Marx 1981). Some of the ways in which this can occur are illustrated by the following examples:

- A bankrobber, interrupted by police, ends up taking hostages and starting a high-speed car chase.
- A rapist commits murder to avoid being identified by his victim.
- A runaway teenager avoids help from ''straight'' people and ends up in the subculture of sex and drugs.
- A man is hospitalized for a nervous breakdown, and then finds that his friends have dropped him and he can't get a job. He has another breakdown.
- Being put in a ''behavioural class'' confirms a child's belief that he's no good, and can only excel at troublemaking.
- A skid-row denizen decides that jail is a better place than the mission or flop-house, especially in winter. She commits a small crime or two, and then gets free housing, protection from the weather, and three meals a day.
- A would-be rebel seeks confrontations with teachers and police to prove to himself and others how tough and fearless he is.
- Some enthusiastic protesters consider themselves martyrs for their cause when they are arrested. For them, the media coverage, the chance to turn the courtroom into a platform for their views, and even the chance to preach to fellow prisoners is a positive thing.
- Tough enforcement of anti-drug regulations tends to drive out the amateur dealers, thus increasing the profits for the few dealers who are strong enough to hang in. This ''crime tariff'' effect has helped to make some cocaine producers powerful and wealthy, just as prohibition strengthened the ''Mafia'' form of organized crime (Morris and Hawkins 1969).
- In trying to control teen promiscuity, adults often interfere with the dissemination of information that could help to control the spread of AIDS.
- When police undercover agents ask for drugs, they may encourage individuals to become suppliers.
- ''Agents provocateurs'' (undercover agents) who join radical political circles may find that these circles encourage them toward more extreme or violent positions.

DEVIANT CONTROLS

Not only can control be deviant (when it is excessive, unfair, or otherwise improper) but many kinds of deviance are actually forms of control (Black 1983).

Murder, assault, and even theft are often motivated by a sense of justice. Men who beat their wives often feel that they "have to" do this to control them (and that controlling them is right); men who assault one another are often attempting to even the score or punish the other for some real or imagined offence. "Police brutality" (when it occurs) is frequently precipitated by actions that the police interpret as disrespectful. Some police officers feel that they have the right to teach deviants to respect them, even when no law has been broken.

Similarly, a great deal of underworld violence represents a form of self-policing by people who cannot turn to legitimate authorities to enforce their contracts, protect their lines of supply, or handle their employee relations. "Turf wars" between suppliers of drugs and other illegal services are often characterized by shootings and arson.

FORMAL AND INFORMAL SOCIAL CONTROLS

Formal controls tend to be written down, and may even take the shape of a systematic "code." The code may be a compilation of past decisions, incorporating some of the informal practices of the group; it may also be a document, premised in high ideals, from which rules have been logically derived. Canada's Criminal Code is an example of the first kind of code. It reflects the decisions of British judges as these stood in the 1800s. Our Criminal Code has evolved both on the basis of *stare decisis* (let the decision stand), by which each case becomes precedent for similar cases, and by occasional adjustments through new legislation. It has no overall logic or structure, contrasting with the more logical and formal codes of most Continental European countries.

There are many other kinds of codes, including school dress codes, sports codes, and codes of behaviour for employees. These range from multi-paged handbooks to simple admonitions such as, "Clean up after yourself! Your mother doesn't work here!"

Informal rules are not usually written down, but they are known by all "insiders." In some groups, these insider's rules may be much more powerful than the rules "on the books." They may regulate appropriate thought, appearance, and action, and may commit individuals to "covering up" for any colleague who is attacked by an outsider. They are ultimately enforced by exclusionary tactics such as "the silent treatment" or denial of access to group resources (see discussion of the Hawthorne studies in Chapter 6 on organizations).

Informal controls, whether over family, neighbourhood, or workplace, usually operate to reinforce conformity to societal standards. Concern over reputation in the community helps to strengthen this control. Informal controls may, however, condone or promote rule infractions and protect guilty members from detection and punishment. That is, informal controls among "insiders" may help to create and sustain conformity to behaviour that outsiders would consider deviant. Examples of this are found at every level, from the street gang and outlaw motor bike club, to the steroid users among athletic competitors, to the illegal price fixing combines of big business. Informal control can also be illustrated by the experiences of "whistle-blowers."

WHISTLE-BLOWERS

Whistle-blowers are people who inform the media or higher authorities about work-place deviance.

> *Whistle-blowers are employees who believe their organization is engaged in illegal, dangerous or unethical conduct. Usually, they try to have such conduct corrected through an inside complaint, but if it is not, the employee turns to government authorities or the media and makes the charge public. Whistle-blowers usually get fired (Sagel 1985).*

Whistle-blowers are rare, in comparison with the number of employees who are aware of waste, fraud, or corrupt practices at work. While the whistle-blower is acting as an agent of control, or attempting to activate control systems, his or her action is often treated (by the company) as deviant. Whistle-blowing frequently leads to the blacklisting, demotion, transfer, or workplace harassment not of the offender but of the whistle-blower, who becomes one of the "walking wounded of conscience."

The case of Karen Silkwood, who went to the newspapers about the improper handling of nuclear materials at a nuclear plant in Oklahoma (and died in a mysterious car accident on her way to meet with a newspaper reporter) has been made into a four-star feature movie (Silkwood 1984). Similarly, the story of a former New York City policeman who revealed corruption within the police force (and was shot) has done well on the big screen (Serpico 1973).

Is the whistle-blower a hero, a martyr, or a villain? The whistle-blower often adheres to a set of values that are not the primary, salient ones in the work place. The whistle-blower is violating the existing order of the organization (criticism is generally supposed to flow from top to bottom, not the other way around), and may (correctly or incorrectly) be accused of undermining organizational morale and effectiveness. From the point of view of the company or department, the whistle-blower is disloyal and deserves to be demoted or expelled. Whistle-blowers stand up for their own standards of right behaviour, regardless of the pressures of the group. Sometimes they are publicly vindicated, as in the cases of Silkwood and Serpico, and sometimes they are not.[16]

SCRAWNY WHISTLE BLOWER MAKES THE TRADING FLOOR TREMBLE

By Stevie Cameron

As if the Vancouver Stock Exchange didn't have enough to depress it these days, it also has Adrian du Plessis hanging grimly around its neck.

Mr. du Plessis hardly fits the picture of the scourge of Howe Street. A scrawny 28-year-old, he sports punkish hair, granny glasses, skinny ties, pointy shoes, wide-padded shoulders and an air of earnestness leavened only by a quick and quirky sense of humor.

What he doesn't look like is a man so disliked and feared by brokers and politicians that he's been sued, fired from one job and investigated by a private detective.

Mr. du Plessis is a whistle blower. For four years he worked as a floor trader on the exchange and then spent nearly a year with *Stockwatch*, a Vancouver publication that follows the market. What he learned shocked him and now he's doing something about it.

This month, he wrote ''Are There Any Ethics on Howe Street?,'' the cover story for *Equity*, a British Columbia business magazine in which he has a monthly column; next month *Vancouver* Magazine is publishing the first feature in a series of background pieces on the VSE. ''It's a roman à clef about the trading floor,'' explained editor Malcolm Parry: ''The names are changed to protect the guilty.''

Mr. du Plessis has contributed to *Globe and Mail* articles and helps reporters from many publications, including *The Sun* and *The Province* in Vancouver and *Maclean*'s Magazine, to break stories about VSE shenanigans. ''He's a zealot,'' explained *Equity* co-editor, Robert Collison. ''He has a mission to reform the system.''

In the late 1970s, when Mr. du Plessis was managing rock bands, times were tough for rock and roll. A friend suggested he try for a job as a board marker at the VSE. ''It was 1980, and the market was taking off. They were pulling guys in off the street,'' Mr. du Plessis said. ''The only requirement was height; you had to be over five feet nine to mark the boards.'' He started the day after he applied and soon graduated to phone boy; a few months later he was promoted to floor trader.

In the VSE culture, floor traders are the ''macho neanderthals'' of the business, as Vancouver *Sun* business columnist Peter O'Neil graphically describes them, and skinny Mr. du Plessis did not look like one of the boys. Stockwatch publisher John Woods loves to tell what happened.

''Phone boys are usually very timid at first, but three hours after Adrian had been out there trading, another trader did a deal behind his back.

"This trader was a loud, wily fellow. Adrian went up one side of him and down the other again and again; it was an extraordinary performance, with never a stutter or a stammer. The guy finally gave up and it never happened again."

Over the next four years, he traded for three companies, Canarim Investment Corp. Ltd., controlled by former VSE chairman Peter Brown, Wolverton and Company and Walwyn Inc. After eight months at Walwyn he was fired.

The Province's stock market reporter, David Baines, recalls the whistle blower telling him a wild tale of being fired for questioning trades. "Within a week the RCMP had arrested some of the key people involved in the trading and promotion of that stock," Mr. Baines says. "That established his credibility for me." (A trial of seven people is under way.)

Mr. du Plessis said he reported the deals to the Mounties. "I was fired the next week." (With real chutzpah, Mr. du Plessis is suing Walwyn for wrongful dismissal.)

John Woods read Mr. Baines' stories about Mr. du Plessis and immediately offered him a job at *Stockwatch*, writing for the weekly edition and assembling data bases for the daily Toronto edition.

While he worked for Mr. Woods, he started giving New Democratic Party MLA Moe Sihota ammunition for Question Period. For example, on Mr. du Plessis' advice, Mr. Sihota questioned the spiralling value of Technigen Platinum Corp., a producer of golf simulators. That led to a brief trading halt on the VSE.

On the day Mr. Sihota raised the issue of Technigen in the Legislature, Canarim's Peter Brown, a major financial backer of the Social Credit Government, pressed Mr. Woods to fire Mr. du Plessis for embarrassing the Government. Mr. Brown had considerable leverage; he owns 45 per cent of Stockwatch and sublets office space to them. (Mr. Woods rehired Mr. du Plessis immediately, telling him to work at home).

A few months ago, Mr. O'Neil tipped Mr. du Plessis that someone had hired a private detective to investigate him. Doing a little snooping of his own, Mr. du Plessis found the man was Patrick Westphal, a former RCMP officer who runs a company called Pro-Techt America Systems, Inc. He phoned Mr. Westphal and asked him who had hired him; all the detective would admit was that it was a "concerned shareholder."

Then Technigen decided to sue Mr. du Plessis. "They sue him but not the vehicles he's publishing in," pointed out *Equity* co-editor Harvey Southam. "But he doesn't back down. We need more people like Adrian who knows what he's talking about; he's a good writer and he's impeccably honest."

Everyone talks about his honesty and his motivation. As *Vancouver* Magazine's Mr. Parry put it, "I think he is the most singularly honest man I've ever met in my life. He is motivated without any sense of personal gain and with only the public good in mind."

Both Mr. O'Neil and Mr. Woods believe he was responsible, through all the dustups he's caused in the Legislature, for the extra $1.4 million given to new B.C. superintendent of brokers Neil de Gelder to hire 12 researchers and to set up a compliance team to track errant stock promoters and brokers.

Now, as Mr. du Plessis considers the free fall of VSE stocks over the past two weeks, he sees the silver lining: "The good thing about the crash," he said, "is it made the bad stocks only cost half as much as they did before."

SUMMARY

Deviance is an integral part of society because it is defined by the salient norms that regulate social life, which, in turn, are based on the core values and beliefs of the society. Deviance is not bad in itself. It is thought of as bad because it challenges the rules. Careful analysis of the actual (not just the intended) consequences of deviance reveals that it may have an important role in creating social cohesion, signalling the problems to be fixed, and helping to adapt the group to social change.

The theories of deviance are numerous. All the disciplines that study human behaviour have contributed to the analysis of deviance. Within each discipline there remains considerable debate over the relative importance of heredity, experience, social structure, and other variables.

Deviance requires both specific behaviour and a label created for that behaviour by the power system of the society. Behaviour emerges from biological, psychological, or psychiatric tensions; it may be a rational or an irrational response to stress, strains, and conflicts in the social order.

Deviance research presents some special practical and moral challenges. Deviants protect themselves from censure and control by a wide variety of defensive techniques. They are often skilled manipulators of false fronts, and their communities are often open only to those with deviant credentials and the right identifiers.

Modern sociologists have managed to penetrate some of these protective guises and have given us some stereotype-breaking glimpses of the underworld social order, the subculture of the delinquent (and the respectable nudist), the individual perspective of the embezzler, and the self-conception of the paid killer and the drug user.

Social control is the means whereby our social behaviour is channeled. It includes internal controls learned as part of socialization, and it includes external controls which range from extreme punishment to the most subtle, subliminal suggestions. Cultures differ in the extent to which they favour controls that are internal or external, and the degree to which controls are based on threats and punishment or promises and rewards. There has been an historical transition from the use of public spectacles of physical punishment toward an emphasis on "treatment" of the causes of deviance. We are currently at a point in history in which the use of institutions (prisons, asylums, "homes," etc.) is declining, and new means of integrating deviants of all kinds into the community are being sought.

We are also reaching a point at which official agencies of control are unable to cope without greater support from individuals and the community. The role of the "whistle-blower" is becoming a matter of great concern in a world in which only the insider knows what is really going on.

The challenge of these changes is forcing us to understand ourselves, our tolerance, and the ways in which communities can create networks of support to meet the challenge of integration and regulation.

ASSIGNMENTS

Do one or more of the following assignments, as instructed by your professor.

1 Read a novel that centres on murder, drug addiction, or some other form of deviance. What theory of deviance does the author use to explain motivation? To what extent are stereotypes of deviants used to tell the story?

2 Observe a selected area of your school, such as the cafeteria, the library, or the bookstore. What kinds of rule-breaking take place there? How is this deviance related to the social organization of activities?

3 Construct a questionnaire in which respondents can reveal how much deviance they have engaged in (or reveal how much they have observed in others or experienced as victims). What kind of questions should be asked? What time period should they cover? What kinds of questions should not be asked?

4 Observe at least three buildings in your area. Which ones offer the most opportunity for crime? (Watch for unsupervised, easy entry; dark, narrow stairwells; apartments that don't provide an overview of play places; and so forth.) Read *Defensible Space*, listed in the Suggested Readings, as an aid to your observations.

5 Choose a moral crusade group to study. What kind of advertising (propaganda) does it use to interest and convince the public?

6 Citizens often have information that would aid regulatory officials

(police, tax investigators, customs officers, etc.), but only rarely do they come forward with this information. Why? What would life be like if we all informed on each other?

7 Take a close look at the lives of a number of people who have been defined as "deviant." How much of the time are they behaving in a deviant fashion? How much of the time are they conforming?

SUGGESTED READINGS

Neil Boyd, *The Last Dance: Murder in Canada*. (Scarborough, Ont.: Prentice-Hall Canada, 1988). Boyd, a criminologist, makes use of case files, police reports, and interviews with forty convicted murderers to shine a light on murders in Canada. The book takes a serious look at the political, social, and psychological contexts of murder.

Roger Caron, *Go-Boy! The True Story of a Life Behind Bars* (Scarborough, Ont.: Nelson, 1978). A grim story with a "happy" ending, this book offers insight into the factors that make for deviant commitments and the ways in which other commitments can come to replace them.

Dianne Francis, *Contrepreneurs*. (Toronto: Macmillan, 1988). Francis documents her case that Canada is a leader in white-collar crime. Her account covers three types of "contrepreneurial" activity: boiler rooms (telemarketing of overpriced or phoney stocks), stock-market swindles (in underregulated stock exchanges), and money-laundering (pulling ill-gotten wealth into the financial system in such a way that its source is disguised). The book gives details of people, places, and events, and calls for better regulation.

David McClintock, *Indecent Exposure: A True Story of Hollywood and Wall Street* (New York: Dell, 1982). McClintock gives a journalist's account of the story of Cliff Roberston and David Begelman, yet another scenario in which the victim gets blamed and the villain gets promoted. The book provides a clear example of why it is so difficult to nail white-collar criminals and why crime statistics seem to show that the upper classes commit fewer crimes than other groups.

Oscar Newman, *Defensible Space: People and Design in the Violent City* (London: Architectural Press, 1972). A pioneering work on the effects of architecture on opportunity for deviance. The hypothesis is that architecture can inspire citizens to defend themselves against crime and deviance. A useful sequel is the same author's *Design Guidelines for Creating Defensible Space* (Washington, D.C.: U.S. Government Printing Office, 1975).

Alexander Kohn, *False Prophets: Fraud and Error in Science and Medicine* (New York: Blackwell, 1986). An expose of "massaged data," plagiarism, and piracy. This book describes the motives, conditions, and pressures that bear on ethical standards. Examples are drawn from many areas of science and medicine, including anthropology, archaeology, and psychology.

Mick Lowe, *Conspiracy of Brothers*. (Toronto: McClelland-Bantam Seal Books, 1988). Subtitled "A true story of murder, bikers and the law," this book takes a biker's-eye view of "the life" among outlaw bikers in Canada. The book tends to downplay the seriousness of the biker's activities, but provides an interesting account of "one percenter" (outlaw) biker characteristics, beliefs, and (deliberately deviant) values.

Lisa Priest, *Conspiracy of Silence*. (Toronto: McClelland and Stewart, 1989). A newspaper journalist's account of the murder of Betty Osborne, a Cree Indian, in The Pas, Manitoba. The author provides a useful account of the ways in which justice works, and sometimes doesn't work, in the North.

Clifford D. Shearing, (ed.), *Organizational Police Deviance: Its Structure and Control* (Toronto: Butterworth, 1981). As long as police are recruited from among human beings, the problem of how to control the controllers will exist. This book gives a revealing picture of the organizational reasons for rule-breaking by police officers.

NOTES

1 The abortion debate offers an excellent example of the importance of labels and precise definitions. Proponents of liberal access to abortion say killing the fetus is not killing a human being and thus cannot be called murder. Many opponents say the fetus is human; therefore, they feel justified in using the label.

2 For a rather different type of social approval of theft, see Peter Maas' *King of the Gypsies* (1973), a readable account of Romany (gypsy) culture.

3 In fact, the differences between the Volstead Act and Canada's provincial temperance act suggest some neat meshing of economic interests. Americans could not legally sell, transport, or manufacture alcoholic beverages, but drinking them was quite legal. Most Canadians were forbidden to drink but could legally manufacture spirits and transport them for sale in some other jurisdictions. Throughout the Prohibition years, many, many ships left Atlantic and Great Lakes ports with cargoes of whisky whose bills of lading claimed they were bound for Mexico or the West Indies. Remarkably, the trips would take only a few days.

4 This is one reason many communities make use of "sunset laws," which have to be passed again every few years. This ensures that the laws on the books reflect current needs — or the current views of the majority.

5 This is not to suggest that moral crusaders are actually "better" than coun-

tercrusaders, or vice versa. Both groups are advocating norms. It is simply that those who make moral rules have the advantage, especially if the rule is in place.

6 Analysts sometimes trace to this source phenomena such as the modern avoidance of people who are dying, and the guilt felt by the parents of handicapped children.

7 When Charles Goring, one of Lombroso's students, compared English criminals with the rest of the population in a more controlled study, he found no significant differences between them (Goring 1913).

8 In an interesting variant of psychodynamic theory, Otto Pollak (1950) has argued that women are more deviant than men, even though crime statistics seem to indicate that the reverse is true. According to Pollak, girls are not more moral than boys, just sneakier. The "normal" development for females is to resolve their problems in passive-dependent ways while males resolve theirs in aggressive-competitive ways. Women learn trickery and manipulation; men learn fighting and pushing. Pollak linked the female's ability to hide her feelings about the sex act from her husband and her sexuality from her children to her greater ability to get away with deceit. This is an example of the ways in which popular stereotypes can acquire "scientific" legitimation.

9 Manifest functions are functions that are openly recognized. Negative manifest functions are often given as the reason for outlawing certain kinds of behaviour.

10 Davis does not consider the morality of this double standard; he simply observes that prostitution stabilizes the system.

11 One change was the so-called Morgentaler amendment, which restricts the owner of a court of appeal to change the verdict when a jury has acquitted the accused. Under Section 613 of the Criminal Code, the court of appeal may order a retrial but may no longer set aside the jury verdict and substitute a guilty verdict. The change is considered to be an important indication of the role of the jury, permitting it to modify the application of law when its letter conflicts with substantive justice (see Stuart 1982).

12 This association is "differential" in that it may vary by frequency, duration, priority (early or late in life), and intensity. Priority refers to how early in life the exposure occurs (and the level of emotion involved in the association). When a person's life includes early, prolonged, and emotional exposure to deviant associations but late, short, and impersonal exposure to conforming associations, the theory predicts that this person will be deviant.

Notice that this theory helps to account for the fact that most people are exposed to deviant values and methods from time to time but do not become deviants.

13 Recent examples include John Dean's *Blind Ambition* (1976) and David McClintock's *Indecent Exposure: A True Story of Hollywood and Wall Street* (1982).

14 The discovery of the new world allowed for the technique of deportation to wild and unsettled lands as a further means of controlling crime, deviance, and political rebellion. In the colonies, recalcitrant deviants were sometimes put in a boat and sent out to sea. If they were lucky, they might reach land again somewhere else.

15 The question of "who polices the police" is an ancient yet continuing one. This issue is well documented in

our literature. Zamiatin's *We*, Huxley's *Brave New World*, and Orwell's *1984* express our abhorrence of total control and domination based on coercion and manipulation (see Howe 1963).

16 For other stories of whistle-blowers see Peter Maas, *Marie: A True Story* (New York: Random House, 1983) and G. Mitchell, *Truth . . . and Consequences: Seven Who Would Not Be Silenced* (New York: Dembner Books, 1981).

9

SOCIAL INSTITUTIONS

Every society encounters certain problems. How they are handled — and even defined — differs across cultures, but everywhere people develop relatively stable patterns to deal with them. These patterns reflect the values, norms, and beliefs of the particular group. Over time, values, belief systems, and coping strategies coalesce into clusters that we identify as **social institutions**.

In simple societies, the spheres of institutions are often not clearly separable. For instance, a council of elders may make all decisions on spiritual, material, and legal matters affecting the group. In modern western society, institutional spheres can be separated for analysis — the family, education, religion, government, and health care are examples. In practice, however, these institutions do not operate in isolation. Rather, they are interactive and interdependent. For example, the legal system depends on the education sector to deliver trained practitioners, such as judges, attorneys, and support staff. Similarly, it is difficult to envision a society in which there is no consonance between the values espoused in families and those inculcated in schools.

Lack of consonance in a society's institutions creates

tension, which may provide an impetus for social change. Institutions both spur and reflect change. However, because tradition creates inertia within institutions and because individuals and groups have vested interests in preserving the status quo, institutional change tends to be slow as well as piecemeal.

Except for the family (which ties a small number of individuals to one another in a primary relationship), institutional sectors in modern western society comprise networks of large organizations that are run along bureaucratic lines. In these organizations, as we noted earlier, rules and regulations govern official conduct, and secondary relationships are the norm, although informal, primary relations often evolve among the individuals who are in frequent contact with one another. Informal ties may facilitate or obstruct interaction within and between institutions. Thus, if a school board's director has cordial relations with senior officials at the provincial ministry of education, funds for an innovative pilot project may be more easily secured.

Individuals who are located in the upper echelons of institutional structures are highly rewarded in terms of pay, power, and prestige. (Not all such individuals actually work for organizations. For instance, physicians are at the pinnacle of the Canadian health-care sector, but many function as independent professionals and work with, but not for, organizations such as hospitals.)

In this chapter, we examine five major social institutions: the family, education, religion, law, and health care. Please note that our discussion does not exhaust the Canadian institutional spheres. Among the major omissions necessitated by considerations of space are the economy and government. We have made frequent reference to the economy throughout this book, particularly in Chapter 5 on work and the division of labour, and the functions of government necessarily enter our discussions of education and law. However, we encourage students to do independent reading on institutional sectors not specifically covered in this overview.

THE FAMILY

In *Brave New World*, Aldous Huxley depicts a society in which the **family** has become obsolete. Pregnancy and giving birth have been replaced by laboratory fertilization of ova and monitoring of fetuses. Infants are raised communally and socialized to assume a position in society commensurate with their programmed genetic endowment. For example, those destined for menial work are systematically deprived of oxygen to stunt their intellectual development.

In Huxley's vision, the state has taken over the fundamental functions of the family, which is defined as a group of people who are related to each other by blood, marriage, or adoption. It is the basic kinship unit of society. The people included in the interactive family network vary *between*, as well as *within*, cultures. There are also variations in the salient relationships: for example, a mother's oldest brother plays a far more significant role in the socialization of children in certain New Guinea tribes than he generally does in western society.[1]

The family performs a variety of functions. Among the most important are the provision of:

- Biological reproduction to ensure continuity of the group.
- Nurture of infants and children.
- Economic activity to meet survival needs.
- Social reproduction of the group's values and norms (socialization).
- Companionship, affection, and emotional support for members.
- Care of the elderly and infirm.

CULTURAL VARIATIONS

The forms used to carry out some of these functions vary cross-culturally. (So do the needs, beyond the basic ones we have just listed, that the family is expected to fulfil.) In western society, it has been the norm for early nurturance and socialization to take place within the basic family unit. However, in some groups these functions are carried out communally, to varying degrees. Among the Hutterites, for example, children sleep in their parents' residence, but from the age of two they are cared for, taught, and disciplined in groups. The main thrust of their socialization stresses that the group takes precedence over the individual and teaches unquestioning acceptance of the Hutterite way of life. Hoesteler and Huntington summarized the world view that underpins this way of life:

> *The community is more important than the individual and governs the activity of the individual, and the corporate group has the power to exclude and to punish, to forgive and to readmit. The German teacher is charged with the formal instruction of the young and he is their primary disciplinarian. The father, as head of the family, supports the discipline of the colony, and the colony can require him to punish his own child in the presence of the group. The older person is required to correct the younger, regardless of his relation to the offender, and self-assertion by the individual against the group is not permitted. The duties of each person are assigned by the community, and tasks may not be chosen or positions aspired to by the individual (1967, 12).*

The agricultural communes of Israel, the kibbutzim, provide another example of communal child rearing. In many such communes, the children have their own sleeping quarters and spend just a few hours daily with their parents. Like the Hutterites, members of the kibbutz hold no private property. The communal socialization of children, the group's most important future resource, fits into this pattern.

Assigning socialization of the young to the whole community rather than to the individual family is a way of minimizing differences among families and of maximizing the homogeneity of the group. The Hutterites have always been a small group surrounded by a largely hostile outside world. The kibbutzim faced the same situation in the early settlements that were established before Israel became a state, and those in areas adjacent to Arab countries still do today. Under such conditions, it becomes vital that individual differences be de-emphasized and that people view themselves as part of a unit that stands and falls together. Communal socialization lays the groundwork for such a perspective.

Using a functionalist perspective, Goode has done a great deal of cross-cultural research on families. He has also focused on how such forces as industrialization and urbanization impinge on the family (*World Revolution and Family Patterns* 1970 is one of his major works).

TYPES OF FAMILIES

Earlier, we noted that interactive networks of family members vary in several ways. Here we focus on differences in household configuration—that is, the family members who share a residence. For a discussion of the Canadian family in historical context see Baker (1984) and Nett (1981). On contemporary families, Eichler's work is informative (1983).

THE EXTENDED FAMILY

In many agricultural societies, the extended family is the **modal type** (the one most prevalent). The extended family is comprised of grandparents, parents, and their children, all of whom share a residence. The parental generation may include brothers, sisters, and their families.

When life expectancy was much shorter than it is today, this family form provided some security for children if their parents died. In an age before government pensions and old age security, adult offspring were insurance that parents would be provided for in old age.[2] The extended family also provides a pool of labour. In societies in which livelihood, even sustenance, is gained in or near the home, each member of an extended family has a personal interest in doing the best job possible (though, obviously, there are individual differences in competence and industriousness). Children have to perform chores from an early age. In some societies, most children are prepared for future work roles by observing their elders in the home and by actually working, rather than by receiving training. Some enter apprenticeships with another family to learn a trade.

In the selection of marriage partners within a society of extended families, a common background and, hence, presumably compatible world views are stressed more than love. An initial attraction between two young people is deemed an added bonus, but the ability of the new wife or husband to fit in with and contribute to the extended family household is the major consideration.

In many societies, including those of the west until the modern era, the importance of economic factors in mate selection was emphasized by the dowry, the sum of material goods (land, money, household goods, cattle) that forecast the contribution of the bride's family to the new union. In some groups in Africa and New Guinea, the groom had to pay his mate's family a bride price (often paid in cattle, pigs, or whatever livestock was basic to the local economy).

When we speak of family or kin, we refer to persons who are related by blood or marriage.

THE NUCLEAR FAMILY

Although there is evidence that the nuclear family, consisting of parents and their children, did exist prior to the industrial era, industrialization and urbanization have played an important part in making it the prevalent form of family organization in western society. Not only has family organization changed; family size has also shrunk steadily over the last century, with a temporary reversal of the trend during the baby boom after the Second World War (see Exhibit 9.1). Exhibit 9.2 suggests one reason — the drop in the birth rate (again excepting the baby boom years). Remaining childless is an option that is being exercised by an increasing number of people (see Veevers' *Childless by Choice*).

We noted earlier that an industrial economy needs a labour force that is willing and able to move to locations where workers are needed. Clearly, it is easier to move three or four people from Halifax to Calgary than to relocate a large family unit.[3]

EXHIBIT 9.1

NUMBER OF PERSONS PER FAMILY IN CANADA

Year	Persons
1986	3.3
1981	3.5
1976	3.1
1971	3.7
1966	3.9
1961	3.9
1956	3.8
1951	3.7
1941[a]	3.9
1931[a]	3.9
1921[a]	4.3

[a]Data exclude Newfoundland, Yukon Territory, and the Northwest Territories.
SOURCE: *Historical Statistics of Canada*, Series A254-259 and 1981 Census of Canada. *Canada Year Book* 1988, 1987.

EXHIBIT 9.2

NUMBER OF CHILDREN EVER BORN PER 1,000 EVER MARRIED WOMEN, 15 YEARS OF AGE AND OVER, CANADA, 1961, 1971 AND 1981

Year	15–19	20–24	25–29	30–34	35–39	40–44	45–54	55–64	65 +	Total
1981	429	687	1,285	1,880	2,330	2,842	6,657	6,190	6,447	2,490
1971	634	910	1,706	2,621	3,158	3,348	3,257	3,049	3,565	2,775
1961	735	1,327	2,178	2,775	3,102	3,231	3,130	3,506	4,038	2,987
1941[1]	529	923	1,587	2,163	2,684	3,368	8,100	8,229	8,236	2,998

[1]Excludes Newfoundland.
SOURCE: *Historical Statistics of Canada*, Series 238-247.
Statistics Canada 1983. 1981 Census of Canada. Nuptiality and Fertility, Catalogue 92-906.

EXHIBIT 9.3

DIVORCE RATES

	100,000 population	100,000 married women age 15 and over
1978	243.4	1,016.1
1979	251.3	1,050.4
1980	259.1	1,084.8
1981	278.0	1,129.2
1982	285.9	1,164.4
1983	275.5	1,125.2
1984	259.5	1,061.9
1985	244.4	1,003.5
1986	300.8	—

SOURCE: Statistics Canada. Vital Statistics, VII, Marriages and Divorces, 1985 (84-205) and *Canada Year Book* 1990.

With the separation of home and work, the nuclear family has become a unit for consuming goods and services paid for with money earned outside the home. In the picture-book North American family, the husband goes out to work while his wife cooks, tends house, cares for the children, and perhaps engages in volunteer activities. In Talcott Parsons' terms, the husband/father is the "instrumental leader," who delineates major family goals—for instance, a bigger house, a trip to the homeland, or university education for the children—and provides the material means for attaining them. The wife/mother is the "expressive leader." She is the main socializer of the children, the font from which her family draws warmth and emotional support.

More recently, it has become more acceptable—even normative—for the North American wife to enter the labour force. Now she is expected to fulfil the traditional wife/mother role while holding down a job. Married women's increased participation in the labour force has wide ramifications. For example, more of the household food budget is spent on eating out. In turn, extensive use of restaurants and fast food outlets creates more service jobs, many of them part time and poorly paid.

The reality of many nuclear families has often not conformed to the ideal, even during the 1950s and 1960s when the rhetoric was resurrected. Death, desertion, or divorce left some parents without mates, many households needed two incomes, and some women were unwilling to abandon careers in which they had heavy personal investment. Nonetheless, the ideal set a norm, and divergence was treated as deviant. In the late 1940s and 1950s, many employers discriminated against women who worked outside the home when their children were young (although they had been glad to hire them when men were in short supply during the Second World War). The film *The Life and Times of Rosie the Riveter* illustrates this. See also Gluck's *Rosie the Riveter Revisited* (1987), a book of oral-history accounts of women who worked in the defence industries of southern California during the war.

With variations along class and ethnic lines, the nuclear family is often child-centred, in the sense that its goals, interaction, and activities tend to revolve around the children. For instance, Little League baseball and hockey involve parents as chauffeurs, coaches, and sometimes, when team selections are made, as rivals. This focus seems to be holding, even with today's increase in mothers who work outside the home.

''Love and marriage go together like a horse and carriage,'' proclaimed a popular song of the 1950s. Love is considered a prerequisite for establishing the modern nuclear family. In popular theory, anyone can fall in love with anyone. However, as Peter Berger noted, the likelihood of meeting a particular person and hence the likelihood of falling in love are influenced by class, religious, and ethnic factors:

In western society, love is seen as the motivating factor in establishing a nuclear family.

In Western countries, and especially in America, it is assumed that men and women marry because they are in love. There is a broadly based popular mythology about the character of love as a violent irresistible emotion that strikes where it will, a mystery that is the goal of most young people and often of the not-so-young as well. As soon as one investigates, however, which people actually marry each other, one finds that the lightning-shaft of Cupid sems to be guided rather strongly within very definite channels of class, income, education, racial and religious background (1963, 35).

SINGLE-PARENT FAMILIES

A **single-parent family** is a domestic unit consisting of one parent and minor children. During the last two decades, such families have become more numerous for several reasons. In Canada, the liberalization of divorce laws and changing expectations of marriage have resulted in a dramatic increase in divorce rates. The divorce rate per 100,000 population was 36.0 in 1961; by 1971 it had climbed to 137.6; and by 1982 to 285.9. By 1985 it had fallen slightly to 244.4 (Canada Year Book 1990). As Ambert commented:

Divorce is a new way of life for Canadians, children as well as adults. It is a social phenomenon that cannot be ignored even if it has not occurred in one's own family. And the same observation can be made about the increase of single-parent families in the aftermath of divorce. Such families are now found in all social classes, a fact that is evident in various types of residential units (1980, 49).

During the last two decades, single-parent families have become more numerous.

The economic consequences of divorce are generally negative for women. Drawing on Weitzman's study, Hewlett notes that "one year after divorce the standard of living of the ex-husband has risen 42 percent while that of the ex-wife—and often her children—has fallen 73 percent" (1986, 66).

Illegitimacy used to be a severe stigma, so most illegitimate children were given up for adoption. As the stigma has lessened, more women have chosen to keep these babies. Some women deliberately conceive a child without intending to get married, so some families start as single-parent ones. In such cases, the urge to bear a child must be powerful because most of these women have to continue to support themselves or must accept social assistance.

Desertion, most often by the father, has swelled the number of one-parent families. Welfare legislation in Canadian jurisdictions limits family benefits to families without an adult male. Hence, men unable to make economic provision for their families may respond to economic incentive by leaving their jobs to ensure their eligibility for benefits.

HYBRID NUCLEAR FAMILIES

In the past, so many women died in childbirth that it was much more usual than it is today for men to be left as widowers. These men often remarried, especially if they had young children, and had second families (giving rise to the mythology surrounding the stepmother). Widows with children also tended to remarry, partly because economic and social pressures made the two-parent family a near necessity.

Nowadays, with divorce increasingly prevalent and a majority of divorced persons remarrying, new family constellations are emerging. For example, one or both partners may bring children from a previous marriage into the household, which may eventually contain his, her, and their children. Children may also spend alternating periods with each divorced parent, both of whom may have remarried.

OTHER CONFIGURATIONS

When we speak of family or kin, we refer to persons who are related by blood or marriage. For young people, living in communal arrangements prior to settling down has long been a common phenomenon. However, unrelated persons may also enter into enduring family-like relationships, in which they must deal with the imperatives that arise from sharing a household. For example, a domestic division of labour must be worked out, as well as the economy of the household and affective relationships. The fact that each member of the household also owes allegiance to his or her own kin group may add complications.

For legal purposes, unrelated persons sharing a household have been treated as individuals rather than as a family unit. In the case of homosexual households, the question has arisen, without being resolved, whether such arrangements should be officially recognized as family units in terms of taxation and health and welfare benefits.

FAMILY REDEFINES ITSELF, AND NOW THE LAW FOLLOWS

By Philip S. Gutis

As a growing number of unmarried couples claim legal rights, governments, courts and private employers are struggling to decide how to define a family.

Last week, the San Francisco Board of Supervisors approved a law that would allow unmarried partners, both heterosexual and homosexual, to register their relationships with the city, in much the same way that a couple applies for a marriage license.

Mayor Art Agnos has said he will sign the bill, making San Francisco the first city to grant legal recognition to unmarried partners. Less certain is whether the city will follow the board's recommendation that unmarried city employees be allowed to extend their health benefits to their partners, an issue that has taken on great importance because of the AIDS epidemic. Such a policy is already in effect in Berkeley, Calif.

In March the Los Angeles City Council passed a law that gives unmarried city employees sick leave to care for a partner and bereavement leave benefits if they have filed a ''domestic partnership'' affidavit. But the recognition of unmarried couples does not extend to people who do not work for the city.

In New York, the state's highest court is now deciding whether the surviving partner of a 10-year gay relationship can be considered a family member and keep the lease to an apartment under rent-control guidelines.

In 1988, 27 per cent, or 24.6 million, of the country's 91.1 million households fit the traditional definition of a family — two parents living with children. In 1970, the proportion was 40 per cent. ''The structure of the family has changed quite a bit since the stereotype of 'Leave It to Beaver' days,'' said Michael Woo, a Los Angeles council member who introduced the measure. The issue not only affects unmarried couples but also handicapped, elderly and other single people living in group homes.

Some groups oppose tinkering with the definition of family, arguing that the effort is not a reaction to a changed environment but an attempt to promote a new social agenda.

''When government begins to legally recognize other kinds of relationships, it educates the citizenry,'' said Gary L. Bauer, the former Reagan Administration domestic affairs adviser who is now president of the Family Research Council, a conservative research group in Washington. ''It says — particularly to the young—that this is a way of living that our society feels to be just as acceptable as married couples.''

Redefining the family is not only a gay rights issue. The New York Court of Appeals recently ruled in a case involving four former mental patients who were living with a family in Brookhaven on Long Island. The town fined the family for having too many unrelated people living in a house zoned for single family use, but the court ruled that for zoning purposes the group was the ''functional equivalent'' of a family.

In another New York case, now awaiting a decision from the Appellate Division of the State Supreme Court, a mother and son are fighting eviction from a rent-controlled apartment in Harlem that they shared with an unrelated man for about 20 years before his death in 1985. In December 1987, a Manhattan Civil Court judge found that although unrelated by blood, marriage or adoption, the mother and son had formed a family with the man and ruled that they could not be evicted.

Still, in most places, gay rights organizations are leading the push for changes in government regulations defining a family. ''That is almost a matter of necessity since there is no identified constituency of unmarried heterosexual couples,'' said Shelly F. Cohen of the Mayor's Lesbian-Gay Task Force in Seattle, where a law similar to the one in Los Angeles was recently proposed.

Although cities are free to extend family benefits to their unmarried employees, they are prohibited by Federal law from requiring that private companies do the same. But some experts believe that broader changes are likely.

''There is a trend toward defining family by functions rather than by structure,'' said Thomas F. Coleman, a member of the California State Task Force on the Changing Family, which was established in 1987 by the state legislature to make recommendations on social, economic and demographic trends. The panel said those functions include: maintaining physical health and safety of members, providing conditions for emotional growth, helping to shape a ''belief system,'' and encouraging shared responsibility.

The private sector has not been immune from pressures to extend the definition of family. The San Francisco Chamber of Commerce has put together a task force to survey its members on policies about unrelated people living together.

''No employer that we know of has extended fringe benefits, such as health care, to people outside the traditional definition of family,'' said Richard Morten, a vice president of the Chamber of Commerce. ''But on a case-by-case basis, certain of our companies are taking a little bit broader interpretation of a family since they know that many of their employees are in nontraditional relationships.''

CLASSIFICATIONS OF MARRIAGE SYSTEMS

In discussing extended and nuclear families, we have mentioned some practices of western societies regarding the selection of marriage partners and the domiciles of young couples. Familiarity with a rather technical vocabulary is helpful when one examines marriage customs and kinship patterns both within, and outside of, one's own culture.

OUT-MARRIAGE AND IN-MARRIAGE

If marriage partners must be chosen from outside the group, as is the case in several Australian tribes, the group is **exogamous**. Most ethnic, racial, and religious groups in our society strive to be **endogamous**—that is, partners are selected from within the group, thus threatening its survival. Generally, out-marriage is discouraged because of the likelihood that a couple's offspring will not be socialized into the ways of the community. Roman Catholics try to ensure against this possibility by insisting that the Catholic partner in a mixed marriage undertake to raise the children within the church. Orthodox Jewish rabbis refuse to marry mixed couples unless the gentile formally converts. Families often encourage children of marriageable age to date within their own ethnic group and socioeconomic class. Marriage across racial lines was illegal in South Africa until 1985 and still is in some other countries.

THE LOCATION OF RESIDENCE

Inherent in the family setting are power relationships. Being located on home territory give obvious advantages to one partner. In western societies today, a young couple generally move into their own apartment or house; in other words, their residence is **neolocal** (literally, ''at a new place''). A shortage of housing or funds may force newlyweds to live with parents or other relatives, but most people view this as an undesirable and thus temporary arrangement.

If extended families are typical in a society, residence for newlyweds may be **patrilocal**—that is, the couple lives with the groom's family. This is the traditional practice in rural India. Quite often, the native villages of the bride and groom are relatively far apart, given limited transportation facilities, and ritual forbids the bride's family from visiting her in her in-laws' house. Hence, the new wife is very much at the mercy of her husband and his family. Awareness of this situation is symbolized by a wedding custom: ''they [the groom and his men] ultimately carry off the bride to their own village, she weeps, clutches her brothers and screams that she is dead'' (Marriott 1969, 176).[4] Alternatively, a couple may move in with the bride's kin, a **matrilocal** arrangement.

Ruth Benedict reported yet another pattern that prevailed among the Dobu of New Guinea. Spouses had to be selected exogamously, from outside one's own village. From marriage until death, the couple spent alternate years in the husband's and the wife's village.

> *Each alternate year one spouse has the backing of his own group and commands the situation. The alternate year the same spouse is a tolerated alien who must efface himself from the owners of his spouse's village (1934, 126).*

This polygamous man has 349 children from 40 wives.

NUMBER OF SPOUSES

In addition to the variations in kinship patterns we have just noted, there are differences in the number of spouses to whom an individual can be married at the same time. In western society, **monogamy**, marriage between one man and one woman, is the rule. When one man may have several wives, the practice is known as **polygyny**.[5] Polygyny is permitted in many societies today, especially in Arab and African countries, but it may be practised by only a fraction of the population. By contrast, **polyandry**, one wife having several husbands, is rare. Anthropologists have discovered only three or four such groups, one of them being the Toada of southern India.

Polygyny and polyandry are the two types of **polygamy**, the practice of being married to more than one person at the same time. It is illegal in western societies; an individual who attempts to become involved in two or more marriages at the same time commits bigamy.

FAMILY RELATIONSHIPS

As we have already suggested, the family is a setting for power relationships. Indeed, the patterned inequalities that are found within the society at large may be reflected in the family. If male dominance is the societal norm, the wife is unlikely to have many legal or actual rights in her marital relationship. When the law ignores children's rights, as was the case in the feudal and early industrial eras, children are left largely at the mercy of their parents.

Today children continue to be controlled by their parents, but that control is not unlimited. For example, compulsory education gives society an entrée into the closed family circle, and legislation in many jurisdictions makes it mandatory to report suspicions of child abuse. Some people believe today's state goes too far in limiting parental control of children — for example, in forcing parents to permit certain actions, such as the giving of blood transfusions, even if they believe them ethically wrong. Other people believe the state does not intervene enough. For example, mothers are usually awarded custody of children, even though the father may be the better parent.

THE FAMILY AS PRIMARY GROUP

Even though its members have unequal power, the family is considered the archetypical primary group. In terms of Parsons' pattern variables, which we discussed in Chapter 5, family relations are expected to be affective and diffuse. The interests of the group are considered to take precedence over those of the individual. Children may forgo more enticing social commitments to be present at their parents' wedding anniversary celebration. Parents give up treats of their own to pay for extras for their youngsters. Many children are socialized to defend siblings against all others. Consideration of the pattern variables in familial relationships warrants two cautions:

- In emotionally charged relationships, the emotions may not be positive. The high incidence of family violence attests to this fact.

- The pattern variables represent an ideal type. In practice, the diffuseness of relationships is not likely to be the same among all family members. One may find it easier to discuss doubts about one's career choice with a favourite brother rather than with one's parents. Individual goals — for example, emigrating to another country — may take precedence over the desire to keep the family together.

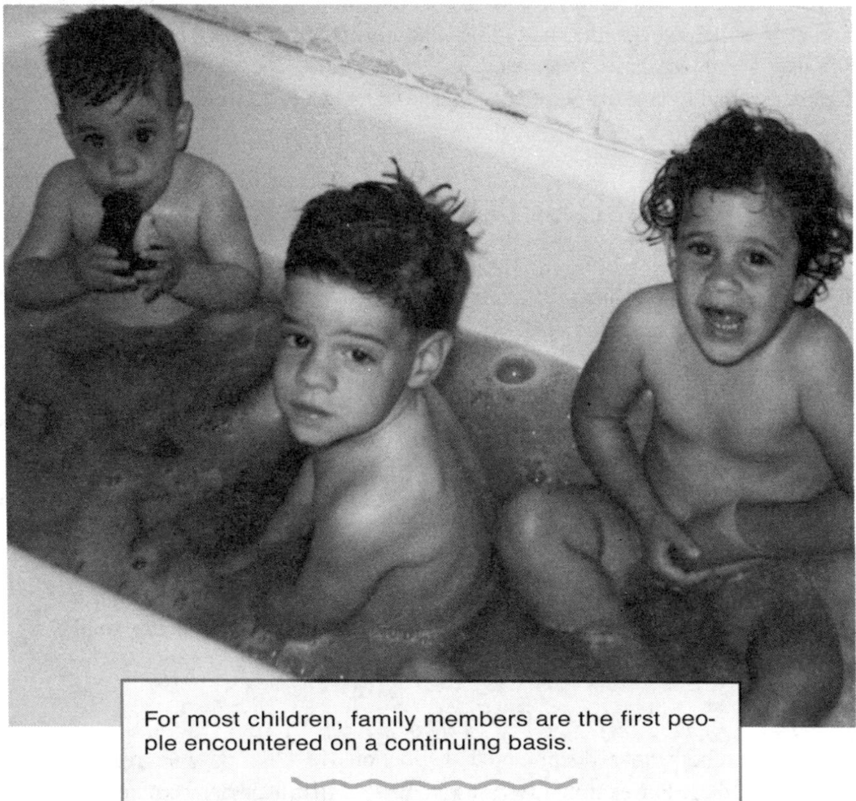

For most children, family members are the first people encountered on a continuing basis.

The family is primary in time, in the sense that, for most children, family members are the first people encountered on a continuing basis. As the studies of Freud, Mead, and Cooley have shown, self-image — whether individuals think of themselves as precious or worthless, as competent or ineffective — is developed against the backdrop of family interaction. Initial impressions of the outside world are also refracted through the prism of the family. Attitudes toward education, work, and leisure, stereotypes of racial and ethnic minorities, and the conception of appropriate gender roles are shaped within the value climate of the family. If children are taught that lying and cheating are wrong but frequently hear the mother shading the truth about her spending habits and the father planning sharp financial transactions, they grow up with the idea that certain kinds of lying and cheating are acceptable. Behaviour patterns—small kindnesses to neighbours, work avoidance or a ''workaholic'' attitude, slighting remarks about members of other religions, political activism—socialize the child to a value system.

This does not mean that the child will necessarily adopt these values. Modern western society is heterogeneous, and behaviour patterns learned in the home often have to compete with conflicting ones encountered in the peer group, in school, and at work. However, the first values and norms, consciously learned or unconsciously absorbed, have an impact on future action. Teenagers and adults often feel compelled to conform to these early precepts or to rebel against them.

INFLUENCES ON THE FAMILY

Like other primary groups, the family is embedded in the context of the larger society. It is located in the class structure and belongs to a particular racial and ethnic group. It is also affected by the myriad variations among individuals and the idiosyncratic modes of interaction that they develop.

CLASS AND ETHNICITY

Statements about ''the North American family'' often obscure class and ethnic differences. Ishwaran has argued:

> *The middle class myth has helped deflect our attention from the poor, as the melting pot myth has blinded us to real and crucial distinctions among ethnic groups with regard to values, patterns and goals (1976, 20).*

Many researchers have documented distinctions in husband-wife relationships along class lines. For example, writing in 1964, Mirra Komarovsky noted:

> *The less-educated couples tend to be more traditional in their ideas about sex-linked interests and about ''rights'' of men to silence and protection from tiresome children and women's trivia. They tend to think that friendship is more likely to exist between members of the same sex, whereas they see the principal marital ties as sexual union, complementary tasks and mutual devotion (1964, 132).*

More than 15 years later, Meg Luxton (1980) heard similar sentiments expressed when she did participant observation of housework among three generations of working-class families in Flin Flon, Manitoba. Couples in the youngest generation were apt to have more egalitarian marriages than their elders, but for the most part husbands had the last word in major decisions and kept aloof from the details of household and child management. Although some of the women received help with the housework, they retained primary responsibility for ensuring that it got done.

In a society such as that of Canada, in which significant power differentials between men and women exist, marriages based on full equality between the partners are likely to be few. However, investigators have found that middle-class families are generally less authoritarian than lower-class families with regard to interaction both between husbands and wives and between parents and children. Skolnick has explained this in terms of the differences in symbolic rewards offered by work requiring brains rather than brawn: ''Men who enjoy respect and power in the business world may have less need than working class men to dominate their wives and children'' (1978, 150).

Even in those middle-class families in which both partners have careers, however, the pattern of male dominance continues in many ways. One example is the tendency for the family to move in response to the husband's career opportunities, at the expense of the wife's. An anecdote illustrates this. A woman who was slated to chair the English department in her high school was called by her husband one lunchtime and asked to make an immediate decision on moving to Winnipeg, where he had been offered a promotion. Not wanting to jeopardize his career, she agreed. As teaching positions were scarce, she was unable to find a suitable one in Winnipeg for several years. However, she finally obtained one at an independent school, where she enjoyed her work. In the following year she was confronted with another transfer for her husband, resignation from her job, and a renewed search for work in Toronto. Since she is competent and highly qualified, she eventually found another post, but her chances for moving up in the educational hierarchy have been minimized.

In their research into the few choices that modern women have, Ann Duffy *et al.* found that:

> *The balancing of full-time wage and domestic labour exacts a personal price. All these women feel stressed from attempting to maintain a traditional maternal role and simultaneously engage in full-time employment. Their individual coping stratgies, on some level, reflect an admission of their deviation from family ideology. Rather than attempting to alter family ideals by pressing for structural alterations in society, these women reinforce traditional stereotypes by attempting to ''do it all.'' Several studies have suggested that employed mothers are physically and emotionally happier, have higher self-esteem and feel less isolated than non-employed mothers, regardless of how low-status and low-paying their jobs are. But this gain is offset by their constant lack of sufficient time and energy to meet personal, work and family demands (Duffy* et al. *1989, 104–5).*

Given the woman's cultural mandate for organizing household and childcare activities, if not necessarily for performing them, the wife's burden is especially heavy. In this connection, feminist Gloria Steinem, the editor of *Ms* magazine, once commented that men like their wives to have "jobettes," income-generating activities that do not reduce a woman's ability and willingness to cater to her spouse.

Has there been any change in very recent years? Hochschild (1989) interviewed 50 San Francisco Bay area families in which both partners worked. She found that, in most cases, women shoulder the bulk of domestic responsibilities, regardless of full-time employment outside the home. Hochschild argues that gender role prescriptions, career expectations, and the absence of adequate childcare facilities are among the important obstacles to any fundamental restructuring of the familial division of labour (see also Duffy and Mandell 1987 for a Canadian perspective). In Hochschild's view, the revolution that propelled women into outside employment "stalled" in the "second shift"—the sphere of domestic work.

WIFE'S CAREER A STRESS-TEST FOR MARRIAGE

By Harvey Fields

It is 6:30 a.m. and my wife just left for work. Three months ago she launched a new career as a stockbroker. Together we concluded it was a good idea. It would boost our income and, perhaps more important, provide a creative outlet for her talents. "We have a solid marriage. You are young and capable. Look around," I advised, "there are all kinds of opportunities."

We reasoned that her time had arrived. Two of our children are at college; a third is a self-sufficient high-school student. For the past 22 years, my wife has cared for our needs, run thousands of errands, driven millions of car-pool miles, looked after our family finances, been there when the plumber arrived to fix our leaking faucets, and at my side, looking radiant, for a constant stream of professional-social obligations.

Now all that has changed, and it's not as easy as I thought it would be. Accommodations have to be made. Worries, doubts, little aching jealousies and resentments, and big ones as well, have emerged. Then, while driving to my office and brooding over this transformation erupting in my life, I happened to hear a commentator announce that new research has determined that husbands with working wives have a shorter life expectancy than those with traditional homemaker wives. Icing on the cake, as they say.

During the first few weeks, certain tasks just fell into place. She could no longer deliver and pick up at the cleaners, or make it to our bank. They are out of her way, but happily right on my route to the office. So are the pharmacy and supermarket.

The supermarket. I love the supermarket, but never during the week, all dressed up in a business suit. Did I feel queasy pushing a cart around on Tuesday afternoon, holding a list written on a pink sheet of paper, with all those women and children staring at me? I did. And I wanted to evaporate when a friend cornered me as I was holding a large box of Tide in one hand and a big bottle of Era Plus in the other. With sympathy pouring from her compassionate brown eyes, she asked: "Is everything all right with Sybil?" By that she meant: "You are supposed to be at your office doing a man's job, and Sybil should be here shopping." Of course I wanted to explain, defend, send her home to read *The Feminine Mystique*, but I didn't.

Instead, I headed for the check-out line gripping my six-pack of beer, hoping to indicate that all the boxes, cans, fruits and vegetables in my cart were simply the unbridled enthusiasm of a mad male on a shopping spree.

When I reached home, her car was not in the driveway. Another trauma. She was always there to greet me at the door with a warm hug and kiss. Now she was late getting home. The house was dark and empty. No sweet aromas of dinner prepared. Just silence, and all those groceries to bring into the house and put away, and bothersome doubts about how our new arrangement will affect us.

It already has, but you grin and bear the first frustrations. A week after she was hired, we sat down to talk about vacation time. I'm tired; it's been a tension-filled year. I need a few weeks to unwind. We've always vacationed together. We would never have considered going off alone. Not us. We are "together" kind of people.

But she's committed to a training program, 16 weeks of rigorous study. She's brimming over with new enthusiasm, and her career demands most of her energy, time and attention. So what about me? A vacation alone? By myself? It hurts, fills me with resentment. What are we married for, anyway?

ETHNICITY

In multicultural societies, like those of Canada and the United States, class differences are cross-cut by ethnic ones (Ishwaran 1980). A family newly arrived from Europe, where the parents themselves are likely to have been socialized in an authoritarian manner, may allow children less freedom and autonomy than a Canadian-born family of similar education and occupational standing.

Differences in family functioning have also been found between anglophones and francophones. For example, during his stay in Cantonville, Quebec, Hughes noted that the goals of the family as a group often superseded those of its individual members, a pattern much less common among the more self-oriented English-speaking group (1971). In looking at parent-adolescent relationships in the mid-1970s, Breton and McDonald found that

> *English-speaking students are still more likely than French-speaking students to report high participation in family decisions and show a high degree of independence in vocational decision-making (1976, 189).*

ECONOMICS AND POWER WITHIN THE FAMILY

The macro factors of class position and ethnic-group membership influence such family dynamics as the domestic division of labour and the ways in which individual members relate to each other; similarly, at the micro level, the economic contribution made by each spouse affects family interaction, specifically the balance of power between the marriage partners. Whether the wife works for pay and, indeed, whether she has marketable skills are important variables. Economic independence reduces personal dependency. (This seems to be one reason some husbands object to their wives' working outside the home.) Furthermore, successful functioning in the work world, even in mundane jobs, enhances self-confidence (see Kessler and McRae 1982).

Studies on family violence have documented that tolerance for abuse is greatest among housebound women without significant earning skills. Some of the reasons are vividly illustrated in *The Burning Bed*, the life story of Francine Hughes, who was acquitted of the crime of killing her husband after enduring years of savage beatings. Married at 16 and with four children born in quick succession, she had left her husband several times; her inability to support herself and her children played a large part in forcing her to go back to the dangers of the home (McNulty 1981).

A wife's earnings augment her power within the family. A husband's loss of earnings, perhaps occasioned by unemployment, both changes and strains relations. Skolnick reported a social worker's account of what happened when unemployment soared in Flint, Michigan:

> *"He's around the house almost all day and he has fixed everything in sight. Something goes out of the family because he's around. He sees the kids when they are dirty and noisy and misbehaving. And they don't pay him the same attention they used to when they greeted him at the door when he came home from work.*
>
> *"He had always had the disciplinary role around the house. He was the boss, the breadwinner. So his relationship with his wife changes. He bosses her around and demands she bring him a beer because he has to prove that he's still the man of the house. In a situation like that, everybody in the house gets bent out of shape" (1978, 152).*

The incidence and severity of wife battering are influenced by the circumstances of a specific family. However, tolerance, and even approbation, of violence against women in general, and against wives in particular, is deeply rooted in history. For example, Greek law (approximately 2500 BC) stipulated that if a woman verbally abused her husband, "her name was to be engraved on a brick which was then to be used to bash out her teeth" (Macleod 1982, 2). In the mid 1400s, Friar Cherubino of Sienna enjoined husbands that "correcting" their wives was an act of Christian charity: "take up a stick and beat her soundly, for it is better to punish the body and correct the soul than to damage the soul and spare the body" (Okun 1986, 3).

Child abuse is an issue that has been increasingly recognized as a social problem in the past twenty years. Although it is a phenomenon that spans all social classes, it may occur disproportionately in homes where parents have the fewest "buffers," such as steady employment, adequate income, personal gratifications, access to periodic relief from childcare duties, and a history of having received decent parenting themselves (Warme and Thomas, 1978). While statistics suggest that child abuse in Canada has increased, it should be noted that greater public awareness and concern have resulted in more diligent statistics-gathering and improved detection of the problem. In a society that places a high value on family privacy, however, it is not an easy matter to ascertain what goes on behind closed doors; thus, the issue of protecting children who are at risk from their own family members is far from being resolved. Nor is there widespread consensus as to what are the acceptable limits of discipline, and what, in fact, constitutes "abuse" (Bakan 1971; Warme 1978). However, while families in higher socioeconomic groups have more "buffers," they also have more "screens"—that is to say, more effective ways of shielding abusive practices from public scrutiny.

Attention has also been directed to abuse at the other end of the age spectrum, namely abuse of the elderly. Because the issue has come to light only recently, and because it is difficult to obtain evidence (there are no specialized protective agencies), the extent of the problem has not been documented.

THE IMPACT OF MODERN ORGANIZATIONS

Discussion of how the spouse's position in the workplace impinges on the domestic sphere reminds us again of the interrelatedness of societal sectors. Canada's welfare state is frequently said to take care of individuals from womb to tomb. As our discussion of the poor has shown, not everyone is taken care of adequately, but specialized public and private organizations certainly have taken over many of the functions formerly performed by the family.

Canadian children may attend a day-care centre or nursery school before being absorbed into the educational system. They must go to school for a long time, and an increasing percentage of the population remains in school past the compulsory age of 15 or 16. At the same time, the school curriculum has expanded far beyond the 3 Rs to encompass areas such as civics, personal hygiene, and sex. Guidance counsellors and psychologists advise young people on vocational choices that used to be discussed in family conclaves. Banks, finance companies, employment agencies, and counsellors perform other services that used to fall within the sphere of the family. The growing number of senior citizens' residences and nursing homes is evidence that many families look to outside organizations for provision of housing and direct care-giving services to their elderly kinfolk.

On the other hand, as more social interaction takes place within organizations in which rationality and impersonality are the rule, the family has become increasingly important as a place where one can relax and be oneself. Ironically, overwhelming reliance for emotional support and renewed psychic energy for all its members may place unrealistic demands on the family and thus undermine its stability.

Moreover, even as children spend more time away from home, parents are increasingly encouraged to feel responsible for their academic and athletic achievements or the lack thereof. Many elementary schools require that the report card be given at a face-to-face conference with the teacher, a practice that is intended to encourage an exchange of information between home and school but that, unless tactfully handled, can be threatening to parents, especially if class or ethnic differences enter the encounter. The media present an assortment of experts who instruct parents on how to produce children who are ambitious but kind, popular but true to their principles, caring, outgoing, bright, and attractive. Since such paragons are hard to come by, parents are left to ponder where they went wrong. If juveniles do get into trouble, the assumption is usually that blame must lie with the family.

The family may now have a reduced number of tasks, but it is expected to perform these to high standards. Failure to meet the standards often results in feelings of inadequacy and guilt. A dual burden that many families have to shoulder is responsibility for adult children whose dependency has been prolonged by the increasing necessity of postsecondary education on the one hand, and responsibility for elderly parents on the other. People are living longer, but late in life they may not be able to look after themselves adequately. Thus, people who are currently in their forties and fifties are often referred to as the "sandwich generation," squeezed between the needs of their parents and those of their children.

SUMMARY

We have defined the family as a kinship group that offers its members at least minimal economic security, affection, and companionship. Despite wide cross-cultural variations, the family everywhere carries out a number of important functions. Notable among these are biological reproduction and social reproduction (socialization) of the group.

Western society places heavy emphasis on the individual; hence early socialization generally takes place in the family unit. However, in nonindustrial societies as well as in certain subcultures of modern societies, children are reared more communally, thus underlining the subordination of the individual to the group.

The modal type of family varies over time and space. In modern western societies, the extended family has for the most part been replaced by the nuclear family and the hybrid nuclear family. Unrelated persons may also enter into enduring, family-like relationships. Although many activities that had previously belonged to the family sphere have now been assumed by outside agencies, such as day-care centres, schools, and even organized sports, the need to provide warmth and emotional support for its members places heavy demands on the family. Recently, single-parent families have become more numerous and more socially acceptable. Their numbers have been swelled by the high incidence of marriage breakdown and divorce.

Mate selection and residence patterns for the newly married also exhibit much cross-cultural diversity. Marriage within the group (endogamy) or marriage outside the group (exogamy) may be the cultural ideal. The couple may live with the groom's family, with the bride's, alternate between the two, or establish their own residence. The extent to which ideal and practice coincide varies across societies.

As western society has become more heterogeneous, marriages that cross class, ethnic, and religious boundaries have become more numerous. Even so, many groups continue to discourage exogamy.

The family is a primary group in the sense of being characterized by close interaction and emotional ties, but it also provides the stage on which power relations are played out. Economic dependence affects power relationships, even within intimate groups. As increasing numbers of women work outside the home, their traditional dependence on their husbands is being attenuated, though it has certainly not been eliminated.

Clearly, there have been changes in the form, organization, and functions of the family. Yet despite predictions of its imminent demise, the family has shown no signs of withering away. Rather, it continues both to reflect and to shape societal values.

ASSIGNMENTS

Do one or both of the following assignments, as instructed by your professor.

1 Do some research on the division of labour in families (not your own). Choose two blue-collar and two white-collar families; one in each category should have the mother working outside the home, and the other should have a mother who is a full-time homemaker. Use a table like the one below to list your findings about the tasks the mother, the father, and the children perform in each case. What similarities and what differences did you find among the four cases? Suggest possible sociological reasons for the differences. What are the limitations of such a study (see Chapter 1)?

	White-collar family	Blue-collar family
Mother works outside home		
Mother is full-time homemaker		

2 Do some library research on a family (or family-like) configuration other than that of father-mother-dependent children. Report what you learn in sociological terms, using material from this section on the family, and from the chapters on culture, socialization and, where applicable, minorities.

SUGGESTED READINGS

David Bakan, *Slaughter of the Innocents: A Study of the Battered Child Phenomenon* (Toronto: CBC Learning Systems, 1971). In a sensitive and sweeping analysis of child abuse, Bakan argues that infanticide has, historically, served the function (as have plagues and wars) of population control. The twists and turns his argument takes will surprise you, as will his provocative analyses of some of the hateful messages embedded in the seemingly benign lullabies and stories that adults pass on to children.

S. Fraser, *My Father's House: A Memoir of Incest and of Healing* (Don Mills: Collins Paperbacks, 1988). After forty years of "forgetting," a prominent Canadian writer remembers, and confronts, her experiences of being sexually abused by her father in childhood and early adolescence. What went on behind closed doors was in stark contrast to the outward respectability of the family.

Janette Turner Hospital, *The Tiger in the Tiger Pit* (Toronto: McClelland and Stewart, 1983). The forthcoming reunion for the 50th wedding anniversary of Edward and Elizabeth Carpenter unleashes a flood of sweet and bitter memories in each of the family members. Edward, the retired principal of a small town high school in Massachusetts, rages against the infirmities and impotence of old age. Elizabeth is determined to reunite the family emotionally as well as physically. The three adult children approach the event with a mixture of trepidation and nostalgia.

Nigel Nicholson, *Portrait of a Marriage* (London: Weidenfeld and Nicholson, 1973). This is a painstaking account of the unconventional marriage of Nicholson's parents, Vita Sackville-West and Harold Nicholson. The 49-year marriage (1913–1962) is described as an extraordinarily successful partnership despite numerous extra-marital relationships, some of them homosexual.

Two of the chapters consist of Sackville-West's journal entries in which she records her turbulent affair with Violet Trefusis. Claiming that, in herself, masculine and feminine tendencies alternatively preponderated, Vita prophesies in 1920 that, in the future, there will be more candour about people possessed of a dual psychology, and that the system of marriage will be reconstructed to accommodate such tendencies.

L.B. Rubin, *Intimate Strangers. Men and Women Together* (New York: Harper and Row, 1983). Rubin examines the impact of socio-cultural factors on personality formation. She argues that different societal expectations for men and women inhibit the development of qualities that would permit real intimacy. Instead, both gender groups grope for the warmth and sharing that, too often, seem to elude them.

Benjamin Schlesinger, *The One-Parent Family in the 1980s* (Toronto: University of Toronto Press, 1985). One sure sign that a social phenomenon is becoming prevalent is when social scientists start writing about it. Single parenthood is not new, but its frequency in Canadian society is increasing. Schlesinger's collection of essays examines various aspects of the one-parent family. The bibliographic material provides ready reference for students interested in doing further research on the subject.

NOTES

1 Notice that here and throughout our discussions of institutions, unless otherwise indicated, we are speaking of what is normative for a given society. There are always exceptions. In some New Guinea families, the maternal uncle is not involved with the children (or perhaps the mother has no brother). In some western families, the maternal uncle assumes considerable responsibility for his nieces and nephews (perhaps their father is dead). But these instances are not the rule in the respective societies.

2 This cultural tradition is one reason that efforts to institute birth control have been largely unsuccessful in such countries as Mexico and India. Children are considered a form of old-age security — quite apart from being deemed proof of virility.

3 Often it is impossible to attract even nuclear families to remote work sites; many resource towns are overwhelmingly populated by single males.

4 The bride may have real cause for concern. Newspaper reports indicate that abuse of daughters-in-law does occur.

5 In some societies, august personages who have a large number of wives keep them in female compounds known as harems. Given the scant attention (sexual and otherwise) the husband in such a situation can pay to all his wives, their fidelity becomes problematic. The husband may, therefore, find it expedient to have the harem guarded by eunuchs.

9B

EDUCATION

That we can write this book and speak of an historical view of education signifies that in the distant past some individuals were able to acquire learning—specifically literacy—that enabled them to record in writing what happened during their lifetimes, how people felt about these events, and what mysteries of the universe they sought to unravel.

Today such records are available from many parts of the world. In the west, the earliest come mainly from classical Greece. There, as in most societies, organized learning was mainly a privilege of the elite, furnishing opportunities for intellectual play as well as supplying practical benefits. The academies of Plato and Aristotle provided a forum in which Greece's brightest and wealthiest young men could engage in stimulating discourse and thereby arrive at insights that would facilitate their understanding of the workings of the universe and point the way to optimum organization of society. However, the perception of intellectual pursuits as desirable filtered down in the society, and some determined and alert individuals of the less privileged classes managed to become literate and proficient at mathematics.

Thus, even 2000 years ago, education provided an avenue for upward mobility. Literacy, the ability to read and write, remained a scarce and precious commodity for centuries. In the Roman empire, slaves who had the skill before being captured, or who contrived to acquire it later, worked as scribes and bookkeepers. Their importance to their masters often enabled them to accumulate enough money to buy freedom.

With the disintegration of the Roman empire, western Europe moved into the dark ages. The vast majority of the population was illiterate. Learning became the purview of the Catholic Church, which supplied the clerks needed by the aristocracy for written communication, records, and bookkeeping.[1] The focus of education was mainly on religious issues, though secular enquiry was kept alive by individuals who managed to stay in touch with each other, eventually through the late mediaeval world's centres of learning, such as those in Paris and Padua. In a culture that made far less distinction than ours between religious and worldly matters, theologians and philosophers tackled problems that today would be considered as falling in the realm of physical or social science. Albertus Magnus (1206?–80) and Roger Bacon (1214–94), both of whom greatly advanced the scientific method, were churchmen who also wrote on philosophy and theology, respectively. Such enquiry blossomed and expanded as the Renaissance marshalled in a new zest for intellectual discovery and for physical exploration of the universe.

Among some Protestant groups that emerged from the Reformation, literacy became highly valued because it enabled people to read god's word without a priestly intermediary. Interestingly, education acquired for such a noneconomic motive has historically bestowed material as well as intrinsic rewards. For example, widespread literacy among Quakers, at a time when this was a rare accomplishment, contributed to the group's importance in the North Atlantic trade. Somewhat analogously, Jews have reaped economic benefits through the ages from book learning that was undertaken in the first place as the prerequisite for study of the Talmud.

FORMAL EDUCATION

We define **formal education** as the process of learning and of being socialized that takes place in specialized organizations such as schools, colleges, technical schools, and universities.

In the western nations, the institution of universal public education roughly coincided with the latter stages of the Industrial Revolution. More sophisticated machinery and the growth of enterprises necessitated written communication and hence a literate work force. Labour laws delaying the age at which children could start work and reducing the length of their work day created a need for a caretaking service, the babysitting function that education continues to perform today. In many cases, church-sponsored schools preceded or co-existed with schools funded from the public purse.

Meanwhile, the Napoleonic Wars (1795–1815) and the American Revolution (1776–83) had spurred the emergence of modern nationalism and the large-scale use of citizen armies to replace hired mercenaries. In public schools, nationalistic feelings could be inculcated and reinforced by such rituals as raising the flag, singing the national anthem, and learning a glorious version of the nation's history.

In the United States, and to a lesser extent in Canada, the schools become important vehicles for assimilating children from different ethnic backgrounds into the mainstream culture of the society.

Educators such as Egerton Ryerson, who was superintendent of education in Upper Canada from 1844 to 1876 and is regarded as the father of Ontario's public schools, described the socializing aspect of education in terms of building character and elevating students to a higher moral plane. By rewarding such qualities as punctuality, neatness, submissiveness, and tolerance for monotonous tasks, the schools began to serve as important agents of socialization for life in the work force. This function was deemed crucial because of the fear that these virtues would not be transmitted through the lower-class family, given that parents had to work long hours for mere survival and that children largely had to fend for themselves. See Prentice (1977), an examination of the attitudes that influenced the Ontario public school system in its early years. The book illustrates how schools were seen as a means for improving society.

In teaching punctuality, neatness, submissiveness, and tolerance for monotonous tasks, the school is an important agent of socialization for the work force.

In brief, from the viewpoint of society, education performs several functions:

- It encourages homogeneity and creates a shared cultural identity.
- It exposes students to nationalistic rituals during the years when they are most impressionable.
- It provides caretaking services.
- Through selective reward and punishment, it reinforces traits needed in an industrial work force.
- It maintains and expands the pool of expertise on which the society can draw. In the absence of such a pool, the society must rely on outside help, such as that provided to third-world countries by Canadian University Students Overseas (CUSO).

Thomas Jefferson believed that education is crucial because ignorance and freedom cannot co-exist in society. He wrote: "If a nation expects to be ignorant and free, in a state of civilization, it expects what never was and never will be."

EDUCATION AND LIFE CHANCES

The word "education" is derived from the Latin *educo*—"I lead out." From the viewpoint of the individual, what does education lead out from? What does it lead to? Ideally, education leads one out of ignorance and the poverty so often associated with it, out of being utterly dependent on forces over which one seems to have no control. Education brings power to exercise some influence over one's own fate. It is no accident that subordinate groups have traditionally been deprived of education or have received an inferior one. During the period before the American Civil War (1861–5), it was an offence in many parts of that country to teach slaves to read and write, and at least until the U.S. Supreme Court outlawed educational segregation in 1954, the schooling blacks received was vastly inferior to that of whites in most parts of the country. The recurrent unrest in South Africa today is focused, in part, on the minimal amount spent on the education of black and "coloured" children compared to the funds allocated to educate white children. Ensuring a lack of education is an effective mechanism for making *actually* inferior a group that has been categorized as such on the basis of ascribed characteristics. Similarly, denying children education in the language of their culture is a symbolic degradation of that culture—and may ultimately destroy it; witness the francophones of Manitoba and the Gaelic-speakers of Great Britain, to name only two of hundreds of historical examples.

Again we recall the close relationship between the organization of the society as a whole and that of its constituent parts. Looking at the way in which education is organized and at the opportunities this organization makes available to individuals, one would expect a highly stratified society to have systems that differ markedly

In South Africa, per capita expenditure on the education of black children is only a fraction of what is spent on white children.

in curriculum and value content for children from different social classes. A likely outcome would be differential opportunities for the students processed in these separate systems. James Coleman, a prominent analyst of education, has described some of the differences between the early British and American systems of education:

> *The emergence of public-tax supported education was not solely a function of industrial development. It was also a function of the class structure in the society. In the United States, without a strong traditional class structure, universal education in publicly-supported free schools became widespread in the early nineteenth century; in England, the "voluntary" schools, run and organized by churches with some instances of state support, were not supplemented by a state-supported system until the Education Act of 1870. Even more, the character of educational opportunity reflected the class structure. In the United States, the public schools quickly became the common schools, attended by representatives of all classes; these schools provided a common educational experience for most American children — excluding only those upper-class children in private schools, those poor who went to no schools and Indians and Southern Negroes who were without schools. In England, however, the class system directly*

> *manifested itself through the schools. The state-supported, or "board schools" as they were called, became the schools of the laboring lower classes with a sharply different curriculum from those voluntary schools which served the middle and upper classes (1968, 10).*

In the early years of public education, equality of opportunity was not a goal in Britain — nor in Canada. Eventually, with the greater democratization of society and, specifically, with universal suffrage, politicians had to appear more responsive to the needs of all citizens. Equality of opportunity for those of equal ability was adopted as a societal objective. Although this equality has not been fully realized in Canadian society, education has been the principal vehicle for upgrading occupational status and, concomitantly, social status.

For the middle class, education is not only a means of moving up. It is also a means of preserving existing status, of avoiding skidding downward. Unlike the scions of the upper class, who can expect large inheritances or a niche in a family enterprise, students from middle-class homes know that their future status will depend on placement in the work world. This placement is increasingly dependent on academic credentials.

During the last decade, as the percentage of students engaged in postsecondary and postgraduate study has risen (see Exhibit 9.4), it has become more difficult to cash in educational credits for immediate jobs and assured career advancement. However, education unquestionably enhances lifetime earnings and decreases the probability of unemployment. Exhibit 9.5 demonstrates the relationship between the level of attained education and the likelihood of unemployment. Notice that since 1975, those with only high school education or less have consistently had higher-than-average unemployment rates, while those with at least some postsecondary education have had lower-than-average rates. Clearly, those with university degrees have fared best, both in relation to other educational groups and in their absolute unemployment rates. However, even this group was sharply affected by the 1982–3 recession, with its unemployment rate jumping from 3.2 percent in 1981 to 5.2 percent in 1983, an increase of more than 60 percent. But the less-educated groups showed nearly as sharp a rise and were much worse off in absolute terms.

EXHIBIT 9.4

SCHOOLING ACHIEVED BY CANADIANS, 1941–81

Percentage of population over 15 years and over

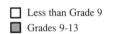

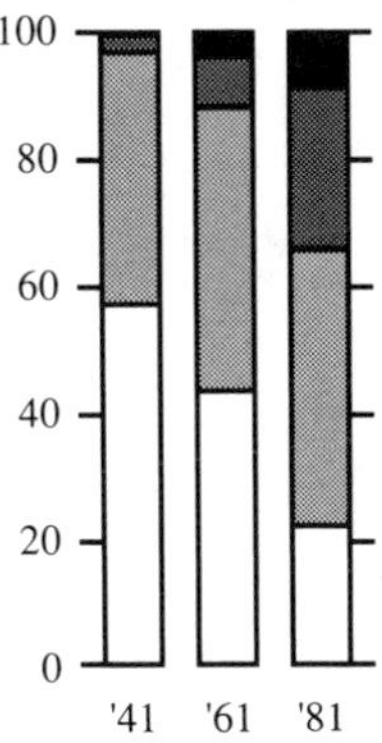

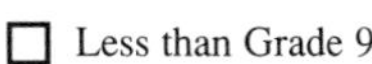

NOTES: 1941 data are estimated.
Notice that by using 15 years of age as the cutoff point for the population studied, the researchers have tilted the results toward the lower categories. Age 15 is under school-leaving age in most provinces and under the usual age for secondary-school completion in all. One can reasonably assume that some young people who fell in the "less than Grade 9" category at the time the data were gathered will end up with secondary-school certificates; a number counted as "grades 9-13" will end up with some postsecondary and even university degrees, and so on. This tilt is an example of the ways presentation of statistics influences our knowledge.

SOURCE: Statistics Canada (1983b, [1]), and The Labour Force (71-001) to Jan. 1989 (table 5).

EXHIBIT 9.5

CANADIANS' UNEMPLOYMENT RATES BY EDUCATIONAL ATTAINMENT

	1975	1976	1977	1978	1979	1980	1981	1982	1983	1984	1985	1986	1987	1988	1989
Total labour force	6.9	7.1	8.1	8.3	7.4	7.5	7.5	11.0	11.9	12.4	12.2	10.7	10.6	8.9	8.4
0-8 years schooling	8.2	7.9	9.4	9.6	8.8	9.0	9.1	13.3	13.5	15.1	15.1	13.7	14.0	12.5	12.6
High school	8.0	8.2	9.3	9.4	8.4	8.6	8.7	12.7	13.9	14.5	14.5	12.9	12.7	10.8	10.0
Some postsecondary education	6.4	6.4	7.5	7.8	6.6	6.4	6.7	10.0	11.7	12.6	11.0	9.5	9.7	7.7	8.3
Postsecondary certificate or diploma	4.3	5.2	5.3	5.8	5.1	5.0	4.9	7.5	8.9	9.2	8.7	7.2	7.2	6.3	5.8
University degree	3.0	3.2	3.4	3.8	3.2	3.1	3.2	4.9	5.2	4.3	5.3	4.8	4.5	4.1	4.0

SOURCE: Statistics Canada (1984c, table 8), and The Labour Force (71-001) to Jan. 1989 (table 5).

Although it is becoming more difficult to cash in educational credits for immediate jobs, education unquestionably enhances lifetime earnings and decreases the probability of unemployment.

Education makes a big difference to a family's income, as shown by Exhibit 9.6. Families headed by persons with only elementary education have half the average income of families whose heads have university degrees ($30,792 as opposed to $61,183). The higher the level of schooling, the higher the average family income. Exhibit 9.7 shows a similar picture for unattached Canadians.

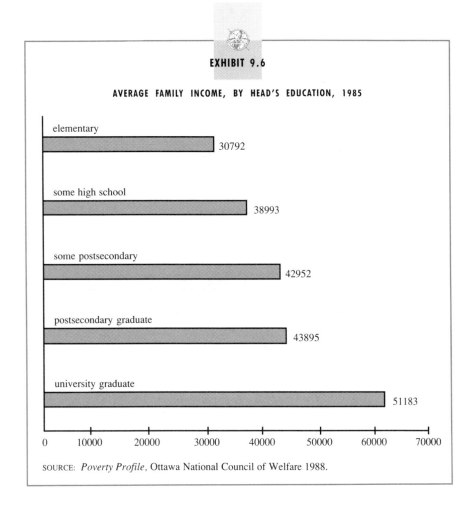

EXHIBIT 9.6

AVERAGE FAMILY INCOME, BY HEAD'S EDUCATION, 1985

elementary 30792

some high school 38993

some postsecondary 42952

postsecondary graduate 43895

university graduate 51183

0 10000 20000 30000 40000 50000 60000 70000

SOURCE: *Poverty Profile*, Ottawa National Council of Welfare 1988.

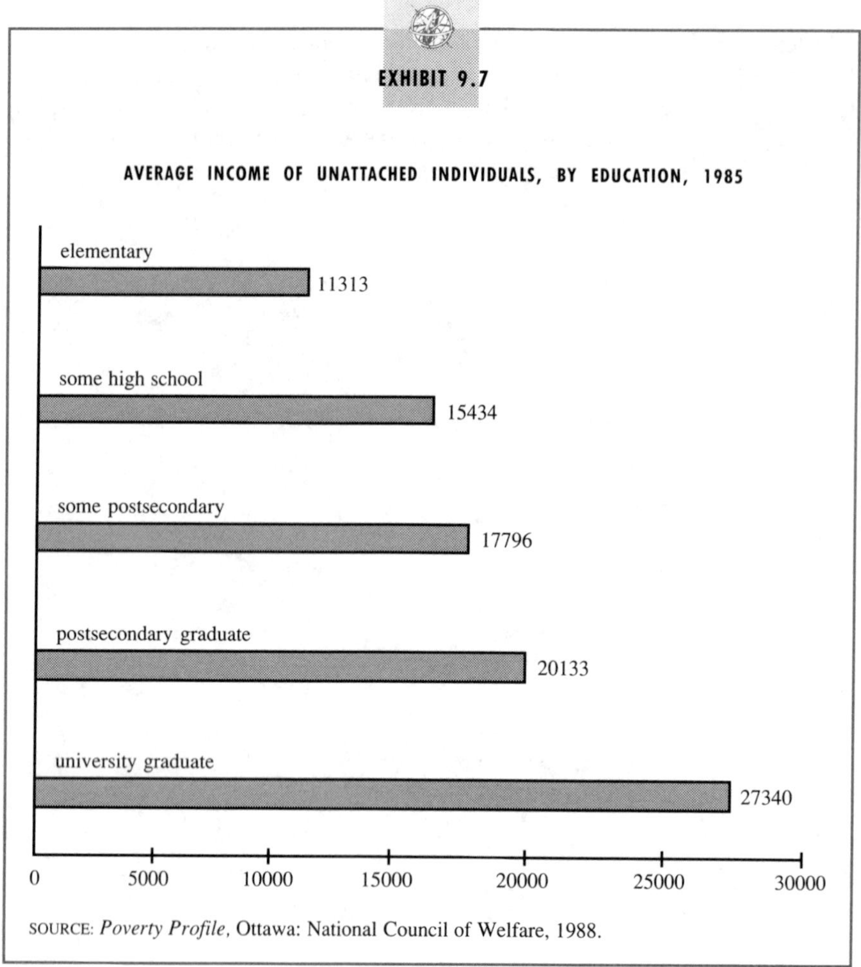

SOURCE: *Poverty Profile*, Ottawa: National Council of Welfare, 1988.

The persistent relationship between education and earnings, and between education and unemployment rates, shows that the concern about drop-out rates is not unjustified. Unlike Sweden or West Germany, for example, Canada does not provide a structured transition from school to work. Thus, many students do not recognize the importance of education and leave school because they see no connection between what they learn at school and their future work. Radwanski's 1987 report documents the high drop-out rates in Ontario. From the viewpoint of society, this represents an underutilization of human capital.

NONMATERIAL REWARDS

Education, of course, yields more than material payoffs. Ideally, it permits an individual to fulfill his or her potential and to rejoice in doing so. Sometimes the thrill and the feeling of power that come with newly acquired knowledge are most apparent among young children. Suddenly, the squiggles on a page form intelligible words that make up a story. Being able to read confers some independence from adults.

ILLITERACY AND ITS COSTS

How serious a problem is illiteracy in Canada today? The 1987 Southam Survey indicated that 24 percent of the population over 18 years of age are illiterate. Of course, there may be disagreement about what constitutes illiteracy. In the Southam survey, respondents had to give correct answers to eight of the ten questions to be categorized as literate. The items ranged from reading instructions on a cough syrup bottle to answering a question on the Charter of Rights and Freedoms.

The costs of illiteracy must be assessed both for the society (untapped potential, less accumulation of cultural capital, lowered productivity) and for those who are illiterate. Since modern societies are oriented to written communications of many kinds, from highway signs to government forms, illiteracy entails both tangible and intangible penalties. How can one find and keep a job, and how much is the job likely to pay? How does one fill out the form for a tax credit? Feelings of isolation, shame, and inadequacy make acknowledgement of illiteracy difficult and the possibility of help remote.

Among immigrants, women who are homebound or work in immigrant job ghettos often have the fewest opportunities to learn English, let alone to acquire literacy skills in the language. *Canadian Women Studies* devoted their 1988 Fall/Winter volume to Women and Literacy (see Suggested Readings). Many of the articles emphasize the role of literacy in women's empowerment—to leave abusive environments, to find more desirable work and, importantly, to think of themselves as people who matter.

BRINGING THEM BACK TO SCHOOL

By Harvey Krahn
and Julian Tanner

By focusing on the "drop-out" issue, the recently published Radwanski Report has drawn public attention to the dissatisfactions of a large minority of Ontario adolescents with the province's education system. Constructive debate over some of the Report's recommendations has begun, although it occasionally appears, as in the case of standardized curriculum material and examinations, that old controversies are being recycled.

However, it may also be useful to reflect on some ideas which are largely absent from the debate. Specifically, the possibility that some of those who have dropped out might still be interested in further education has not been addressed. Thus, while the Report concerns itself with keeping young people in school, it ignores the equally important question of how those who have already left might be enticed to return.

Three years before Radwanski, we conducted a similar study in Edmonton. Many of our findings — based on semi-structured interviews with 162 young people who had left school without completing grade 12 — parallel those reported by Radwanski.

Most notably, we also found that while respondents gave a variety of reasons for dropping out, school-based and family-related factors (in that order) were most important.

When identifying school-related problems, these young people were most likely to say simply that they disliked school or that it was all too boring. A large number said they had been skipping too many classes, no doubt for the same reasons.

The most commonly mentioned family-related reason involved problems getting along with parents; dropping out (and leaving home) was a dramatic solution. While some sample members stated they had left school to take a job or because they wanted to find one, such reasons were less common.

But what struck us at the time — and even more so now, given the emphasis of the Radwanski Report — was not the magnitude of adolescent alienation from the school system, but the very opposite. Given that drop-outs, by definition, are the education system's most estranged clients, it was surprising to find how committed to education many of them remained.

Many of our respondents were rather ambivalent about their decision to leave school. We asked them if they felt, in retrospect, that dropping out of school had been a good or a bad thing. Roughly equal proportions answered "good," "bad," or "both good and bad." Listening to these young people elaborate their answers, it was apparent that often it was a bit of both: a case of short-term gain for long-term pain.

As one sample member commented: "Well, at first I thought it was a good thing because I was going to be moving on to something. Right now, I don't know."

On the one hand, these individuals saw dropping out as an immediate solution to the various problems they had encountered in school or at home. On the other hand, these benefits were more than tempered by a growing awareness that the lack of a high school diploma, if it had not already done so, could well cause problems in the not too distant future.

Another respondent stated the case clearly: "Well, it was bad because I lost some years. But it was good because then I knew exactly what education was when I went out to fill out the applications for jobs, you know. Some jobs you have to have high school and you just don't find a good job without a high school diploma."

For young people supposedly deeply alienated from the education system, a surprisingly large number were still receptive to the idea of more education in the future. When asked, "Would you like to get more education?", 70 per cent answered positively, 24 per cent said "maybe," and only 6 per cent were certain that they had been through enough school. There is very little evidence here of a deep and lasting antagonism towards the idea of schooling among these early school leavers.

By presenting a picture of drop-outs as adolescents frustrated with and alienated from school, Radwanski unintentionally conceals a basic similarity between them and those who remain in school. What the two groups have in common is a pragmatic view of school as a place where qualifications are acquired in order to maximize job opportunities.

Our findings do not dispute the conclusion that frustration and alienation were present when these individuals quit school. But they do highlight a continuing recognition of the importance of education among those who dropped out. Neither the belated acknowledgement of the value of education nor the doubts expressed about the decision to quit school are sentiments one would expect among unambiguously alienated young people.

Reasons for our informants' ambivalence and regret about dropping out were not hard to find. The experience of trying to find employment without a grade 12 diploma proved, in many cases, to be dispiriting.

One of the sample members reflected as follows on his labour market experiences: "Yeah, I learned a few things. I learned about how hard work is, like a real tough job. Like I never really knew. I thought, you know, construction and stuff like that wouldn't be too bad, but then it gets to you. It's hard."

While this respondent was learning about unskilled manual labour, the work experience of many others did not extend beyond part-time, low-paying jobs in the service sector. Jobs in restaurants and fast-food outlets, and as retail sales clerks, were mentioned frequently, along with extended periods of unemployment. The consequent disillusionment with work, and with unemployment, forced a re-evaluation of attitudes towards education.

THE EDUCATIONAL SYSTEM IN CANADA

The structure of the educational system and the manner in which it operates are closely intertwined. Under Canada's federal political system, the provinces are responsible for education at the primary and secondary levels. School boards act under provincial or territorial guidelines. Hence, when we talk about "Canadian" schools,[2] we are, in fact, referring to schools directed by the appropriate ministries or departments of ten provinces and two territories and by a large number of school boards. Private schools may operate in any province and grant diplomas provided they meet the regulations and standards set by the province or territory. They are independent of the public system, are managed privately by an individual association or corporation, and charge fees, but they usually closely follow the curriculum and diploma requirements of the relevant department or ministry of education.

Through the Department of Indian Affairs and Northern Development (DIAND), the federal government is responsible for the education of status Indians and Inuit children. Every province except Newfoundland has federal schools, and they are operated either by DIAND or by Indian bands or tribal councils. As well, the federal government may pay for the education of native children in provincial schools. The issue of native education is currently in flux, as native peoples are seeking greater control in terms of location of schools, language of instruction, and content of curriculum.

The main sources for financing secondary and elementary schools are provincial funds and municipal property taxes. Each ministry of education, headed by an elected politician, sets educational goals in light of the province's overall priorities and the resources available to meet them. Translating these goals into action — to use the formal term, **operationalizing** them — is left to the bureaucratic officials (civil servants) of the ministries concerned. General policies are handed down by the ministries and form the basis for adaptations made by the school board officials, who are elected, appointed, or both, depending on jurisdiction; their decisions are implemented by hired administrators, including principals. Within provincial guidelines, most school boards have a fair degree of autonomy. For example, the trustees of the Etobicoke Board of Education may decide to increase local taxes in order to continue remedial programs no longer funded by the province of Ontario. The Board's authority is limited. In 1985, British Columbia required its local boards to reduce their budgets and removed the trustees of two school districts that refused. For an interesting analysis of the evolution of the Canadian educational system in contrast with the American system (less centralized) and those of western Europe and Japan, see Pike 1988.

EXHIBIT 9.8

TEACHERS IN POSITIONS OF ADDED RESPONSIBILITY, PUBLIC ELEMENTARY SCHOOLS, 1978 AND 1986

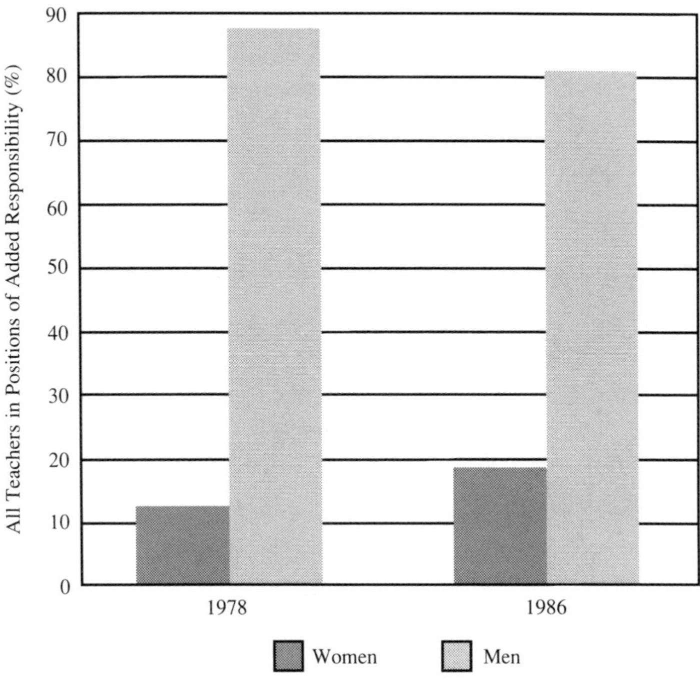

NOTE: "Positions of Added Responsibility" includes principals, vice-principals, and department heads.

SOURCE: September School Reports, 1978 and 1986.

Teachers in Positions of Added Responsibility, Public Elementary Schools, 1978 and 1986

	1978		1986	
Position	Female	Male	Female	Male
Principal	166	2 325	285	2 108
Vice-principal	176	963	328	898
Department head	133	232	120	187
SUBTOTAL	475	3 520	733	3 193
PER CENT OF TOTAL	11.9	88.1	18.7	81.3

SOURCE: September School Reports, 1978 and 1986.

EXHIBIT 9.9

TEACHERS IN POSITIONS OF ADDED RESPONSIBILITY, PUBLIC SECONDARY SCHOOLS, 1978 AND 1986

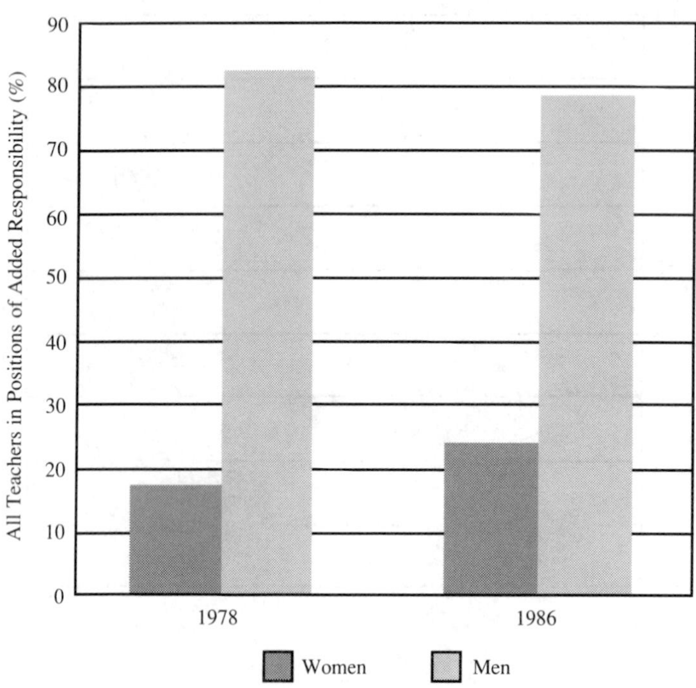

NOTE: "Positions of Added Responsibility" includes principals, vice-principals, and department heads.

SOURCE: September School Reports, 1978 and 1986.

Teachers in Positions of Added Responsibility, Public Secondary Schools, 1978 and 1986

	1978		1986	
Position	Female	Male	Female	Male
Principal	17	560	45	530
Vice-principal	59	759	121	722
Department head	1 328	5 406	1 602	5 063
SUBTOTAL	1 404	6 725	1 768	6 315
PER CENT OF TOTAL	17.3	82.7	21.9	78.1

SOURCE: September School Reports, 1978 and 1986.

CONFESSIONAL SCHOOLS

The intricacies of the Canadian educational system are made even more complex by the existence in some provinces of publicly supported separate school systems — usually Roman Catholic — and the practice in others of providing public funds for private schools. This support of confessional education has existed in Canada since the 19th century.

> *Fundamental to the creation of a system of free and universal education was the notion, then common, that education and religion were inseparable and that the state had a responsibility to foster, wherever possible, a harmonious relationship between them. Religion in education was important, even essential, to both Protestants and Catholics* (The Canadian Encyclopedia *1985, 1677*).

The British North America Act (now incorporated in the Constitution Act of 1982) guaranteed separate, publicly funded Protestant and Catholic systems in Ontario and Quebec. Ontario's Protestant system became its present public system. Provincial funding for its Catholic system was extended in the mid-1960s, from the end of elementary school to the end of grade 10 (roughly, the official school-leaving age of 16), and, in June 1984, to the end of high school. Both enlargements caused considerable public discussion.

Some people believe continuation of tax-supported confessional schools fans prejudice, retards the assimilation of cultural groups whose religious identity is strong, is unfair to denominations not entitled to schools in particular jurisdictions, and is expensive because of duplicated services. Supporters invoke Canada's multicultural tradition, point out that, historically, separate schools have protected minorities in some provinces, and claim that competing systems spur each other to better performance.[3]

THE LANGUAGE OF EDUCATION

In provinces such as Quebec, New Brunswick, Nova Scotia, Ontario, and Manitoba, the alternatives in public schooling are also cross-cut along language lines. Historically, most francophone schools were Catholic and most anglophone schools Protestant (an exception being the Catholic schools in Ontario, partly created to serve Irish immigrants and guaranteed in the British North America Act as a trade-off for the guarantee of anglophone Protestant schools in Quebec). Historically, too, the question of the language of instruction has been a contentious one in Canada. Manitoba, for instance, joined Confederation as a bilingual province, with guarantees for both English- and French-language schools, but in 1890, after two decades of controversy, the government set English as the sole language of instruction.[4]

Today the situation is more complex, but the question of the language of instruction can still raise political — and emotional — temperatures. As we said in Chapter 7 on minority groups, parts of Quebec's series of language laws have been aimed at reducing the number of children, especially immigrant children, eligible for the English-language schools. Ontario boards, public and separate (Catholic), offer French schools "where numbers warrant;" the interpretation of that phrase and demands for separate (francophone) facilities as well as curricula have split several communities and have given rise to litigation. Controversy has also erupted in some New Brunswick and Nova Scotia communities. Alternatively, in recent years, French immersion classes have proved enormously popular with middle-class anglophone families, even in such nonfrancophone cities as Calgary and Vancouver.

The vehemence with which people fight for and against schools that are confessional and/or taught in a minority language suggests they well understand that schools are engaged in passing on values as well as knowledge (Olson and Burns 1983).

INDEPENDENT SCHOOLS

Private or independent schools have traditionally catered to a miniscule proportion of the Canadian population, yet they have played an important part in socializing the children of the elite to assume their intended roles. Porter (1965), Clement (1975), and numerous other analysts of Canadian society have commented on the overrepresentation of private-school graduates in key economic, professional, and political positions.

During recent years, enrolment in private schools has grown significantly, even as the overall school-age population has decreased. From 1971/2 to 1982/3, public-school enrolment declined by over 16 percent while private school enrolment increased by 50.5 percent (Statistics Canada 1988). Public school enrolment declined 1.4 percent from 1982/3 to 1986/7. Private school enrolment was 10.5 percent in 1986/7 (Statistics Canada 1988).

Several factors have contributed to this development. In the 1960s and 1970s, the Civil Rights Movement, the women's liberation movement, and the emergence of the "flower children" both reflected and heightened the urge to cast off traditional restraints. "Open" schools became geared to providing "self-actualization" for the individual student, rather than adhering to standard curricula. Discipline became more relaxed, and teachers assumed the guise of "resource persons" rather than authority figures. Parents who were dissatisfied with these changes and who could afford it opted to send their children to those independent schools that were slower to institute changes, in part because such schools had to be responsive to the generally conservative leanings of their boards of governors.[5]

As the competition has become more intense to gain entrance to the postsecondary programs most likely to lead to well-paid, secure employment, the shift to independent schools has become more pronounced. Small classes and the power to enforce academic and disciplinary standards are seen as promoting achievement. In one survey of delegates from women's guilds attached to 13 independent schools in Ontario, all the respondents listed academic achievement as a prime reason for sending their children to such schools. The belief that independent schools enforced stricter behavioural standards and were "character-building" also ranked as important motives. Almost 40 percent of the respondents reported no prior association with a private school among their immediate kin. The push of dissatisfaction with public education and the perceived advantages of private schools had induced them to enrol their children in the latter (Lundy 1982).

The demand for alternatives to public schools has resulted in the mushrooming of new private ones. In many cases, these schools' sales pitch is the promise to realize students' full potential and enhance their achievements, thus giving them an edge in the academic contest. Students in public-school are almost equally divided between elementary (grades one to six) and secondary (grades seven to twelve)—43.5 and 42.7 percent respectively — while 57.6 percent of students in private schools are at the same secondary level (Statistics Canada 1988). In 1986/7, 69.2 percent of public school students were in elementary schools and 30.8 percent were in secondary schools. For independent schools, the percentages were 62.8 and 37.2 (Statistics Canada 1988). It may well be that parents view the financial investment as more worthwhile in the later years of schooling, since high school achievement has become a crucial determinant of vocational opportunities.[6]

POSTSECONDARY EDUCATION

In our discussion of the functions education performs for society, we noted that it creates, maintains, and expands the pool of expertise upon which the society can draw. As Canadian society has become more highly industrialized and urbanized, an increased percentage of the labour force has moved to the professional, technical, and administrative sectors (look back to Exhibits 5.1 and 5.2). This shift has occurred in conjunction with the explosive growth of postsecondary institutions since the end of the Second World War, bringing Canada to a position among western nations that is second only to the United States in terms of the proportion of 20- to 24-year-olds enrolled in post-secondary education.

The growth was fuelled by the confluence of several trends. Economists and social scientists were calling for investment in human resources to ensure continued prosperity and technological advancement. The baby-boom cohorts were passing through the school system, looking for further education which was to provide the key to the good life. The federal and provincial governments, riding a buoyant economy, made available scholarships, student grants, and loans to broaden access to postsecondary education. They also provided capital funding for colleges and new universities, and increased operating grants. Academics were recruited from the United States and Britain to staff the expanded system.

Another trend becomes evident from closer examination of the statistics. In 1961, 7.5 percent of Canadians aged 18 to 24 were enrolled in university programs; among females, the percentage was 3.9, compared to 11.2 among males. By 1982, overall participation had increased to 12.8 percent, and the difference between males and females had shrunk to two percentage points — 13.8 compared to 11.8 percent (Council of Ontario Universities 1983). Much of the overall increase, then, is the result of the much higher participation of women.

Part-time students, too, have played a large part in bolstering university enrolments. Between 1962/3 and 1982/3, their number increased from 11,904 to 87,155 — a rise of 732.1 percent. During the same period, full-time enrolment increased by 447.9 percent (Statistics Canada 1984b). In 1987, overall part-time enrolment was 286,207, with the overwhelming majority of students being at the undergraduate level (Statistics Canada 1989). Shorter working hours, smaller families coupled with improved domestic technology, awareness of the importance of advanced education, and the desire to utilize opportunities that may not have been previously open to individuals jointly created this trend.

The foregoing discussion should alert you to the fact that broad-range statistics, such as those documenting changes in overall university enrolment, may conceal important information about the groups that comprise the total. In fact, the new constituencies of women and part-time students account for a significant proportion of increased university enrolment. Full-time male enrolment increased only slightly.

REGIONAL DIFFERENCES IN CANADIAN SCHOOLS

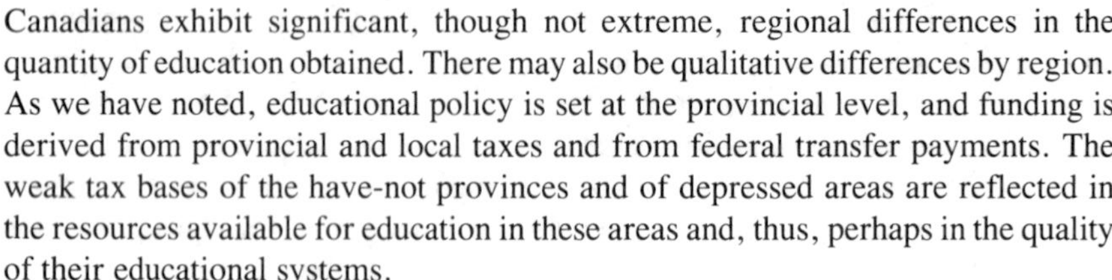

Canadians exhibit significant, though not extreme, regional differences in the quantity of education obtained. There may also be qualitative differences by region. As we have noted, educational policy is set at the provincial level, and funding is derived from provincial and local taxes and from federal transfer payments. The weak tax bases of the have-not provinces and of depressed areas are reflected in the resources available for education in these areas and, thus, perhaps in the quality of their educational systems.

Tomorrow Is School and I Am Sick to the Heart Thinking about It is an account of the two years a young couple, Jan and Don Sawyer, spent teaching at Hoberly Cove, an outport community in Newfoundland. There was little by way of books or sports equipment:

> *Carrying copies of my new texts, I wandered across the hall to where the library had been shown on the floor plan. I walked in the door and froze in disbelief. The room was tiny, only about twelve feet square. Along the back wall were almost bare shelves; a low counter ran under*

> *the large, multi-paned window in the north wall. The rest of the room was filled with desks. ''We don't really use it as a library,'' Calvin told me later. ''We just don't have enough room. We mostly have to use it as a classroom'' (1979, 34).*

The principal and teachers rationalized the sparse supply of books:

> *''These kids don't know how to do a real research paper anyway, so that's all they need just now. Anyway, there's a public library in town'' (1979, 35).*

Lack of adequate facilities, combined with teachers' low evaluation of the students, contributed to a pattern of failure and hopelessness:

> *During the school year after we left Hoberly Cove, ninety percent of the students in my former grade nine class either dropped out of school or failed grade ten. Of the thirty grade nines in school at the end of my last year, only three graduated from grade ten. A similarly high dropout failure rate, though not as extreme, occurred in the other grades as well (1979, 203).*

The Sawyers' experience was not an isolated one, nor is it outdated. In November 1984, five Newfoundland agencies associated with education released a study showing that only half the students who enter that province's school systems actually graduate. Even this is a sizeable improvement on earlier rates:

> *Economic conditions are probably related to dropout rate. From the early 1960's to the late 1970's, as the standard of living in rural Newfoundland rose, huge sums were spent on new schools, teacher training and upgrading. Not surprisingly, the study found that the percentage of students graduating from Newfoundland schools climbed from 22 percent in 1965 to 49 percent in 1980, and then seems to have levelled off (Roche 1984, 8).*

Employment prospects within Newfoundland are generally bleak. Yet those of its citizens who are without educational credentials have little hope of improving their position by moving to other parts of North America, because technological advances have steadily eroded the demand for unskilled workers.

Poor schools and chaotic conditions in the classroom and the schoolyard are by no means confined to Newfoundland. In *Cries from the Corridor* (see Suggested Readings), Peter McLaren describes his experiences in an urban Ontario school:

> *At the half-hour mark, I told the kids it was time to go outside. Sandwich wrappings flew everywhere in the delicate stampede out the door.*

Once outside, I breathed a sigh of relief—that is, until I heard screams coming from the sand pit. A big red-headed kid had tied a piece of glass to the end of a broken hockey stick and was gleefully charging a terrified pack of fleeing behinds. He held a garbage-pail lid as a shield, and wore an inverted plastic funnel as a helmet. I took the weapon from this miniature Don Quixote, which he didn't like at all.

"Gimmie back my spear, you son-of-a-bitch!"

"Sorry, weapons aren't allowed on school property," I said crisply.

"Hand it over or I'll break your ass, man!"

I pried the glass off the end of the stick, and threw it over the fence.

"You're new here," the kid drawled, "ain't ya, turkey?"

That afternoon, as I was pulling out of the school parking lot, I glanced down at the dashboard. The eight-track stereo I kept locked in my car was missing (1980, 41).

EDUCATION FOR EXCEPTIONAL CHILDREN

The situation of exceptional children highlights both the fatefulness of where one grows up and the limitations of public education. Mass education systems are primarily geared to educating the average child. Schools in regions low in funds or numbers have fewer facilities to diagnose and teach gifted children or children with learning disabilities, emotional disorders, and physical or mental disabilities.

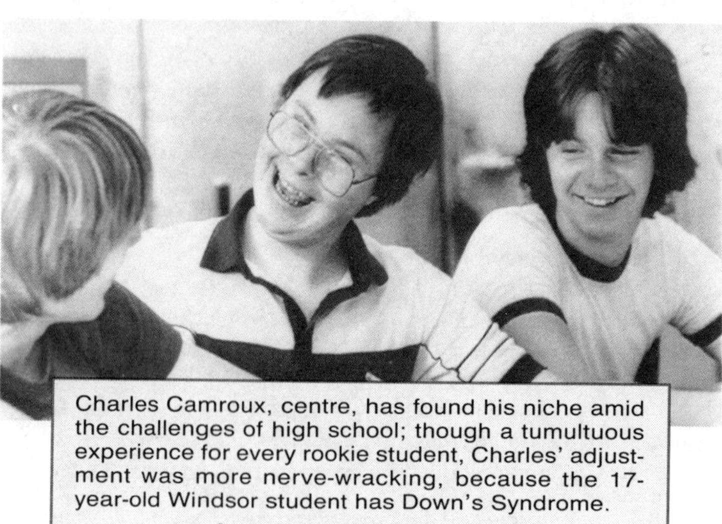

Charles Camroux, centre, has found his niche amid the challenges of high school; though a tumultuous experience for every rookie student, Charles' adjustment was more nerve-wracking, because the 17-year-old Windsor student has Down's Syndrome.

Efforts are made to help many of these children. The most far-reaching is Ontario's Bill 82, passed in 1982. It requires that each child be provided with adequate education, regardless of exceptional qualities. This well-intentioned law encounters two problems. First, ''adequacy'' may be differently defined by different interest groups — for example, by the parents of a multi-disabled student and by the local school board. Second, even minimal implementation requires the availability of a cadre of experts, such as psychologists, psychometrists, social workers, and special teachers. Hence the program is bound to be more manageable and more accessible in Toronto, Hamilton, and Ottawa than in remote northern communities.

In the less populous and poorer provinces, exceptional children are unlikely to do well. For instance, a child with a reading disability may be labelled ''retarded.'' Such a classification can set into motion a self-fulfilling prophecy: teachers gear down their expectations and efforts, and the child comes to think of himself or herself as dull and performs accordingly. Again, however, we must inject a note of caution. We are talking about probability. A learning-disabled child may not be diagnosed in a highly sophisticated school system, whereas such a disability may be noticed by an alert teacher in a small country school.

NOW LISTEN AND LEARN, DOG-FACED REPROBATE!

By A. Trevor Hodge

Everybody has their own way of getting ready for the annual back-to-school ritual. My own preparation is simple. I read a bit of Libanius. After all, come a few days and I'll be back in there lecturing to another bunch of students, and it always helps me to keep my perspective if I read how they did it in ancient Athens.

Not that they had universities, in the modern, organized sense, but they weren't too far off the general idea. Athens was recognized as an intellectual centre, particularly during the Roman Empire, and it was a fairly standard thing for intellectual Romans to send their children there (or to Antioch or other cities in the East) to get an education.

There were no degrees but the place was full of individual scholars giving lecture courses, and all you had to do was sign up. You could even go and live in their homes — in their day, both Plato and Aristotle ran this kind of private residential institution, part school and part boarding house. Plato's house was called ''Academy'' because it was alongside a small shrine to a local Athenian hero, Academos, and the name has stuck ever since.

Modern scholars often refer loosely to the whole set-up as the University of Athens, and you can see why, considering that many European universities actually began in this informal way; indeed, living with the professor was the origin of the college system at Oxford and Cambridge.

As for Libanius, he may not have been one of the third century's best professors but he was certainly one of the gabbiest. His memoirs give us a good insight into what "back to school" meant in ancient Athens.

For the new student it started as soon as he got off the boat at Pireaus — unless, of course, he'd had the good sense to get off at the previous stop and sneak into town. This is because the boat was met by hordes of second- and third- year students, intent on grabbing any newcomer and enrolling him by hook or by crook with their particular professor.

Hook was represented by intellectual persuasion: "Friend, have I got a deal for you! Prof. Lysicrates still has a few places open, and I may be able to get you in."

Crook took the form of kidnapping and imprisonment by force in some abandoned warehouse, with solicitous enquiries as to whether the new student was interested in the continued good health of his kneecaps.

Either way, Prof. Lysicrates wound up with another student.

It would be nice to record that this was all in the name of academic excellence. In fact, it was a matter of money. The professor was paid directly by his students and while an apple for the teacher is all very well, it's not in the same league as cold hard cash.

So, professors very often put their older students on commission, giving them a discount on their tuition if they could "recruit" a newcomer or two.

Still, there were drawbacks to the system. For example, the recruits tended to overlook paying their fees, even when Dad had sent Junior the money — there were always a lot of taverns between Dad's house and the professor's.

The worst off were professors of philosophy. The ancients had a very clear mental picture of what a philosopher was like. He was dirty, ragged and lived in a hovel if not actually an old barrel, despised the world, and, in particular, money. This meant that if he was bilked of his fees, it was nearly impossible for him to collect.

The great jurist Ulpian, one of the founders of Roman law, gave it as his legal opinion that philosophers suing for collection of their fees should be denied judgment on the grounds that by suing they proved they were not philosophers, and hence were guilty of misleading advertising.

Small wonder that some cities invited professors from abroad to come and teach there, putting them on permanent salary. It was the closest the ancient world came to tenure, and was sometimes the only way of getting the big names to come and stay.

With the start of classes, the professor's troubles were far from over. Libanius' complaints have a familiar ring: The students we get nowadays! He had a job even getting them into the lecture theatre. When he was due to start, there they were, all hanging about outside singing folk songs and talking about girls.

When he did get them in, it wasn't much better. "They keep whispering about jockeys at the races, or ballerinas and comic actors; or last week's public riot — or next week's. Some keep blowing their noses with both hands." (No handkerchiefs, remember.) "Others sit stock-still, with no reaction to my brilliance and wit." And to think the worst I had was a student who sat in the front row of my class reading a motorcycle magazine.

Of course, you'll be asking the obvious question. Libanius asked it, too, and came up with a very satisfactory answer: "But, you may say, maybe it's my fault, my lectures aren't as good as they used to be. Not a bit of it! The older students, who have been around for some time, *they* say I'm surpassing myself; my lectures have always been outstandingly excellent, but now they're even better than before."

For dealing with such doubtful customers, the professor has in his armoury a repertoire of deterrents, many of which I have considered with a personal interest. The satirist Lucian tells us of a professor who, in a difference of opinion with a student, hurled himself bodily upon the miscreant "and would have chewed his nose from his face, had the boy's friends not intervened."

Unfortunately, most of my students seem to come from the football team, and I would tend to favor Libanius' ultimate weapon — expulsion. "Ha! Shameless, dog-faced reprobate, have you not been thrown out from the Holy Place of Learning, as defiling the Temple of the Muses?"

Can you see any student facing up to it — getting thrown out of university, slinking home with his tail between his legs with a thing like that hanging over his head? Of course not. That's why every year, before classes start, I like to read a bit of Libanius. It soothes the nerves.

EDUCATION AS CAUSE AND EFFECT

Whether one focuses on the fate of groups or on the destiny of individuals, education can be viewed as both cause and effect. To express this idea in sociological terminology, we say that education can be treated as an **independent variable** (cause) or as a **dependent variable** (effect). Theodorson and Theodorson have defined these concepts as follows:

> *An independent variable . . . is one whose occurrence or change results in the occurrence or change in another variable (the dependent*

variable). In terms of the cause-effect schema, the independent variable is the cause.

A dependent variable . . . occurs or changes in a regular, determinable pattern related to the occurrence of or changes in another variable or variables (1969, 457).

Whether a sociologist treats education as cause or effect depends on the conceptual framework adopted. In Chapter 4 on stratification, we cited John Porter's work on the relationship between a family's socioeconomic position and its children's educational attainment. Porter viewed socioeconomic position as the independent (causal) variable that influences how much education (dependent variable) one is likely to receive.

On the other hand, numerous studies have treated education as an independent variable, affecting, for example, attitudes toward minority groups, child-rearing practices, and degrees of political participation. In Exhibit 9.5 earlier in this chapter, we showed the level of education as the independent variable affecting the unemployment rate of individuals.

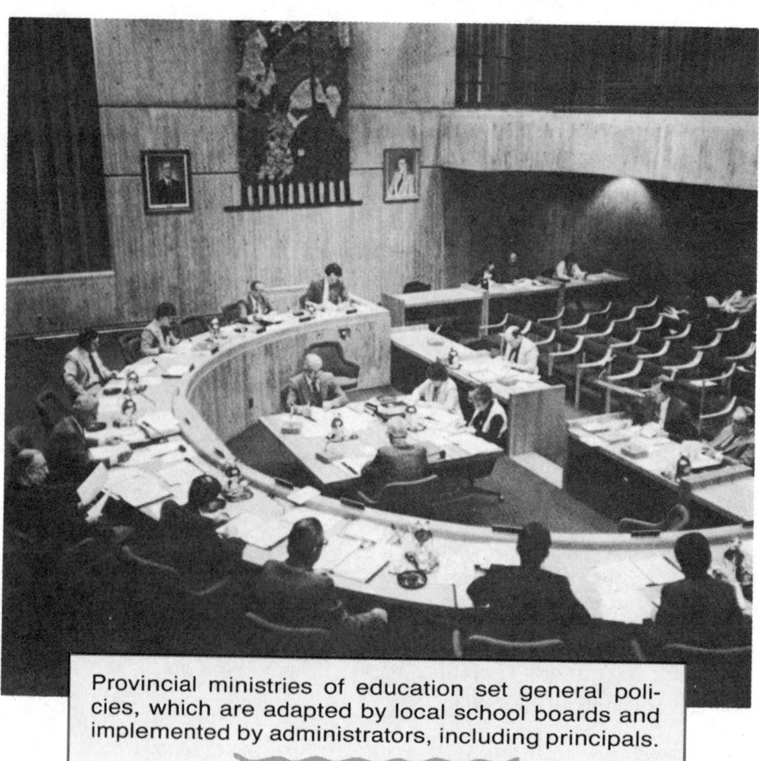

Provincial ministries of education set general policies, which are adapted by local school boards and implemented by administrators, including principals.

EDUCATION AND SOCIAL STRATIFICATION

The complex relationships between social stratification and education have received a great deal of attention from social scientists. In an American study, James Coleman *et al.* (1966) and Christopher Jencks *et al.* (1972) investigated, on a national scale, the extent to which educational opportunity was equal and how students' family backgrounds impinged on their schooling. Both studies found that background played an important role in achievement at school. Similar evidence was found in Canada (Anisef 1973/4; Anisef, Paasche, and Turrittin 1980; Breton 1972; Wright 1970). Breton (1972) looked at students whose test scores for ability placed them in the bottom third of their cohorts. Of those from upper-class families, 72 percent were in academic programs, compared to 38 percent of those from lower-class families.

Wright's study (1970) was sparked by a brief presented to the Toronto Board of Education by a group of mothers from a public-housing development. They asked why so many of their children were being placed in vocational rather than academic classes. The board surveyed the 106,921 students who were in the school system in April 1970, to investigate whether a student's place of birth, mother tongue, and the occupation of the head of the household in which he or she resided affected placement. No clear relationship emerged between foreign birth or non-English mother tongue and placement. However, the occupation of the head of the household was strongly related to placement, especially at the secondary-school level. Only 0.5 percent of the children of "accountants, engineers, lawyers, etc." were in special vocational classes; 89.7 percent were in five-year academic programs.[7] For the children of "labourers, taxi drivers, etc.," the respective proportions were 9 and 46.5 percent. Students whose parents were on public assistance fared worst: 28.6 percent were in vocational classes and only 21.4 percent in five-year academic programs. Wright summarized the findings:

> *The pattern of results is easy to describe in terms of occupation. Starting with the categories "Unemployed" and "Welfare," then "Housewife" (mother only) and from there moving on an occupational scale from labourer to professional, there is a steady change in the proportions found by grade, programme and special class, the children of professionals being the most likely to be found in 5-year programmes and the least likely to be average or in a special class (1970, 49).*

In a panel study of Ontario students who graduated from Grade 12 in 1973,[8] Anisef, Paasche, and Turrittin (1980) commented on the importance of the high school program in postsecondary achievement. Of the respondents who had been in academic high school programs, 40 percent graduated from university, compared with 4.1 percent of students who had been in commercial programs and 7.4 percent of those who had been in technical and vocational programs. The findings for the whole of Ontario were consonant with those cited earlier for Toronto:

Respondents who chose academic programmes were disproportionately selected from upper middle class sectors of Ontario society (1980, 65).

Earlier in this chapter, we noted that educational opportunity is influenced by the geographic region in which one is raised. The Anisef, Paasche, and Turrittin study supported and expanded on this argument:

The overall rate of post-secondary experience was found to vary by as much as 21% (highest in Toronto and lowest in small towns and rural areas). Insofar as a majority of young persons must expect to leave home to enroll in post-secondary institutions, and insofar as rural areas are disproportionately populated by lower socio-economic families, rural people suffer a double hardship in terms of gaining access to and financing their post-secondary education. In terms of occupational consequences, our analysis suggests greater job opportunities exist for city people than for rural people, and that the former group held down relatively more prestigious jobs (1980, 383–4).

SOCIOECONOMIC STATUS AND EDUCATION: WHY THE LINKS?

Researchers are virtually unanimous in finding that socioeconomic position ranks high among the factors that impinge on education. They disagree on the reasons for the variations in performance by students from different class backgrounds. We will examine some of the arguments put forward.

GENETIC DIFFERENCES

A social Darwinist has a simple explanation: through biological selection, the ''fittest'' have attained an advantaged socioeconomic position. Their superior qualities are genetically transmitted to their offspring and manifest themselves in high academic performance.

Such an argument seems dubious, since it cannot be tested empirically. There is no way of completely separating the respective impact of nature and nurture. No achievement tests exist for newborn babies, and those performed on very young children have proven quite unreliable because children mature at different rates. In any case, the performance of even a one-year-old is a function of both native endowment and environment. As studies of institutionalized children have shown, lack of attention, stimulation, and love retards physical and mental development (Bowlby 1951).

It is a premise of democracy that intellectual endowment is randomly distributed in the population, regardless of race, gender, or class. No scientific evidence exists to contradict this belief.

CULTURAL DEPRIVATION

Some educators and social scientists agree that lower-class children perform poorly in school because they bring with them few verbal skills, their home environments offer few stimulating experiences, such as books, pictures, and travelling, and the parents do not encourage learning.

Several of the teachers interviewed by Hall and Carlton in their study of ''Albertown'' responded in this vein:

> *There's a small minority, about twenty per cent . . . no matter what you do it is negated outside school. From Kindergarten on we give them special attention, but there's only about a five per cent result (1977, 49).*
>
> *Kids reflect the attitudes of the parents; they don't want to be at school; see the school as a hindrance . . . authoritarian figures putting restrictions on them (1977, 48).*

One teacher noted, ''Parents care, but are ill-equipped.'' In our view, such a position has validity. Imagine a child bringing home an assignment for a report on dinosaurs. Middle-class parents in an urban setting might take the child to a museum; even in a small town, they would likely point to the research section of the local library or discuss what is known about extinct species generally. Minimally educated parents may be equally anxious for their child to do well but lack both awareness of what resources are available and facility in using them. Thus, for the lower-class child to produce an assignment as good as that of the middle-class child likely requires greater ability or a higher level of motivation.

Hall and Carlton comment on the variation in skill levels:

> *In sum, variation in skill levels, both within and between schools, appears to owe a great deal to factors lying entirely outside the school. If there is heterogeneity in skill attained within the school it is in some large part because the community outside the schools is heterogeneous, crucially influential, and beyond the reach of the educational system. This is the first parameter which has to be recognized in explaining any skill deficiencies which may be visible at the outcome of elementary schooling, or indeed in higher levels of education (1977, 51).*

THE HIDDEN CURRICULUM

By Sandro Contenta

When the bell rings at the end of each school day, Ontario's students take home lessons much more lasting than anything they learned in math or science class.

''In a competitive society, for somebody to win, someone else has to lose. Kids learn that very quickly,'' says Queen's University sociologist Alan King, a respected authority on Ontario's school system.

King and others call it the ''hidden curriculum''—a largely unacknowledged and, for students, virtually invisible process with lifelong effects.

The hidden curriculum works like this:

Schools are organized like factories, sorting students for the best and worst jobs. Education experts say the system uses the wrong yardsticks to determine who wins, puts too much pressure to perform on even the top students, and strips the losers of their self-esteem.

The most graphic example? Streaming.

☐ Students in the basic, or vocational, ''stream'' are prepared for trades. But 79 per cent drop out and fall into low-skilled jobs before getting a Grade 12 diploma.

☐ Those at the general level are bound for community college. Sixty-two per cent, however, never graduate.

☐ University-bound students are in the advanced stream. Only 12 per cent drop out.

'Selling dope'

In interviews with The Star, students had their own ways of describing the impact of the hidden curriculum.

☐ ''I failed kindergarten. I mean, can you believe that?'' says Adam Sawyer, a student at Central Etobicoke High School, that city's only vocational school.

☐ ''My family always says, 'Make up your own mind,' but I'm not allowed to screw up,'' says university-bound Becky Rosen, a top student at North Toronto Collegiate.

☐ ''If you're in a level 6 (advanced) school, you're going somewhere,'' says Peter McGovern, a vocational student at Brockton High School in Toronto. ''If you're in a basic-level school, half are going somewhere, but the other half are hitting the skids—unless you can make it on your own by selling dope.''

The classroom clocks at Toronto's West Park High School used to be set 10 minutes behind standard time.

Yet another symbol of a school system out of step with society?

Maybe.

But the official reason for the time lag reveals something at least as disturbing: the consequences of dealing with basic-level students whose self-respect has been badly eroded.

The clocks were turned back to ''give students a sense of success by helping them get to class on time,'' says Ron Kendall, former principal of West Park.

''We would say to them, 'Look, you can do it, you can do it!' ''

Kendall says every little bit helps when dealing with basic-level students struggling for dignity.

The school's job is to prepare them for the workplace. But teachers compare much of their work to that of doctors in a hospital ward trying to control a mass hemorrhage of self-esteem.

"Our whole program is based on addressing and helping kids who have been wounded," says Ken Hanson, vice-principal at Brockton.

It may start with a child failing in elementary school — a quick and lasting lesson in winning and losing — and ends in a job as a bus boy or factory worker, or in some other low-skilled position.

Lack of dignity

Of 15 students in Grade 11 and 12 auto body shop at Brockton, only two had not failed a grade or more in elementary school.

All blamed themselves.

American sociologists Richard Sennett and Jonathan Cobb have argued that, in the long run, self-blame coupled with a lack of dignity helps perpetuate social inequality.

Numbed with losing while watching others succeed, such youths accept their stations in life without demanding a bigger share of the pie, the scientists say.

People also find dignity outside of their work — with their friends, hobbies or families. But students understand that above all, society judges people not by who they are but by what they do.

"If a doctor and a mechanic walk into a restaurant and there was only one table left, who do you think would get it?" asks vocational student Sawyer.

SCHOOLS AS MIDDLE-CLASS INSTITUTIONS

The cultural-deprivation argument attributes a passive, non-interventionist role to the schools. The assumption that students' performance substantially mirrors their social-class position negates the ideology that education's function is to "lead out." Can you see that this very negation can be construed as a lack of political will to transform the social order? In western countries, education has traditionally been seen as a force for reducing poverty and promoting social equality. To achieve these goals, a school must exert a strong effect that is independent of the student's home environment.

Consequently, some analysts blame the schools for not being an effective tool for bringing about social change. They argue that most teachers are middle-class individuals who espouse the middle-class values that are dominant in society. Children who have been socialized to similar values at home and exhibit the attitudes and behaviour the schools hold dear are off to a good start.

Richer has enlarged on this theme:

I am suggesting that certain middle class characteristics, notably the tendency to defer gratification, the greater concern with inter-individual competition, the tendency towards an analytical goal orientation, the greater reliance on verbal rather than physical skills, and the greater likelihood of responding to non-material rewards, ensures a rather distinct advantage from the first days of formal schooling (1982, 362).

In this view, the schools act as a selection agency, culling those destined for educational success. Middle-class children start with certain advantages. Not all, of course, will succeed. Children of any class who exhibit desirable traits are rewarded with attention and praise from the teacher. Over time, the children develop a self-image that incorporates rewarded attitudinal behaviour patterns. This theory is consonant with Cooley's concept of the looking-glass self, which suggests that people come to see themselves as they think others see them (see Chapter 3 on socialization).

Teachers may not initiate this process deliberately; they simply reinforce conformity to the schools' manifest and hidden curriculum. Sennett and Cobb reported on their observations in an elementary school in a working-class district of Boston:

What happens is that the teachers act on their expectations of the children in such a way as to make the expectations become reality. Here is how the process worked in one second-grade class at Watson School—unusual in that it was taught by a young man. In this class there were two children, Fred and Vincent, whose appearance was somewhat different from that of the others: their clothes were no fancier than the other children's but they were pressed and seemed better kept; in a class of mostly dark Italian children, these were the fairest-skinned. From the outset the teacher singled out these two children, implying that they most closely approached his own standards for classroom performance. To them he spoke with a special warmth in his voice. He never praised them openly by comparison to the other children, but a message that they were different, were better, was spontaneously conveyed (1972, 81).

Sennett and Cobb went on to say that over the course of the year, the two boys had less and less contact with the other children but were doing the best work in the class. Fred and Vincent, as well as their classmates, were acting on the assumption, probably neither conscious nor articulated, that they were moving in a different direction.[9]

In brief, those who attribute the limited academic success of working-class children to the middle-class biases pervading the schools argue that teachers consciously and unconsciously favour children who are clean, polite, nicely spoken, and able to make interesting and articulate responses in the classroom. Since working-class children usually do not have the same opportunities as their middle-class peers to develop these attributes and since the behaviour expected of them at home may differ from the school's expectations, their chances of succeeding at school are reduced.

SCHOOLS AS AGENCIES OF CAPITALIST SOCIETY

Marxists and others who take the conflict perspective argue that, far from being intended to "lead out," schools are primarily geared to maintaining the status quo by preparing students for their class-based destiny. Martell argued along these lines:

> *How, then, do our schools prepare kids to fit into these various levels of working-class and middle-class employment? Primarily, it seems to me, the job is done by setting up a social system within the schools, in which the social relationships the kids experience are the same they will later experience in factories and offices. This transplanted social system in the schools is there when the kids arrive. In order to survive in it, the kids have to fit in (and are fitted in) to that level of the system for which their already developed public character has prepared them. That is, by the time they reach school, they already have a way of living within the society as they experience it, and that way of living or behaving — including forms of resistance, acquiescence and local community life—is appropriate to a certain stream or grouping within the social system (1974, 18).*

Looking at the role schools play in American society, Bowles and Gintis advanced similar arguments, stating flatly that experiences in the educational system imbue students with values appropriate to their future societal roles:

> *The educational system is an integral element in the reproduction of the prevailing class structure of society. The educational system certainly has a life of its own, but the experience of work and the nature of the class system are the bases upon which the educational values are formed, social justice assessed, the realm of the possible delineated in people's consciousness, and the social relations of the educational encounter historically transformed (1976, 126).*

In a social order that is based on inequality, the schools, as part of that order, reinforce and transmit inequality. They are structured so that success is less easily attainable for those of working- and lower-class origins.

Mothers are not only expected to get their children to school on time, properly fed and clothed, but also to oversee homework assignments. If remedial work is necessary, part of the responsibility is shifted to the home. The research of Smith and Griffith documents the reliance of the school system on mothering work at home (Smith 1987).

Note that ultimately this situation reflects decisions regarding the allocation of societal resources. Extra school personnel could be hired to carry out some of the tasks that are now performed by parents (mainly by mothers) as unpaid work in the home. To the extent that middle-class parents are better equipped to do this work, in terms of time and expertise, their children are advantaged. Thus, the transmission of class position is facilitated and the status quo is perpetuated.

Importantly for the stability of society, the schools use a variety of strategies to reconcile students to their fate so that their expectations become aligned with their achievements. Bowles and Gintis argued:

> *By rendering the outcome (educational attainment) dependent not only on ability but also on motivation, drive to achieve, perseverance and sacrifice, the status allocation mechanism acquires heightened legitimacy. Moreover, such personal attributes are tested and developed over a long period of time, underlining the apparent objectivity and achievement orientation of the stratification system. . . . Frequent failures play an important role in gradually bringing a student's aspirations into line with his or her probable career opportunities. By the time most students terminate schooling, they have been put down enough to convince them of their inability to succeed at the next highest level. Through competition, success, and defeat in the classroom, students are reconciled to their social positions (1976, 106).*

Clearly, not all students move smoothly along their allotted channels. For those with exceptional ability, motivation, and some luck, schooling does pave the way out and up. Ironically, the very existence and visibility of those few individuals reaffirms the credo of equal opportunity. Many of those who were able to move up through education have internalized this credo and profess it. If they managed to succeed, why can't others?

Education facilitates successful functioning in the established society. However, it is also potentially revolutionary, in that individuals become empowered to question the status quo and acquire political consciousness. As Freire observes: ''To exist, humanly, is to *name* the world, to change it'' (1972, 61).

ILLITERACY IS COSTLY

By Margot Gibb Clark

A year ago, Tracy LeQuyere, 33, couldn't read. If he took the subway, he'd count the stops. In a restaurant, he ordered whatever the person with him asked for.

He had never paid income tax and didn't know what a social insurance number was. He had a friend take his driving test and get his license.

In Canada, where an adult is defined as functionally illiterate if he has completed less than nine years of schooling, there are 3.73 million such people. Some can read words, but not well enough to function at work. Others, like Mr. LeQuyere, cannot read at all.

"Illiteracy cannot be linked to lack of intelligence," says a 1983 UNESCO report on the problem in Canada. "Illiterates have to be very adept at covering up their difficulties and devising methods of coping in a print-oriented society."

Mr. LeQuyere didn't even tell his new wife. "How she picked up on it was one day when I was putting oil into the antifreeze in the car, or vice versa, something really stupid.

"She stood there and said 'hello, are you here, what are you doing?'

"When I told her, she didn't believe me." Before that, he says, she had just considered him lazy or bossy when he asked her to do things for him.

"I remember just about everything was difficult before. If I saw the word ketchup on a bottle I could read it, but put 'ketchup' on a wall with nothing else around it and who knows. It might be Kentucky."

Yet Mr. LeQuyere managed to hide his illiteracy all through his adult life, even for two months in a new job which required some writing.

This work involved approaching employers to see if they had work for ex-offenders under the HELP program, set up to keep people in work and out of prison. A former convict himself, he considers it his first real job. He had just met the woman who is now his wife and she told him matter-of-factly that if he wasn't working, she couldn't continue to see him. "I knew I wanted to be with her. It was the first time in my life I had ever really wanted to work."

Coincidentally, at the same time a welfare worker gave him a brochure about HELP, and he was hired as a field worker, searching out jobs for others. "I thought it was a joke. I had hardly worked a day in my life and now I'm going to be finding people jobs?" But he did.

"You had to come in with a book in the morning and write down a daily report (of employers seen). I used to copy the date off a piece of paper we kept in the office for clients to sign in on.

"I'd had my wife read me our brochure. I'd give employers copies and say 'It's simple, read this.' Then I'd take their business card and write down their name, address and phone and put the time I was there.

"Then one day my boss said, 'there's a piece of paper missing from your report. Would you just sit down over there and write it out?' I sat down and hummed and hawed and went red. He nicely pulled up on it and said 'Don't worry about it now.' I went home that night and got my wife to write up the report."

But his boss also quietly alerted staff at Frontier College, Canada's oldest adult literacy program, with which HELP is affiliated. Shortly afterward when Mr. LeQuyere was there on business, a tutor approached him and asked him if he'd like to learn to read.

"Upstairs in a little room at Frontier, my whole new world began," he says. "It's as simple as that."

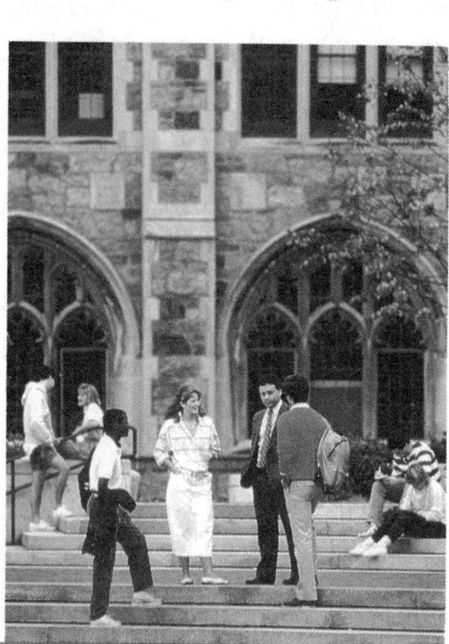

Socioeconomic background strongly influences the ease with which university graduation can be achieved.

SOCIOECONOMIC STATUS AND EDUCATION: SOME CONCLUSIONS

With the exception of the deterministic argument, which we deem invalid, we concede some explanatory power to each of the viewpoints presented. However, no one view adequately explains the relationship between socioeconomic origin and educational attainment. In progressing through the educational system from kindergarten to university graduation, students must cross several junctures. Anisef and his colleagues found that once a university degree has been achieved, that "whether an individual has a higher or lower SES [socioeconomic status] background is of little further consequence" (1980, 209) in how he or she is likely to fare in postgraduate studies or in the work world.

As has been emphasized throughout this section, socioeconomic background strongly influences the ease with which university graduation can be achieved. This is an expression of education as a dependent variable, with socioeconomic status as the independent variable. In turn, we have noted that education also serves as an independent variable, influencing socioeconomic status.

Exhibit 9.10 shows that in the vicious circle that entraps the poor, education serves as both an independent and a dependent variable. It performs similar functions in perpetuating affluence. In our society, these circles are neither closed nor inevitable because both downward and upward mobility can occur intergenerationally. For large numbers of individuals, education has paved the way for upward mobility.

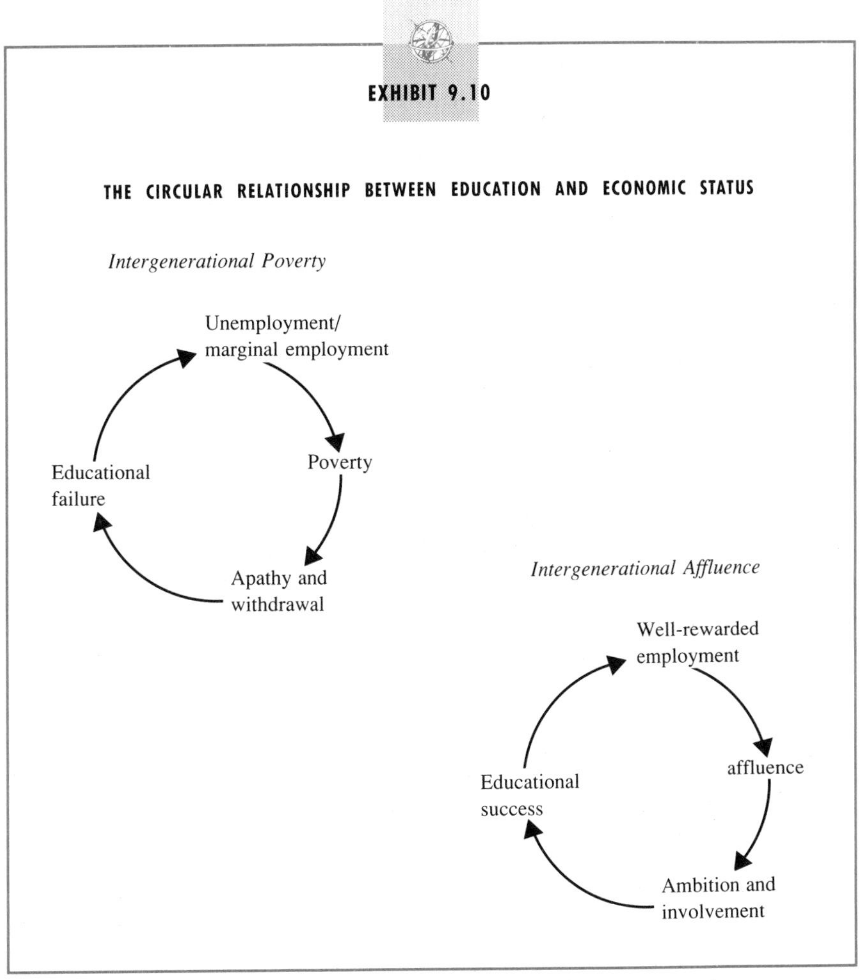

SUMMARY

The acquisition of learning and literacy and the joy of intellectual enquiry have a long history, but mass education in formal settings is a relatively recent phenomenon. Education has met important functions for society as well as for individuals. As countries industrialized, a literate work force became essential; moreover, education transmitted such values as punctuality, reliability, and discipline. For countless men and women, education has provided an escape from poverty and ignorance. For others, lack of education or educational failure has been socially disabling.

In Canada, the organization of educational systems is both complex and highly diversified. Education is a provincial responsibility and is often divided along religious and linguistic lines. Hence, the quality of education is variable.

During the 1950s and 1960s, tremendous expansion occurred at all levels of the educational apparatus in response to the entry of the baby boomers and to the credo that higher education is the route to continued prosperity.

Since education is such a pivotal institution and since it is heavily financed by public funds, much concern has been aroused by the repeated finding that children from disadvantaged backgrounds have poor academic performance relative to that of other students. This phenomenon arouses concern because it is a flagrant contradiction of both the ideology of equal opportunity and the belief that education "leads out."

ASSIGNMENTS

Do one or both of the following assignments, as instructed by your professor.

1 Attend a meeting of the Home and School Association in your community. Take note of the issues on the agenda and analyse the meeting using a sociological perspective. Did any of the items involve institutional sectors other than education and the family?

2 Do some library research regarding the advantages and disadvantages of educating children at home rather than at school. (Historically, this practice was followed in the upper classes. Recently, some middle-class parents have demanded the right to educate their own children at home.) To track down sources, you may wish to enlist the aid of such people as your instructor, a reference librarian, or an official in your local school board or ministry of education.

SUGGESTED READINGS

Canadian Woman Studies/les cahiers de la femme, *Women and Literacy* (Toronto: v. 9 nos. 3 and 4, Fall/Winter 1988). This issue of "Canadian Woman Studies/les cahiers de la femme" will give you an understanding of the experiences of women, in various parts of the world, who are disadvantaged by their inability to read and write. The articles also describe some of the imaginative programs, often linked to other services, that have been designed to help women acquire the literacy skills they need for a more independent life. Many programs in Canada have been influenced by the writings of Paolo Freire, and by work carried out in the Third World, such as the Nicaragua literacy crusade. When you have located this journal in the library, take the opportunity to browse through some of the other issues.

Paulo Freire, *Pedagogy of the Oppressed* (Harmondsworth: Penguin Books, 1972). This is a classic argument for education as a subversive activity (as opposed to that which merely transmits information and established values). On the basis of his experience in Latin America, Freire urges that the aim of a liberating education must be to create an awareness of selfhood and the capacity to view critically the social context of one's life. How else can one contemplate changing conditions of oppression? "Problem-posing education does not and cannot serve the interests of the oppressor. No oppressive order could permit the oppressed to begin to question: Why?" Freire's work, including *Cultural Action for Freedom*, has influenced literacy campaigns in both Third World and modern nations.

Ivan Illich, *Deschooling Society* (New York: Harper and Row, 1971). Focusing on education, Illich argues that in all areas of life individuals in modern western societies are in danger of being swallowed up by institutions that keep growing in size and number. In his view, a great deal of learning could be acquired more cheaply and more effectively outside formal educational institutions. He also warns against the "hidden curriculum" of schools, which imbues students with conservative worldviews that entrench opposition to fundamental change. Even though one may not agree with this passionate indictment of western society, Illich's views are thought-provoking.

P. McLaren, *Cries from the Corridor* (Toronto: Methuen, 1980). The high-rise dwellings along Toronto's Jane/Finch corridor contain large numbers of polyglot, low-income, often single-parent families. *Cries from the Corridor* is McLaren's account of his three years' experience in a local junior high school, where he found that the lesson plans advocated in teachers' college did not spark the interest of streetwise kids, who frequently came to school hungry and who might be ignored, neglected, or abused at home. The book is a plea for adapting schools to the needs of children, rather than trying to squeeze children into prefabricated slots.

NOTES

[1] Notice that the word "clerk" is derived from "cleric."

[2] Technically, all Canadian universities and many colleges and other postsecondary institutions are private schools. In fact, most policy is set by the provinces and they jealously guard their autonomy in this area. A sizeable amount of funding for postsecondary education comes from the federal government, through the Established Program Funding mechanism, but the allocation is done provincially. The provinces also administer the program whereby the federal government pays the interest on loans to qualified postsecondary students.

[3] Although the rules vary from jurisdiction to jurisdiction, a determined parent can often find ways to transfer children from one system to another, no matter what the family's religious preference.

[4] Until well after the Second World War, however, some schools in francophone districts continued to teach in both languages, hiding the French textbooks when provincial school inspectors were present.

[5] By contrast, some private schools pride themselves on innovation and flexibility of curriculum.

[6] In 1982–3, 8 percent of Canada's enrolment was in the pre-elementary level, 43 percent in the elementary level, 45 percent in the secondary level, and 4 percent in special education.

[7] The five-year (Grade 13) programs were geared almost exclusively to university preparation.

[8] A panel study is one in which the same subjects are studied at several different points in time.

[9] William Foote Whyte noted similar divisions among the "college boys" and "corner boys" in his participant observation study of Boston's north end (1943).

9c RELIGION

Thus far in our examination of societal institutions, each institution has revealed paradoxes. The family is the archetypical primary group, but for most people, it also provides an introduction to unequal power distribution, in this case among family members. Formal education can be viewed as a vehicle for reducing inequality, but the greater opportunities for advanced education enjoyed by the children of the privileged consolidate their advantaged position.

Religion also presents contradictory images. The quest for peace on earth stands in sharp contrast to the blood that has been shed in the name of religion throughout history. Religion has justified persecution of minority groups, from Christians during the days of the Roman empire, to Jews and Protestants during the Inquisition, to Baha'ists in the Middle East today. Religious fervour has fuelled conflicts, such as the English Civil War and the 30-Years War (1618–48) and continues to set people against each other today, in India as in Northern Ireland. It has also been used throughout the centuries to justify political and cultural colonization, such as western Europe's takeover of the Americas and the Arabs' sweep of the Middle East, northern Africa, and the Iberian Peninsula in the seventh and eighth centuries.

Like the family, religion is a universal institution. There are vast differences in the form of religious rituals and in the content of belief systems, but sociologists and historians have no knowledge of any group that does not possess some form of religion.

The root of the word "religion" is *ligio* ("I tie" — as *liga*ments tie muscle to bone). Durkheim's definition focused on the tying aspect of religion:

> *A religion is a unified system of beliefs and practices relative to sacred things, that is to say, things set apart and forbidden — beliefs and practices which unite, in one single moral community called a Church, all those who adhere to them (1954 [1912], 47).*

His concern was not with how individuals experience religion but, rather, with the communal bonds forged by joint participation in religious activities.

By contrast, Yinger defined religion in terms of the function it provides for the individual: "a system of beliefs and practices by which people struggle with the ultimate problems of life" (1964, 358). We might add that it helps people to accept the inevitability of death, both for themselves and for their loved ones.

Historically, religion has played an important part in legitimating and supporting existing social orders. The doctrine that kings were god's anointed on earth and ruled by divine right ultimately converted insubordination to the king into insubordination to god. Hence, civil disobedience became a very serious offence. On the other hand, the growing conviction among clergy and laity that the corruption of the mediaeval church violated "true" religion spurred the Protestant Reformation, which resulted in fundamental societal change.

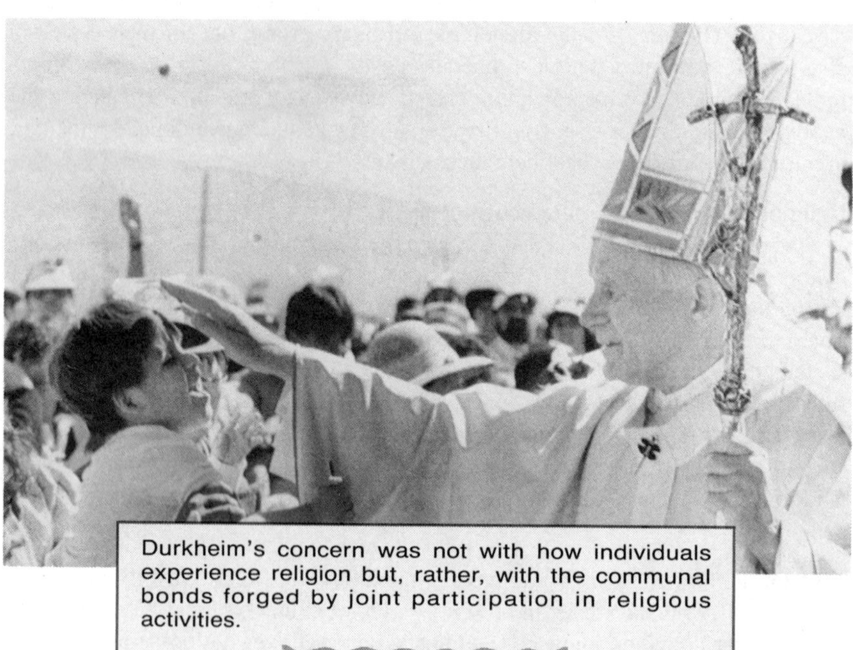

Durkheim's concern was not with how individuals experience religion but, rather, with the communal bonds forged by joint participation in religious activities.

RELIGION AND EARLY SOCIOLOGICAL THOUGHT

Given the important role played by religion, it is hardly surprising that early sociologists made it an object of study.[1] Here, we will provide a brief overview of the ways Marx, Durkheim, and Weber looked at religion.

Marx viewed religion as an ''opiate'' that relieves the present deprivations of the oppressed with visions of future glory.

THE ''OPIATE OF THE MASSES''

Consonant with his conception of the economy as the substructure of other societal institutions, Marx viewed established religion as legitimating a given social system. By teaching that acceptance of one's earthly fate and faithful performance of religious obligations are pleasing to god and conducive to eternal salvation, religion helps to contain potentially explosive forces, he said. For the oppressed masses, religion becomes an ''opiate'' that assuages present deprivations with visions of future glory.

Religion, Marx argued, is a tool the dominant group uses to cajole subordinated groups into passivity. Such a view is shared by many — though not all — modern social scientists. For example, Glenn described how, for most of their history, the black churches of the American south have served to pacify their flocks:

> *The emotionalism and the strong otherworldy orientation of this traditional religion of American Negroes have made the Negroes' subordinate status more bearable. The religious services have provided tension release, excitement and escape in an existence characterized by hardship, drudgery and vicissitudes of various kinds. The focus upon the afterlife has promised the Negro "pie in the sky by and by when you die" and has had a soporific and diversionary influence. This type of Negro religion has not encouraged efforts for the improvement of the status of the Negro in the here and now and has tended to reconcile him to an inferior status. From emancipation almost to the present, the Negro church was the main influence in orienting Negroes to the dominant white population, and there is almost unanimity among scholars of American race relations that the overall influence of the church has been more toward acquiescence and docility than toward rebelliousness and protest (1964, 629).*

In the short run, such psychic relief may facilitate survival in a dehumanizing environment. Like a narcotic, religion eases the pain but does not remove its cause. In the long run, accommodation retards the struggle for change.

A SOURCE OF COHESION

As we noted in Chapter 1, Durkheim was a functionalist in the sense that he analysed practices and instructions in terms of the functions they perform for the group. By providing common sacred symbols, Durkheim argued, religion underpins unity and separates the in-group from the out-group. Old Testament references to "idol worshippers" and to the "uncircumcised," for example, re-emphasized group boundaries.

Durkheim noted that objects are inherently neither sacred nor profane (ordinary). Sacredness is bestowed on them when they are given ritual significance in group worship (Coser 1977). The cow is sacred to Hindus but not to Christians or Moslems; a wafer of bread becomes sacred to many Christians as a symbol of Christ's body. Possession and commonality of sacred symbols are reinforced by **positive rituals** — occasions when group members gather to reaffirm their commonality, thus strengthening mechanical solidarity. Confirmation, the Hindu initiation rite,[2] and the pilgrimage to Mecca are examples of positive rituals. If such ritual occasions are no longer observed, the cohesiveness of the group and the individual's adherence to it are weakened. Therefore, most religions insist on some minimal participation and attendance. For instance, a Roman Catholic must take communion at least once a year.

Disintegrative tendencies were prevalent in 19th-century Europe. Durkheim realized that the old social regulators—custom, tradition, and religion—had become weakened. Insofar as the stability of the social order depended on these regulators, the social scientist's task was to find alternative foundations. Durkheim envisioned a rationally-based ethic that would replace religiously-based ones. In his words: ''We must discover the rational substitutes for these religious notions that for a long time have served as the vehicle for the most essential moral ideas'' (1961, 9).

In many ways, the modern ''isms'' — nationalism, communism, and fascism — have assumed religious signficance. Indeed, the official opposition to traditional religion in the Soviet Union can be seen as an attempt to eliminate all other faiths (but communism)—though *glasnost* has brought a softening of this opposition.

Both Marx and Durkheim saw religion as a basis for social stability. For Marx, this stability obscured the opposing interests of ruler and ruled, seducing the latter into passivity by expectations of a glorious afterlife in which injustice would be corrected and the last would become the first. For Durkheim, however, social order was a prerequisite for human happiness and creative endeavour. To the extent that religion — or its rational substitutes — contributed to this state of affairs, he believed it fulfilled a positive function for society.

A POTENTIAL AGENT OF CHANGE

Central to Weber's view of religion were two aspects of his overall theoretical stance. First, he insisted that phenomena be viewed in their historical context. Thus, he believed it essential to examine the parts played by specific religions in given societies at specific points in time. (In this respect, Weber followed in the tradition of Marx and the school of German historical scholarship.) Second, one of Weber's prime concerns was to unravel the effect of people's ideas on their actions.

In tracing the rise of capitalism in England, Marx had focused on the confluence of economic factors without actually analysing the values that had propelled individuals to engage in the behaviour that had fostered the transformation from fuedalism to capitalism. Weber ''was most respectful of Marx's contribution [but] refused to see in ideas simple reflections of material interests'' (Coser 1977, 228). He undertook a series of studies on how religious ideas had influenced earlier civilizations:

> *Weber took advantage of the fact that history has left us with the record of its own sociological experiments. Several large-scale civilizations had developed in relative isolation from each other: the West, China and India, among others. By tracing out economic developments in each, Weber attempted to hold constant the material pre-conditions for western-style capitalism. This enabled him to focus on religious ideology, in each society, to see if it had independent effects. Compar-*

> *ative method, then, may be called a sociological equivalent of experimentation (Birnbaum 1953, 135).*

Weber argued that, although many material preconditions for the development of capitalism had been present in India and China, Hinduism and Confucianism did not provide values supportive of its development. By contrast, ascetic Protestantism, specifically Calvinism, had "elective affinity" with a capitalistic economic orientation.

Calvinist doctrine espoused hard work in this world, "the lord's vineyard," but it condemned luxury and any "indulgence of the flesh." Since the money earned with all this hard work could not be spent, it was reinvested, promoting technological innovation that led to greater productivity and thus freed funds for more research, further innovation, and growing productivity, in an endless spiral.

In *The Protestant Ethic and the Spirit of Capitalism*, Weber did not posit that Protestantism had caused capitalism, but he did address the vital role religion had played in its emergence:

> *The Protestant Ethic discouraged consumption, especially of luxuries; at the same time, it unloosed the impulse to acquire. The great campaigns of the devout against the temptations of the flesh and indulgence were struggles as well against irrational spending and for rational saving. Thus capital accumulates through a compulsion to save. And from accumulated capital and the impulse to accumulate more, production escalates higher and higher. Capitalism flourishes (Hansen 1976, 157).*

Religious values that help to undermine one social order may provide moral justification for a succeeding one. As we have noted, ascetic Protestantism emphasized relentless labour and self-denial for the greater glory of god. Over time, the material success which ensued from this combination came to be seen as a sign of divine approval. By extension, poverty became a symbol of having failed to please god. In this sense, religious ideology came to be used to legitimate economic distinctions under capitalism. As Birnbaum has noted:

> *In his later years [Weber] discussed the class basis of religion in the following terms. Religions of privileged, ruling strata emphasize this-worldly values. Members of such strata feel intrinsically worthy because of their present social positions, and their religious beliefs justify the social system that allowed them such elevation. Members of underprivileged and oppressed strata, far from feeling worthy in terms of what they are, emphasize the importance of what they will* become. *They emphasize otherworldly values, and their religions depict a future salvation entailing a radical transformation of society's present relationships (1953, 133).*

To the extent that the endeavours of the underprivileged are geared to achieving salvation in the next world, rather than to altering their position in this one, religion becomes an impediment to change.

History has provided many instances, however, in which religion has functioned as a dynamic for change — from early Christianity to the present-day revival of Islamic fundamentalism in Iran. By analysing the relationship between religion and social change, specifically in terms of ascetic Protestantism and the rise of capitalism, Weber augmented Marx's analysis of how capitalism evolved in the west. However, he did not lose sight of the influence economic position wields on religious ideology.

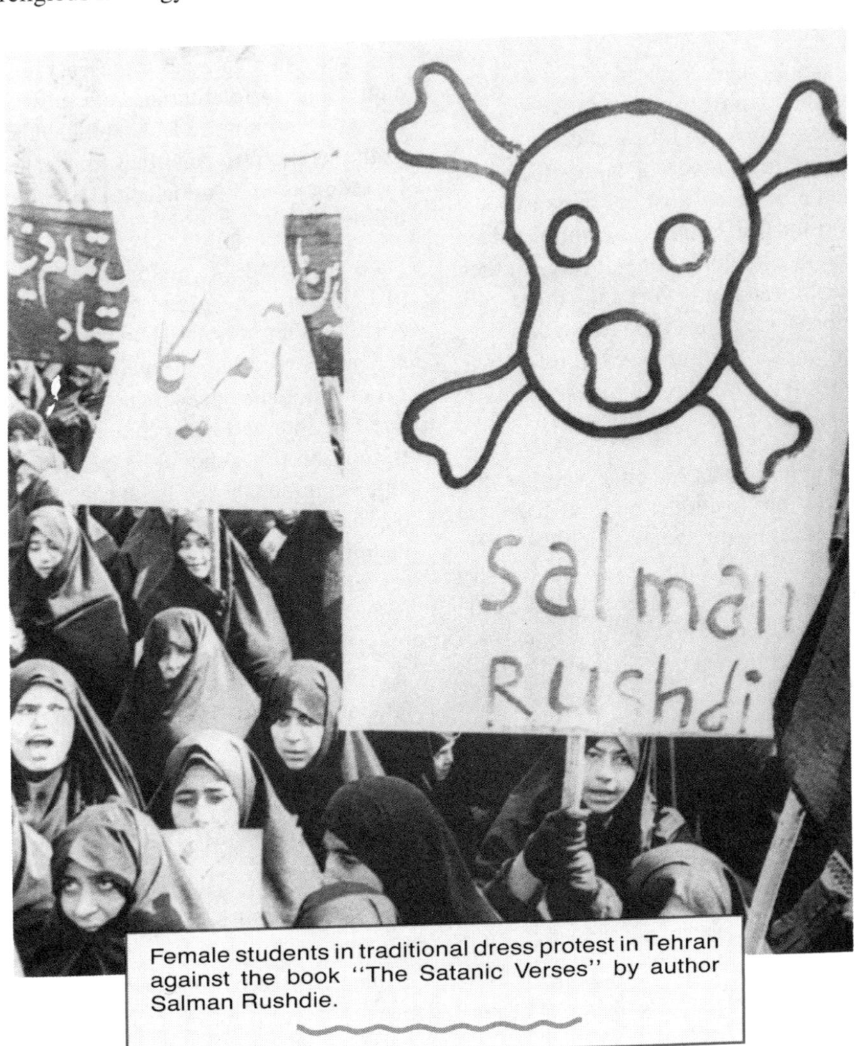

Female students in traditional dress protest in Tehran against the book "The Satanic Verses" by author Salman Rushdie.

HOW KILLING TURNS INTO DOGMA WHEN RELIGION, STATE ARE ONE

By Amos Perlmutter

The furor — both carefully calculated and calibrated as well as hysterical — in the Muslim world over Salman Rushdie's *The Satanic Verses* is a potentially murderous example of Islam's shrill intolerance and an illustration of the danger of fundamentalism when it embodies the power of a political state and organization.

Islam as such, with all of its schisms, offshoots and splinters, remains a religion — a way of life, a code of ethics, a particular mode of human behavior and existence — just the same as Judaism and Christianity. In addition to having in common a tone of piety in their scriptural framework, all three religions have at one time or another been noted for outbursts of intolerance, authoritarianism and schismatic convulsions.

Despite a history spotted with spontaneous persecutions, none of the three great religions' founders, philosophers and theologians ever officially preached a doctrine of specific assassination, as did the Ayatollah Ruhollah Khomeini when he called for the death of Rushdie, his publishers and any others who may have had something to do with the publication of his novel.

Murder, assassination and mass executions become official doctrine when religion becomes tied to the state, when it becomes the state, and religious intolerance mixes with pervasive xenophobia and a political struggle for supremacy between the secular and theological forces.

There is historical precedent for the kind of behavior we are witnessing in Khomeini's Iran. The Spanish Inquisition is one case in point: In the name of Spanish imperial ambition and national unity, a highly systematic and elaborate effort at mass murder, exile, torture, excommunication and forced conversion took place, wrapped in a thin gauze of legality as represented by church law. A totalitarian state authority, which dominated and exploited the Catholic church, sanctified its crimes by religious motivation and a claim to holiness.

State-organized Islam is not the Islam of believers, the pious followers of Allah. Rather, it is an Islam dominated and submerged into a secular political system. But it is the doctrine, the practice and international behavior of the Islamic state that should be questioned and examined here. In the name of Islam, the state condones and decrees the most vicious acts of fundamentalist terrorism. Khomeini's followers believe that they have achieved the ideal Islamic state. What they have achieved is another in a long line of totalitarian states — a danger to the rest of the world.

This Islamic state hungers to gain revenge on its "oppressors," its Christian, Western and Soviet masters of time past. The function of the Islamic-dominated state is to annihilate and eradicate the non-believers, the foreigners and the blasphemers, which is one of the reasons why *The Satanic Verses* is such an ideal target. Islam at its most fundamental is totally intolerant. It cannot abide ridicule, irreverence or what it perceives as blasphemy. This is true in its approach to art, even if it is unfamiliar with the work itself, which is surely the case here.

ORGANIZED RELIGION AND SOCIAL CONCERNS

Historically, religious groups have helped to bring about social reform (gradual change) through their charitable work with the poor, the orphaned, the aged, and those disadvantaged in other ways. Religious organizations have not only provided immediate relief to the needy; by publicizing their plight, these groups have also aroused public concern and influenced social-welfare policies.[3] The reformist call of people associated with religious groups has often assumed added weight because it has invoked higher values espoused in the society at large, even if frequently violated in practice.

In present-day Canadian society, for example, the Jewish community is very active in the provision of social services, mainly (but by no means exclusively) to its own members. Survivors of the Holocaust and, recently, immigrants from the Soviet Union and from Middle Eastern countries have been assisted in becoming established, both economically and socially.

In considering the role religion has played in the change process, it should be noted that by reducing the worst excesses of deprivation and injustice, religiously sponsored charity and reform have indirectly helped to maintain a given social order by reducing pressure for revolutionary change.

SACRED TO SECULAR

In Chapter 2, we noted that western societies have moved from the small, homogeneous Gemeinschaft to the large, heterogeneous Gesellschaft. One aspect of this transformation is a change from a dominant sacred orientation to a predominantly secular one, a process generally described as secularization. In a **sacred society**, there is much concern with the supernatural, and events are explained in terms of the prevailing belief system, whose tenets are not subject to question. Similarly, social relationships, as between ruler and ruled or parents and children, tend to be viewed as absolute and unchallengeable. In a secular society, the supernatural is accorded far less importance; primary values are rational and utilitarian, and change and innovation are welcomed (Theodorson and Theodorson 1969, 373).

The sacred orientation that prevailed in Europe during the Middle Ages meant that virtually all issues sooner or later came within the jurisdiction of the Roman

Catholic Church. Galileo's claim that the earth was just one of the planets that revolved around the sun was treated, not as an empirical observation to be confirmed or denied by further research, but as a heresy that cast god's word into doubt. In Bertolt Brecht's dramatization of the episode, one of Galileo's accusers captures the presumed threat:

> *They make heaven and earth no longer exist. No earth, for it is a star in heaven. No heaven, for it is many earths. There is no longer any difference between above and below — between the eternal and the mortal. We know we die. Now they tell us heaven will die too. It is written—there are stars, sun, moon and the earth below. But that man says the earth is a star! There are only stars! We will live to see the day when these heretics say—there are no men and animals, there are only animals, man is an animal (1981, 39).*

The minor ups and downs of daily life were also subject to sacred interpretation. In societies such as that of 17th-century England, misfortunes might be blamed on witches:

> *It was dangerous, if you were an old woman, a beggar perhaps, of disagreeable appearance, to curse your uncharitable or unkind neighbour, or even to allow your lips and what Hannah Woolley called "that slippery glib member the tongue" to move in some possible version of a curse. For then if your neighbour suffered a loss, grief or other form of injury, you might be suspected of having caused it . . . with the aid of the devil. It would be suggested either that he had brought about the injury himself or that he had endowed you, as his partner, with the powers to do so (Fraser 1984, 104).*

A sacred orientation held sway in rural Quebec until well into the 20th century. The power of the Catholic Church was reinforced by its control over the educational system and by the ethnic and religious homogeneity of the population. Loyalty to the church was not cross-cut by other institutional loyalties, and local priests felt free to tell their parishioners what was acceptable and unacceptable in many realms. Hughes quoted from a curé's sermon in the 1930s:

> *"There were races last Sunday, and there are races announced for next Sunday. I speak to you as Catholics. Not as to Protestants, or people of other religions, who can discuss, each for himself, what his minister says. I am not discussing. I am telling you, as your pastor and rightful moral leader and guide, the will of your Infallible Church. God reveals to His Church His Will; and His rightful representative, the Pope, and your bishop, and finally we, your pastors, tell you. God's representatives know these moral questions better than you do; it is their rightful prerogative, and it is for you to listen.*

"So, dust is blowing over the fields of the western provinces.[4] *Generally, such things are the just punishment of God. Your children will beg their bread — if they do not live and practice what God wills" (1971, 100–1).*

In a **secular society**, there is supposed to be clear separation between church and state. What individuals believe and whether they belong to a formal religion or engage in religious practices are matters that do not affect their status as citizens. In fact, questions pertaining to religious affiliation have had to be removed from government and employment forms as contravening human-rights legislation.

At times, the separation has been breached, as it was in the case of John Scopes, a Tennessee schoolteacher who had been teaching Darwin's theory of evolution, which holds that, over a very long time, the human species evolved from a lower animal species. In 1925, Scopes was accused of violating a state statute that made it unlawful to "teach any theory that denies the story of the Divine Creation of man as taught in the Bible, and to teach instead that man has descended from a lower order of animals" (*Encyclopedia Americana* 1981, 397). In a much-publicized trial, Scopes was convicted of the charge and fined $100, but the conviction was reversed on a technicality in order to prevent an appeal against the law from being brought to the U.S. Supreme Court. Not until 1968 did the Court strike down the Tennessee law, and similar laws in Arkansas and Mississippi, on the grounds that they violated the U.S. constitutional ban against the establishment of religion. It is interesting that with the recent resurgence of a conservative worldview, creationists (those who insist on the literal truth of the biblical account of creation) have made a strong comeback, particularly in the United States but also in Canada.

The relationship between church and state is an issue that is very much alive. For a discussion of the interaction of politics and religion in many countries, see Shupe and Hadden (1988).

SECULAR SOCIETY GAVE COUPLE THEIR NICHE: THE WEDDING BUSINESS

By Andrew van Velzen

A probation officer and his wife have found a novel way of marrying people who do not belong to an organized religion or who prefer not to get married in a church. Edward and Ruth Simmons have formed a company called *Weddings* and opened up chapels in Hamilton and Burlington, Ont.

Mr. Simmons said he came up with the idea when he saw couples being married in the courts. "They would go in happy and come out with a stunned look on their faces. I don't think they realized the abruptness of the proceedings. That really bothered me," he said. "I talked it over with Ruth and we decided to do something about it. We were up for new challenges and we have always been in the business of helping people.''

Before he became a probation officer, Mr. Simmons had been a Protestant minister as well as a school trustee. Ruth Simmons is a kindergarten teacher.

He said the couple first looked into the legalities of setting up a wedding chapel, then took a mortgage out on their home and rented the bottom floor of a building in downtown Hamilton in early 1980. They renovated the place and performed their first weddings in May of that year. This spring, they expanded to nearby Burlington and are opening a chapel in Kitchener, Ont.

Mr. Simmons said they originally looked at the chapels as a hobby.

''We always expected it would pay for itself but, in fact, it has made money,'' he said. The company uses the services of five ministers and five organists, who all get paid on a per-wedding basis.

The chapels are popular, Mr. Simmons contends, because many people — despite their secular lifestyles—need a spiritual experience at certain points in their lives such as when marrying.

Religion doesn't always meet the needs of a secular society, he added. In many cases, a place of worship won't marry couples who don't belong to it, people who have been divorced, couples that have been living together and those who have crossed religious barriers.

Mr. Simmons is still a licenced minister and performs many of the ceremonies himself. *Weddings* offers five different ceremonies: four religious and one secular. The rituals are open to change: at one recent marriage someone read a Shakespearean sonnet; at another, the bride and groom, maid of honor and the best man all wore brand-new blue-jeans. Simmons has also conducted weddings on boats.

The company has performed weddings for couples from every religion, Mr. Simmons reckoned, and has a special ceremony for situations such as a marriage between a Jew and a non-Jew. ''I've often had the family of the Jewish person thank me — the ceremony satisfied both sides,'' he said.

Weddings allows couples to bring in their own minister. ''We've had people bring justices of the peace in as well,'' Mr. Simmons said.

The company offers a basic package, which includes use of the chapel, services of a licenced minister, an organist, choice of one of five ceremonies, souvenir booklet, marriage-preparation seminar and a rehearsal, for $290.

There's a simplified wedding that doesn't include features such as an organist or rehearsal. It runs to $170.

The company also offers wedding stationery at a reduced rate, Mr. Simmons said.

The company advertises in the Hamilton Spectator and the Burlington Post as well as using some direct-mail promotion.

It has expanded its range of services to include dedications. ''The reason for the dedications is just like the reason for the weddings,'' Mr. Simmons said. ''Couples are not involved in organized religion but want God in the life of their child.''

The Bar Mitzvah ceremony demonstrates the passing of Jewish traditions from generation to generation and reflects the way religion promotes group solidarity.

THE MEETING OF NEEDS

Whether religion is central to a society or not, everywhere it meets certain needs, both for the group and for individuals:

- It enhances solidarity among the members of the group and supports its values and norms. At the micro level, this effect is expressed by the aphorism ''a family that prays together, stays together.'' Even in societies in which several religious groups co-exist, religion in general buttresses such institutions as the family and the law. Acts that are deemed undesirable, even if they do not contravene formal laws, are defined as sins. To the extent that individuals identify with a religion, its ethical content may deter them from engaging in such antisocial acts. In this way, social control is reinforced. Because societies depend on their members' willing co-operation, such reinforcement is especially important, since it is primarily based on internalized values, rather than on external surveillance.

- Membership in a religious group may be an integral part of individual identity. The relative importance of such membership depends on structural as well as individual variables. One structural variable is the centrality of religion in a particular society at a particular time. For the early Christians or the Huguenots of 16th-century France, religion was a crucial aspect of identity, since membership in these forbidden groups exposed one to the risk of torture and death. For many people in Canada today, even for those who are regular churchgoers, religion has far less impact on identity.

  Another such structural variable is the nature of the religious group itself. For the Hutterite or the Hassidic Jew, every facet of life is pervaded by religion. Distinctive clothing is a public manifestation of membership in the religious group, so the first identifier others recognize in such an individual is a religious one.

  Membership in such an all-embracing group permits little variation in personal commitment. Those who do not conform are expelled. Many other religious communities, however, permit differences in the extent to which religion impinges on personal identity. A man who attends church only for christenings, weddings, and funerals may identify himself as an engineer, a husband, a father, a Canadian, and a resident of Ottawa before considering that he is a member of the United Church.

- Religion provides explanations for the mysteries encountered in human existence, thus making the world more comprehensible. Often, deities or supernatural beings are endowed with human characteristics. For example, the Bible describes god's anger at the corruption of the people of Sodom and Gomorrah as if it were a father's anger toward his wayward children.

  Religion is an approach to understanding the world that requires the individual to accept certain phenomena on faith. By contrast, science seeks understanding through empirical verification. In today's secular societies, scientific activities are carried out for the most part without regard to their compatibility with faith. The late mediaeval and early Puritan scientists, far from treating science and religion as incompatible, saw their efforts as leading to a clearer understanding of the lord's creation. In a study of science in 17th-century England, Merton quoted the physicist Robert Boyle, who left in his will the following message for the Fellows of the Royal Society:

  > *"Wishing them also a happy success in their laudable attempts, to discover the true Nature of the Works of God; and praying that they and all other Searchers into Physical Truths, may cordially refer their Attainments to the Glory of the Great Author of Nature, and to the Comfort of Mankind" (Quoted in Merton 1968, 630).*

- The prescriptions and proscriptions that underpin religion's social control provide the individual with a guide for everyday conduct. Opinions, attitudes, and actions can be justified in terms of the religious code, which establishes what is right and what is wrong. For example, a devout Catholic physician categorically excludes performing an abortion unless the pregnant woman's life is in dire peril.

- Practical conditions change, but certain aspects of human existence do not. Everyone in every age must cope with fear and anxiety and with the inevitability of death. The belief of many religions in a life after death, in which present injustices will be corrected, makes bearable what otherwise would not be. Acceptance "that the Lord giveth and the Lord taketh away" affirms that there are happenings in the universe that are beyond human understanding but also holds out hope of an eventual reunion with loved ones.

  The persistence of religion in societies in which it is suppressed or discouraged by the state seems to indicate that it meets fundamental human needs that are not fully met by such secular belief systems as communism.

This list of the functions performed by religion is by no means exhaustive, but these functions do meet *universal* needs of groups and individuals.

CHURCH AND SECT

Christian religions are numerically dominant in Canada today. According to the 1981 census, more than 90 percent of the 24 million Canadians reported themselves as belonging to a Christian religion (see Exhibit 9.11).

This apparent homogeneity conceals great diversity, especially in the Protestant category, which subsumes such mainstream denominations as Anglicans and Presbyterians, as well as smaller groups, such as the Society of Friends (Quakers) and the Christadelphians.

One of the most frequent distinctions social scientists make in studying religious organizations is between **church** and **sect**. A church has a bureaucratized structure, a hierarchy of authority, and a professional priesthood. Services are conducted by the minister or priest in a ritualized manner, with congregational participation at prescribed intervals, as in the singing of hymns and the interjection of "amen."

EXHIBIT 9.11

CANADIANS BY RELIGIOUS PREFERENCE, 1981

	Number	% of total
Catholic	1 402 605	47.35%
Protestant	9 914 580	41.17
Eastern Orthodox	361 560	1.50
Eastern non-Christian	305 890	1.27
Jewish	296 425	1.23
Parareligious	13 450	0.05
No religious preference	1 783 530	7.40

NOTE: Any of the religions listed in the table could be separately disaggregated. A number of the denominations or religions listed under "Protestant" could possibly be otherwise classified. The Eastern Orthodox group subsumes the Greek Orthodox group and a number of National Orthodox groups, such as Antiochian Christian, Armenian, Romanian, Russian, Serbian, Ukrainian and Orthodox, n.o.s. Historically, the terms Greek Orthodox and Eastern Orthodox are considered to be equivalent, but the latter term is used in the 1981 Census only to indicate the presence of responses to the religion question where Greek Orthodox was either not indicated or was overwritten by a more specific National Orthodox Church group. The Jewish main group is the only group that does not contain subgroups. The Eastern non-Christian main group is composed of Baha'i, Buddhist, Hindu, Islam and Sikh, as well as Confucian, Taoist and Other Eastern non-Christian. The parareligious group is the smallest of all of the main groups and contains religions such as Fourth Way, New Thought-Unity-Metaphysical and Theosophical groups. Finally, the last main group is "no religious preference," which combines agnostics, atheists, "no religion," and "other nonreligious."
SOURCE: Adapted from Statistics Canada (1983d, table 1).

A sect represents a breaking away from an established church. Typically, it has a loose, nonbureaucratic structure, no clear-cut hierarchy of authority, and a lay priesthood composed of those who have heard a "call." Worship is spontaneous (though a general pattern may evolve over time), with extensive participation by the congregation. The Holy Rollers are a dramatic example:

> *They sang with all the strength that was in them, and clapped their hands for joy. . . . Something happened to their faces and their voices, the rhythm of their bodies, and to the air they breathed, it was as though wherever they might be became the upper room, and the Holy Ghost were riding on air (Baldwin 1953, 8-9).*

A major difference between church and sect is in the social-class base of the membership. Members of churches tend to be middle and upper class or to have aspirations for upward mobility. Typically, sects appeal to the socially disinherited. By strict adherence to group norms, sect members can feel part of the elect, who may be poor in material goods but are rich in spirit.

> *Because the sect is lower class, its appeal rests on providing an exclusive fellowship of the elect for those who are denied access elsewhere and on supplying an ideology of escape and other-worldly salvation for those who find this world oppressive. Much of the sect's emphasis on doctrinal purity and the total ideology is designed to provide a new framework for self-evaluation for those who are evaluated so demeaningly by prevailing standards (Demerath and Hammond 1969, 71).*

Demerath and Hammond (1969) have argued that because the sect provides the salient status for many of its members, they are willing to let it influence every aspect of their lives. A Jehovah's Witness accepts the group's ban on smoking, drinking, receiving blood transfusions, and celebrating birthdays, even the birth of Christ (Christmas). Historical support for this contention is provided by Clark's research, reported in *Church and Sect in Canada*. He found that with the growth of towns and the expansion of trade in the early 1800s, the Baptist restriction on private conduct became irksome and thus unacceptable to many adherents in the Maritimes; the result was "increasing defection of Baptists to religious denominations commanding greater prestige and making fewer demands with respect to private conduct" (1948, 244). For many middle-class people, religion is one of several statuses, and the church must, therefore, permit the individual some leeway in everyday life.

Clark has also outlined differences in the ways church and sect relate to the larger society:

> *The church seeks the accommodation of religious organization to the community; the welfare of society is something for which it feels responsible. The sect emphasizes the exclusiveness of religious organization; the worldly society is something evil of no concern to the spiritually minded. While no sharp line can be drawn between the two forms of religious organization (the church always contains some of the attributes of the sect while the sect is never "pure," completely otherworldly in character), within the church the spirit of accommodation tends to dominate, within the sect the spirit of separation. It is the difference in outlook, in attitude of mind, which is so important in setting the one off from the other (1948, xii).*

"Moses" Thériault, above, attracted a following, primarily of women, to the Northern Ontario bush. Thériault combined a back-to-nature philosophy with charismatic leadership.

Theodorson and Theodorson have defined a **cult** as lacking structure and having a loosely defined membership. In contrast to most other religious groups, a cult is something no one is born into. Adherence to beliefs and practices is voluntary, and there is no system of enforcing discipline (1969, 91). A cult is usually headed by a **charismatic leader**, an individual whose claim to authority is based on personal qualities, rather than on position in an organization. Cults are attractive to isolates in society, people who have never been integrated into a community or whose social relationships have atrophied.

The Hare Krishna movement and Jim Jones' People's Temple meet many, but not all, criteria for cults. The latter rigidly enforced discipline for some years, preceding the group's mass suicide in Guyana in 1978. An affidavit given by a member who escaped from Jonestown and returned to the United States, referred to:

> *. . . the armed guards in Jonestown, the near impossibility of leaving, the harsh working conditions, the inadequate diet, the terror and brutal punishment, and finally, the ritual White Night rehearsals for mass suicide (Kilduff and Javers 1978, 122).*

Generally, neither sects nor cults have long lifespans. Those that persist tend to lose many of their sectlike or cultlike characteristics, becoming more structured and bureaucratized. When the original charismatic leader is replaced, the new leader derives authority from his office rather than from his personality. Denominations that are currently within the religious mainstream, such as the Baptists and Methodists, began their existence as sects (Clark 1948). It is worth remembering that Christianity itself began as a sect.

A cautionary note must be injected. Pointing to differences among church, sect, and cult tends to obscure their similarities and to blur the differences among groups that are slotted into one of these broad categories. Not all sects have a predominantly lower-class membership, for example. The Jesus People, an offshoot of the hippie movement of the 1960s, were largely young, middle-class white individuals who became disenchanted with conventional middle-class goals and were perhaps fearful of being unable to attain them (Mauss and Petersen 1983). They felt comfortable in the sect, which de-emphasized worldly achievement and a rational approach to religious issues, stressing instead simple faith and unconditional surrender to Jesus.

TODAY'S YOUTH: THE SCAPEGOATS

By John Tower

Now, as in the past, some religious perspectives offer clear-cut solutions to complex problems; this leaflet, distributed in the subway, exemplifies such a perspective:

There are millions of people wondering what has gone wrong with the younger generation of today.

Parents look at their children getting into drugs, being rebellious, not seeming to have any real direction in life and they say to themselves, what is wrong with these kids today.

Well the shocking fact is that the blame for the way that the kids are today rests squarely on the shoulders of the older generation, the parents and grandparents.

The parents and especially the grandparents lived in a world of much less crime and violence, a world in far better shape than ours. And the reason it was in far better shape is because the people used to be God fearing. Because they were God fearing they feared to do wrong and consequently did wrong much less of course.

Consequently the world obviously was a much better place because of it.

As the world began moving away from God, and referring to God as an old superstition, etc., and began becoming progressive and modern, the crime and violence rate not surprisingly began climbing in direct proportion to the degree society discarded God.

The grandparents and parents slowly allowed society to manipulate them in this same direction and as a result they too became deceived by this doctrine of progress despite the decline of society proving the opposite to be true.

As a result they passed less and less of the fear of God onto their children with its obviously desirable results because they themselves were not living it anymore.

This regrettable cycle increased with each generation until we arrived at today's sorry state of affairs, virtual total moral anarchy.

So we see that members of the young generation of today are directionless and Anarchistic because their parents failed to pass onto them direction in life in the form of Godliness and the guidance it automatically brings.

The parents knew first hand the benefits of a Godly society because they had lived in one but they failed in their duty as parents to pass it on.

Then they have the audacity and nerve to look down at the kids blaming the kids for what they themselves caused.

So we must place the blame for why the kids are the way they are today where the blame really belongs not on the poor kids but on the wayward older generation who had the knowledge of what made a good society but turned away from it.

The solution is obvious: society must return to God and godliness contained in the ages old wisdom of the Bible.

When society doesn't think it needs the wisdom of the Bible anymore it inevitably moves slowly into a state of moral anarchy where anything goes as in today's chaotic self destructive society.

RESPONSES TO SECULARIZATION: A NEW PERSPECTIVE

Stark and Bainbridge have done a great deal of work in the sociology of religion, both in terms of theoretical formulations and empirical research. In *The Future of Religion*, they argue that:

> *The process of secularization is self-limiting and generates two countervailing processes. One of these is religious revival. Religious organizations that are eroded by secularization abandon a substantial market demand for less worldly religion, a demand that produces breakaway sect movements. Thus, out of secularization is born revival as protest groups form to restore vigorous otherworldliness to a conventional faith.*
>
> *Secularization also stimulates religious innovation. Not only do worldly churches prompt new religious groups, which seek to revive faith, but secularization also prompts the formation of new religious*

> *traditions. New religions constantly appear in societies. Whether they make any headway depends on the vigour of the conventional religious organizations. When new faiths that are better adapted to current market demand spring up, older faiths are eclipsed. Thus did Christianity, Islam, Buddhism, and other great world faiths wrest dominant market positions from the older faiths (1985, 2).*

In other words, as established religions themselves become secularized, they are no longer able to meet the needs of some of their members (for example, assurance that there is life after death in which they will be reunited with their loved ones). Niches are created for groups that purport to *revive* the original traditions, as well as for innovative movements, those that offer a new amalgam of beliefs, rituals, and practices.

Stark and Bainbridge do not view sects and cults (revivals and innovative movements, respectively) as lying on the same continuum. Rather:

> *Sects, being schismatic movements, begin life as religious organizations and thus their status as religious movements is clear. However, many cults do not develop into full-blown religious movements. Therefore, it is necessary to survey more closely the range of cults to identify various forms, only some of which fall within the scope of a theory of religious movements (1985, 26).*

They view the formation of both sects and cults as *responses* to secularization, which are likely to occur at different stages of the process. When established churches are still relatively strong, disaffected members are more likely to look for solutions within the same tradition. Hence, Stark and Bainbridge hypothesized that the formation of sects would occur when church membership is still strong. On the other hand, cult membership would be high where conventional churches are weak, since cults represent a radical alternative to established churches. Findings on the correlation between church membership and the prevalence of sects and cults strongly supported the hypotheses. Nock notes:

> *What they have shown clearly is that cults are strongest where irreligion is strongest. On the other hand, sects tend to be strongest in regions in which irreligion is weak. In North America this means that ratios of cult membership are highest by far on the Pacific coast, second highest in the Rocky Mountain region, and weakest in the East. This finding holds for both Canada and the United States (1987, 516).*

Although Stark and Bainbridge examined whether the negative correlation between the strength of conventional religious traditions and the presence of cults also holds for Canada, they did not use census data. Nock replicated this part of their study using 1981 census data. His findings confirmed a high correlation between "irreligion" (expressed in the census as "no religious preference") and "cult receptivity.'' The latter ranges from a high in British Columbia to a low in Quebec and Newfoundland. ''The hypothesis that cults benefit from irreligion and apostasy from the conventional religions seems to be strongly sustained'' (Nock 1987, 519).

Findings regarding ''sect receptivity'' are not as clear-cut. Whether this receptivity coincides with a high or low degree of irreligion varies with the nature of the sect. Nock commented:

> *This part of the study is as yet tentative and incomplete. However, it does seem that the areas of greatest strength for Evangelical conversionist sects are much more widely dispersed across the general population than for cults. However, revolutionist sects, at least in Canada, tend to vary positively with cults and regions of high irreligion. This is a distinction which should be looked into more closely in the context of the United States (1987, 523).*

It is one of the challenging and exciting aspects of intellectual endeavour that no findings, no ''conclusions,'' are ever truly conclusive. Existing evidence is juxtaposed with fresh data, and new hypotheses are formulated, tested, and modified in an ongoing process. In offering a reinterpretation of the relationships of adherence to religious traditions, secularization, and receptivity to sects and cults, Stark and Bainbridge have brought a new fillip to the scholarly debate on the ''future of religion'' and limits to secularization.

RELIGION AND STATUS

Weber argued that religious values influence economic conduct — as in the relationship he posited between the Protestant ethic and the emergence of capitalism. Here, then, religion is treated as an independent (causal) variable. On the other hand, Weber also noted that members of the privileged strata tend to belong to religions that stress the values of this world, an emphasis that is useful in consolidating their position. In this instance, membership in a religious group is a dependent variable, influenced by socioeconomic status.

In his study of the corporate elite, Porter (1965) took the latter tack and noted the overrepresentation of Anglicans and Presbyterians and the underrepresentation of Catholics in this group in modern Canada.[5] Supporting data from the 1981 census show that there are differences in educational attainment among various religious groups (see Exhibit 9.12).[6]

EXHIBIT 9.12

HIGHEST LEVEL OF SCHOOLING ATTAINED BY CANADIANS OF VARIOUS RELIGIONS

		Education		
	Total population 15 and over	Grade 9	Secondary school certificate	Bachelor's degree or higher
Anglican	1 748 090	16.11%	12.33%	8.76%
Baptist	479 395	21.14	11.33	6.48
Catholic	7 646 005	27.81	14.73	6.46
Pentecostal	209 295	26.29	10.77	2.87
Salvation Army	83 410	32.96	10.29	2.56
Jewish	211 325	14.60	11.23	25.34
No religious preference	1 144 195	11.57	11.44	16.20

NOTE: From the ten levels of school shown in the original table, we have reproduced only three, choosing to indicate a minimal, intermediate, and high level of schooling. All 10 levels in the original added across each category to 100 percent.

SOURCE: Statistics Canada (1981a).

Such statistical information does not tell us to what extent religious values influence educational attainment or whether people with given levels of education are *attracted* to particular religious groups. Since the majority of people are born into a religion, we can speculate that religious values affect educational attainment. However, since religion may be either an ascribed or an achieved characteristic, it may be that individuals are attracted to different religions as they become more highly educated. It is interesting that the proportion of university graduates among those reporting no religious preference is second only to their proportion in the Jewish group. These figures lend some support to the contention that religion provides one way of interpreting the world. With education, more individuals become aware of alternative interpretations and may then find religion less compelling.

Tomes used 1981 census data on native-born males ages 25 to 64 who were working in 1980 to examine the relationship between religion and earnings. His specific focus was on Jews, and he found that, on average, they earned 12.7 percent more than Protestants. However, as he noted, Jews are overwhelmingly urban, "95 percent live in Canada's 13 largest cities, and 70 percent in the two largest ones: Toronto and Montreal" (1985, 247). Hence, to some degree, he hypothesized, Jews' higher earnings reflect the higher wages available in urban centres. And when he compared urban Jews with urban Protestants, the earning differential in favour of Jews declined to 7.25 percent, "equivalent to the payoff from 1.8 years of schooling" (1985, 247). As we noted in Exhibit 9.12, Jews as a group have the highest level of postsecondary education among the Canadian population.

Hitherto, research on the association between religion and earnings has focused on males. Tomes made a preliminary examination of women workers and found the converse of his findings for males: on average, Jewish women earn less than Protestant or Catholic women (1985, 249). Again, we remind you that significant variations occur *within* groups. Furthermore, the fact that the *average* earnings of Jews are higher does not mean that there are no poor Jews or that a given Jewish male earns more than his Protestant or Catholic counterpart.

THE MASS MEDIA AND RELIGION

When future historians focus on the second half of the 20th century, a phenomenon that will undoubtedly attract their attention is the intrusion of the mass media into all areas of life. Margaret Mead aptly noted that "TV more than any other medium gives models to the American people—models for life as it is, or should, or can be lived" (quoted in Goethals 1981, 134). Religion concerns itself with the way "life should be lived," and the way for spreading the religious message through television was paved by a long history of using radio broadcasting.[7] Furthermore, there is a strong tradition of evangelical revivals in North America.[8] The Methodist movement in the 18th century and the urban revivals led by the Salvation Army at the turn of this century are examples. It is hardly surprising, therefore, that evangelical denominations are using the mass media to promote modern revivals and that TV religion has a strongly evangelical flavour. What is new is the medium; the message has been stated many times before.

Oral Roberts, a prominent electronic minister, has explained why he decided to use television as his pulpit:

> *The previous twenty years God had said, "Go into all the world and preach the Gospel to every creature" . . . . Now as I struggled with this great need, deep inside I heard God say: "*GO INTO EVERYMAN'S WORLD*" . . . . Well, I didn't know how so I said, "How God?" In my heart God spoke: "Do it through weekly and quarterly television programs" (1974, 91).*

Roberts' claim to personal communion with god, by extension, renders his own pronouncements true beyond challenge.

Sociologists want to find out what electronic religion offers that large numbers of people need and seem unable to find in conventional religious institutions. Hendricks pinpointed one area:

> *In an impersonalized world where people are reduced to numbers, where life seems part of a programmed assembly line, the electronic church offers "someone up there who likes you," and who will do special things for you (1984, 64).*

Traditionally, evangelical religion has appealed most strongly to those whose critical skills have not been developed by higher education, and to disadvantaged groups generally. The minimally educated and those trapped in monotonous work are most apt to perceive themselves as faceless numbers and to be attracted to the apparent intimacy of TV religion.

> *Too many of the local churches and their ministers across our nation don't really care. In particular, they don't care about the very people —the elderly, the infirm, the socially retarded, the "unappealing"— who most often have to turn to media religion with their unfilled needs and unhealed hurts (Quebedeaux 1982, 170).*

TV evangelism is big business in Canada and the United States. For instance, Mironowicz (1985, 11) reported that official tax receipts were issued for donations received from Canada in the following amounts:

Worldwide Sect of God	$12 171 230	1983
100 Huntley Street	11 660 127	1984
Rex Humbard Associates	1 886 824	1983

In her article "Faith, Hope and Charitable Donations," Mironowicz argued that many of these donations came from people who had to deprive themselves of basic necessities in order to send money. Yet, she pointed out, electronic religion brings considerable solace to some:

> *Mildred is a lonely woman. Near 60, she lives by herself in the Moss Park low-income apartment complex in Toronto. God has become the centre of her life — and comes right into her living room through television evangelist Rex Humbard's broadcasts and constant correspondence . . . . She felt good when her TV pastor talked to her, and considered it her moral obligation to send him money. The people on the evangelical broadcasts she watched so religiously were like family to her (1985, 1).*

It would seem that the weakening of communal and family ties and the anonymity of working in large organizations and living in cities have left a void in the lives of many. For some, it is being filled by TV religion, and they are willing to expend scant material resources to feel part of a caring, spiritual community.

It will be interesting to see how revelations of corruption and hypocrisy on the part of some TV evangelists affect the popularity of electronic religion. Jim and Tammy Bakker were found guilty of diverting funds from the PTL (Praise the Lord) Foundation for personal use. Jimmy Swaggart, who publicly proclaimed the virtues of chastity and a "clean" life, was observed to be consorting with prostitutes.

Jim Bakker appears in a taped message, saying that he and wife Tammy resigned as heads of the PTL television ministry to thwart a hostile takeover of PTL and not because he was blackmailed in a sex scandal.

BAKKER AIDES SENTENCED TO MORE THAN 17 YEARS

By Associated Press

Two of Jim Bakker's former aides were sentenced to more than 17 years in jail and fined $500,000 each on tax evasion charges yesterday as a minister appealed to the television evangelist to repent.

"Greed, lust and power. It happens. It happens to the best of us," Rev. Alan Foor, a United Church minister from Beavertown, Pa., declared at Mr. Bakker's fraud trial. "Jim and (his wife) Tammy had better look at the humble lifestyle of Jesus Christ.''

In a separate courtroom, former Bakker aides David and James Taggart received their sentences for using church credit cards to buy furs, jewels and a condominium at the Trump Tower in New York.

The two men said Mr. Bakker's PTL ministry had known about the purchases.

David Taggart, 32, the evangelist's former personal assistant, was sentenced to 18 years and five months in jail and fined $500,000. His brother James, the former PTL interior decorator, was sentenced to 17 years and nine months, and fined $500,000.

Both men were convicted in July on five counts of tax evasion and conspiracy, charges that carry a maximum penalty of 25 years.

Assistant U.S. Attorney David Brown said Federal Judge Robert Potter imposed the maximum penalty allowed under new federal sentencing guidelines. He praised the sentences, saying they send a message that white-collar criminals face the same penalties as those who commit crimes such as bank robbery.

Mr. Bakker, on trial in the same courthouse, is accused of overselling subscriptions for a time-share scheme at the PTL's huge Heritage USA theme park, 20 kilometres from Charlotte. In return for $1,000, buyers were entitled to three nights of lodging annually for the rest of their lives at a park hotel.

Testifying yesterday, Mr. Foor said his subscription was for a hotel that was never completed, and he was not able to obtain a refund of the $1,000 fee.

''I feel robbed and cheated,'' he said. ''I do forgive them for the drug and sexual thing, but I have a hard time dealing with the misuse of money.''

Tammy Faye Bakker entered hospital at one point to obtain treatment for abuse of prescription drugs. Mr. Bakker was forced to resign from PTL after it was revealed he had had an affair with church secretary Jessica Hahn.

Mr. Foor said that after Mr. Bakker resigned he made ''dumb excuses . . . about millions of dollars in ministry money unaccounted for and said the devil got into the computer.

''How dumb does he think we are that he can pass everything off on the devil question?''

Appearing earlier, former PTL budget director Mark Burgund said the ministry tried to get a $50-million loan in Switzerland after local banks refused because its cheques kept bouncing.

He said an unidentified Swiss corporation agreed to make the loan on condition that the ministry set up a company in Switzerland and transfer all PTL assets to it.

The condition was not acceptable, he said, so PTL turned down the offer.

Mr. Bakker could face 120 years in jail and a $5-million fine if convicted on all of the 24 counts of fraud and conspiracy he faces.

SUMMARY

Even our cursory overview demonstrates the contradictory role of religion. It has frequently acted as a pacifier, the function on which Marx focused when he called it the opiate of the people. On the other hand, religious fervour has been the wellspring of revolutionary change and the rationale for many colonial conquests. Religious groups have relieved the misery of individuals and have often been in the vanguard of social reform. However, such reform activities have not led to a *restructuring* of the social order but have often helped to buttress the status quo.

Each of sociology's founders addressed the role of religion in society. Marx recognized the function it performs in maintaining stability. Durkheim, too, focused on the contribution religion makes to social order by bolstering cohesion among group members. However, while ties are strengthened among members of the in-group, differences *among* religious groups are sharpened and aggression against out-group members is often justified. Weber drew attention to the part religious values have played in generating or discouraging societal change.

One aspect of the transformation from Gemeinschaft to Gesellschaft has been a shift from a religious (sacred) to a secular orientation. In the latter view, the mysteries of the world can eventually be unravelled by rational analysis and scientific investigation. Another notable characteristic of a secular society is increased separation between church and state.

Although significant variations exist among individual Christian religions, they can be ordered into typologies that differentiate them along several dimensions. One such typology identifies cult, sect, and church. Stark and Bainbridge regard the formation of sects and cults as responses which occur at different stages of the secularization process.

By building on the tradition of evangelism, TV religion has become an influential presence on the religious scene. Electronic religion has an especially strong appeal for those who, for one reason or another, feel themselves outside the social mainstream.

ASSIGNMENTS

Do one or both of the following assignments, as instructed by your professor.

1 In *Nostalgia for the Absolute* (see Suggested Readings), read Steiner's analysis of the debate between those who put their faith in science and those who argue that science must be checked because it endangers the survival of humanity. Would you agree with the position he himself takes, or would you opt for innocence?

2 Watch several religious programs on

television. Note what values they espouse and what codes of behaviour they advocate. If you have a religious affiliation, compare and contrast the values and behavioural norms enunciated on TV with those put forward by your own group.

SUGGESTED READINGS

Margaret Craven, *I Heard the Owl Call My Name* (New York: Dell Publishing, 1973). In this gentle novel set in British Columbia, a young Anglican clergyman goes to minister to an Indian village that does not welcome his notions of what is best for native peoples. Ultimately, persuasion works in the other direction, and he slowly develops a deep appreciation of their interpretation of what is important in the universe.

T.S. Eliot, *Murder in the Cathedral* (London: Faber and Faber, 1967). The clash between church and state culminated in the murder of Thomas Beckett, Archbishop of Canterbury, in the year 1170. But is this just a historical drama? In his introduction to the program notes for the Canadian Stratford Festival's 1988 performance, Timothy Findley argued that Eliot's play is as much a commentary on the present as on the past:

What were you doing when you heard that Kennedy had been shot? Which Kennedy do you mean? you are forced to ask. Now, as we approach the latter days of the most sophisticated century in human history, this is how we count our awareness of time. By recalling what we were doing when presidents and senators and priests have been murdered. *What were you doing when they killed Indira Ghandi? Where were you when they tortured Jacobo Timerman, turned the key on Martha Kunsa, kidnapped Terry Waite?*

Edmund Gosse, *Father and Son* (Harmondsworth: Penguin, 1979). First published in 1907, this is the fascinating account of a lonely childhood stamped by the religious fanaticism of an unbending Plymouth Brethren faith. It is also Gosse's account of the relationship with his father, a well-known natural scientist who lost all professional respectability by his implausible attempts to reconcile the religious doctrine of creation with the theory of natural selection promulgated by his colleague and friend, Charles Darwin. Gosse describes the relationship between father and son as a "struggle between two temperaments, two consciences and almost two epochs. Of the two human beings here described, one was born to fly backward, the other could not help being carried forward."

George Steiner, *Nostalgia for the Absolute* (Toronto: CBC Publications, 1974). In five provocative essays, originally a series of radio broadcasts, Steiner argues that the decay of Christian theology and dogma has left a vast emptiness that "modern mythologies" have attempted to fill. The mythologies he discusses may surprise you: Marxism, Freudian psychology, the anthropology of Levi-Strauss, the current "cults of unreason" (such as astrology, clairvoyance, and the belief in UFOs) and, finally, the modern call for a retreat from science.

Arthur Miller, *The Crucible* (Markham, Ont.: Penguin Books Canada, 1977; first published 1953). Miller's play deals with what he has called "one of the strangest and most awful chapters in human history," the Salem witchcraft trials in Puritan New England in the late 1600s. Because the play appeared in 1953, it was immediately understood as providing an analogy for the political persecutions of the McCarthy era in the United States, when many North Americans viewed communism as the greatest menace to the prevailing belief system. Revivals of the play have shown, however, that *The Crucible* is a moving defence of freedom of conscience applicable to many periods, including the present.

NOTES

1 Comte did not systematically address the question of religion; however, in his latter, eccentric years, he founded the "religion of humanity" with himself as its "pope" (Coser 1977, 38–9).

2 The Hindu initiation rite, conducted by the guru (teacher and divine inspirer), permits the individual to create a link between his or her inner self and the universe.

3 For example, the Moral and Reform Council of Canada, an interfaith council of churches at the turn of the century, evolved to become the Social Service Council of Canada in 1913.

4 Dust storms devastated agriculture on the Prairies during the 1930s. They are explained here as god's punishment for people's neglect of religious obligations.

5 Specifically, 25.5 percent of the economic elite were Anglicans, a group that constituted 14.7 percent of all Canadians. The respective representation of Presbyterians and Catholics in the elite was 11.3 and 10 percent, compared with a representation in the overall population of 8.6 and 43 percent (1965, 289–90).

6 Education, occupation, and income are the variables most frequently used to calculate socioeconomic status.

7 In fact, radio preaching changed politics in western Canada in the 1930s. William Aberhart, founder of the Social Credit party, blended religion and economic doctrine in radio sermons that swept the party to power in Alberta in 1935.

8 Garrett defines as "evangelical" a theological stance that claims: (1) the complete reliability and formal authority of scripture in matters of faith and practice; (2) the necessity of *personal* faith in Jesus Christ as saviour from sin and consequent commitment to him as lord; and (3) the urgency of seeking actively the conversion of sinners to Christ (1983, 61).

9D LAW

Institutions may appear simple and their functions straightforward, but critical examination reveals that neither impression is correct. The **law** provides an illustration of this phenomenon. If asked to give a spontaneous description of the law, most people would respond promptly in terms of its prohibitions. Yet the law is actually an institution that performs complex, and sometimes apparently contradictory, functions.

The law does restrict the freedom of individuals to do just what they want, but it also safeguards their freedom to go about their business undisturbed. The law may impede changes desired by a sizeable proportion of the population, such as free access to abortion or the right to smoke marijuana in the privacy of one's home. On the other hand, it enforces changes many people have resisted, such as equal division of family assets between husband and wife in the event of a divorce, school integration in the American south, and the use of French as an official language in the provinces of New Brunswick and Manitoba.

The law exerts a pervasive influence on everyday life, but most people become conscious of this only when they have violated some prohibition or seek redress for some harm, such as not receiving money that is due or having a car damaged by an unmarked hole in the road.

THE EVOLUTION OF MODERN LAW

Briefly speaking, law is the formal regulation of "the relationship of a society's individual members to each other and to society as a whole" (*Canadian Encyclopedia* 1985, 984).[1] Many societies do not differentiate between law and religion. In ancient Palestine, Judaic law regulated not only the obligations of human beings to god but also relationships among human beings. Thus, the Book of Numbers (35:173) distinguishes between premeditated murder and killing someone by accident, stipulating appropriate retribution in each instance.

Theocracy (literally, "government by god") is not confined to ancient history. Several Middle Eastern countries today appear to be returning to traditional Islamic law. Although England was never a theocracy in recorded times, complete separation between the domain of religion and the domain of law was slow in being instituted. As late as the 17th century, a person who had been excommunicated could not testify in court (Black 1976, 114). In the Puritan colony of Massachusetts in the same century, conflict existed between religious and secular law and, by extension, between the clergy and lawyers. (See *The Crucible* in the Suggested Readings.) There,

> *the morality of lawyers was questioned by the clergy, for in biblical terms there was only one right side to an argument, whereas the lawyer would argue either side of any case for a fee, and indeed considered his professional ethics on this issue as a positive and desirable aspect of his profession (Krause 1971, 24–5).*

Here, the Supreme Court gathers in Ottawa for the swearing-in ceremony of Justice Beverley McLachlin in 1989.

THE ROOTS OF MODERN LAW

The system of law in present-day western societies is rooted in Roman law and in Anglo-American common law. Thus it combines two quite different approaches. One is **civil law**, based on the systematic and logically coherent laws of the Roman Empire, laws which were to be valid for the Empire as a whole, regardless of the cultural differences between the subject nations. Civil law codes have been developed in most Western European countries; they can be found in places as diverse as Scotland, Latin America, parts of Africa, and Turkey. Civil law codes are always written and enacted by the legislature of the country.[2]

The other system of law is **common law**, based on the customs of the English people. Under common law, the basic principle is *stare decisis* (let the decision stand). Each case that is decided becomes a precedent for similar cases that may arise. While this system does not rule out the eventual development of logically-related laws, it is precedent, not logic, which is decisive.

Common law originated in England, and is used in most English-speaking parts of the world. In England, the common law has never been enacted by the legislature, despite many attempts to codify it and give it a more consistent, logical form. In Canada, as in many former British Colonies, a ''codifications'' of the common law has become part of the enacted law of the land.

ROMAN LAW

The Romans were the first to develop a code of law that was substantially separate from religious prescriptions and proscriptions. Many of the philosophical underpinnings of Roman law, however, were derived from Greek culture.[3] The Greeks had provided a method of logical analysis, and the Romans used it to develop a legal code that could be employed to cope with the problems of a growing state and, eventually, with those of a rapidly expanding empire.

It is interesting that the Twelve Tablets, the first Roman legislation known to us, were enacted in the fifth century BC after repeated pleadings by the plebeians for clear limits on the power of the patrician magistrates.

> *Many plebeians were small and poor people, often heavily indebted to the patricians. The procedure for enforcement of obligations, as in all primitive law, was harsh. It might lead to slavery and death for the debtor and his family. The magistrates who supervised the enforcement were members of the same class as the creditors. It was therefore only natural that the plebeians were interested in a clear statement of the limits to which creditors might go, and to which magistrates might allow them to go, in enforcing their claims (Wolff 1983, 320).*

Over the next thousand years or so, law was elaborated and codified, reaching a height of development in the second and third centuries AD. The writings of prominent jurists of this classical period of Roman jurisprudence (the science and philosophy of law) were excerpted and compiled in *The Digest*, published during the reign of the Emperor Justinian in 533 AD.

By that time, the Roman empire had been divided into east and west — Justinian was emperor of the eastern part, Byzantium, and in the west, Roman civilization was being overrun by "the primitive tribal civilization of the Goths, the Vandals, the Franks, the Saxons, and other Germanic peoples. After the sixth century Roman law survived in the West only in fragments" (Berman 1983, 401).

Although it was nearly 600 years until Europe rediscovered Roman law, scholars regard it as "one of the strongest formative forces in the development of Western civilization" (Wolff 1983, 319). Most civil-law countries in the modern world can trace their legal systems back to the Romano-Barbarian codes, such as the Code of Alaric II (the *Brevarium Alaricianum*), which emerged among the Germanic peoples as they incorporated the Roman law into their own customs. National codes began to be adopted in the 17th and 18th centuries, the most famous of which is the Code Napoleon, or Code Civil, of France.

COMMON LAW

After the failing Roman empire abandoned England in the fifth century AD, a confused time ensued, about which historians know relatively little. Much of the island was taken over by Angles, Jutes, and Saxons from the north, and no single power emerged for centuries. The northerners brought with them their tradition of settling many disputes by blood feuds, whereby the injured party or his kin "would seek revenge by further killing, by maiming or by seizing goods" (Parker 1983, 31). Such feuds proceeded without a trial or other attempt to prove guilt.[4] Feuding eventually occurred more rarely as the tribes realized that it sapped their resources and made them less able to ward off attacks from external enemies.[5]

In the early ninth century, power in England was technically consolidated in one overlord, but these successive Anglo-Saxon kings never had effective authority throughout the whole country. Although there were many types of courts and tribunals, there existed no coherent legal system backed by the power of the crown. The slack was taken up by the Catholic Church, which had arrived during the most lawless days and gradually became an equal partner in dealing with antisocial behaviour. Acts such as murder, rape, and robbery were treated as sins.

> *The more serious the sin, the more likely that the Church would demand public penance with weeping, wailing and the donning of sackcloth and ashes. The sinner was excommunicated, and this was a close analogue to the idea of outlawry which was the secular method of treating the worst wrongdoers. The ex-communicant was ostracized and deprived of the offices of the Church. The outlaw was cast out of the community and could be killed on sight (Parker 1983, 30).*

With the Norman Conquest in 1066, each king of England became more successful in centralizing power. The administration of justice was an important component of royal power. Common law (that is, law universal throughout the realm) began to develop with the separation of ecclesiastical (church) and lay courts and the institution of travelling magistrates whose authority came from the Crown.

Once an English king had consolidated his power, he used it to impose various taxes and levies on the barons. The latter became increasingly resentful as these levies became more burdensome. For example, landowners who wished to avoid military service had to pay scutage, even though no campaign was in progress. These resentments came to a head during the reign of King John, who was greedier than his predecessors and widely disliked. Stephen Langdon, a noted theologian and archbishop of Canterbury during the early part of the 13th century, believed that ''just as there was a canon law to govern the internal polity of the church and its relations to the lay world, there should be a recognized system of law to rule the affairs of secular states'' (*Encylopedia Americana* 1973, 123). Accordingly, he formulated the demands of a group of rebellious barons. In 1215, they succeeded in extracting a grant of various liberties from the king. These liberties were incorporated into a formal charter, the **Magna Carta**.

King John was forced to sign the first detailed definition of the relationship between the king and the barons; the agreement outlined the responsibilities of each to each other.

Intended to safeguard individuals from arbitrary royal action, the Magna Carta

> *contained the first detailed definition of the relationship between the king and the barons, outlining the mutual responsibilities of both. It guaranteed the reform of certain royal abuses and regularized the judicial system. It established permanent courts of common pleas, laid down rules for court procedure, guaranteed freedom of commerce, and set up a system of standard weights and measures (Deming 1970, 36).*

Perhaps most importantly, the Magna Carta guaranteed that

> *no freeman shall be arrested and imprisoned, or dispossessed or outlawed, or banished, or in any way molested; nor will we [the king—in other words, the government] set forth against him, nor send against him, unless by the lawful judgment of his peers and by the law of the land.*

In the beginning, these safeguards did not extend to the unfree agricultural population. However, as people gained freedom, the guarantees of the charter extended to them as well. The charter challenged absolute royal power and proclaimed that the king was subject to the law of the land. For several hundred years, the nobility, and later parliament, battled with English monarchs until this principle was firmly established.

CANADIAN LAW

From these two systems—Roman and British—emerged the law of today's western world. Both traditions are strong in Canada. Our laws reflect our historical connection to both France and Britain. By 1670, the French settlements on the St. Lawrence were ruled by Colbent's civil code (enacted in France), while the English traders and settlers (such as those brought in by the Hudson's Bay Company) had brought with them the common-law traditions of England.

The conflict between these two systems did not end with the ''conquest'' of New France, since Britain found it necessary to allow her new French-speaking subjects to maintain their customs, rather than risk having them join the rebellious colonists to the south. The Quebec Act of 1774 enshrined this compromise. The legacy of this decision is apparent from the fact that Quebec still has noncriminal laws based on the French civil code. These civil laws have been given modern form in a Quebec code drawn up in 1866 and partly amended in 1981.[6]

Criminal law in Canada began with a draft compilation of English common law made by Sir James Fitzjames Stephens. Although this was never adopted in England, the Canadian government used it as the basis for our criminal code of 1892. The Criminal Code of Canada has undergone periodic revisions since then that have helped to eliminate its inconsistencies and that have adapted the rules to changing times. Amendments have dealt with issues such as drunken driving, hate propaganda, and the hijacking of aircraft. In practice, the anglophone jurisdictions have greatly modified their common law with statutes and other legislation, while Quebec has passed many laws that are not part of the code and has modified others by judges' interpretations. All Canadian jurisdictions have had an increasing number of legally binding rules set by regulatory agencies.

Thus, the laws of the land truly reflect a mingling of the two great legal traditions of western history.

LAW IN DEMOCRATIC SOCIETIES

Having provided a brief overview of how the foundations of the Canadian legal order evolved, we will define law and examine some of its functions.

According to Black:

> *Law is governmental social control. It is, in other words, the normative life of a state and its citizens, such as legislation, litigation, and adjudication (1976, 2).*

The type of norms for conduct which we call *laws* are rules enforced by representatives of the state, in the name of the state. Thus, for law to exist, a social group must have an authority above the kinship level. This authority may range from an elected government to a hereditary tribal council, from the most democratic of popular governments to the most authoritarian of coercive ones.

The powers of this authority may be extensive. In matters involving criminal offences in most of the world today, the conflict between offender and victim is no longer a personal matter between two private parties. Rather, the crime is an offence against the state authority itself. It is often a further offence—against the state—for the victim to not report the offence or to refuse to testify against an offender. For example, in 1984, an Ontario woman was jailed for a week because she refused to testify against a man accused of having raped her. The state becomes a third party that takes over the work of punishment and restitution. Its representatives, such as lawmakers and law enforcers, decide whether the victim has any participation in whatever legal proceedings ensue. Often, any fines levied are paid to the state rather than to the injured party.

THE FUNCTIONS OF LAW

In discussing the functions of law, it is especially important to distinguish between the ideal and the actual. As we will show later in the chapter, powerful groups may subvert and thwart certain functions of the law. Here, we are presenting an ideal version.

What are some of the functions law performs for society and for individuals?

- *Upholding public order*. Law serves to maintain public order. In the process of socialization, members of a society internalize many of its formal and informal rules governing conduct, so that continuous external enforcement is not needed — indeed, it would be impracticable. Nonetheless, awareness that laws exist, and that transgressing them may bring punishment, keeps many would-be offenders on the straight and narrow.

  Another aid to public order is the resolution of disputes through recourse to official agencies (courts, tribunals) in which impartial judges make decisions on the basis of existing laws and precedents. If all parties acknowledge the fairness of such laws and of the manner in which they have been adjudicated, even a loser may be satisfied with an outcome. The outcome of a personal feud or vendetta, on the other hand, is unpredictable, depending as it does on the characteristics and mood of the parties involved. Thus, resolution of conflict by due process of law lends predictability and stability to social life.

  At the global level, agencies such as the United Nations and the International Court at The Hague are intended to replace feuds amongs nations—wars—with peaceful resolutions. Ideally, such dispute-solving takes into account the interests of all parties, rather than being based on inflamed national passions. Although no international body has yet managed to prevent war, some dispute-solving mechanisms, such as the commissions used by the nations that have signed the General Agreement on Tariffs and Trade, have succeeded in stopping a number of bitter economic (as well as other) quarrels.

- *Establishing the obligations of people to one another*. Laws govern co-operative action among organizations and individuals, even among those that have no personal contact. Property is bought and sold, contracts are let for building highways and schools, goods are transported by air, land, and sea. The parties involved in such transactions are safeguarded by contracts that can be enforced in law and that stipulate compensation in case the conditions of the agreement are not met (for example, if goods are not delivered).

- *Protecting rights*. Law is the arbiter between the rights of the individual and those of the community. Waddams has referred to law as "the knife-edge on which the delicate balance is maintained between the individual on the one hand and the society on the other" (1983, 2). Should smoking be prohibited in public places? Such a rule protects everyone against having to breathe smoke-laden air but infringes on the rights of the individual smoker. Should the vaccination of children against infectious diseases be compulsory, even though it is contrary to the religious beliefs of some parents or to their views regarding health practices?

In a democracy, the law enshrines the rights and freedoms of individuals: for instance, freedom of movement, freedom of speech, the right to vote, freedom of religion. Such rights may be curtailed in the event of a national emergency, as when the federal government invoked the War Measures Act in October 1970, following the kidnapping of British trade commissioner James Cross and Quebec cabinet minister Pierre Laporte, and the murder of the latter.[7] Even then, Canadians maintained the right under law to debate the necessity of this drastic abridgement of individual freedoms. For an interesting discussion of individual and group rights, see Berger's *Fragile Freedoms: Human Rights and Dissent* (1981).

It is rule by law that ultimately protects the citizen against tyranny, as Charles I eloquently expressed prior to his execution (by order of the British parliament) in 1649:

> *For the people truly I desire their liberty and freedom as much as anybody whomsoever, but I must tell you that their liberty and freedom consist in having of government — those laws by which their life and their goods may be most their own.*

In democratic societies, individuals are assured not only rule by law (procedures which are fair), but also equality before the law (results which are fair). Such equality is rare, even in modern societies. In South Africa, members of different races are clearly not equal before the law; indeed, some of the most repressive legislation, such as that restricting freedom of movement, impinges mainly on blacks. In Islamic countries, the testimony of men and women does not carry equal weight. Even when equality before the law is guaranteed, it is not always achieved in practice. In Canada, Native Indians and Inuit, among others, have complained of, and documented, cases of unequal treatment.

- *Regulating life in society.* Law is the instrument by which governments carry out their regulatory role in accordance with societal values. For collectivities, such as public and private organizations, as well as for individuals, law then provides a framework within which everyday life can proceed. If the law prohibits betting away from the race track, the law-abiding person is spared the dilemma of whether or not to place a bet. The company that has advertised a product with the guarantee of ''satisfaction or your money back'' must honour its promise or face possible legal consequences.[9] If legislation prohibits discrimination based on race, gender, or religion in the provision of employment or accomodation, those found guilty of such discrimination are subject to sanctions. Notice that law regulates both the public and the private domains to a significant extent. As society has moved from a Gemeinschaft, in which tradition and custom provide rules for conduct, to a Gesellschaft, in which the emphasis is on formal contracts and agreements, the sheer number of laws (formal rules and regulations) has increased, and the areas of everyday life that they touch have become more extensive. In a society like Canada's, in which people interact fleetingly and impersonally with many other people and organizations, informal arrangements confirmed by a handshake cannot ensure that each party will carry out its obligations.

Employees at Ontario Hydro headquarters must leave the office to smoke since an anti-smoking bylaw was implemented in Toronto in 1988.

CIVIL LIBERTIES AND CANADA'S WAR MEASURES ACT

By Janet Enright

On Oct. 19, 1970, three days after Prime Minister Pierre Elliot Trudeau introduced the War Measures Act in the House of Commons, a dozen members of an environmental organization — which was to become Greenpeace — staged a demonstration in downtown Vancouver. The demonstration had nothing to do with the Front de Libération du Québec members who had kidnapped Quebec Labor Minister Pierre Laporte and British Trade Commissioner James Cross. The Greenpeacers wanted the city to make Granville Street a pedestrian mall, and they had gathered on the steps of the courthouse to make their demands known.

But by the time the demonstrators had assembed, they were already out-numbered by a squad of motorcycle policemen wearing riot gear and armed with the act's powers of detention without charge. The protesters dispersed quickly. Recalled Hilda Thomas, then a candidate for Vancouver city council, who was participating in the action: "We had to decide whether to go or stay and have our heads broken. It was a real demonstration of how quickly a society, through the use of force, can intimidate people and prevent political expression."

The hammer blow of the War Measures Act was aimed at Quebec. And because many Canadians perceived the crisis as a Quebec problem, they were slow to realize that their normal civil liberties had been suspended throughout a difficult 48-day period.

The process of learning that fact began at 5:15 a.m. on Oct. 16, when a spokesman for Trudeau announced the proclamation of the War Measures Act. At 11 a.m. Trudeau made his announcement to the Commons. The Tories protested the act's extensive powers but agreed that action was necessary. When the Commons voted on Monday, Oct. 19, only 16 members of the House, all members of the NDP, failed to approve its sweeping powers of arrest, search and seizure without warrant and detention without trial. And most Canadians supported the government's move. Indeed, a survey by the Canadian Institute of Public Affairs, conducted the day after the act came into force, showed that 37 per cent of Canadians believed the government was "not tough enough."

The impact of the act was immediate and pervasive. Army regiments were deployed to Quebec City, Montreal and Ottawa, and across Canada all RCMP detachments, including the training academy in Regina, were put on full alert in case FLQ members bombed federal government buildings in other parts of Canada. More than 450 arrests, most of them in Montreal, were carried out by RCMP and provincial police. Soldiers performed simple guard duties and remained calm. Indeed, on Halloween night one soldier guarding cabinet minister Robert Andras's Ottawa house handed out candies to masked youngsters.

But only a handful of Canadians protested what they perceived to be an infringement of their rights and freedoms. In Winnipeg on Oct. 17, 200 young people marched down Portage Avenue yelling "Hypocrite Trudeau." Across Canada newspapers applauded the measure, with only a few columnists speaking out against the act, including Robert Hunter of *The Vancouver Sun*, George Bain of *The Globe and*

Mail and W.A. Wilson of *The Montreal Star*. As well, at several Canadian universities students denounced the act. Forbidden to publish the FLQ's manifesto, four student newspapers did so anyway and either had their pages deleted or were prohibited from distributing. Yet police took no action against at least seven other student papers which printed excerpts of the manifesto.

Aside from those isolated actions there was almost no criticism of the act. Even Canada's French-speaking communities outside Quebec supported the government's tough stand. Winnipeg lawyer Rheal Teffaine, who was 31 when the kidnappings occurred, recalls that many of Manitoba's francophones trusted Trudeau because he was Québécois.

A few officials, such as Vancouver Mayor Thomas Campbell, even attempted to use the sweeping powers of the act to deal with unrelated problems. On Oct. 17, Campbell told reporters he wanted to use the legislation to rid his city of drug pushers and hippies. Said Campbell: "Draft dodgers had better start dodging — get out of here, boy, because we're going to pick you up." Campbell never carried through on his threats. But on Oct. 26, Vancouver police took into custody seven members of the Vancouver Liberation Front — recently described to *Maclean's* by Vancouver journalist *Maclean's* by Vancouver journalist Bob Hunter as "just a bunch of drug-crazed Maoists" — after they received complaints that group members were handing out leaflets and pamphlets criticizing the War Measures Act. The seven were released shortly after.

In Manitoba flamboyant Joe Borowski, highways minister in the NDP government of the time and now better known for his anti-abortion stand, sent Trudeau a telegram. It read: "Thank you for initiating the War Measures Act. When you catch the abductors, execute the bastards."

Still, the act did have a few lasting effects. Said June Callwood, vice-president of the Canadian Civil Liberties Association: "It probably energized the later debate on our Charter of Rights and Freedoms. It turned people around and made them more skeptical of authority."[8]

For most Canadians the experience only underlined one of the country's strongest national characteristics — deference to authority.

THE ADMINISTRATION AND ENFORCEMENT OF LAW

In Canada, as in many western countries, law is divided into criminal and civil law.[10] Under **criminal law**, the prosecution of the accused (the defendant) is conducted by the state — in Canada, in the name of its titular head, the Queen. (Notes of court proceedings refer, for example, to "Regina vs. Smith.") Murder, rape, burglary, and assault are examples of offences under the Criminal Code, which is uniform across the country. Civil law deals with disputes between two or more private parties. The state arbitrates but is not actually a party to the proceedings. The plaintiff, which is the party bringing the action, seeks redress against the defendant for such offences as nonperformance of contract, breach of promise, or encroachment on property. Tourists who buy a prepaid package tour and find themselves stranded without accommodation, a patient who believes improper care by a doctor has resulted in bodily harm, a man who is bitten by his neighbour's dog — any of these people may bring action for damages against the individual or company deemed responsible for the damage.

LAW ENFORCEMENT AND ADJUDICATION

The plethora of laws, rules, and regulations is administered and enforced by complex bureaucratic organizations, all of which have their own specialized staff. Almost everyone has dealings with some of these agencies, such as the driver's license bureau, the passport office, and Revenue Canada. For most Canadians, the police are the principal contact with law-enforcement officials. In the case of minor offences, the contact need go no further. For instance, many traffic violations can be settled by pleading guilty to the offence and sending the assessed penalty to the provincial court by the stipulated date.

Canada has three types of police force: municipal, provincial, and federal. Large cities, such as Halifax and Vancouver, have their own municipal police forces, while small towns and rural areas are served by either provincial or federal police. Only Ontario and Quebec maintain a provincial police force. The other eight provinces and the territories contract for use of the federal force, the Royal Canadian Mounted Police. The RCMP comes under the jurisdiction of the solicitor general, whose ministry also controls federal penitentiaries.

THE COURTS

Canadian courts, too, are divided into several levels. As in other institutional sectors, there are interprovincial variations in how the court system is structured. Our discussion here focuses mainly on the Ontario system.

Minor civil cases are heard in small claims court, whose judges are appointed by the province. The amounts of money involved are relatively small, and procedures are simplified, so neither party needs to be represented by a lawyer. A case might involve a claim for damages against a dry cleaner who shrank a customer's garment.

The provincial court is divided between the family courts and the criminal courts and is staffed by provincially appointed judges or magistrates. The family court decides such matters as custody, adoption, and whether a mother charged with child neglect should be allowed to keep her child and if so, under what conditions. A motorist who wishes to contest a speeding ticket argues his case, with or without a lawyer, in the criminal court, which has jurisdiction over minor criminal offences.

Every province has a superior court (for example, the Supreme Court of British Columbia, the Court of Queen's Bench in Alberta, the Quebec Superior Court). It is empowered to administer all law within the province except "insofar as a statute specifically gives exclusive jurisdiction over some particular subject matter to another tribunal" (Waddams 1983, 147).[11] Major civil disputes, as well as serious criminal cases, are heard in the province's supreme court. Decisions may be appealed to its Court of Appeal. Superior court judges are appointed by the federal government, and lower court judges are appointed by the provincial government. As a result of controversy over political patronage in the appointment of judges, there is now an emphasis on universalistic criteria (professional achievement) rather than on particularistic criteria (personal links to political parties).

The ultimate arbiter of law in the country is the Supreme Court of Canada, staffed by nine federally appointed judges, three of whom must be from Quebec. The judges are chosen from the top jurists in the country. The court may agree to hear civil or criminal cases adjudicated by a lower court (the criterion is whether an important legal principle is at stake). It also rules on constitutional questions, such as disputes among provincial governments or between the federal government and one or more provincial governments. Thus, it adjudicated the question of whether offshore oil resources were owned by Canada or by the province of Newfoundland, and it declared certain sections of Quebec's language act (Bill 101) unconstitutional because they violated the Charter of Rights and Freedoms. Since the Supreme Court is Canada's highest tribunal, no further avenues of appeal exist once it has handed down its decision.

Unlike the United States Supreme Court, the Canadian Court has traditionally not been actively involved in issues related to government policy. However, with the patriation of the Constitution and the creation of a Charter of Rights and Freedoms, the Canadian Supreme Court will likely assume a more active role both in constitutional issues and in decisions concerning the rights of individuals. However, the Supreme Court's 1989 ruling that struck down the abortion law put this difficult issue back into the political arena.

THE COURTS AND LEGISLATION

In democracies, laws are passed by elected governments. The function of the courts is to administer these laws by ruling on their applicability to specific cases and by assessing penalties within the range laid down for a particular offence. For instance, if armed robbery carries a prison sentence of three to ten years, the judge can sentence the convicted robber to a three-, four-, or ten-year term but cannot arbitrarily impose a life sentence.

The Canadian Charter of Rights, entrenched in the repatriated Constitution, was signed by Queen Elizabeth II in 1982.

In theory, then, courts do not legislate. In practice, the higher courts, and certainly the Supreme Court, do engage in lawmaking when they overturn previous decisions and thereby invalidate the law on which these decisions have been based.[12] The 1954 decision of the U.S. Supreme Court outlawing schools segregated for black and white students is a dramatic example. In 1896, the Court had ruled that "separate but equal" facilities for blacks and whites were acceptable. The southern states had quickly proceeded to entrench segregation between the races, without much worry about equality. With one fell swoop, the unanimous 1954 decision removed the underpinning from a whole web of laws sanctioning segregation—in schooling, in public transportation and accommodation, and in sports and cultural facilities.

THE DILEMMA OF INTERPRETATION

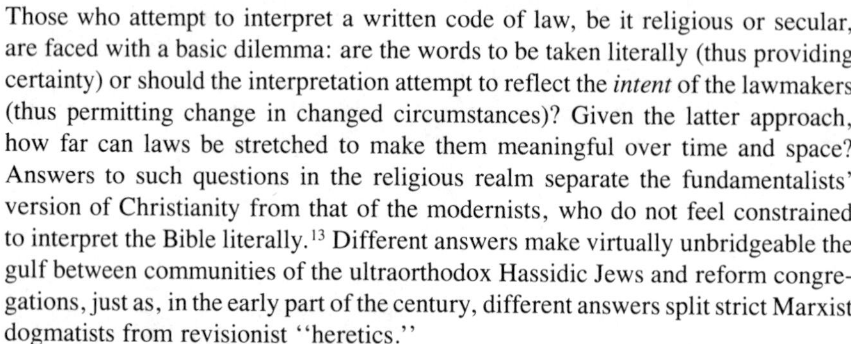

Those who attempt to interpret a written code of law, be it religious or secular, are faced with a basic dilemma: are the words to be taken literally (thus providing certainty) or should the interpretation attempt to reflect the *intent* of the lawmakers (thus permitting change in changed circumstances)? Given the latter approach, how far can laws be stretched to make them meaningful over time and space? Answers to such questions in the religious realm separate the fundamentalists' version of Christianity from that of the modernists, who do not feel constrained to interpret the Bible literally.[13] Different answers make virtually unbridgeable the gulf between communities of the ultraorthodox Hassidic Jews and reform congregations, just as, in the early part of the century, different answers split strict Marxist dogmatists from revisionist ''heretics.''

The courts, too, must meet the challenge of steering an even course between certainty and change:

> *Certainty and change—these are the essential needs of a legal system. Obviously, they both cannot be given full scope; in their pure forms they are antagonistic poles. Neither one can be made the exclusive concern of the legal system: without certainty the law becomes not a chart to govern conduct, but a game of chance; with only certainty, the law is as the still waters in which there are only stagnation and death. Inherent in every system of law is the antimony between certainty and change. The law must be stable and yet it cannot stand still; that is the great juristic paradox which no legal system has as yet been able to resolve in a wholly satisfactory manner (Schwartz 1954, 346).*

THE DILEMMA OF SOCIAL CONSENSUS

Laws reflect societal values, but in a heterogeneous society like Canada's, not all laws can reflect the values of all groups. The controversy surrounding laws on abortion is an example. The pro-choice groups argue that any law is too restrictive and that the decision whether to bear a child should rest only with the woman concerned. On the other hand, pro-life factions believe that abortion is murder and, as such, should be categorically forbidden.

It is important, however, that laws reflect the values and beliefs of large numbers of the society's members, and that laws not meeting these criteria be changed or eliminated. The reason is exemplified in the widespread flouting of the Prohibition laws of the 1920s. As explained in Chapter 8, many Canadians and Americans did not consider the manufacture, sale, and consumption of alcohol deviant or offensive. Accordingly, enforcement of alcohol-related laws became very difficult and caused widespread popular resentment until they were rescinded in the 1930s.

If some laws are continually disregarded with relative impunity, there is danger that the disregard will spread to all laws—"What's the point of stopping for a red light when there is no traffic?" Ultimately, such practices would lead to anarchy, a society without law and, in the words of Thomas Hobbes, life would revert to being "nasty, brutish and short." In the religious as in the secular realm, lawgivers seek to maintain consonance between the substance of the laws and beliefs of right and wrong held by the members of a group.

FETAL RIGHTS

By Catherine Tolton

Although the constitutional status of the unborn is in dire need of clarification, a Supreme Court of Canada decision on Chantal Daigle's appeal that addresses the rights of the fetus would go far beyond the narrow confines of abortion.

It would amount to a sweeping constitutional pronouncement affecting everything from embryo transplants, contraception, surrogate parenthood and prenatal surgery to the right of a critically ill pregnant woman to a natural death or to life-saving treatment.

A conflict between woman and fetus is unavoidable when a fetus is accorded rights, particularly regarding such reproductive technologies as *in vitro* fertilization, the freezing of embryos and surrogacy.

If, for example, an ovum fertilized outside the womb is accorded the same constitutional status as the fetus within a woman, the possibilities that *in vitro* fertilization offers to childless couples might be denied because of the legal uncertainty created by the disposal of ova that are fertilized but not implanted. Could the state insist that all embryos created outside the human body be returned to some woman's womb or be frozen to await future implantation?

A further maze of legal issues arises in surrogate motherhood. Who are the legal guardians of the unborn child and at what point do the parents who "commission" a fetus actually become its guardians? If, for example, the implanted embryo has no genetic relationship to the woman carrying it, what are her rights versus those of the commissioning parents if fetal surgery or some other intrauterine procedure is advised, or a caesarian section is recommended? Could the couple authorize something over her objections?

Broader questions for all childbearing women are raised by the injunction that was granted and then overturned in the Barbara Dodd case, in which child-welfare legislation was used to protect a fetus from an abortion. At what point in gestation is it permissible to apprehend a fetus, what degree of risk or harm would justify intervention and what are the rights of the pregnant woman?

Not only could such legislation be used to deny a woman an abortion or life-saving surgery; a fetus in British Columbia was recognized in a bid to force a woman to have a caesarian section. On judicial review the decision was set aside, but in what other ways might such laws be used to force pregnant women to submit to other medical procedures?

Furthermore, could evidence that drugs or alcohol (taken weeks, months or years before a pregnancy) might harm a fetus be invoked to justify regulating the behaviour of all fertile women?

Is it possible that the state could ultimately require only planned pregnancies, to avoid the possibility of such harm to the fetus? The nightmare of enforcing such restrictions would probably stop them being introduced, but such ghoulish possibilities may not be that far-fetched.

Where there is an inherent conflict between a woman's right to pursue a particular lifestyle and the fetus's right to be free of damaging substances, the key issue will be whether the state can establish a sufficient level of fetal rights to justify curtailing the freedom of pregnant women.

Child-welfare legislation might also be used to override a parent's deeply held religious convictions. Could a pregnant Jehovah's Witness be compelled to accept a blood transfusion for the physical welfare of her unborn child?

In general, women's health care could be seriously compromised by a ruling that a fetus is a person under the constitution. If a medical procedure that saves a woman's life harms her unborn child, would it constitute an abortion and the killing of a protected life?

This could arise with the removal of an ectopic pregnancy before it ruptures the fallopian tubes and threatens the woman's life; dilation and curretage when miscarriage is imminent and inevitable; inducing labor or early delivery to protect the woman; appendectomy that might induce a miscarriage, and radiation treatment of a pregnant woman with cancer when it could harm the fetus.

Even the legality of home births may be suspect, considering there is an increase in risk to the fetus.

Under law a dying pregnant woman can refuse measures designed simply to prolong, rather than save, her life. But if the fetus's right to life is perceived as paramount, a woman may lose her right to die a natural death with dignity.

In the United States, even though the rights of the unborn are not constitutionally entrenched, concerns for the rights of the dying pregnant woman have already arisen in two distinct ways. One involves keeping a brain-dead woman alive artificially long enough for her fetus to be delivered with a good chance at a healthy life. The other is when death is imminent but the woman is conscious and mentally alert — should she be kept alive against her wishes to benefit the fetus?

The entire debate about whether a fetus is a person serves only to obscure the critical underlying issues. To what extent will our society respect the right of a woman to make fundamental personal decisions, and who has the right to determine the values that govern those decisions? Underlying these choices are difficult questions about life, death and the appropriate circumstances in which to choose one over another.

The importance life has for us extends far beyond mere physical existence into the realm of values that imbue our lives with meaning: human dignity, freedom from bodily invasion, the freedom to make one's own choices, equality. Confining the court's consideration to the abortion context could obscure some of the fundamental issues that are at stake.

LEGAL EXPERTISE IN A COMPLEX SOCIETY

We have noted that the complexity of society gives rise to more and more law. Closely associated with this trend is the growth of the legal profession. As Krause has noted:

> *In complex societies of the past and present the critical rules of social life are codified and their meaning enforced by more sanctions than simple disapproval. Wherever the division of labor has reached the point where such legal rules are necessary, a body of experts on their proper application and use arises (1971, 147).*

Reliance on experts is a salient characteristic of complex societies and one reason their expertise is highly rewarded (see the discussion of the professions in Chapter 5). You cannot think of health care without thinking of physicians. Analogously, the law requires the participation of lawyers.[14] All parties to a civil suit are likely to be represented by lawyers, except in small claims court. In the criminal courts, Crown attorneys prosecute on behalf of the state. Other lawyers may defend the accused; in fact, anyone accused of a serious offence under the Criminal Code has the *right* to be defended by a lawyer. (The state provides defence lawyers—legal aid—for people who cannot pay for their own.)

Tribunals and commissions, such as the provincial human-rights and securities commissions, all employ lawyers to draw up, interpret, and apply regulatory statutes. Lawyers mediate in relationships among corporations and in those between the state and organizations, between organizations and individuals, and between the state and individuals.

Befitting their broad areas of involvement, lawyers are a highly specialized profession. Some deal only with taxation or patent law, others with international law or real estate. Most individuals utilize lawyers' services at least occasionally, as when they buy or sell a house, draw up a will, or seek a divorce. Some people may choose to handle such matters themselves, but most, rightly or wrongly, heed the adage: *be your own lawyer and have a fool for a client.*

STRATIFICATION WITHIN THE LEGAL PROFESSION

Throughout the book, we have stressed that the structure of Canadian society as a whole, one that is stratified by classes defined in terms of power relations, is reflected in each societal sector. In a sophisticated study of the Toronto bar, Hagan, Huxter and Parker (1988) analyse the legal profession in terms of class divisions, and in terms of power relations between classes.

They divide the profession into ten classes, ranging from ''capitalists'' (senior partners in elite firms having over 30 employees, who participate directly in major decisions) through ''small employers'' (those with two or more employees) to the ''working class'' (lawyers who are employees with little or no autonomy). The latter are usually recent graduates; only two percent of lawyers who had been in practice for more than six years were categorized as working class.

In theory, the professional firm is a ''collegium of equals;'' in practice, large firms clearly operate as capitalist enterprises whereby the surplus from the workers' labour accrues to the owners:

> *To determine billing rates, the top firms generally use a formula: they double associates' salaries and divide by 1,000. Thus, a new associate who is paid $43,500 per year would be billed to the client at a rate of $87 per hour. If that associate bills 2,500 hours in a year (a large but fairly typical figure), he will generate $217,500 in revenue for the firm. Generously assuming that overhead per associate (rent, secretarial, etc.) is about the same as the associate's salary of $43,500, the firm is left with $130,000 in profit per new associate (Stewart 1983, 376—quoted by Hagan, Huxter and Parker 1988, 37).*

The researchers found women to be over-represented at the bottom of the legal hierarchy, a finding that can in part be explained by the recentness of women's entry on a large scale into the profession:

> *Overall, more than 60 percent of all women lawyers now in the Toronto legal profession are in an underclass of semi-autonomous employees, workers, and the surplus population. The comparable figure for men lawyers is almost half this. Of course, women are newer entrants into the profession, and if time in the profession is taken into account, our data indicate that women may be getting to the top of the profession in increasing numbers. Nevertheless, women are still overrepresented at the bottom of the profession, especially if the underclass is broadly defined and includes persons not employed full-time. Beyond this, we found evidence that clients more than employers may be the primary*

> *sources of gender-based discrimination, with women practicing on their own particularly susceptible to such experiences (Stewart 1988, 52).*

Although they are moving up, it appears that women professionals must not only deal with the potential for discriminatory practices on the part of employers, but also with prejudice and discrimination by potential clients whose views of "professionals" are influenced by gender stereotypes. In recent years, there has been a furor in some Canadian universities over the hiring and promotion of female law professors, and over gender-related curriculum matters.

Previous studies (Carlin 1962, Heinz and Laumann 1982, Smigel 1964, 1969) showed that Jewish lawyers, despite their relatively large numbers, were sparsely represented in elite firms. In the present study, too, Jews were found to be underrepresented in the capitalist class—less than one percent, compared with 8.3 percent of white Anglo-Saxon Protestant (WASP) lawyers. However, the situation is changing:

> *About equal proportions of Jewish and WASP lawyers hired in the 1980s are now in large (33.4% and 33.5%, respectively) and elite firms (15.7% and 18.9%, respectively). Note that if our data stopped in the early 1970s, as previous data sets have, our conclusions would be quite different. Indeed, they would parallel those of Heinz and Laumann. These recent changes in patterns of entry into the profession may have important long-term consequences (1988, 39).*

These findings again point to the growing importance of achievement over ascription in modern society. If firms want to survive, and thrive, in a competitive environment, they must recruit the most able, rather than those with the most "suitable" ascribed characteristics. However, the findings also show how long it takes for change to percolate through the system; it will be years before junior lawyers become senior partners whose decisions have far-reaching consequences. Furthermore, there is no guarantee that the road will be open all the way for outsiders. Evidence from industry points to a "glass ceiling" that makes it very difficult for women as well as for blacks to reach the top corporate echelons. Will the situation be different for minorities in the legal profession?

EQUALITY BEFORE THE LAW

Where social inequality exists, it is likely to manifest itself in all areas of life. In Chapter 5 on work and Chapter 9B on education, we noted that Canadian society does not fully meet in practice the societal ideal of equal opportunity for people of equal ability. A similar picture emerges vis-à-vis the ideal that all citizens are equal before the law when one examines the experiences of individuals who are differently situated in the hierarchy of society.

Conflict theorists view the law as a tool of social control by which dominant groups seek to perpetuate their privileged position:

> *The law in capitalist societies is structured* a priori *on the basis of social class. It is structured in a way that determines at the outset that lower-class people will predominate among its violators, at least in the case of criminal law. Pretensions of equality before the law, that is, of fairness in legal processing, should not obscure this fact. As Anatole France once remarked, "The law in all its majestic equality, forbids the rich as well as the poor to sleep under bridges on rainy nights, to beg in the streets and to steal bread" (Greenaway 1980, 254).*

It is a moot point whether law is deliberately structured to give advantages to the advantaged, or whether these advantages are a latent function (one neither intended nor anticipated) of membership in the higher classes. However, evidence certainly exists that lower-class people (especially young, lower-class males), homosexuals, hippies, and members of visible minorities are likely to be more closely watched by the police than middle-aged, middle-class suburbanites, and are less likely to be given the benefit of the doubt if caught in an apparent misdemeanour. Several studies have found that a similar pattern prevails after individuals have been formally charged and are being processed through the legal machinery.

We have already noted that, for a majority of people, contact with the law means contact with police officers. Parker has commented that police response to certain conduct is frequently influenced by the social characteristics of the actors:

> *There are too many instances of police officers whose perceptions of reasonable suspicion or bases of decision to arrest have been distorted by their prejudices. They take the attitude that anyone with a beard, long hair, from a particular ethnic group or riding a motorcycle and wearing a leather jacket should be watched more often and more closely. Too often police officers believe that the discretion to invoke the criminal process can be exercised more precipitously in such cases (1983, 347).*

In his study of Crow Lake, a railway town in northwestern Ontario, Stymeist found that native peoples were subject to discriminatory treatment:

> *Most arrests in Crow Lake are for public intoxication. Ontario Provincial Police cars park outside the entrance to the Crow Lake Hotel, the town's largest central pub, for an hour or so before and after the pub closes. The waiters will ask a drunk white man, who is perhaps a relative, friend or steady customer, if he wants to call a cab. The cab*

> *will arrive at the back door of the hotel and the man in question will leave unseen. Many Indians, however, are arrested as they leave the pub, and some have been arrested for public drunkenness as they were climbing the stairs to their rooms in the hotel (1977, 79).*

Contrary to the legal maxim that a person is presumed innocent until proven guilty, the police often appear to presume members of minority groups guilty until they can establish their innocence. It must be emphasized, however, that such treatment of out-groups reflects not necessarily the prejudices of police officers but rather the attitudes of many members of the society. In the Crow Lake situation, waiters could have ordered cabs for Native Indians as they did for white people. Community members could have objected to the arrest of Indians for public drunkenness while they were on private (hotel) property.

Certain types of people are more likely to come under suspicion than others.

Many factors affect the ways in which people in law enforcement view groups and individuals. Vincent's study of the Windsor police force revealed that the police tend to evaluate groups in terms of how much difficulty members are likely to cause and how predictable their behaviour is deemed. New immigrants engender suspicion because they are little-known entities:

> *The increased heterogeneity of the city's population makes his [the police officer's] work more difficult because he does not know what to expect when confronted by people from widely diverse cultures which are relatively unknown to him. His lack of information about these cultures sometimes makes it difficult for him to understand the actions and motivations of these new residents (1979, 106).*

Although a number of occupational groups are clustered in the institutional sector of law and, therefore, have overarching common interests, they may also come in conflict with one another. (Similarly, the united front presented to outsiders by a family or by the teaching profession may conceal significant internal dissension.) An example is the difference between the attitudes of the police and those of other legal groups toward the treatment of people who have been charged with crimes.

Police officers do much of the dirty work of law enforcement, such as defusing domestic and public disputes and arresting suspected lawbreakers. Accordingly, they are likely to have abrasive contact with the public and to attract a great deal of popular resentment. In turn, police officers resent their "bad guy" image, particularly since they perceive that much of their effort is nullified at the higher echelons of law enforcement. One of Vincent's respondents clearly expressed this frustration:

> *You're damned right I'm frustrated. All those lawyers, Crowns [Crown attorneys], and judges, they all went to law school together. They eat and drink together and pal around together. They try to make a fool out of you in the courtroom. They aren't interested in justice, just the buck. So why should I break my butt all the time when I know the case is going to be thrown out on a technicality or, they arrange amongst themselves to have a plea-cop and a reduced sentence. Some of them will even drop the case in the middle because the poor slob can't come up with the dough (1979, 96–7).*

Contrary to the belief prevailing among many police officers and the public generally, "there is virtually no evidence that judges, in Canada or elsewhere, have become more lenient" in recent years (Snider 1982, 432). In his survey of the American justice system, Silberman (1980) found no trend toward leniency in the penalties imposed.

EXHIBIT 9.13

SENTENCED ADMISSIONS, 1986–87

Province	Total number	Rate per 100,000 population	Percent female	Percent native	Median age
Newfoundland	1 839	32	3	5	29
Prince Edward Island	1 662	131	5	3	29
Nova Scotia	2 965	34	4	4	26
New Brunswick	3 610	51	3	4	28
Quebec	16 825	26	7	2	28
Ontario	45 306	50	7	9	27
Manitoba	6 239	59	9	56	27
Saskatchewan	6 731	67	9	64	25
Alberta	19 227	81	9	30	26
British Columbia	10 524	36	6	18	28
Yukon	560	238	6	60	26
Northwest Territories	781	150	5	90	24
Canada	116 269	46	6	17	27

SOURCE: Statistics Canada, Adult Correctional Services in Canada.

However, there is evidence that members of different social groups do not fare equally during the various stages of legal proceedings. As Exhibits 9.13 and 9.14 suggest, the young and people too poor to pay fines seem over-represented in provincial and federal prisons. Other studies have suggested further differences in application of the law. For example, Greenaway has commented:

> *While it may not be absolutely certain that discretion always works to the disadvantage of lower-class defendants, investigation and processing of so-called white collar crimes is often conducted so as to keep high status law violators out of the courts. In her examination of legislation—municipal, provincial and federal—affecting corporate conduct in Canada, Snider (1978) points out that procedures often dictate that past infractions be ignored if such violations are remedied or if future compliance is assured. Attrition rates for such offenses tend therefore to be much higher than rates for normal, that is, predominantly lower-class, crimes. If someone burglarizes your house and is apprehended in circumstances which would clearly yield a conviction, it would not be common for the offender to be released by the police on the promise that stolen articles will be returned and that the offender will go straight (1980, 259).*

EXHIBIT 9.14

INMATES ADMITTED TO PROVINCIAL CUSTODY FOR FINE DEFAULT

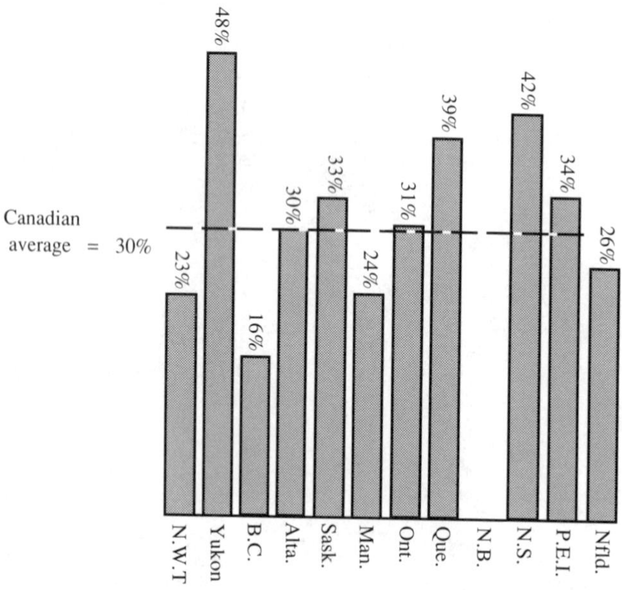

NOTES:

1. Fine-default admissions refer to those persons who, if their original sentence of fine payment had been satisfied, would not have been required to serve a term of custody. Excluded are those offenders who defaulted on their fine but who were also sentenced to custody in addition to the fine.
2. New Brunswick data not available.

SOURCE: Statistics Canada (1988, 85).

Large corporations and powerful individuals, guided by expert lawyers, are clearly better equipped to negotiate their way through the bureaucratic maze of the legal system than an unemployed youth charged with breaking and entering.

That the powerful fare better under the law is by no means new. Some 2600 years ago, the Greek philosopher Solan noted, "Laws are like spider's webs which, if anything small falls into them they ensnare it, but large things break through and escape." Two hundred years later, Plato remarked, "Everywhere there is one principle of justice, which is the interest of the stronger" (quoted in Ericson and Baranek 1982, 216). The same idea is expressed in the popular aphorism, "might makes right."

Mann and Lee have presented the argument even more strongly, noting that corporations that cause massive environmental pollution, or jeopardize their workers' lives in unsafe work environments, may incur only minor penalties: "When corporations kill, there may be a fine, or only a warning. When individuals kill, they are imprisoned" (1979, 21). For an interesting discussion of environmental rights and environmental crime, see the Law Reform Commission of Canada's working paper, *Crimes Against the Environment* (1985).

"When corporations kill, there may be a fine, or only a warning. When individuals kill, they are imprisoned."

Despite evidence that some people are more equal than others before the law, it would be misleading to dismiss the concept of equality before the law as simply a myth. On the contrary, the ideal is a crucial safeguard of individual rights because departures from the guarantee of equality are deviant and subject to appeal. If infringements of the principle of equality are major, it is likely that they will be corrected, even though the process may take a long time. Thus, the severe legal disabilities blacks had suffered in the American south, such as having their fate decided by all-white, often hostile, juries, were eventually remedied—in part, if not totally.

Totalitarian states make no distinction between the legal system and the state as represented by the government. Thus, the law does not and cannot act as arbiter between the state and its members. In democracies, the state and its agencies are theoretically bound by law in the same way as the individual citizen. Despite the considerable evidence of violations of this principle (see *The RCMP vs. the People* in the Suggested Readings), the state's responsibility to observe the law is no hollow obligation. When Richard Nixon, as President of the United States, sought to place his personal ambitions and the aims of his administration above the law, the investigation following the Watergate break-in and subsequent revelations of official malfeasance ultimately led to his resignation. The decision by the RCMP to use illegal means to obtain information about ''potentially subversive'' organizations, such as the Parti Québécois, led the Quebec government to appoint the Keable Commission to investigate RCMP action within the province. In 1977, the federal government appointed the McDonald Commission to examine undue curtailment of individual rights in the name of national security. Mann and Lee cited a statement made by Quebec Justice James Hugessen:

> *Much has been made, in the present case, of national security and state secrets, but we must not forget that in principle we live in an open and democratic society. Even the security of the state can and must be the subject of informed debate among all citizens (1979, 258).*

SUMMARY

Our overview has shown the gradual separation of religious law from secular law and the elaboration and increasing importance of law as an institutional sphere in western societies. Law has major functions in maintaining social order, in protecting groups and individuals from arbitrary acts of others and of the state, and in establishing the obligations of people, one to another.

The drafting, administration, and adjudication of law depend on a cadre of experts. A delicate balancing act is necessary to ensure that laws reflect changes in the values of society while at the same time promoting predictability and stability. The law must safeguard societal interests without riding roughshod over those of individual citizens. A major challenge is to ensure equality before the law in a society in which significant inequality persists. Inequality manifests itself in all phases of the legal process: in the treatment likely to be received from the police, in the probability of being formally charged, and in the courts' disposition. The ideal of equality before the law is not consistently met in practice, but appeal procedures are available to limit the potential for unjust treatment.[15]

Like other professions, the legal profession is internally stratified. There is evidence that position in the legal hierarchy is affected by gender and ethno-cultural characteristics. A recent study of the bar shows that access is becoming more open, though obstacles have not disappeared.

Law has come to pervade almost every aspect of daily living. At the societal level, law is crucial in defining relationships among institutions, groups, and individuals.

ASSIGNMENTS

Do one or both of the following assignments, as instructed by your professor.

1 Spend a morning or afternoon in a provincial court or a police station. Use a "sociological window" as you watch the proceedings. Carefully record what you see; then use the ideas you have gleaned from this course to interpret your observations.

2 Over a one-week period, keep track of all references in your newspaper to the Canadian Charter of Rights. Identify the issues that are raised, and discuss them (with the help of material from this section on law, and the chapters on stratification, work, and minorities).

SUGGESTED READINGS

J. Batten, *Lawyers* (Toronto: Gage, 1984). Batten is a lawyer turned free-lance writer. He sets out to discover what lawyers do and reports it with a flair for the dramatic. *Lawyers* illustrates the diversity of legal work, and of the conditions under which this work is performed.

Batten spirits the reader from the circuit riders (fliers) of the Arctic, to the boardrooms of Toronto, and to the relative calm of rural practice in southwestern Ontario. Because Batten focuses on prominent lawyers, and on their stellar rather than their routine cases, the practice of law probably comes across as more glamorous and exciting than it is for most lawyers most of the time.

Ian Greene, *The Charter of Rights* (Toronto: Lorimer, 1989). Greene offers a good, basic introduction to Canada's Charter of Rights. Greene presents a balanced view of the costs and benefits that the provisions of the Charter will entail, and describes some of the cases to which it has been applied.

M. Harris, *Justice Denied* (Toronto: Macmillan of Canada, 1986). How can a gross miscarriage of justice remain unremedied for eleven years in a country like Canada, whose legal system is committed to the proposition that everyone is innocent until proven guilty? In the case of Donald Marshall, a Micmac Indian accused of killing a black youth, several factors coalesced. The police were desperate to get a conviction, the investigating officer in charge was unethical, Marshall had a reputation as a young tough, and his friends were sufficiently scared to give the perjured testimony the police and the prosecutor wanted to hear.

In *Justice Denied*, Harris reconstructs the context as well as the actual events surrounding the murder of Sandy Seale, Marshall's conviction, and his eventual vindication. Note that if there had still been capital punishment in Canada, Marshall might have been executed.

Arthur Koestler, *Darkness at Noon* (Harmondsworth: Penguin, 1940). In a democratic society, legal institutions act as intermediaries between the state and its citizens. Those accused of wrongdoing are deemed innocent until proven guilty. In totalitarian societies, such as Stalinist Russia or Nazi Germany, the state and the law are one. No institutional safeguards exist to protect individuals.

Arthur Koestler, who fought against Franco's side in the Spanish Civil War, was sympathetic to Communist ideals but became deeply disillusioned with the ways in which these ideals were subverted in practice. *Darkness at Noon* is Koestler's chilling account of the show trial of a former party functionary who is accused of betraying the regime and plotting to kill its leader. Although the book is a work of fiction, many such trials actually took place in Russia during the purges of the 1930s.

Elsie Gregory MacGill, *My Mother, the Judge: A Biography of Helen Gregory MacGill* (Toronto: The Ryerson Press, 1955). This is the biography of a suffrage leader who became the first female jurist in British Columbia. Elsie Gregory MacGill was appointed to the Juvenile Court of British Columbia in 1917, and served for 23 years. The author is MacGill's daughter, a pioneer in aeronautical engineering in Ontario.

E. Mann and **J.A. Lee**, *The RCMP vs. the People* (Don Mills, Ont.: General Publishing, 1979). Mann and Lee provide a short history of the Royal Canadian Mounted Police and trace the route by which the force has reached its hallowed position in Canadian society. The authors argue that, in the name of national security, the RCMP has repeatedly broken the law. Further, they raise grave concerns about the secrecy with which the force has been allowed to operate in our supposedly open society. They see no easy answers to the age-old question of "who shall guard the guardians?"

NOTES

1 A more complete definition appears later in the chapter.

2 Students should be aware that "civil law" has another, quite different meaning (the opposite of "criminal law"), as discussed later in this chapter.

3 In a letter to the editor of the *Globe and Mail* (February 18, 1989), Gerald Owen comments on the *graphe paranomon*, a constitutional safeguard in Athenian democracy which, in Mr. Owen's words "went beyond anything in the Canadian Charter or the U.S. Constitution." This provision allowed any Athenian citizen to "launch a criminal indictment against any other citizen who had proposed in the Assembly a measure inconsistent with the laws, at any time up to a year after the proposal had been passed."

4 Such feuding has never completely died out. A famous more recent example is the feud between the Hatfields and the McCoys, large, closely knit clans living

at the time of the American Civil War on what is now the West Virginia/Kentucky state border. After intermittent feuding, armed hostilities erupted when John Hatfield sought to elope with Rosanna McCoy; Ellison Hatfield was shot and subsequently died. When three McCoy brothers were taken to jail in connection with the shooting, they were ambushed by a posse of Hatfields and murdered. The feuding continued until 1888, when the Kentucky authorities crossed the West Virginia border and seized and convicted several Hatfields.

Finally, the communities grew tired of the disruptions caused by the feuding, and co-operated with the law authorities to put an end to it (*Encyclopedia Americana* 1973, 853).

5 Consideration of these lawless days makes it easier to understand the rise of feudalism; people were willing to exchange freedom for protection by a strong landowner who could assemble a fighting band. A number of modern scholars believe that it was this period that gave rise to the legends of King Arthur and the round table; he may have been an exceptionally wise leader who tried to substitute the rule of law for the rule of might.

6 Quebec's entire civil code has been rewritten, but only some portions relating to family law have been enacted since 1981. Experts expect other parts to be enacted in the future.

7 The kidnappings, which came at a time of considerable unrest in Quebec, were the work of a radical group, the Front de Libération du Québec; it also published a manifesto challenging all established authority in the country and the province. Declaring a state of "apprehended insurrection," the federal government sent troops to Montreal and used its powers under the War Measures Act to authorize arrests and detentions without charges being laid. Some 450 individuals suspected of being radical separatists were jailed in this fashion in Quebec; most were released with no further legal action.

8 The War Measures Act was replaced, in July 1988, by The Emergencies Act, which is subject to the Charter of Rights and Freedoms, and which provides more specific and limited restrictions of civil liberties according to the type of emergency that occurs.

9 During the past decade, substantial fines have been levied, even against such large corporations as Eaton's and Sears, for false advertising.

10 Additional, important categories of Canadian law are: (1) constitutional law, which regulates the powers of government and their division among the various levels of government; and (2) administrative law, which governs administrative agencies, from workers' compensation boards to licensing authorities, and provides means whereby individuals can seek remedies if they think such agencies have been unfair.

11 These matters include labour disputes, most of which are reserved for special tribunals, as well as cases involving maritime law, copyright, patent, and trademark law, and federal taxation; the latter cases go to the Federal Court of Canada, which has both a trials and an appeals division.

12 In Canada, as Waddams has explained, "Decisions of superior courts are binding on lower courts. The Supreme Court of Canada is not bound by its own previous decisions and several times in recent years has overruled them" (1983, 114). The same is true of the U.S. Supreme Court.

13 The Scopes monkey trial is a case in point—see Chapter 9C on religion.

14 In Quebec, the legal profession is divided into *notaires* and *avocats*. *Notaires*, who have no precise counterparts in English Canada, draft or receive acts and contracts that need authentication, such as those for real estate transactions. *Avocats* act where the parties (including the state) dispute the relevant law or facts (*The Canadian Encyclopedia*, 1985, 1282).

[15] Donald Marshall, a Nova Scotia Indian found guilty of murder in the early 1970s, was retried in 1983. The evidence on which he had originally been convicted was found to have been false, and he was acquitted. He subsequently received monetary compensation, though this could not restore the decade he had spent in prison (see Suggested Readings: *Justice Denied*).

9E HEALTH CARE

In contemporary Canadian society, health is considered a cardinal social value. Think for example of compulsory inoculation against certain diseases, the prevention of which is seen as too important for society as a whole to be left to individual choice. Health is also seen as a vital matter for individuals. Access to **health care** is viewed as an individual right, enshrined in legislation in the wake of the Second World War, and most recently in the 1984 Canada Health Act. Here, as in other social institutions, it is an ongoing social and political challenge to ensure that legal rights are translated into practice. Meeting this challenge continues to be elusive. (Monique Begin was federal minister of health when the 1984 act was passed; her book *Medicare: Canada's Right to Health* is an interesting account of the political struggles involved.)

At the beginning of this chapter, we referred to the interdependence and interrelatedness of institutions. The health care field provides an apt illustration. It has a strong link with religion in that, historically, health care facilities, notably hospitals, had religious affiliations. In Canada, linkages with government and legal agencies are strong, since such agencies regulate the conditions under which health care is dispensed. For example, persons diagnosed as carriers of an infectious disease, such as typhoid fever, must be reported to the appropriate authorities. Staff for health care are trained in educational institutions. Such training must be flexible and adaptable since, spurred by technological advances, the division of labour in the health care sector, as in society generally, is becoming ever more complex. Specialties such as respiratory technology, intensive nursing care, or neonatology (problems of the newborn) have evolved only in the latter part of this century.

An historical perspective on the development of hospitals, and the role relationships within them, demonstrates how ways of dealing with health and illness have changed.

HOSPITALS—ORIGINS AND CHANGES

It is thought that temples were the first organizations to provide resident facilities for healing the sick. In the Greek and Roman empires, temples were erected in honour of Asclepius, the god of medicine. Patients were housed in these temples, and attended by disciples of the cult. The emblem of the cult was a snake wound around a staff; patients were licked by the sacred snakes, a practice believed to provide a cure for their illnesses. This symbol is still associated with medicine today.

St. Paul had extolled the virtues of "faith, hope and charity," and pronounced charity as the greatest of the three. When the emperor Constantine accepted Christianity and declared it to be the state religion of the Roman Empire, he put into practice his commitment to charity by instructing the Bishops to build a hospital in each cathedral city (Council of Nicea, 325 AD). Early institutions fulfilled medical as well as social functions in the care of the sick and the needy. Moreover, by emphasizing that "it is more blessed to give than to receive," these charitable endeavours provided an opportunity for the faithful to earn eternal salvation through extending financial support.

In the mediaeval period, hospitals were common throughout Europe and Britain as well as in Byzantium, the eastern part of the Roman empire. During the Crusades, groups of knights, particularly the Knights of St. John (an order still familiar to us by the red cross emblem and St. John's Ambulance first aid courses),[1] founded hospitals all along the routes of the Crusaders. Rosen describes the proliferation of hospitals in Europe:

> *By the end of the fifteenth century . . . Europe was covered with a network of hospitals. For example, in England alone, by the middle of the fourteenth century, there were more than six hundred institutions of this kind, ranging in size from numerous small foundations caring for a dozen or so persons to the great establishments like St. Peter's and St. Leonard's of York. Developments on the Continent were similar. According to the chronicler Giovanni Villani, Florence in 1300, with a population of some ninety thousand inhabitants, had thirty hospital and welfare establishments capable of providing medical aid and shelter to more than a thousand sick and needy people. They were staffed by more than three hundred monks and other nursing personnel. . . . Paris at the beginning of the fourteenth century is reported to have had about forty hospitals and as many leper houses (1963, 9).*

Hospitals gradually passed from religious to secular control, though they continued to be staffed by religious orders. In Britain, consolidation of the nation state resulted in the control, by civil authorities, of several sectors which had previously fallen under religious jurisdiction. Also, there was continuing concern that the funds donated to hospitals were being diverted to other purposes (such as the creation of religious benefices). As the number of the poor, and poverty-related problems, increased with the Enclosure Acts and the migration of landless peasants to the burgeoning towns, private charity alone became incapable of meeting the demand for services. The Reformation ushered in more punitive attitudes toward poverty and the poor — giving them succour was no longer seen as the surest way to salvation in the hereafter.[2]

In the late 19th century, aided by the discoveries of Lister and Pasteur, hospitals began to adopt antiseptic and aseptic methods. These innovations all but banished the dreaded "hospitalism" (the danger of exposure to infections that might be more deadly than one's original illness), and transformed the hospital from a place dedicated to the sick poor to one utilized by all classes of society (Bloom 1965, 150–1).

Florence Nightingale's efforts to upgrade nursing from an unskilled occupation frequently practised by women of "doubtful virtue" to a profession[3] staffed by trained personnel, were being put into practice in North America. At least in Canada, this transition did not proceed smoothly; training programs were not supervised, and their quality varied. In many cases, nursing trainees became unpaid workers rather than students. Coburn notes:

> *Student nurses were completely at the mercy of the expedience of hospitals whose operations went unchallenged by provincial authorities. Since no accreditation procedure was necessary, there was no limit on the size of a hospital or the quality of its program. Very small hospitals (under twenty-five beds) advertised for students without regard to their educational background; consequently, many students had not finished public school before they began their training. Furthermore, these small hospitals generally had no qualified nursing instructors. Two or three years of sporadic lectures from doctors, who often made no attempt to adjust their medical terminology, was accepted as nursing education. At the end of this time, the graduates left their cloistered existence with nervous exhaustion, a nursing certificate and no job (1987, 449).*

The requirements for becoming a physician also changed. Historically, physicians were trained through apprenticeships. This gradually shifted as a system of formal education was introduced. In the United States, a large number of privately-owned medical schools sprang up, many of which could grant degrees even though they had no connection with a university. The result was that those entitled to call themselves physicians varied significantly in their knowledge and expertise.

Proprietary medical schools could not grant degrees in Canada. "Though university affiliations were easily come by, the number of proprietary schools was automatically limited by the number of universities" (Kett 1981, 199). Thus, in Canada, medical education may have been of a higher calibre, but it was less accessible than in the United States.

HEALTH CARE IN CONTEMPORARY SOCIETY

It took a long time for the hospital to evolve from a (usually) last stop for the indigent sick to an institution from which patients from all walks of life can expect to leave healthy, or at least healthier. Breakthroughs in science and technology during the last 150 years played a major role in increasing utilization of hospitals, both on an in-patient and out-patient basis. Sophisticated diagnostic and treatment equipment are unaffordable by solo practitioners — think of dialysis machines or hyperbaric chambers — and hospitals are the only places where such equipment can be made available to those who need it. Torrance notes:

> *After the war [WW II], the Canadian hospital industry was transformed. The pent-up demand for new facilities and technology exploded. Doctors and patients began to use hospitals as never before. In the eight years following the war, total expenditures in Ontario grew by 250 percent, wages and salaries by 300 percent (Torrance 1987, 482).*

In this chapter, our discussion must be confined to general hospitals. We would, however, refer interested students to the extensive literature on mental hospitals.[4] In the last few years there has also been a growing movement toward specialized care of the terminally ill.[5] One reason for the development of hospices and similar facilities has been the realization that hospitals, committed to the conventional medical goals of curing and healing, are not well-suited to provide proper physical and emotional care to dying patients.

As suggested above, there are different types of health care institutions. Within each type of institution, there is a high degree of specialization in terms of the functions performed. A large teaching hospital such as Vancouver General Hospital would have out-patient, emergency, and intensive care facilities as well as a range of medical and surgical services: internal medicine, pediatrics, neurosurgery, obstetrics, cardiology, to name just a few.

The tasks performed on the wards, in operating theatres, and in emergency departments are made possible by a broad support structure. A range of laboratory and X-ray facilities provides diagnostic support. Occupational and physical therapy programs assist in getting patients back on their feet. Food for patients on restricted diet regimens must be prepared; patients' social and religious needs are attended to by social workers, psychologists, and clerics. The premises must be kept clean, adequately heated, and ventilated, and security has to be maintained.

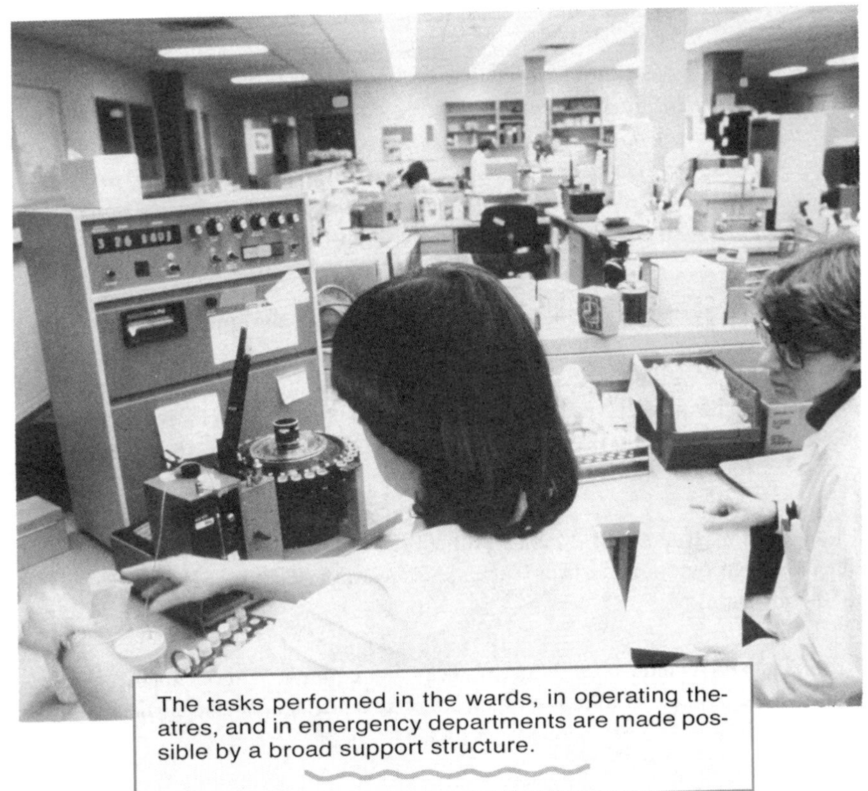

The tasks performed in the wards, in operating theatres, and in emergency departments are made possible by a broad support structure.

The hospital is a microcosm of society, reflecting and reinforcing its vertical divisions through task specialization, and its horizontal differentiation by way of internal stratification. Torrance describes the hospital hierarchy as follows:

> *Sociologically, there are three main "castes" of hospital workers with virtually impenetrable status and mobility barriers between them. The top caste is composed of doctors who are "in but not of" the hospital and a few high-ranking administrators; the second caste includes semi-professionals and technicians, such as nurses, dietitians, physiotherapists and lab personnel; and the third is formed of non-professional service workers who form the invisible underside of the industry. Although this last group makes up from one-third to one-half of the hospital labour force, little is known about them (1987, 491).*

For many years the concentrated power of the medical profession encountered few challenges either from within the hospital or from society at large. Freidson argued that this power inhered in the relationship between the medical profession and the state:

> *The foundation on which the analysis of a profession must be based is its relationship to the ultimate source of power and authority in modern society—the state. In the case of medicine, much, though by no means all, of the profession's strength is based on legally supported monopoly over practice. This monopoly operates through a system of licensing that bears on the privilege to hospitalize patients and the right to prescribe drugs and order laboratory procedures that are otherwise virtually inaccessible. It is the state that grants this monopoly, the exact form of which varies widely throughout the world (1970, 83).*

Recently, however, other health professionals, such as chiropractors, nurses, and midwives, have staked a claim to greater autonomy (see, for example, *Chiropractors: Do They Help?* which describes the long and bitter struggle to break through the barriers the medical profession had erected to prevent chiropractors from practising independently [Kelner, Douglass and Oswald 1986].) No longer content to "watch silently," nurses are seeking more input into hospital decision-making.

It is interesting to note differences in the 1950 and 1976 Codes for Professional Nurses set out by the American Nurses' Association (Rothman 1987, 73–4). The 1950 code states:

> (6) A nurse recommends or gives medical treatment without medical orders only in emergencies and reports such action to a physician at the earliest possible moment.
>
> (7) The nurse is obligated to carry out the physician's orders intelligently, to avoid misunderstanding or inaccuracies by verifying orders and to refuse to participate in unethical procedures.

No mention is made of physicians or of the relationship between nurses and physicians in the 1976 code. With respect to the nurse's mandate, the code states:

> (6) The nurse exercises informed judgment and uses individual competence and qualifications as criteria in seeking consultation, accepting responsibilities, and delegating nursing activities to others.

The official code does not determine what nurses actually *do*, but sets out their Association's view of what they *ought to do*. Clearly, the nursing profession is attempting to strengthen its autonomy.

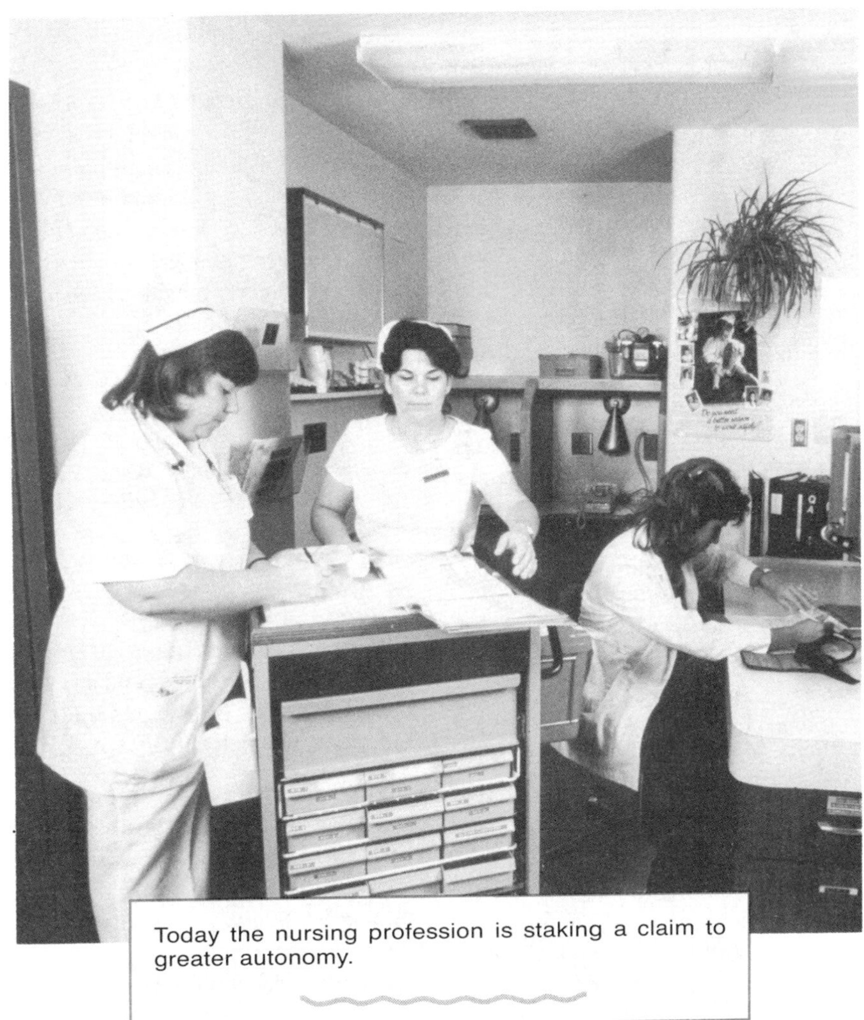

Today the nursing profession is staking a claim to greater autonomy.

OVERWORKED NURSES SAY ''ENOUGH IS ENOUGH''

By Christie McLaren

It is 4 a.m. in a big-city hospital. In one room a patient's intravenous line is running dry; the man in 2B is overdue for a shot of painkiller; the woman in 3A needs to go to the bathroom; someone down the hall is confused and crying out.

There is only one nurse on this ward. What does she do first?

This dilemma is no fantasy; it happens every day in Canadian hospitals. And nurses say they have had enough.

This summer, rank-and-file nurses battling for better contracts in British Columbia and Quebec are rebelling even against their union leaders. Although the unrest is not new — previous strikes prove that nurses have been unhappy for more than a decade — it is deepening. Why?

The health-care system is gobbling up money at an alarming rate, yet nurses say they are undervalued and underpaid; required to work under poor and even dangerous conditions; frightened by deteriorating patient care; patronized by doctors; responsible if anything goes wrong; and, above all, powerless to change the system. Many nurses are at the end of their rope.

"We're not prepared to carry the system on our backs any more," said Pat Savage, president of the 20,000-member B.C. Nurses' Union.

Despite major advances in medical care, drugs and technology that keep people alive longer, nursing leaders across Canada say patients are getting less personal attention and suffering more than they did 25 years ago.

"They go home thinking: 'I've done what I could, but it wasn't enough,' " said Dr. Judith Ritchie, president of the Canadian Nursing Association (whose doctorate is in nursing). "I think that's what's made them so militant—they're scared. We are in a job that's high-risk for error."

There are actually more nurses per patient than there were a generation ago. But they are able to give patients less tender loving attention, because as the population ages and medical science advances, the people occupying hospital beds are sicker and require much more complex care — involving more drugs, more technology and more paperwork—than in the past.

Overworked nurses worry that they will make a mistake that could end their career. "None of us like doing half-assed jobs," said Judy Watts, executive director of the Registered Nurses Association of Ontario.

Kathleen Connors, president of the National Federation of Nurses' Unions, said in Halifax that nurses risk their health working in dangerous conditions, yet their complaints go unheeded by employers.

Waste-anesthetic gases in operating rooms and recovery rooms have been linked to higher rates of miscarriage and birth defects. In many hospitals, nurses must mix anti-cancer drugs without proper equipment to protect them from dangerous dust. In every province, Ms Connors says, nurses exposed to AIDS and infectious hepatitis have to fight for hospitals to buy good-quality latex gloves instead of cheap, less effective brands.

And hospital associations concede that a high rate of back injuries among nurses — 45 per cent of the total in Ontario — is a serious unresolved problem.

Altogether, nursing "has become more difficult at a time when women are less and less willing to accept difficult situations,'' Ms Watts said.

In the face of these frustrations, a general duty nurse rarely makes more than $36,000 a year, noted Jenniece Larsen, director of the school of nursing at the University of Manitoba.

''The tragedy is if you work at Safeway, you can make more money.''

However, the deep discontent among Canada's 210,000 nurses has less to do with pay than with frustration over one of the major dilemmas facing governments: how to manage a $47.8-billion health-care system whose costs are spiralling out of sight.

While doctors are pushing hard for Ottawa and the provinces to put more money into the latest equipment, procedures, and medicines to treat the ill in acute-care institutions, nurses argue just as strongly that governments could save money by treating more chronically ill people in community clinics and in their homes, and by emphasizing health promotion and the prevention of disease.

They say they have watched governments and hospitals bow to demands from doctors and the public for high-tech wizardry and surgery without evaluating its cost-effectiveness, while reducing nurses, physiotherapists and other staff.

Dr. John O'Brien-Bell, president of the Canadian Medical Association, acknowledged that doctors and nurses have different approaches: ''The whole system is in turmoil, and in the centre of all this are the nurses and the doctors, and their interests and our interests tend to be competitive at times.''

He said doctors have also advocated more health promotion, but it will only postpone the spending of money. Meanwhile, it is the duty of doctors to lobby for the latest medical care (partly because they are increasingly subject to lawsuits if they do not provide the most advanced treatment), and it is up to governments to decide what society needs.

Nearly 20 studies about nurses' unhappiness in the past three years have called for the same solutions: control the use of medical services; examine how the health-care dollar could be better spent; pay nurses more, give them more decision-making power, and allow them to pursue higher education and be rewarded for it.

''The question is, who's really listening?'' Ms Connors asked. ''I think the fact that the issues haven't been addressed indicates . . . the words have been falling on deaf ears.''

In the end, nurses say, they lack influence because they are women.

''The issue is one of power,'' Ms Connors said. ''And we know who has the power in health care—the doctors and governments.'' Nurses ''in many, many cases are still seen as the physician's handmaiden — the subservient, silent Florence Nightingale.''

Nurses still feel obliged to bite their tongue when doctors ignore their training or knowledge of individual patients, leaders say, although that is slowly starting to change.

Doctors continue to exert greater influence than nurses over hospital spending, as evidenced by the way they have been included in the decision-making structure.

Most hospital boards of directors have a permanent advisory committee of doctors, as well as physicians on other key committees and sometimes on the board itself. By contrast, few if any hospitals have nursing advisory committees, nor do they have nurses on other committees or the board.

In fairness, provincial governments are searching valiantly for ways to contain high medical costs, and many are beginning to recognize that nurses should play a bigger role. Nova Scotia's Royal Commission on Health Care is examining nurses' concerns. In December the Alberta government ordered provincial hospitals to appoint nurses to their boards, and the Alberta Hospital Association is considering the establishment of nursing advisory committees in each hospital. In Ontario, new government regulations will oblige hospitals to put nurses on key budget advisory committees by Sept. 30.

Although these changes are too late for hundreds of disillusioned nurses who have already quit the profession, in the past there have always been more to take their place. But last year, for the first time, Statistics Canada recorded a drop in the number of nurses employed in the field—210,506 versus 210,773 in 1987. Although Quebec gained 1,000 nurses, Ontario lost 3,600.

If the trend continues, nursing leaders such as Dr. Ritchie predict "a very dismal future" for the profession and for hospitals, which will be forced to close more beds. Nurses who stay face a rocky period as they fight to win more money and recognition and to sell their vision of health care to the public, perhaps through information picket lines.

The movement "is still in its infancy," Ms Connors said. "Nurses have been called the sleeping giant of the health-care system. Everybody should know the giant is waking up."

Now that nurses have discovered they can roar, union leaders say, they will not be silenced by stiffer fines, penalties or even jail terms that governments may throw at them.

"It's not going to stop nurses . . . from speaking out," said Heather Smith of the United Nurses of Alberta, "because we're not talking just about wages and working conditions; we're talking about the health-care system and the failure to address the needs of patients in the system.

"In many ways it's becoming a crusade."

Nurses want to leave a message with governments, Dr. Ritchie said: "If the health-care system is in crisis, you fix it. We're not going to pay for it with our lives."

Today, many questions are being raised about health care. Is it appropriate for physicians to dominate the setting of priorities in health-related issues? Would the public be better served by more programs aimed at the prevention of illness (such as the ParticipAction program for the promotion of a healthy lifestyle)? Is private delivery (fee-for-service) of publicly-funded health care the most efficient arrangement? Does the monopoly that highly-trained and highly-paid physicians have on performing relatively simple tasks (such as taking a Pap smear) needlessly escalate health care costs that are already high in North America? In Canada, $16.3 billion was spent on health care in 1986–7, an increase of 7.8 percent over 1985–6 (Statistics Canada 1988). Even if this rate of growth were deemed acceptable, are there more effective ways of *delivering* health care than via large-sale organizations? These questions illustrate the axiom that different ways of defining a problem (in this case, power relations, cost, mode of delivery) invite different types of solutions. When you read items about health care in the newspaper, try to identify how the problem is defined.

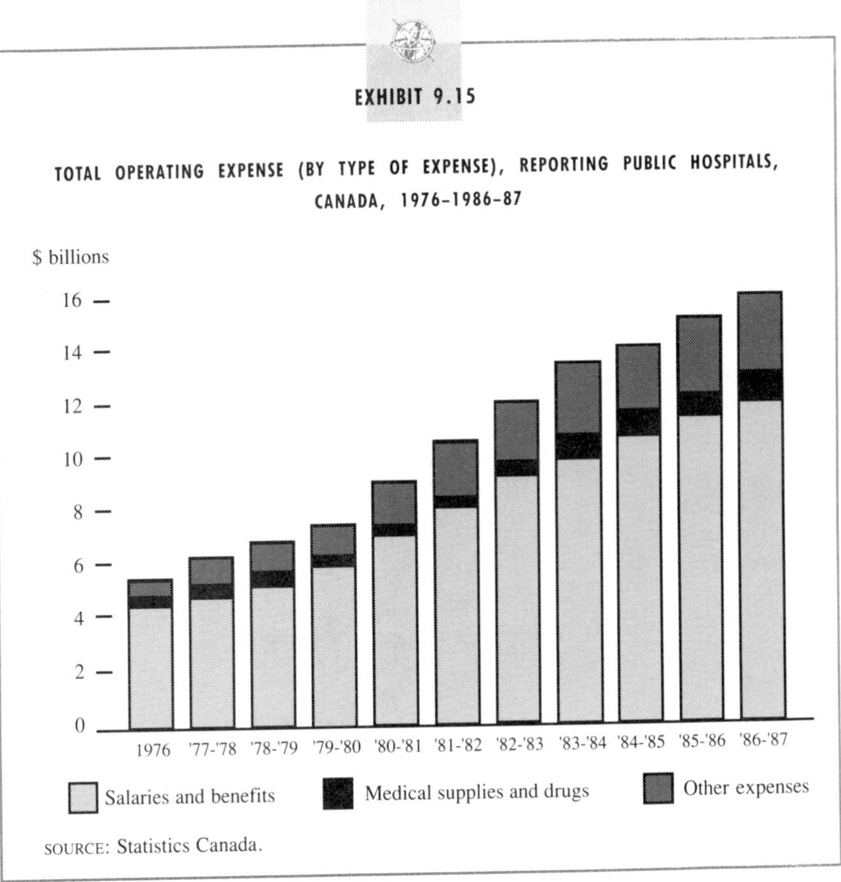

SOURCE: Statistics Canada.

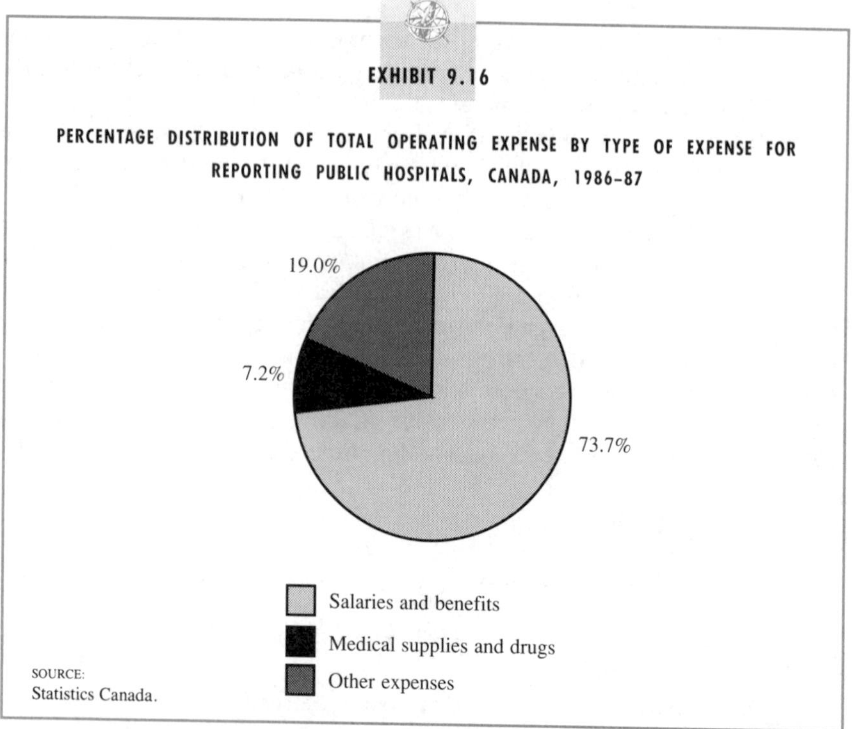

GENDER DISTRIBUTION OF HEALTH CARE PERSONNEL

Examination of the gender distribution of health care personnel demonstrates the preponderance of males among physicians, the group wielding the greatest power, but also shows that some changes are taking place.

EXHIBIT 9.17

HEALTH CARE WORKERS (NUMBERS)

	Male	Female
Paid workers in Medicine and Health	94,000	491,000
Physicians	37,745	10,175
Nurses (registered, graduate, and in training)	11,025	223,455

SOURCE: Statistics Canada 1989.

Among all workers employed in health care, women outnumber men by more than five to one, but women are concentrated in nursing, and other paramedical and service occupations. They constitute only 21.2 percent of physicians. The lower mean age of female physicians shows that significant numbers of women have entered the medical profession recently. Among women doctors, 53.1 percent are in the age category 15 to 34; for males the figure is 26.6 percent. At the other end of the age spectrum, among those 55 and over, the percentages for males are 25.7 and for women 7.9 (Statistics Canada 1989).

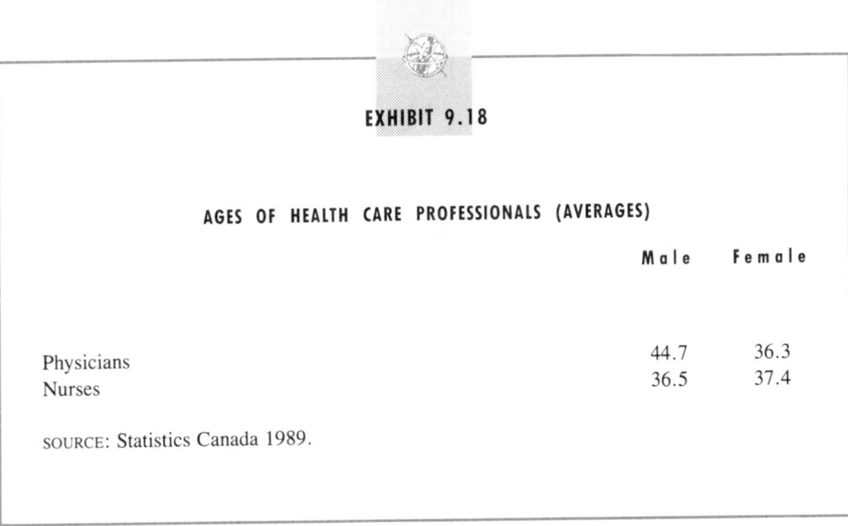

EXHIBIT 9.18

AGES OF HEALTH CARE PROFESSIONALS (AVERAGES)

	Male	Female
Physicians	44.7	36.3
Nurses	36.5	37.4

SOURCE: Statistics Canada 1989.

The increasing number of female physicians may have beneficial consequences for the health care of women. There is evidence that many women have been short-changed by having to depend on male physicians who have dismissed their health concerns as trivial.

In terms of earnings, women doctors lag far behind their male counterparts, and they are catching up very slowly. In 1980, their income was 60.2 percent of male physicians', and by 1985 it had risen to 63.1 percent. In part, the difference is related to women's fewer years of practice. Women are also sparsely represented in high-paying specialties such as surgery and pathology.

It is interesting that male nurses, who constitute less than five percent of the profession, had higher mean earnings than female nurses. However, the gap narrowed between 1980 and 1985. One reason for the slight earning differences between male and female nurses may be that males are more likely to have a baccalaureate degree.

EXHIBIT 9.19

PERSONAL INCOME OF HEALTH CARE PROFESSIONALS

		1980	1985
Physicians (full-time)	male	$85,622	$90,562
	female	51,681	57,126
Nurses	male	27,033	26,282
	female	25,816	26,111

EXHIBIT 9.19

SOURCE: Statistics Canada, Cat. 93-116.

Again, we draw students' attention to the fact that in a society in which gender stratification is present, it is likely to be found in all social institutions, albeit in varying degrees. Can you think of examples in support of this statement, and of exceptions to it?

HOW IS HEALTH CARE DISTRIBUTED?

Health care facilities — general hospitals, mental hospitals, clinics — are service organizations. Likewise, the primary responsibility of health care professionals is to provide service to their clients. To what extent is health care geared to its clientele in practice? How do women fare? Do individuals at different socioeconomic levels and members of various racial and ethnic groups have equal *access* to available services?

Given the vastness of Canada and the fact that large parts of it are sparsely populated, and therefore sparsely serviced, geographic location significantly affects access. Think of the difficulty of transporting a burn victim from the Arctic to an appropriate hospital, and compare this with the relative ease of obtaining proper treatment in Calgary or London. Another example is the variation in access to abortion. A resident of Timmins, where the local hospital is under Catholic auspices, would probably have to travel 400 kilometres south to North Bay to avail herself of this service. If the woman is poor, or has children who need care, this could represent a major undertaking.

Native peoples are especially disadvantaged in terms of access, both because they generally live in remote areas and because they are culturally ill-equipped to deal with the bureaucratic steps that are frequently involved in utilizing what services do exist. Understandably, they are often distrustful and wary about how these things work. Grescoe notes:

> *Parents of native children express this sort of distrust to the staff of the Children's Clinic in Winnipeg. ''I think it's a fairly widespread belief that we experiment on their children,'' said Dr. Ferguson of the clinic's out-patient department. ''They're totally vulnerable to the medical system. They don't have any 'ins.' If your kid has a heart murmur, you'll phone around and get the best heart man. But Indians aren't part of the health system. Their ignorance of health matters is abysmal, and it's not their fault'' (Gescoe 1987, 131).*

Since the end of World War II, Toronto has become a polyglot city in which only 68 percent of residents cited English as their mother tongue in the 1981 Census. Yet, in a study of ''Access to Health and Social Services for Members of Diverse Cultural and Racial Groups,'' Doyle and Visano found that 81 percent of service providers stated that information about services was available in English only, and 87 percent believed that the public was ill-informed about existing services (1987, 61). Eighty-two percent believed that the ways in which services are delivered are inappropriate for some cultures (1987, 71).

In examining the views of service consumers (clients), Doyle and Visano begin by commenting that:

> *There has been a striking paucity of systematic studies of the perspectives of consumers. Our literature review revealed that the most common feature of extant studies concerns the examination of consumers of small agencies. Little attention has been given to consumers within an overall range of health and social services. Although the power of consumers continues to be a matter of contemporary concern, the prevailing assumption that all consumers who come to agencies are served equally has not been subjected to extensive empirical examination (1987, 105).*

In their own study, Doyle and Visano found that consumers had scant knowledge of what services are available. What they did know was usually gleaned from family and friends, whose own information might be incomplete, inaccurate, or both. Before one can gain access to a service, one must know of its existence. Even so, 85 percent of consumers reported an ''overall favourable appraisal of agencies.'' Women were more likely to be positive than men (95 percent compared with 75 percent) and variations existed among racial and ethnic groups. Thus, 86 percent of Latin-Americans, 76 percent of Anglo-Saxons, but only 62 percent of Blacks expressed positive sentiments (1987, 156). Unfortunately, Doyle and Visano do not separate health care and social service agencies in reporting their data.

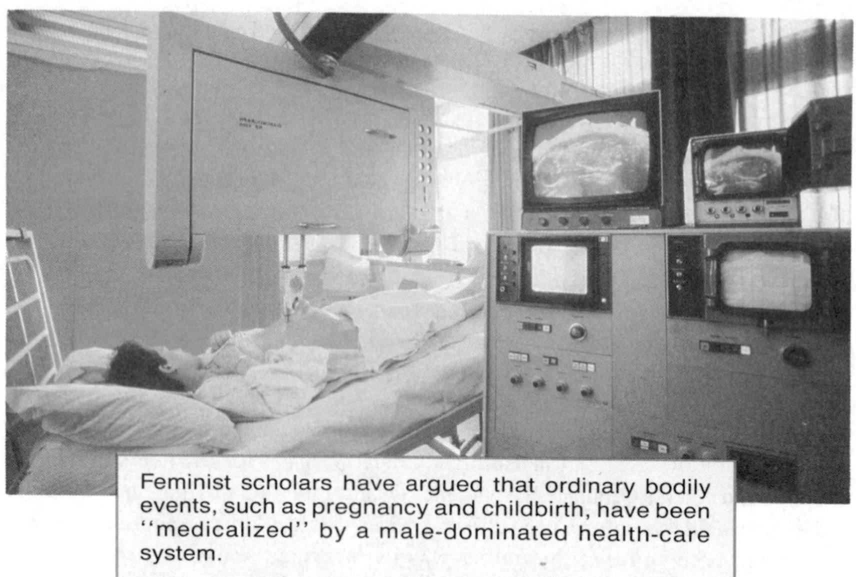

Feminist scholars have argued that ordinary bodily events, such as pregnancy and childbirth, have been "medicalized" by a male-dominated health-care system.

In what respects can health care be considered a "women's issue?" Feminist scholars have argued that definitions of illness may be viewed as patriarchal forms of social control over women, serving to restrict their participation in society. Ordinary bodily events such as menstruation, pregnancy, childbirth, and menopause have been "medicalized" by a male-dominated health-care system. Pirie (1988) calls for research on the ways in which medical labels become accepted by women themselves (see Ehrenreich and English 1989; Boston Women's Health Collective 1984; Oakley 1986). Institutions, whether education, law or health, are primarily geared to serve those who are part of mainstream society. In Canada, this society is often treated as if it were comprised of middle-class anglophones (except in Quebec). Services to meet the needs of those who do not fall into this category frequently lag far behind the demand for them.

In *Getting Doctored*, Shapiro suggests that members of minority groups are not the only ones who are not adequately served by the health care system but, rather, that this is a widespread experience:

> *Patients are alienated in their relationships to the institutions of medicine, such as hospitals, which are intimidating and confusing, and to medical services, which are rarely designed to maximize patient convenience and accessibility. That these institutions and services are not rationally arrayed according to what is socially most appropriate — the needs of consumers — can be attributed to the bureaucracies that control them, which are subject to the influence of groups seeking to advance their own particular economic or other interests (1978, 194).*

We are not suggesting that negative experiences are the norm. For every "horror story" one can cite accounts of outstanding efforts to help clients. Rather, we point to the problems inherent in the delivery of health care via large organizations in which the individual patient may fall through the cracks. Furthermore, control over what services are available, and the ways in which they are offered, rests with the service providers. Freidson comments:

> *In health above all, but also in law, education, welfare, and to a degree religion, the market is restricted to that which is licensed, certified, accredited, or otherwise officially approved, and control over the definition of services is held by those who control the* production *of services rather than those who consume them (1970, 169).*

We have pointed to imperfections in access to health care, and in the quality of service. However, these shortcomings are relative to what are considered desirable standards in Canada. On a global comparative basis, Canada's health care would rank among the best. Nevertheless, the politics of health care continue to provoke controversy.

IS MEDICARE UNAFFORDABLE OR UNDERFUNDED?

By Desmond Morton

As governments on both sides of the border get set to tackle their respective deficits, mounting medicare costs will be common targets. Business leaders, eager to set a cost-cutting agenda, are already telling Canadians that our universal health insurance scheme is beyond our means. Since the elderly are major users of health care, Canada's rapidly aging population will either send our medicare costs soaring or will force governments to cut our existing services to tatters.

Certainly medicare costs have escalated far beyond the expectation of Justice Emmett Hall and his 1961 Royal Commission on Health Services. Wealthy Ontario now devotes a third of its spending on health services, more than double the share in 1970. Most provinces have a similar experience. Politicians and taxpayers alike have good reason to get the most out of the health-care dollar.

The United States currently spends between 10 and 11 per cent of its gross national product (GNP) on a health system few Canadians envy. That is twice the 1960 share. Until medicare took effect around 1970, Canadians had always spent more of their GNP on health; since then, the proportion has stayed between 7 and 8 per cent.

The reason is simple. Whether or not universality makes sense for old age pensions or family allowances, it is a great basis for an insurance system. A tax-supported system gives governments strong incentives to control costs while health-care providers, especially since the National Health Act of 1984, have no alternative way of getting paid.

If an aging population and high-tech medicine really mean higher costs, Canadians should rejoice that they already have in place a far more cost-effective system than their American neighbours.

Nor does it necessarily follow that medical research and an aging population have to lead to soaring health costs. ''Salvage surgery'' — organ transplants and the like—are expensive but costs are coming down with increasing experience. Medical research can also save billions. The aged will add more to the health-care bill — about 1.5 to 2 per cent a year when the baby boomers of the '50s turn gray in the next century. The elderly need nursing and home care but they use less dentistry!

What medicare's enemies are really saying is not that costs are out of control; the real complaint from the provinces is that governments are too tight-fisted. In their own interests, argues University of British Columbia economist Robert Evans, the providers are right.

U.S. doctors, laboratories and pharmaceutical companies earn much more than their Canadian counterparts and hospital corporations have become a rich growth stock. If Ottawa and the provincial governments are holding down health care spending, the pressure is on to create holes in the system so extra-billing, private alternative insurance and user fees can siphon post-tax income into the health industry.

Yet, as Evans argues, Canadians stand to gain nothing from breaches in our system of universal medicare. If Canadians really want more of their GNP spent on health care, they will get far better value for money by tickling government's political antennae. The American alternative should be visible enough as a warning.

Even by so-called market tests, the case for higher health spending is not very good. Physicians have borne most of the brunt of health cost control, with income rising about 3 per cent per year under the U.S. trend. Their bitterness is understandable and audible but it has not kept medical schools from being the target for many of Canada's brightest students. Doctors' incomes demand respect but we should distinguish between claims that our health system is collapsing and the usual heated rhetoric of collective bargaining.

Indeed, the growing number of Canadian doctors — ''guests at the health-care feast''—is one of the real sources of medicare cost escalation. While doctors' incomes have been restrained, their growing numbers absorb a rising share of medicare expenditure, together with pressure to enhance the acute-care hospitals where they do their most remunerative work. One result is that the less glamorous services really needed by an aging population, from home help to nursing homes, have often been neglected or underfunded. The proper supply and remuneration of medical ''person power'' is one of the tough issues Canadians will have to address.

Another, Evans argues, is just what medicare should cover for an aging population. The Hall Commission was clear enough that universal insurance would only pay for ''medically necessary'' services. Cosmetic surgery has rarely qualified. But what should? Who decides what is ''medically necessary?'' As professionals, physicians insist that they are the only qualified judges. Does a fee-for-service payment system ever affect their judgment? Are all procedures necessary or even beneficial? If expert opinion regards a service as useless or even harmful, but the doctor and patient want it, who should be the arbiter? Most likely it will be newspaper editors, looking for a human interest story that puts ''authority'' in a bad light.

These are issues Evans thinks Canadians should be debating as the age-bulge of the year 2000 approaches. We should also be considering the proper limits for health care. Medicare finances health, not happiness, but for the lonely, ailing old person, is there always a distinction? While we wrestle with this problem, active treatment beds are occupied by elderly invalids and others, less fortunate, die in solitary squalor.

With these problems to address it would be mischievous folly for Canadians to waste time on issues we resolved a generation ago, just because our U.S. neighbours failed to do so. To quote Evans: ''What distinguishes the Canadian situation . . . is that our solution to the earlier problem, of funding and delivering health care, narrowly defined, has been one of the more successful in the world in reconciling and striking compromises among equity, access, quality and affordability.''

Instead, we have 10 years to become leaders in funding and delivering the best possible health system for elderly Canadians. The issues are tough but solvable.

SOME CURRENT DILEMMAS

Monitoring professionals whose work is technical and not easily evaluated by the layman-client has always been problematic. In theory, the practitioner is regulated by standards internalized in the course of professional socialization. What happens if the standards are poorly internalized and violated in the course of practice? Moreover, there are variations in standards among professional schools.

In private practice, the physician and patient interact on a one-to-one basis. The weight of expertise lies with the doctor. The dependency of patients has increased with the availability of new medical techniques. Who is to specify the qualifications needed to employ them? In the summer of 1989, a woman died of complications following liposuction (a procedure by which fat is literally sucked out from under the skin). In the ensuing enquiry, it was revealed that procedures not paid for by OHIP (Ontario Health Insurance Plan) can be carried out at any location deemed acceptable by a medical practitioner, who need not be a specialist. The Ministry of Health is now collaborating with the Ontario Medical Association to tighten control over qualifications.

AIDS has created multiple dilemmas. How do health care institutions deal with AIDS, and what are the responsibilities of other institutions, such as education? In what ways can people living with AIDS (or PWAS) be treated so as to preserve their privacy and dignity while at the same time ensuring adequate measures are taken to check the spread of the disease? (For recent studies on AIDS in Canada, see Harkness 1989; Ornstein 1989.)

As a member of the Special Advisory Committee on AIDS, appointed by the Ontario government, Dr. Fanning wrote in her 1983 report:

> *Health planners today are frequently confronted with issues such as diminishing resources in the face of increasing needs, shifts in disease patterns in the community requiring reallocation of health care resources or periodic short-lived epidemics with an identifiable control measure. However, the problem of emergence of a new disease which is lethal, utilizes tremendous health care resources and is spreading in uncontrolled epidemic proportions with no known treatment or cure is seldom faced today (quoted in O'Malley 1986, 129).*

"I enjoy sex,
but I'm not ready
to die for it."

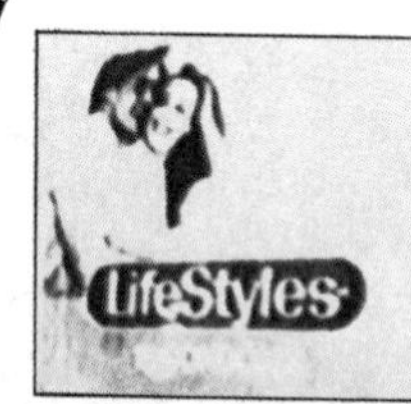

In North America and Europe by 1990, the majority of people with AIDS were homosexuals and drug addicts (and their mates and newborns); some activists believe AIDS research would receive more money if this majority were heterosexual.

CONFERENCE CONDEMNS TRADING IN ORGANS

By Paul Taylor

An international conference of doctors and public health officials yesterday condemned the buying and selling of human organs for transplants carried out in underdeveloped countries.

George Abouna, a surgeon from Kuwait, told the conference that citizens of his country travel to India to buy a kidney for $20,000 and only 5 to 10 per cent of the money is given to the donor.

He also told the conference that payment programs seriously undermine the development of voluntary programs.

Others expressed fears that the buying and selling of organs could spread to industrialized nations if the acute shortage of donors persists.

For a wide variety of reasons, organ supply has not kept pace with demand. In Canada, for instance, each year about 3,000 people die whose vital organs would be suitable for transplants.

These potential donors would be more than enough to meet transplant needs. For example, they would provide 6,000 kidneys, immediately wiping out the backlog of 4,000 Canadians waiting for transplants.

Yet only about 20 per cent of the 3,000 end up becoming organ donors.

''And in the past two years, there has been no increase in the donation rate in Canada,'' said Calvin Stiller, a chairman of the transplant unit at University Hospital in London, Ont.

He noted that these low donor rates fly in the face of public opinion polls that indicate most people are in favor of transplants.

He said the latest poll, in 1986, showed that 88 per cent of Canadians would donate the organs of a deceased relative if they were asked by hospital employees to do so. And 63 per cent replied they would be willing to donate their own organs when they die.

Dr. Stiller, one of the organizers of the conference, said he believes the medical profession is partly at fault for the shortage of donors. Hospital workers and doctors, he said, simply do not bother to ask families for the organs of potential donors.

''It's considered more of a burden than a responsibility'' to ask bereaving family members for permission for the vital organs.''

William Brady, a board member at London's University Hospital, agreed that ''people are not given an opportunity to donate.''

Dr. Stiller said doctors will have only themselves to blame if the shortage persists.

''If we don't solve it as a medical crisis, it will become a social crisis and people will take actions which are undesirable.''

Questions surrounding the rights of mother and fetus have highlighted the interconnectedness of law, religion, and health care. Whether deliberate termination of pregnancy is seen as a medical procedure or as murder is pitting pro-choice and pro-life groups in a bitter fight both in Canada and in the United States. In the United States, the 1989 Supreme Court Decision in Webster vs. Medical Services has made access to abortion much more difficult, a curtailment that will disproportionately affect poor women.

There is no consensus on the right to be born, nor on the right to die. Are medical personnel obliged to take "heroic" measures (for example, maintaining a terminally ill patient on life-support systems) even if the patient and the next-of-kin oppose this? Should the mandate to preserve life take into account the *quality* of life to be preserved, such as for those in long-term comas?

Technology is a pivotal factor in many of these dilemmas. In the abortion controversy, technology can be used to buttress either argument. On the one hand, the fetus is now viable at a much earlier stage of gestation; on the other hand, a pregnancy can be terminated relatively safely even during the second trimester. Eichler (1989) raises a number of intriguing questions about the social consequences of new reproductive technologies. For example:

> *What are the long-term consequences of having undergone intensive treatment for infertility unsuccessfully?*
>
> *What has been the effect of preconception contracts for the production of children (so-called surrogate arrangements) on siblings, birth mothers, husbands of birth mothers, fathers and wives of fathers? Grandparents of all involved parties?*

Is our society facing situations similar to those reported in *Brave New World*?

Health care is confronted with a host of dilemmas, many of which have wide ramifications. We have touched on just some of these. They are dilemmas precisely because there are no clear-cut answers, and in some cases no answers at all.

From "Doonesbury" by G.B. Trudeau.

SUMMARY

In this chapter, we have traced the evolution of hospitals from religious to largely secular institutions. Discoveries in epidemiology and in aseptic treatment methods transformed hospitals from repositories for the dying poor to healing institutions used by all classes of society.

The trend toward specialization in society is reflected in, and reinforces, the complex structure of health care organizations. There are distinct types of hospitals, among which general hospitals exhibit the greatest internal differentiation in terms of functions performed and personnel employed.

The training of physicians and nurses has become increasingly scientific and demanding, a far cry from the apprenticeships of physicians and the lack of any formal training for nurses in the days before Florence Nightingale. New specialties in health care are constantly emerging, such as respiratory technologists or laboratory technicians focused on one or two sub-specialties. The dominance physicians have exercised in the hospitals and in health care decisions generally is being challenged by other workers in the field, notably by nurses, and also by the public — the health care consumers.

The health care sector has absorbed more and more public money, a state of affairs that is setting alarms ringing both in Canada and in the United States. Though the Canadian health care system is one of the best in the world, there is inequity of access, and the nature and delivery of services are not well suited to the needs of certain groups, such as native peoples and non-English speaking immigrants.

The health care sector is faced with serious dilemmas, such as control over the quality of services, especially those delivered by solo practitioners removed from peer scrutiny. AIDS has been compared to the plague that infiltrated Europe during the Middle Ages — and no major breakthrough has been made in the fight against the disease. Not just the health care sector, but the larger society is beset by the medical-legal-moral ramifications of abortion and of prolonging the lives of the terminally ill. In part, these dilemmas have been sharpened by advancements in technology that present previously non-existent options.

ASSIGNMENTS

Do one or more of the following assignments, as instructed by your professor.

1 We have listed a few of the dilemmas facing health care today. Add at least three others. State in what ways they constitute dilemmas, and why you consider them significant.

2 Interview a physician or a nurse who has been in practice for at least twenty years. Ask your respondent to describe, in as much detail as possible, in what ways his or her work

has changed during that period. Pose specific questions to elicit your respondent's view of the role played by technology in these changes.

3 In this chapter, we have discussed ways in which the official goal of equal access to health care is not being met. Think of the ways in which the risks to health are also unequally distributed among certain occupational groups.

SUGGESTED READINGS

Peter Conrad and **Rochelle Kern** (eds.), *The Sociology of Health and Illness: Critical Perspectives* (New York: St. Martin's Press, 3rd ed., 1989). The 42 articles in this textbook cover a wide range of health-care issues, and will introduce you to a variety of perspectives on the relationships between social structures and illness. Why do some behaviours (for example, alcoholism or premenstrual syndrome) acquire the status of "disease" while others do not? What group interests are involved in the labelling process? How does it happen that individuals come to accept these labels? The book is likely to challenge your thinking about the social and cultural meanings of illness.

H. Green, *I Never Promised You a Rose Garden* (New York: Holt, Rinehart and Winston, 1964). What does it feel like to be a talented teenager who finds life so terrifying that it becomes imperative to create one's own world, one peopled by fantasy characters with whom it is safe to communicate?

I Never Promised You a Rose Garden describes Debbie Blau's relationship with an exceptionally sensitive therapist, and her slow, painful victory over schizophrenia. Even in the relatively benign setting of the private mental hospital, individuals become depersonalized into "problems." When the patients fantasize with one another about creating the "perfect" hospital, one requirement remains constant — each physician, nurse, and ward attendant must spend a week as an inmate.

B.A. Mason, *Spence and Lila* (New York: Harper and Row, 1988). Married for over forty years, with children and grandchildren, Spence and Lila must cope with Lila's hospitalization for a series of life-threatening medical problems.

The state-of-the-art technology, the doctors' explanations couched in incomprehensible jargon, and the continuing invasion of hospital routines and procedures are totally bewildering for the Culpeppers. They are sustained by their children's love, and by Lila's determination to return to her garden, her canning and pickling.

The book moves skillfully between two universes: the warmth of a close-knit family and the impersonality of a large institution. It also raises the question of what happens to those who must deal with old age and sickness without a cushion of support.

M. O'Malley, *Doctors* (Toronto: Macmillan of Canada, 1983). Physicians play a central part in the drama of life and death, and this role has endowed them with a mystique attached to few other occupations.

O'Malley assembles a pastiche of Canadian doctors, focusing on their personalities, their specialties, and their ways of interacting with patients. The book is intended for popular consumption and makes interesting reading. It also illustrates the diverse activities carried out by individuals fitting into the general occupational classification of "physician."

NOTES

1 The Hospitallers were founded as a religious order in the 11th century. Their first hospital was built in Jerusalem to take care of sick pilgrims. During the Crusades, the Hospitallers performed valuable medical services for the wounded. Grateful patients frequently bequeathed parts of their estates to the Order. Having access to both funds and personnel, the Hospitallers became powerful, dedicated to healing the sick and fighting the Muslims. Charles V bestowed Malta on them, a territory they successfully defended against repeated attacks from the Ottoman Empire. The Knights ruled Malta until 1798, when Napoleon wrested it from them during his victorious Peninsula campaign.

2 The Elizabethan Poor Law (1601) was administered through parish overseers and provided relief for the aged, the sick, and the infant poor. The able-bodied had to earn their keep in workhouses—a fate universally dreaded because of the conditions in these establishments. Workhouses persisted until well into the 19th century, and are vividly depicted in several of Dickens' novels.

3 Strictly speaking, nursing is not a full-fledged profession because it lacks some of the attributes of professions, notably self-regulation and autonomy in task performance. Generally, nurses receive instructions from physicians. However, nurses are vigorously pursuing attainment of full professional status; educational requirements have been raised, and nurses' associations are lobbying for greater autonomy.

4 See, for example: Eaton 1986, *The Sociology of Mental Disorders*; Morrissey, Goldman and Klerman 1980, *The Enduring Asylum*; Shortt 1986, *Victorian Lunacy*; Stanton and Schwartz 1954, *The Potentials*.

5 See, for example: Manning 1984, *The Hospice Alternative: Living with Dying*; Munley 1983, *The Hospice Alternative*.

10

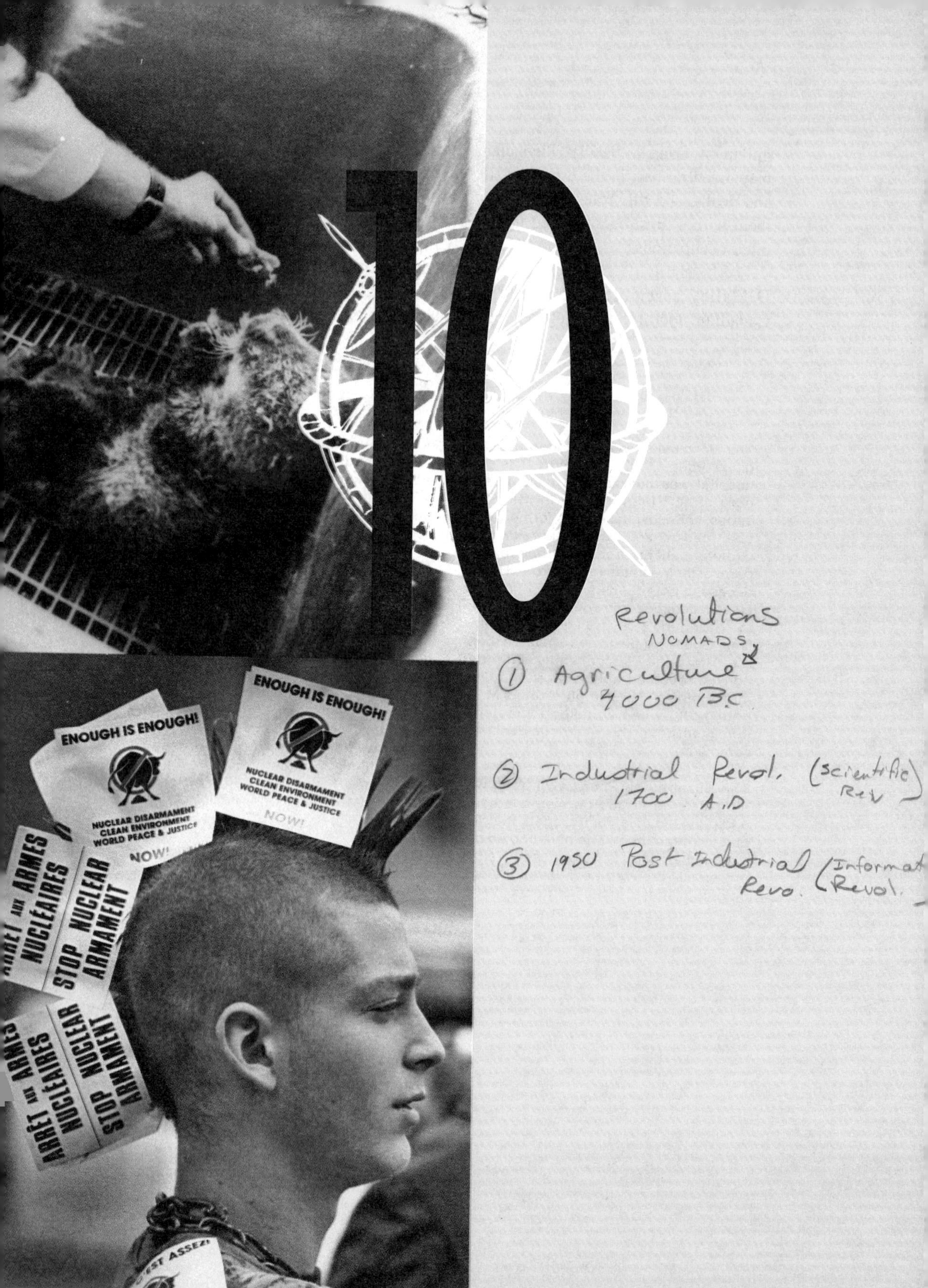

Revolutions
NOMADS
① Agriculture 4000 B.C.
② Industrial Revol. (scientific Rev)
1700 A.D
③ 1950 Post Industrial Revo. (Informat Revol.

SOCIAL CHANGE

Come gather 'round people
Wherever you roam
And admit that the waters
Around you have grown
And accept it that soon
You'll be drenched to the bone,
If your time to you is worth savin'
Then you better start swimmin'
Or you'll sink like a stone,
For the times they are a-changin'.
The line it is drawn
The curse it is cast
The slow one now will
Later be fast.
As the present now
Will later be past
The order is rapidly fadin'
And the first one now
Will later be last
For the times they are a-changin'.

Bob Dylan

HERACLITUS: "You do not step into the same river twice."

PARMENIDES: "Whatever is, is eternal and unchanged."

Both continuity and change are fundamental, "normal" features of human society, and the study of social life must seek to account for both phenomena. The historical record reveals much stability and consistency in the way human beings have arranged their lives, and it also reveals many discontinuities and drastic alterations.

This chapter focuses on social change. Our examination of the phenomenon is not, however, confined to this portion of the book. The dynamic perspective we have sought to adopt in the other chapters has drawn attention to the ways in which cultures, societies, stratification systems, belief systems, institutions, and so on have undergone transformation—sometimes suddenly because of crisis and sometimes over a long period of time.

Although change is the hallmark of today's world, it is not new. It is unlikely that preliterate peoples lived fixed, placid lives, free from dislocation and upheaval. Certainly, a flood of changes in the social order has come tumbling through the centuries since that time. What is peculiar to the 20th century and particularly to the past few decades is the scale, the diversity, and the dizzying pace of change (see Exhibit 10.1). Furthermore, to a greater extent than ever before, change has become institutionalized, with many societal resources devoted to forecasting behaviour, predicting outcomes, and developing policies for *planned* change.

Consider the span of your life to date. If you were born in the western world, you have probably experienced a rather stable existence. And yet your world has been radically transformed in a variety of ways. Evoking the "horse and buggy" days is not the prerogative only of old people. You have "horse and buggy" days, too. Take the year 1967, when Canada celebrated her one hundredth birthday.

In the Canada of 1967 there were no hand calculators, no digital watches, no videos, cassettes, Walkmans, push-button phones, or cable TV. Gas was cheap, since the cartel of the Organization of Petroleum Exporting Countries had not yet been established, and Japanese cars were rare. There was no Diet Pepsi, no McDonald's, no frozen pizzas nor microwave ovens to heat them in. A single mother rarely considered keeping her baby; there was little overt homosexuality and definitely no gay militancy; and AIDS had not emerged as a much-publicized and ominous threat to health. The bilingualism bandwagon was barely under way, and federal funding of postsecondary education had begun, only that year, to accommodate the baby-boom entrants. There was national hospital insurance but no universal medicare. The term PCBS was not in the lay vocabulary, and there was no widespread concern about depleting precious natural resources or destroying the physical environment. Major league baseball had not yet arrived in Canada, and the electrifying moment of the first "giant step for mankind" on the moon had not yet occurred. The technologies of transportation and communication had begun to knit the nations of the earth, economically and politically, into a more perilous and disorderly state of interdependence than ever before. The world was already living under the shadow of potential annihilation, but the nuclear arsenals had not yet reached their present terrifying size and sophistication.

EXHIBIT 10.1

THE INCREASING SPEED OF CHANGE

Carl Sagan demonstrates the rapidly increasing speed of change. He has worked out a ''year-long'' calendar using a scale in which one second equals 475 terrestrial years. The cosmos begins on January 1; here is what happens after noon of the last day of the ''year.'' The symbol ~ denotes ''approximately.''

DECEMBER 31

~ 1:30 PM	Origin of *Proconsul* and *Ramapithecus*, probable ancestors of apes and men
~ 10:30 PM	First humans
11:00 PM	Widespread use of stone tools
11:46 PM	Domestication of fire by Peking man
11:56 PM	Beginning of most recent glacial period
11:58 PM	Seafarers settle Australia
11:59 PM	Extensive cave painting in Europe
11:59:20 PM	Invention of agriculture
11:59:35 PM	Neolithic civilization; first cities
11:59:50 PM	First dynasties in Sumer, Ebla and Egypt; development of astronomy
11:59:51 PM	Invention of the alphabet; Akkadian Empire
11:59:52 PM	Hummurabic legal codes in Babylon; Middle Kingdom in Egypt
11:59:53 PM	Bronze Metallurgy; Mycenaean culture; Trojan War; Olmec culture; invention of the compass
11:59:54 PM	Iron metallurgy; First Assyrian Empire; Kingdom of Israel; founding of Carthage by Phoenicia
11:59:55 PM	Asokan India; Ch'in Dynasty China; Periclean Athens; birth of Buddha
11:59:56 PM	Euclidean geometry; Archimedean physics; Ptolemaic astronomy; Roman Empire; birth of Christ
11:59:57 PM	Zero and decimals invented in Indian arithmetic; Rome falls; Moslem conquests
11:59:58 PM	Mayan civilization; Sung Dynasty China; Byzantine Empire; Mongol invasion; Crusades
11:59:59 PM	Renaissance in Europe; voyages of discovery from Europe and from Ming Dynasty China; emergence of the experimental method in science
Now: The first second of New Year's Day	Widespread development of science and technology; emergence of a global culture; acquisition of the means for self-destruction of the human species; first steps in spacecraft planetary exploration and the search for extraterrestrial intelligence

SOURCE: Sagan (1977, 16).

The instability and precariousness of this modern condition of interdependence lends urgency to the task of studying change and understanding its processes and outcomes. The hope is that it can be both more accurately predicted and, to whatever extent possible, brought under more rational control.

Wilbert Moore has summarized the characteristics of (present-day) change:

> *For any given society or culture, rapid change occurs frequently or "constantly."*
>
> *Changes are neither temporally nor spatially isolated — that is, changes occur in sequential chains rather than as "temporary" crises followed by quiet periods of reconstruction, and the consequences tend to reverberate through entire regions or virtually the entire world.*
>
> *Thus, because contemporary change is probable "everywhere" and its consequences may be significant "everywhere," it has a dual basis.*
>
> *The proportion of contemporary change that is either planned or issues from the secondary consequences of deliberate innovations is much higher than in former times.*
>
> *Accordingly, the range of material technology and social strategies is expanding rapidly and the net effect is additive or cumulative despite the relatively rapid obsolescence of some procedures.*
>
> *The normal occurrence of change affects a wider range of individual experience and functional aspects of societies in the modern world — not because such societies are in all aspects more "integrated" but because virtually no feature of life is exempt from the expectation or normality of change (1974, 2).*

Do people welcome change or fear it? Habit and customs exert a powerful influence, and novelty is not always welcomed with open arms. Nisbet observed:

> *Most of us do everything we can, of course, to shore up the old ways. Such is the shock of enforced social change that most people will often employ what the nineteenth-century English philosopher called "fictions." No matter how extreme the need for change in our old ways, we adopt, in effect, verbal, legal, religious, or other fictions through which we convince ourselves that change of behaviour is not needed, that the old and cherished, if properly understood, can continue despite all overt evidence of its unsuitability. Much of the world's literature consists, basically, of justifications and rationalizations of practices that have become obsolete or even injurious. . . . Few of us are altogether immune to the practice of creating fictions, by which we so often prop up what should be dismantled (1970, 317–8).*[1]

Prizing what is familiar and unchanging is bolstered by the assumption that stable conditions are a necessity for the human spirit to thrive and achieve its potential. "For how but in order and ceremony," queried Yeats, who knew all too well the pain and the inevitability of change, "can beauty and truth be born?" Yet we know that some of the most creative periods in history have occurred when migrations, conquest, and expanded trading patterns have given rise to the collision of ideologies, value systems, and social structures.

THERE'S NO PLACE TO DUMP THE TRASH

By Tom Spears

Where do you put 5,000 tonnes of garbage a day?

In two dumps that are fast filling up, that's where.

Metro's booming economy has produced a garbage glut, an incredible 3.3 million tonnes of garbage a year from Metro, York and Durham.

That's 471,000 truckloads a year — 1,700 a day — rumbling to Maple and Pickering with our garbage.

The Brock West dump (off Brock Rd. in the north end of Pickering) will have to close sometime in the summer or fall next year. The Keele Valley dump in Maple may last until 1993, but no longer.

It may even have to close next summer because dumps have to be lined with clay to stop contaminants from leaching into nearby groundwater, and they're running out of clay at the dump. Metro has asked to expropriate nearby land to mine more clay, but Maple residents are kicking up a fuss over this and may succeed in blocking it.

Metro, understandably, is in a flap over its garbage crisis.

In The Star's survey, 25.3 per cent of respondents ranked garbage as the most important environmental problem facing Metro. Only air pollution ranked higher, with 37.1 per cent of people polled.

Metro works commissioner Bob Ferguson shocked the city in April when he announced that all garbage collection could be cancelled next summer if the Keele Valley dump closes.

If there's no place to truck it, the garbage will just have to lie on people's lawns, uncollected, he said.

There is no interim solution to pull Metro out of its garbage crisis during the search for a permanent replacement for the dumps, he said.

The only way around this is for the province to pass a special law giving Metro the right to expropriate the land where it wants to get clay, Alderman Richard Gilbert said.

But he warned that Queen's Park may be afraid to harm its image by backing Metro against its weaker neighbours.

Metro could stretch the life of its dumps by up to a year by turning away all garbage from businesses, which comes in on private trucks.

It could do this by boosting the amount charged private garbage haulers from $83 a tonne to $2,500 or more, Gilbert said.

It takes several years to get approval for a new dump site, since a proposed site's neighbours always force an environmental assessment hearing. Metro can't wait that long.

"If they get in there they're going to be there for 20 years," she said.

Meanwhile, nobody has any clear idea of where the new dump should go.

In fact, the only person who seems to want our garbage is Theo Jewell, Mayor of Kapuskasing, who figures his town can make some money from all that garbage 840 kilometres (520) miles south.

He sees his town getting a chunk of the potentially profitable recycling business along with the garbage, and thereby sharing in the southern prosperity that has so far bypassed Kapuskasing.

THEORIES OF CHANGE

Ordinary speech is full of garden-variety theories of change, which generally fall into two categories—the optimistic and the pessimistic. You are familiar with the reassurances that "every cloud has a silver lining" and that "every day, in every way, we're getting better and better." At the same time, you are accustomed to hearing about "the good old days," a sentiment usually accompanied by the gloomy observation that "the world is going to the dogs." Where some see decay and loss, others see growth and progress. Still others liken changing features of social life to features of the human life cycle.

These ordinary notions are reflected in the scholarly works of a number of social theorists.

As we have noted in other chapters, early social theorists were concerned with ambitious historical analyses of society (or civilization) as a whole, rather than with examining a specific social group or institution. They sought to explain society in terms of what had occurred in the past. A metaphor that has permeated social thought over a period of 2500 years, from the works of Heraclitus in ancient Greece to those of Pitirim Sorokin in the 20th century, is that of society as an organism, a living, growing, purposeful part of nature.

The Greeks and Romans saw social, physical, and biological reality in terms of relentless, continuous change, and they were preoccupied with questions about origins, stages of growth, causes, and purpose. Christianity adopted the same metaphor of growth but shifted it to the realm of the sacred: the universe, created by god, was unfolding according to his purpose. The Renaissance, the Enlightenment, and especially the 19th-century base of modern science did nothing to dispel this analogy between the social world and the ever-evolving world of nature. It has had, in fact, a deep influence on present-day functionalist theory in sociology.

In Chapter 1, we referred briefly to Comte's Law of Three Stages. Comte viewed society as emerging in a linear ascent from the theological to the metaphysical to the "positive" (scientific) stage. An understanding of the ways in which these stages unfolded would, he argued, make it possible "for man to influence the course of his own civilization" (1877, 572).

Comte's was an optimistic view. So, too, was that of Herbert Spencer (1820–1903). Each phase of social growth or evolution was, Spencer argued, marked by increasing complexity, greater differentiation among functions, and greater interdependence among society's various parts. He envisaged this evolutionary process as leading to more stability, to less conflict—in other words, to a more rational, humane, and orderly universe. Consequently, Spencer was opposed to collective action (such as state education and state medicine) which would interfere with natural processes and artificially preserve society's weakest members.

By contrast, Oswald Spengler (1880–1936) took a pessimistic perspective. He viewed the history of civilization as proceeding in cycles, analogous to the development of the single organism: birth, childhood, maturity, senescence (old age), and death. The end of each cycle returned a culture to its beginnings. For Spengler, the west had passed its stage of maturity and was well into its phase of decline, with the death of western civilization an inevitability.

SOCIAL DARWINISM

In Chapter 3 on socialization, we referred to the impact of Darwin's evolutionary theory on social thought. Viewing human beings as subject to the biological law of survival of the fittest has consequences for the ways in which social phenomena are explained. One can rationalize differences between the rich and the poor, the successful and the unsuccessful, the powerful and the weak, on the basis of the notion that the poor, the unsuccessful, the weak are less fit than the others. A belief in biological determinism does not promote the view that the structure of society can—or should—be changed, since it is seen as natural.

Throughout this book we have indicated how, in one form or another, biological determinism has been pervasive in much of western thought, and we have encouraged you to reject the assumptions of social Darwinism because they have been used to justify social inequality and to resist change.

CHANGE AS A DIALECTIC

The theory of Marx (see Chapter 1) was also one of progress, but it posited conflict and dialectical change rather than linear progress. Change, according to Marx, comes about as the result of internal contradictions which every social system develops. Thus, as we noted, one reason why the feudal system collapsed was that the emerging capitalist mode, abetted by technological developments, required a labour force that was not tied to the land.

Marx viewed the events of each historical epoch as centering upon the struggle, between a dominant group and exploited groups, for a share of societal rewards. He saw the power of the dominant group as stemming from its control over the means of producing the goods and services society requires. The ultimate struggle in the capitalist system would, Marx argued, occur between owners and workers, and this confrontation would finally (though he did not specify when) lead to a better, classless society. In a sense, one can say that Marx, too, was a romantic optimist.

THE CUMULATIVE WEIGHT OF HUMAN ACTION

Weber challenged Marx's preoccupation with economic factors, arguing that, in the case of capitalism, economic changes were preceded by changes in the value system of western society. Thus, he gave the Protestant ethic a central place in his explanation of the emergence of capitalism. As we have emphasized, Weber did not ignore the importance of economic factors; rather, he insisted on a broader view that took into account the interplay of many factors. In this insistence, exemplified in his own work, he has been influential in helping sociology to reject narrow, deterministic explanations.

Weber viewed cultural change as a process of ever-increasing rationalization—for example, in the transition from magic to science and in the transfer of work from a primary-group setting to that of a large, impersonal bureaucracy. He was firmly opposed to any view of social change that hypothesized the existence of one inevitable social force. Rather, he believed that a great many individuals must make a great many decisions. Think of the dramatic decline in the Quebec birth rate. By itself, the availability of reliable birth control methods could not produce change. For this to occur, many women, for whatever reasons, had to decide to practise birth control. Cumulatively, such decisions would lead to social change. Since change is the central feature of the modern world, social scientists are compelled to seek explanations for it. In doing so, they tend to use the functionalist perspective, the conflict perspective, or a combination of both.

HOW IS STABILITY ACHIEVED?

In Chapter 1, we explained that present-day functionalist theory is rooted in the tradition of Durkheim, who was greatly concerned with the problem of social order. Recall that his concept of organic solidarity was of a group characterized by a high degree of social differentiation (manifested in a highly specialized division of labour) and a high degree of interdependence.[2]

Here, the metaphor of society as a complex organism is clear. In such a differentiated system, the various parts must perform their functions properly if society as a whole is to operate coherently. Likewise, a change in one part has consequences for other parts as well as for the whole. Thus, if one identifies a change in some aspect of social life — say, a change in the way work is performed — one can be alert to adjustments and transformations in other aspects of society — for example, changes in the extent of deviant behaviour or changes in family life. Durkheim strictly rejected, however, evolutionary theory that posited stages through which society *must* pass: "The stages that humanity traverses successively do not engender one another" (1950 [1895], 117). In other words, chronology does not imply causation; antecedent states do not by nature produce subsequent ones.

Modern functionalism, too, rejects sweeping evolutionary notions. However, like Durkheim, functionalists today treat society as a system of interdependent parts. Central to this view is the concept of equilibrium. To maintain continuity and balance in society, certain "functional requisites" must be met. For example, the young must be socialized to accept the moral precepts of society. In Chapter 9B on education, we noted the view that schools socialize children to accept middle-class values, such as deferred gratification, competitiveness, and verbal rather than physical proficiency. Another functionalist view, which we outlined in Chapter 4 on stratification, argues that rewards (pay, power, prestige) must be distributed unevenly to ensure that society's most important tasks are accomplished.

Any model encourages certain questions and discourages others. An equilibrium model invites the question, "How do things persist?" It tends to inhibit the question, "How do things change?" Observed change is interpreted as an occurrence which will require complementary changes in the system as a whole in order to re-establish equilibrium. Thus, when a mobile labour force is required by a society, functionalists seek to identify the new arrangements (functional alternatives) developed to perform the functions that the extended family used to fulfil.

THE OUTCOME OF STRUGGLE

Conflict theorists look at change in terms of the struggle between vested interest groups and those who challenge the existing order. For instance, corporations seek to continue to minimize expenditures on pollution control, while environmentalists assert the priority of protection over profit.

Ralf Dahrendorf has argued that confict theory provides the most useful paradigm for analysing forces of interruption and change. Conflict, he stated, can be a positive thing.

> *The clash of values and interests, the tension between what is and what some groups feel ought to be, the conflict between vested interests, and new strata and groups demanding their share of power, wealth and status, have been productive of vitality; note for example the contrast between the "frozen world" of the Middle Ages and the burst of creativity that accompanied the thaw that set in with the Renaissance (1973, 68).*

At a less general level, Dahrendorf noted, such a view raises doubts about the approach of the Human Relations School (which we discussed in Chapter 5 on work), with its stress on harmony. If a social system fails to allow for the open expression of conflict, the likelihood of violent eruptions is increased. This applies to all levels of systems. In the case of South Africa, the muzzling of conflict has led to escalating confrontations.

Even violence does not always lead to change but may be only a temporary disruption.

> *While violence is a pervasive feature of Latin American politics, revolution, or the fundamental transformation of society, is rare. An isolated rebellion may be put down, a leader may be assassinated or perhaps just replaced, but control of the economic bases of power is not changed nor is the hierarchy of society affected. In short, there is no restructuring of society (Warme 1985, 2).*

This observation draws attention to the fact that change cannot be easily predicted; rather, it must be studied in specific contexts at specific times and places.

Some changes are on a small scale, while others involve large-scale transformations. Moore defines small-scale change as

> *changes in the characteristics of social structures, that, though comprised within the general system identifiable as a society, do not have any immediate and major consequences for the generalized structure (society) as such (1974, 48).*

Small-scale changes will not have major consequences in the short run, but if they are numerous and persistent, they are likely to effect more general changes within society over the long run.

In examining social change, it is also important to distinguish between **readjustment** (modification without a change of kind) and **change of type** (an actual transformation of kind). The society of an urban, industrialized nation-state such as Canada clearly differs in type from that of a primitive tribe. Changes in type may be less common than they seem at first. In Chapter 2 on culture, we contrasted an 1898 Ontario school board list of obligations for a teacher with a list of duties outlined in the 1983 Ontario Education Act. We noted that although the earlier conception of the role had been modified significantly by 1983, still the two lists have many basic similarities. Today's teachers are still governed by moral expectations and still have little organizational control over their work. Can one really say, then, that the role of the teacher has undergone a change of *type*? Would it be truer to say that certain adjustments have occurred to suit modern conditions?

Moore (1974) has advocated the view of society as a "tension-management system," a model that permits the identification of tensions likely to produce change. The participation of women in the labour force, for example, produces tensions between their domestic roles and their career roles. This alerts the sociologist to the possibility that change may occur, though it does not predict *what* change. One possible outcome is the reorganization of the division of labour within the home. Another is the reorganization of work itself, to accommodate female participation in a way that allows women to meet domestic obligations. So far, however, the increased presence of women in managerial positions has not led to basic changes in industry. According to a study by Symons (1986), women have tended to adapt to the corporate world rather than trying to change it. What changes will occur in the long run is a question that sociologists will be able to answer only after-the-fact.

Another possible source of change-producing tension is the increasing access to higher education afforded immigrant groups in Canada. Education has traditionally been an avenue of upward mobility for some second- and third-generation immigrants. With the recent expansion of postsecondary education, more such people are entering colleges and universities. Once young people have been socialized to ways of seeing the world that differ drastically from the outlook of their parents, a severe strain on family life is probable.

In every chapter of this book, we have pointed to changes in Canadian society. Yet it can be argued that Canadian society has persisted, over time, in a remarkably stable, orderly way with few alterations to its structure. Both perspectives are true.

We now turn to an examination of several major areas of change in modern society. As we have noted, change is a constant feature of almost every area of social life today. The changes we have chosen to explore — out of the nearly endless list of possibilities — are among those bringing fundamental alterations to Canadian society, particularly society as students are likely to encounter it.

CONTINUITY AND CHANGE: THE STATUS OF WOMEN

History is sparsely dotted with powerful women. Most of them were born into their positions — that is, their status was ascribed. Cleopatra, Elizabeth I, and

Queen Victoria come to mind. The vast majority of women have been powerless, subject to potential abuse by men because of their inferior physical strength and their inability to control reproduction through contraception. Legal discrimination has often denied them even personhood. In the late 1800s, the British jurist William Blackstone ruled that "women become incorporated and consolidated with their husbands." Therefore, "a man cannot grant anything to his wife for the grant would be to suppose her separate existence" (Gavron 1966).[3]

It is precisely because, historically, the fate of women has been dependent on men that it is difficult to make statements about women as a group. Often they are still deemed to be incorporated with their husbands. Social columns refer to "Mrs. John Brown, the former Barbara Smith," as though Barbara Smith no longer exists. A further difficulty in making generalizations about women is that, to a greater degree than other individuals lumped into groups, women are divided by class membership, and this status depends largely on the position of the individual woman's father and, if she is married, on that of her husband. Women are further separated by ethnicity, religion, and language. The heroine of Rayfield's *Maria in Markham Street* (1972) would perceive little in common with a young female lawyer or even with the aspiring executive's wife who chooses to stay at home with young children.

Despite these differences, social scientists make general statements about the status of women. As with any generalization, they lose a certain amount of detailed information, indicative of diversity, in the interest of identifying commonalities. For wide-ranging discussions of women's historical position in Canada see Prentice (1988) and Burt, Code, and Dorney (1988). The latter volume contains examinations of how women have fared in some of the institutional spheres we discussed in the previous chapter.

POWERFUL CABINET MINISTER "JUST NELLIE" IN TERRITORIES

By Julia Necheff

Nellie Cournoyea recounts the tale quite humbly, but she seems to derive satisfaction from telling southerners of her upbringing in the harsh Arctic wilderness.

Cournoyea (pronounced CORN-yay), 49, is a cabinet minister in the Northwest Territories, a 10-year veteran of the territorial government. She shoulders a formidable load of a different sort nowadays, carrying the high-profile portfolios of energy, mines and resources; health; and public works.

"You had to do everything, including pack caribou, look after fish nets, go out hunting," she recalls.

The second-oldest in the family, she says there was no such thing as women's work and men's work.

"It was really equal, sometimes too equal," Cournoyea adds with a dry laugh.

The daughter of a Norwegian trapper and an Inuvialuit woman, Cournoyea grew up near the western Arctic community of Aklavik in the Mackenzie River Delta.

DOWN TO EARTH

Although a powerful politician in the North, widely known and well respected, she's completely without pretension. And there's a steely quality to Cournoyea; you get the feeling she doesn't suffer fools gladly.

Cournoyea says her upbringing was character-building. But she stresses it was no different from other northerners who grew up in the early 1950s.

"People might come into the Arctic and they might see problems," she says. "But they don't realize there's a whole strength and dignity out there. It didn't come from nowhere. It came from people surviving in a very challenging environment."

HANDED JOBS

Cournoyea is an integral part of an eight-member cabinet led by government leader Dennis Patterson. The Northwest Territories has undergone a major transition recently, taking over full responsibility from the federal government for the N.W.T. Power Corp. and for health care. Those new responsibilities were handed to Cournoyea.

Until a recent cabinet reorganization, she was also in charge of highways and the Public Utilities Board, and oversaw a review of the territorial Workers' Compensation Board. Referring to her diverse duties, one of her staff quipped that Cournoyea was the minister of "ice roads, AIDS, condoms and gas."

Cournoyea and the Patterson government face pressing issues. One is to consolidate control over the Territories' bountiful natural resources, also handed over by Ottawa in principle last year in the Northern Accord.

Cournoyea says improving transportation in the North is another key demand. But costs in the inhospitable, vast territory "are so exorbitant," she says.

MANY CONCERNS

As health minister she must grapple with complex social problems including alcoholism, drugs and AIDS, as well as poor nutrition among natives who have dropped their traditional food in favor of unhealthy "junk food."

"The real issue is to try to get people to look after themselves."

She also cites a growing concern over northern pollution. A recent study found that airborne pollution from industrialized areas in Southern Canada and other countries had contaminated the natural food supplies of remote Inuit communities.

With so much to do, Cournoyea's day begins with meetings at 7:00 a.m. and often lasts until midnight, but she doesn't consider herself a workaholic. Asked whether she ever feels overwhelmed by her numerous responsibilities, she says flatly: "I don't get overwhelmed." Divorced after a few years of marriage, Cournoyea has two children and two grandchildren.

She also has to fit in visits to her constituents in her far-flung Tuktoyaktuk riding. It covers about 900,000 square kilometres of tundra and sea ice.

Her constituents have placed a great deal of confidence in her, she says. But although she carries much political authority, they don't place her on a pedestal. ''Nobody's in awe of me,'' Cournoyea says. ''I'm just Nellie.''

WOMEN AS A MINORITY GROUP

It can be argued that women constitute a minority group in terms of the definition supplied in Chapter 7. This was true in the early days of Canadian society and is still true today, despite pronounced changes in societal rules and despite the evolution of **feminism**, that is to say, heightened consciousness of women's rights to equality with men, giving due weight to biological differences. The ''women's liberation movement'' — a term one hears used at various times optimistically, cynically, derisively, wistfully, militantly — was sparked in the 1960s as part of the general contemporary movement to articulate the rights of minority groups and to bring an end to discrimination. No one would say that changes have not occurred in the lives of women or that these changes have not reverberated throughout the social structure in a number of ways. However, the position of women relative to men has not been substantially altered.

Since women are a numerical majority in Canada, the concept of them as a minority group may be startling. Yet consider their situation in light of the criteria for a minority group (discussed in more depth in Chapter 7):

- A social category defined by the majority as incompetent or inferior on the basis of presumed physical, cultural, and/or behavioural differences from the majority. (In the case of women, the basis of discrimination is **sexism**. It is their differences from male characteristics and norms which are viewed negatively.)
- The experience by the group of both systemic discrimination and restriction of rights.
- Occupation of a subordinate, disadvantaged, and stigmatized position within society, as a consequence of structural discrimination.

Women are often set apart as a social category judged ''incompetent or inferior on the basis of presumed differences'' (see Kanter 1989). For example, they may be denied opportunities for top corporate positions on the grounds that they are too emotional to handle such positions. ''A male executive will pound the table when things are not being done right, a woman will burst into tears,'' the president of a large corporation told one of the authors during an interview (Lundy 1977). When asked whether he had actually seen a woman behave in this manner, the respondent replied that this had not occurred in his company, but he had been told of several instances in which it had.

Kanter has made a similar point:

> *Perhaps the most pervasive stereotype of women in organizations is that they are "too emotional," whereas men hold the monopoly on rational thought. Women represent the antithesis of the rational manager. They were considered by some people in a* Harvard Business Review *survey to be "temperamentally unfit for management" (1977, 25).*

Being viewed as "too emotional" does, indeed, hamper women's corporate advancement. At the same time, it has been argued that emotion and sensitivity can play a positive role in the work place, since a more humane organization may be a more effective one. (Refer to the discussion of women in organizations, Chapter 6).

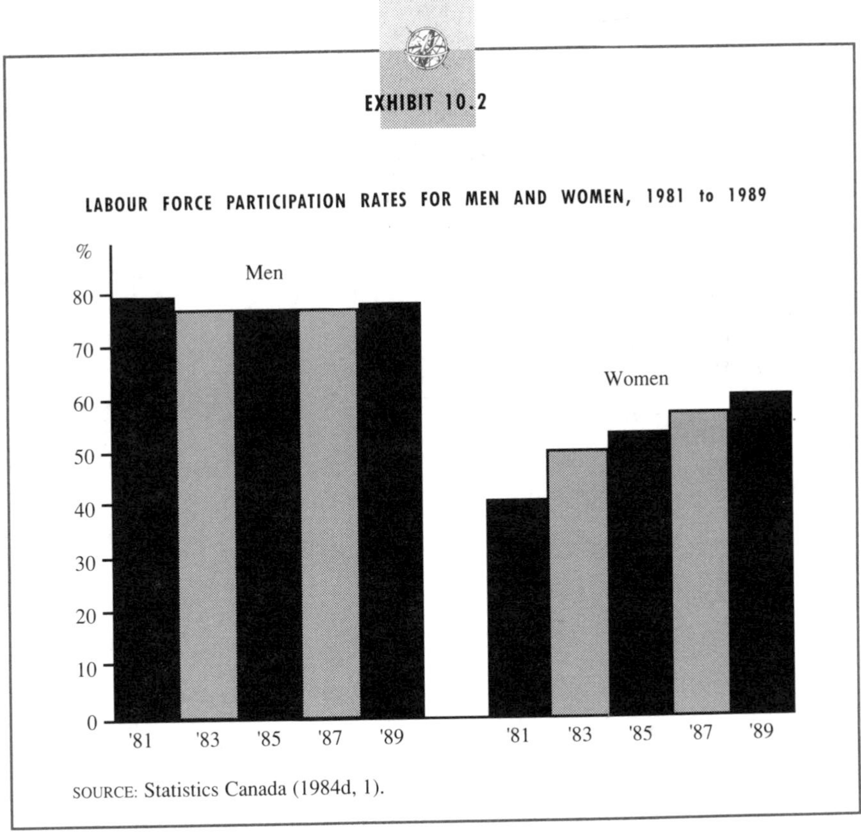

The experience of discrimination is a feature of minority-group status. Negative stereotypes rationalize discrimination that restricts opportunities for women. In Chapter 4 on stratification, we noted the fatefulness of economic position for all other spheres of life. In the past, economic discrimination against women had been legally entrenched. For example, until the Second World War, female teachers were obliged to resign when they got married; the same rule applied at IBM until the mid-1950s. Even though such overt discrimination has now been outlawed, its effects persist at a time when women have entered the labour force in unprecedented numbers.

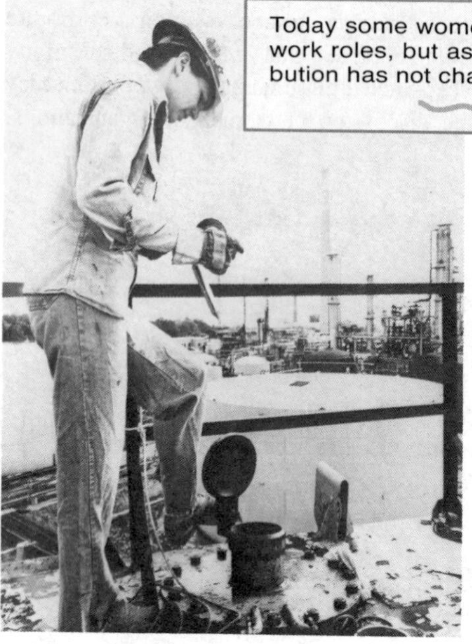

Today some women have moved into nontraditional work roles, but as a group, their occupational distribution has not changed greatly.

The rapid, massive increase in the labour-force participation of women has not appreciably changed their occupational distribution (see Exhibit 10.2). A 1982 study of women in the work place noted:

> *There are now some women in almost all paid jobs, but most are at the bottom of the heap doing women's work at women's wages — the picture that emerges is one of pervasive and often debilitating ghettoization (Canadian Advisory Council on the Status of Women 1982).*

Statistics Canada reports that the average 1987 earnings of women who worked full time year round were $21,012, compared with $31,865 for men. To put the matter differently, the average female wage was 65.9 percent of the average male wage; as shown in Exhibit 10.3, this ratio represented only a small improvement in 15 years.

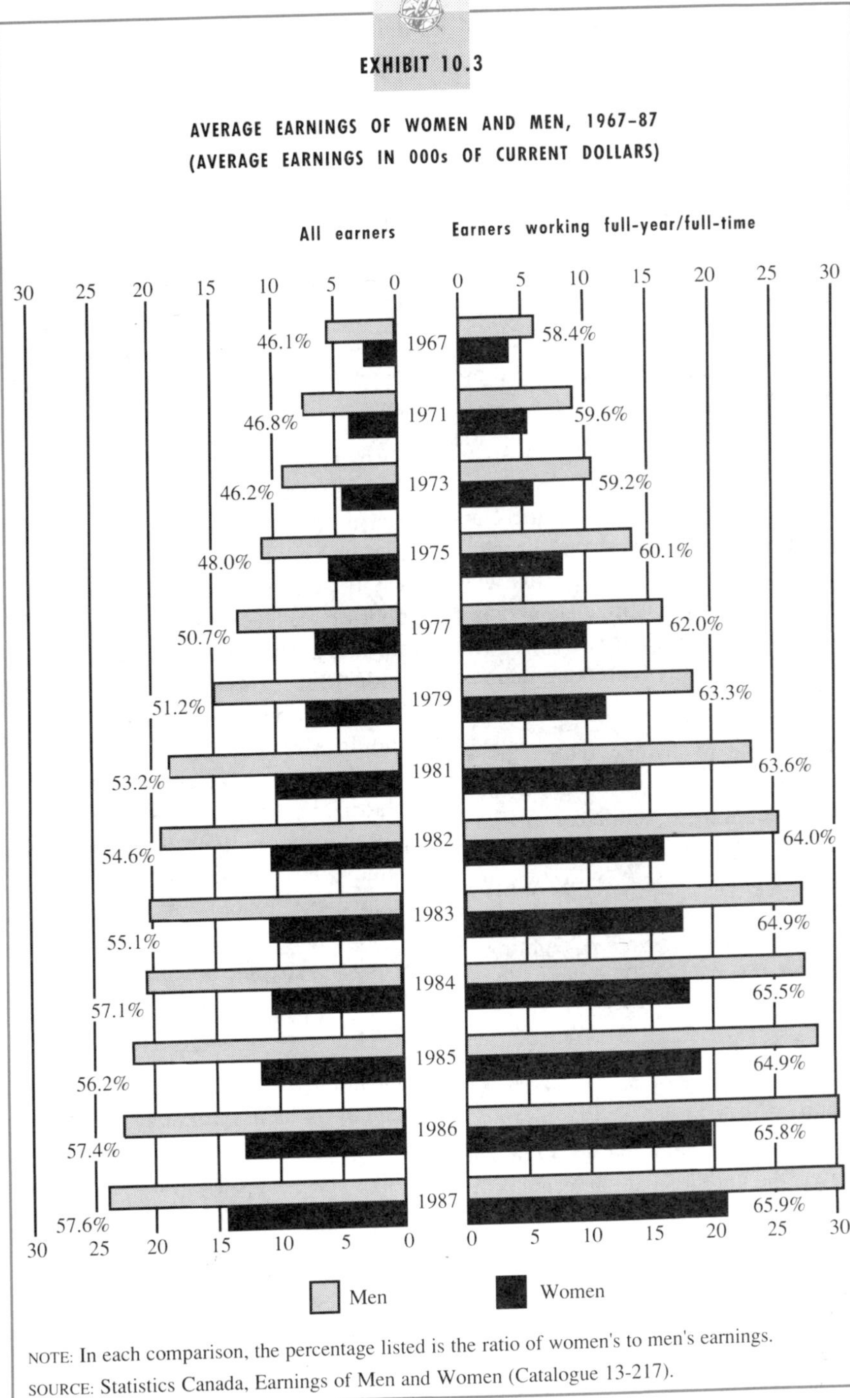

NOTE: In each comparison, the percentage listed is the ratio of women's to men's earnings.

SOURCE: Statistics Canada, Earnings of Men and Women (Catalogue 13-217).

"MOMMY TRACK" ROW DIVIDING WOMEN

By Jennifer Lewington

Felice Schwartz has sparked a row that reverberates from the U.S. playpen to the boardroom. Unfortunately, so far, the debate pits women against each other. The New York consultant, a long-time champion of women in the executive suite, says employers should spot and promote single females committed to the fast-track, putting those who stop to have children on a slower course in middle-management — the so-called "Mommy track."

Writing in a recent issue of the Harvard Business Review, the 64-year-old founder of Catalyst Inc. says that corporations should distinguish between women as "career-primary" and "career and family," treating them as two distinct groups.

"The secret to dealing with (career-primary) women is to recognize them early, accept them, and clear artificial barriers from their path to the top," she writes. By contrast, those who opt for husbands and families are willing to trade off the pressure of fighting to the top for more free time with the family.

"She's very smart, she's talented, she's committed to her career," Ms Schwartz says of the "career and family" woman, "and she's satisfied to stay at the middle level, at least during the early child-rearing years."

The article, which baldly states that women cost more to employ than men, has spawned news stories and commentaries, mostly written by women, in the leading U.S. daily and business press. However, the debate is a narrow one, confined to looking at women as the cause of, and the solution to, their failure to break into the ranks of upper management, still the preserve of white males. In reality, the two-track thesis is a side-show that detracts from the main event — equal employment opportunities for men and women at all levels of the corporate ladder.

By her own admission, Ms Schwartz talks the language of the corporate boardroom, encouraging chief executives to pick the best recruits, many of whom increasingly are women, from a pool of management graduates that is shrinking with the birth rate. Armed with these "new facts of life," Ms Schwartz argues that chief executives should hire and cultivate ambitious women bound for the fast-track as readily as they do male graduates poised for a run to the top rung. At the same time, she urges businesses to adopt more flexible work arrangements to keep talented, though less driven, females who trade off a little less career for a little more family life in the early years.

The fallacy of Ms Schwartz's two-track remedy is its assumption that companies will know in advance who will choose the briefcase or the baby—and stick to one route or the other. For their part, many women work out of economic necessity, often trapped in low-paying jobs as the family's sole breadwinner, without the luxury of choosing between a career and the "Mommy track." At worst, the two-track approach smacks of latent discrimination, giving employers an excuse to promote working fathers and single women at the expense of equally competent females who have children.

The argument for the "Mommy track" plays to the old rules of corporate life which dictate that employees fit the pinstripe profile or flee. However, some large U.S. corporations are adjusting to the new rules that recognize the new economic realities of the 1990s: two-income families and single, working mothers are here to stay. Motivated more by efficiency than altruism, these blue-chip companies are experimenting with ways to keep their best people — including mothers on the fast track — with better day care, parental leave, job-sharing and part-time work for senior managers. Such creative approaches give the company and its employee a shared stake in staying together for the long-term.

These experiments are still the exception. In time, though, they may prove the rule if companies see the long-term reward of keeping highly prized employees, men and women, who opt out temporarily to rear children.

That way, men and women of merit will have an equal shot at the keys to the executive washrooms.

It would be simplistic to attribute women's disadvantaged position in the work world solely to discrimination. However, discrimination has been a key factor in keeping women close to the bottom.[4] Epstein has observed, "No matter what sphere of work women are hired for or select, like sediment in a wine bottle they seem to settle at the bottom" (1970, 2).

Are women deprived of political, economic, and social power? As consumers, they exert considerable economic influence by virtue of their domestic role, yet their economic power is constrained by their depressed position in the labour market. Individual women, of course, do have high earnings or control a great deal of inherited wealth; they are, however, the exception.

Enfranchisement is a prerequisite for political power. Originally, women's quest for the vote was spurred in the United States by their participation in the movement against slavery, and in that country and Canada by their attempts to have the consumption of alcohol prohibited. Once the franchise had been won, however, North American women made few concerted efforts to seek political power or even to use their votes to improve the overall position of women.[5] Today, though some Canadian women hold high political office, they are much more likely to have an honorific post, such as governor-general or lieutenant-governor, than to stand a chance of being elected prime minister or provincial premier. The Civil Rights Movement following the Second World War, however, eventually provided new impetus and led women to a heightened awareness of the inequities they themselves faced. This consciousness was articulated in a book by Betty Friedan (1921–), *The Feminine Mystique* (1963), which became a landmark of the women's liberation movement, and in Kate Millett's *Sexual Politics* (1970).

Astronaut Roberta Bonar, the second Canadian to rocket into space, is a pilot and medical doctor who holds degrees in neurobiology, experimental pathology, and agriculture.

Today many women continue to be denied social power and human dignity. Most dramatically, this is denied to victims of family violence. By taking inadequate measures to combat such violence, our society condones it, at least tacitly. Inadequate funds to provide shelter for abused women and children were further reduced during the 1981–2 economic recession, and most of these services continue to be underfunded.[6]

Typically, violations against minority-group members are treated more lightly than offences against other individuals. For a long time, assaults by whites against blacks went unpunished in the American south (see *A Gathering of Old Men* in the Suggested Readings for Chapter 7). In his study of Crow Lake (1975), Stymeist found that whites could abuse Indians with relative impunity. Analogously, assaults on women, including rape, have generally been punished leniently, if at all. It is questionable whether women receive protection equal to men's under the law.

Those who hold power in a group, whether it be a family, an organization, or a society, define issues and decide priorities. As Hall has said of organizations:

> *Power holders shape and decide what are issues and what are non-issues. . . . If an organizational member believes that something is a burning issue, it will only* become *one in the organization if power holders also define it as such (1982, 148).*

Because women have had little power, their demands in such areas as childcare, maternity leave, contraception, access to abortion, and regulation of pay differentials have been given a low priority. Similar observations can be made about other minority groups, such as the disabled. Many disabled individuals, especially those with multiple disabilities, languish in institutions because there is no appropriate accommodation for them to live independently.

Nevertheless, the changing rate of female participation in the labour force has had a ripple effect, providing an impetus for change in other parts of the social structure. The manufacturing and service industries are responding to women's changing needs through the creation of jobs, goods such as fast foods, and facilities geared to accommodating new family arrangements. Banting has noted that the women's movement "has created a powerful political constituency with a commitment to social intervention in a variety of forms . . . " (1987, 318). For a discussion of the contemporary women's movement in Canada, see Adamson *et al.* (1988).

Canadian women, as a subordinate group, have made real gains in the past 25 years. It remains to be seen whether they will be able to consolidate and build on these gains. Some action has been taken to implement the employment equity called for in Abella's 1984 Report. Legislation has been passed on Equal Pay for Work of Equal Value, but interpretation and implementation of this legislation remain thorny issues.

"WHAT WILL TOMORROW BRING . . . ?"

By M. Baker

Partly because of their limited experience in life and their receptiveness to romantic portrayals of men/women, marriage, and family life in novels, magazines, and television programs, most girls in our study painted a very rosy picture of their personal lives at age thirty. They generally expected to be married to the same man, to have two normal healthy children, to live in a house they owned near their parents and siblings, and to have a loving husband with a professional job. In their leisure time, they expected to watch television, play with their children, have intimate conversations with their husband in front of the fireplace, and to travel to exotic places on their holidays. None of the girls expected to have an unemployed husband, and none who wanted to have a career anticipated anything other than minor sexual discrimination in promotion. Very few anticipated divorce.

Considering the high rate of recent marriages ending in divorce, many adolescent women should expect to be self-supporting in the future. After divorce, women usually are granted custody of the children and husbands do not often pay child support after the first few years. Although no one likes to think that her marriage could end prematurely, the reality of divorce has to be accepted and adolescents should be able to prepare themselves for that eventuality. Remaining in the labour force as long as possible during adult life, and upgrading qualifications at regular intervals, may improve the financial situation of women whose marriages end.

While a few girls in this study seemed to be aware of what life realistically could be like in 10 or 15 years, most saw their future in the following sequence: high school, college or university, paid work, marriage, children, and return to the work force. They expected to find professional or clerical positions immediately after their schooling was complete, and work for pay until their children were born. After their children were in school, they expected to re-enter the labour force and to experience no difficulty finding paid work; few child care problems were anticipated.

The boys in our study were somewhat more realistic in that they knew they had to work to support their families and seemed to see their work as lifelong, requiring long-range plans. However, their expectations for full employment and professional work were more optimistic than present employment statistics indicate. Although the boys in our study were not much more realistic than the girls, they may be penalized less than girls for their lack of realism. Women still have to contend with employment discrimination, shifting priorities of paid work and work at home and a society which sees the husband as the main breadwinner.

THE INFORMATION AGE

A proliferation of computer-related technologies has transformed the human capacity to obtain, store, manipulate, and communicate information. It is often said that the computer has brought about an electronic revolution and that the West now lives in an **information age**.[7] The significance of this transition is discussed by Valaskakis and Sendell (1980).

Information has become a highly valued commodity, and where one stands in respect to its flow is critical. For example, if a large corporation has the means to be the first to discover that government is planning to spend money on the expansion of transportation services in the north, that firm has an advantage over its competitors.

It is also true that the capacity to produce information has outstripped the ability to control it, especially since computer technology now permits not only the formation of data banks but also data linkage (the mingling and manipulation of information from a variety of data sources). An astonishingly thorough profile of an individual can be created from various sources of partial information.

In the Gemeinschaft, sustained interaction with a relatively small group of people meant that everyone knew everyone else's business. It is unlikely that privacy was ever a consideration. The emergence of the Gesellschaft brought greater anonymity and the ability to keep the various spheres of one's life separate from each other. Privacy has thus come to be valued as a basic right worth protecting. Placing privacy in jeopardy is a significant threat in the information age.[8]

The notion of privacy of information is based on the assumption that all information about you belongs, in a very basic way, to *you*. You can choose to disclose it or to keep it secret, as you see fit. That is the key to an effective right to privacy: the individual's ability to control the circulation of information relating to himself or herself, an ability necessary for maintaining social relationships and for retaining personal freedom.

Think of a ''zone of privacy'' surrounding a person, like the plastic bubble built for the child whose own immune system could not protect him from infection. The important question is just how large this zone should be. There is always a tension between what is necessary for individual well-being and what is in the best interests of the social collectivity. In any democratic society, the balance achieved is never frozen once-and-for-all but is constantly being negotiated.

The technological ability to handle vast amounts of information is already available to governments and large organizations in the private sector. As this technology is being produced more and more cheaply, it is also becoming available to small organizations, public and private, and to households. Widened access to information confers many advantages, but it also entails greater and greater risks to privacy.

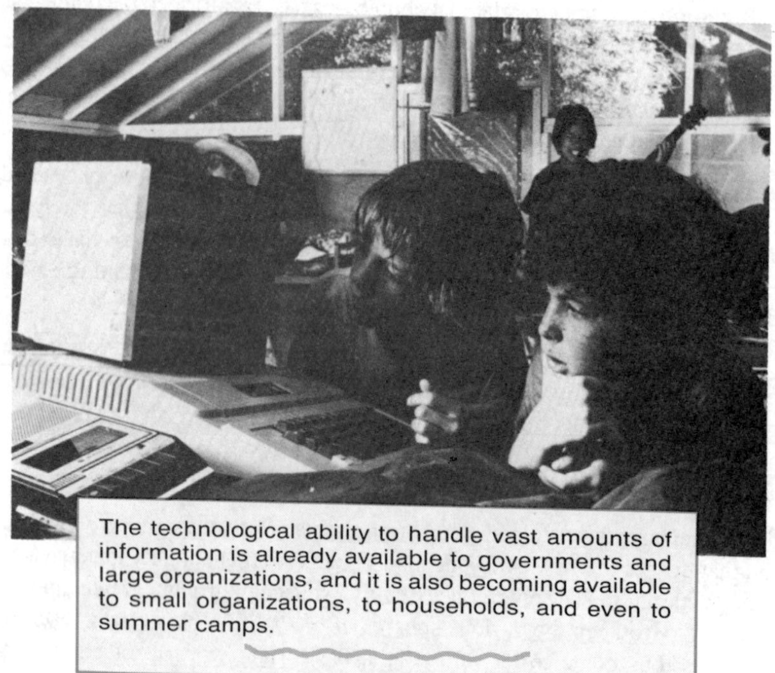

The technological ability to handle vast amounts of information is already available to governments and large organizations, and it is also becoming available to small organizations, to households, and even to summer camps.

THE COMPUTER AND THE FIRM

We have said that information is a valued commodity. It has, for example, commercial value for a variety of firms. Manufacturers who want to target their advertising effectively find it useful to gather information about your tastes and buying habits. Automobile insurance firms in Ontario spend several million dollars annually to purchase information that the provincial government has collected in connection with the issuing of drivers' licenses. Credit bureaus gather data to prepare reports on where you are employed, where you live, and how quickly you pay your bills; they sell this information to firms that make decisions about applications for such things as credit, insurance, jobs, or rental dwellings. The files these agencies prepare may be large and contain an assemblage of both facts and opinions, including your neighbours' opinions of your general character. Few firms tell an individual why an application has been rejected.

Similar information has, of course, been collected for similar purposes over many decades. The modern—and increasingly dangerous—difference is the exponential increase in banks of available information and the concomitant decrease in the cost of gathering data. Firms that once would have found the cost of obtaining such information prohibitive can now do so for a pittance.

People have a right to know what is in their own files, but many do not ask. Few complain to government consumer bureaus about violations of their rights. In addition, a confusing mass of government regulations addresses this type of activity. Thus, regulatory confusion and lack of public awareness have combined to permit the marketing of information in what has been called an open season on privacy.

The use of information about individuals is not confined to potential retailers of goods and services. Firms also gather detailed information about their own employees in the interests of bureaucratic efficiency. For example, managers may be in a hurry to identify, among their employees, those who have specific skills. However, in the process of seeking that information in the records, they may also obtain access to information concerning such things as an employee's financial condition, insurance-policy beneficiaries, state of health, and so on. Such information, even if seen inadvertently, may affect decisions with regard to promotion or firing. Is this, then, an invasion of the privacy of employees?

Employers can also use the computer to increase the efficiency of the work process itself through the techniques of mechanized surveillance.[9] Machines can monitor a typist's speed, how many calls an operator is handling, or how often a worker leaves his or her post. These practices have brought loud protests from unions, on the grounds that they dehumanize the workplace in the interests of raising productivity.

THE COMPUTER AND THE HOUSEHOLD

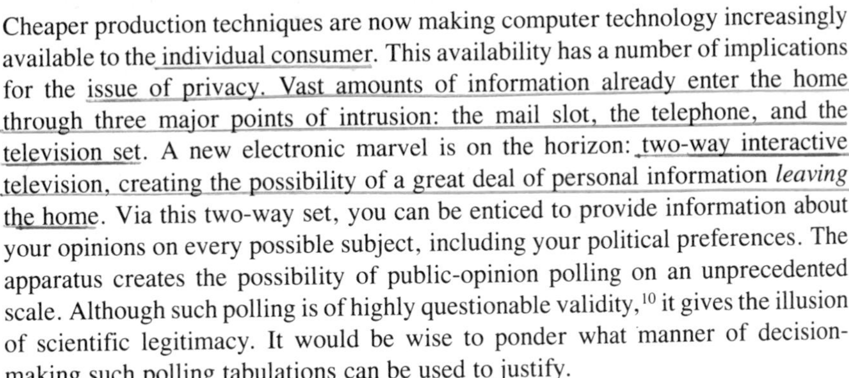

Cheaper production techniques are now making computer technology increasingly available to the individual consumer. This availability has a number of implications for the issue of privacy. Vast amounts of information already enter the home through three major points of intrusion: the mail slot, the telephone, and the television set. A new electronic marvel is on the horizon: two-way interactive television, creating the possibility of a great deal of personal information *leaving* the home. Via this two-way set, you can be enticed to provide information about your opinions on every possible subject, including your political preferences. The apparatus creates the possibility of public-opinion polling on an unprecedented scale. Although such polling is of highly questionable validity,[10] it gives the illusion of scientific legitimacy. It would be wise to ponder what manner of decision-making such polling tabulations can be used to justify.

In addition, interactive TV will compile enormous amounts of data on your consumer habits. And since it will involve the use of credit accounts, such as VISA, it will increase the points of access to information on your finances (and, of course, encourage the use of purchasing on credit).

The proponents of interactive TV point to its unquestionable convenience and claim that financial privacy will be respected. However, the ethics of computer use in the private sector have not yet been clearly articulated. In fact, the area of computer crime has only recently begun to be studied, and very few legislative recommendations have resulted. Since the technology itself is in such a constant state of change, it is difficult for society to anticipate the possibilities for using these systems in ways that harm others and infringe on privacy. Data-bank robberies are already a concern. Some time ago, a group of adolescents from a New York private school attempted to tap into 21 Canadian data systems as a lark. They succeeded in entering the data banks of Bell Canada, Canada Cement La Farge, Honeywell, Concordia University, the Universities of Toronto, Alberta, and Waterloo, and two federal government bureaus, and they destroyed the files of two other firms. This incident is only one of many that have raised concerns about the vulnerability of data banks to intrusion, whether done with caprice or with serious intent.

That interactive TV will catch on seems likely.[11] That it and other computer-related innovations will change society is equally certain—think of the far-reaching effects of the printing press, the telegraph, the telephone, and every other advance in the gathering, recording, and transmitting of information. It cannot be doubted that some of the changes will be beneficial, but there may also be dangers inherent in the widespread use of computers and related machines.

THE COMPUTER AND THE GOVERNMENT

Government has always played a large role in Canada, promoting immigration, facilitating the creation of a vast infrastructure of transportation and communications, and assisting the private sector in a variety of other ways in the development of the economy. Since the Great Depression, its role has expanded enormously, particularly at the federal level.

During the later years of the Depression, when many provincial and municipal governments were teetering on the edge of bankruptcy, federal governments, both Conservative and Liberal, attempted to provide relief for citizens who could find little or no work. Many of these efforts initially encountered difficulties because of the jurisdictional provisions of the British North America Act, but federal unemployment insurance was established in 1940. Meanwhile, with the coming of the Second World War, the federal government assumed vast responsibilities for economic planning under its constitutional mandate to maintain "peace, order and good government."

By the end of that period, the notion that government activity is a positive thing had become entrenched in the national psyche. The consequence of this notion has been burgeoning public-service bureaucracies to accommodate new regulatory functions and to pursue the task of providing a more uniform standard of well-being for Canadians across the country. Roughly half of the Gross National Product now passes through government hands at the federal, provincial, and municipal levels.

Obviously, the more citizens ask government to do for them, the more it needs to know about them. Thus, it has become the largest repository of information about individual Canadians. Decisions crucial to individuals are made on the basis of this information. Who, for instance, is worthy of mother's allowance or qualifies for unemployment insurance? Who deserves a disability pension?

Some of this information is referred to as "personally sensitive," especially that which falls in such areas as health, education, employment, social services, and law enforcement and corrections. For example, the Ontario Student Assistance Program requires applicants to submit data concerning their work and study history, their marital status, their residency and citizenship history, their parents' residency and citizenship history, the duration and nature of the educational program in which they're enrolled, their own, and their spouse's, income and assets, and, in many cases, the income and assets of their parents. Since 1978, applicants have also been required to submit forms empowering the release of tax information on themselves, their spouses, and often their parents. This means the mandatory transfer of entire tax returns, which had formerly been defined as confidential and to be used for one purpose (taxation) only. The statements of assets contain information not normally found on any other record, such as details regarding real estate investments, personal property, and business holdings. Although the forms for the release of tax information assure the signator that it "will be treated in strictest confidence" and used "solely for the purpose of administering the Ontario Student Assistance Program," the transfer of information increases the number of people who have access to it.

Few people would object to Ontario's stated purpose for demanding tax information of OSAP applicants: to enable the ministry "to award financial assistance fairly to all students according to need." Most other government information-gathering has aims that ostensibly are equally laudable. For instance, tax and unemployment records can be of assistance in tracking down fathers who default on child-support payments.

In other words, there is no conspiracy here. Government *routinely* collects and stores data on individuals in order to carry out its normal, socially approved functions. Yet one must ask how the government's need to know is balanced against the individual's right to privacy.

A number of North American and European jurisdictions have adopted privacy-protection laws in recent years. In the spring of 1983, the Canadian government passed Bill C-43, known as the Privacy Act.[12] It defines a zone of privacy for individuals in two major ways:

- Setting out conditions for the collection, storage, and disposal of personal information.
- Providing a code for the use and the disclosure of the information.

The act also requires that the Index of Personal Information be available to the public, in such places as libraries, government information offices, and post offices. There are approximately 1500 federal data banks currently listed in this index. You can ask to see the information collected about yourself, and you can appeal to the federal courts if access is denied. Furthermore, personal data can only be disclosed to someone else with your permission.

The legislation does, then, make an attempt to safeguard privacy. However, there are significant loopholes. Twenty-two data banks are exempt from access.[13] If you are alleged to have engaged in activities defined as potentially harmful to the national welfare, you can be denied access to your file.

Even in the information age, Canadians possess only a vague notion of what is involved in the issue of privacy, and they are less vigilant about its protection than are Americans or Europeans.

CRIMINALIZE THEFT OF CITIZENS' DATA, PRIVACY HEAD SAYS

By Graham Fraser

Privacy Commissioner John Grace has called upon the federal government to make the theft of its information about citizens a criminal offence.

"The Privacy Act gives an implicit commitment that personal information will be held confidential," Mr. Grace said in an interview yesterday. He said that a recent Supreme Court judgment had undermined that concept.

However, he made it clear that the legislation he had in mind would not affect a case such as that involving Global Television reporter Doug Small, who was charged with possession of a stolen document as a result of his obtaining a summary of April's federal budget before it was officially released.

Mr. Grace said his concern was the unauthorized use of personal information in government files, such as that collected by the Canadian Security and Intelligence Service or the Royal Canadian Mounted Police.

In his annual report, published yesterday, Mr. Grace said that there is "a gap in the law which Parliament should close," pointing out that "significant amounts of personal information are held by governments in paper files and . . . compromise of such information by outsiders cannot be ruled out."

The Privacy Commissioner was particularly concerned about the implications of a Supreme Court decision last year overturning a conviction of theft based on the photocopying of a document.

The case, known as Stewart versus Her Majesty the Queen, arose when a consultant offered to pay a security guard for photocopying the names and addresses of the 600 employees of the Constellation Hotel in Toronto on behalf of a union trying to mount an organizing drive.

The case "did not receive the public attention it deserved," Mr. Grace wrote. "Had the information been sensitive health or financial records and not a mere list of names involved in a commonplace labor dispute, the outcry would have been enormous — and deservedly so."

The consultant was charged with fraud, and acquitted, but the Ontario Court of Appeal found him guilty of counselling theft, and two of the judges argued that Parliament should broaden the criminal definition of property.

In May of 1988, the Supreme Court of Canada overruled the appeal court's decision.

"One cannot be deprived of confidentiality because one cannot own confidentiality. One enjoys it," Mr. Justice Antonio Lamer wrote in the unanimous judgment.

"Confidential information is not of a nature such that it can be (taken) because, if one appropriates confidential information without taking a physical object, for example by memorizing or copying information . . . the alleged owner is not deprived of the uses or possession thereof," Judge Lamer wrote.

"The only thing that the victim would be deprived of is the confidentiality of the information. In my opinion, confidentiality cannot be the subject of theft because it does not fall within the meaning of 'anything,' " the Supreme Court ruling said.

"That really scared me," Mr. Grace said yesterday. In his report, he wrote that "these observations have alarming implications for the information society in general and the Privacy Act in particular."

He pointed to the discrepancy between two Supreme Court decisions on privacy, and warned that "terrible personal tragedy" could result from the unauthorized disclosure of RCMP investigation records, security service surveillance reports, or Health Department medical files.

"Yet, the court seems to have said that records could be memorized—or copied—without any criminal sanctions as long as documents are not physically appropriated," Mr. Grace wrote.

"I don't think the Criminal Code is up to date in this regard," Mr. Grace said, noting that the Supreme Court judgment called on Parliament to legislate.

The commissioner said he was disturbed at changes in the Income Tax Act that have made it obligatory for Canadians to disclose their social insurance number when they open a bank account.

"In the complexity and detail of the amendments to the Income Tax Act, the extension of the SIN and its significance was missed by members of Parliament, the media, and, yes, the

Privacy Commissioner's Office.''

Noting that it is now a punishable offence to refuse to provide a SIN, Mr. Grace wrote that ''another precedent is established here. Until these income tax amendments, Canadians were required by law to give their SINs only to the federal government. Now they must confess their SINs to banks, trust companies, stockbrokers, credit unions, whenever and wherever they make what looks like an interest-bearing investment. Welcome to the computer society.''

Mr. Grace used his report to warn of the increasing danger to personal privacy represented by computer data banks, and, as a result, the greater importance of privacy legislation.

''Without privacy legislation or working, effective voluntary codes, there is no opportunity to see and correct one's file,'' he wrote. ''Without privacy legislation or enforced codes, there is nothing to stop the frightening growth industry in the sale and exchange of computerized information, of data chronicling personal consumption habits (traced through credit card orders) and charitable or political contributions.''

He raised the question of power.

''Who's in control here? Is it individuals of their own information?'' he asked. ''Or is it personal information collectors and traders with their marvellous machines? To become a 'data subject' should not mean becoming any less a human being.''

Mr. Grace pointed to the fact that one company has transferred Bell Canada's telephone directories onto laser disks along with the coordinates of each household within one metre on a grid map of Canada, the names of neighbours, electoral districts and the length of time the occupant had been at that address.

''All this information is in the public domain. But add credit card or banking information, if such information was to be made available by fair means or foul, and the result is profiling of the population on a mass, systematic scale,'' he wrote. ''It is a marketer's dream—a privacy nightmare.''

TECHNOLOGY AND CHANGE

The simplest definition of technology is ''applied science.'' It refers to all the physical problem-solving activities that human beings have developed to cope with their environment.

In this sense, technology is as old as human history, with each major new technological discovery bringing about far-reaching changes in the way social life is organized. Just as the plough brought drastic changes to mediaeval agriculture, so, too, has the transistor had a major effect on the modern economy. As Simmonds noted about the discovery of the transistor in Bell Telephone's research laboratories:

> *The impact of this development was not only on the telephone system but on the whole economy. The influence of the transistor went far beyond the telephone system into radios and stereos, into computers, accounting and information systems; defence generals thanked God for it; for airlines and air controllers, it led to greater safety and improved regularity of service; and even car manufacturers are finding its descendants of value.*
>
> *In cold analytical language, the characteristic that defines a major new technology is that it forces the majority of companies and/or consumers to respond positively to it. They respond by changing their patterns of expenditure or their allocations of time or both: their habits change (1981, 53–4).*

Today's technological revolution has been greeted with both optimism and pessimism. Few disagree that it will involve profound societal dislocations. Fear centres on issues ranging from the possibility of nuclear warfare to the more immediate issue of job loss. To the extent that people are aware of the marvels that this revolution promises, there is a great deal of optimism. There is a sense that it will advance the frontiers of knowledge in unimaginable ways, transforming current ways of doing things and of seeing things, and expanding people's contact with the rest of the world and with outer space.

The economic significance of the new technologies lies in the transformations they are bringing to the processes of production. These changes, say many experts, give hope for unprecedented economic growth. The sociological perspective prompts questions such as: how will the new technologies be implemented? What impact will they have on the social organization of work? How will the costs and benefits of growth be distributed?

THE MICRO-CHIP REVOLUTION

The miniaturized computer or **micro-chip** may constitute the most important agent of change in modern society. Its advent

> *means technological change that pervades every aspect of our lives. The chip can program a micro-wave oven to cook a roast while you are out, give individually paced instruction to your child at school,*

command the robots that are taking over routine factory work, monitor warehouse stock, take voice dictation of letters and print them by word processor, provide 24-hour automated banking services, monitor the chronically ill for changes in condition — even release and clasp the binding on downhill skis (Speirs 1983).

It is impossible to imagine all the potential applications of this technology. Yet it is certain that such applications will unite the globe in a single complex economic system, radically changing current economies. What this will mean for existing cultures, not to mention political systems, is an important question.

EXHIBIT 10.4

HOME MACHINERY

Televisions	99%
Telephones	98%
Cassette or tape recorders	70%
Cable television	69%
Microwave ovens	54%
VCRs	52%
Cable converters	41%
Home computers	13%
Pay television	11%
Compact disc players	8%
Camcorders	3%

SOURCE: Statistics Canada 1988.

Year by year, Canadian households are becoming more and more new tech. Microwave ovens and VCRs, which were considered luxury items only a few years go, are now commonplace. Newer electronic products—such as CD players and camcorders (video camera cassette recorders) — are gradually entering the home. The three interrelated cornerstones for an expanding range of technological systems and services in the home are a telephone, a television and a computer. Above are the percentages of Canadian households that have these new — and some not-so-new — technologically advanced items.

Royal Bank Reporter, Fall, 1989

Think about the potential effects of **robotics**, just one aspect of computer technology. Robots can be programmed to perform delicate microsurgical procedures and they can manipulate heavy machinery. The optimists point out that robots can operate in environments hazardous to humans, such as the ocean bed, outer space, and nuclear or chemical plants, and that they can relieve human beings of mind-numbing, monotonous assembly-line work. The pessimists count the jobs that will be lost. For example, robots have, since their inception, replaced tens of thousands of autoworkers.

Moreover, the fifth-generation computer behaves in ways that have long been said to reflect intelligence; it can understand something of the world around it and can use this understanding to reason, deduce, estimate, and plan. Such a computer gathers information about its environment through vision, speech recognition, touch, and manipulation, as well as through more conventional devices such as typewriters, touch-sensitive screens, and magnetic tape. It stores, organizes, and integrates data along with other general knowledge in its memory bank. Then, it uses all the pertinent information to arrive at a solution to a problem. What it replaces is not human muscle but, rather, many functions of the human brain. One such computer devises methods for a robot to move objects around in a room; another is able to identify problems in train locomotives, and repair them; a third, appropriately named PUFF, can diagnose lung problems and make treatment recommendations. An awesome type of artificial intelligence computer system

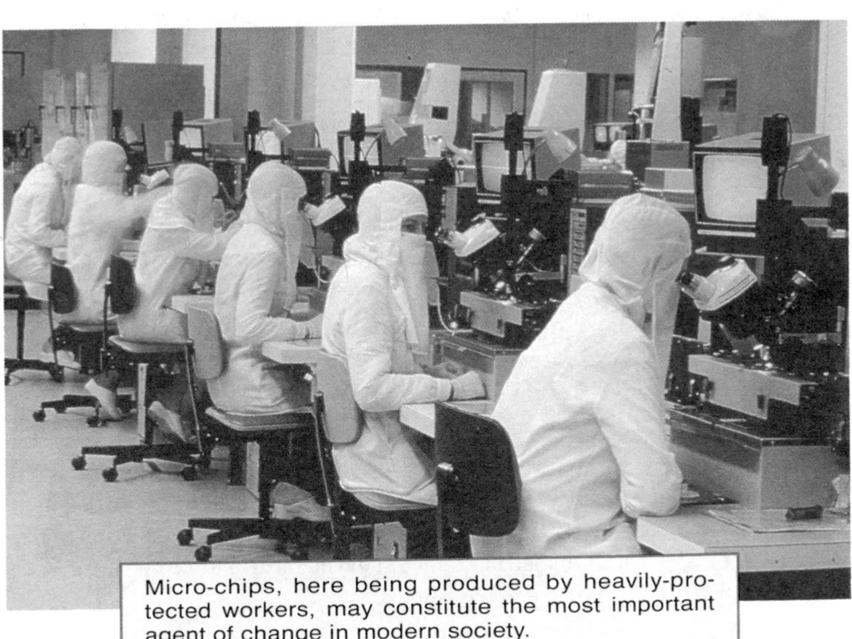

Micro-chips, here being produced by heavily-protected workers, may constitute the most important agent of change in modern society.

attempts psychologically accurate discussion with human beings. For example, a Yale program called ABDUL can respond to statements about Middle East politics using either an Arab or an Israeli point of view. Another, appropriately named MAGPIE, poses questions as a shrewish wife would:

> WIFE: *Where were you last night?*
> HUSBAND: *I went bowling with the boys.*
> WIFE: *I thought you hated bowling.*
> HUSBAND: *It's okay when I have some company.*
> WIFE: *Aren't I company?*
>
> *(Strauss 1984, 19).*

It is important to note the implications that computer technology has for a great variety of human work (see Menzies, 1989). Computer systems will provide a substitute not only for routine tasks now performed by factory and office workers, but also for the complicated, decision-making responsibilities of professionals. In other words, jobs at all levels of the occupational structure are threatened. Where will these workers go? The primary and secondary sectors of the economy already employ fewer than one-third of all Canadian workers, and it is predicted that manufacturing could employ only 5 percent by the year 2000. As Speirs has noted:

> *That puts the burden of absorbing the technologically unemployed on the service sector — government, finance and trade — which already employs 70 per cent of Canadian workers. Unfortunately, the service sector is beginning to show signs of saturation as government restraints put the brakes on spending and on economic growth (1983, 12).*

On the other hand, computers have the capacity to bring vast improvements to the physical condition of human life. And, like other technological breakthroughs, they are creating previously unknown jobs. (Your great-grandparents, for example, would never have imagined newscasters, much less videotext page creators.) These jobs are not only providing new career opportunities for young people but are inducing workers in other fields to seek retraining so that they can transfer into the computer field.[14]

THE BIOTECHNICAL REVOLUTION

The technological applications of the biological sciences are referred to as **biotechnology**. This field involves the altering of phenomena in the natural world and the creation of new combinations of "building blocks." The interdisciplinary science base of biotechnology includes chemical and biological engineering, microbiology, applied genetics, molecular biology, biochemistry, toxicology, forest and foods chemistry, physiology, and parasitology.

The use of bacteria to transform natural substances is an endeavour with an ancient history, dating from the first making of fermented drinks, cheese, and yoghurt.

Yoxen noted:

> *For thousands of years people from many cultures have used biological processes, in a controlled fashion, to make foods, dyes, drugs, fuels, adhesives, paper and fertilizers. Many of these procedures lie at the heart of traditional industries like brewing or the manufacture of dairy products.*
>
> *Into this complex of traditional crafts, household routines and long established industrial practices has now come the dynamism of high technology and advanced laboratory research. Not only are traditional micro-organisms like moulds and yeasts being geared up to much higher levels of productivity, but new organisms are being built in order to carry out all kinds of hitherto inconceivable tasks. Bacteria can now make human proteins, excrete plastic, manufacture antifreeze, extract metal from their ores or accumulate them from sea water, and turn human sewage into food. Add to that what yeasts can do (principally, they can make alcohols from all kinds of improbable materials), what moulds can do (which is a great deal more than just putting the blue veins into Stilton), what cultured plant, animal and human cells can do, and you have the makings of a revolution (1983, 14–5).*

Food production is one major affected area, and with it, there will be alterations in the social division of labour. Substitutes for human milk can now be produced in enormous quantities. What will this mean for infant nutrition and the traditional cultural patterns of child care? New sweeteners, such as high-fructose corn syrup and aspartame, are now being manufactured. What will be the effect on sugar economies such as Cuba's? In the plant world, research is leading to new hybrids such as triticale, a cross between wheat and rye. How will the availability of grains that can grow in salty soils change the traditional uses of land areas?

In other cases, waste material, including human sewage, is being used as a food source for bacteria, producing compact forms of protein-rich substances that are edible when mixed with plasticizers, flavourings, binding agents, preservatives, and dyes. Professor Moo Young, at the University of Waterloo, developed a process that can transform forestry waste, sawdust, wood chips, and twigs into a basic food substance. Factories using such processes will replace land as the site of production — with a transfer of capital from land and agricultural labour to chemical plants. Social changes are inevitable when patterns of food production change so radically.

Biotechnology is also affecting the world of medicine. For example, medical substances that can be extracted, at great expense, from human or mammalian organs (insulin for diabetes, interferon for cancer research) can now be made more cheaply from bacteria. Genetic engineering can also increase the yields of antibiotics from the moulds that produce them. Society has much to gain from these

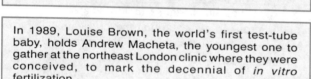

Surrogate mother Mary Beth Whitehead holds her daughter Melissa Stern at a youth centre in New Jersey during her second weekly visit since the state supreme court renewed them.

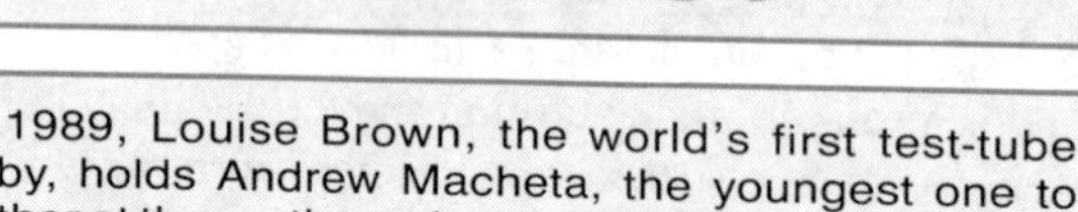

In 1989, Louise Brown, the world's first test-tube baby, holds Andrew Macheta, the youngest one to gather at the northeast London clinic where they were conceived, to mark the decennial of *in vitro* fertilization.

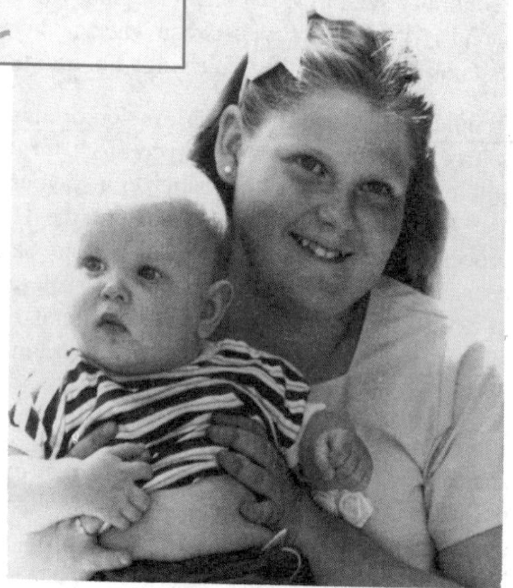

advances. But will the commercial push of pharmaceutical companies serve not only to meet the demand for new wonder drugs but also to create such a demand? The social consequences have yet to be explored.

Animal genetic engineering is another area of biotechnology that is making headway. For instance, the international trade in frozen cow embryos, which can be implanted in other cows, is now worth millions of dollars. At first, it was only possible to combine organisms within the same species or closely-related species. Now experimentation is leading to the reality both of mixing genes, such as those of rabbits and mice, and of putting human genes into bacteria.

The potential of this type of experimentation begins to read like science fiction. Its long-term prospects defy the present ability to forecast. As Yoxen has stated:

> *In a mere seven or eight years biotechnology has grown from being an esoteric research topic of university scientists into the foundations of a new industrial movement, a new wave of investment, commercialization and production. . . . This is not just a change of technique, it is a new way of seeing. It is now possible to think of making organisms to a specification to carry out particular industrial tasks. The limitations of species can be transcended by splicing organisms, combining functions, dovetailing abilities and linking together chains of properties. The living world can now be viewed as a vast organic Lego kit inviting combinations, hybridization and continual rebuilding. Life is manipulability (1983, 15).*

If the universe can indeed be moved around like building blocks, what are the implications for human life? What will be the impact of this kind of scientific breakthrough on the human environment and on consumption, health, work, and leisure? Some people predict that biotechnology will greatly reduce poverty, hunger, and illness in the world; others stress its potential for creating new hazards and large-scale social dislocations.

SCIENTISTS SHOULD NOT TURN FROM TWISTED NAZI GENETICS

By David Suzuki

Last fall, I was invited to attend a meeting of the organizing committee of the Couchiching Conference. Each year, experts from various areas meet at Lake Couchiching, Ont., to discuss a specific topic. This year, the conference will focus on DNA and genetic engineering, a timely topic in view of the tremendous advances in molecular genetics and the proposal to decipher the entire genetic blueprint of a human cell.

The Couchiching committee focused on the technology of DNA manipulation and its future implications. But the very important questions have to do with what scientists and people in power will do with the unprecedented ability to alter the genetic makeup of life forms. The only way to anticipate that comes from looking backward.

Early in this century a brand new science — genetics — uncovered the laws of heredity. Scientists were understandably excited and exuberant about the potential to apply this knowledge for the benefit of mankind. Direct results of this enthusiasm in the United States were the imposition of immigration restrictions against people considered "inferior," the sterilization of mental patients and the prohibition in many states of interracial marriages.

In Germany, where culture and science were at a peak, doctors and scientists, using genetics, applied studies of the inheritance of *physical* characteristics in fruitflies and corn plants to *behaviour* and *intelligence* in people. They concluded that human beings could be "perfected" through selective breeding and the elimination of "defectives." The Nazi Race Purification programs seemed to represent the application of some of the most "progressive" ideas in science.

I discussed this at the Couchiching committee meeting and suggested that doctors and scientists of that earlier time — especially geneticists — had, in their intoxication with new findings, popularized the notion of the overriding importance of heredity in human behavior and sold it to Hitler's National Socialists. It led inexorably to the horrors of the Holocaust for which scientists must therefore acknowledge some responsibility. Two of the committee members (one a molecular biologist, both Jews) were outraged. They denied the possibility that scientists have to bear some of the blame for the excesses of Nazi action, and called me "hysterical."

This selective memory of science's history amounts to a cover-up and a revisionism that only ensures that it could happen again. This is particularly disturbing when today's budding scientists must specialize earlier and have virtually no knowledge of the history and philosophy of their disciplines, while geneticists are once more anxious to apply their powerful techniques. However, to even suggest there is an unpleasant part of science's past is interpreted as opposition to science. Three years ago, in a review of a television program I did that included some history of genetics, a Globe and Mail science writer wrote:

"You are of the clergy, a scientist who left the monastery/laboratory to reform the world's understanding of his faith, and who now may well be on the way to becoming a heretic. (Some of your fellow geneticists think that.)" When questions are raised, the accusation of heresy is a powerful way to enforce dogma or excommunicate the centre. The reluctance to face up to the past becomes understandable. But there are exceptions.

Benno Muller-Hill is a professor of

molecular biology in Cologne, West Germany. Few texts in molecular biology and genetics fail to mention his work. While at Harvard University, working with Walter Gilbert (who later was awarded a Nobel Prize), Prof. Muller-Hill carried out a classic experiment that allowed the isolation and purification of a protein molecule, called a *repressor*, that controls gene activity.

Only a few copies of the repressor are present per cell, so the Muller-Hill/Gilbert experiment was a scientific tour de force. Prof. Muller-Hill's lab went on to collect sufficient quantities of the material to determine the primary structure of the protein.

Prof. Muller-Hill, a scientist of world-class stature who continues to do research, has for the past decade also studied the history of genetics in Nazi Germany.

One of his articles, entitled Genetics After Auschwitz appeared in Holocaust and Genocide Studies, Volume 2, Number 1 (1987). It is a document that is at once chilling and agonizing — an unflinching look by a scientist at the role of scientists in the Holocaust.

The article begins: ''The past must be recollected and remembered before it can be evaluated. — It is particularly difficult for scientists. Science is oriented to the present — only today's results exist. Only new data or new theories bring glory, honor and money for new research. Reflection on the past almost excludes the reflecting scientist from the ranks of present-day science.'' He summarizes his studies this way: ''The rise of genetics is characterized by a gigantic process of repression of its history.'' Later, he writes, '' . . . geneticists have refused — and even now refuse — to acknowledge their history.'' Organizers of the Couchiching meeting should pay attention to this man. Next week, I will discuss Prof. Muller-Hill's article in detail.

WHO WILL MANAGE TECHNOLOGICAL CHANGE?

Who will control the development of these new technologies? If decisions are left to the market, control will be in the hands of giant corporations — for example, chemical, oil, food, seed, and pharmaceutical companies — which are propelled by the profit motive. Are such decisions too important to be left to commerce?

It is often said that technological change is sweeping over us like a relentless tidal wave. This fatalistic view implies that there is nothing that can be done about it. It also obscures the fact that the impact of technology will differ from one society to another and from one societal sector to another. Should the harnessing of technological change in order to serve societal goals be a matter of greater public concern? Earlier we noted that the proportion of change that is ''either planned or issues from the secondary consequences of deliberate innovations'' is much higher today than in previous times (Moore 1974, 2). We thus speak of change that is organized, or *institutionalized*. A certain degree of centralized or co-ordinated planning is characteristic of most democratic nations. This means that how the costs and benefits of change are to be distributed can be negotiated in the political arena. As Yoxen observed:

> *New technologies, processes and products have to be dreamt, argued, battled, willed, cajoled and negotiated into existence. They arise through endless rounds of conjecture, experiment, persuasion, appraisal and promotion. They emerge from chains of activity, in which at many points their form and existence is in jeopardy. There is no unstoppable process that brings invention to the market. If this view is correct, then the scale, pace and social impact of the biotechnological revolution must be open to negotiation. There must be alternative pathways (1983, 29).*

What Yoxen said with reference to the biotechnological revolution is applicable to technological change in general. It supports the Weberian view that change is the product of human decision-making. It also reflects the modern view that change can be structurally planned and, perhaps, controlled in accordance with negotiated priorities.

SPENDING ON MILITARY VERSUS ENVIRONMENTAL SECURITY

By G.H. Brundtland

The world spent well over $900 billion on military purposes in 1985, more than $2.5 billion a day. The real cost is what the same resources might otherwise be used for:

- An Action Plan for Tropical Forests would cost $1.3 billion a year over the course of five years. This annual sum is the equivalent of half a day of military expenditure worldwide.
- Implementing the UN Action Plan for Desertification would cost $4.5 billion a year during the last two decades of this century—the equivalent of less than two days of military spending.
- One of the greatest environmental hazards in the Third World is lack of clean water for household use, contributing to 80 percent of disease. The UN Water and Sanitation Decade, although given only a small fraction of support needed, would have cost $30 billion a year during the 1980s. This is the approximate equivalent of 10 days of military spending.
- To supply contraceptive materials to all women already motivated to use family planning would cost an additional $1 billion per year on top of the $2 billion spent today. This additional $1 billion is the equivalent of 10 hours of military spending.

SUMMARY

A major theme of this book is the co-existence of continuity and change in society. In areas such as socialization, the division of labour, the distribution of societal rewards, and the relationships between minority and dominant groups, we have noted that the thrust for change has often clashed with the weight of tradition, inertia, and the interests of groups intent on maintaining things as they are.

In this chapter we have reviewed evolutionary, cyclical, and dialectical theories of change. Most sociologists today study change from either a functionalist or a conflict perspective, or a combination of the two approaches. While functionalists are primarily interested in the mechanisms of adjustment that contribute to social stability, conflict theorists focus on the opposition between groups that seek to maintain their position of dominance and groups attempting to change their condition.

We have singled out three areas of change for detailed examination:

- The position of women with respect to their legal rights, their role in the family, and their participation in the labour force. Here, as elsewhere, a dynamic feedback process takes place whereby transformations in one area reverberate in others.
- The explosive growth of information and of the ability to gather, conserve, disseminate, and interpret it. More than ever before, information is a precious commodity; hence, governments, corporations, and individuals vie for access to information that is of particular interest to them. However, there has been a lag in the ability to control the flow of information, thus jeopardizing privacy.
- The technological revolution, which has brought the wonders of the micro-chip and biotechnology.

What distinguishes change in the modern world is its accelerating pace and its magnitude, facilitated by a rapidly expanding knowledge base, a heavy investment in technological innovation, and an increasing emphasis on rational decision-making to *change*.

ASSIGNMENTS

Do one or more of the following assignments, as instructed by your professor.

1 Review the vignettes at the beginning of Chapter 1, and the sociological questions derived from them. Using material in the book, outline how you might go about exploring these questions. Do the vignettes suggest other questions to you?

2 Select two major societal changes that have taken place since the year of your birth. Explore the chain of effects that these changes have initiated in various areas of social life.

3 Search your memory to make a list

of the information you have released about yourself in the last year. Remember such things as application forms, consumer surveys, and forms connected with opening a bank account.

(a) What kind of information did you release?
(b) To whom?
(c) For what purpose?
(d) What guarantees of confidentiality, if any, were provided for you?

Investigate the protection of privacy guaranteed to individuals in your province.

4 What view of change is presented by Bob Dylan's song of the 1960s, "The Times They Are a-Changin'?" Do you think that Dylan's predictions have become reality? Select a new song, analyse the lyrics, and compare them with the point of view expressed by Dylan.

5 Examine the 1899 list of a teacher's duties (Chapter 5) and do some research on a teacher's duties in your community today. What does the comparison tell you about continuity and change in the role of the teacher?

SUGGESTED READINGS

Jane Austen, *Pride and Prejudice* (New York: Airmont Books, 1962; originally published 1813). Jane Austen portrays life in 18th-century provincial England. The Bennet family was genteel but far from rich, and for its five daughters, hopes for a good life were tied to making advantageous marriages. No appealing alternatives were available to such women; spinsters stayed at home or, in case of financial need, became paid companions to rich ladies.

In many ways, the world of *Pride and Prejudice* is far removed from ours, yet the realism of Austen's writing highlights the commonalities of the human condition.

Neil Bissoondath, *A Casual Brutality* (Toronto: Macmillan of Canada, 1988). The story of a tight-knit Indian family, whose grandson comes to Toronto to study medicine and marries a Canadian, is played out against the violent changes occurring in Casaquemada.

Casaquemada is a tiny fictitious West Indian island that gains independence from Britain and, for a while, becomes oil-rich. Sudden prosperity exacts a high price: long-standing racial antagonisms intensify and fresh needs, unsatisfiable for many, are created. When the money dries up, old and new hatreds erupt.

Gro Harlem Brundtland, *Our Common Future: Report of the World Commission on Environment and Development* (Oxford: Oxford University Press, 1987). Run, don't walk, to your nearest library or bookstore, and get a copy of this report. It is anything but dry. Mandated in 1983 by the General Assembly of the United Nations to formulate "a global agenda for change," the Commission undertook a massive examination of the intricate relationship between the state of the environment and economic growth in the context of an increasingly international economy. The result is a compelling analysis of a downward spiral which can only be reversed by changes in political choices, institutional and legal arrangements, business practices, and the actions of individuals. The wide-ranging reports deals with such issues as population growth, the nightmarish conditions created by urban concentration, food security, economic threats to ecological systems, Third World debt, and the ultimate environmental threat—nuclear war.

Friedrich Durrenmatt, *The Physicists* (New York: Grove Press, 1964). Who is mad and who is sane? Durrenmatt's black comedy takes place in an asylum where three men attempt to confound their caretakers and each other by posing as lunatics. All three are famous physicists who are keenly aware of the lethal changes that scientific knowledge—*their* knowledge—can bring to the world. In attempting to convince the others that, paradoxically, the only way to exercise social responsibility is to retreat permanently from society, one of them says, "We have to take back our knowledge and I have taken it back. There is no other way out. . . . "

J. Houston, *The White Dawn* (New York: Harcourt Brace Jovanovich, 1971). When change is thrust on a group rapidly, and without consideration for its values and way of life, the results may be disastrous. Houston gives a fictionalized account of events following the rescue by Inuit hunters of three whalers lost in an arctic storm.

Nursed back to health in the Inuit's igloos, the whalers introduced their hosts to exciting, strange customs that rode roughshod over established Inuit ways.

Arthur Miller, *Death of a Salesman* (New York: The Viking Press, 1949). "Times change and we change in them," goes a Latin saying. Willy Loman, Miller's salesman, has not changed with the times. He harkens back to a period in which business was conducted through personal ties and jocular relationships. The Loman family is a close one; his wife and sons love Willy and seek to shield him from harsh reality, but ultimately he feels unable to continue living in a world that no longer seems familiar.

Edward Yoxen, *The Gene Business: Who Should Control Biotechnology?* (London: Pan Books, 1983). Edward Yoxen has a mission: to explain to non-scientists the social and political issues involved in the current explosion of biotechnology. Using case studies, Yoxen carefully describes the ways in which biotechnology is in the process of transforming the agriculture and food industries, medicine, and the production of energy and chemicals. He argues convincingly that the establishment of priorities must not be left exclusively to scientists and corporations, since the decisions that are made will have profound effects on many aspects of social life.

NOTES

1 Nisbet illustrated the rather amusing side of this human tendency with an historian's story:

> *During World War II in Britain . . . time and motion studies were made of gun crews in the artillery. . . . In one such study of a gun crew numbering five men, two of the men simply stood at attention for three seconds, then resumed the work necessary to the next firing. This was puzzling. The men themselves could not explain it, it was a part of the technique they had learned in gunnery school. Neither the officers nor the instructors at gunnery school could explain it either. All any of them knew was that the three-second standing at attention was "a necessary" part of the process of firing the highly mechanized piece of artillery. One day, an old, long-retired artillery colonel was shown the time and motion pictures. . . . "Ah," he said when the performance was over. "I have it. The two men are holding the horses."*
>
> *Not for close to half a century had horses drawn artillery, but they once had—holding the horses while the gun fired was necessary. The horses disappeared from the artillery, but the way of behaviour went on. We laugh, and say the story is one more illustration of military inertia. . . . But the history of the academic, legal, medical and engineering professions is not different, except in details. Nor is the rest of society different (1970, 318).*

2 Recall, too, that this state parallels Tönnies' Gesellschaft.

3 Recall, too, that even as late as 1929, a decade after Canadian women had the vote in all jurisdictions except Quebec—women had to appeal to the British Privy Council for a ruling that they were persons and thus eligible to serve in the Senate.

4 We explored some of the other factors, many of which are interrelated, in Chapter 5 on work.

5 Many individual women, of course, strove mightily for a wide range of social changes, and their many successes helped to improve the situation of a variety of groups and to lessen, bit by bit, stereotypes of women as incompetent, dependent creatures. The point is that women exhibited little consciousness of themselves as a class or group cross-cutting other group divisions, and their efforts were not necessarily devoted to bettering the condition of women *qua* women.

6 Such shelters have never been provided in many rural areas of the country.

7 To give just one example of the scope of the change we are talking about, consider the Domesday Book, the first census of property, inhabitants, and domestic animals in most of England in 1085–6. Ordered by William the Conqueror (who wanted a record of the lands he controlled), the data, which do not include London, Winchester, or the northern counties, took a virtual army of clerks two years to collect and are still the main source of statistical and other information on the period. Dissemination was limited by the need to copy by hand the two volumes, totalling 1660 pages. Getting similar information today would be a simple matter of accessing the regular census database and having the computer print out the appropriate portions (cross-indexed in a manner convenient for the researcher). The print-out could, of course, be photocopied many times.

8 Privacy of information is only one of several types of privacy, but it is the one that concerns us here.

9 See, for example, a discussion of computer control of airline clerks in Nash and Krzaniwski (1984).

10 The lack of validity arises because it is difficult to ensure that the respondents are a representative sample and that they are not answering frivolously or in a manner designed to stuff the ballot box.

11 Pilot projects have already been run in both Canada and the United States. The technology is a logical extension of the kind used for banking machines.

12 Notice that this legislation does not confront the issue of information abuse in the private sector. It concerns only the regulation of federal government data banks.

13 Exemptions are based on a number of considerations. For example, information is not released if it would injure the government's conduct of international affairs.

14 For example, a course at Centennial College, Scarborough, Ontario, designed to train technicians to tend robots — roboticians, as they are called — attracted graduate engineers, a teacher, a millwright, salesmen, a lumbermill worker, a child-care worker, and a helicopter mechanic (Strauss 1982, 18).

APPENDIX: WRITING AN ESSAY

Writing is a central skill in the acquisition of knowledge. Writing and learning are inextricably connected. That is, you learn to write *while* you are writing to learn. Often you do not know what you want to say until you have made a first attempt to write it down. As you write, you "discover" what you mean or want to say. Then, with the thoughts on the page, you can rethink what you have said before trying to express it in a revised form. (In fact, the word "revised" comes from the Latin for "see twice.") Writing, then, permits you to find meaning and to establish firmer ownership over your thoughts.

Thus, the ability to write is not acquired overnight, once and for all at a particular stage of your education. Rather, it is a skill to be developed, improved, and honed over a lifetime as you progress to more complex ways of thinking.

The academic essay is a particular form of writing, which begins with a problem or question that calls for resolution through research, study, and the presentation of evidence. It requires you to formulate a central idea (often referred to as a thesis) tying all the evidence together in response to the problem. The way the evidence is linked in support of the central idea is called the argument, an argument that you formulate in order to persuade a reader. As the writer of an essay, you are cast in the role of the courtroom lawyer arguing a case. The argument runs as a single thread throughout the essay and does not permit the inclusion of anything that would not support, clarify, or elaborate your central idea. The academic essay is, thus, a very disciplined form of thinking and writing.

GETTING STARTED

Faced with a task, most people worry in a rather general way about getting it done before actually buckling down to confront it. The longer you procrastinate, however, the larger the job looms. Something that is, in fact, quite manageable may grow into a major stumbling block, for the worry becomes diffuse and is hard to allay.

Students say that this is often true of writing essays. The problem can be minimized by focusing on a sequence of tasks, as described below.

CHOOSING THE TOPIC

If you have been given a list of topics from which to choose, make that choice almost immediately. Once you have committed yourself, you have only one topic to worry about, instead of five or six.

An assignment that reads "Write an eight-page essay on a subject of your choice" appears seductively simple but is one of the most difficult assignments of all because it leaves the field so open, obliging you to create a topic with appropriate limits.

Choosing your own topic does provide an opportunity to study something that interests you. However, it is wise to avoid a controversial issue about which you already hold strong opinions. You may fall into the trap of overstating your argument and presenting evidence in an excessively emotional way. Readers, like juries, are likely to dismiss this type of argument.

Limiting your topic is necessary, because you cannot write a short paper on a general subject such as ''Part-time Work.'' *What* is it about part-time work that interests you? Perhaps you are curious about whether part-time workers are unionized. *Who* are the part-time workers that interest you most? Perhaps health-care workers. *Where?* In Canada? In a particular province? Perhaps you want to have a look at the situation in Saskatchewan. *When?* In the 1940s? In the last decade? Now your topic may look something like this: ''The unionization of Saskatchewan part-time health-care workers in the 1980s.'' At this point, you are ready to turn your topic into a question that you can address in your essay, such as ''What have been the obstacles to the unionization of these part-time health care workers?''

ANALYSING THE ASSIGNMENT

Your instructor may provide you with a topic rather than requiring you to create one. Before you rush off to read for an essay, it is important that you understand precisely what you are being asked to write about. Your first task, then, is to work carefully through the terms of the assignment. Make sure that you do not miss any dimension of the question. Use whatever method of analysis works best for you. For example, you can underline, circle, and define all of the key words. Or, if you have the kind of mind that tends to order things into a series of subtasks, reduce the assignment to a list of questions. Perhaps you like to map things out in a more visual way, playing with the relationships among the various parts of the question. You might come up with a rather messy-looking diagram that makes sense to you. Whatever your method, devoting some time to this phase of the project is a good investment.

WHAT ARE YOUR RESOURCES?

An essay assignment is not just an extra task designed to keep you busy. Rather, it's an opportunity for you to ''try on for size'' the material of the course. Place the question squarely in the context of the course, using as your primary resources the vocabulary, concepts, and theories that you have been acquiring along the way. Recall from Chapter 1 of this book the examination of different ways various disciplines, such as history, sociology, and economics, would approach the issue of unemployment among young people. The questions posed by sociologists would not be the same as those posed by economists, even though both might be examining the same phenomenon. If your essay is for a sociology class, you need to respond to your assignment in sociological terms, asking sociological questions. Further, we have shown that within a single discipline, such as sociology, there are different ways of defining a problem, depending on one's theoretical perspective. Be aware of these differences in considering your essay problem and in gathering the information for it.

After analysing the assignment, you may think that the next step is to research in the library, but you are not quite ready for that. First, ask yourself what you *already* know that will help you to undertake this essay. The contents of your lecture notes and course readings have provided you with basic analytical tools and perhaps some specific information. Other courses may also have given you useful data. This information will be easy to retrieve if you have taken a little time throughout each course to edit your lecture notes, culling out the basic concepts as you go along. (Leaving a wide margin on each page of notes facilitates this process.)

Our book can assist you in a number of ways, once you know what you are looking for. Think of key terms associated with your topic. Can you find any of them in the *Subject Index*? If so, track them down in the text to see the context in which these terms are used. If they appear in several different chapters, you might pick up some hints about the sociological dimensions of your topic. Under what headings are these terms used? Are there any *glossary* terms in the passages under those headings? Check the glossary for other terms that might also be useful. Are there any references to sociological studies in the passages you have located? Look them up in the list of *References* at the back of the book to see whether the book titles seem appropriate to your topic: Use the *Author-Title Index* to find out whether the authors are mentioned in other parts of our book as well. If so, have a look at those passages. Remember that there are *Suggested Readings* at the end of each chapter. One of them might be relevant to your question.

Review the major sociological perspectives introduced in Chapter 1. Which one might yield the most interesting approach to your topic? Remember that each perspective invites certain types of explanation and de-emphasizes others.

There is no ''one best way'' to go about this process of exploration. Just allow yourself the flexibility to search for clues by going back and forth between the chapters and the glossary, indexes and list of references.

LIBRARY RESEARCH

The subject of the assignment now dictates what particular information you need to track down. Usually, you need to do some library research to gather information.

Become familiar with the library at your earliest opportunity, so it does not remain a forbidding mystery. Some libraries offer tours with explanations of how the catalogue system works, where the journals are located, and so on. Reference librarians are also there to assist you in locating appropriate material and to identify the general indexes and encyclopaedias that might be relevant (for example, *Social Sciences Index*, Sociological Abstracts, and *The Encyclopedia of the Social Sciences*).

SCANNING POTENTIAL MATERIAL

Once you have collected some books you think may be useful, there are a number of ways to determine whether they are actually relevant to your topic. Scan the following:

- *The table of contents*. Does it show specific aspects of the general topic in which you are interested?
- *The index*. Is your topic mentioned here? Does the author make only passing reference to it, or is it dealt with extensively?
- *The introduction to the book*. Does the author indicate that he or she deals with the topic in a way that coincides with your interests? In a sociological work, watch for indications of the author's theoretical perspective.
- *The bibliography*. Does the author's research material seem to include the particular topic you are investigating? This bibliography may also lead you to other useful sources of information. Choose the most recent references first, and see what sources those have used.

Journal articles may begin with an abstract that states the essence of the author's argument. Otherwise, scan the introductory paragraphs and the conclusion to determine the article's usefulness.

NOTE-TAKING

When taking notes from books, journals, magazines, or newspapers, be sure to record the source of your material each time. This will save a great deal of backtracking later. Record the title, author, page number, place of publication, publisher, and date of publication. This information will go into your citations and bibliography, if you eventually use the material for your essay. Placing each note on a separate file card makes it easier to organize your bibliography later.

If you want to record the author's words, instead of just summing up (paraphrasing) the ideas, make sure that you copy the words exactly. Taking liberties with someone else's words is one of the deadly sins in the academic world.

Even when you are not actively working on your paper, the topic you are wrestling with will, no doubt, be simmering on a back burner of your mind. Thoughts about the topic may occur to you at the most unlikely times—on the bus, at the dinner table, or while reading for another course. It is useful to have a systematic way of capturing these ideas at the time that they occur to you. If you carry around a small notepad, you can jot down ideas in short form for future reference, since you cannot rely on their returning to you, like obedient children when summoned, at the time you sit down to write the essay. You may be surprised how quickly such ideas accumulate, and they will give you confidence when you are ready to begin writing.

WRITING THE ESSAY

As we have already noted, your assignment may have been given to you in the form of a general topic (such as ''part-time work''). As we noted earlier, *within* this general topic, you must identify a problem that requires resolution, a question that calls out for an answer you are prepared to defend. Being driven by a ''sense of problem'' is somewhat like having a chicken bone stuck in your throat: something must be done about it!

The *thesis* of your essay is the answer to the question you have identified. It is the essence of your argument, a position for which you will present supporting (and possibly refuting) evidence throughout the essay.

Thus, when you have settled on an answer to the question your assignment raises, you can begin working on an outline of an argument that supports your answer (thesis). Unless your instructor requires a formal outline, you are not obliged to prepare one. However, it is wise to sketch out at least a skeleton of your argument—a plan for presenting your evidence—so that when you are writing, you do not lose sight of the essential points that will buttress your case. Writing and thinking almost never proceed in a simple linear fashion that is policed by an outline. You will find yourself moving back and forth between the thesis and ideas for the argument, modifying each as you go along. Linda Flower has aptly called writing a ''mental three-ringed circus.''

In organizing the essay, state your thesis or central idea and the essence of your argument in your introductory paragraph. An essay is not a whodunnit that entices the reader onwards with the promise of major revelations somewhere near the end. Just as you, when doing library research, want to know right from the beginning what a journal article is about, your reader, too, deserves to learn your point from a quick reading of your introduction. He or she will then be compelled to read on, not to learn *what* your central idea is, but *why* you believe it to be accurate.

The decision as to what evidence is important to advancing your case is determined by the question ''What do my readers need to know in order to understand and accept my thesis?'' Imagining that you have your readers by the hand and are leading them through the argument, step by step, is useful for ensuring that you are developing that argument in a clear, logical, and persuasive way. It will prevent you from darting about randomly in your notes for something to say next and will also facilitate clear transitions from paragraph to paragraph. If you include quotations, tables, or charts in your essay, integrate them into the text by explaining their significance for your thesis. No essay should contain "orphan information," unattached to the sentences that come before and after it.

You are the gatekeeper of your paper, the one who makes the decisions as to what should be allowed to stay and what should be excluded. With each piece of information you have gathered, ask yourself sceptically, "So what? Does it add anything to what I have already argued? Does it relate directly to my thesis? Have I already said this in another way?" It is always hard to discard data and ideas that you have painstakingly gathered but, inevitably, not everything you have read in preparation for the essay will be applicable when you write it. Deciding what to exclude is as important as deciding what to include.

A dictionary and a thesaurus are good to have on hand when you are writing. The latter provides synonyms for words, so that you can enlarge your vocabulary and avoid boring repetition.

ACKNOWLEDGING YOUR SOURCES

It is important to let your reader know where the material in your paper comes from. First, it is dishonest to represent someone else's words as your own, even if you have not used direct quotations from another author. To borrow someone else's ideas or information without acknowledgement is called *plagiarism*, and it is considered a serious academic offence, a breach of intellectual honesty.

If you quote someone else's words directly, cite the author and page number, or put the complete reference in a footnote.[1] If you paraphrase the author's words, do the same. Perhaps you are merely summing up the author's general argument in the book or article. In that case, you must still acknowledge your source in accordance with the method of referencing that you have chosen to adopt. Second, the interested reader may want to consult your sources, and it is your job to make this possible.

If your instructor does not specify the form of acknowledging sources, consult a writing manual for optional forms of citation and for the bibliography that is presented at the end of the paper. A bibliography essentially provides your reader with a map of the territory that you have covered in writing the essay. Whatever form you choose, use it consistently.

In our book, we have chosen to use the referencing method used in many academic journals. Instead of using numbered footnotes, we insert the author's name, and date of publication, in the text itself. For example, in the chapter on Organizations, we say: "Kanter (1977) argues that individuals, aspirations, and expectations are influenced by the 'opportunity structure' they encounter in the work environment." In this example, since we are referring to her general argument rather than to a specific passage in Kanter's book, and are not using a direct quotation, we do not cite a page number. If you look for Kanter in the alphabetical list of references (bibliography) at the back of our book, you will find the author's name, date of publication, title of book, place of publication, and the name of the publishing firm:

Kanter, R.M.
1977 *Men and Women of the Corporation*.
New York: Basic Books.

Notice that some authors have multiple entries; these references are listed in chronological order, beginning with the earliest date of publication.

CHANGING YOUR MIND

The first completed version of an essay is called the first draft. Once you have written it, you can work on refining your argument and making it more coherent. You may even find that, in the course of writing the initial draft, you have actually changed your focus or the position you wish to take on the problem raised by the assignment. When you think about it, changing your mind means that you, as an individual and a thinker, have taken a significant step during the process of writing. This is what we mean when we say that you write to learn.

EDITING AND PROOFREADING

When you are satisfied that your second (or third or fourth!) draft is the version you want to submit, it is time for careful editing. Review the paper thoroughly to eliminate distractions for the reader: incorrect spelling; grammatical errors; awkward, convoluted, or incomplete sentences; words that are colloquial (those that come from casual speech), jargon, or words so heavy or pedantic that they intrude upon the page. Certainly, take the risk of trying out new words from time to time, but as a general rule, choose language that is simple and straightforward.

Even if someone else types your essay, you are responsible for the final product.

WHAT'S NEW?

You may well say, "But I'm just a student. My ideas all come from what I have read or from my professor. How can I possibly write something original at this stage?"

Yes, the theories and concepts that you employ do originate with other people, the "experts" of your discipline. Likewise, most of your information comes from other people's research. However, the way you bring these elements together in support of your argument is unique. The synthesis — the interplay of ideas and information — is yours and reflects your ability to assimilate information, think about it in theoretical terms, and advance a sound argument. As we said at the beginning, writing permits you to discover meaning and to establish firmer ownership over your thoughts. It can be an adventure.

SUGGESTED READINGS

Peter Elbow, *Writing Without Teachers*. (London: Oxford, 1973).
Elbow's purpose is to dispel people's worries about writing. If you tend to get stuck in the ''getting started'' stage, this short book may be helpful.

Margrit Eichler, *Nonsexist Research Methods: A Practical Guide*. (Winchester, Mass.: Allen and Unwin, Inc., 1987).
Sexist biases can infect both thinking and writing. Eichler offers a set of guidelines for how to identify them and to avoid them.

The Sociology Writing Group, UCLA, *A Guide to Writing Sociology Papers*. (Los Angeles: University of California Press, 1986).
The authors take you through all stages of the essay-writing process, and discuss ways of handling various kinds of sociological data.

Linda Flower, *Problem-solving Strategies for Writing*. 3rd ed. (New York: Harcourt Brace Jovanovich, 1989).
Flower has done a great deal of research on the writing strategies of both expert and novice writers. Her book is a lively introduction to the ''academic discourse community'' and suggests imaginative strategies for formulating, and thinking through, a problem.

Christopher Ricks and **Leonard Michaels** (eds.), *The State of the Language*. 2nd ed. (Berkeley: University of California Press, 1990).
This is a book to have fun with, although it is by no means just a funny book. What is the disease called ''infomania?'' The contributors examine the state of the English language as it is written and spoken at the end of the 1980s, and find it wanting.

NOTES

1 We use our footnotes to expand or qualify ideas or information given in the text.

SUGGESTED FILMS

CULTURE

The Hutterites
27 min. sd. col. 1984. Distributor: Magic Lantern Films (Oakville, Ontario).
Explores the communal principles that underlie North American Hutterite communities.

Number Our Days
29 min. sd. col. 1978. Distributor: McNabb & Connolly (Toronto, Ontario).
Documents the lives of a community of Jewish senior citizens living in Venice, California. Based on the field research of Barbara Myerhoff.

Songs in Minto Life
29 min. sd. col. 1986. Distributor: Native American Broadcasting Consortium (Lincoln, Nebraska).
Shows how the musical traditions of Athabaskan Indians in the Alaska interior are integral to the community's cultural organization.

SOCIALIZATION

Anybody's Son Will Do (War Series)
57 min. sd. col. 1983. Distributor: National Film Board of Canada (Toronto, Ontario).
Follows a group of young recruits through basic training at an American marine base in South Carolina.

Coming of Age (Strangers Abroad Series)
52 min. sd. col. 1985. Distributor: Thomas Howe (Vancouver, British Columbia).
Assesses the contribution of Margaret Mead to contemporary ideas about how an individual is shaped by society.

The Pinks and the Blues (Nova Series)
59 min. sd. col. 1980. Distributor: Marlin Motion Pictures (Mississauga, Ontario).
Probes the subtle ways in which parents and teachers influence children's ideas about sex roles.

STRATIFICATION

28 Up
136 min. sd. col. 1985. Distributor: Thomas Howe (Vancouver, British Columbia).
Examines the relationship between economic background and career and family choices made by a group of British children who were interviewed at the ages of 7, 14, 21, and 28 years of age.

Maids and Madams
53 min. sd. col. 1985. Distributor: DEC Films (Toronto, Ontario).
Examines the situation of black women in South Africa who work as maids for white women.

WORK AND ORGANIZATIONS

Class of Promise
43 min. sd. col. 1985. Distributor: National Film Board of Canada (Toronto, Ontario).
Considers the potential impact of women executives on business culture by examining the career expectations of female students in the University of Western Ontario's M.B.A. programme, and the experience of its recent female graduates.

Clockwork
25 min. sd. col. 1981. Distributor: California Newsreel (San Francisco, California).
Links the time-study research of Frederick Taylor to the development of modern assembly-line production.

Loose Bolts
29 min. sd. col. 1973. Distributor: Merrimak Films (Franklin Lake, New Jersey).
Interviews with employees on the assembly-line at a Ford automotive plant convey their reactions to this well-paying but dehumanizing work.

MINORITIES

Cree Hunters of the Mistassini
58 min. sd. col. 1974. Distributor: National Film Board of Canada (Toronto, Ontario).
Three Cree families show how the James Bay Hydroelectric Project will disrupt hunting practices and therefore weaken Indian cultural identity.

The Disability Myth, Part One: Segregation
53 min. sd. col. 1981. Distributor: Lauron Productions (Toronto, Ontario).
Shows the frustrations that disabled people face in their struggle to become part of the community.

Ethnic Notions
56 min. sd. col. 1987. Distributor: California Newsreel (San Francisco, California).
Demonstrates how racial stereotypes are perpetuated by analysing the image of blacks presented over the past 150 years in newspapers, magazines, cartoons, comic books, motion pictures, and television.

Legacy of Injustice
29 min. sd. col. Distributor: TVOntario (Toronto, Ontario).
Joy Kogawa, a Japanese-Canadian who was interned during World War II,

describes her experience and the public discussion about compensation for the victims.

No Way! Not Me
31 min. sd. col. 1987. Distributor: National Film Board of Canada (Toronto, Ontario).
Feminist Rosemary Brown shows Toronto high school students how the educational choices available to women have contributed to the feminization of poverty.

Proud Women, Strong Steps
30 min. sd. col. 1987. Distributor: DEC Films (Toronto, Ontario).
Recounts the hardships of married immigrant women who work in low-paying, hazardous jobs and are responsible for home and child care.

DEVIANCE

Clockwork Orange
137 min. sd. col. 1971. Distributor: Criterion Pictures (Toronto, Ontario).
An adaptation of the Anthony Burgess' novel in which a sadistic young man is subjected to a form of mind control in order to change his behaviour.

Democracy on Trial: The Morgentaler Affair
59 min. sd. col. 1984. Distributor: National Film Board of Canada.
A docudrama that details the complexities of the successful court challenges brought by Dr. Henry Morgentaler against Canada's abortion laws.

Prison Mother, Prison Daughter
87 min. sd. col. 1986. Distributor: Canadian Broadcasting Corporation (Toronto, Ontario).
Follows two women, one a first-time offender, the other a repeat offender, during their internment in the Kingston Prison for Women and release on parole.

SOCIAL INSTITUTIONS

FAMILY

Stepdancing: Portrait of a Remarried Family
27 min. sd. col. 1987. Distributor: Kinetic Films (Toronto, Ontario).
Presents the problems that confront members of remarried families through their own words.

EDUCATION

Don't Pass Us By
26 min. sd. col. 1987. Distribution: TVOntario (Toronto, Ontario).
Illiteracy is examined through the testimonies of individuals who are learning to read as adults.

Starting from Nina: The Politics of Learning
30 min. sd. col. 1978. Distributor: DEC Films (Toronto, Ontario).
Shows that different groups in society have different educational requirements. Refers to the ideas of Paulo Freire, who argued that education is not politically neutral.

RELIGION

Behind the Veil . . . Nuns
130 min. sd. col. 1984. Distributor: National Film Board of Canada (Toronto, Ontario).
Cross-cultural look at the status of nuns that traces their position in the church hierarchy back through the history of Christianity.

LAW

Inside the Jury Room
58 min. sd. col. 1987. Distributor: Visual Education Centre (Toronto, Ontario).
Documents the deliberations of an American jury as it delivers a not-guilty verdict to a man accused of the illegal possession of a firearm. In making its decision, the jury disregards the factual evidence in favour of community values.

SOCIAL CHANGE

Rising Up Strong: Women in the 80's, Part 1
29 min. sd. col. 1981. Distributor: DEC Films (Toronto, Ontario).
Encourages women in the work force to act collectively to improve wage levels and child-care facilities.

Computers in Context
33 min. sd. col. 1986. Distributor: California Newsreel (San Francisco, California).
Show how some Scandinavian companies have benefitted from the use of computer systems that enhance rather than replace skilled workers.

Quel Numéro?/What Number?
78 min. sd. col. 1985. Distributor: DEC Films (Toronto, Ontario).
Describes the negative effect of the electronic revolution on female grocery clerks, secretaries, postal workers, and telephone operators.

Shift Change (Reckoning: The Political Economy of Canada Series)
57 min. sd. col. 1987. Distributor: National Film Board of Canada/TVOntario (Toronto, Ontario).
Weighs the impact of new technologies on Canadian workers and their families.

Pandora's Box (Life Revolution Series)
52 min. sd. col. 1987. Distributor: TVOntario (Toronto, Ontario).
Examines the moral dilemma posed by genetic engineering.

GLOSSARY

Absolute deprivation: A definition of poverty that refers to the individual's capacity to obtain the basic necessities of life, such as food, clothing, and shelter. *Cf.* relative deprivation.

Acculturation: The process by which groups or individuals who are in contact exchange cultural traits and acquire new ones.

Achieved status: A status attained through the individual's actions. Examples are education, occupation, and marital status. *Cf.* ascribed status.

Affirmative action: One method that may be chosen to facilitate employment equity; it entails special measures to compensate a group for past discrimination. It may be a short-term measure to hire or promote members of one group at a faster rate than those in other groups.

Agencies of control: Those organizations which function to identify, classify, and respond to deviance within the society. These agencies include police and welfare organizations, as well as churches, schools, and rehabilitation hospitals.

Agents of socialization: The people with whom the individual interacts in the process of socialization, *q.v.* Parents, peers, and teachers are examples.

Alienation: Estrangement, an individual's sense of powerlessness, meaninglessness, and isolation from society as a whole. In Marxian analysis, alienation on several levels is the inevitable results of workers' being separated from the other means of production and performing highly specialized and thus meaningless tasks.

Anomia: Merton's term for normlessness resulting from the disjunction between culturally established goals and the legitimately available means to achieve them.

Anomie: Normlessness, a lack of clarity about values and established rules for conduct. In Durkheim's analysis, this state arises when a person socialized to one set of values must live in a world in which they no longer apply.

Anticipatory socialization: The process by which individuals prepare themselves for roles to which they aspire but which they do not yet occupy.

Ascribed status: A status assigned to individuals, usually at birth, based on the social categories to which they belong. Examples are gender, race, religion, and age. *Cf.* achieved status.

Atavism: Qualities that are characteristic of a genetic throwback to a more primitive stage of development; Lombroso argued that criminals demonstrated atavism in physique and behaviour.

Authority: Power that is legitimated and institutionalized. *Cf.* charismatic, rational-legal and traditional authority.

Behaviourism: The theory that human beings are almost infinitely plastic, within the bounds of basic biological needs, and are conditioned to behave in various ways; behaviour is a matter of stimulus and response.

Biological determinism (social Darwinism): The theory that each person is born with a certain temperament and with certain abilities, which can be changed only within a narrow range; thus, socialization has a limited role in human development, and the genetic endowment of individuals and groups is the major determinant of how they will fare.

Biotechnology: The technological applications of the biological sciences.

Bourgeoisie: In Marxian analysis of society, the class whose members own and control the means of production.

Bureaucracy: A hierarchical organization designed to accomplish stated goals. Each position carries with it specific authority, rights, and duties, is clearly related to other positions on an organizational chart, and is filled on the basis of achievement. Procedures are standardized and recorded in writing.

Caste society: A stratified society in which each stratum is a closed group that determines virtually every aspect of the individual's life; assignment to a stratum is ascribed and hereditary, and rigid taboos regulate interaction among members of difference castes.

Centralization: The allocation of decision-making power. In a highly centralized organization, all major decisions are made at the top, and lower-level ''decisions'' are constrained by the policies that are already laid down.

Change of type: An actual transformation of kind.

Charismatic authority: Authority legitimated by the extraordinary personal qualities of a leader (Greek: charisma = grace). *Cf.* rational-legal and traditional authority.

Charismatic leader: A leader whose claim to authority is based on personal qualities, rather than on position in an organization.

Chicago School: A group of sociologists who worked at the University of Chicago in the 1920s. They and their students pioneered studies of occupations and control theories of deviance.

Church: A religious organization with a bureaucratized structure, a hierarchy of authority, and a professional priesthood; worship is ritualized. *Cf.* sect.

Civil law: (1) Laws specified in codes, statutes, ordinances, and the like. In this sense of the word, the antonym is common law, *q.v.* (2) Law regulating relations between two or more private parties; the state arbitrates disputes but is not party to them. The antonym here is criminal law, *q.v.*

Class: The social position and life chances derived from the individual's or family's relation to the processes of production in the society.

Class society: A stratified society in which each stratum is made up of families and individuals who have similar socioeconomic status. Strict Marxists argue that economic criteria (relationship to the means of production) are the only determinants of social position in a class society; others add prestige, power, lifestyle, and attitudes.

Common law: Unwritten law, applied by courts throughout the entire nation or society, based on previous judicial decisions.

Communication: A process that involves the transmission of information. Within organizations, formal as well as informal ('the grapevine') communication takes place. Formal communication can be divided into vertical communication (between hierarchical levels) and horizontal communication (within hierarchical levels).

Competition: A model of majority-minority relations in which members of the dominant groups view their inferiors with hostility as potential competitors for societal rewards. Spatial segregation is common, reducing opportunities for informal mixing, but the rules for interaction may be fuzzy. Minority-group status is not the exclusive determinant of an individual's place in the division of labour. The antonym is paternalism, *q.v.*

Complex organization: A formal, structured group formed to reach a specific goal or goals; the rules are explicit, and there is a set of clearly designated roles.

Complexity: Horizontal and vertical differentiation within an organization. The ways in which tasks are subdivided constitutes horizontal differentiation. The number of hierarchical levels makes up vertical differentiation.

Conflict: A struggle among groups or individuals. Conflicts revolve around such issues as the allocation of resources, and the introduction, perpetuation or elimination of certain practices.

Conflict perspective: One of the major perspectives or orientations of sociology. It stresses the effect of power on relationships between competing status groups or between classes. Theorists using this perspective emphasize conflict rather than consensus, and constant societal change rather than stability.

Control theory: A theory of social control that focuses on bonds to society. It assumes deviance is common and asks why there is not more of it.

Counterculture: A subculture formed as a protest against the mainstream values and norms.

Criminal law: The body of law that prohibits various actions, making them offences against the state and imposing sanctions for such conduct; the state, not the victim, is the plaintiff in a prosecution under criminal law. The antonym is civil law, *q.v.*, definition 2.

Cult: A group that is usually, but not necessarily, religious. Cults lack structure, have a loosely defined membership, and are in a state of tension with the social environment.

Cultural capital: The body of formal and informal knowledge and social skills that enables people to cope successfully with their environment.

Cultural diffusion: The exchange of the material and symbolic elements of culture that occurs when two societies come in contact. Diffusion may be rapid or slow and may be more in one direction than in the other, but it always occurs.

Cultural mosaic: A society in which racial, ethnic and religious groups maintain a distinct identity, rather than being absorbed into a "melting pot."

Cultural relativism: Acknowledgement of and respect for cultural diversity; the belief that other people's cultures are as good as one's own, even if they involve very different values and norms. The antonym is ethnocentrism, *q.v.*

Culture: A society's or group's shared way of life. It includes knowledge, beliefs, arts, morals, laws, customs, and symbols.

Culture lag: The delay between changes in material culture (technological change) and related adjustments in other aspects of social life.

Deinstitutionalization: A process by which long-term commitment of individuals to asylums, prisons, or reformatories is phased out and those individuals are returned to the streets, or to smaller community-based programs.

Dependent variable: A variable whose occurrence or change is regarded as the effect of the occurrence or change of another variable, called the independent variable, *q. v.*

Deviance: Behaviour that violates salient norms.

Deviant: A person designated as one who typically violates salient norms.

Deviantizing: The process whereby a type of behaviour is designated deviant. *Cf.* labelling.

Dialectic: A process of change in which contradictions arise in a system (thesis). Ultimately, the contradictions (antithesis) become so strong that the system cannot survive. From the remnants of the old system and its opposite, a new amalgam emerges (synthesis). Marx argued that this process, originally conceived by Hegel as explaining the evolution of ideas, occurred in economic systems. Thus, Marx said, capitalism emerged as the synthesis of the remnants of feudalism (thesis) and its contradictions (antithesis).

Differential association: A social learning theory that emphasizes the learning of definitions favourable to breaking the law.

Discrimination: The unequal treatment of individuals or groups on the basis of their falling into some category.

Disidentifiers: Self-image signals intentionally used to deny belonging within a social group (membership) or category (type of person). Disidentifiers are chosen to counteract an undesired image of the self.

Division of labour: The basis on which tasks are allocated to individuals in a group.

Education: *See* formal education.

Elites: Powerful and prestigious groups that exert a pervasive influence on the ways in which society operates.

Endogamy: Marriage within one's own group, based on race, religion, ethnicity, or other social characteristics.

Estate society: A stratified society in which each stratum is clearly separated from the others but comprises a variety of occupations and socioeconomic levels.

Ethnicity: A shared cultural tradition and self-consciousness as a group that distinguishes a subgroup, usually one based on imputed common ancestry.

Ethnocentrism: The view that one's own culture is inherently superior to other cultures. The antonym is cultural relativism, *q. v.*

Exogamy: Marriage outside one's own religious, ethnic, or other group.

Extended family: A family comprising people who are related to each other by blood or marriage; in addition to the father, mother, and unmarried children (the nuclear family), it includes other relatives: grandparents, siblings of the father or mother, or polygamous mates and their children, or some combination thereof. The family members usually live in one dwelling place.

External social control: Control which is experienced as coming from others or the built environment. External control operates mainly through the likelihood of detection, the awareness of penalties, and the assessment of the efforts/risks involved in deviation from the norm.

Family: The basic kinship unit of society: a group of people related to each other by blood, marriage, or adoption. It generally provides the group with biological reproduction, the nurture and socialization of children, economic activity to meet survival needs, care of the elderly and infirm, and emotional support for individuals.

Feminism: The belief in the economic, political, and social equality, with due respect to biological differences, of women and men, and a commitment to changes in the structure and functioning of society to eliminate inequality in the institutional treatment of men and women.

Feminization of poverty: Women's increasing risk of poverty, a risk which is greater than that borne by men.

Folkways: Informal norms, usually not encoded in law, that change frequently. Violation of folkways may bring criticism or reprimand but is not as harshly sanctioned as violation of mores.

Formal communication: A form of communication occuring in organizations that can be divided into (1) **vertical communication**, which takes place *between* the levels of the hierarchy, and (2) **horizontal communication**, which occurs *within* the levels of the organization.

Formal education: The process of learning and socialization that takes place in specialized institutions, such as schools, colleges, technical schools, and universities.

Formal organization: A collectivity that has explicitly stated objectives and is governed by rules and regulations. The system of roles and the rights and obligations attached to each role are clearly defined.

Formal social control: Control which is official within the particular social setting. Formal controls are characteristic of secondary groups and organizations, and are usually codified or posted in some way, so that even strangers may be aware of them. Typical formal controls are official regulations supported by fines or suspensions.

Formalization: The extent to which procedures are routinized in an organization (manner and order of task performance, hours of work), and the degree of tolerance for deviation from such rules.

Functionalism: One of the major perspectives or orientations of sociology. It views society as a system each of whose components contributes to supporting the others and maintaining the whole. Its proponents tend to explain behaviour and institutions in terms of their function within the social system and thus focus on the mechanisms by which society coheres.

Gemeinschaft: One of Tönnies' ideal types of society. It is a small, homogeneous, usually rural community with a high degree of self-sufficiency, simple division of labour, shared values, and personal relationships overlapping several spheres of life. The orientation is sacred. Ascribed status is salient. The opposite is the Gesellschaft, *q.v.*

Gender inequality: Power relations between the sexes, usually with men in a dominant and women in a subordinate position (*Cf.* patriarchy).

Gender socialization: Socialization that inculcates in the child the values, attitudes, and patterns of behaviour deemed desirable for men or women in a society.

Geographic mobility: Movement from one location to another. Often such movement is undertaken by those who want to move up or maintain their place in the socioeconomic hierarchy.

Gesellschaft: One of Tönnies' ideal types of society. It is large, heterogeneous, and urban, with a highly specialized division of labour, a diversity of world views, and segmented personal relationships. Achieved status is normatively salient. The orientation is secular. *Cf.* Gemeinschaft.

Ghettoization: Segregation and confinement of groups, generally on the basis of race, religion, ethnicity, class, gender, age or some combination of these variables.

Goal displacement: The phenomenon whereby goals are shunted aside to maintain organizational routines. Thus, waking patients to accommodate nursing shift changes is an example of displacement of a hospital's primary goal of optimal patient care.

Health care: The patterned ways of pursuing the social goal of treating illness and promoting health among members of society.

Horizontal mobility: Movement among jobs at roughly the same socioeconomic level.

Human Relations School: An approach to management based on the idea that developing better human relations in the workplace (by providing pleasant surroundings, involving workers in minor decisions) will lessen alienation and thus increase productivity. The founder was Elton Mayo in the 1920s.

Hypothesis: A tentative statement about the relationship between two or more variables.

Ideal type: A general model or prototype of a phenomenon that posits what it would be like if all the characteristics attributed to the phenomenon were present in pure form. An ideal is an abstract — an idea — and never exists in its pure form in reality. It is used as a measuring device.

Idealist: A person who regards society's values, beliefs, and attitudes — its ideas — as the substructure.

Identifiers: self-image signals intentionally used to indicate belonging within a social group (membership) or category (type of person). Identifiers, unlike stigmata, are chosen, not imposed by others.

Ideology: A set of beliefs that provides moral justification for a social, economic, or political system.

Independent variable: A variable whose occurrence or change is regarded as the cause of the occurrence of change of another variable, called the dependent variable, *q.v.*

Influence: The ability to persuade, rather than coerce, individuals or groups to change their opinions, attitudes, or actions.

Informal communication: Networks such as the "grapevine" through which workers compensate for a lack of information from official sources in an organization.

Informal organization: The everyday norms and practices that, while not appearing in its blueprint, are nevertheless an integral part of an organization's functioning. These practices may either facilitate productivity or else subvert organizational goals.

Informal social control: A control which is practised within the group and which may even conflict with formal social controls in the same setting. Informal controls are usually uncodified yet are recognizable by members of the group. Typical informal controls are group customs supported by gossip, ridicule, and other forms of peer pressure.

Information age: The present age in which the proliferation of computer-related technology has transformed the human capacity to obtain, store, manipulate, and communicate information. Since information is a highly valued commodity, this enlargement of capacity is changing society.

Institution: *See* social institution.

Intergenerational mobility: Vertical mobility between one generation and the next of a family.

Internal social control: Control which is experienced as coming from within the individual's personality—it is experienced as the fulfillment of values and the avoidance of guilt.

Intragenerational (career) mobility: Vertical (upward or downward) mobility within one's own work life, accomplished by change in occupation or by career movement. Marriage, too, can provide an avenue for intragenerational mobility.

Labelling: The practice of defining groups, individuals, or activities on the basis of one overriding characteristic, thus obscuring internal differences.

Law: The formal regulation of relations among the individual members of a society and between individuals and the society as a whole. The institution of law comprises the society's methods of legislation, litigation, and adjudication.

Leadership: A relational concept that is distinguished from the concept of power in that it entails persuasion, influence, and innovativeness of ideas.

Looking-glass self: In Cooley's theory of socialization, the basis of self-perception; it is determined by the way the individual imagines he or she appears to others.

Macro-level sociology: The study of relationships of large social groups.

Magna Carta: An agreement between King John of England and that country's barons, signed in 1215. The inclusion of a list of rights for the aristocracy, to which John was forced to assent, established the principle that the authority of the state is not absolute but subject to the rule of law. The rights listed in this "great charter," today much expanded and extended to all citizens, are regarded as the source of fundamental human rights under Anglo-American law.

Majority: The dominant group in society, holding disproportionate power and access to desired goods and services. In the definition used in this book, a sociological majority may be a small numerical minority. *Cf.* minority.

Margin of tolerance: The extent to which the commission of an act that is normally disapproved escapes censure; a gray area in which rule enforcement is suspended. This will vary according to such factors as time, place, and the characteristics of the rule violator.

Master status: *See* salient status.

Material reward: Money or other tangible reward (for example, board and lodging).

Materialist: A person who believes that economic institutions form the substructure of the other societal sectors. The antonym is idealist, *q.v.*

Matrilocal residence: The custom of a married couple living with the wife's family.

Means of production: The factors that must be combined to produce any kind of economic goods. The three means are land (any natural resource), labour, and capital (factories, machinery, and other technological devices, as well as the money to buy more).

Mechanical solidarity: Durkheim's term for the social bond created by the common experience of people living in small, homogeneous communities, engaged in similar work and hence in similar lifestyles and thus coming to hold the same values and beliefs.

Melting pot: The rapid assimilation of recent immigrants into their new society. This concept has been a longstanding ideal underlying immigration policy in the United States. *Cf.* cultural mosaic.

Micro-chip: A miniature electronic circuit mounted on a tiny piece of material (often silicon). These circuits are the base of modern computer technology.

Micro-level sociology: The study of relationships within and between small social groups.

Minority: A group stigmatized and discriminated against by the dominant majority on the basis of presumed physical, cultural, and/or behavioural differences from the norm. In the definition used in this book, a sociological minority may be a numerical majority in the society. *Cf.* majority.

Modal type: The form or type of social phenomena most prevalent in a given society.

Monogamy: The practice of being married to only one person at a time.

Moral crusade: Becker's term for a campaign, often led by moral entrepreneurs, to build up public support for new definitions of what is right and what is deviant.

Moral entrepreneurs: Becker's term for people who invest in the moral uplift of imposing or preserving a "better" way of life, usually by attempting to bring about new laws or to enforce current ones.

Mores: The norms salient in a particular culture, as opposed to folkways or to rules merely on the books. They are often the basis of law, and breaking them may bring severe sanctions. Also called salient norms.

Neolocal residence: The custom of a married couple's establishing its own household, separate from the parental household of either mate.

Norms: The formal or informal rules of everyday behaviour; the concrete ways in which values are put into practice. Norms are divided into mores and folkways, *q.v.*

Nuclear family: A family that comprises a father, a mother, and their unmarried children; they share a dwelling place with each other but usually with no one else.

Operationalizing: The translation of a goal into action. For example, the goal of minimizing the trauma of separation for young children who must be hospitalized is translated into the practice of allowing a parent to stay overnight with the child.

Organic solidarity: Durkheim's term for the social bond created by the interdependence of people living in societies that have a highly specialized division of labour. Lifestyles and, thus, values and beliefs may vary among groups, but each needs the others to survive.

Organization: *See* formal organization, social organization.

Organizational culture: The culture that subsumes an organization's values, norms, folkways, symbols, rituals, and traditions. "The way things are done around here" is the shorthand definition of this term.

Organizational subculture:

Party: In Weber's analysis of social stratification, a group that participates in the political sphere.

Paternalism: A model of majority-minority relations in which members of the dominant group regard the inferiors as irresponsible, like children who need a father's guidance; docility brings kindness and treats, but only menial tasks are allotted to the inferiors. The two groups live in close proximity but interaction is ritualized. The antonym is competition, *q.v.*

Patriarchy: Literally rule by the father or head of the household. The system that entrenches male dominance in society (*Cf.* gender inequality).

Patrilocal residence: The custom of a married couple living with the husband's family.

Pattern variables: Talcott Parsons' term for his construct of opposite, typical ways in which people relate to each other in specific kinds of situations. The variables are ascription/achievement, affectivity/affective neutrality, diffuseness/specificity, particularism/universalism, and collectivity orientation/self-orientation. For each pair, the first listed is typical of primary groups and the Gemeinschaft, the second of secondary groups and the Gesellschaft.

Peer group: A group of individuals who occupy roughly similar statuses in a society and who tend to identify with each other.

Polyandry: The practice of one woman being married to two or more men simultaneously.

Polygamy: The practice of being married to more than one person simultaneously.

Polygyny: The practice of one man being married to two or more women simultaneously.

Positive rituals: Occasions when group members gather to reaffirm their commonality, thus strengthening mechanical solidarity. Canada Day celebrations, college graduation ceremonies, and weddings are common examples.

Power: The ability to impose one's will on others. Access to resources that make possible attainment of one's objectives.

Prejudice: Pre-judgement of an individual, based on stereotyping.

Primary deviance: Deviance that is not the result of social reaction to previous deviance. *Cf.* secondary deviance.

Primary group: A group of people, usually few in number, who have face-to-face contact, know who the other members of the group are, engage in several kinds of joint activities, and hold common values and beliefs. Emotion, which may be positive or negative (love or hate), frequently plays a part in interaction. *Cf.* secondary group.

Primary sector: The activity of an economy that produces useful or saleable goods directly from natural resources; farming, fishing, and mining are examples.

Profession: A high-status occupation staffed by a cadre of experts who have exclusive competence in a specific type of knowledge.

Proletariat: In Marxian social analysis, the class whose members do not own or control the means of production and hence have nothing to sell but their labour.

Qualitative methods: Research methods that yield nonnumerical data. Participant observation and in-depth interviewing are examples.

Quantitative methods: Research methods to obtain numerical data by way of enumeration or measurement. Census-taking and survey research are examples.

Race: A set of genetic physical characteristics, such as skin and eye pigmentation, used to categorize human beings in a socially significant way.

Racism: Discrimination on the basis of race.

Rational-legal authority: Authority (typical of bureaucracies) that is vested in the office.

Readjustment: *Cf.* change of type.

Reference group: A group that provides a model of values, attitudes, and behaviour that an individual seeks to adopt or to emulate.

Relative deprivation: A definition of poverty that refers to the individual's economic well-being in relation to community standards.

Religion: A unified system of beliefs and practices relative to sacred things and the mysteries of the universe. From a communal viewpoint, its function is to unite adherents in the moral community of a church. For individuals it provides a way of coping with the ultimate problems of life, including the inevitability of death.

Resocialization: Socialization aimed at stripping the individual of his or her identity and replacing it with a new one.

Robotics: The construction, maintenance, and supervision of a complex automatic device that performs tasks and functions once regarded as requiring human labours.

Role: The pattern of behaviour that is associated with a particular status.

Role conflict: A clash between the obligations accruing from two or more roles.

Role model: A person whose role behaviour provides another with a standard for determining the socially acceptable behaviour and attitudes for filling that role.

Sacred society: A society oriented to the supernatural; the primary beliefs and values are viewed as absolute. The antonym is secular society, *q.v.*

Salient norms: The norms that reflect the most cherished social values, in contrast to rules "on the books," which can be ignored with impunity. *See also* mores.

Salient status: The status that is the source of an individual's social identity, overriding his or her other statuses. Also called master status.

Scientific management: A movement to enhance labour productivity, spearheaded by F.W. Taylor, "father of the assembly line." This approach assumed that the interests of workers and employees could be reconciled if pay were tied to productivity.

Secondary deviance: Deviance caused by societal reaction to deviance (or the belief that deviance has occurred). The stigma produces a change in status, and the resulting secondary deviance is a role knowingly played by the deviant. *Cf.* primary deviance.

Secondary group: A relatively impersonal group; the focus is on some objective common to members, who may not meet or know each other. *Cf.* primary group.

Secondary sector: The manufacturing (goods-producing) activity of an economy.

Sect: A religious group that has split off from a church. It has a loose, non-bureaucratic structure, no clear-cut hierarchy of authority, and worship is spontaneous.

Secular society: A society oriented to the tangible world; the primary values are rational and utilitarian, and innovation is welcomed. The antonym is sacred society, *q.v.*

Self-fulfilling prophecy: A phenomenon in which the prediction of an event, such as deviance, becomes its cause. The beliefs about an individual or group may be internalized (by the individual or the group members) and ultimately manifest themselves in behaviour.

Sexism: Prejudice and discrimination on the basis of sex.

Significant others: The agents of socialization in Mead's I/me theory. They are people important to the individual at various life stages who transmit the parts of the culture they deem relevant to successful functioning in society.

Single-parent family: A domestic unit comprising one parent and minor children. *Cf.* nuclear family.

Social control: A general term for all those techniques and strategies which are employed for the purpose of regulating human behaviour.

Social Darwinism: *See* Biological determinism.

Social distance: The degree of separateness between individuals or groups. Separateness is often gauged by a social-distance scale in which the measure ranges from willingness to have a person of a particular social type (for example, religious, racial, or class) in intimate family association, to unwillingness to have a person of this type enter the country.

Social institution: A patterned way of accomplishing an important social goal or solving an important social problem. The institution emerges from the interaction of a particular group's beliefs, value system, and coping strategies.

Social organization: A stable and predictable pattern of social relationships within a group or society that is based on social roles, rules for conduct, and shared meanings.

Social structure: The crystallization of patterned relationships which, themselves, are influenced by the values and norms of a particular society.

Socialization: The process of transmitting a culture's patterns of thinking and acting to newcomers to the group. Basic socialization occurs in childhood, but the individual must also be socialized to some extent every time he or she enters a new group or assumes a new role.

Status: (1) A culturally defined position in the social structure. Each individual occupies many statuses, which may be ascribed or achieved. (2) In Weber's analysis of social stratification, prestige or social honour.

Status inconsistency: A phenomenon in which a person has the characteristics of more than one status level and these statuses are not compatible (for example, a clergyman who is a member of a nudist colony).

Stereotype: An overgeneralized view of a category of people based on beliefs validated by emotion rather than reason.

Stigma: A mark of discredit or unworthiness; the opposite of a status symbol. The impact of a stigma on social identity varies both with the severity of the stigma and with the way it is perceived in a particular society.

Stratification: The division of a group into horizontal layers (strata); rewards differ for individuals in different strata.

Structural mobility: Socioeconomic (often occupational) mobility brought about by changes in the economy that facilitate or constrict opportunities for occupational advance.

Subculture: A group existing within mainstream society but differing from it in patterned ways. Ethnolinguistic groups offer common examples in Canada.

Surplus value: In Marxist theory, it is the difference between the wages paid to workers and the actual value of what they produce. This surplus is appropriated by the capitalists.

Symbol: A sign that has shared meaning for members of a group.

Symbolic interactionism: One of the major perspectives or orientations of sociology. Focusing on the micro level, it emphasizes individual actors' interpretations of situations. According to this perspective, interaction is both prompted and mediated via symbols.

Symbolic reward: Power, prestige, or some other nonmaterial reward.

System: An arrangement of interrelated and interdependent parts.

Tertiary sector: The service-producing activity of an economy. "Services" may be personal (for example, hairdressing), sales, financial (for example, banking), technological (for example, research and repairs), and so on.

Total institution: An institution that controls every aspect of an individual's existence. Prisons and boarding schools are examples.

Traditional authority: As exemplified by monarchies, authority that is legitimized by an ascribed position.

Values: Cultural themes that designate goals worth striving for and lay out standards for evaluating behaviour. *Cf.* norms.

Verstehen: The social researcher's attempt to grasp the frame of mind of subjects, thus making it possible to give causal interpretations of behaviour. The word means ''understanding'' in German.

Vertical mobility: Movement (or the ability to move) up and down a social hierarchy. The fact that a society permits vertical mobility does not mean that everyone actually moves.

Vertical mosaic: A society in which racial and ethnic groups are hierachically ranked. John Porter coined the term to describe Canadian society.

Whistle-blowers: A person who reports on deviance within the workplace to the public, or to external authorities.

REFERENCES

Abella, R.
1984 *Equality in Employment: A Royal Commission Report*. Ottawa: Ministry of Supply and Services.

Abella, I. and H. Troper
1983 *None is Too Many: Canada and the Jews of Europe, 1933-48*. Tor.: Lester & Orpen Dennys.

Acker, J.
1980 "Women and Stratification: A Review of Recent Literature." *Contemporary Sociology* 9.

Adams, Howard
1979 "Canada from the Native Point of View." In J.L. Leonard, ed., *Two Nations: Many cultures*. Scarborough, Ontario: Prentice-Hall of Canada.

Adamson, N., N. Briskin and M. McPhail
1988 *Feminists Organizing for Change: The Contemporary Women's Movement in Canada*. Don Mills, Ontario: Oxford University Press Canada.

Agnew, N.M. and S. Pyke
1987 *The Science Game*. 4th ed. Englewood Cliffs, N.J.: Prentice-Hall.

Akyeampong, E.
1987 "Involuntary Part-Time Employment in Canada, 1975-1986." *Canadian Social Trends* (Autumn).

Alger, Horatio, Jr.
1973 *Silas Snobden's Office Boy*. New York: Doubleday. First published in *Argosy*, 1889-1890.

Ambert, A.M.
1980 *Divorce in Canada*. Toronto: Academic Press.

Ames. H.B.
1972 *The City below the Hill*. Toronto: University of Toronto Press. First Published 1897.

Anderson, G.M.
1981 "Networks, Education, and Occupational Success." In K.L.P. Lundy and B.D. Warme, eds., *Work in the Canadian Context*. Toronto: Butterworth.

Angelou, M.
1971 *I Know Why the Caged Bird Sings*. New York: Bantam.

Anisef, P.
1973, 1974 *The Critical Juncture*. Toronto: Ontario Ministry of Colleges and Universities.

Anisef, P., J.G. Paasche and A.H. Turrittin
1980 *Is the Die Cast?* Toronto: Ontario Ministry of College and Universities.

Anthony, P.D.
1977 *The Ideology of Work*. London: Tavistock Publications.

Arendt, Hannah
1964 *Eichmann in Jerusalem: A Report on the Banality of Evil*. New York: Viking.

Armstrong, P. and H. Armstrong
1983 *A Working Majority: What Women Must Do for Pay*. Ottawa: Canadian Advisory Council on the Status of Women.
1984 *The Double Ghetto*. Revised ed. Toronto: McClelland and Stewart.

Austen, Jane
1962 *Pride and Prejudice*. New York: Airmont Books. First published 1813.

Baar, Ellen
1983 "Patterns of Selective Accentuation Among Niagara Mennonites." *Canadian Ethnic Studies* 15 (2): 77-91.

Bakan, D.
1971 *Slaughter of the Innocents: A Study of the Battered Child Phenomenon*. Toronto: CBC Learning Systems.

Baldwin, J.
1953 *Go Tell It on the Mountain*. New York: Knopf.
1964 *Blues for Mr. Charlie*. New York: Dial Press.

Baker, M., (ed.)
1984 *The Family: Changing Trends in Canada*. Toronto: McGraw-Hill Ryerson.

Banting, K.G.
1987 "The Welfare State and Inequality in the 1980s," *Canadian Review of Sociology and Anthropology* 24 (3, Aug.).

Barnard, C.
1938 *The Functions of the Executive*. Cambridge, Mass.: Harvard University Press.

Batten, J.
1984 *Lawyers*. Toronto: Gage.

Beattie, C.
1975 *Minority Men in a Majority Setting*. Toronto: McClelland and Stewart.

Beaud, M.
1983 *A History of Capitalism 1500-1980*. New York: Monthly Review.

Beccaria, Cesare
1819 *An Essay on Crimes and Punishments*. Philadelphia: Nicklen.

Becker, H.S., *et al.*
1961 *Boys in White*. Chicago: University of Chicago Press.
Becker, Howard S.
1963 *Outsiders: Studies in the Sociology of Devince*. New York: Free Press.
1964 *The Other Side: Perspectives on Deviance*. New York: Free Press.
1967 *Social Problems*. New York: Wiley.
Benedict, Ruth
1934 *Patterns of Culture*. New York: Mentor.
Bennett, J.W.
1967 *Hutterian Brethren: The Agricultural, Economic and Social Organization of a Communal People*. Palo Alto, California: Stanford University Press.
Berger, Peter
1963 *Invitation to Sociology*. New York: Doubleday.
Berger, T.R.
1977 *Northern Frontier, Northern Homeland: The Report of the Mackenzie Valley Pipeline Inquiry*. Ottawa, Supply and Services Canada.
1981 *Fragile Freedoms: Human Rights and Dissent*. Toronto: Clarke, Irwin.
Berman, H.J.
1983 "The Origins of Western Legal Science." In J.C. Smith and D.V. Weisstub, eds., *The Western Idea of Law*. Toronto: Butterworth.
Birnbaum, N.
1953 "Conflicting Interpretations of the Rise of Capitalism: Marx and Weber," *The British Journal of Sociology* 9: 1 25-41.
Bissoondath, N.
1988 *A Casual Brutality*. Toronto: Macmillan of Canada.
Black, Donald
1976 *The Behavior of Law*. New York: Academic Press.
1983 "Crime as Social Control," *American Sociological Review* 48 (Feb.): 34-45.
Blauner, R.
1964 *Alienation and Freedom: The Factory Worker and His Industry*. Chicago: University of Chicago Press.
Blishen, B.R. and H.A. McRoberts
1967 "A Revised Socio-Economic Index for Occupations in Canada," *Canadian Review of Sociology and Anthropology* 13: 71-9.
Blishen, B.R., W.K. Carrol and C. Moore
1987 "The 1981 Socioeconomic Index for Occupations in Canada," *The Canadian Review of Sociology and Anthropology* 24 (4, Nov.).
Bloom, S.W.
1965 *The Doctor and His Patient*. New York: Free Press.
Blumer, H.
1987 *Symbolic Interactionism: Perspective and Method*. Berkeley: University of California Press.
Boston Women's Health Collective
1984 *The New "Our Bodies, Ourselves*." New York: Anchor Books.
Bottomore, T.B., (ed.)
1956 *Karl Marx: Selected Writings in Sociology and Social Philosophy*. London: Watts.
Bowes, Angus H.
1956 "The Ataractic Drugs: The present position of chlorpromazine, frenqual, pacatal and reserpine in the psychiatric hospital," *American Journal of Psychiatry* 113: 530-39.
Bowlby, J.
1951 *Maternal Care and Mortality*. World Health Organization Monograph 2. Geneva: WHO.
Bowles, S. and H. Gintis
1976 *Schooling in Capitalist America*. New York: Basic Books.
Bowra, C.M.
1985 *The Greek Experience*. Toronto: McClelland and Stewart.
Boyd, Neil
1988 *The Last Dance: Murder in Canada*. Scarborough, Ontario: Prentice-Hall Canada.
Boydell, C.L., C.F. Grindstaff and P.C. Whitehead
1972 *Deviant Behaviour and Societal Reaction*. Toronto: Holt, Rinehart and Winston.
Braverman, H.
1974 *Labour and Monopoly Capital: The Degradation of Work in the Twentieth Century*. New York: Monthly Review Press.
Brecht, Bertolt
1981 *The Life of Galileo*. London: Eyre Methuen. Originally published in German, 1939.
Breton, R.
1972 *Social and Academic Factors in the Career Decisions of Canadian Youth*. Ottawa: Information Canada.
Breton, R. and J. McDonald
1976 "Aspects of Parent-Adolescent Relationships: The Perceptions of Secondary School Students." In K. Ishwaren, ed., *The Canadian Family*. Rev. ed. Toronto: Holt, Rinehart and Winston.

Bronfenbrenner, U.
1958 "Socialization and Social Class through Time and Class." In E.E. Maccoby, T.M. Newcomb, and E.L. Hartley, eds., *Readings in Social Psychology*. 3rd ed. New York: Holt, Rinehart and Winston.

Brown, M.
1974 *Seated Labour: A Study of Homework*. London: Low Pay Unit.

Brundtland, G.H.
1987 *Our Common Future: Report of the World Commission on Environment and Development*. Oxford: Oxford University Press.

Burman, P.
1988 *Killing Time, Losing Ground: Experiences of Unemployment*. Toronto: Wall and Thompson.

Burnet, J. and H. Palmer, (eds.)
1988 *Generations: A History of Canada's People*. Toronto: McClelland and Stewart.

Burt, S., L. Code and L. Dorney, (eds.)
1988 *Changing Patterns: Women in Canada*. Toronto: McClelland and Stewart.

Callwood, J.
1986 *Twelve Weeks in Spring*. Toronto: Lester and Orpen Dennys.

Campbell, R.M. and L.A. Powell
1989 *The Real Worlds of Canadian Politics: Cases in Process and Policy*. Peterborough: Broadview Press.

Canadian Advisory Council on the Status of Women
1982.

The Canadian Encyclopedia
1985 Edmonton: Hurtig.

Caplan, P. 1985 *Class and Gender in India*. London and New York: Tavistock.

Carcopino, J.
1962 *Daily Life in Ancient Rome: The People and the City at the Height of the Empire*. Translated by E.O. Lorimer. London: Penguin.

Carlin, J.
1962 *Lawyers on Their Own*. New Brunswick, N.J.: Rutgers University Press.

Caron, Roger
1978 *Go-Boy! The True Story of a Life Behind Bars*. Don Mills, Ontario: Nelson.

Carson, Rachael
1962 *The Silent Spring*. Greenwich, Conn.: Fawcett Publications.

Chance, N.A.
1966 *The Eskimo of North Alaska*. New York: Holt, Rinehart and Winston.

Chatwin, Bruce
1987 *The Songlines*. Markham, Ontario: Penguin Books Canada.

Christopher, R.
1989 *Crashing the Gates: The De-Wasping of America's Power Elite*. New York: Simon and Schuster.

Cicourel, Aaron V.
1969 *The Organization of Juvenile Justice*. New York: John Wiley & Sons.

Clairmont, D.H. and D.W. Magill
1974 *Africville*. Toronto: McClelland and Stewart.

Clark, S.D.
1948 *Church and Sect in Canada*. Toronto: University of Toronto Press.

Clarke, J.N.
1981 "The Clergy's Decline: A Historical Perspective on the Declining Power of Anglican and United Church Clergy." In K.L.P. Lundy and B.D. Warme, eds., *Work in the Canadian Context: Continuity Despite Change*. Toronto: Butterworth.

Clement, W.
1975 *The Canadian Corporate Elite*. Toronto: McClelland and Stewart.
1977 *Continental Corporate Power*. Toronto: McClelland and Stewart.
1981 *Hardrock Mining*. Toronto: McClelland and Stewart.

Clinard, Marshall and Peter Yeager
1983 *Corporate Ethics and Crime: The Role of Middle Management*. London: Sage.

Cloward, Richard and Lloyd Ohlin
1960 *Delinquency and Opportunity: A Theory of Delinquent Gangs*. New York: Free Press.

Coates, M.L.
1988 "Part-Time Employment: Labour Market Flexibility and Equity Issues." in *Research and Current Issues Series No. 50*. Kingston: Industrial Relations Centre, Queen's University.

Coburn, J.
1987 " 'I See and Am Silent:' A Short History of Nursing in Ontario, 1850-1930." In D. Coburn *et al.*, eds., *Health and Canadian Society*. 2nd ed. Toronto: Fitzhenry and Whiteside.

Codere, Helen
1961 "Kwakiutl." In E.H. Spicer, ed., *Perspectives on American Indian Culture Change*. Chicago: University of Chicago Press.

Cohen, M.G.
1988 *Women's Work, Markets, and Economic Development in Nineteenth-Century Ontario.* Toronto: University of Toronto Press.
Cohen, Albert K.
1963 *Delinquent Boys: The Culture of the Gang.* Glencoe, Ill.: Force Press.
1966 *Deviance and Control.* Englewood Cliffs, N.J.: Prentice-Hall.
Cole, S.
1980 *The Sociological Method.* 3rd ed. Boston: Houghton Mifflin.
Coleman, J.R.
1971 *Blue Collar Journal: A College President's Sabbatical.* Philadelphia: J.B. Lippincott.
Coleman, J.S.
1963 *The Adolescent Society: The Social Life of The Teenager and Its Impact on Education.* New York: Free Press.
1968 "The Concept of Equality of Educational Opportunity," *Harvard Educational Review* 38: 7-22.
Coleman, James, *et al.*
1966 *Equality of Educational Opportunity.* Washington: U.S. Department of Health, Education and Welfare, Office of Education.
Coles, R.
1964 *Children of Crisis.* Boston: Little Brown.
Collins, R. and M. Makowsky
1984 *The Discovery of Society.* 3rd ed. New York: Random House.
Comte, Auguste
1877 *Systems of Positive Polity.* London: Longmans, Green and Company.
Connell, R.W., *et al.*
1982 *Making the Difference.* Sydney: Allen and Unwin.
Conniff, Richard
1982 "21st Century Crime Stoppers," *Science Digest* 90 (8, Aug.): 60-5
Conrad, Peter and Rochell Kern, (eds.)
1989 *The Sociology of Health and Illness: Critical Perspectives.* 3rd ed. New York: St. Martin's Press.
Cook, Shirley J.
1969 "Canadian Narcotics Legislation, 1908-1923: A Conflict Intrpretation," *The Canadian Review of Sociology and Anthropology* 6 (1).
Cooke, K.
1986 *Report of the Task Force on Child Care.* Ottawa: Status of Women, Canada.
Cooley, C.H.
1902 *Human Nature and the Social Order.* New York: Scribner's.
Corbett, G.A.
1981 *Bernardo Children in Canada.* Peterborough, Ont.: Woodland Publishing.
Coser, Lewis A.
1962 "Some Functions of Deviant Behavior and Normative Flexibility," *American Journal of Sociology* 68 (Sept.): 171-81.
Council of Ontario Universities 1983.
Craven, Margaret
1973 *I Heard the Owl Call My Name.* New York: Dell Publishing.
Croll, D.A.
1982 *Poverty Line Update.* Ottawa: Senate Report.
Currie, D.
1988 "Re-thinking What We Do and How We Do It: Study of Reproductive Decisions," *The Canadian Review of Sociology and Anthropology* 25 (2): 231-253.
Dahrendorf, Ralf
1959 *Class and Class Conflict in Industrial Society.* Palo Alto, California: Stanford University Press.
1973 "Toward a Theory of Social Conflict." In Amitai Etzioni and Eva Etzioni-Halevy, eds., *Social Change: Sources, Patterns and Consequences.* New York: Basic Books.
Daniels, Arlene Kaplan
1970 "Normal Mental Illness and Understandable Excuses: The Philosophy of Combat Psychiatry," *American Behavioral Scientist* 14: 169-78; excerpts reprinted in Earl Rubington and Martin S. Weinberg, eds., *Deviance: The Interactionist Perspective.* 4th ed. New York: Macmillan, 1981.
Daudlin, R.
1984 Special Committee on Visible Minorities in Canadian Society, *Equality Now.* Ottawa: Queen's Printer.
Davis, Kingsley
1961 "The Sociology of Prostitution." In Robert K. Merton and Robert Nisbet, eds., *Contemporary Social Problems.* New York: Harcourt Brace and World.
Davis, K. and W.E. Moore
1945 "Some Principles of Stratification," *American Sociological Review* 10: 242-9.
Deal, Terrence E. and A.A. Kennedy
1982 *Corporate Cultures: The Rites and Rituals of Corporate Life.* Reading, Mass.: Addison-Wesley.
Dean, John
1976 *Blind Ambition.* New York: Simon & Schuster.

Demerath, N.J., III and P.E. Hammond
1969 *Religion in Social Context*. New York: Random House.
Deming, R.
1970 *Man and Society*. New York: Dell Publishing.
Dickens, Charles
1978 *Oliver Twist*. Oxford University Press. First published 1837.
Deitz, Mary Lorenz
1983 *Killing for Profit: The Social Organization of Felony Homicide*. Chicago: Nelson-Hall.
Dillard, Annie
1987 *An American Childhood*. New York: Harper and Row.
Doctorow, E.L.
1989 *Billy Bathgate*. New York: Random House.
Dollard, J., N.E. Miller, L.W. Doob, O.H. Mower and R.S. Sears
1939 *Frustration and Aggression*. New Haven, Conn.: Yale Unversity Press.
Dominion Bureau of Statistics
1963 *University Student Expenditure and Income in Canada, 1961*. 2 vols. Ottawa.
Doyle, R. and L. Visano
1987 *A Time for Action*. Toronto: Social Planning Council of Metropolitan Toronto.
Drummond, R.J.
1986 "Government and Employment in the Canadian Federal System." In K.L.P. Lundy and B.D. Warme, eds., *Work in the Canadian Context: Continuity Despite Change*. 2nd ed. Toronto: Butterworths.
Duffy, A., N. Mandell and N. Pupo
1989 *Few Choices: Women, Work and Family*. Toronto: Garamond Press.
Dulude, L.
1978 *Women and Aging: A Report on the Rest of our Lives*. Ottawa: Canadian Advisory Council on the Status of Women.
Durkheim, Emile
1947 *The Division of Labor in Society*. Trans. by G. Simpson. Glencoe, Ill.: Free Press. First published 1893.
1950 *The Rules of Sociological Method*. Trans. by Sarah A. Soloway and John H. Mueller; ed. by George E.G. Catlin. Glencoe, Ill.: Free Press. First published 1895.
1952 *Suicide*. London: Routledge and Kegan Paul. First publsihed 1897.
1954 *The Elementary Forms of Religious Life*. New York: Free Press. First published 1912.
1961 *Moral Education*. New York: Free Press.
Durrenmatt, Friedrich
1964 *The Physicists*. New York: Grove Press.
Eaton, W.W.
1986 *The Sociology of Mental Disorders*. 2nd ed. New York: Praeger.
Ehrenreich, Barbara and Deirdre English
1989 "The Sexual Politics of Sickness." In P. Conrad and R. Kern, eds., *The Sociology of Health and Illness: Critical Perspectives*. 3rd ed. New York: St. Martin's Press.
Eichler, Margrit
1985 "And the Work Never Ends: Feminist Contributions," *Canadian Review of Sociology and Anthropology* 22 (5): 619-44.
1983 *Families in Canada*. Toronto: Gage.
1987 *Non-sexist Research Methods: A Practical Guide*. Winchester, Mass.: Unwin Hyman Inc.
Elbow, Peter
1973 *Writing Without Teachers*. London: Oxford.
Eliot, T.S.
1967 *Murder in the Cathedral*. London: Faber and Faber.
Encyclopedia Americana
1973 International edition. New York: Americana Corporation.
Epstein, Cynthia Fuchs
1970 *Women's Place*. Berkeley, Calif.: University of California Press.
Ericson, R.V.
1981 *Making Crime: A Study of Detective Work*. Toronto: Butterworth.
Ericson, R.V. and P.M. Baranek
1982 *Ordering of Justice: A Study of Accused Persons as Defendants in the Criminal Process*. Toronto: University of Toronto Press.
Erikson, Erik H.
1963 "The Eight Stages of Man," a chapter in *Childhood and Society*. 2nd ed. New York: Norton.
Ermann, M. David and R.J. Lundman, (eds).
1978 *Corporate and Government Deviance*. New York: Oxford University Press.
Etzioni, A.
1965 "Dual Leadership in Complex Organizations," *American Sociological Review* 30 (5, Oct.).
Fisher, Matthew
1989 "Two Cormie firms wilfully broke law, U.S. regulator rules," *The Globe and Mail*, Toronto, May 19.
Flower, Linda
1989 *Problem-Solving Strategies for Writing*. 3rd ed. New York: Harcourt Brace Jovanovich.

Flynn, Robert
1985 "Assessing the Effectiveness of Deinstitutionalization: Substantive and Methodological Conclusions from the Research Literature." In *Deinstitutionalization: Costs and Effects*. Ottawa: Canadian Council on Social Development.

Ford, R.C., B.R. Armandi and C.P. Heaton
1988 *Organizational Theory: An Integrative Approach*. New York: Harper & Row.

Forman, F.J. with C. Sowton
1989 *Taking our Time: Feminist Perspectives on Temporality*. Oxford, U.K.: Pergamon Press.

Foucault, M.
1965 *Madness and Civilization*. New York: Random House.
1976 *Discipline and Punish*. London: Allan Lane.

Fowler, Norman
1979 *After the Riots: The Police in Europe*. London: Davis Poynter.

Fox, B.J. and J. Fox
1987 "Occupational Gender Segregation in the Canadian Labour Force 1931-81," *The Canadian Review of Sociology and Anthropology* 24 (3, August).

Francis, Dianne
1988 *Contrepreneurs*. Toronto: Macmillan of Canada.

Fraser, A.
1984 The Weaker Vessel. London: Weidenfeld and Nicholson.

Fraser, S.
1988 *My Father's House: A Memoir of Incest and Healing*. Don Mills, Ontario: Collins Paperbacks.

Freeman, David
1972 *Creeps*. Toronto: University of Toronto Press.

Freidson, E.
1970 *Professional Dominance: The Social Structure of Medical Care*. New York: Aldine Publishing.

Freire, P.
1972 *Pedagogy of the Oppressed*. Harmondsworth: Penguin.

Fretz, J. Winfield
1989 *The Waterloo Mennonites: A Community in Paradox*. Waterloo, Ontario: Wilfrid Laurier University Press and Conrad Grebel College.

Friedan, Betty
1963 *The Feminine Mystique*. Harmondsworth: Penguin.

Fry, Alan
1970 *How a People Die; A Novel*. Toronto: Doubleday.

Gaines, E.
1983 *A Gathering of Old Men*. New York: Knopf.

Gallese, L.R.
1985 *Women Like Us*. New York: Morrow.

Gambino, R.
1981 *Bread and Roses*. New York: Seaview Books.

Ganley, Elaine
1989 "Taxi 'hot seat' a crime stopper?" *The Globe and Mail*, Toronto, October 23.

Garrett, J.L. and E.G. Hinson
1983 *Are Southern Baptists "Evangelicals?"* Macon, Ga.: Mercer University Press.

Gavron, H.
1966 *The Captive Wife*. London: Routledge and Kegan Paul.

Gedge, Pauline
1977 *Child of the Morning*. Agincourt, Ontario: Gage.

Gerth, H.H. and C.W. Mills, (eds.)
1946 *From Max Weber: Essays in Sociology*. New York: Oxford University Press.

Glenn, N.
1964 "Negro Religion and Negro Status in the United States." In *Religion, Culture, and Society*. L. Schneider, ed. New York: Wiley.

Gluck, S.B.
1987 *Rosie the Riveter Revisited*. Boston: Twayne Publishers.

Glueck, Sheldon and Eleanor Glueck
1956 *Physique and Delinquency*. New York: Harper and Row.

Goethals, G.T.
1981 *The T.V. Ritual: Worship at the Video Altar*. Boston: Beacon Press.

Goffman, Erving
1962 *Asylums*. Chicago: Aldine Publishing.
1963 *Stigma: Notes on the Management of a Spoiled Identity*. Englewood Cliffs, N.J.: Prentice-Hall.

Gold, R.L.
1964 "In the Basement—The Apartment Building Janitor." In P.L. Berger, ed., *The Human Shape of Work*. New York: Macmillan.

Goldenberg, S.
1987 *Thinking Sociologically*. Belmont: Wadsworth.

Gonick, Cy.
1978 *Out of Work*. Toronto: James Lorimer and Company.

Goode, W.J.
1957 "Community within a Community: The Professions," *American Sociological Review* 22: 194-200.
1970 *World Revolution and Family Patterns*. Glencoe: Free Press.

Goring, Charles
1913 *The English Convict*. London: H.M. Stationery Office.

Gosse, Edmund
1979 *Father and Son*. Harmondsworth: Penguin. First published 1907.

Grabb, E.G.
1984 *Social Inequality: Classical and Contemporary Theorists*. Toronto: Holt, Rinehart and Winston.

Grayson, J.P.
1986 *Plant Closures and De-Skilling: Three Case Studies*. Ottawa: Science Council of Canada.

Green, H.
1964 *I Never Promised You a Rose Garden*. New York: Holt, Rinehart and Winston.

Greenaway, W.K.
1980 "Crime and Class." In J. Harp and J.R. Hofley, eds., *Structured Inequality in Canada*. Toronto: Prentice-Hall of Canada.

Greene, Ian
1989 *The Charter of Rights*. Toronto: Lorimer.

Greenwood, E.
1957 "Attributes of a Profession," *Social Work*. 2 July, pp. 44-55.

Grescoe, P.
1987 "A Nation's Disgrace." In D. Coburn *et al.*, eds., *Health and Canadian Society*. 2nd ed. Toronto: Fitzhenry and Whiteside. 127-140.

Griessman, B. Eugene
1975 *Minorities: A Text with Readings in Intergroup Relations*. Hinsdale, Illinois: Dryden Press.

Gusfield, Joseph R.
1963 *Symbolic Crusade: Status Politics and the American Temperance Movement*. Urbana, Ill.: University of Illinois Press.

Hagan, J., M. Huster and P. Parker
1988 "Class Structure and Legal Practice: Inequality and Mobility among Toronto Lawyers," *Law and Society Review*. 22 (1).

Hall, E.T.
1959 *The Silent Language*. Garden City: Doubleday.

Hall, G.S. and G. Lindzey
1963 *Theories of Personality*. New York: Wiley.

Hall, O. and R. Carlton
1977 *Basic Skills at School and Work*. Toronto: Ontario Economic Council.

Hall, R.H.
1975 *Occupations and the Social Structure*. Englewood Cliffs, N.J.: Prentice-Hall.
1982 *Organizations: Structure and Process*. 3rd ed. Englewood Cliffs, N.J.: Prentice-Hall.
1987 *Organizations: Structures, Processes and Outcomes*. 4th ed. Englewood Cliffs, N.J.: Prentice-Hall.

Hammond, Phillip E., (ed.)
1964 *Sociologists at Work*. New York: Basic Books.

Hansen, D.A.
1976 *An Invitation to Critical Sociology*. New York: Free Press.

Harkness, Jon
1989 "The Economic Costs of AIDS in Canada," *Canadian Public Policy* 15 (4, Dec.): 405.

Harp, J. and J.R. Hofley, (eds.)
1971 *Poverty in Canada*. Scarborough: Prentice-Hall of Canada.

Harris, M.
1986 *Justice Denied*. Toronto: Macmillan of Canada.

Harvey, E.B. and R. Kalwa
1983 "Occupational Status Attainments of University Graduates: Individual Attributes and Labour Market Effects Compared," *Canadian Review of Sociology and Anthropology* 20 (4): 435-53.

Hawkesworth, J.
1973 *Upstairs, Downstairs*. New York: Dell.

Heinz, J.P. and E.D. Laumann
1982 *Chicago Lawyers: The Social Structure of the Bar*. New York: Russell Sage Foundation and American Bar Foundation.

Hendricks. W.
1984 "The Theology of the Electronic Church," *Review and Exposition* 81: 59-76.

Henry, F. and E. Ginzberg
1985 *Who Gets the Work? A Test of Racial Discrimination in Employment*. Toronto: The Urban Alliance on Race Relations and the Social Planning Council of Metropolitan Toronto.

Herberg, E.N.
1989 *Ethnic Groups in Canada*. Scarborough, Ontario: Nelson Canada.

Heron, C.
1989 *The Canadian Labour Movement*. Toronto: Lorimer.

Hershi, Travis
1969 *Causes of Delinquency*. Berkeley: University of California Press.
Hewlett, S.
1986 *A Lesser Life*. New York: William Morrow and Company Inc.
Historical Statistics of Canada 1983 Ottawa: Ministry of Supply and Services.
Hochschild, A.
1989 *The Second Shift*. New York: Viking.
Hoesteler, J.A. and G.E. Huntington
1967 *The Hutterites in North America*. New York: Holt, Rinehart and Winston.
Hooton, Earnest Albert
1939 "Crime and the Man." In B. Rosenberg, I. Gerver and F.W. Howton, eds., *Mass Society in Crisis: Social Problems and Social Pathology*. New York: Macmillan.
Hospital, Janet Turner
1983 *The Tiger in the Tiger Pit*. Toronto: McClelland and Stewart.
Houston, J.
1971 *The White Dawn*. New York: Harcourt Brace Jovanovich.
Howe, Irving
1963 "Orwell's *1984*," in Irving Howe, ed., *The Fiction of Anti-Utopia*. New York: Harcourt Brace Jovanovich.
Howe, L.K.
1978 *Pink Collar Workers*. New York: Avon Books.
Hughes, Everett C.
1945 "Dilemmas and Contradictions of Status," *American Journal of Sociology* 50 (March): 353-9.
1958 *Men and Their Work*. New York: Free Press.
1971 *French Canada in Transition*. Chicago: University of Chicago Press.
Humphries, L.
1979 *Tearoom Trade*. 2nd ed. Chicago: Aldine.
Hunter, A.A.
1981 *Class Tells*. Toronto: Butterworths.
Huws, U.
1984 *The New Homeworkers*. London: Low Pay Unit.
Huxley, Aldous
1984 *Brave New World*. London: Penguin. First published 1932.
Iacocca, L.
1984 *Iacocca*. Toronto: Bantam.
Ignatieff, Michael
1978 *A Just Measure of Pain: The Penitentiary in the Industrial Revolution, 1750-1850*. New York: Columbia University Press.
Illich, Ivan
1971 *Deschooling Society*. New York: Harper and Row.
Ishwaran, K., (ed.)
1976 *The Canadian Family*. Rev. ed. Toronto: Holt, Rinehart and Winston.
1980 *Canadian Families: Ethnic Variations*. Toronto: McGraw-Hill Ryerson.
Jarvik, L., V. Klodin and S.S. Matsuyama
1973 "Human Aggression and the Extra Y Chromosome," *American Psychologist* August.
Jarvis, G.K.
1972 "Canadian Old People as Deviant." In C.L. Boydell, C.F. Grindstaff and P.C. Whitehead, eds., *Deviant Behaviour and Societal Reaction*. Toronto: Holt, Rinehart and Winston.
Jencks, Christopher, *et al.*
1972 *Inequality: A Reassessment of the Effect of Family and Schooling in America*. New York: Harper & Row.
1979 *Who Gets Ahead?* New York: Basic Books.
Johnson, L.C. and R.E. Johnson
1982 *The Seam Allowance: Industrial Home Sewing in Canada*. Toronto: Women's Press.
Kahne, H.
1985 *Re-Conceiving Part-Time Work: New Perspectives for Older Workers and Women*. Totowa, New Jersey: Rowan and Allanheld.
Kallen, Evelyn
1982 *Ethnicity and Human Rights in Canada*. Toronto: Gaye.
1989 *Label Me Human: Minority Rights of Stigmatized Canadians*. Toronto: University of Toronto Press.
Kanter, R.M.
1989 *Deceptive Distinctions*. New Haven: Yale University Press.
Kanter, R.M. and B. Stein
1979 *Life in Organizations: Workplaces as People Experience Them*. New York: Basic Books.
Kelner, M., O. Hall and I. Coulter
1980 *Chiropractors: Do They Help?* Toronto: Fitzhenry and Whiteside.
Kennedy, L.
1985 *The Airman and the Carpenter*. London: Collins.
Kessler, R.C. and J.A. McRea
1982 "The Effect of Wives' Employment on the Mental Health of Men and Women," *American Sociological Review* 47: 216-27.

Kett, J.F.
1981 "American and Canadian Medical Institutions 1800-1870." In S.E.D. Shortt, ed., *Medicine in Canadian Society*. Montreal: McGill-Queen's University Press.

Kilduff, M. and R. Javers
1978 *The Suicide Cult*. New York: Bantam.

King, A.R.
1967 *The School at Mopass*. New York: Holt, Rinehart and Winston.

Kirby, S. and S. McKenna
1989 *Experience, Research and Social Change: Methods from the Margins*. Toronto: Garamond Press.

Kluckhohn, Clyde and A.L. Kroeber
1963 *Culture: A Critical Review of Concepts and Definitions*. New York: Vintage Books.

Knight, G.
1981 "Work Orientation and Mobility Ideology in the Working Class." In K.L.P. Lundy and B.D. Warme, eds., *Work in the Canadian Context: Continuity Despite Change*. Toronto: Butterworths.

Koestler, Arthur
1940 *Darkness at Noon*. Harmondsworth: Penguin.

Kogawa, Joy
1981 *Obasan*. Toronto: Lester and Orpen Dennys.

Kohn, M.L.
1963 "Social Class and Parent-Child Relationships," *American Journal of Sociology* 68: 471-80.

Kohn, Alexander
1986 *False Profits: Fraud and Error in Silence and Medicine*. New York: Blackwell.

Komarovsky, M.
1964 *Blue Collar Marriage*. New York: Random House.

Kostash, M.
1987 *No Kidding: Inside the World of Teenage Girls*. Toronto: McClelland and Stewart.

Krahn, H.J. and G.S. Lowe
1988 *Work, Industry and Canadian Society*. Scarborough, Ontario: Nelson Canada.

Krause, E.A.
1971 *The Sociology of Occupations*. Boston: Little Brown.

Krauter, J.K. and M. Davis
1978 *Minority Canadians: Ethnic Groups*. Toronto: Nelson Canada.

Kreiner, P.
1987 *Contact Prints*. Toronto: Doubleday Canada.

Kroeber, T.
1962 *Ishi in Two Worlds*. Berkeley and Los Angeles: University of California Press.

Labour Canada
1986 *Women in the Labour Force, 1985-86 Edition*. Ottawa: Supply and Services Canada.

Laurence, Margaret
1964 *The Stone Angel*. Toronto: McClelland and Stewart.

Law Reform Commission of Canada
1985 "Crimes Against the Environment," *Working Paper 44*.

Lawrence, P.R. and J.W. Lorseh
1968 *Organizations and Environment*. Cambridge: Harvard University Press.

Lederer, William J. and Eugene Burdick
1958 *The Ugly American*. New York: W.W. Norton.

Lee, Harper
1960 *To Kill a Mockingbird*. Philadelphia: Lippincott.

Lemert, Edwin M.
1951 *Social Pathology*. New York: McGraw-Hill.
1967 *Human Deviance, Social Problems, and Social Control*. Englewood Cliffs, N.J.: Prentice-Hall.

Lenski, G.E.
1966 *Power and Privilege: A Theory of Social Stratification*. New York: McGraw-Hill.

Lewis, Oscar
1955 "Peasant Culture in India and Mexico." In McKim Marriott, ed., *Village India*. Chicago: University of Chicago Press.
1959 *Five Families*. New York: Basic Books.

Li, P.S.
1988 *The Chinese in Canada*. Toronto: Oxford University Press.

Liebow, E.
1967 *Tally's Corner: A Study of Negro Streetcorner Men*. Boston: Little Brown.

Lindsay, C. and S. Donald
1988 "Income of Canada's Seniors," *Canadian Social Trends* (Autumn).

Lombroso, Cesare
1895 *The Female Offender*. London: Unwin.
1911 "Introduction" to Gina Lombroso Ferrero, *Criminal Man According to the Classification of Cesare Lombroso*. New York: Putnam.
1918 *Crime, Its Causes and Remedies*. Boston: Little Brown. Originally published in French, 1899.

Lowe, G.S.
1981 "The Administrative Revolution in the Canadian Office." In K.L.P. Lundy and B.D. Warme, eds., *Work in the Canadian Context: Continuity Despite Change*. Toronto: Butterworths.
1987 "Jobs, Class and Gender in the Canadian Office," *Labour/Le Travail* 10 (Autumn).

Lowe, Mick
1988 *Conspiracy of Brothers*. Toronto: McClelland-Bantam Seal Books.

Lower, A.R.M.
1977 *Colony to Nation: A History of Canada*. Toronto: McClelland and Stewart.

Lowrie, R.H.
1948 *Social Organization*. New York: Rinehart.

Lundberg, F.
1969 *The Rich and the Super Rich: A Study of the Power of Money Today*. New York: Bantam.

Lundy, K.L.P.
1972 "The Toronto Chapter of the National Secretaries Association." Unpublished MA thesis, University of Toronto.
1977 "The Effect of Organizational Setting on Secretary-Executive Interaction." Ph.D. thesis, University of Toronto.
1982 "Who Sends Their Children to Private School and Why?" University of Toronto.

Lundy, K.L.P. and B.D. Warme
1981 *Work in the Canadian Context: Continuity Despite Change*. 2nd ed. Toronto: Butterworths.

Lundy, L.A.
1969 "Learning the Ethical Norms of Practitioner-Client Relationships at a School of Social Work." D.W.S. thesis, Univèrsity of Toronto.

Luxton, M. and H. Rosenberg
1980 *More than a Labour of Love*. Toronto: Women's Educational Press.
1986 *Through the Kitchen Windows: The Politics of Home and Family*. Toronto: Garamond Press.

Lykken, David
1982 "Fearlessness: Its Carefree Charm and Deadly Risks," *Psychology Today*. September, pp. 20-27.

Maas, Peter
1975 *King of the Gypsies*. New York: Viking.
1985 *Marie: A True Story*. New York: Praeger.

MacGill, E.G.
1955 *My Mother, the Judge: A Biography of Helen Gregory MacGill*. Toronto: The Ryerson Press.

MacKay, Harry and Howard Clifford
1982 "Choices for Day Care," *Policy Options* 3 (3).

Mackenzie, Robert
1983 "Anguish of Being Homosexual Led Him to Shoplift: Charron," *Toronto Star*, 30 May.

MacKinnon, Malcolm H.
1981 "The Industrial Worker and the Job: Alienated or Instrumentalized?" In Lundy, K. and B. Warme, eds., *Work in the Canadian Context: Continuity Despite Change*. 2nd ed. Toronto: Butterworths.

MacLennan, Hugh
1945 *Two Solitudes*. Toronto: Macmillan of Canada.

Mann, E.
1967 *Society behind Bars: A Sociological Scrutiny of the Guelph Reformatory*. Toronto: Social Science Publishers.

Mann, W.E. and J.A. Lee
1979 *The RCMP vs. the People*. Don Mills, Ontario: General Publishing.

Manning, M.
1984 *The Hospice Alternative: Living with Dying*. London: Souvenir Press.

Mantoux, P.
1961 *The Industrial Revolution in the Eighteenth Century*. London: Jonathan Cape.

Marchak, P.
1981 "Labour in a Staples Economy." In K.L.P. Lundy and B.D. Warme, eds., *Work in the Canadian Context: Continuity Despite Change*. Toronto: Butterworths.

Marriott, M.
1969 "Little Communities in an Indigenous Civilization." In McKim Marriott, ed., *Village India*. Chicago: University of Chicago Press.

Marshall, V.H.
1987 *Aging in Canada: Social Perspectives*. 2nd ed. Toronto: Fitzhenry and Whiteside.

Martell, G., (ed.)
1974 *The Politics of the Canadian Public School*. Toronto: Lorimer.

Martin, Leslie
1986 "Women Workers in a Masculine Domain: Jobs and Gender in a Yukon Mine." In Lundy and Warme, eds., *Work in the Canadian Context: Continuity Despite Change*. 3rd ed. Toronto: Butterworths.

Marx, Gary T.
1981 "The Ironies of Social Control," *Social Problems* 28 (Feb.).

Marx, K.
1932 *The Communist Manifesto*. New York: Modern Library. First published 1848.

Marx, Karl and F. Engels
1932 *The Communist Manifesto*. New York: Modern Library. First published 1848.

Mason, B.A.
1988 *Spence and Lila*. New York: Harper and Row.

Matza, David
1964 *Delinquency and Drift*. New York: John Wiley & Sons.
1969 *Becoming Deviant*. Englewood Cliffs, N.J.: Prentice-Hall.

Mauss, A.L. and D.W. Petersen
1973 "The Cross and the Commune: An Interpretation of the Jesus People." In R.R. Evans, ed., *Social Movements*. Chicago: Rand McNally.

Mayo, E.
1945 *The Social Problems of an Industrial Civilization*. Cambridge, Mass.: Harvard University Press.

McClintock, David
1982 *Indecent Exposure: A True Story of Hollywood and Wall Street*. New York: Dell.

McIntosh, Mary
1971 "Changes in the Organization of Thieving." In Stanley Cohen, ed., *Image of Deviance*. Harmondsworth: Penguin Books.

McLaren, P.
1980 *Cries from the Corridor*. Toronto: Methuen.

McLeod, L.
1982 *Wife Battering in Canada: The Vicious Circle*. Ottawa: Canadian Government Publishing Centre.

McNulty, F.
1981 *The Burning Bed*. New York: Bantam.

McRoberts, K.
1988 *Quebec: Social Change and Political Crisis*. 2nd ed. Toronto: McClelland and Stewart.

McRoberts, R. and D. Posgate
1980 *Quebec—Social Change and Political Crisis*. Rev. ed. Toronto: McClelland and Stewart.

Mead, G.H.
1934 *Mind, Self and Society*. Chicago: University of Chicago Press.

Menzies, Heather
1989 *FastForward and Out of Control*. Toronto: Macmillan Canada.

Merton, Robert K.
1968 *Social Theory and Social Structure*. Glencoe, Ill.: Free Press.

Merton, Robert K., G.K. Reader and P.L. Kendall, (eds.)
1987 *The Student Physician*. Cambridge, Mass.: Harvard University Press.

Miller, Arthur
1949 *Death of a Salesman*. New York: The Viking Press.
1977 *The Crucible*. Markham, Ontario: Penguin Books Canada. First published 1953.

Miller, D.C. and W.H. Form
1980 *Industrial Sociology: Work in Organizational Life*. 3rd ed. New York: Harper and Row.

Miller, G.
1978 *Odd Jobs: The World of Deviant Work*. Englewood Cliffs, N.J.: Prentice-Hall.

Miller, Walter P.
1958 "Lower Class Culture as a Generating Milieu of Gang Delinquency," *Journal of Social Issues* 14 (Summer): 5-19.

Millett, Kate
1970 *Sexual Politics*. New York: Doubleday.

Mills, C.W.
1956 *White Collar*. New York: Oxford University Press.
1956 *The Power Elite*. New York: Oxford University Press.
1959 *The Sociological Imagination*. New York: Oxford University Press.

Ontario Minister's Advisory Committee on the International Year of Shelter for the Homeless
1987 *More than Just a Roof: Action to End Homelessness in Ontario*. Toronto: Ministry of Housing.

Mironowicz, M.
1985 "Faith, Hope and Charitable Donations," *Globe and Mail*, 18 April.

Mitchell, G.
1981 *Truth . . . and Consequences: Seven Who Would Not Be Silenced*. New York: Dembner Books.

Moore, Wilbert E.
1974 *Social Change*. Englewood Cliffs, N.J.: Prentice-Hall.

Morgan, G.
1986 *Images of Organization*. Beverly Hills, Calif.: Sage.

Morris, J.
1974 *Conundrum*. New York: Harcourt Brace Jovanovich.

Morris, Norvall and Gordon Hawkins
1969 "The Overreach of the Criminal Law," *Midway* (9, Winter).
1970 *The Honest Politician's Guide to Crime Control*. Chicago: University of Chicago Press.
Morrissey, J.P., H.H.Goldman and L.V. Klerman, (eds.)
1980 *The Enduring Asylum*. New York: Gruene and Stratton.
Munan, H. 1988 *Culture Shock*. Singapore: Times Books International.
Munley, A.
1983 *The Hospice Alternative*. New York: Basic Books.
Myrdal, Gunnar
1944 *An American Dilemma*. New York: Harper.
Naipaul, V.S.
1968 *An Area of Darkness*. Markham, Ontario: Penguin Books Canada.
Nash, Peggy and Cheryl Krzaniwski
1984 "Electronic Imprisonment," *Our Times* 3 (5): 18-20.
National Council of Welfare
1979 *Women and Poverty*. Ottawa.
1988 *Poverty Profile*. Ottawa: Minister of Supply and Services
National Institute of Mental Health
1970 *Report on the XXY Chromosomal Abnormality*. (US) Public Health Service Publication 2103, Rockville, M.D.: NIMH.
Naylor, G.
1983 *The Women of Brewster Place*. London: Penguin.
Nett, E.
1981 "Canadian Families in Socio-Historical Perspective," *Canadian Journal of Sociology* 5 (3): 239-60.
Nettler, Gwynn
1982 *Criminal Careers*. 4 vols. Cincinnati, Ohio: Anderson Publishing.
Newman, Oscar
1972 *Defensible Space: People and Design in the Violent City*. London: Architectural Press.
Newman, Peter C.
1975 *The Canadian Establishment*. Toronto: McClelland and Stewart.
1978 *Bronfman Dynasty*. Toronto: McClelland and Stewart.
1981 *The Acquisitors*. Toronto: McClelland and Stewart.
Nicholson, Nigel
1973 *Portrait of a Marriage*. London: Weidenfeld and Nicholson.
Nisbet, Robert A.
1970 *The Social Bond*. New York: Albert A. Knopf.
Nock, D.A.
1987 "Cult, Sect and Church in Canada: A Re-Examination of Start and Bainbridge," *The Canadian Review of Sociology and Anthropology* 24 (4): 514-25.
Novak, Michael
1971 *The Rise of the Unmeltable Ethnics: Politics and Culture in the Seventies*. New York: Macmillan.
Oakley, Ann
1986 "Feminism, Motherhood, and Medicine: WHO CARES?" In Juliet Mitchell and Ann Oakley, eds., *What is Feminism?* Oxford: Basil Blackwell Ltd.
Ogburn, W.F.
1922 *Social Change*. New York: Viking Press.
Okun, L.
1986 *Women Abuse: Facts Replacing Myths*. New York: State University of New York Press.
Olson, P. and G. Burns
1983 "Politics, Class and Happenstance: French Immersion in a Canadian Context," *Interchange* 14 (1).
O'Malley, M.
1983 *Doctors*. Toronto: Macmillan of Canada.
1986 *Hospital*. Toronto: Macmillan of Canada.
Ontario Education Act
1985 Toronto: Queen's Printer.
Ornstein, Michael
1989 *AIDS in Canada: Knowledge, Behaviour and Attitudes of Adults*. Toronto: Institute for Social Research, York University.
Osberg, Lars
1981 *Economic Inequality in Canada*. Toronto: Butterworths.
Palmer, B.D.
1986 *The Character of Class Struggle: Essays in Canadian Working Class History, 1850-1985*. Toronto: McClelland and Stewart.
Parker, G.
1983 *An Introduction to Criminal Law*. 2nd ed. Toronto: Nelson Canada.
Parrilo, V.N.
1980 *Strangers to These Shores*. Boston: Houghton Mifflin.
Parsons, T.
1937 *The Structure of Social Action*. New York: Free Press.

1951 *The Social System*. New York: Free Press.
1960 *Structure and Process in Modern Societies*. New York: Free Press.

Perrow, Charles
1986 *Complex Organizations: A Critical Essay*. New York: Random House.

Peters, T.J. and R.H. Waterman, Jr.
1984 *In Search of Excellence*. New York: Harper and Row.

Pfohl, Stephen
1985 *Images of Deviance and Control: A Sociological History*. New York: McGraw-Hill.

Pike, R.M.
1988 ''Education and the Schools.'' In J. Curtis and L. Tepperman, eds., *Understanding Canadian Society*. Toronto: McGraw-Hill Ryerson.

Pineo, P.C. and J. Porter
1967 ''Occupational Prestige,'' *Canadian Review of Sociology and Anthropology* 4: 24-40.

Pirie, Marion
1988 ''Women and the Illness Role: Re-thinking Feminist Theory,'' *Canadian Review of Sociology and Anthropology* 25 (4): 628-48.

Platt, Anthony
1969 *The Child Savers*. Chicago: University of Chicago Press.

Pollack, Otto
1950 *The Criminality of Women*. Philadelphia: University of Pennsylvania Press.

Polsky, Ned
1969 *Hustlers, Beats and Others*. New York: Anchor Books.

Ponting, J.R.
1988 ''Native-White Relations.'' In J. Curtis and L. Tepperman, eds., *Understanding Canadian Society*. McGraw-Hill Ryerson.

Porter, John
1965 *The Vertical Mosaic: An Analysis of Social Class and Power in Canada*. Toronto: University of Toronto Press.

Porter, John, M.R. Porter and B. Blishen
1973 *Does Money Matter? Prospects for Higher Education*. Toronto: Institute for Behavioural Research.

Posner, J.
1980 ''Old and Female: The Double Whammy.'' In V.H. Marshall, ed., *Aging in Canada: Social Perspectives*. Toronto: Fitzhenry and Whiteside.

Poulantzas, N.
1978 *Classes in Contemporary Capitalism*. London: Verso.

Powell, Brian and James Martin
1980 ''Economic Implications of Canada's Aging Society.'' In V.H. Marshall, ed., *Aging in Canada*. Toronto: Fitzhenry and Whiteside.

Prentice, A.
1977 *The School Promoters: Education and Social Class in Mid-Nineteenth Century Upper Canada*. Toronto: McClelland and Stewart.

Prentice, A., *et al.*, (eds.)
1988 *Canadian Women: A History*. Toronto: Harcourt Brace Jovanovich, Canada.

Priest, Lisa
1989 *Conspiracy of Silence*. Toronto: McClelland and Stewart.

Quebedeaux, R.
1982 *By What Authority?* San Francisco: Harper and Row.

Radwanski, G.
1987 *Ontario Study of the Relevance of Education and the Issue of Dropouts*. Toronto: Ministry of Education.

Rayfield, J.R.
1970 *Maria in Markham Street: The Role of Italian Women in a Central City Neighbourhood*. Ethnic Studies Committee: Unpublished.

Reitz, J.S.
1980 *The Survival of Ethnic Groups*. Toronto: McGraw-Hill Ryerson.

Rendell, R.
1978 *A Judgement in Stone*. London: Avon Books.

Richardson, R.J.
1988 '' 'A Sacred Trust:' The Trust Industry and Canadian Economic Structure,'' *The Canadian Review of Sociology and Anthropology* 25 (1, Feb.): 1-22.

Richer, S.
1982 ''Equality to Benefit from Schooling: The Issue of Educational Opportunity.'' In P. Forcese and S. Richer, eds., *Social Issues*. Scarborough, Ont.: Prentice-Hall.

Richler, Mordecai
1969 *The Apprenticeship of Duddy Kravitz*. Toronto: McClelland and Stewart.

Richmond, Anthony H. and Warren E. Kalbach
1980 *Factors in the Adjustment of Immigrants and Their Descendants*. Ottawa: Statistics Canada.

Ricks, Christopher and Leonard Michaels, (eds.)
1990 *The State of the Language*. 2nd ed. Berkeley: University of California Press.

Riley, M.W.
1988 *Sociological Lives*. Newbury Park: Sage Publications.
Rinehart, J.
1987 *The Tyranny of Work: Alienation and the Labour Process*. 2nd ed. Toronto: Harcourt Brace Jovanovich, Canada.
Roberts, O.
1974 *Twelve Greatest Miracles of My Ministry*. Tulsa, Okla: Pinoak Publications.
Roche, P.
1984 "Bleak Dropout Picture Calls for Dramatic Change," *Globe and Mail*, 10 November.
Roethlisberger, F.J. and W.J. Dixon
1939 *Management and the Worker*. Cambridge, Mass.: Harvard University Press.
Rogoff, N.
1953 *Recent Trends in Occupational Mobility*. Glencoe, Ill.: Free Press.
Rosen, G.
1963 "The Hospital: Historical Sociology of a Community Institution." In E. Freidson, ed., *The Hospital in Modern Society*. London: The Free Press.
Ross, David P.
1980 *The Canadian Fact Book on Income Distribution*. Ottawa: The Canadian Council on Social Development.
1981 *The Working Poor*. Toronto: Lorimer.
Ross, E.A.
"Social Control," *American Journal of Sociology* 1: 513-35.
Rothman, R.
1987 *Working: Sociological Perspectives*. Englewood Cliffs, N.J.: Prentice-Hall.
Roy, Gabrielle
1947 *The Tin Flute*. Toronto: McClelland and Stewart.
1982 *The Fragile Lights of Earth*. Toronto: McClelland and Stewart.
Royal Commission on Bilingualism and Biculturalism
1969 *Report*. Vol. 3, *The Work World*. Ottawa: Queen's Printer.
Rubin, Lillian
1977 *Worlds of Pain: Life in the Working-Class Family*. New York: Basic Books.
1983 *Intimate Strangers: Men and Women Together*. New York: Harper and Row.
Ryan, T.J.
1972 *Poverty and the Child: A Canadian Study*. Toronto: McGraw-Hill Ryerson.
Sagan, Carl
1977 *The Dragons of Eden*. New York: Random House.
Sagel, J. Frederic
1985 "Time for a whistle-blower law," *The Globe and Mail*, Toronto, January 14.
1984 "Blowing the whistle," *Ontario Lawyer's Weekly* (Dec. 7).
Samenow, Stanton E.
1984 *Inside the Criminal Mind*. New York: Times Books.
Sampson, Anthony
1984 *The Seven Sisters: The Great Oil Companies and the World They Shaped*. Toronto: Bantam.
Sawyer, D.
1979 *Tomorrow Is School and I Am Sick to the Heart Thinking about It*. Vancouver: Douglas and McIntyre.
Schein, E.H.
1978 *Career Dynamics: Matching Individual and Organizational Needs*. Reading, Mass.: Addison-Wesley.
Scheleff, Lion Shaskolsky
1981 "The Relevance of Classical Criminology Today." In Israel Barak-Glantz and C. Ronald Huff, eds., *The Mad, the Bad, and the Different*. Lexington, Mass.: Lexington Books/Heath.
Schlesinger, Benjamin
1985 *The One Parent Family in the 1980's*. Toronto: University of Toronto Press.
Schur, Edwin M.
1965 *Crimes Without Victims*. Englewood Cliffs, N.J.: Prentice-Hall.
1979 *Interpreting Deviance*. New York: Harper and Row.
1980 *The Politics of Deviance: Stigma Contests and the Uses of Power*. Englewood Cliffs, N.J.: Prentice-Hall.
Schwartz, B.
1953 *The Supreme Court*. New York: Ronald Press.
Schwenger, C.W.
1974 "Keep the Old Folks at Home," *Canadian Journal of Public Health* 65.
Segal, Erich
1989 *Doctors*. New York: Bantam.
Selznick, Philip
1957 *Leadership in Administration: A Sociological Interpretation*. New York: Harper & Row.
Sennett, R. and J. Cobb
1972 *The Hidden Injuries of Class*. New York: Random House.

Shapiro, M.
1978 *Getting Doctored: Critical Reflections on Becoming a Physician*. Kitchener, Ontario: Between the Lines.
Shaw, Clifford R.
1966 *The Jack Roller: A Delinquent Boy's Own Story*. Chicago: University of Chicago Press. First published 1930.
Shaw, George Bernard
1965 *Pygmalion: A Romance in Five Acts*. Harmondsworth: Penguin. First published 1913.
Shearing, Clifford D., (ed.)
1981 *Organizational Police Deviance: Its Structure and Control*. Toronto: Butterworths.
Sheldon, W.H.
1948 *Varieties of Delinquent Youth: An Introduction to Constitutional Psychiatry*. New York: Harper and Row.
Shortt, S.E.D.
1986 *Victorian Lunacy*. Cambridge, U.K.: Cambridge University Press.
Shupe, A. and J.K. Hadden, (eds.)
1988 *The Politics of Religion and Social Change: Religion and the Political Order*. Toronto: McClelland and Stewart.
Silberman, C.E.
1980 *Criminal Violence, Criminal Justice*. New York: Vintage Books.
Sills, David L.
1980 *The Volunteers*. Salem, N.H.: Ayer Co. Publications. First published 1957.
Silzer, Kent
1985 "Deinstitutionalization of Psychiatrically Disabled Persons." In *Deinstitutionalization: Costs and Effects*. Ottawa: Canadian Council on Social Development.
Simmonds, Clive
1981 "The Next Wave in Technology," *Policy Options* 2 (5).
Simmons, Jerry L.
1969 *Deviants*. California: Glendessary Press.
Skolnick, A.
1978 *The Intimate Environment: Exploring Marriage and the Family*. 2nd ed. Boston: Little Brown.
Smigel, E.O.
1964 *The Wall Street Lawyer*. Glencoe, Ill.: Free Press.
1969 "The Wall Street Lawyer Reconsidered," *New York* 36 (August 18).
Smith, B.
1943 *A Tree Grows in Brooklyn*. New York: Harper and Row.
Smith, D.E.
1987 *The Everyday World as Problematic: A Feminist Sociology*. Milton Keynes: Open University Press.
Snider, L.
1982 "The Criminal Justice System." In D. Forcese and S. Richer, eds., *Social Issues*. Scarborough, Ont.: Prentice-Hall of Canada.
Sociology Writing Group, (The), U.C.L.A.
1986 *A Guide to Writing Sociology Papers*. Los Angeles: University of California Press.
Speirs, Rosemary
1983 "The Chip: Killing Jobs and Creating Peasants," *Globe and Mail*, 1 January.
Spergel, Irving
1964 *Racketville, Slumtown and Haulberg: An Exploratory Study of Delinquent Subcultures*. Chicago: University of Chicago Press.
Spradley, J.P. and B.J. Mann
1975 *The Cocktail Waitress*. New York: John Wiley.
Stanton, A.H. and M.S. Schwartz
1954 *The Mental Hospital*. New York: Basic Books.
Stark, R. and W.S. Bainbridge
1985 *The Future of Religion*. Berkeley: University of California Press.
Steiner, G.
1974 *Nostalgia for the Absolute*. Toronto: CBC Publications.
Steur, F.B., J.M. Applefield and R. Smith
1971 "Televised Aggression and Interpersonal Aggression of Pre-school Children," *Journal of Experimental Child Psychology* 11: 442-7.
Stewart, J.B.
1983 *The Partners: Inside America's Powerful Law Firms*. New York: Simon and Schuster.
Stouffer, S.A.
1950 *The American Soldier*. Princeton, N.J.: Princeton University Press.
Strauss, Stephen
1982 "Getting All Ready for Robot Invasion," *Globe and Mail*, 11 November.
1984 "Human Ideas from Computer," *Globe and Mail*, 19 January.
Struthers, J.
1983 *No Fault of Their Own: Unemployment and the Canadian State 1914-1941*. Toronto: University of Toronto Press.
Stuart, Don
1982 *Canadian Criminal Law: A Treatise*. Toronto: Carswell.

Stymeist, David
1975 *Ethics and Indians*. Toronto: Peter Martin Associates.

Such, P.
1973 *Riverrun*. Toronto: Clarke Irwin.

Sudnow, David
1965 "Normal Crimes: Sociological Features of the Penal Code in a Public Defender Office," *Social Problems* 12: 255-76.

Sutherland, Edwin H.
1961 *White Collar Crime*. New York: Holt, Rinehart and Winston.

Swingewood, A.
1984 *A Short History of Sociological Thought*. London: Macmillan

Sykes, Gresham and Davis Matza
1957 "Techniques of Neutralization: A Theory of Delinquency," *American Sociological Review* 22 (December): 664-70.

Symons, Gladys
1986 "Careers and Self-Concepts: Managerial Women in French and English Canada." In K.L.P. Lundy and B.D. Warme, eds., *Work in the Canadian Context: Continuity Despite Change*, 2nd ed. Toronto: Butterworths.

Talbott, J.E., (ed.)
1980 *State Mental Hospitals: Problems and Potentials*. New York: Human Sciences.

Task Force on Human Relations
1977 *Now Is Not Too Late*. Toronto.

Taylor, F.W.
1919 *Shop Management*. New York: Harper and Row.

Tepperman, L.
1975 *Social Mobility in Canada*. Toronto: McGraw-Hill Ryerson.

Terkel, Studs
1972 *Working*. New York: Avon Books.

Theodorson, G.A. and A.A. Theodorson
1969 *A Modern Dictionary of Sociology*. New York: Crowell.

Tomes, N.
1985 "Religion and the Earnings Function," *American Economic Review: Papers and Proceedings*.

Torrance, G.M.
1987 "Hospitals as Health Factories." In D. Coburn *et al.*, eds., *Health and Canadian Society*. 2nd ed. Toronto: Fitzhenry and Whiteside. 479-500.

Townsend, R.
1984 *Further Up The Organization: How To Stop Management From Stifling People and Strangling Productivity*. New York: Knopf.

Truzzi, Marcello
1971 "Lilliputians in Gulliver's Land: The Social Role of the Dwarf." In Marcello Truzzi, ed., *Sociology and Everyday Life*. Englewood Cliffs, N.J.: Prentice-Hall.

Tuchman, B.
1978 *A Distant Mirror*. New York: Alfred A. Knopf.

Tumin, M.
1953 "Some Principles of Stratification: A Critical Analysis," *American Sociological Review* 18: 387-93.
1967 *Social Stratification*. Englewood Cliffs, N.J.: Prentice-Hall.

Turrittin, J.
1981 "Doing Domestic: Work Relationships in a Particularistic Setting." In K.L.P. Lundy and B.D. Warme, eds., *Work in the Canadian Context: Continuity Despite Change*. Toronto: Butterworths.

Tylor, E.B.
1970 *Primitive Culture*. 2nd ed. Gloucester: Smith.

Valaskakis, R. and Peter Sendell
1980 *Industrial Strategy and the Information Economy: Towards a Game Plan for Canada*. Montreal: Gamma.

Van den Berghe, Pierre
1967 *Race and Racism*. New York: Wiley.

Vaz, E.W.
1976 *Aspects of Deviance*. Scarborough: Prentice-Hall of Canada.

Veevers, J.E.
1980 *Childless by Choice*. Toronto: Butterworths.

Vincent, C.L.
1979 *Policeman*. Toronto: Gage.

Waddams, S.M.
1983 *Introduction to the Study of Law*. 2nd ed. Toronto: Carswell.

Walby, S.
1988 *Gender Segregation at Work*. Milton Keynes: Open University Press.

Wallace, Ernest and E.A. Hochel
1952 *The Comanches: Lords of the South Plains*. Norman, Okla.

Wallace, J.
1983 *Part-time Work in Canada: Report of the Commission of Inquiry into Part-time Work.* Ottawa: Minister of Supply and Services.

Wallis, W.A. and M.V. Roberts
1962 *The Nature of Statistics.* New York: Free Press.

Walshok, M.L.
1981 *Blue-Collar Women.* Garden City, N.J.: Anchor Books.

Warme, B.D.
1979 "Breaking the Cycle of Child Abuse," *Status of Women News* 5 (5).

Warme, B.D. and K.L.P. Lundy
1988 "Erosion of an Ideal: The 'Presence' of Part-Time Faculty," *Studies in Higher Education* 13 (2).

Warme, B.D. and S. Thomas
1978 "Wednesday's Parent and the Role of the Para-Professional." In M.A. Beyer-Gammon (ed.), *Violence in Canada.* Toronto: Methuen.

Warme, Paul
1985 "Political Stability and Instability in Latin America." York University. Unpublished.

Warner, W. Lloyd, *et al.*
1963 *Yankee City.* New Haven: Yale University Press. Abridged edition.

Weber, M.
1958 *The Protestant Ethic and the Spirit of Capitalism.* New York: Scribner's Sons. First published 1904-5.

Weingarten, Murray
1959 *Life in a Kibbutz.* Jerusalem: Jerusalem Post Press.

Weisser, Michael
1982 *Crime and Punishment in Early Modern Europe 1350-1850.* 2nd ed. Sussex, U.K.: The Harvester Press.

Weitzman, Lenore J.
1985 *The Divorce Revolution: The Unexpected Social and Economic Consequences for Women and Children in America.* New York: Free Press.

Whyte, W.F.
1943 *Street Corner Society: The Social Structure of an Italian Slum.* Chicago: University of Chicago Press.

Wolff, H.J.
1983 "Roman Law." In J.C. Smith and D.V. Weisstub, eds., *The Western Idea of Law.* Toronto: Butterworths.

Woodsworth, J.S.
1972 *Strangers Within Our Gates.* Toronto: University of Toronto Press. First published 1909.

Woodward, J.
1965 *Industrial Organizations: Theory and Practice.* London: Oxford University Press.

Wright, E.N.
1970 *Student's Background and Its Relationship to Class and Programme in School.* Toronto: Toronto Board of Education.

Wright, P.J.
1979 *On a Clear Day You Can See General Motors.* Grosse Point: Wright Enterprises.

Yinger, M.
1970 *The Scientific Study of Religion.* New York: Macmillan.

Yochelson, Samuel and Stanton Samenow
1976 *The Criminal Personality.* New York: Aronson.

Yoxen, Edward
1983 *The Gene Business: Who Should Control Biotechnology?* Burgary Suffold: Richard Clay (The Chaucer Press).

Zeitlin, I.M.
1973 *Rethinking Sociology: A Critique of Contemporary Theory.* Englewood Cliffs, N.J.: Prentice-Hall.

Zerker, S.F.
1982 *The Rise and Fall of the Toronto Typographical Union 1832-1932: A Case Study of Foreign Domination.* Toronto: University of Toronto Press.

CREDITS

Permission to reprint copyrighted material is gratefully acknowledged. Information that will enable the publisher to rectify any error or omission will be welcomed.

Statistics Canada material reproduced by permission of the Minister of Supply and Services Canada.

CHAPTER 1

''Jobless teenagers are put to work,'' by David Crane, *Toronto Star*, April 7, 1985. Reprinted with permission—The Toronto Star Syndicate.

''Suicide rates in Canada vary from province to province. What makes the difference?'' article originally titled ''Jumping to conclusions,'' by Sean Fine, *The Globe and Mail*, Toronto, March 4, 1989.

''Anti-poverty group opposes Games,'' by Sean Fine, *The Globe and Mail*, Toronto, June 3, 1989.

''Scientific side of opinion poll doesn't stand up,'' by Conrad Winn, *The Globe and Mail*, Toronto, September 9, 1987.

CHAPTER 2

Excerpt from ''Scenes From an Arranged Marriage,'' by Allan Abel, *Toronto* Magazine, June 1989.

Excerpt from ''Red Sox one up on Jays,'' *The Globe and Mail*, Toronto, June 5, 1989

''Symbols mean all have same 'language,' '' by Jonathan Berry, *The Globe and Mail*, Toronto, November 5, 1983. Reprinted with permission of the author.

Excerpt from ''Seven bridges for seven berbers,'' by Peter Dax, *New York Times*, September 3, 1989.

''Brazil seeks to bury Millennia-old culture,'' by David Suzuki, *The Globe and Mail*, Toronto, October 29, 1988. Reprinted with permission of the author.

Excerpt from ''For every North American Indian who begins to disappear, I also begin to disappear,'' by Wilfred Pelletier *et al.*, The Neewin Publishing Co. Ltd., Toronto, 1971, pages 6-9.

CHAPTER 3

Adaptation of ''The Little Engine That Could,'' from *Sharing Time* by Bernadette Bouchard *et al.* (Starting Points in Language Arts series). Toronto: Ginn and Company, 1977, pages 56-62. Reproduced courtesy of the publisher.

Excerpt from ''The New Executive Father,'' by Rona Maynard. The Globe and Mail, *Report on Business Magazine*, Toronto, 5 (9) March, 1989.

Excerpt from ''Vision of quality day care in Ontario clouded by race for space,'' by Ann Rauhala and Andrew McIntosh, *The Globe and Mail*, Toronto, February 8, 1989.

''cathy'' by Cathy Guisewite, Universal Press Syndicate, Kansas City, 1985.

Excerpt from ''Does punishing children cause a violent society?'' by Janet Watts, *The London Observer*, October 16, 1988.

''No boys in math classes so girls can make passes,'' by Regina Hickl-Szabo, *The Globe and Mail*, Toronto, October 26, 1984.

CHAPTER 4

Excerpt from ''Rich city, Poor city,'' by Peter Cheney and Kim Zarzour, *The Toronto Star*, March 11, 1989. Reprinted with permission—The Toronto Star Syndicate.

''Doonesbury,'' by G.B. Trudeau, Universal Press Syndicate, Kansas City, 1984.

Excerpt from ''8,500 poor huddle together in city-within-a-city,'' by June Callwood, *The Globe and Mail*, Toronto, November 14, 1987. Reprinted with permission of the author.

Excerpt from ''Four sisters project a haven of sanity and response,'' by June Callwood, *The Globe and Mail*, Toronto, November 14, 1987. Reprinted with permission of the author.

''Consortium of indifference frustrates Lewis,'' by Jim Cody, *The Guardian*, Charlottetown, June 30, 1989.

''Endless poverty likely future of poor children, study shows,'' by Graham Fraser.

CHAPTER 5

Exhibit 5.2: Statistics Canada. The Labour Force. Jan. 1989, p. B-27.

Excerpt from ''Garment industry needs to mend its ways,'' by June Callwood, *The Globe and Mail*, Toronto, September 13, 1989. Reprinted with permission of the author.

''They Own The Place,'' by Frederick Ungeheuer, *Time* Magazine, February 13, 1989. Copyright 1989, The Time Inc. Magazine Company. Reprinted with permission.

''Most derelicts want jobs, Montreal study shows,'' by André Picard, *The Globe and Mail*, Toronto, June 26, 1989.

''Irving Inc. says 'People working part-time shouldn't benefit,' '' *The Canadian Press*, November 3, 1988.

Excerpt from ''New job-sharing is catching on . . . ,'' by Violet Johnstone, *The Daily Telegraph*, London, England, May 14, 1989.

''He Works, She Works 'Nine to Five': But What Different Impressions They Make!'' *Paths to Power*, by Natasha Josefowitz.

CHAPTER 6

''Hands Across the Workplace,'' by Marguerite Michaels. Copyright 1989, The Time Inc. Magazine Company. Reprinted with permission.

Excerpt from ''Environment groups face a crisis of identity,'' by Craig McInnes, *The Globe and Mail*, Toronto, July 15, 1989.

Excerpt from ''An uphill battle: Voluntary affirmative action plans don't seem to be working,'' by Ann Rauhala, *The Globe and Mail*, Toronto, August 20, 1988.

Excerpt from ''Managerial class gets roughed up,'' by Steven Prokesch, *New York Times*, March 22, 1987.

CHAPTER 7

Excerpt from ''Homosexual Rights: A Moderate Majority Accepts Gays,'' by Nora Underwood, *Macleans* Magazine, January 2, 1989.

''Native bands sign mutual defence treaty.'' Copyright *The Toronto Star*, July 8, 1989.

Excerpt from ''Japanese Canadians win apology to 'cleanse' past,'' *The Toronto Star*, September 23, 1988. Reprinted with permission — The Toronto Star Syndicate.

Excerpt from ''South African blacks taught from childhood that 'equality' is not for them,'' article originally titled ''South Africa's child victims,'' by Emil Sher, *The Globe and Mail*, June 16, 1989.

Excerpt from ''New pension law won't bring needed reforms,'' by John Deverell, *The Toronto Star*, June 1989. Reprinted with permission — The Toronto Star Syndicate.

''Seeking full rights in the work force,'' by Susan Reid, *The Toronto Star*, June 6, 1989. Reprinted with permission — The Toronto Star Syndicate.

CHAPTER 8

Excerpt from ''Canadian Narcotics Legislation: An Example,'' *Aspects of Deviance*, by E.W. Vaz. Copyright 1967 by Prentice-Hall of Canada, Ltd.

''Police arrest 6 Santas, 2 elves during protest against war toys,'' by Janice Hass, *The Globe and Mail*, Toronto, December 19, 1988.

''Insults fly as TV hosts defend right to be kinky,'' *The Globe and Mail*, Toronto, April 14, 1989. Copyright *The Associated Press*, New York.

Excerpts from ''Deviance Disavowal and Stigma Management: A Study of Obesity,'' by Alexander Himelfarb and John Evans, *Decency & Deviance*, Jack Haas and Bill Shaffir, eds., 1974, pages 222-25. The Canadian Publishers, McClelland and Stewart.

''Nigeria's gruesome war on crime,'' by Angela Cobbina, *Gemini News Service*, London, England, September 21, 1986.

Excerpt from ''The U.S. debate on 'crackdown' is a contest to see who can propose more spending,'' by Colin Mackenzie, *The Globe and Mail*, Toronto, September 9, 1989.

"Scrawny whistle blower makes the trading floor tremble," by Stevie Cameron, *The Globe and Mail*, Toronto, October 29, 1987.

"Bakker aides sentenced to more than 17 years," *Reuters New Agency*, New York, September 9, 1989.

CHAPTER 9A

"Family redefines itself, and now the law follows," by Philip S. Gutis, *New York Times*, May 28, 1989. Copyright 1987/89 by The New York Times Company. Reprinted with permission.

Excerpts from "Wife's career a stress-test for marriage," by Harvey Fields, *New York Times*, January 1, 1984. Copyright 1984 by The New York Times Company. Reprinted with permission.

CHAPTER 9B

"Bringing Them Back to School," by Harvey Krahn and Julian Tanner, *Policy Options Magazine*, Halifax, Nova Scotia, March 1989.

"Now listen and learn, dog-faced reprobate," by A. Trevor Hodge, Dept. of Classics, Carleton University. *The Globe and Mail*, Toronto, September 4, 1989.

Excerpt from "The hidden curriculum," by Sandro Contents, *The Toronto Star*, June 13, 1989. Reprinted with permission — The Toronto Star Syndicate.

Excerpt from "Illiteracy is costly," article originally titled "Back to Basics," by Margot Gibb Clark, *The Globe and Mail*, Toronto, November 3, 1984.

CHAPTER 9C

"How killing turns into dogma when religion, state are one," by Amos Perlmutter, *The Toronto Star*, Toronto, February 21, 1989.

Excerpt from "Secular society gave couple their niche: the wedding business," by Andrew Van Velzen, *The Globe and Mail*, Toronto, August 14, 1989. Reprinted with permission of the author.

"Today's Youth: The Scapegoats," by John Tower.

CHAPTER 9D

"Civil Liberties and Canada's War Measures Act," by Janet Enright *et al.*, *Maclean's* Magazine, October 21 ,1985.

"Fetal rights," by Catharine Tolton, *The Globe and Mail*, Toronto, August 4, 1989. Reprinted with permission of the author.

Exhibit 9.14: Statistics Canada, Jan. 1988. Adult Correctional Services in Canada, 1986-7 (85-211.)

CHAPTER 9E

"Overworked nurses say 'enough is enough,'" by Christie McLaren, *The Globe and Mail*, Toronto, July 29, 1989.

Exhibit 9.16: Statistics Canada, June 1988. Catalogue 83-217.

"Is medicare unaffordable or underfunded?" by Desmond Morton, *The Toronto Star*, January 9, 1989. Reprinted with permission of the author.

"Conference condemns trading in organs," by Paul Taylor, *The Globe and Mail*, Toronto, August 25, 1989.

"Doonesbury," by G.B. Trudeau, United Press Syndicate, Kansas City, 1987.

CHAPTER 10

Excerpt from "The Times They Are A-Changin' " by Bob Dylan © 1963, 1964 WARNER BROS. INC. All Rights Reserved. Used with permission.

"The Increasing Speed of Change," from *The Dragons of Eden: Speculations on the Evolution of Human Intelligence*, by Carl Sagan. New York: Random House, 1977. Reproduced by permission of Alfred A. Knopf, Inc.

Excerpt from "There's no place to dump the trash," by Tom Spears, *The Toronto Star*, Thursday May 19, 1989. Reprinted with permission — The Toronto Star Syndicate.

Excerpt from "Powerful cabinet minister 'just Nellie' in territories," by Julie Necheff, *The Guardian*, Charlottetown, P.E.I., June 30, 1989.

" 'Mommy track' row dividing women," by Jennifer Lewington, *The Globe and Mail*, Toronto, March 22, 1989.

Excerpt from "What will tomorrow bring . . ." *A Study of the Aspirations of Adolescent Women* by M. Baker. Ottawa: Canadian Advisory Council on the Status of Women, 1985. Reprinted with permission.

"Criminalize theft of citizens' data, privacy head says," by Graham Fraser, *The Globe and Mail*, July 13, 1989.

Exhibit 10.4: "Home Machinery," *Royal Bank Reporter*, Fall 1989.

"Scientists should not turn from twisted Nazi genetics," by David Suzuki, *The Globe and Mail*, January 9, 1988. Reprinted with permission of the author.

PHOTOGRAPHS AND ILLUSTRATIONS

Dorothy and Neil Brown, page *449*

Canada Wide Feature Services Ltd., pages *85, 271, 274, 287, 344, 399, 493*

Canadian Pacific Corporate Archives, page *269*

Canapress Photo Service, pages *29, 49 upper, 55, 74, 191, 209, 211, 214, 216, 219, 229, 244, 246, 265, 308, 315, 335, 351, 353, 356, 418, 438, 443, 454, 462, 468, 478, 481, 489, 518, 524 lower, 542, 544, 560 upper, 560 lower;* with special thanks to consultant Paulee Kestin.

Canapress/Uniphoto Worldwide Service—Representative/Laurie J. Taylor, pages *78, 91/R. Open, 168, 223, 329/Stefan Richter*

Etobicoke Board of Education, page *422*

The Globe and Mail, page 320/*James Lewcun*

The Granger Collection, New York, page *122*

Historical Pictures Service, Chicago, page *19*

The Image Bank Photo Service—Representative/Tony Lever, pages *"0"/Zao Longfield, 44/Lawrence Fried, 60 lower/Larry Dale Gorden, 180/Ted Russell, 182/Jeff Smith, 186/Janeart Ltd., 196/Alvis Upitis, 198/Merrel Wood, 204/Walter Bibikow, 242/Stephen Derr, 252/Hans Wolf, 557/P. Thomann*

L. Lundy, page *53*

Magnum, pages *383, 401*

Masterfile Photo Service—Representative/Mary Fiumano, pages *368 upper, 368 middle, 368 lower, 432/Gabe Palmer, 503/Al Harvey, 505/Larry Mulvehill*

Miller Services, pages *102, 135, 378*

National Ballet of Canada/Andrew Oxenham, page *49 lower*

The Observer, London, page *101*

Reuter, page *525/Peter Jones*

Don Summerhayes, page *54*

Sygma, pages *82, 89, 191, 311, 318, 374, 404, 439, 548*

The Toronto Star, pages *112 upper and lower/Andrew Stawicki, 299, 301/Scott Gardner*

UPI/Bettmann Archive, pages *60 upper, 120, 157, 471*

UPI/Bettmann Newsphotos, pages *9, 11, 16, 66*

Mike Ware, page *377*

B. Warme, page *385*

York University Photography, page *26*

AUTHOR-TITLE INDEX

SUBJECT INDEX